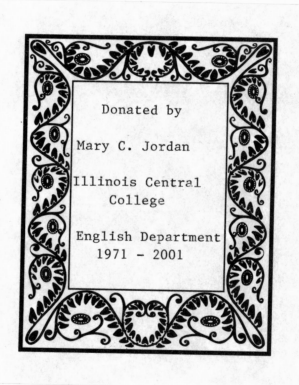

THE ART OF THE
MYSTERY
STORY

A Collection of
Critical Essays

Edited and with a commentary by

HOWARD HAYCRAFT

New Edition with Index

BIBLO and TANNEN
NEW YORK
1976

Reprinted, 1975, with the permission of Curtis Brown, Ltd.
by

BIBLO & TANNEN BOOKSELLERS & PUBLISHERS, INC.

63 Fourth Avenue / New York, N.Y. 10003

Library of Congress Cataloging in Publication Data

Haycraft, Howard, 1905-   ed.
   The art of the mystery story.

   Reprint of the 1946 ed. published by Simon and
Schuster, New York, with the index from the ed. copy-
righted in 1947 published by Grosset & Dunlap, New York.
   1. Detective and mystery stories--History and crit-
icism. 2. Detective and mystery stories--Bibliography.
I. Title.
PN3448.D4H28 1975   808.3'872   75-28263
ISBN 0-8196-0289-2

FOREWORD

THE PURPOSE of this book is to bring together under one cover a
representative selection of the best critical and informative writing
about the modern mystery-crime-detective story, from Poe to the
present time. Ever since the day some five years ago that I ventured
to perpetrate a history of detective fiction,* lovers of this variety
of literature have been writing me of the need for such a book.
Concurrently, the last few years have witnessed in the public prints
an outpouring of serious critical discussion of the once-lowly whodunit and its relations-by-marriage unequalled in any comparable
period in the 100-year history of the genre. In view of these circumstances, it seemed to my publishers and myself that the time had
arrived for the compilation of the first and definitive anthology
devoted solely to this aspect of the subject. It is our hope that the
resulting volume will serve equally well the uses of pleasure and
reference.

In choosing the material to be included, I have been guided by a
few simple but necessary rules-of-thumb which it may be helpful
to state. Except for certain historically obligatory selections in the
opening section, I have tried diligently throughout the volume to
avoid material that repeated too closely either the information or
themes found in other selections. That this unavoidably ruled out
many otherwise fine essays and articles is the occasion of sincere
sorrow. (The anthologist's life, as every member of the profession
will testify, is a constant succession of hard choices and regret at
never having the space to include everything and everybody he
would like.) Some exclusions based on types of subject matter were
also found necessary. Thus, appreciations of individual authors
have had to be omitted as not quite germane to the principal consideration (with two exceptions only: Poe and Doyle) and, likewise,
selections however excellent in themselves that were believed too

---

* *Murder for Pleasure: The Life and Times of the Detective Story* (New York:
Appleton, 1941; London: Davies, 1942).

limited, specialized, or recondite for the general reader's interest. Articles of a purely "How-To-Write-It" nature have been avoided, both because this is a book for readers rather than writers of detective stories, and because there is already a satisfactory collection of such pieces available in the volume *Writing Detective and Mystery Fiction,* edited by A. S. Burack (Boston: The Writer, Inc., 1945). On the other hand, a chapter from Marie F. Rodell's textbook *Mystery Fiction: Theory & Technique* (New York: Duell, Sloan & Pearce, 1943) has been given space because of the interest of its subject matter to lay as well as professional readers.

So much for the principles of selection. The final choices for inclusion simply represent (as they must in any anthology) the editor's best judgment as to what the putative reader of the book would like to find in it. Taste being the variable thing it is, anyone else performing the same task would doubtless have chosen differently in many instances; quite possibly more wisely. I can only hope that the reader who is disappointed by the omission of some personal favorite will be reimbursed by the discovery of new material and delights he knew not of.

In addition to the formal acknowledgments at the end of the book, I wish to thank specially those authors, critics, and editors who so generously wrote original essays for this volume and thereby increased inestimably whatever value it may possess: Erle Stanley Gardner, Craig Rice, Anthony Boucher, Lee Wright, Isabelle Taylor, Richard Mealand, Ken Crossen, "Judge Lynch," and Isaac Anderson. To several of these, and to Ellery Queen and James Sandoe, I am additionally indebted for invaluable editorial advice and assistance.

New York City
July, 1946

CONTENTS

4. THE LIGHTER SIDE OF CRIME

5. CRITICS' CORNER

6. DETECTIVE FICTION vs. REAL LIFE

7. PUTTING CRIME ON THE SHELF

8. WATCHMAN, WHAT OF THE NIGHT?

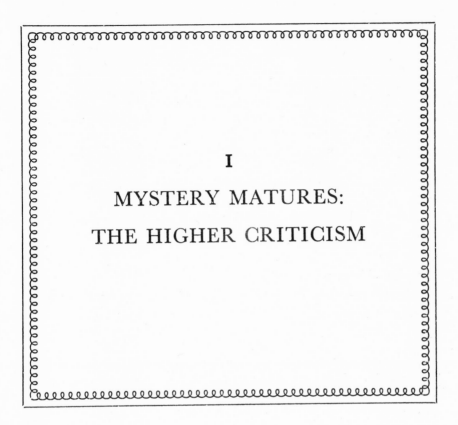

I

MYSTERY MATURES:
THE HIGHER CRITICISM

It is a literary truism that criticism follows creation. In the case of the modern detective-crime-mystery story, criticism—as distinguished from the reviewing of individual works—took an inordinately long time to catch up to original performance. Poe wrote the first police story, as we know it, in 1841. Yet the earliest critical discussion of the genre as such that your editor has been able to discover appeared in the London Saturday Review for May 5, 1883. A pallid and pointless effort at best, this unsigned pioneer editorial contained no thought more critically memorable or worth repeating than the daring pronouncement that "for a long time past, fictitious detectives and their achievements have more or less interested the readers of novels."

As time went forward, published comment of a somewhat analytical nature about the detective story and its kin became more frequent, though for a good many years scarcely more significant.

There were exceptions. The chapter on "The Literature of Crime Detection" in F. W. Chandler's The Literature of Roguery *(Boston: Houghton Mifflin, 1907) was an early landmark, mature and informed beyond its time, though of little present-day interest. And G. K. Chesterton's essays beginning around the turn of the century (one of which opens this volume) remain as fresh and immediate today as when they were written. But on the whole it must be said that the development of any competent body of detective story criticism did not occur until the mid-1920's—since which date the anthologist in the field suffers only from an embarrassment of riches.*

In this opening section, then, the reader will find ten chronologically-arranged selections representing what, by some slight imaginative license, may be called the Higher Criticism of the subject. Six of the chosen ten are virtually obligatory: prefaces, introductions, and chapters from the outstanding critical anthologies and full-length historical works devoted to police fiction in its several aspects. The remaining four—and here the problem of selection was infinitely more difficult—are random essays and magazine articles chosen from several hundred possible candidates to illustrate the nature and evolution of detective story criticism through the years.

Ladies and gentlemen, the Higher Critics.

A Defence of Detective Stories

(1902)

By G. K. Chesterton

Gilbert K. Chesterton (1874–1936), world-renowned English man-of-letters, is justly beloved by devotees of police fiction as the creator of Father Brown, the little priest-detective who is one of the true immortals of modern crime literature. But G.K.C. was also one of the earliest and in his writings still remains one of the most brilliant critical apologists for the detective story as a literary form. The present essay, one of a number on the topic from his pen, is the source of several of his most frequently quoted dicta on the subject. It appeared in his The Defendant *(London: R. B. Johnson; New York: Dodd, Mead, 1902) and marks what is probably the first serious and perceptive application of the critical method to the genre; certainly the earliest by any major literary figure.*

IN ATTEMPTING to reach the genuine psychological reason for the popularity of detective stories, it is necessary to rid ourselves of many mere phrases. It is not true, for example, that the populace prefer bad literature to good, and accept detective stories because they are bad literature. The mere absence of artistic subtlety does not make a book popular. Bradshaw's Railway Guide contains few gleams of psychological comedy, yet it is not read aloud uproariously on winter evenings. If detective stories are read with more exuberance than railway guides, it is certainly because they are more artistic. Many good books have fortunately been popular; many bad books, still more fortunately, have been unpopular. A good detective story would probably be even more popular than a bad one. The trouble in this matter is that many people do not realize that there is such a thing as a good detective story; it is to them like speaking of a good devil. To write a story about a burglary is, in their eyes, a sort of spiritual manner of committing it. To persons of somewhat weak sensibility this is natural enough; it must be confessed that many detective stories are as full of sensational crime as one of Shakespeare's plays.

There is, however, between a good detective story and a bad detective story as much, or, rather more, difference than there is between a good epic and a bad one. Not only is a detective story a perfectly legitimate form of art, but it has certain definite and real advantages as an agent of the public weal.

The first essential value of the detective story lies in this, that it is the earliest and only form of popular literature in which is expressed some sense of the poetry of modern life. Men lived among mighty mountains and eternal forests for ages before they realized that they were poetical; it may reasonably be inferred that some of our descendants may see the chimney-pots as rich a purple as the mountain-peaks, and find the lamp-posts as old and natural as the trees. Of this realization of a great city itself as something wild and obvious the detective story is certainly the 'Iliad.' No one can have failed to notice that in these stories the hero or the investigator crosses London with something of the loneliness and liberty of a prince in a tale of elfland, that in the course of that incalculable journey the casual omnibus assumes the primal colours of a fairy ship. The lights of the city begin to glow like innumerable goblin eyes, since they are the guardians of some secret, however crude, which the writer knows and the reader does not. Every twist of the road is like a finger pointing to it; every fantastic skyline of chimney-pots seems wildly and derisively signalling the meaning of the mystery.

This realization of the poetry of London is not a small thing. A city is, properly speaking, more poetic even than a countryside, for while Nature is a chaos of unconscious forces, a city is a chaos of conscious ones. The crest of the flower or the pattern of the lichen may or may not be significant symbols. But there is no stone in the street and no brick in the wall that is not actually a deliberate symbol—a message from some man, as much as if it were a telegram or a post-card. The narrowest street possesses, in every crook and twist of its intention, the soul of the man who built it, perhaps long in his grave. Every brick has as human a hieroglyph as if it were a graven brick of Babylon; every slate on the roof is as educational a document as if it were a slate covered with addition and subtraction sums. Anything which tends, even under the fantastic form of the minutiæ of Sherlock Holmes, to assert this romance of detail in civilization, to emphasize this unfathomably human character in flints and tiles, is a good thing. It is good that the average man should fall into the habit of looking imaginatively at ten men in the street even if it is only on the chance that the eleventh might be a notorious thief. We may dream, perhaps, that it might be possible to have another and higher romance of London, that men's souls have stranger adventures than their bodies, and that it would be harder and more exciting to hunt their virtues than to hunt their crimes. But since our great authors (with the admirable exception of Stevenson) decline to write of that thrilling mood and moment when the eyes of the great city, like the eyes of a cat, begin to flame in the dark, we must give fair credit to the popular literature which, amid a babble of pedantry and preciosity, declines to regard the present as prosaic or the common as commonplace. Popular art in all ages has been interested in contemporary manners and costume; it dressed the groups around the Crucifixion in the garb of Florentine gentlefolk or Flemish burghers. In the last century it was the custom for distinguished actors to present Macbeth in a powdered wig and ruffles. How far we are ourselves in this age from such conviction of the poetry of our own life and manners may easily be conceived by anyone who chooses to imagine a picture of Alfred the Great toasting the cakes dressed in tourist's knickerbockers, or a performance of 'Hamlet' in which the Prince appeared in a frock-coat, with a crape band round his hat. But this instinct of the age to look back, like Lot's wife, could not go on for ever. A rude, popular literature of the romantic possibilities of the modern city was bound to arise. It has arisen in the popular detective stories, as rough and refreshing as the ballads of Robin Hood.

There is, however, another good work that is done by detective stories. While it is the constant tendency of the Old Adam to rebel against so universal and automatic a thing as civilization, to preach departure and rebellion, the romance of police activity keeps in some sense before the mind the fact that civilization itself is the most sensational of departures and the most romantic of rebellions. By dealing with the unsleeping sentinels who guard the outposts of society, it tends to remind us that we live in an armed camp, making war with a chaotic world, and that the criminals, the children of chaos, are nothing but the traitors within our gates. When the detective in a police romance stands alone, and somewhat fatuously fearless amid the knives and fists of a thieves' kitchen, it does certainly serve to make us remember that it is the agent of social justice who is the original and poetic figure, while the burglars and footpads are merely placid old cosmic conservatives, happy in the immemorial respectability of apes and wolves. The romance of the police force is thus the whole romance of man. It is based on the fact that morality is the most dark and daring of conspiracies. It reminds us that the whole noiseless and unnoticeable police management by which we are ruled and protected is only a successful knight-errantry.

The Art of the Detective Story

(1924)

By R. Austin Freeman

For many years most writing by partisans of the detective story assumed an unconsciously defensive if not actually apologetic tone. This state of affairs still largely persisted when the late respected R. Austin Freeman (1862–1943) first published the famous essay which follows in Nineteenth-Century and After (London) *for May 1924—although the beginnings of a more positive and assertive position will be discerned in his observations. As the creator of Dr. Thorndyke and the acknowledged founder and dean of modern scientific police fiction, no one was better qualified than Dr. Freeman to state the case on behalf of the "pure", or rigidly logical detective story, genus Britannicum. Some of the more formalistic rules he advocates no longer hold today, even in England. Nevertheless, many a long-suffering reader will wish that more present-day authors would study and take to heart Dr. Freeman's still-valid statement of fundamentals.*

THE STATUS in the world of letters of that type of fiction which finds its principal motive in the unravelment of crimes or similar intricate mysteries presents certain anomalies. By the critic and the professedly literary person the detective story—to adopt the unprepossessing name by which this class of fiction is now universally known—is apt to be dismissed contemptuously as outside the pale of literature, to be conceived of as a type of work produced by half-educated and wholly incompetent writers for consumption by office boys, factory girls, and other persons devoid of culture and literary taste.

That such works are produced by such writers for such readers
is an undeniable truth; but in mere badness of quality the detective story holds no monopoly. By similar writers and for similar
readers there are produced love stories, romances, and even historical tales of no better quality. But there is this difference: that,
whereas the place in literature of the love story or the romance
has been determined by the consideration of the masterpieces of
each type, the detective story appears to have been judged by its
failures. The status of the whole class has been fixed by an estimate formed from inferior samples.

What is the explanation of this discrepancy? Why is it that,
whereas a bad love story or romance is condemned merely on
its merits as a defective specimen of a respectable class, a detec-
tiv story is apt to be condemned without trial in virtue of some
sort of assumed original sin? The assumption as to the class of
reader is manifestly untrue. There is no type of fiction that is
more universally popular than the detective story. It is a familiar
fact that many famous men have found in this kind of reading
their favourite recreation, and that it is consumed with pleasure,
and even with enthusiasm, by many learned and intellectual
men, not infrequently in preference to any other form of fiction.

This being the case, I again ask for an explanation of the contempt in which the whole genus of detective fiction is held by
the professedly literary. Clearly, a form of literature which arouses
the enthusiasm of men of intellect and culture can be affected by
no inherently base quality. It cannot be foolish, and is unlikely
to be immoral. As a matter of fact, it is neither. The explanation
is probably to be found in the great proportion of failures; in the
tendency of the tyro and the amateur perversely to adopt this difficult and intricate form for their 'prentice efforts; in the crude
literary technique often associated with otherwise satisfactory productions; and perhaps in the falling off in quality of the work of
regular novelists when they experiment in this department of
fiction, to which they may be adapted neither by temperament
nor by training.

Thus critical judgment has been formed, not on what the detective story can be and should be, but on what it too frequently

was in the past when crudely and incompetently done. Unfortunately, this type of work is still prevalent; but it is not representative. In late years there has arisen a new school of writers who, taking the detective story seriously, have set a more exacting standard, and whose work, admirable alike in construction and execution, probably accounts for the recent growth in popularity of this class of fiction. But, though representative, they are a minority; and it is still true that a detective story which fully develops the distinctive qualities proper to its genus, and is, in addition, satisfactory in diction, in background treatment, in characterization, and in general literary workmanship is probably the rarest of all forms of fiction.

The rarity of good detective fiction is to be explained by a fact which appears to be little recognized either by critics or by authors; the fact, namely, that a completely executed detective story is a very difficult and highly technical work, a work demanding in its creator the union of qualities which, if not mutually antagonistic, are at least seldom met with united in a single individual. On the one hand, it is a work of imagination, demanding the creative, artistic faculty; on the other, it is a work of ratiocination, demanding the power of logical analysis and subtle and acute reasoning; and, added to these inherent qualities, there must be a somewhat extensive outfit of special knowledge. Evidence alike of the difficulty of the work and the failure to realize it is furnished by those occasional experiments of novelists of the orthodox kind which have been referred to, experiments which commonly fail by reason of a complete misunderstanding of the nature of the work and the qualities that it should possess.

A widely prevailing error is that a detective story needs to be highly sensational. It tends to be confused with the mere crime story, in which the incidents—tragic, horrible, even repulsive—form the actual theme, and the quality aimed at is horror—crude and pungent sensationalism. Here the writer's object is to make the reader's flesh creep; and since that reader has probably, by a course of similar reading, acquired a somewhat extreme degree of obtuseness, the violence of the means has to be progressively increased in proportion to the insensitiveness of the subject. The sportsman in the juvenile verse sings:

> I shoot the hippopotamus with bullets made of platinum
> Because if I use leaden ones his hide is sure to flatten 'em:

and that, in effect, is the position of the purveyor of gross sensationalism. His purpose is, at all costs, to penetrate his reader's mental epidermis, to the density of which he must needs adjust the weight and velocity of his literary projectile.

Now no serious author will complain of the critic's antipathy to mere sensationalism. It is a quality that is attainable by the least gifted writer and acceptable to the least critical reader; and, unlike the higher qualities of literature, which beget in the reader an increased receptiveness and more subtle appreciation, it creates, as do drugs and stimulants, a tolerance which has to be met by an increase of the dose. The entertainments of the cinema have to be conducted on a scale of continually increasing sensationalism. The wonders that thrilled at first become commonplace, and must be reinforced by marvels yet more astonishing. Incident must be piled on incident, climax on climax, until any kind of construction becomes impossible. So, too, in literature. In the newspaper serial of the conventional type, each instalment of a couple of thousand words, or less, must wind up with a thrilling climax, blandly ignored at the opening of the next instalment; while that *ne plus ultra* of wild sensationalism, the film novel, in its extreme form is no more than a string of astonishing incidents, unconnected by any intelligible scheme, each incident an independent "thrill," unexplained, unprepared for, devoid alike of antecedents and consequences.

Some productions of the latter type are put forth in the guise of detective stories, with which they apparently tend to be confused by some critics. They are then characterized by the presentation of a crime—often in impossible circumstances which are never accounted for—followed by a vast amount of rushing to and fro of detectives or unofficial investigators in motor cars, aeroplanes, or motor boats, with a liberal display of revolvers or automatic pistols and a succession of hair-raising adventures. If any conclusion is reached, it is quite unconvincing, and the interest of the story to its appropriate reader is in the incidental matter, and not in the plot. But the application of the term "detective story" to works of this kind is misleading, for in the essential qualities of the type of fiction properly so designated they are entirely deficient. Let us now consider what those qualities are.

The distinctive quality of a detective story, in which it differs from all other types of fiction, is that the satisfaction that it offers to the reader is primarily an intellectual satisfaction. This is not to say that it need be deficient in the other qualities appertaining to good fiction: in grace of diction, in humour, in interesting characterization, in picturesqueness of setting or in emotional presentation. On the contrary, it should possess all these qualities. It should be an interesting story, well and vivaciously told. But whereas in other fiction these are the primary, paramount qualities, in detective fiction they are secondary and subordinate to the intellectual interest, to which they must be, if necessary, sacrificed. The entertainment that the connoisseur looks for is an exhibition of mental gymnastics in which he is invited to take part; and the excellence of the entertainment must be judged by the completeness with which it satisfies the expectations of the type of reader to whom it is addressed.

Thus, assuming that good detective fiction must be good fiction in general terms, we may dismiss those qualities which it should possess in common with all other works of imagination and give our attention to those qualities in which it differs from them and which give to it its special character. I have said that the satisfaction which it is designed to yield to the reader is primarily intellectual, and we may now consider in somewhat more detail the exact nature of the satisfaction demanded and the way in which it can best be supplied. And first we may ask: What are the characteristics of the representative reader? To what kind of person is a carefully constructed detective story especially addressed?

We have seen that detective fiction has a wide popularity. The general reader, however, is apt to be uncritical. He reads impartially the bad and the good, with no very clear perception of the difference, at least in the technical construction. The real connoisseurs, who avowedly prefer this type of fiction to all others, and who read it with close and critical attention, are to be found among men of the definitely intellectual class: theologians, scholars, lawyers, and to a less extent, perhaps, doctors and men of science. Judging by the letters which I have received from time to time, the enthusiast *par excellence* is the clergyman of a studious and scholarly habit.

Now the theologian, the scholar and the lawyer have a common characteristic: they are all men of a subtle type of mind. They find a pleasure in intricate arguments, in dialectical contests, in which the matter to be proved is usually of less consideration than the method of proving it. The pleasure is yielded by the argument itself and tends to be proportionate to the intricacy of the proof. The disputant enjoys the mental exercise, just as a muscular man enjoys particular kinds of physical exertion. But the satisfaction yielded by an argument is dependent upon a strict conformity with logical methods, upon freedom from fallacies of reasoning, and especially upon freedom from any ambiguities as to the data.

By schoolboys, street-corner debaters, and other persons who are ignorant of the principles of discussion, debates are commonly conducted by means of what we may call "argument by assertion." Each disputant seeks to overwhelm his opponent by pelting him with statements of alleged fact, each of which the other disputes, and replies by discharging a volley of counterstatements, the truth of which is promptly denied. Thus the argument collapses in a chaos of conflicting assertions. The method of the skilled dialectician is exactly the opposite of this. He begins by making sure of the matter in dispute and by establishing agreement with his adversary on the fundamental data. Theological arguments are usually based upon propositions admitted as true by both parties; and the arguments of counsel are commonly concerned, not with questions of fact, but with the consequences deducible from evidence admitted equally by both sides.

Thus the intellectual satisfaction of an argument is conditional on the complete establishment of the data. Disputes on questions of fact are of little, if any, intellectual interest; but in any case an argument—an orderly train of reasoning—cannot begin until the data have been clearly set forth and agreed upon by both parties. This very obvious truth is continually lost sight of by authors. Plots, i.e., arguments, are frequently based upon alleged "facts"—physical, chemical, and other—which the educated reader knows to be untrue, and of which the untruth totally invalidates conclusions drawn from them and thus destroys the intellectual interest of the argument.

The other indispensable factor is freedom from fallacies of reasoning. The conclusion must emerge truly and inevitably from the premises; it must be the only possible conclusion, and must leave the competent reader in no doubt as to its unimpeachable truth.

It is here that detective stories most commonly fail. They tend to be pervaded by logical fallacies, and especially by the fallacy of the undistributed middle term. The conclusion reached by the gifted investigator, and offered by him as inevitable, is seen by the reader to be merely one of a number of possible alternatives. The effect when the author's "must have been" has to be corrected by the reader into "might have been" is one of anti-climax. The promised and anticipated demonstration peters out into a mere suggestion; the argument is left in the air and the reader is balked of the intellectual satisfaction which he was seeking.

Having glanced at the nature of the satisfaction sought by the reader, we may now examine the structure of a detective story and observe the means employed to furnish that satisfaction. On the general fictional qualities of such a story we need not enlarge excepting to contest the prevalent belief that detective fiction possesses no such qualities. Apart from a sustained love interest—for which there is usually no room—a detective novel need not, and should not, be inferior in narrative interest or literary workmanship to any other work of fiction. Interests which conflict with the main theme and hinder its clear exposition are evidently inadmissible; but humour, picturesque setting, vivid characterization and even emotional episodes are not only desirable on aesthetic grounds, but, if skilfully used, may be employed to distract the reader's attention at critical moments in place of the nonsensical "false clues" and other exasperating devices by which writers too often seek to confuse the issues. *The Mystery of Edwin Drood* shows us the superb fictional quality that is possible in a detective story from the hand of a master.

Turning now to the technical side, we note that the plot of a detective novel is, in effect, an argument conducted under the guise of fiction. But it is a peculiar form of argument. The problem having been stated, the data for its solution are presented inconspicuously and in a sequence purposely dislocated so as to conceal their connexion; and the reader's task is to collect the data, to rearrange them in their correct logical sequence and ascertain their relations, when the solution of the problem should at once become obvious. The construction thus tends to fall into four stages: (1) statement of the problem; (2) production of the data for its solution ("clues"); (3) the discovery, i.e., completion of the inquiry by the investigator and declaration by him of the solution; (4) proof of the solution by an exposition of the evidence.

1. The problem is usually concerned with a crime, not because a crime is an attractive subject, but because it forms the most natural occasion for an investigation of the kind required. For the same reason—suitability—crime against the person is more commonly adopted than crime against property; and murder— actual, attempted or suspected—is usually the most suitable of all. For the villain is the player on the other side; and since we want him to be a desperate player, the stakes must be appropriately high. A capital crime gives us an adversary who is playing for his life, and who consequently furnishes the best subject for dramatic treatment.

2. The body of the work should be occupied with the telling of the story, in the course of which the data, or "clues," should be produced as inconspicuously as possible, but clearly and without ambiguity in regard to their essentials. The author should be scrupulously fair in his conduct of the game. Each card as it is played should be set down squarely, face upwards, in full view of the reader. Under no circumstances should there be any deception as to the facts. The reader should be quite clear as to what he may expect as true. In stories of the older type, the middle action is filled out with a succession of false clues and with the fixing of suspicion first on one character, then on another, and again on a third, and so on. The clues are patiently followed, one after another, and found to lead nowhere. There is feverish activity, but no result. All this is wearisome to the reader and is, in my opinion, bad technique. My practice is to avoid false clues en-

tirely and to depend on keeping the reader occupied with the narrative. If the ice should become uncomfortably thin, a dramatic episode will distract the reader's attention and carry him safely over the perilous spot. Devices to confuse and mislead the reader are bad practice. They deaden the interest, and they are quite unnecessary; the reader can always be trusted to mislead himself, no matter how plainly the data are given. Some years ago I devised, as an experiment, an inverted detective story in two parts.* The first part was a minute and detailed description of a crime, setting forth the antecedents, motives, and all attendant circumstances. The reader had seen the crime committed, knew all about the criminal, and was in possession of all the facts. It would have seemed that there was nothing left to tell. But I calculated that the reader would be so occupied with the crime that he would overlook the evidence. And so it turned out. The second part, which described the investigation of the crime, had to most readers the effect of new matter. All the facts were known; but their evidential quality had not been recognized.

This failure of the reader to perceive the evidential value of facts is the foundation on which detective fiction is built. It may generally be taken that the author may exhibit his facts fearlessly provided only that he exhibits them separately and unconnected. And the more boldly he displays the data, the greater will be the intellectual interest of the story. For the tacit understanding of the author with the reader is that the problem is susceptible of solution by the latter by reasoning from the facts given; and such solution should be actually possible. Then the data should be produced as early in the story as is practicable. The reader should have a body of evidence to consider while the tale is telling. The production of a leading fact near the end of the book is unfair to the reader, while the introduction of capital evidence—such as that of an eye-witness—at the extreme end is radically bad technique, amounting to a breach of the implied covenant with the reader.

3. The "discovery," i.e., the announcement by the investigator of the conclusion reached by him, brings the inquiry formally to an end. It is totally inadmissible thereafter to introduce any new

---

* *The Case of Oscar Brodski.*

matter. The reader is given to understand that he now has before him the evidence and the conclusion, and that the latter is contained in the former. If it is not, the construction has failed, and the reader has been cheated. The "discovery" will usually come as a surprise to the reader and will thus form the dramatic climax of the story, but it is to be noted that the dramatic quality of the climax is strictly dependent on the intellectual conviction which accompanies it. This is frequently overlooked, especially by general novelists who experiment in detective fiction. In their eagerness to surprise the reader, they forget that he has also to be convinced. A literary friend of mine, commenting on a particularly conclusive detective story, declared that "the rigid demonstration destroyed the artistic effect." But the rigid demonstration was the artistic effect. The entire dramatic effect of the climax of a detective story is due to the sudden recognition by the reader of the significance of a number of hitherto uncomprehended facts; or if such recognition should not immediately occur, the effect of the climax becomes suspended until it is completed in the final stage.

4. Proof of the solution. This is peculiar to "detective" construction. In all ordinary novels, the climax, or denouement, finishes the story, and any continuation is anti-climax. But a detective story has a dual character. There is the story, with its dramatic interest, and enclosed in it, so to speak, is the logical problem; and the climax of the former may leave the latter apparently unsolved. It is then the duty of the author, through the medium of the investigator, to prove the solution by an analysis and exposition of the evidence. He has to demonstrate to the reader that the conclusion emerged naturally and reasonably from the facts known to him, and that no other conclusion was possible.

If it is satisfactorily done, this is to the critical reader usually the most interesting part of the book; and it is the part by which he—very properly—judges the quality of the whole work. Too often it yields nothing but disappointment and a sense of anti-climax. The author is unable to solve his own problem. Acting on the pernicious advice of the pilot in the old song to "Fear not, but trust in Providence," he has piled up his mysteries in the hope of being able to find a plausible explanation; and now, when he comes to settle his account with the reader, his logical assets are nil. What claims to be a demonstration turns out to be a mere specious attempt to persuade the reader that the inexplicable has been explained; that the fortunate guesses of an inspired investigator are examples of genuine reasoning. A typical instance of this kind of anti-climax occurs in Poe's "Murders in the Rue Morgue" when Dupin follows the unspoken thoughts of his companion and joins in at the appropriate moment. The reader is astonished and marvels how such an apparently impossible feat could have been performed. Then Dupin explains; but his explanation is totally unconvincing, and the impossibility remains. The reader has had his astonishment for nothing. It cannot be too much emphasized that to the critical reader the quality in a detective story which takes precedence of all others is conclusiveness. It is the quality which, above all others, yields that intellectual satisfaction that the reader seeks; and it is the quality which is the most difficult to attain, and which costs more than any other in care and labour to the author.

Crime and Detection
(1926)
By E. M. Wrong

With the publication of a collection of short stories called Crime
and Detection (*London & New York: Oxford University Press,
1926*), *detective story criticism finally left off apologizing and took
the offensive. Not only was this anthology the first on the subject
to be compiled in accordance with critical principles; its succinct
Introduction, here reproduced, by E. M. Wrong (1889–1928)
marked the earliest attempt at a purposive historical and analytical survey and summation of the medium. Together with the essays by Willard Huntington Wright and Dorothy Sayers which
follow, it constituted for several years substantially all the scholarship on the subject that was to be found between covers. Unlike
his two confrères, who were themselves detective story writers,
of the first rank, Mr. Wrong was a layman. The son of the Canadian scholar G. M. Wrong, he was by profession an historian, a
Fellow and Tutor of Magdalen College, Oxford; he died at the
untimely age of thirty-nine. So far as is known, the present essay
was his sole contribution, critical or creative, to the literature of
detection. If there are often wide gaps in the discussion, if the
consideration of the subject seems almost exclusively British, it
must be remembered that Mr. Wrong was primarily introducing
a collection of stories chosen for English readers, and that when
he made his study the Golden Age of the American detective story
was only just beginning.*

THE DETECTIVE story is of respectable antiquity if we judge it by
its remote forebears, though it is recent times only that have made

it into a branch of art. Two early examples lie in the Apocrypha: in one, Daniel's cross-examination saves Susanna from the false witness of lecherous elders; in the other, the same Daniel establishes the deceitfulness of Bel's priests. The modern reader, accustomed to subtlety of plot and tangled clues, finds these tales elementary, for the crimes that they record are so obvious that Daniel unravels them by the simplest of methods. Yet, as the pace of the detective story must always be set by the criminal and not by the detective, and since Daniel did solve both cases submitted to him, we are probably justified in regarding him as the remote ancestor of Sherlock Holmes and Dr. Thorndyke.

A story of crime and of unusual methods to discover the culprit can be found in Herodotus. An enterprising Egyptian with his brother robbed the royal treasury by a secret entrance; the brother was laid by the heel in a trap, whereon the hero cut off his head to prevent identification. A few days later he fuddled the guardians of the body with drink, stole and buried the corpse. He ended by escaping from the king's daughter turned prostitute to extort a confession; he was pardoned and married the princess, having proved himself a bolder and more successful, though possibly a cruder, Raffles than any of recent times. Here are the twin themes of detection and crime sketched in their essentials. Why was there no flowering under the Roman Empire, when an urban population sought amusement in the butchery of the circus, and might have been more cheaply appeased by stories of law-breaking and discovery? Perhaps a faulty law of evidence was to blame, for detectives cannot flourish until the public has an idea of what constitutes proof, and while a common criminal procedure is arrest, torture, confession, and death.

Whatever the cause, the art of detective fiction lay for centuries untouched, and its effective history is crowded into the last eighty years. Defoe would have made an admirable detective writer had he been drawn to the subject, for his love of piling detail on detail would have concealed all relevant clues from the ordinary reader while leaving them in plain view the whole time. Balzac flirted effectively with crime in Vautrin, but his criminal was much abler than his police. Our ancestors indeed took a great interest in homicide. The stir made by Eugene Aram, by Burke

and Hare, shows that, as does De Quincey's famous essay on murder. But it was sensation rather than reasoning that they sought,
and crude sensation is better provided by real crimes than by imaginary. So the detective story was left for modern times to develop into an art with a technique and a code of its own.

There are still some, though fewer than a few years ago, who
deny that it is or can become an art. They stand in their contention partly on the illiteracy and bad logic of many detective
stories, partly on the nature of the theme. But artistic achievement must be judged by the best, not by the average, or else the
popularity of any form that attracts incompetent practitioners
would lower its place. Robert Montgomery injured not poetry but
himself. As to the theme, the detective story is obviously not concerned with any very exalted actions, but *The Ring and the Book*
finds its subject in the Old Bailey of Rome, and Agamemnon's
quarrel with Achilles did not spring from lofty motives. Some
criticize detective fiction because it is not realistic, gives inadequate scope for character drawing, looks chiefly to one thing only,
and that mechanism. That is its nature, but there can be an art
of plot as well as an art of the mimicry of life; art is not limited
to realism but can show itself in diverse forms.

Detective fiction as we know it begins with Poe. When one
studies the slightness, the lack of effort, in the three stories that
Poe wrote between 1841 and 1845 and then turns to the multiply-
ing progeny of his invention, the effect is impressive indeed. Poe
set for all time one of the two lines on which the detective story
has grown—a private investigator chronicled by an unimaginative friend; he did this in three stories only, and then he either
wearied of the game or his audience was unresponsive, and he
turned from the rich pocket of gold into which he had dipped
his hand to other and more barren fields. He had begun one of
the two orthodox traditions of to-day, but it was not developed
and made popular for over forty years—not in fact till 1887, when
Sir Arthur Conan Doyle published *A Study in Scarlet*.

It was the other and less rigorous form that flourished till Sherlock Holmes was to revive the Dupin canon, and its leading English follower was Wilkie Collins. In 1860 *The Woman in White*
made a happy connexion between villainy and detection; in 1868

came *The Moonstone,* more orthodox because more of a pure puzzle. The criminal theme attracted Dickens, worn-out though he was with popular lecturing, and in the autumn of 1869 he began what some regard as potentially his greatest novel. The first number of *Edwin Drood* appeared in April 1870; two months later Dickens was dead, and his mystery had not got as far as the discovery of the corpse. There are some who even deny that there is a corpse to be discovered, and speculation rages still over the identity of Datchery. Whatever the secret, every lover of detective fiction would sooner have the unwritten chapters than all the lost books of Livy.

Meanwhile a considerable development went on in France. Gaboriau wrote his police tales between 1866 and 1873, Fortuné du Boisgobey took up the theme between 1872 and 1889. Stories of crime became common in England and America largely, it appears, through the influence of Collins and Gaboriau. That they were popular in the 'eighties, even before Sherlock Holmes, Anna Katharine Green's stories show, and if further proof is wanted it can be found in Stevenson's unsurpassed romance, *The Wrong Box.* We read there that Gideon Forsyth had written a detective tale called *Who Put Back the Clock?,* and that only three copies of it had passed into circulation—if the British Museum can be called circulation when the work is secreted behind a false catalogue entry. Now Forsyth's way of disposing of a troublesome grand piano does not stamp him as a man of great penetration of mind, and we know moreover that his attempt at musical composition was an echo of "Tommy, Make Room For Your Uncle"; he had in fact no originality. He would assuredly not have tried the detective form of composition had it not been popular. *The Wrong Box* appeared in 1889, and Forsyth's literary adventure must have been at least a year or two earlier, perhaps in 1887, the great year when Sherlock Holmes broke upon the world.

Sir Arthur Conan Doyle's name must stand, in the history of the detective story, only a little lower than Poe's. He wedded plots nearly as elaborate as Gaboriau's to the methods and tradition of Poe; from the marriage was produced Sherlock Holmes, to become in a few years a universally recognized character of English speech. *Vixere fortes ante Agamemnona,* but we have forgotten them, and tend to think of the pre-Holmes detectives as of the pre-Shakespearian drama; to call them precursors only. Holmes was a really great achievement. From him dates the expansion of the last thirty years, and the crystallizing of one type of detective story. The canon is not exclusive but it is fixed; a friend of the detective tells the tale, as he did in Poe; he sees or can see all that the detective does, but never understands what deductions to draw from the facts. Thus the chief relevant incidents are in reality concealed from the reader though there is an ostentatious parade of openness. The detective's friend acts in the dual capacity of very average reader and of Greek chorus; he comments freely on what he does not understand.

For a time it seemed that this might become the only accepted form of detective fiction. Mr. Morrison followed it in Martin Hewitt, softening the detective's eccentricities, making him more of a business man, and giving him a less striking coadjutor than Dr. Watson. Dr. Austin Freeman took the same line with Thorndyke, improving on Sherlock's science, raising the narrator to average intelligence, and providing mysteries more cunning and obscure. Miss Christie's Poirot follows the tradition, though he distrusts the laboratory and relies on "the little grey cells" of his brain; he is assisted by the most admirably foolish of all Watsons, Captain Hastings. But some writers have revolted against the domination of a Boswell-Watson, and have preferred to tell their stories in the third person. A school has arisen modelled more on the Collins-Gaboriau tradition than on that of Dupin-Holmes, and the technique of the art has of late widened considerably.

This second school divides itself unequally into two parts. Most of its adherents concern themselves with external clues; industry and mobility take the place of the instantaneous deduction loved of Holmes; Mr. Mason's Hanaud is a fine example of this kind, though he is like Holmes in one way—while his actions are not described by his admirer, only such actions are recorded as his admirer has seen. Better examples of the new mode are the painstaking sleuths of Mr. Crofts, who by careful inquiry and a lavish use of transport facilities explode the most detailed alibis known to fiction—alibis moreover that might easily go unquestioned in court. Mr. Bentley's Trent worked chiefly on similar lines, although he refrained from arresting the suspect because his judgement of character made him come to doubt the evidence of his eyes.

A less common and rather more subtle type is that of the intuitionist detective. England knows only two of these worth mention, Mr. Chesterton's Father Brown and Mr. Bailey's Mr. Fortune. Father Brown needs no lengthy method of proving guilt for he can guess the secret of the crime from his wide knowledge of sin. Mr. Fortune feels atmosphere more keenly than any other detective, and is marvellously accurate in his judgement of character. These men leap to conclusions while others limp behind. Those who like them like them very much indeed, even though they admit that many of the crimes discovered by Father Brown were impossible, and think Mr. Fortune perhaps too ready to assume the responsibility of granting life or death. They are at any rate the most brilliant talkers among modern detectives, not only in what they say but also in their pregnant silences.

Some other detectives share their intuitional ability, though none possess it in as high degree as these two. Miss Christie's Poirot, Mr. Mason's Hanaud, are at times helped by it; so is Mr. Bramah's Max Carrados, who combines in one person all the remarkable abilities of all the blind men of history. Mr. Milne's Antony Gillingham has a visual memory that brings almost the same result as intuition. Yet all these last depend mainly on external things, and are detectives of exploration rather than of instinct.

Forsyth found, Stevenson tells us, that "it is the difficulty of the police romance that the reader is always a person of such vastly greater ingenuity than the writer." This remains the cardinal problem, but it has been fairly met and defeated many times. Technique has improved so that things once permissible can be no longer allowed, and there is now a kind of code of what is fair play to the reader. Yet even so the old problem is still too often evaded. Clues are given that are meant only to mislead, and whose existence is never explained. Criminal and victim, one or both, will behave as no sane person would; corpses turn out to be alive, and secret passages provide a surfeit of alibis. Father Knox's *The Viaduct Murder* was difficult to solve largely through improbable false clues, concealed passages, and inept action by the murderer which made his actions unlike those of the ordinary sensible man; eventually he was hanged through his own stupidity. That happens, it is true, often enough in real life, but art should be better than actuality.

The detective story has now joined the novel of realism and the tale of passion as fit and proper reading for evenings and holidays, and its most devoted adherents are found principally among the highly educated. Partly this is because the modern age prides itself on its ingenuity. It enjoys mechanism and is attracted by the neatness of a good mystery. Economy, tidiness, completeness— these are qualities possessed by every good tale of detection, and they are qualities conspicuously lacking in some forms now much cried up, especially in Russian novels and English *vers libre*. Reacting against works of art with little beginning and no end but only a yawning middle, and in some measure rebelling against the discrepancies so common in real life, we go for solace to the detective of fiction. His appeal is chiefly intellectual, but there must be some emotion in it too, or else our sympathy might lie as much with the hunted as with the avenger of society. Yet the heart must be less moved than the brain or our pleasure will be the less.

A detective story involves a problem which must nearly always be criminal, the guilty man must be discovered by the detective and brought to justice unless his breach of the law was technical rather than moral. Commonly the matter is not taken beyond arrest, and this for various reasons. Sometimes the chain of evidence that satisfies a reader would fail to convince a jury, or might not even stand the rules of cross-examination; when this seems likely the criminal sometimes commits suicide once his capture is certain. Even when this objection to a trial does not exist an author seldom brings his culprit into court. The atmosphere of a trial would not accord well with the feelings roused by the chase, and the sight of a remorseless system grinding to pieces the man who has, after all, provided half our entertainment, might swing our sympathy to his side. Even arrest is dispensed with at times; a confession is enough for Father Brown, who is concerned more with laying bare the heart of man than with the crude matter of punishment. In fact the detective is not often a sociologist, and tends to shun the drab side of crime, its atonement. The number of criminals in fiction who come to their end by accident or suicide is very great, and points to some laxity by the detective after he has made his arrest.

Of the crimes to be detected murder must always come first, for it is more mysterious and dramatic than any other. Yet one cannot hold that every detective story must centre round homicide, for that would rule out many of our best stories. In the early days of detective fiction murders and attempted murders were much rarer than they are to-day. Only one of Poe's three tales was about murder, and the killers of Marie Roget remained in fact undiscovered. Sherlock Holmes and Martin Hewitt were more often consulted about small crimes than are the chief modern practitioners. Time has in fact exalted murder, which used to be only one of several offences, to a position of natural supremacy.

There are good reasons for this. What we want in our detective fiction is not a semblance of real life, where murder is infrequent and petty larceny common, but deep mystery and conflicting clues. Murder has removed one party to the secret, and so is essentially more mysterious than theft. Moreover, it involves an intenser motive than any other peace-time activity: the drama is keyed high from the start for the murderer is playing for the highest stake he has, and can reasonably be expected to tangle the evidence even to the committing of a second murder. The law places murder in a category by itself, not necessarily because it is more wicked than other crimes—the murder of a blackmailer appeals to us, at least in fiction, as a beneficent act—but because it is more desperate and final. When the death of a man is compassed either the victim or the slayer is generally a villain, and either the motives or incidents of the deed, save when it is due to animal passion or to drink, are nearly always interesting. The motive for robbery, covetousness, is almost too common; most of us know it well. Hatred that is strong enough to bring murder is familiar enough to be intelligible to nearly every one, yet far enough from our normal experience to let us watch as detached observers, for we do not feel that it is our own crimes that are unmasked. So for many reasons murder is advisable, though not necessary. The author, if he withholds its appeal, must give us compensation in some other way. This is admirably done in Mr. Croft's *The Ponson Case,* where three excellent alibis make accidental death more than tolerable.

One temptation the detective novelist does well to avoid; many have walked into it and few have escaped with their artistry unblemished. It is that of including in the same book a Napoleon of crime and a Wellington of detection, drawing a master-villain who controls a huge organization of iniquity and impartially directs robbery, forgery, blackmail, and murder. It is an attractive theme, for it provides an explanation of the most improbable crimes, since anything may be part of a campaign against civilization. Yet it does not do, for all that. A small objection is that a man with the intellectual resources of the master-criminal would naturally take to politics or business rather than to crime. A greater one is that we never have the organization or the motives of the captain of evil exposed to us; we see him only in sporadic operation and near his fall, his true greatness we have to take on faith. Greatest of all is the fact that were the enemy the intellectual prodigy he is painted, he would begin operations by snuffing out the detective before the detective knew of his existence. Moriarty could have had Holmes murdered a number of times if he had not stayed his hand until Holmes's plans were nearly complete. In fact one suspects Holmes, whose reasoning was not always perfect, of exaggerating both the power and brains of the Professor of Mathematics. And lastly, the detective who fights a universal provider of crime has to make more use than is quite proper of the official police. The final struggle is one of organization against organization; it is never really described for us, and we get instead violent but often clumsy attempts to kill the detective when the time for that is over, and the criminal's real danger has shifted from Baker Street to Scotland Yard.

Criticism of the Moriarty theme does not mean that the criminal must play a lone hand and be passive once his work is accomplished. He may have a gang, provided it does not grow into a departmental store, and he may attempt the life of the detective.

A counter-attack makes the problem dynamic rather than static, and gives life to the story. The greatest master of tales where the criminal fights to the end is Dr. Austin Freeman: in *The Silent Witness* he achieved a unique success, an unsuspected man fearing that his identity was known made detection possible by his needless struggle. Such a war is better than a tame pursuit.

Tales of giant conspiracy against civilization share many of the defects of the master-criminal theme. Like it they have a pleasant side—they make the detective run for his life. We may get a little tired of the security of our detectives who take the money while the criminal runs the risk. So we are glad to see him fleeing either because his particular Moriarty is after him or because he has trespassed on some vast design against the state or society in general. A good chase described by the fugitive, though it falls a little outside the ordinary scope of detective fiction, is in some ways better than the plain narrative of pursuit, and Mr. Buchan's *The Thirty-Nine Steps* and *The Power House* contain such hunts in classic perfection. Possibly it is unfair to complain that the revelation of such mysteries when it comes is never quite up to the chase. The spy story has been well developed on the lines of pursuit of the pursuer before and during the war; when peace made the Teuton innocuous, author and reader turned for similar enjoyment to Russian communist agents. They have on the whole brought a poor return. We knew what the spy wanted, he had an intelligible purpose; but these new conspirators, supposedly subtle and dangerous, never quite convince. What do they hope for? Their organization is generally far too large for their secret, which in itself never is convincing. In an attempt to explain conduct that is sometimes foolish, always unusual, the author may tell us that these villains work from a pure passion for "evil," it is for this that they abduct, assassinate, and rob. But this "evil" remains inexplicable, and we can only guess its power from the dark deeds of its apostles. So intellect though reluctant will creep in and complain that the mystery does not explain the action. It is, one may remark, time for a pause in subtle Bolshevik plots; the other side should have a chance, and there is room for a tale of the unmasking of a dastardly capitalist intrigue by some bright spark in the labour movement. Mr. Wells in *When the*

Sleeper Awakes approaches such a theme, and Mr. Baines in *The Black Circle* comes very near it.

From the habits of the great detectives of fiction it is possible to draw some general rules, provided they are not made too dogmatic to cramp genius. The relations of an investigator to the police have varied a good deal since Poe. Dupin and Holmes were private citizens with an extreme contempt for their salaried rivals. Dupin retired or died soon after his failure to solve the Marie Roget problem; Holmes continued in occasional practice till 1914, and gradually established a more friendly relationship with Scotland Yard. The greatest detective now in business, Thorndyke, works freely with the police, and has always been willing to use them as his instruments. Mr. Bailey's Fortune has gone further and become himself an official, though it is not easy to define his exact position; he has a freer hand than most civil servants enjoy. Mr. Mason's Hanaud goes further still and has never engaged in genuine private practice. The tendency is clear, it is towards greater laxity and away from a rigid convention. Yet the detective should be careful, lest he become swallowed up in the government machine and lose the freedom to take a case when and as he will.

When the tale follows the Poe canon and the story is told by the detective's Boswell, certain obvious advantages follow. The narrative of an eye-witness attains a dramatic quality more easily than does an impersonal record. The clues can, as we have seen, be described not as they really are, but as they appear to a man of average, or generally less than average, intelligence. This parade of openness pleases while it deceives. Yet if there is a Boswell he must be present at all times, and this may prove inconvenient. The intuitionist detective like Father Brown or Mr. Fortune would only be hampered by him. It is true that they often need companions, partly as foil, partly to share in the conversation. But they get assistance as it is required, Fortune from the police, Father Brown from Flambeau, who was a prosperous thief till he reformed and became an unsuccessful detective. Mr. Bramah's Max Carrados generally operates with a private investigator called Carlyle, who is competent in a normal divorce case but quite at sea against subtlety.

The habit of running in couples, generally very ill-matched couples, at first sight appears strange. Why should a client seek out Holmes in some very private affair, and never object to Watson's presence at the most intimate revelations—guessing (as he must) that Watson's help will be negligible? But man in general likes telling his secrets to an interested audience, and there is more difficulty in checking confidences than in extorting them. Moreover, a great detective's help can only be obtained on his terms, and if he insists on companionship he must have it.

Dupin began the practice of instantaneous deduction; Holmes continued it, became over-confident, and was rather lucky that his occasional *non sequiturs* avoided exposure. A criminal who had grasped his methods could have defeated him. Holmes knew which way a bicycle had gone because the back wheel's impression was deeper than that of the front wheel; the fact is true but, save possibly on a hill, contributes nothing to the question of direction. Holmes guessed that two persons, not three, had drunk out of three glasses because all the lees were in the third, but two clever men could have drunk from all three and avoided this, or three might thus have masqueraded as two. Many have discerned a weakening in Holmes's powers as he grew older, and attributed this to a fall over a cliff at the hands of Moriarty. But in fact he never had such a fall, and if he deteriorated it was probably through his long addiction to cocaine.

What one loves in Holmes, in truth, is not his logic but his habits and his colleague. No detective has been so successfully eccentric as he was. None has had as satisfactory a companion as Watson, who is not quite the fool he is often thought. Once, as Mr. Vernon Rendall points out,* Watson deceived Holmes and induced him at St. Luke's College to detect an imaginary bit of cribbing for a scholarship examination. Watson is in fact a remarkable person, and his stories, like Boswell's *Johnson,* are the records of not one but two great men. His brain remains consistently a trifle below the average; his restraint, devotion, and character are constantly above it, and his medical practice is obliging if not lucrative.

Holmes dabbled in science, but his knowledge therein bears the

---

* Vernon Rendall, *The London Nights of Belsize,* 1917, pp. 147–57.

same relation to Thorndyke's as his pocket magnifying-glass to the latter's research case. In Thorndyke we have complete use of all the resources of the laboratory, coupled with a logic that is safer than that of Holmes because it is less cock-sure. The chief blemish in Thorndyke is the deplorable habit his associates possess of falling in love in the course of an investigation. The record of detection should in general be as cold as a scientific experiment, and to mix romance with it is in some measure to spoil it. A detective ought to remain single or at least not obtrude his own family affairs on us, and the same applies to the victim, the criminal, and the associate, save only when a love affair forms an integral part of the mystery. For in a detective story the true beauty is in mass and line, not in irrelevant ornament without structural value: that should be left for the realists to exploit.

Few other detectives need specific mention, but it may be worth pointing out that Miss Christie's Poirot has twice been mistaken on a point of English law. He thinks that arrest for a crime relieves a man who is discharged of all further risk, and he may find his tasks easier in future if he learns that only trial and acquittal have this result.

One last problem remains: should a detective tell all, lay bare his clues as they are found, with all their significance, or may he keep them secret till the revelation scene when all is made clear? Real life could give but one answer; the detective would have to explain the position from day to day, else with his death from murder or accident the fears of the criminal would perish. But in fiction it is another matter, and almost the only detectives who take us fully into their confidence are those of Mr. Crofts. Holmes was extremely secretive; Thorndyke makes a parade of openness but keeps his special knowledge, on which the meaning of his clues depends, to himself; Hanaud not only conceals all that he can, but even starts every quest with some special information not known to the reader. Father Brown may only see what his companions see, but it is by no means described as he sees it. Lord Gorell's Humblethorne and Evelyn Temple * let us know what they know as they learn it, and so to some extent does Mr. Bentley's Trent, but all these investigators were proved wrong, so

* *In the Night.*

their honesty was a subtle kind of deception. If the rules of art are made by the artists, a detective is entitled to secrecy provided it is not too flagrant.

The detective story has proved capable of high development and has become a definite art; the same cannot be said of the tale of crime with the criminal as hero. Why is there this difference? Why is Holmes a greater figure than the late Raffles?

There are several reasons. A detective thrives on difficulties, cannot be great without them, but does not make his own. A criminal is in a different position. The better criminal he is, the more thoroughly he plans his campaign, every chance is allowed for, all goes smoothly, and as a result there should be no story. An account of his greatest successes would be as even and undramatic as the life of a stockbroker. Therefore many crime stories have by the nature of things to deal with episodes that should never have occurred were the criminal a true superman; the author may cry 'Here is a great though misguided intellect,' but our reason stirs uneasily. Then there is the question of morality. Perhaps art in general should have no moral purpose, but the art of the detective story has one and must have; it seeks to justify the law and to bring retribution on the guilty. The criminal must be unmasked, the detective represents good and must triumph. To make a hero of the criminal is to reverse the moral law, which is after all based on common sense, for crime is not in fact generous and open but mean. Robin Hood may have robbed the rich and given to the poor, but his accounts were never audited, and the proportion of his charity to his thefts remains obscure. Raffles stole principally from unpleasant people, but steal he did; not even success can make robbery appeal to us as a truly noble career. Is the criminal then to try other crimes than theft? Blackmail hardly provides a fitting career for a hero, and we are driven back on murder. Now it is possible for murderers to show courage and resource, to be less mean than the pickpocket or forger. But murder to be successful must be selfish, the victim cannot be given a chance, so a narrative of successful murders, like a narrative of successful robbery, leaves us at the end with a bad taste in our mouth. If each murder is to be done from the highest motives (as those by Mr. Wallace's Four Just Men) it will not be easy for there to be enough of them to keep our interest and approval. Even the Four Just Men began public life by killing a fairly harmless Secretary of State to prevent the Cabinet, of which he was but one member, from carrying a bill through Parliament. We might wink at this if we disapproved of the bill, but can it be called justice? Was this the only way? After all, if we are to regard murder as just, we must credit the murderer with an omniscience that we deny to our courts of law. Even if he thinks himself omniscient has he any business to act on his own opinion, regardless of the consequences to the innocent?

It is probably for some such reasons that the crime story has on the whole been a failure as compared with the tale of detection. Even Raffles, supposed to be a Bayard of crime, did many mean things, and caused great unhappiness to innocent policemen and amiable wives. If we analyse him we find that he took to crime because he preferred it to honest work, for it is futile to assure us that a man of his abilities could not have supported himself in a more orthodox way. Morally Raffles stood much lower than the Bunny he despised and led astray; Bunny was not an admirable citizen; but he had as great courage as his leader and seducer and far greater unselfishness. Mr. Barry Pain's Constantine Dix was a better man than Raffles for he had the decency to play a lone hand, and to spend his non-professional hours in trying to stop others walking down the road he had taken. Yet even he, a good man save for his profession, does not quite do as a hero. In fact the tale of crime is best seen from the detective's angle.

The Great Detective Stories
(1927)
By Willard Huntington Wright

Willard Huntington Wright (1888–1939) brought to detective story criticism a mind and pen trained in professional evaluation of literature and the arts. As "S. S. Van Dine" he was also qualified to speak on the subject as a foremost if controversial American practitioner of the form. But this identity was still a closely guarded secret when, under his legal name, he published his anthology The Great Detective Stories *(New York: Scribner's, 1927) with its detailed historical Introduction, reprinted here. In the early 1920's Wright suffered a severe illness, brought on by overwork in his profession as a critic of the arts. Forbidden by his physician to do any "serious" reading, he lightened the months of a long convalescence by assembling and analyzing a 2,000-volume library of detective fiction and criminology. To this fortuitous circumstance we owe not only the Philo Vance novels by Van Dine but also the essay which follows. Many of Wright's more dogmatic observations—his opposition to all "style" in the detective novel is an extreme case in point—have been invalidated by the passage of time; but this consideration should not be allowed to overshadow his scholarly pioneer work in the historical aspects of the subject.*

I

THERE IS a tendency among modern critics to gauge all novels by a single literary standard—a standard, in fact, which should be applied only to novels that patently seek a niche among the

33

enduring works of imaginative letters. That all novels do not aspire to such exalted company is obvious; and it is manifestly unfair to judge them by a standard their creators deliberately ignored. Novels of sheer entertainment belong in a different category from those written for purposes of intellectual and æsthetic stimulation; for they are fabricated in a spirit of evanescent diversion, and avoid all the deeper concerns of art.

The novel designed purely for entertainment and the literary novel spring, in the main, from quite different impulses. Their objectives have almost nothing in common. The mental attitudes underlying them are antipathetic: one is frankly superficial, the other sedulously profound. They achieve diametrically opposed results; and their appeals are psychologically unrelated; in fact, they are unable to fulfil each other's function; and the reader who, at different times, can enjoy both without intellectual conflict, can never substitute the one for the other. Any attempt to measure them by the same rules is as inconsistent as to criticize a vaudeville performance and the plays of Shakespeare from the same point of view, or to hold a musical comedy to the standards by which we estimate the foremost grand opera. Even Schnitzler's *Anatol* may not be approached in the same critical frame of mind that one brings to Hauptmann's *The Weavers;* and if *The Mikado* or *Pinafore* were held strictly to the musical canons of *Parsifal* or *Die Meistersinger,* they would suffer unjustly. In the graphic arts the same principle holds. Forain and Degas are not to be judged by the æsthetic criteria we apply to Michelangelo's drawings and the paintings of Rubens.

There are four distinct varieties of the "popular," or "light," novel—to wit: the romantic novel (dealing with young love, and ending generally either at the hymeneal altar or with a prenuptial embrace); the novel of adventure (in which physical action and danger are the chief constituents: sea stories, wild-west yarns, odysseys of the African wilds, etc.); the mystery novel (wherein much of the dramatic suspense is produced by hidden forces that are not revealed until the dénouement: novels of diplomatic intrigue, international plottings, secret societies, crime, pseudoscience, specters, and the like); and the detective novel. These types often overlap in content, and at times become so intermingled in subject-matter that one is not quite sure in which category they primarily belong. But though they may borrow devices and appeals from one another, and usurp one another's distinctive material, they follow, in the main, their own special subject, and evolve within their own boundaries.

Of these four kinds of literary entertainment the detective novel is the youngest, the most complicated, the most difficult of construction, and the most distinct. It is, in fact, almost *sui generis,* and, except in its more general structural characteristics, has little in common with its fellows—the romantic, the adventurous, and the mystery novel. In one sense, to be sure, it is a highly specialized offshoot of the last named; but the relationship is far more distant than the average reader imagines.

II

If we are to understand the unique place held in modern letters by the detective novel, we must first endeavor to determine its peculiar appeal: for this appeal is fundamentally unrelated to that of any other variety of fictional entertainment. What, then, constitutes the hold that the detective novel has on all classes of people—even those who would not stoop to read any other kind of "popular" fiction? Why do we find men of high cultural attainments—college professors, statesmen, scientists, philosophers, and men concerned with the graver, more advanced, more intellectual problems of life—passing by all other varieties of best-seller novels, and going to the detective story for diversion and relaxation?

The answer, I believe, is simply this: the detective novel does not fall under the head of fiction in the ordinary sense, but belongs rather in the category of riddles: it is, in fact, a complicated and extended puzzle cast in fictional form. Its widespread popularity and interest are due, at bottom and in essence, to the same factors that give popularity and interest to the cross-word puzzle. Indeed, the structure and mechanism of the cross-word puzzle and of the detective novel are very similar. In each there is a problem to be solved; and the solution depends wholly on mental processes—on analysis, on the fitting together of apparently unrelated parts, on a knowledge of the ingredients, and, in some measure, on guessing. Each is supplied with a series of overlapping clues to guide the solver; and these clues, when fitted into place, blaze the path for future progress. In each, when the final solution is achieved, all the details are found to be woven into a complete, interrelated, and closely knitted fabric.

There is confirmatory evidence of the mechanical impulse that inspires the true detective novel when we consider what might almost be called the dominant intellectual *penchant* of its inventor. Poe, the originator of the modern detective story, was obsessed with the idea of scientific experimentation. His faculty for analysis manifested itself in his reviews and in the technicalities of his poetry; it produced "Maelzel's Chess-Player"; it led him into the speculative ramifications of handwriting idiosyncrasies in "A Chapter on Autography"; it brought forth his exposition of cryptograms and code-writing in "Cryptography"; and it gave birth to his acrostic verses. His four analytic stories—"The Murders in the Rue Morgue," "The Mystery of Marie Rogêt," "The Gold-Bug," and "The Purloined Letter"—were but a literary development, or application, of the ideas and problems which always fascinated him. "The Gold-Bug," in fact, was merely a fictional presentation of "Cryptography." (Incidentally, the number of detective stories since Poe's day that have hid their solutions in cipher messages is legion.)

There is no more stimulating activity than that of the mind; and there is no more exciting adventure than that of the intellect. Mankind has always received keen enjoyment from the mental gymnastics required in solving a riddle; and puzzles have been its chief toy throughout the ages. But there is a great difference between waiting placidly for the solution of a problem, and the swift and exhilarating participation in the succeeding steps that lead to the solution. In the average light novel of romance, adventure, or mystery, the reader merely awaits the author's unraveling of the tangled skein of events. True, during the waiting period he is given emotion, wonder, suspense, sentiment and description, with which to occupy himself; and the average novel depends in large measure on these addenda to furnish his enjoyment. But in the detective novel, as we shall see, these qualities are either subordinated to ineffectuality, or else eliminated entirely. The reader is immediately put to work, and kept busy in every chapter, at the task of solving the book's mystery. He shares in the unfoldment of the problem in precisely the same way he participates in the solution of any riddle to which he applies himself.

Because of this singularity of appeal the detective novel has gone its own way irrespective of the *progressus* of all other fictional types. It has set its own standards, drawn up its own rules, adhered to its own heritages, advanced along its own narrow-gage track, and created its own ingredients as well as its own form and technic. And all these considerations have had to do with its own isolated purpose, with its own special destiny. In the process of this evolution it has withdrawn farther and farther from its literary fellows, until to-day it has practically reversed the principles on which the ordinary popular novel is based.

A sense of reality is essential to the detective novel. The few attempts that have been made to lift the detective-story plot out of its naturalistic environment and confer on it an air of fancifulness have been failures. A castles-in-Spain atmosphere, wherein the reader may escape from the materiality of every day, often gives the average popular novel its charm and readability; but the objective of a detective novel—the mental reward attending its solution—would be lost unless a sense of verisimilitude were consistently maintained,—a feeling of triviality would attach to its problem, and the reader would experience a sense of wasted effort. This is why in cross-word puzzles the words are all genuine: their correct determination achieves a certain educational, or at least serious, result. The "trick" cross-word puzzle with coined words and purely logomachic inventions (such as filling four boxes with e's—e-e-e-e—for the word "ease," or with i's—i-i-i-i—for the word "eyes," or making u-u-u-u stand for the word "use") has never been popular. The philologic realism, so to speak, is dissipated. A. E. W. Mason has said somewhere that Defoe would have written the perfect detective story. He was referring to Defoe's surpassing ability to create a realistic environment.

This rule of realism suggests the common literary practice of endowing *mises en scène* with varying emotional pressures. And here again the detective novel differs from its fictional confrères; for, aside from the primary achievement of a sense of reality, atmospheres, in the descriptive and psychic sense, have no place in this type of story. Once the reader has accepted the pseudo-actuality of the plot, his energies are directed (like those of the detective himself) to the working out of the puzzle; and his mood, being an intellectual one, is only distracted by atmospheric invasions. Atmospheres belong to the romantic and the adventurous tale, such as Poe's "The Fall of the House of Usher" and Scott's *Ivanhoe,* and to the novel of mystery—Henry James's *The Turn of the Screw* and Bram Stoker's *Dracula,* for instance.

The setting of a detective story, however, is of cardinal importance. The plot must appear to be an actual record of events springing from the terrain of its operations; and the plans and diagrams so often encountered in detective stories aid considerably in the achievement of this effect. A familiarity with the terrain and a belief in its existence are what give the reader his feeling of ease and freedom in manipulating the factors of the plot to his own (which are also the author's) ends. Hampered by strange conditions and modes of action, his personal participation in the story's solution becomes restricted and his interest in its sequiturs wanes. A detective novel is nearly always more popular in the country in which it is laid than in a foreign country where the conditions, both human and topographic, are unfamiliar. The variations between English and American customs and police methods, and mental and temperamental attributes, are, of course, not nearly so marked as between those of America and France; and no sharp distinction is now drawn between the English and the American detective tale. But many of the best French novels of this type have had indifferent sales in the United States. Gaston Leroux's *The Mystery of the Yellow Room, The Perfume of the Lady in Black,* and *The Secret of the Night* have never had their deserved popularity in this country because of their foreign locales; but *The Phantom of the Opera,* by the same author, which is a sheer mystery story, has been a great success here, due largely to that very unfamiliarity of setting that has worked against the success of his detective novels.

III

In the matter of character-drawing the detective novel also stands outside the rules governing ordinary fiction. Characters in detective stories may not be too neutral and colorless, nor yet too fully and intimately delineated. They should merely fulfil the requirements of plausibility, so that their actions will not appear to spring entirely from the author's preconceived scheme. Any closely drawn character analysis, any undue lingering over details of temperament, will act only as a clog in the narrative machinery. The automaton of the cheap detective thriller detracts from the reader's eagerness to rectify the confusion of the plot; and the subtly limned personality of the "literary" detective novel shunts the analytic operations of the reader's mind to extraneous considerations. Think back over all the good detective stories you may have read, and try to recall a single memorable personality (aside from the detective himself). And yet these characters were of sufficient color and rotundity to enlist your sympathetic emotions at the time, and to drive you on to a solution of their problems.

The style of a detective story must be direct, simple, smooth, and unencumbered. A "literary" style, replete with descriptive passages, metaphors, and word pictures, which might give viability and beauty to a novel of romance or adventure, would, in a detective yarn, produce sluggishness in the actional current by diverting the reader's mind from the mere record of facts (which is what he is concerned with), and focussing it on irrelevant æsthetic appeals. I do not mean that the style of the detective novel must be bald and legalistic, or cast in the stark language of commercial documentary exposition; but it must, like the style of Defoe, subjugate itself to the function of producing unadorned verisimilitude. No more is gained by stylizing a detective novel than by printing a cross-word puzzle in Garamond Italic, or Cloister Cursive, or the Swash characters of Caslon Old-style.

The material for the plot of a detective novel must be commonplace. Indeed, there are a dozen adequate plots for this kind of story on the front page of almost any metropolitan daily paper. Unusualness, *bizarrerie*, fantasy, or strangeness in subject-matter is rarely desirable; and herein we find another striking reversal of the general rules applying to popular fiction; for originality and eccentricity of plot may give a novel of adventure or mystery its main interest. The task confronting the writer of detective fiction is again the same confronting the cross-word-puzzle manufacturer—namely, the working of familiar materials into a difficult riddle. The skill of a detective story's craftsmanship is revealed in the way these materials are fitted together, the subtlety with which the clues are presented, and the legitimate manner in which the final solution is withheld.

Furthermore, there is a strict ethical course of conduct imposed upon the author. He must never once deliberately fool the reader: he must succeed by ingenuity alone. The habit of inferior writers of bringing forward false clues whose purpose is to mislead is as much a form of cheating as if the cross-word-puzzle maker should print false definitions to his words. The truth must at all times be in the printed word, so that if the reader should go back over the book he would find that the solution had been there all the time if he had had sufficient shrewdness to grasp it. There was a time when all manner of tricks, deceits, and far-fetched devices were employed for the reader's befuddlement; but as the detective novel developed and the demand for straightforward puzzle stories increased, all such methods were abrogated, and to-day we find them only in the cheapest and most inconsequential examples of this type of fiction.

In the central character of the detective novel—the detective himself—we have, perhaps, the most important and original element of the criminal-problem story. It is difficult to describe his exact literary status, for he has no counterpart in any other fictional genre. He is, at one and the same time, the outstanding personality of the story (though he is concerned in it only in an *ex-parte* capacity), the projection of the author, the embodiment of the reader, the *deus ex machina* of the plot, the propounder of the problem, the supplier of the clues, and the eventual solver of the mystery. The life of the book takes place in him, yet the life of the narrative has its being outside of him. In a lesser sense, he is the Greek chorus of the drama. All good detective novels have had for their protagonist a character of attractiveness and interest, of high and fascinating attainments—a man at once human and unusual, colorful and gifted. The buffoon, the bungler, the prig, the automaton—all such have failed. And sometimes in an endeavor to be original an otherwise competent writer, misjudging the psychology of the situation, has presented us with a farcical detective or a juvenile investigator, only to wonder, later on, why these innovations failed. The more successful detective stories have invariably given us such personalities as C. Auguste Dupin, Monsieur Lecoq, Sherlock Holmes, Dr. Thorndyke, Rouletabille, Dr. Fortune, Furneaux, Father Brown, Uncle Abner, Richard Hannay, Arsène Lupin, Dawson, Martin Hewitt, Max Carrados and Hanaud—to name but a few that come readily to mind. All the books in which these characters appear do not fall unqualifiedly into the true detective-story category; but in each tale there are sufficient elements to permit broadly of the detective classification. Furthermore, these Œdipuses themselves are not, in every instance, authentic sleuths: some are doctors of medicine, some professors of astronomy, some soldiers, some journalists, some lawyers, and some reformed crooks. But their vocations do not matter, for in this style of book the designation "detective" is used generically.

We come now to what is perhaps the outstanding characteristic of the detective novel: its unity of mood. To be sure, this is a desideratum of all fiction; but the various moods of the ordinary novel—such as love, romance, adventure, wonder, mystery—are so closely related that they may be intermingled or alternated without breaking the thread of interest; whereas, in the detective novel, the chief interest being that of mental analysis and the overcoming of difficulties, any interpolation of purely emotional moods produces the effect of irrelevancy—unless, of course, they are integers of the equation and are subordinated to the main theme. For instance, in none of the best detective novels will you find a love interest,—Sherlock Holmes in mellow mood, holding a lady's hand and murmuring amorous platitudes, would be unthinkable. And when a detective is sent scurrying on a long-drawn-out adventure beset with physical dangers, the reader fumes and frets until his hero is again in his armchair analyzing clues and inquiring into motives.

In this connection it is significant that the cinematograph has never been able to project a detective story. The detective story, in fact, is the only type of fiction that cannot be filmed. The test of popular fiction—namely, its presentation in visual pictures, or let us say, the visualizing of its word-pictures—goes to pieces when applied to detective stories. The difficulties confronting a motion-picture director in the screening of a detective tale are very much the same as those he would encounter if he strove to film a crossword puzzle. The only serious attempt to transcribe a detective story onto the screen was the case of *Sherlock Holmes;* and the effort was made possible only by reducing the actual detective elements to a minimum, and emphasizing all manner of irrelevant dramatic and adventurous factors; for there is neither drama nor adventure, in the conventional sense, in a good detective novel.

IV

The origin of the detective novel need not concern us greatly. Like all species of popular art, its beginnings are probably obscure and confused. Enthusiastic critics have pointed to certain tales in the Old Testament (such as Daniel's cross-examination of the elders in the story of Susanna) as examples of early crime-detection. But if we were to extend our search into antiquity we would probably find few ancient literatures that would not supply us with evidence of a sort. Persian sources are particularly rich in stories that might be drawn into the detectival category. The Turkish and the Sanscrit likewise furnish material for the ancient-origin theory. And, of course, the Arabian *The Thousand Nights and a Night* offers numerous exhibits of criminological fiction. Herodotus, five centuries B.C., recounted what might be termed a detective tale in the story of King Rhampsinitus's treasure-house—a story of a skilfully planned theft, the falsifying of clues (no less an act than decapitation), the setting of traps for the criminal, the clever eluding of these snares, and—what should delight the modern romanticist—a "happy ending" when the scalawag wins the hand of the princess. This ancient Greek tale, by the way, might also be regarded as the inspiration for the common modern device of having a crime committed in a locked and sealed room. But even the story of Rhampsinitus was not solely Egyptian: Charles Johnston, of the Royal Asiatic Society, has variously traced it, both in its general plot and its details, to the Thibetan, the Italian, and the Indian. And we may find it, in its essentials, retold in modern English and staring at us, in gaudy wrappers, from the shelves of our favorite bookstore. Another tale of Herodotus to which might be traced the prevalent cipher-message device of the nineteenth-century detective-story writer is the one which relates of the code pricked by Histiaios on the bald head of his slave in order to convey a secret message to Aristagoras. Chaucer has retold, in "The Tale of the Nun's Priest," a story from Cicero's *De Divinatione;* and the *Gesta Romanorum* has long been a mine of suggestions for the modern writer of crime-mystery fiction.

Antiquity unquestionably was familiar with all manner of tales and legends that might be academically regarded as the antecedents of the modern detective story; and it is interesting to note that the current connotation of the word *clue* (or *clew*) is derived from the thread with which Ariadne supplied Theseus to guide him safely from the Cretan labyrinth after he had slain the Minotaur. However, all such genealogical researches for the remote forebears of the modern crime story may best be left to the antiquary, for they are irrelevant to our purpose, which is to trace the origin and history of the specialized branch of literary form called the detective novel. While many such tales may be unearthed in the ancient records of imaginative narrative, they did not become unified into a type until toward the latter half of the nineteenth century; and it is from that time that the entire evolution of this literary genre has taken place.

It would be possible, no doubt, to find indications of the later detective novel in many books during the early decades of the last century. Poe, however, is the authentic father of the detective novel as we know it to-day; and the evolution of this literary type began with "The Murders in the Rue Morgue" (1841), "The Mystery of Marie Rogêt" (1842), "The Gold-Bug" (1843), and "The Purloined Letter" (1845). In these four tales was born a new and original type of fictional entertainment; and though their structure has been modified, their method altered, their subject-matter expanded, and their craftsmanship developed, they remain to-day almost perfect models of their kind; and they will always so remain, because their fundamental psychological qualities—the very essence of their appeal—embody the animating and motivating forces in this branch of fiction. One can no more ignore their basic form when writing a detective novel to-day than one can ignore the form of Haydn when composing a symphony, or the experimental researches of Monet and Pissarro when painting an impressionist painting.

For fifteen years after Poe there was little detective-story fiction of an influential nature. Desultory and ineffectual attempts were made to carry on the Auguste Dupin idea, chiefly in France, where Poe's influence was very great. Perhaps the most noteworthy is to be found in Dumas' *Le Vicomte de Bragelonne* (1848) where D'Artagnan enacts the rôle of detective. But even here the spirit of adventure overrides the spirit of deduction,—*Le Vicomte de Bragelonne* is, after all, a sequel to *Les Trois Mousquetaires.* Five years later, in 1853, came Dickens's *Bleak House;* and in this novel appeared England's first authentic contribution to modern detective fiction. This novel, to be sure, contains many elements which to-day would not be tolerated in a strict detective story; and its technic, as was inevitable, is more suited to the novel of manners; but Inspector Bucket (who, by the way, was drawn from Dickens's personal friend, Inspector Field of the Metropolitan Police Force of London) is a character who deserves to rank with Dupin and the famous fictional sleuths who came later. In *The Mystery of Edwin Drood* (which unfortunately remained unfinished at the time of Dickens's death in 1870) we have a straightaway detective story which might almost be used as a model for this type of fiction.

But ten years of criminal waters, so to speak, had passed under the detectives' bridge when *The Mystery of Edwin Drood* appeared; and Dickens cannot be regarded as, in any sense, a precursor, or even developer, of the crime-mystery technic. In 1860 Wilkie Collins's *The Woman in White* had been published; and *The Moonstone* had followed eight years later, two years before the world was aware of the mysterious murder of Edwin Drood and the ensuing unresolved melodrama amid the picturesque purlieus of old Rochester and the opium dens of Shadwell. Indeed, it was Wilkie Collins who carried on the tradition of Poe in England, and, by giving impetus to the detective-story idea and purifying its technic, paved the way for Gaboriau. Sergeant Cuff, though we hear his name but seldom to-day, deserves a larger and more conspicuous niche among the literary immortals of crime detection, for few of his later brethren have proved themselves more efficient than did he when called upon to solve the mystery of the great diamond which Colonel Herncastle had secured. But Collins, because of the nature of his numerous other books, will always be classed as a dealer in adventures and mysteries, despite his contributions to the evolution of strictly problematic crime literature. At that early date the analytical crime story was not considered worthy of any writer's entire time and energy.

V

It was not until the appearance of Gaboriau's *L'Affaire Lerouge* (*The Widow Lerouge*) in 1866, that the first great stride in the detective novel's development was taken. This book was the first of a long series of detective novels by Gaboriau, in which the protagonist, Monsieur Lecoq, proved himself a worthy successor to Poe's Auguste Dupin. If we call Poe the father of detective fiction, Gaboriau was certainly its first influential tutor. He lengthened its form along rigid deductional lines, and complicated and elaborated its content. *Le dossier No. 113* (*File No. 113*), published in 1867, has deservedly become a classic of its kind; and *Monsieur Lecoq*, which appeared in 1869, will, despite the remarkable fact that the criminal in the end outwits and eludes the sleuth, always remain one of the world's foremost detective stories. With Gaboriau's *L'Argent des autres* (*Other People's Money*), published posthumously in 1874 (Gaboriau died in 1873), the detective novel was permanently launched, and during the past fifty years it has taken a conspicuous and highly popular place in the fictional field.

But though Gaboriau remains to-day the foremost writer of detective fiction during the period following Poe and Collins, mention should in justice be made of that other French exponent of the *roman policier,* Fortuné du Boisgobey, whose name is often bracketed with Gaboriau's. Boisgobey was a prolific writer of detective fiction, and his work had the undoubted effect of popularizing this type of story in France. Moreover, there is no doubt that he influenced Conan Doyle, if, indeed, Doyle did not go to him for actual suggestions. Boisgobey's first detective work was *Le Forçat colonel,* which appeared in 1872; and this was followed by *Les gredins, La tresse blonde, Les Mystères du nouveau Paris, Le billet rouge, Le Cri du Sang, La bande rouge,* and others. *La main froide* was published as late as 1889.

Five years after the death of Gaboriau another writer of detective tales entered the field—the American, Anna Katharine Green —and this author has hewed to the line for nearly half a century, producing a large number of some of the best-known detective novels in English. *The Leavenworth Case,* which appeared in 1878, had a tremendous popularity; but its importance lay in the fact that it went far toward familiarizing the English-speaking public with this, as yet, little-known genre, rather than in any inherent contribution made by it to the genre's evolution. This book and the numerous other detective novels written by the same author appear to many of us to-day, who have become accustomed to the complex, economical and highly rarified technic of detective fiction, as over-documented and as too intimately concerned with strictly romantic material and humanistic considerations. However, their excellent style, their convincing logic, and their sense of reality give them a literary distinction almost unique in the American criminal romance since Poe; and Mrs. Rohlf's detective, Ebenezer Gryce, is as human and convincing a solver of mysteries as this country has produced. There is little doubt that the novels of Anna Katharine Green have played a significant part in the historical evolution of the fiction of crime detection: certainly no roster of the foremost examples of this branch of literature would be complete without the inclusion of such books of hers as *Hand and Ring, Behind Closed Doors, The Filigree Ball, The House of the Whispering Pines,* and *The Step on the Stair.*

A book which played a peculiar part in the history of the detective novel is *The Mystery of a Hansom Cab* by Fergus Hume. This story, based on the technic of Gaboriau and influenced by the writings of Anna Katharine Green, represents what is perhaps the greatest commercial success in the history of modern detective fiction, and throws an interesting light on the English public's avidity for this type of literary diversion during the closing years of the nineteenth century. *The Mystery of a Hansom Cab* has sold over half a million copies to date, and the record of its early editions is eloquently indicative of the fact that the detective novel as a definite genre had, even at that time, made a place for itself in the Hall of Letters. The book, however, added nothing new to the technic or the subject-matter of detective fiction, but adhered sedulously to the lines already laid down.

Not until the appearance of *A Study in Scarlet* in 1887 (which, incidentally, was the same year in which *The Mystery of a Hansom Cab* appeared), and *The Sign of Four* in 1890, did the detective novel take any definite forward step over Gaboriau. In these books and the later Sherlock Holmes vehicles Conan Doyle brought detective fiction into full-blown maturity. He adhered to the documentary and psychological scaffolding that had been erected by Poe and strengthened by Gaboriau, but clothed it in a new exterior, eliminating much of the old decoration, and designing various new architectural devices. In Doyle the detective story reached what might be termed a purified fruition; and the numerous changes and developments during the past two decades have had to do largely with detail, with the substitution of methods, and with variations in documentary treatment—in short, with current modes.

But in as vital, intimate, and exigent a type of entertainment as detective fiction, these modes are of great importance: they mark the distinction between that which is modern and up-to-date and that which is old-fashioned, just as do the short skirt and the long skirt in sartorial styles. The Sherlock Holmes stories are now obsolescent: they have been superseded by more advanced and contemporaneously alive productions in their own realm. And the modern detective-story enthusiast would find it hard sledding to read Gaboriau to-day—even *Monsieur Lecoq* and *Le dossier No. 113*. Poe's four analytic tales are a treasure-trove for the student rather than a source of diversion for the general reader. The romantic and adventurous atmosphere we find in "The Gold-

Bug" has now been eliminated from the detective tale; and the long introduction to "The Murders in the Rue Morgue" (really an *apologia*), and the unnecessary documentation in "The Mystery of Marie Rogêt," act only as irritating encumbrances to the modern reader of detective fiction. Even in "The Purloined Letter"—the shortest of the four stories—there is a sesquipedalian and somewhat ponderous analysis of philosophy and mathematics, which is much too *ritenendo* and *grandioso* for the devotees of this type of fiction to-day.

VI

The first detective of conspicuous note to follow in the footsteps of Sherlock Holmes was Martin Hewitt, the creation of Arthur Morrison. Hewitt is less colorful than Holmes, less omnipotent, and far more commonplace. He was once, Mr. Morrison tells us, a lawyer's clerk, and some of the dust of his legal surroundings seems always to cling to him. But what he loses in perspicacity and incredible gifts, he makes up for, in large measure, by verisimilitude. His problems as a whole are less melodramatic and bizarre than those of Holmes, except perhaps those in *The Red Triangle;* and his methods are not as spectacular as those of his Baker Street predecessor. An obvious attempt has been made by Mr. Morrison to give to detective fiction an air of convincing reality; and by his painstaking and even scholarly style he has sought to appeal to a class of readers that might ordinarily repudiate all interest in so inherently artificial a type of entertainment.

In R. Austin Freeman's Dr. Thorndyke the purely scientific detective made his appearance. Test tubes, microscopes, Bunsen burners, retorts, and all the obscure paraphernalia of the chemist's and physicist's laboratories are his stock in trade. In fact, Dr. Thorndyke rarely attends an investigation without his case of implements and his array of chemicals. Without his laboratory assistant and jack-of-all-trades, Polton,—coupled, of course, with his ponderous but inevitable medico-legal logic—he would be helpless in the face of mysteries which Sherlock Holmes and Monsieur Lecoq might easily have clarified by a combination of observation, mental analysis, and intuitive genius. Dr. Thorndyke is an elderly, plodding, painstaking, humorless and amazingly dry sleuth, but so original are his problems, so cleverly and clearly does he reach his solutions, and so well written are Dr. Freeman's records, that the Thorndyke books rank among the very best of modern detective fiction. The amatory susceptibilities of his recording coadjutors are constantly intruding upon the doctor's scientific investigations and the reader's patience; but even with these irrelevant impediments most of the stories march briskly and competently to their inevitable conclusions. Of all the scientific detectives Dr. Thorndyke is unquestionably the most convincing. His science, though at times obscure, is always sound: Dr. Freeman writes authoritatively, and the reader is both instructed and delighted.

Craig Kennedy, the scientific detective of Arthur B. Reeve, on the other hand, is far less profound: he is, in fact, a pseudo-scientist, utilizing all manner of strange divining machines and speculative systems, and employing all the latest "discoveries" in the realm of fantastic and theoretic physical research. He is not unlike a composite of all the inventors and ballyhoo doctors of science who regularly supply sensational research copy for the Sunday Supplement magazines. But Mr. Reeve's stories, despite their failure to adhere to probability and to the accepted knowledge of recognized experimenters in the scientific fields, are at times ingenious and interesting, and there is little doubt that they have had a marked influence on modern detective fiction. They are unfortunately marred by a careless journalistic style. Among the many Craig Kennedy volumes may be mentioned *The Poisoned Pen, The Dream Doctor, The Silent Bullet* and *The Treasure-Train* as containing the best of Mr. Reeve's work.

Better written, conceived with greater moderation, and clinging more closely to human probabilities, are John Rhode's novels dealing with Dr. Priestley's adventures—*Dr. Priestley's Quest, The Paddington Mystery,* and *The Ellerby Case.* Dr.—or, as he is generally referred to in Mr. Rhode's text, Professor—Priestley has many characteristics in common with Dr. Thorndyke. He is a schoolman, fairly well along in years, without a sense of humor, and inclined to dryness; but he is more of the intellectual scientist, or scientific thinker, than Dr. Freeman's hero. ("Priestley,

cursed with a restless brain and an almost immoral passion for the
highest branches of mathematics, occupied himself in skirmishing
round the portals of the universities, occasionally flinging a bomb
in the shape of a highly controversial thesis in some ultra-scientific
journal.") His detective cases to date have been few, and he suffers
by comparison with the superior Dr. Thorndyke.

VII

The purely intellectual detective—the professor with numerous scholastic degrees, who depends on scientific reasoning and
rarefied logic for the answer to his problems—has become a popular figure in the fiction of crime detection. His most extravagant
personification—what might almost be termed the *reductio ad
absurdum* of this type of super-sleuth—is to be found in Jacques
Futrelle's Professor Augustus S. F. X. Van Dusen, PH.D., LL.D.,
F.R.S., M.D., etc. The first book to recount the criminal mysteries that came under Professor Van Dusen's observation was *The
Thinking Machine,* later republished as *The Problem of Cell 13;*
and this was followed by another volume of stories entitled *The
Thinking Machine on the Case.* These tales, despite their improbability—and often impossibility—nevertheless constitute attractive diversion of the lighter sort.

G. K. Chesterton's Father Brown—a quiet, plain little priest
who is now definitely established as one of the great probers of
mysteries in modern detective fiction—is also what might be
called an intellectual sleuth, although the subtleties of his analyses depend, in large measure, on a kind of spiritual intuition—
the result of his deep knowledge of human frailties. Although
Father Brown does not spurn material clues as aids to his conclusions, he depends far more on his analyses of the human heart
and his wide experience with sin. At times he is obscure and symbolic, even mystical; and too often the problems which Mr. Chesterton poses for him are based on crimes that are metaphysical
and unconvincing in their implications; but Father Brown's conversational gifts—his commentaries, parables and observations—
are adequate compensation for the reader's dubiety. The fact that
Father Brown is concerned with the moral, or religious, aspect,

rather than the legal status, of the criminals he runs to earth, gives Mr. Chesterton's stories an interesting distinction.

Similar in methods, but quite different in results, are the excellent stories by H. C. Bailey setting forth the cases of Dr. Reginald Fortune. Dr. Fortune is an adjunct of Scotland Yard, a friend and constant companion of Stanley Lomas who is a chief of the Criminal Investigation Department. Like Father Brown, Dr. Fortune is highly intuitional; and his final results depend on logic and his knowledge of men rather than on the evidential and circumstantial indications of the average official police investigation. And like Father Brown he has a gift for conversation and repartee that makes even the most sordid and unconvincing of his cases interesting, if not indeed fascinating. In addition, he is a man of amazing gifts, with a wide range of almost incredible knowledge; but so competent is Mr. Bailey's craftsmanship that Dr. Fortune rarely exceeds the bounds of probability. He has, in fact, in a very short time (the first Fortune book, *Call Mr. Fortune,* appeared in 1919) made a permanent and unquestioned place for himself among the first half-dozen protagonists of detective fiction.

Hercule Poirot, Agatha Christie's pompous little Belgian sleuth, falls in the category of detectival logicians, and though his methods are also intuitional to the point of clairvoyance, he constantly insists that his surprisingly accurate and often miraculous deductions are the inevitable results of the intensive operation of "the little gray cells." Poirot is more fantastic and far less credible than his brother criminologists of the syllogistic fraternity, Dr. Priestley, Father Brown and Reginald Fortune; and the stories in which he figures are often so artificial, and their problems so far fetched, that all sense of reality is lost, and consequently the interest in the solution is vitiated. This is particularly true of the short stories gathered into the volume *Poirot Investigates.* Poirot is to be seen at his best in *The Mysterious Affair at Styles* and *The Murder on the Links.* The trick played on the reader in *The Murder of Roger Ackroyd* is hardly a legitimate device of the detective-story writer; and while Poirot's work in this book is at times capable, the effect is nullified by the dénouement.

Of an entirely different personality, yet with dialectic methods broadly akin to Father Brown's and Dr. Priestley's, is Colonel

Gore in Lynn Brock's *The Deductions of Colonel Gore* and *Colonel Gore's Second Case*. Colonel Gore, though ponderous and verbose, is well projected, and the crimes he investigates are well worked-out and admirably, if a bit too leisurely, presented. The various characterizations of the minor as well as the major personages of the plots, and the long descriptions of social and topographical details, tend to detract from the problems involved; but the competency of Mr. Brock's writing carries one along despite one's occasional impatience. This fault is not to be found in Ernest M. Poate's *Behind Locked Doors* and *The Trouble at Pinelands*. But Mr. Poate errs on the side of amatory romance, and in *Behind Locked Doors* he introduces a puppy love affair which both mars and retards what otherwise might have been one of the outstanding modern detective novels. Even as it stands it must be given high rank; and the figure of Dr. Bentiron—an eccentric but lovable psychopathologist—will long remain in the memory of those who make his acquaintance.

No list of what we may call the deductive detectives would be complete without the name of A. E. W. Mason's admirable Hanaud of the French Sûreté. Hanaud may almost be regarded as the Gallic counterpart of Sherlock Holmes. The methods of these two sleuths are similar: each depends on a combination of material clues and spontaneous thinking; each is logical and painstaking; and each has his own little tricks and deceptions and vanities. The two Hanaud vehicles, *At the Villa Rose* and *The House of the Arrow,* are excellent examples of detective fiction, carefully constructed, consistently worked out, and pleasingly written. They represent—especially the latter—the purest expression of this type of literary divertissement; and Hanaud himself is a memorable and engaging addition to the great growing army of fictional sleuths. The psychological methods of crime detection, combined with an adherence to the evidences of reality, are also followed in S. S. Van Dine's *The Benson Murder Case* and *The "Canary" Murder Case,* wherein Philo Vance, a young social aristocrat and art connoisseur, enacts the rôle of criminologist and investigator.

Although the blind detective is a comparatively recent innovation in crime-mystery fiction, his methods belong necessarily to the logic-*cum*-intuition school, despite the fact that all his processes and conclusions are accounted for on strictly material and scientific grounds. In the various attempts at novelty made by recent detective-story writers the sightless crime specialist has been frequently introduced, so that now he has become a recognized and accepted type. The most engaging and the most easily accepted of these unique detectives is Ernest Bramah's Max Carrados, who made his appearance in a volume bearing his name for title in 1914. To be sure, he was endowed with gifts which recalled the strange powers of the citizens of H. G. Wells's *The Country of the Blind,* but so accurately and carefully has Mr. Bramah projected him that he must be given a place in the forefront of famous fictional sleuths. Far more miraculous, and hence less convincing, is the blind detective, Thornley Coiton, who appears in a book which also bears his name for title, by Clinton H. Stagg.

As soon as the detective story became popular it was inevitable that the woman detective would make her appearance; and to-day there are a score or more of female rivals of Sherlock Holmes. The most charming and capable, as well as the most competently conceived, is Violet Strange, who solves eight criminal problems in Anna Katharine Green's *The Golden Slipper.* Lady Molly, in *Lady Molly of Scotland Yard* by the Baroness Orczy, is somewhat more conventional in conception but sufficiently entertaining to be regarded as a worthy deductive sister of Violet Strange. George R. Sims, in *Dorcas Dene, Detective,* has given us a feminine investigator of considerable quality; and Arthur B. Reeve's Constance Dunlap has resources and capabilities of a high, even if a too melodramatic, order. Millicent Newberry, in Jeanette Lee's *The Green Jacket,* is an unusual and appealing figure—more a corrector of destinies, perhaps, than a detective. And Richard Marsh's Judith Lee, in a book called simply *Judith Lee,* while not technically a sleuth, happens upon the secret of many crimes through her ability as a lip-reader.

VIII

So individual and diverse has become the latter-day fictional detective that even a general classification is well-nigh impossible. In Robert Barr's *The Triumphs of Eugène Valmont* we have an

Anglicized Frenchman of the old school who undertakes private investigations of a too liberal latitude to qualify him at all times as a crime specialist; but, despite his romantic adventurings and his glaring failures, he unquestionably belongs in our category of famous sleuths if only for the care and excellence with which Mr. Barr has presented his experiences. Then there is the fat, commonplace, unlovely and semi-illiterate, but withal sympathetic and entertaining, Jim Hanvey of Octavus Roy Cohen's book, *Jim Hanvey, Detective,* who knows all the crooks in Christendom and is their friend; the nameless logician in the Baroness Orczy's *The Old Man in the Corner* and *The Case of Miss Elliott,* who sits, shabby and indifferent, at his café table and holds penetrating post mortems on the crimes of the day; Malcolm Sage, of Herbert H. Jenkins's *Malcolm Sage, Detective,* a fussy, bespectacled bachelor who runs a detective agency and uses methods as eccentric as they are efficient; Lord Peter Wimsey, the debonair and deceptive amateur of Dorothy L. Sayers's *Whose Body?*; Jefferson Hastings, the pathetic, ungainly old-timer of the Washington Police, whose mellow insight and shrewd deductions make first-rate reading in *The Bellamy Case, The Melrose Mystery* and *No Clue!* by James Hay, Jr.; and Inspectors Winter and Furneaux—that amusing and capable brace of co-sleuths in Louis Tracy's long list of detective novels.

The alienist detective is not a far cry from the pathologist detective, and though there have been several doctors with a flair for abnormal psychology who have enacted the rôle of criminal investigator, it has remained for Anthony Wynne to give the psychiatrist a permanent place in the annals of detection. In his Dr. Hailey, the Harley Street specialist, (the best of whose cases is related in *The Sign of Evil,*) we have an admirable detective character who mingles neurology with psychoanalysis and solves many crimes which prove somewhat beyond the ken of the Scotland Yard police. It was Henry James Forman, however, I believe, who gave us the first strictly psychoanalytical detective novel in *Guilt* —a story which, despite its unconventional ending and its singularity of material, makes absorbing reading.

The reporter sleuth—or "journalistic crime expert"—has become a popular figure in detective fiction on both sides of the

Atlantic, and to enumerate his various personalities and adventures would be to fill several small-type pages with tabulations. Most famous of this clan is Rouletabille of Gaston Leroux's excellent detective novels, although J. S. Fletcher has created an engaging rival to the little French reporter in the figure of Frank Spargo who solves the gruesome mystery in *The Middle Temple Murder.* Another reporter detective of memorable qualities and personality is Robert Estabrook in Louis Dodge's *Whispers;* and very recently there has appeared a book by Harry Stephen Keeler —*Find the Clock*—in which a Chicago reporter named Jeff Darrell acquires the right to sit among the select company of his fellow detective-journalists.

One of the truly outstanding figures in detective fiction is Uncle Abner, whose criminal adventures are recounted by Melville Davisson Post in *Uncle Abner: Master of Mysteries,* and in a couple of short stories included in the volume, *The Sleuth of St. James's Square.* Uncle Abner, indeed, is one of the very few detectives deserving to be ranked with that immortal triumverate, Dupin, Lecoq and Holmes; and I have often marveled at the omission of his name from the various articles and criticisms I have seen dealing with detective fiction. In conception, execution, device and general literary quality these stories of early Virginia, written by a man who thoroughly knows his *métier* and is also an expert in law and criminology, are among the very best we possess. The grim and lovable Uncle Abner is a vivid and convincing character, and the plots of his experiences with crime are as unusual as they are convincing. Mr. Post is the first author who, to my knowledge, has used the phonetic misspelling in a document supposedly written by a deaf and dumb man as a proof of its having been forged. (The device is found in the story called "An Act of God.") If Mr. Post had written only *Uncle Abner* he would be deserving of inclusion among the foremost of detective-fiction writers, but in *The Sleuth of St. James's Square,* and especially in *Monsieur Jonquelle,* he has achieved a type of highly capable and engrossing crime-mystery tale. The story called "The Great Cipher" in the latter book is, with the possible exception of Poe's "The Gold-Bug," the best cipher story in English.

Another distinctive detective, but one of an entirely different character, is Chief Inspector William Dawson of Bennett Copplestone's *The Diversions of Dawson* and *The Lost Naval Papers*—the latter a series of secret-service stories. There is humor in Mr. Copplestone's delineation of Dawson, but the humor is never flippant and does not, in any sense, detract from the interest of the cases in which this rather commonplace, but none the less remarkable, Scotland Yard master of disguise plays the leading rôle. In fact, the humor is so skilfully interwoven in the plots, and is presented with such consummate naturalness, that it heightens both the character drawing of Dawson and the fascination of the problems he is set to solve. The literary quality of Mr. Copplestone's books is of a high order, and goes far toward placing them among the best of their genre that England has produced. Dawson, for all his shortcomings and conventional devices, is a figure of actuality, with the artificial mechanics of his craft reduced to a minimum.

John Buchan's Richard Hannay, who runs through a series of novels (*The Thirty-Nine Steps, Greenmantle, Mr. Standfast* and *The Three Hostages*), is a figure of unforgettable attraction—slow-moving yet shrewd, sentimental yet efficient—although only in the last named of the four books does he play a strictly detectival rôle, his other "cases" being of a purely adventurous or secret-service nature. A delightful type of detective—debonair, whimsical, yet withal penetrating—is Antony Gillingham of A. A. Milne's *The Red House Mystery*—one of the best detective stories of recent years, as well developed as it is well written. I regret that Mr. Milne has seen fit to let his reputation as a writer of detective tales rest on this single volume. Philip Trent, the somewhat baffled nemesis of E. C. Bentley's *Trent's Last Case,* is highly engaging, despite the fact that his elaborate deductions, based on circumstantial evidence, lead him woefully astray. Mr. Bentley's book, though unconventional in conception, is, in its way, a masterpiece. Another detective deserving of mention alongside of Antony Gillingham and Philip Trent is Anthony Gethryn, the solver of the criminal riddle in Philip MacDonald's entertaining book, *The Rasp*—which, incidentally, is Gethryn's sole vehicle of deduction.

IX

Eden Phillpotts has written some of the best detective stories in English. Not only has he proved himself a student of this type of literary entertainment, but he has brought to his task a life-long experience in the craft of writing. *The Grey Room* was the first of his essays in this field, and, for all its unconventionality of structure, immediately took its place among the leading mystery stories of the day. This was followed by *The Red Redmaynes* (a more elaborately worked-out detective novel), *A Voice from the Dark,* and *Jig-Saw.* Both in craftsmanship and ingenuity Mr. Phillpotts's detective tales—all of which are of a high order—seem intimately related to the novels of Harrington Hext—*The Thing at Their Heels, Who Killed Cock Robin?, The Monster,* and *Number 87.* (The last is a scientific mystery story rather than a straight detective novel.) *Who Killed Cock Robin?* is of conventional pattern and technic, but its adroitness entitles it to the first rank; *The Monster,* for sheer cleverness and suspense, has few equals in contemporary detective fiction; and *The Thing at Their Heels,* though ignoring the accepted canons of detective-story writing, must be placed in this category with an asterisk of distinction marking it.

A popular and prolific novelist who has long been regarded as a detective-story writer is E. Phillips Oppenheim; but while he has written several books of detective stories, they represent his secondary work, and have little place in a library devoted to the best of crime-problem fiction. Mr. Oppenheim is primarily a writer of mystery romances and stories of diplomatic intrigue; the latter, in fact, are his forte. Even in his best-known so-called detective books—such as *Peter Ruff, The Double Four, The Yellow Crayon,* and *The Honorable Algernon Knox, Detective*—the complications of international diplomacy and of the secret service greatly overbalance the criminological research and deductions that are essential to the true detective story. *Nicholas Goade, Detective* comes nearer to the detectival technic than any of Mr. Oppenheim's other books; but aside from its being a careless and inferior work, it is filled with irrelevancies of a romantic and adventurous nature. Nor are its criminal problems of any particular originality.

Among the most entertaining and adroitly written of modern detective novels must be placed Ronald A. Knox's two semi-satirical books, *The Viaduct Murder* and *The Three Taps*. These stories attain to a high literary level, and though the amateur detective of the first fails in his deductions, and the "murder" in the second proves to be a disappointment—both of which devices are contrary to all the accepted traditions of the detective-story technic—these two books sedulously and intelligently follow the clues of their problems to a logical solution, and unflaggingly hold the reader's interest and admiration. Two other writers of marked literary capacity have tried their hand at the detective novel—Arnold Bennett and Israel Zangwill—with entertaining, if not wholly satisfactory, results. Mr. Bennett's *The Grand Babylon Hotel*, though a detective story only through association and implication, contains several adventures that bring the book broadly within the detective category. Mr. Zangwill's *The Big Bow Mystery* is more in line with the tradition of the detective novel, despite the fact that its theme contraverts one of the basic principles of crime-problem fiction.

Mrs. Belloc Lowndes has made two interesting and noteworthy contributions to criminal literature: indeed, any review of the more important detective stories would be incomplete without an inclusion of her *The Chink in the Armour* and *The Lodger*, the latter dealing with the famous Jack-the-Ripper murders. Burton E. Stevenson has also given us several first-rate detective novels of orthodox pattern—*The Halladay Case, The Gloved Hand, The Marathon Mystery*, and *The Mystery of the Boule Cabinet*—the last being particularly well conceived and executed. Edgar Wallace has written too much and too rapidly, with too little attention to his problems and too great an insistence on inexpensive "thrills," to be included in the roster of the ablest detective-tale authors; but *The Clue of the New Pin*—one of his earlier books—should be mentioned here because of the ingenious device used by the criminal to escape detection. Arthur E. McFarland's *Behind the Bolted Door?* is another detective novel which contains an entirely novel (so far as I know) device; and the interest of the story is markedly enhanced by Mr. McFarland's journalistic competency as a writer and his thorough familiarity with the various factors of his locale. Marion Harvey's *The Mystery of the Hidden Room* is likewise noteworthy because of the criminal device employed; and it should be added that the deductive work done by Graydon McKelvie is at times extremely clever. The four Ashton Kirk novels by John T. McIntyre—*Ashton Kirk, Investigator, Ashton Kirk, Secret Agent, Ashton Kirk, Special Detective,* and *Ashton Kirk, Criminologist*—are a bit extravagant both in characterization and plot, but they may be justly mentioned here because of their strict adherence to the Sherlock Holmes tradition and their occasional ingenuity of structure.

X

Fashions in detectives have changed greatly during the past decade or so. Of late the inspired, intuitive, brilliantly logical super-sleuth of the late nineteenth century has given place to the conservative, plodding, hard working, routine investigator of the official police—the genius of Carlyle's definition, whose procedure is based largely on a transcendent capacity of taking trouble. And it must be said that this new thoroughgoing and unimaginative detective often has a distinct advantage, from the standpoint of literary interest, over the flashy intellectual detective of yore. He is more human, more plausible, and often achieves a more satisfactory solution of the criminal mysteries to which he is assigned. The reader may follow him as an equal, and share in his discoveries; and at all times a sense of reality, even of commonplace familiarity, may be maintained by the author—a sense which is too often vitiated by the inspirational methods of the older detective.

The most skilful exponent of this style of detective story is Freeman Wills Crofts. His *The Cask* and *The Ponson Case* are masterpieces of closely-wrought construction, and, with *The Groote Park Murder, Inspector French's Greatest Case* and *The Starvel Hollow Tragedy*, stand as the foremost representatives of their kind—as much as do the novels of Gaboriau and the Holmes series of Conan Doyle. Indeed, for sheer dexterity of plot Mr.

Crofts has no peer among the contemporary writers of detective fiction. His chief device is the prepared alibi, and this he has explored with almost inexhaustible care, weaving it into his problem with an industry matched only by the amazing industry of his sleuths.

A. Fielding has devoted his talents to this new mode of detective fiction with a success but little less than Mr. Crofts'. In *The Footsteps that Stopped* he has worked out an intricate problem along the painstaking lines of investigation characteristic of the actual methods of Scotland Yard; and in both *The Eames-Erskine Case* and *The Charteris Mystery* he has successfully followed these same methods. *The Detective's Holiday*, by Charles Barry, is another good example of the plodding, naturalistic detective technic, enlivened by a foil in the presence of a typical French detective of contrasting subtlety and emotionalism. And Henry Wade's *The Verdict of You All* is a first-rate story conceived along the same lines; but it breaks away from all tradition in the climax, and turns its dénouement into an ironical criticism of legal procedure—a device which had a famous precedent in *The Ware Case* by Gordon Pleydell. Two earlier capable examples of the detective novel of industrious routine are A. W. Marchmont's *The Eagrave Square Mystery* and Mark Allerton's *The Mystery of Beaton Craig*.

In the same classification with Crofts, Fielding and Wade belongs J. S. Fletcher, the most prolific and popular of all the current writers of detective fiction. Mr. Fletcher, however, carries his naturalism so far in the projection of his plots that his detectives are too often banal and colorless; and in many of his books the solution of the crime is reached through a series of fortuitous incidents rather than through any inherent ability on the part of his investigators. Mr. Fletcher writes smoothly, and his antiquarian researches—which he habitually weaves into the fabric of his plots—give an air of scholarship to his stories. But his problems and their solutions are too frequently deficient in drama and sequence, and his paucity of invention is too consistently glaring to be entirely satisfactory. This may be due to the frequency with which his books appear: I believe he has published something like four a year for the past eight or ten years;

and such mass production is hardly conducive of conceptional care and structural ingenuity. But Mr. Fletcher has none the less played an important part in the development of the detective novel, if for no other reason than that he has, by his fluent style and authoritative realism, given an impetus to the reading of this type of novel among a large class of persons who, but a few years ago, were unfamiliar with the literature of crime detection. Mr. Fletcher's earlier books are his best; and I have yet to read one of his more recent novels that equals his *The Middle Temple Murder* published ten years ago.

It will be noted that the great majority of detective stories I have selected for mention are by English authors. The reason for the decided superiority of English detective stories over American detective stories lies in the fact that the English novelist takes this type of fiction more seriously than we do. The best of the current writers in England will turn their hand occasionally to this genre, and perform their task with the same conscientious care that they confer on their more serious books. The American novelist, when he essays to write this kind of story, does so with contempt and carelessness, and rarely takes the time to acquaint himself with his subject. He labors under the delusion that a detective novel is an easy and casual kind of literary composition; and the result is a complete failure. In this country we have few detective novels of the superior order of such books as Bentley's *Trent's Last Case*, Mason's *The House of the Arrow*, Crofts' *The Cask*, Hext's *Who Killed Cock Robin?*, Phillpotts's *The Red Redmaynes*, Freeman's *The Eye of Osiris*, Knox's *The Viaduct Murder*, Fielding's *The Footsteps That Stopped*, Milne's *The Red House Mystery*, Bailey's Mr. Fortune series, and Chesterton's Father Brown stories, to mention but a scant dozen of the more noteworthy additions to England's rapidly increasing detective library.

XI

In the foregoing brief resumé of the detective fiction which followed upon the appearance of the Sherlock Holmes stories I have confined myself to English and American efforts. We must not, however, overlook the many excellent detective stories that have come out of France since the advent of Monsieur Lecoq. The Gallic temperament seems particularly well adapted to the subtleties and intricacies of the detective novel; and a large number of books of the *roman policier* type have been published in France during the past half century, most of them as yet untranslated into English. The foremost of the modern French writers of detective fiction is Gaston Leroux; in fact, the half dozen or so novels comprising the *Aventures Extraordinaires de Joseph Rouletabille, Reporter* are among the finest examples of detective stories we possess. *Le Mystère de la Chambre Jaune (The Mystery of the Yellow Room), Le Parfum de la Dame en Noir (The Perfume of the Lady in Black), Rouletabille chez le Tsar (The Secret of the Night), Le Château Noir, Les Étranges Noces de Rouletabille, Rouletabille chez Krupp* and *Le Crime de Rouletabille (The Phantom Clue)* represent the highest standard reached by the detective novel in France since the literary demise of Lecoq, and contain a variety of ideas and settings which gives them a diversity of appeal. Rouletabille is engagingly drawn, and his personality holds the reader throughout.

More popular, and certainly more ingenious, though neither as scholarly nor as strictly orthodox, are the famous Arsène Lupin stories of Maurice Leblanc. Lupin in the records of his earlier adventures is a shrewd and dashing criminal—*"un gentleman-cambrioleur"*—and therefore quite the reverse of the regulation detective; but he indulges in detective work—in deductions, in the following of clues, in the subtleties of logic, and in the solution of criminal problems—which is as brilliant and traditional as that of any fictional officer of the Sûreté. In his more recent escapades he gives over his anti-legal propensities, and becomes a sleuth wholly allied with the powers of righteousness. Some of the best and most characteristic examples of conventional modern detective stories are to be found in *Les Huit Coups de l'Horloge*. To the solution of the criminal problems involved in this book Lupin brings not only a keen and penetrating mind, but the fruits of a vast first-hand experience with crime.

Germany's efforts at the exacting art of detective-story writing are, in the main, abortive and ponderous. An air of heavy officialdom hangs over the great majority of them; and one rarely finds the amateur investigator—that most delightful of all detectives— as the central figure of German crime-problem stories. The hero is generally a hide-bound, system-worshiping officer of the *Polizei;* and sometimes as many as three detectives share the honor of bringing a malefactor to justice. Even the best of the Germanic attempts at this literary genre read somewhat like painstaking official reports, lacking imagination and dramatic suspense. There is little subtlety either in the plots or the solutions; and the methods employed are generally obvious and heavy-footed. Characteristic of the German detective story are the books of Dietrich Theden—*Der Advokatenbauer, Die zweite Busse, Ein Verteidiger,* and a volume of short stories entitled *Das lange Wunder.* And among the other better-known works of this type might be mentioned J. Kaulbach's *Die weisse Nelke,* P. Weise's *Der Rottnerhof,* R. Kohlrausch's *In der Dunkelkammer,* and P. Meissner's *Platanen-Allee Nr. 14.* Karl Rosner, the author of *Der Herr des Todes* and *Die Beichte des Herrn Moritz von Cleven,* is also one of the leading German writers of detective stories.

The Austrian authors who have devoted their energies to crime-problem fiction follow closely along German lines, though we occasionally find in them a lighter and more imaginative attitude, although here, too, a stodgy officialism and a reportorial brevity detract from the dramatic interest. Balduin Groller is perhaps the most capable and inventive of the Austrian detective-story writers: his Detektiv Dagobert is perhaps Austria's nearest approach to Sherlock Holmes. Adolph Weissl (who was, I believe, a former official of the Vienna police) also has an extensive reputation as a writer of detective stories. His best-known, perhaps, are *Schwarze Perlen* and *Das grüne Auto.* The latter has been translated into English under the title of *The Green Motor Car.*

The other European countries are also far behind France and England in the production of this kind of narrative entertainment. Russia is too deeply sunk in Zolaesque naturalism to be interested in sheer literary artifice, and the detective novel as a genre is unknown to that country. Only in occasional stories do we find even an indication of it, although when a Russian author does turn his hand to crime detection he endows his work with a convincing realism. Italy's creative spirit is not sufficiently mentalized and detached to maintain the detective-story mood; but Olivieri, in *Il Colonnello,* and Ottolengui, in *Suo Figlio,* have given us fairly representative examples of the detective tale; and Luigi Capuana has written several stories which may broadly be classed as "detective." The Pole, Carl von Trojanowsky, has written, among other books, *Erzählungen eines Gerichtsarztes;* but this work cannot qualify wholly as detective fiction. There are, however, certain indications that the Scandinavian countries may soon enter the field as competitors of France and England and America. A Swedish writer, under the *nom de guerre* of Frank Heller, has had a tremendous success in Europe with a series of novels setting forth the exploits of a Mr. Collin—a kind of Continental Raffles—and several of his books have been translated into English: *The London Adventures of Mr. Collin, The Grand Duke's Finances, The Emperor's Old Clothes, The Strange Adventures of Mr. Collin,* and *Mr. Collin Is Ruined.* They are not, however, true detective novels; but the germ of the species is in them, and they indicate an unmistakable tendency toward the Poe-Gaboriau-Doyle tradition. Far more orthodox, and with a firmer grasp of the principles of detective-fiction technic, are the books of the Danish writer, Sven Elvestad—*Der rätselhafte Feind, Abbe Montrose, Das Chamäleon* and *Spuren im Schnee.* Elvestad also writes detective stories under the name of Stein Riverton. Then there is the popular Norwegian author, Oevre Richter Frich, whose detective, Asbjorn Krag, is almost as well known in Norway as Holmes is in England.

XII

So much confusion exists regarding the limits and true nature of the detective story, and so often is this genre erroneously classified with the secret-service story and the crime story, that a word may properly be said about the very definite distinctions that exist between the latter type and the specialized detective type. While the secret-service story very often depends on an analysis of clues and on deductive reasoning, and while it also possesses a protagonist whose task is the unearthing of secrets and the thwarting of plots, these conditions are not essential to it; and herein lies a fundamental difference between the secret-service agent and the regulation detective. The one is, in the essence of his profession, an adventurer, whereas the other is a *deus ex machina* whose object it is to solve a given problem and thereby bring a criminal to book. No matter how liberally the secret-service story may have borrowed from the methods of detective fiction, its growth has been along fundamentally different lines from those of detective fiction; and during the past few decades it has developed a distinctive technic and evolved a structure characteristically its own. It is true that famous fictional detectives have, on occasion, been shunted successfully to secret-service work (like Dawson in *The Lost Naval Papers,* Hannay in *Greenmantle* and *The Thirty-Nine Steps,* Max Carrados in "The Coin of Dionysius," and even Sherlock Holmes in an occasional adventure); but these variations have, in no wise, brought the secret-service story into the strict category of detective fiction. That the appeals in these two literary types are often closely related, is granted; but this fact is incidental rather than necessary.

The best and truest type of secret-service story may be found in the writings of William Le Queux—in *The Invasion, Donovan of Whitehall, The Czar's Spy,* and *The Mystery of the Green Ray,* for instance. And the novels of E. Phillips Oppenheim contain many of the most capable and diverting stories of this type to be found in English. Lord Frederick Hamilton has introduced a welcome element of novelty into the secret-service formula by way of his P. J. Davenant series—*Nine Holiday Adventures of Mr. P. J. Davenant, Some Further Adventures of Mr. P. J. Davenant, The Education of Mr. P. J. Davenant,* and *The Beginnings of Mr. P. J. Davenant.* Robert Allen, in *Captain Gardiner of the International Police,* has given us a first-rate secret-service-adventure book; and J. A. Ferguson, in *The Stealthy Terror,* has created noteworthy entertainment in this field. One of the best of recent secret-service romances is J. Aubrey Tyson's *The Scarlet Tanager;* and in *The Unseen Hand* Clarence Herbert New has written a series of diplomatic adventures which rank high as fictional secret-service documents. But for all the superficial similarity between these books and the detective adventures of the official and un-official peace-time sleuths, the secret-service narrative has played no part in the narrow and intensive process of the detective story's evolution; and in its more rigid projections it differs radically from the definite and highly specialized form of detective fiction.

This is likewise true of the crime story wherein the criminal is the hero—for example, the stories of Raffles by E. W. Hornung, and the early adventures of Maurice Leblanc's Arsène Lupin. Both in appeal and technic the detective tale and the criminal-hero tale are basically unlike. The author of the latter must, first of all, arouse the reader's sympathy by endowing his hero with humanitarian qualities (the picturesque Robin Hood is almost as well known to-day for his philanthropy as for his brigandage); and, even when this lenient attitude has been evoked, the intel-lectual activity exerted by the reader in an effort to solve the book's problem is minimized by the fact that all the knots in the tangled skein have been tied before his eyes by the central char-acter. Moreover, there is absent from his quest that ethical en-thusiasm which is always a stimulus to the follower of an upright detective tracking down an enemy of society—a society of which the reader is a member and therefore exposed to the dangers of anti-social plottings on the part of the criminal. The projection of oneself into the machinations of a super-criminal (such as Wyndham Martin's Anthony Trent) is a physical and adventur-ous emotion, whereas the cooperation extended by the reader to his favorite detective is wholly a mental process. Even Vautrin, Balzac's great criminal hero, does not inspire the reader with emo-tions or reactions in any sense similar to those produced by Dupin, Monsieur Lecoq, Holmes, Father Brown, or Uncle Ab-ner. And for all the moral platitudes of Barry Pain's Constantine Dix and the inherently decent qualities of Louis Joseph Vance's Lone Wolf—both of whom had the courage to war upon society single-handed—we cannot accept them in the same spirit, or with the same sense of partnership, that we extend to the great sleuths of fiction, who have the organized police of the world at their back. The hero of detective fiction must stand outside of the plot, so to speak: his task is one of ferreting out impersonal mysteries;

and he must come to his work with no more intimate relationship to the problem than is possessed by the reader himself.

XIII

The subject-matter of a detective story—that is, the devices used by the criminal and the methods of deduction resorted to by the detective—is a matter of cardinal importance. The habitual reader of the detective novel has, during the past quarter of a century, become a shrewd critic of its technic and means. He is something of an expert, and, like the motion-picture enthusiast, is thoroughly familiar with all the devices and methods of his favorite craft. He knows immediately if a story is old-fashioned, if its tricks are hackneyed, or if its approach to its problem contains elements of originality. And he judges it by its ever shifting and developing rules. Because of this perspicacious attitude on his part a stricter form and a greater ingenuity have been imposed on the writer; and the fashions and inventions of yesterday are no longer used except by the inept and uninformed author.

For example, such devices as the dog that does not bark and thereby reveals the fact that the intruder is a familiar personage (Doyle's "Silver Blaze" and the Baronness Orczy's "The York Mystery"); the establishing of the culprit's identity by dental irregularities (Freeman's "The Funeral Pyre," Leblanc's *Les Dents de Tigre*, and Morrison's "The Case of Mr. Foggatt"); the finding of a distinctive cigarette or cigar at the scene of the crime (used several times in the Raffles stories, in Knox's *The Three Taps*, Groller's *Die feinen Zigarren*, and Doyle's "The Boscombe Valley Mystery"); the cipher message containing the crime's solution (Wynn's *The Double Thirteen*, Freeman's "The Moabite Cipher" and "The Blue Scarab," and Doyle's "The Adventure of the Dancing Men"); the murdering—generally stabbing—of a man in a locked room after the police have broken in (Chesterton's "The Wrong Shape," Zangwill's *The Big Bow Mystery*, and Caroline Wells's *Spooky Hollow*); the commission of the murder by an animal (Poe's "The Murders in the Rue Morgue," Doyle's "The Speckled Band" and *The Hound of the Baskervilles*); the phonograph alibi (Freeman's "Mr. Pointing's Alibi" and Doyle's "The Adventure of the Mazarin Stone"); the shooting of a dagger from a gun or other projecting machine to avoid proximity (Freeman's "The Aluminium Dagger" and Phillpotts's *Jig-Saw*); the spiritualistic séance or ghostly apparition to frighten the culprit into a confession (McFarland's *Behind the Bolted Door?* and Phillpotts's *A Voice from the Dark*); the "psychological" word-association test for guilt (Kennedy's *The Scientific Cracksman* and Poate's *Behind Locked Doors*); the dummy figure to establish a false alibi (MacDonald's *The Rasp* and Doyle's "The Empty House"); the forged fingerprints (Freeman's *The Red Thumb Mark* and *The Cat's Eye,* and Stevenson's *The Gloved Hand*),—these, and a score of other devices, have now been relegated to the discard; and the author who would again employ them would have no just claim to the affections or even the respect of his readers.

G. K. Chesterton, in his introduction to a detective story by Walter S. Masterman, gives a list of many of the devices that have now come to be regarded as antiquated. He says: "The things he [Mr. Masterman] does not do are the things being done everywhere to-day to the destruction of true detective fiction and the loss of this legitimate and delightful form of art. He does not introduce into the story a vast but invisible secret society with branches in every part of the world, with ruffians who can be brought in to do anything or underground cellars that can be used to hide anybody. He does not mar the pure and lovely outlines of a classical murder or burglary by wreathing it round and round with the dirty and dingy red tape of international diplomacy; he does not lower our lofty ideas of crime to the level of foreign politics. He does not introduce suddenly at the end somebody's brother from New Zealand, who is exactly like him. He does not trace the crime hurriedly in the last page or two to some totally insignificant character, whom we never suspected because we never remembered. He does not get over the difficulty of choosing between the hero and the villain by falling back on the hero's cabman or the villain's valet. He does not introduce a professional criminal to take the blame of a private crime; a thoroughly unsportsmanlike course of action, and another proof of how professionalism is ruining our national sense of sport. He does not introduce about six people in succession to do little bits of the same small murder, one man to bring the dagger, and another to point it, and another to stick it in properly. He does not say it was all a mistake, and that nobody ever meant to murder anybody at all, to the serious disappointment of all humane and sympathetic readers. . . ."

But, strangely enough, Mr. Masterman does something much worse and more inexcusable than any of the things Mr. Chesterton enumerates,—he traces the crime to the detective himself! Such a trick is neither new nor legitimate, and the reader feels not that he has been deceived fairly by a more skilful mind than his own, but deliberately lied to by an inferior. To a certain extent Gaston Leroux is guilty of this subterfuge in *The Mystery of the Yellow Room;* but here Rouletabille, and not the guilty detective, is the central nemesis; and it is the former's ingenious probing and reasoning that unmasks the culprit. A similar situation is to be found in the story called "The Cat Burglar" in H. C. Bailey's *Mr. Fortune, Please,* and also in *The Winning Clue* by James Hay, Jr. In Israel Zangwill's *The Big Bow Mystery* the device is again used; but here it is entirely legitimate, for the situation consists of a specified and recognized battle of wits. A variation of this trick is resorted to in one of Agatha Christie's Poirot books—*The Murder of Roger Ackroyd*—but without any extenuating circumstances.

In this connection it should be pointed out that a certain "gentleman's agreement" has grown up between the detective-story writer and the public—the outcome of a definite development in the relationship necessary for the projection of this type of fiction. And not only has the reader a right to expect and demand fair treatment from an author along the lines tacitly laid down and according to the principles involved, but an author who uses this trust for the purpose of tricking his co-solver of a criminal problem immediately forfeits all claim to the reading public's consideration.

A word in parting should be said in regard to the primary theme of the detective novel, for herein lies one of its most important elements of interest. Crime has always exerted a profound fascination over humanity, and the more serious the crime the greater has been that appeal. Murder, therefore, has always been an absorbing public topic. The psychological reasons for this morbid and elemental curiosity need not be gone into here; but the fact itself supplies us with the explanation of why a murder mystery furnishes a far more fascinating *raison d'être* in a detective novel than does any lesser crime. All the best and most popular books of this type deal with mysteries involving human life. Murder would appear to give added zest to the solution of the problem, and to render the satisfaction of the solution just so much greater. The reader feels, no doubt, that his efforts have achieved something worth while—something commensurate with the amount of mental energy which a good detective novel compels him to expend.

The Omnibus of Crime

(1928-29)

By Dorothy L. Sayers

If some enterprising editor or publisher should undertake to assemble a collection of the best literary criticism of all types and topics, and wished to include the finest single piece of analytical writing about the detective story, it is almost certain that the choice would go to the Introduction by Dorothy L. Sayers to the memorable anthology known in her native England as Great Short Stories of Detection, Mystery, and Horror *and in America as the first* Omnibus of Crime *(London: Gollancz, 1928; New York: Payson & Clarke, 1929). Authoritative without being didactic, concise but comprehensive, Miss Sayers' critique contains in its relatively brief compass virtually all that was to be said about the detective story up to the date of its composition. It is the present editor's great regret that space will not permit the inclusion, also, of Miss Sayers' admirable prefatory remarks to her second omnibus (England, 1931; America, 1932) in which she forecast with remarkable accuracy the trend toward the novel of psychology and character which has been the outstanding technical development in the crime-detective story of the 1930's and 1940's. . . . As to Miss Sayers' qualifications for her task, it is surely unnecessary to introduce the creator of Lord Peter Wimsey, the author who has been most frequently called (pace Edmund Wilson and Raymond Chandler) the most distinguished living exponent of her art, to an audience of detective story readers.*

THE art of self-tormenting is an ancient one, with a long and honourable literary tradition. Man, not satisfied with the mental confusion and unhappiness to be derived from contemplating the cruelties of life and the riddle of the universe, delights to occupy his leisure moments with puzzles and bugaboos. The pages of every magazine and newspaper swarm with cross-words, mathematical tricks, puzzle-pictures, enigmas, acrostics, and detective-stories, as also with stories of the kind called "powerful" (which means unpleasant), and those which make him afraid to go to bed. It may be that in them he finds a sort of catharsis or purging of his fears and self-questionings. These mysteries made only to be solved, these horrors which he knows to be mere figments of the creative brain, comfort him by subtly persuading that life is a mystery which death will solve, and whose horrors will pass away as a tale that is told. Or it may be merely that his animal faculties of fear and inquisitiveness demand more exercise than the daily round affords. Or it may be pure perversity. The fact remains that if you search the second-hand bookstalls for his cast-off literature, you will find fewer mystery stories than any other kind of book. Theology and poetry, philosophy and numismatics, love-stories and biography, he discards as easily as old razor-blades, but Sherlock Holmes and Wilkie Collins are cherished and read and re-read, till their covers fall off and their pages crumble to fragments.

Both the detective-story proper and the pure tale of horror are very ancient in origin. All native folk-lore has its ghost tales, while the first four detective-stories in this book hail respectively from the Jewish Apocrypha, Herodotus, and the Æneid. But, whereas the tale of horror has flourished in practically every age and country, the detective-story has had a spasmodic history, appearing here and there in faint, tentative sketches and episodes, until it suddenly burst into magnificent flower in the middle of the last century.

EARLY HISTORY OF DETECTIVE FICTION

Between 1840 and 1845 the wayward genius of Edgar Allan Poe (himself a past-master of the horrible) produced five tales, in which the general principles of the detective-story were laid down for ever. In "The Murders in the Rue Morgue" and, with a certain repulsive facetiousness, in "Thou Art the Man" he achieved the fusion of the two distinct genres and created what we may call the story of mystery, as distinct from pure detection on the one hand and pure horror on the other. In this fused genre, the reader's blood is first curdled by some horrible and apparently inexplicable murder or portent; the machinery of detection is then brought in to solve the mystery and punish the murderer. Since Poe's time all three branches—detection, mystery, and horror—have flourished. We have such pleasant little puzzles as Conan Doyle's "Case of Identity," in which there is nothing to shock or horrify; we have mere fantasies of blood and terror—human, as in Conan Doyle's "The Case of Lady Sannox," * or supernatural, as in Marion Crawford's "The Upper Birth," † most satisfactory of all, perhaps, we have such fusions as "The Speckled Band," ‡ or "The Hammer of God," § in which the ghostly terror is invoked only to be dispelled.

It is rather puzzling that the detective-story should have had to wait so long to find a serious exponent. Having started so well, why did it not develop earlier? The Oriental races, with their keen appreciation of intellectual subtlety, should surely have evolved it. The germ was there. "Why do you not come to pay your respects to me?" says Æsop's lion to the fox. "I beg your Majesty's pardon," says the fox, "but I noticed the track of the animals that have already come to you; and, while I see many hoof-marks going in, I see none coming out. Till the animals that have entered your cave come out again, I prefer to remain in the open air." Sherlock Holmes could not have reasoned more lucidly from the premises.

Cacus the robber, be it noted, was apparently the first criminal to use the device of forged footprints to mislead the pursuer, though it is a long development from his primitive methods to the horses shod with cow-shoes in Conan Doyle's "Adventure of the Priory School." ‖ Hercules's methods of investigation, too, were rather of the rough and ready sort, though the reader will not

---

* Conan Doyle: *Round the Red Lamp.*
† Marion Crawford: *Uncanny Tales.*
‡ Conan Doyle: *Adventures of Sherlock Holmes.*
§ G. K. Chesterton: *The Innocence of Father Brown.*
‖ Conan Doyle: *Return of Sherlock Holmes.*

fail to observe that this early detective was accorded divine honours by his grateful clients.

The Jews, with their strongly moral preoccupation, were, as our two Apocryphal stories show, peculiarly fitted to produce the *roman policier.** The Romans, logical and given to law-making, might have been expected to do something with it, but they did not. In one of the folk-tales collected by the Grimms, twelve maidens disguised as men are set to walk across a floor strewn with peas, in the hope that their shuffling feminine tread will betray them; the maidens are, however, warned, and baffle the detectives by treading firmly. In an Indian folk-tale a similar ruse is more successful. Here a suitor is disguised as a woman, and has to be picked out from the women about him by the wise princess. The princess throws a lemon to each in turn, and the disguised man is detected by his instinctive action in clapping his knees together to catch the lemon, whereas the real women spread their knees to catch it in their skirts. Coming down to later European literature, we find the Bel-and-the-Dragon motif of the ashes spread on the floor reproduced in the story of Tristan. Here the king's spy spreads flour between Tristan's bed and that of Iseult; Tristan defeats the scheme by leaping from one bed to the other. The eighteenth century also contributed at least one outstanding example, in the famous detective chapter of Voltaire's *Zadig.*

It may be, as Mr. E. M. Wrong has suggested in a brilliant little study,† that throughout this early period "a faulty law of evidence was to blame, for detectives cannot flourish until the public has an idea of what constitutes proof, and while a common criminal procedure is arrest, torture, confession, and death." One may go further, and say that, though crime stories might, and did, flourish, the detective-story proper could not do so until public sympathy had veered round to the side of law and order. It will be noticed that, on the whole, the tendency in early crime-literature

---

* In "Bel and the Dragon" the science of deduction from material clues, in the popular Scotland Yard manner, is reduced to its simplest expression. "Susanna," on the other hand, may be taken as foreshadowing the Gallic method of eliciting the truth by the confrontation of witnesses.

† Preface to *Tales of Crime and Detection*. World's Classics. (Oxford University Press, 1926.)

is to admire the cunning and astuteness of the criminal.* This must be so while the law is arbitrary, oppressive, and brutally administered.

We may note that, even to-day, the full blossoming of the detective-stories is found among the Anglo-Saxon races. It is notorious that an English crowd tends to side with the policeman in a row. The British legal code, with its tradition of "sportsmanship" and "fair play for the criminal" is particularly favourable to the production of detective fiction, allowing, as it does, sufficient rope to the quarry to provide a ding-dong chase, rich in up-and-down incident. In France, also, though the street policeman is less honoured than in England, the detective-force is admirably organised and greatly looked up to. France has a good output of detective-stories, though considerably smaller than that of the English-speaking races. In the Southern States of Europe the law is less loved and the detective story less frequent. We may not unreasonably trace a connection here.

Some further light is thrown on the question by a remark made by Herr Lion Feuchtwanger when broadcasting during his visit to London in 1927. Contrasting the tastes of the English, French, and German publics, he noted the great attention paid by the Englishman to the external details of men and things. The Englishman likes material exactness in the books he reads; the German and the Frenchman, in different degrees, care little for it in comparison with psychological truth. It is hardly surprising, then that the detective-story, with its insistence on footprints, bloodstains, dates, times, and places, and its reduction of character-drawing to bold, flat outline, should appeal far more strongly to Anglo-Saxon taste than to that of France or Germany.

Taking these two factors together, we begin to see why the detective-story had to wait for its full development for the establishment of an effective police organisation in the Anglo-Saxon countries. This was achieved—in England, at any rate—during the early part of the nineteenth century,† and was followed about

* e.g. "The Story of Rhampsinitus; Jacob and Esau;" "Reynard the Fox;" "Ballads of Robin Hood." etc.

† In a letter to W. Thornbury, dated February 18, 1862, Dickens says: "The Bow Street Runners ceased out of the land soon after the introduction of the new police. I remember them very well. . . . They kept company with thieves and such-like,

the middle of that century by the first outstanding examples of the detective-story as we know it to-day.*

To this argument we may add another. In the nineteenth century the vast, unexplored limits of the world began to shrink at an amazing and unprecedented rate. The electric telegraph circled the globe; railways brought remote villages into touch with civilisation; photographs made known to the stay-at-homes the marvels of foreign landscapes, customs, and animals; science reduced seeming miracles to mechanical marvels; popular education and improved policing made town and country safer for the common man than they had ever been. In place of the adventurer and the knight errant, popular imagination hailed the doctor, the scientist, and the policeman as saviours and protectors. But if one could no longer hunt the manticora, one could still hunt the murderer; if the armed escort had grown less necessary, yet one still needed the analyst to frustrate the wiles of the poisoner; from this point of view, the detective steps into his right place as the protector of the weak—the latest of the popular heroes, the true successor of Roland and Lancelot.

EDGAR ALLAN POE: EVOLUTION OF THE DETECTIVE

Before tracing further the history of detective fiction, let us look a little more closely at those five tales of Poe's, in which so much of the future development is anticipated. Probably the first thing that strikes us is that Poe has struck out at a blow the formal outline on which a large section of detective fiction has been built up. In the three Dupin stories, one of which figures in the present collection, we have the formula of the eccentric and brilliant private detective whose doings are chronicled by an admir-

---

much more than the detective police do. I don't know what their pay was, but I have do doubt their principal complements were got under the rose. It was a very slack institution, and its head-quarters were the Brown Bear, in Bow Street, a public house of more than doubtful reputation, opposite the police-office." The first "peelers" were established in 1829.

* The significance of footprints, and the necessity for scientific care in the checking of alibis, were understood at quite an early date, though, in the absence of an effective detective police, investigations were usually carried out by private persons at the instigation of the coroner. A remarkable case, which reads like a Freeman Wills Crofts novel, was that of R. *v.* Thornton (1818).

ing and thick-headed friend. From Dupin and his unnamed chronicler springs a long and distinguished line: Sherlock Holmes and his Watson; Martin Hewitt and his Brett; Raffles and his Bunny (on the criminal side of the business, but of the same breed); Thorndyke and his various Jardines, Ansteys, and Jervises; Hanaud and his Mr. Ricardo; Poirot and his Captain Hastings; Philo Vance and his Van Dine. It is not surprising that this formula should have been used so largely, for it is obviously a very convenient one for the writer. For one thing, the admiring satellite may utter expressions of eulogy which would be unbecoming in the mouth of the author, gaping at his own colossal intellect. Again, the reader, even if he is not, in R. L. Stevenson's phrase, "always a man of such vastly greater ingenuity than the writer," is usually a little more ingenious than Watson. He sees a little further through the brick wall; he pierces, to some extent, the cloud of mystification with which the detective envelops himself. "Aha!" he says to himself, "the average reader is supposed to see no further than Watson. But the author has not reckoned with me. I am one too many for him." He is deluded. It is all a device of the writer's for flattering him and putting him on good terms with himself. For though the reader likes to be mystified, he also likes to say, "I told you so," and "I spotted that." And this leads us to the third great advantage of the Holmes-Watson convention: by describing the clues as presented to the dim eyes and bemused mind of Watson, the author is enabled to preserve a spurious appearance of frankness, while keeping to himself the special knowledge on which the interpretation of those clues depends. This is a question of paramount importance, involving the whole artistic ethic of the detective-story. We shall return to it later. For the moment, let us consider a few other interesting types and formulæ which make their first appearance in Poe.

The personality of Dupin is eccentric, and for several literary generations eccentricity was highly fashionable among detective heroes. Dupin, we are informed, had a habit of living behind closed shutters, illumined by "a couple of tapers which, strongly perfumed, threw out only the ghastliest and feeblest of rays." From this stronghold he issued by night, to promenade the streets and enjoy the "infinity of mental excitement" afforded by quiet observation. He was also given to startling his friends by analysing their thought-processes, and he had a rooted contempt for the methods of the police.

Sherlock Holmes modelled himself to a large extent upon Dupin, substituting cocaine for candlelight, with accompaniments of shag and fiddle-playing. He is a more human and endearing figure than Dupin, and has earned as his reward the supreme honour which literature has to bestow—the secular equivalent of canonisation. He has passed into the language. He also started a tradition of his own—the hawk-faced tradition, which for many years dominated detective fiction.

So strong, indeed, was this domination that subsequent notable eccentrics have displayed their eccentricities chiefly by escaping from it. "Nothing," we are told, "could have been less like the traditional detective than"—so-and-so. He may be elderly and decrepit, like Baroness Orczy's Old Man in the Corner, whose characteristic habit is the continual knotting of string. Or he may be round and innocent-looking, like Father Brown or Poirot. There is Sax Rohmer's Moris Klaw,* with his bald, scholarly forehead; he irrigates his wits with a verbena spray, and carries about with him an "odically-sterilised" cushion to promote psychic intuition. There is the great Dr. Thorndyke, probably the handsomest detective in fiction; he is outwardly bonhomous, but spiritually detached, and his emblem is the green research-case, filled with miniature microscopes and scientific implements. Max Carrados has the distinction of being blind; Old Ebbie wears a rabbit-skin waistcoat; Lord Peter Wimsey (if I may refer to him without immodesty) indulges in the buying of incunabula and has a pretty taste in wines and haberdashery. By a final twist of the tradition, which brings the wheel full circle, there is a strong modern tendency to produce detectives remarkable for their ordinariness; they may be well-bred walking gentlemen, like A. A. Milne's Antony Gillingham, or journalists, like Gaston Leroux's Rouletabille, or they may even be policemen, like Freeman Wills Crofts' Inspector French, or the heroes of Mr. A. J. Rees's sound and well-planned stories.†

---

* Sax Rohmer: *The Dream Detective.*
† A. J. Rees: *The Shrieking Pit; The Hand in the Dark;* (with J. R. Watson) *The*

There have also been a few women detectives,* but on the whole, they have not been very successful. In order to justify their choice of sex, they are obliged to be so irritatingly intuitive as to destroy that quiet enjoyment of the logical which we look for in our detective reading. Or else they are active and courageous, and insist on walking into physical danger and hampering the men engaged on the job. Marriage, also, looms too large in their view of life; which is not surprising, for they are all young and beautiful. Why these charming creatures should be able to tackle abstruse problems at the age of twenty-one or thereabouts, while the male detectives are usually content to wait till their thirties or forties before setting up as experts, it is hard to say. Where do they pick up their worldly knowledge? Not from personal experience, for they are always immaculate as the driven snow. Presumably it is all intuition.

Better use has been made of women in books where the detecting is strictly amateur—done, that is, by members of the family or house-party themselves, and not by a private consultant. Evelyn Humblethorne † is a detective of this kind, and so is Joan Cowper, in *The Brooklyn Murders*.‡ But the really brilliant woman detective has yet to be created.§

While on this subject, we must not forget the curious and interesting development of detective fiction which has produced the *Adventures of Sexton Blake,* and other allied cycles. This is the Holmes tradition, adapted for the reading of the board-school boy and crossed with the Buffalo Bill adventure type. The books are written by a syndicate of authors, each one of whom uses a set of characters of his own invention, grouped about a central

---

Hampstead Mystery; The Mystery of the Downs, etc. Messrs. Rees and Watson write of police affairs with the accuracy born of inside knowledge, but commendably avoid the dullness which is apt to result from a too-faithful description of correct official procedure.

 * e.g. Anna Katharine Green: *The Golden Slipper;* Baroness Orczy: *Lady Molly of Scotland Yard;* G. R. Sims: *Dorcas Dene;* Valentine: *The Adjusters;* Richard Marsh: *Judith Lee;* Arthur B. Reeve: *Constance Dunlap;* etc.

 † Lord Gorell: *In the Night.*

 ‡ G. D. H. & M. Cole.

 § Wilkie Collins—who was curiously fascinated by the "strong-minded" woman —made two attempts at the woman detective in *No Name* and *The Law and the Lady.* The spirit of the time was, however, too powerful to allow these attempts to be altogether successful.

and traditional group consisting of Sexton Blake and his boy assistant, Tinker, their comic landlady Mrs. Bardell, and their bull-
dog Pedro. As might be expected, the quality of the writing and
the detective methods employed vary considerably from one author to another. The best specimens display extreme ingenuity,
and an immense vigour and fertility in plot and incident. Nevertheless, the central types are pretty consistently preserved throughout the series. Blake and Tinker are less intuitive than Holmes,
from whom however, they are directly descended, as their address in Baker Street shows. They are more careless and reckless
in their methods; more given to displays of personal heroism and
pugilism; more simple and human in their emotions. The really
interesting point about them is that they present the nearest modern approach to a national folk-lore, conceived as the centre for
a cycle of loosely connected romances in the Arthurian manner.
Their significance in popular literature and education would
richly repay scientific investigation.

Edgar Allan Poe: Evolution of the Plot

As regards plot also, Poe laid down a number of sound keels
for the use of later adventurers. Putting aside his instructive excursion into the psychology of detection—instructive, because we
can trace their influence in so many of Poe's successors down to
the present day—putting these aside, and discounting that atmosphere of creepiness which Poe so successfully diffused about
nearly all he wrote, we shall probably find that to us, sophisticated
and trained on an intensive study of detective fiction, his plots
are thin to transparency. But in Poe's day they represented a new
technique. As a matter of fact, it is doubtful whether there are
more than half a dozen deceptions in the mystery-monger's bag
of tricks, and we shall find that Poe has got most of them, at any
rate in embryo.

Take, first, the three Dupin stories. In "The Murders in the
Rue Morgue," an old woman and her daughter are found horribly
murdered in an (apparently) hermetically sealed room. An innocent person is arrested by the police. Dupin proves that the police
have failed to discover one mode of entrance to the room, and

deduces from a number of observations that the "murder" was committed by a huge ape. Here is, then, a combination of three typical motifs: the wrongly suspected man, to whom all the superficial evidence (motive, access, etc.) points; the hermetically sealed death-chamber (still a favourite central theme); finally, the *solution by the unexpected means.* In addition, we have Dupin drawing deductions, which the police have overlooked, from the evidence of witnesses (superiority in inference), and discovering clues which the police have not thought of looking for owing to obsession by an *idée fixe* (superiority in observation based on inference). In this story also are enunciated for the first time those two great aphorisms of detective science: first, that when you have eliminated all the impossibilities, then, whatever remains, *however improbable,* must be the truth; and, secondly, that the more *outré* a case may appear, the easier it is to solve. Indeed, take it all round, "The Murders in the Rue Morgue" constitutes in itself almost a complete manual of detective theory and practice.

In "The Purloined Letter," we have one of those stolen documents on whose recovery hangs the peace of mind of a distinguished personage. It is not, indeed, one of the sort whose publication would spread consternation among the Chancelleries of Europe, but it is important enough. The police suspect a certain minister of taking it. They ransack every corner of his house, in vain. Dupin, arguing from his knowledge of the minister's character, decides that subtlety must be met by subtlety. He calls on the minister and discovers the letter, turned inside out and stuck in a letter-rack in full view of the casual observer.

Here we have, besides the reiteration, in inverted form,* of aphorism No. 2 (above), the method of *psychological deduction* and the solution by the formula of the *most obvious place.* This

---

* "The business is very simple indeed, and I make no doubt that we can manage it sufficiently well ourselves; but then I thought Dupin would like to hear of it because it is so excessively *odd.*"

"Simple and odd," said Dupin.

"Why, yes; and not exactly that either. The fact is, we have all been a good deal puzzled because the affair *is* so simple, and yet baffles us altogether."

"Perhaps it is the very simplicity of the thing which puts you at fault," said Dupin.

The psychology of the matter is fully discussed in Poe's characteristic manner a few pages further on.

trick is the forerunner of the diamond concealed in the tumbler of water, the man murdered in the midst of a battle, Chesterton's "Invisible Man" (the postman, so familiar a figure that his presence goes unnoticed) * and a whole line of similar ingenuities.

The third Dupin story, "The Mystery of Marie Rogêt," has fewer imitators, but is the most interesting of all to the connoisseur. It consists entirely of a series of newspaper cuttings relative to the disappearance and murder of a shopgirl, with Dupin's comments thereon. The story contains no solution of the problem, and, indeed, no formal ending—and that for a very good reason. The disappearance was a genuine one, its actual heroine being one Mary Cecilia Rogers, and the actual place New York. The newspaper cuttings, were also, *mutatis mutandis,* genuine. The paper which published Poe's article dared not publish his conclusion. Later on it was claimed that his argument was, in substance, correct; and though this claim has, I believe, been challenged of late years, Poe may, nevertheless, be ranked among the small band of mystery-writers who have put their skill in deduction to the acid test of a problem which they had not in the first place invented.†

Of the other Poe stories, one, "Thou Art the Man," is very slight in theme and unpleasantly flippant in treatment. A man is murdered; a hearty person, named, with guileless cunning, Goodfellow, is very energetic in fixing the crime on a certain person. The narrator of the story makes a repulsive kind of jack-in-the-box out of the victim's corpse, and extorts a confession of guilt from—Goodfellow! Of course. Nevertheless, we have here two more leading motifs that have done overtime since Poe's day: the trail of false clues laid by the real murderer,‡ and the *solution by way of the most unlikely person.*

The fifth story is "The Gold Bug." In this a man finds a cipher which leads him to the discovery of a hidden treasure. The cipher is of the very simple one-sign-one-letter type, and its solution, of the mark-where-the-shadow-falls-take-three-paces-to-the-east-and-dig

---

* G. K. Chesterton: *The Innocence of Father Brown.*

† Sir Arthur Conan Doyle's successful efforts on behalf of George Edalji and Oscar Slater deserve special mention.

‡ See also "The Story of Susanna."

variety. In technique this story is the exact opposite of "Marie Rogêt"; the narrator is astonished by the antics of his detective friend, and is kept in entire ignorance of what he is about until *after* the discovery of the treasure; only then is the cipher for the first time either mentioned or explained. Some people think that "The Gold Bug" is Poe's finest mystery-story.

Now, with "The Gold Bug" at the one extreme and "Marie Rogêt" at the other, and the other three stories occupying intermediate places, Poe stands at the parting of the ways for detective fiction. From him go the two great lines of development— the Romantic and the Classic, or, to use terms less abraded by ill-usage, the purely Sensational and the purely Intellectual. In the former, thrill is piled on thrill and mystification on mystification; the reader is led on from bewilderment to bewilderment, till everything is explained in a lump in the last chapter. This school is strong in dramatic incident and atmosphere; its weakness is a tendency to confusion and a dropping of links—its explanations do not always explain; it is never dull, but it is sometimes nonsense. In the other—the purely Intellectual type—the action mostly takes place in the first chapter or so; the detective then follows up quietly from clue to clue till the problem is solved, the reader accompanying the great man in his search and being allowed to try his own teeth on the material provided. The strength of this school is its analytical ingenuity; its weakness is its liability to dullness and pomposity, its mouthing over the infinitely little, and its lack of movement and emotion.

INTELLECTUAL AND SENSATIONAL LINES OF DEVELOPMENT

The purely Sensational thriller is not particularly rare—we may find plenty of examples in the work of William Le Queux, Edgar Wallace, and others. The purely Intellectual is rare indeed; few writers have consistently followed the "Marie Rogêt" formula of simply spreading the *whole* evidence before the reader and leaving him to deduce the detective's conclusion from it if he can.

M. P. Shiel, indeed, did so in his trilogy, *Prince Zaleski,* whose curious and elaborate beauty recaptures in every arabesque sentence the very accent of Edgar Allan Poe. Prince Zaleski, "victim of a too importunate, too unfortunate Love, which the fulgor of the throne itself could not abash," sits apart in his ruined tower in "the semi-darkness of the very faint greenish lustre radiated from an open censer-like *lampas* in the centre of the domed encausted roof," surrounded by Flemish sepulchral brasses, runic tablets, miniature paintings, winged bulls, Tamil scriptures on lacquered leaves of the talipot, mediæval reliquaries richly gemmed, Brahmin gods, and Egyptian mummies, and lulled by "the low, liquid tinkling of an invisible musical-box." Like Sherlock Holmes, he indulges in a drug—"the narcotic *cannabis sativa:* the base of the *bhang* of the Mohammedans." A friend brings to him the detective problems of the outside world, which he proceeds to solve from the data given and (except in the final story) without stirring from his couch. He adorns his solutions with philosophical discourses on the social progress of mankind, all delivered with the same melancholy grace and remote intellectual disdain. The reasoning is subtle and lucid, but the crimes themselves are fantastic and incredible—a fault which these tales have in common with those of G. K. Chesterton.

Another writer who uses the "Marie Rogêt" formula is Baroness Orczy. Her *Old Man in the Corner* series is constructed precisely on those lines, and I have seen a French edition in which, when the expository part of the story is done, the reader is exhorted to: "Pause a moment and see if you can arrive at the explanation yourself, before you read the Old Man's solution." This pure puzzle is a formula which obviously has its limitations. Nearest to this among modern writers comes Freeman Wills Crofts, whose painstaking sleuths always "play fair" and display their clues to the reader as soon as they have picked them up. The intellectually minded reader can hardly demand more than this. The aim of the writer of this type of detective-story is to make the reader say at the end, neither: "Oh well, I knew it must be that all along," nor yet: "Dash it all! I couldn't be expected to guess that"; but: "Oh, of course! What a fool I was not to see it! Right under my nose all the time!" Precious tribute! How often striven for! How rarely earned!

On the whole, however, the tendency is for the modern educated public to demand fair play from the writer, and for the Sensational and Intellectual branches of the story to move further apart.

Before going further with this important question, we must look back once more to the middle of the last century, and see what development took place to bridge the gap between Dupin and Sherlock Holmes.

Poe, like a restless child, played with his new toy for a little while, and then, for some reason, wearied of it. He turned his attention to other things, and his formula lay neglected for close on forty years. Meanwhile a somewhat different type of detective-story was developing independently in Europe. In 1848 the elder Dumas, always ready to try his hand at any novel and ingenious thing, suddenly inserted into the romantic body of the *Vicomte de Bragelonne* a passage of pure scientific deduction. This passage is quite unlike anything else in the Musketeer cycle, and looks like the direct outcome of Dumas' keen interest in actual crime.*

But there is another literary influence which, though the fact is not generally recognised, must have been powerfully exerted at this date upon writers of mystery fiction. Between 1820 and 1850 the novels of Fenimore Cooper began to enjoy their huge popularity, and were not only widely read in America and England, but translated into most European languages. In *The Path-finder, The Deerslayer, The Last of the Mohicans,* and the rest of the series, Cooper revealed to the delighted youth of two hemispheres the Red Indian's patient skill in tracking his quarry by footprints, in interrogating a broken twig, a mossy trunk, a fallen leaf. The imagination of childhood was fired; every boy wanted to be an Uncas or a Chingachgook. Novelists, not content with following and imitating Cooper on his own ground, discovered a better way, by transferring the romance of the woodland tracker to the surroundings of their native country. In the 'sixties the generation who had read Fenimore Cooper in boyhood turned, as novelists and readers, to tracing the spoor of the criminal upon their own native heath. The enthusiasm for Cooper combined magnificently with that absorbing interest in crime and detection which better methods of communication and an improved

---

* He published a great collection of famous crimes.

police system had made possible. While, in France, Gaboriau and Fortuné du Boisgobey concentrated upon the police novel pure and simple, English writers, still permeated by the terror and mystery of the romantic movement, and influenced by the "Newgate novel" of Bulwer and Ainsworth, perfected a more varied and imaginative genre, in which the ingenuity of the detective problem allied itself with the sombre terrors of the weird and supernatural.

The Pre-Doyle Period

Of the host of writers who attempted this form of fiction in the 'sixties and 'seventies, three may be picked out for special mention.

That voluminous writer, Mrs. Henry Wood, represents, on the whole, the melodramatic and adventurous development of the crime-story as distinct from the detective problem proper. Through *East Lynne*, crude and sentimental as it is, she exercised an enormous influence on the rank and file of sensational novelists, and at her best, she is a most admirable spinner of plots. Whether her problem concerns a missing will, a vanished heir, a murder, or a family curse, the story spins along without flagging, and, though she is a little too fond of calling in Providence to cut the knot of intrigue with the sword of coincidence, the mystery is fully and properly unravelled, in a workmanlike manner and without any loose ends. She makes frequent use of supernatural thrills. Sometimes these are explained away: a "murdered" person is seen haunting the local churchyard, and turns out never to have been killed at all. Sometimes the supernatural remains supernatural, as, for instance, the coffin-shaped appearance in *The Shadow of Ashlydyat*. Her morality is perhaps a little oppressive, but she is by no means without humour, and at times can produce a shrewd piece of characterisation.

Melodramatic, but a writer of real literary attainment, and gifted with a sombre power which has seldom been equalled in painting the ghastly and the macabre, is Sheridan Le Fanu. Like Poe, he has the gift of investing the most mechanical of plots with an atmosphere of almost unbearable horror. Take, for example, that scene in *Wylder's Hand* where the aged Uncle Lorne appears —phantom or madman? we are not certain which—to confront the villainous Lake in the tapestried room.

" 'Mark Wylder is in evil plight,' said he.

" 'Is he?' said Lake with a sly scoff, though he seemed to me a good deal scared. 'We hear no complaints, however, and fancy he must be tolerably comfortable notwithstanding.'

" 'You know where he is,' said Uncle Lorne.

" 'Aye, in Italy; everyone knows that,' answered Lake.

" 'In Italy,' said the old man reflectively, as if trying to gather up his ideas, 'Italy. . . . He has had a great tour to make. It is nearly accomplished now; when it is done, he will be like me, *humano major*. He has seen the places which you are yet to see.'

" 'Nothing I should like better; particularly Italy,' said Lake.

" 'Yes,' said Uncle Lorne, lifting up slowly a different finger at each name in his catalogue. 'First, Lucus Mortis; then Terra Tenebrosa; next, Tartarus; after that Terra Oblivionis; then Herebus; then Barathrum; then Gehenna, and then Stagnum Ignis.'

" 'Of course,' acquiesced Lake, with an ugly sneer. . . .

" 'Don't be frightened—but he's alive; I think they'll make him mad. It is a frightful plight. Two angels buried him alive in Vallombrosa by night; I saw it, standing among the lotus and hemlocks. A negro came to me, a black clergyman with white eyes, and remained beside me; and the angels imprisoned Mark; they put him on duty forty days and forty nights, with his ear to the river listening for voices; and when it was over we blessed them; and the clergyman walked with me a long while, to-and-fro, to-and-fro upon the earth, telling me the wonders of the abyss.'

" 'And is it from the abyss, sir, he writes his letters?" enquired the Town Clerk, with a wink at Lake.

" 'Yes, yes, very diligent; it behoves him; and his hair is always standing straight on his head for fear. But he'll be sent up again, at last, a thousand, a hundred, ten and one, black marble steps, and then it will be the other one's turn. So it was prophesied by the black magician.' "

This chapter leads immediately to those in which Larkin, the crooked attorney, discovers, by means of a little sound detective work of a purely practical sort, that Mark Wylder's letters have indeed been written "from the abyss." Mark Wylder has, in fact,

been murdered, and the letters are forgeries sent abroad to be
despatched by Lake's confederate from various towns in Italy.
From this point we gradually learn to expect the ghastly moment
when he is "sent up again at last" from the grave, in the Black-
berry Dell at Gylingden.

> "In the meantime the dogs continued their unaccountable yell-
> ing close by.
> " 'What the devil's that?' said Wealden.
> "Something like a stunted, blackened branch was sticking out
> of the peat, ending in a set of short, thickish twigs. This is what it
> seemed. The dogs were barking at it. It was, really, a human hand
> and arm. . . ."

In this book the detection is done by private persons, and the
local police are only brought in at the end to secure the criminal.
This is also the case in that extremely interesting book *Checkmate* (1870), in which the plot actually turns upon the complete
alteration of the criminal's appearance by a miracle of plastic
surgery. It seems amazing that more use has not been made of this
device in post-war days, now that the reconstruction of faces has
become comparatively common and, with the perfecting of asep-
tic surgery, infinitely easier than in Le Fanu's day. I can only call
to mind two recent examples of this kind: one, Mr. Hopkins
Moorhouse's *Gauntlet of Alceste;* the other, a short story called
"The Losing of Jasper Virel," by Beckles Willson.* In both stories
the alterations include the tattooing of the criminal's eyes from
blue to brown.

For sheer grimness and power, there is little in the literature
of horror to compare with the trepanning scene in Le Fanu's *The
House by the Churchyard*. Nobody who has ever read it could
possibly forget that sick chamber, with the stricken man sunk in
his deathly stupor; the terrified wife; the local doctor, kindly and
absurd—and then the pealing of the bell, and the entry of the
brilliant, brutal Dillon "in dingy splendours and a great draggled
wig, with a gold-headed cane in his bony hand . . . diffusing a
reek of whisky-punch, and with a case of instruments under his
arm," to perform the operation. The whole scene is magnificently

---

* *Strand Magazine,* July 1909.

written, with the surgeon's muttered technicalities heard through the door, the footsteps—then the silence while the trepanning is proceeding, and the wounded Sturk's voice, which no one ever thought to hear again, raised as if from the grave to denounce his murderer. That chapter in itself would entitle Le Fanu to be called a master of mystery and horror.

Most important of all during this period we have Wilkie Collins. An extremely uneven writer, Collins is less appreciated today than his merits and influence deserve.* He will not bear comparison with Le Fanu in his treatment of the weird, though he was earnestly ambitious to succeed in this line. His style was too dry and inelastic, his mind too legal. Consider the famous dream in *Armadale,* divided into seventeen separate sections, each elaborately and successively fulfilled in laborious detail! In the curious semi-supernatural rhythm of *The Woman in White* he came nearer to genuine achievement, but, on the whole, his eerieness is wire-drawn and' unconvincing. But he greatly excels Le Fanu in humour, in the cunning of his rogues † in characterdrawing, and especially in the architecture of his plots. Taking everything into consideration, *The Moonstone* is probably the very finest detective story ever written. By comparison with its wide scope, its dove-tailed completeness and the marvellous variety and soundness of its characterisation, modern mystery fiction looks thin and mechanical. Nothing human is perfect, but *The Moonstone* comes about as near perfection as anything of its kind can be.

In *The Moonstone* Collins used the convention of telling the story in a series of narratives from the pens of the various actors concerned. Modern realism—often too closely wedded to externals—is prejudiced against this device. It is true that, for example, Betteredge's narrative is not at all the kind of thing that a butler

---

* In the British Museum catalogue only two critical studies of this celebrated English mystery-monger are listed: one is by an American, the other by a German.

† Collins made peculiarly his own the art of plot and counter-plot. Thus we have the magnificent duels of Marion Halcombe and Count Fosco in *The Woman in White;* Captain Wragge and Mrs. Lecount in *No Name;* the Pedgifts and Miss Gwilt in *Armadale.* Move answers to move as though on a chessboard (but very much more briskly), until the villain is manœuvred into the corner where a cunningly contrived legal checkmate has been quietly awaiting him from the beginning of the game.

would be likely to write; nevertheless, it has an ideal truth—it is the kind of thing that Betteredge might think and feel, even if he could not write it. And, granted this convention of the various narratives, how admirably the characters are drawn! The pathetic figure of Rosanna Spearman, with her deformity and her warped devotion, is beautifully handled, with a freedom from sentimentality which is very remarkable. In Rachel Verinder, Collins has achieved one of the novelist's hardest tasks; he has depicted a girl who is virtuous, a gentlewoman, and really interesting, and that without the slightest exaggeration or deviation from naturalness and probability. From his preface to the book it is clear that he took especial pains with this character, and his success was so great as almost to defeat itself. Rachel is so little spectacular that we fail to realise what a singularly fine and truthful piece of work she is.

The detective part of the story is well worth attention. The figure of Sergeant Cuff is drawn with a restraint and sobriety which makes him seem a little colourless beside Holmes and Thorndyke and Carrados, but he is a very living figure. One can believe that he made a success of his rose-growing when he retired; he genuinely loved roses, whereas one can never feel that the great Sherlock possessed quite the right feeling for his bees. Being an official detective, Sergeant Cuff is bound by the etiquette of his calling. He is never really given a free hand with Rachel, and the conclusion he comes to is a wrong one. But he puts in a good piece of detective work in the matter of Rosanna and the stained nightgown; and the scenes in which his shrewdness and knowledge of human nature are contrasted with the blundering stupidity of Superintendent Seagrave read like an essay in the manner of Poe.

It is, of course, a fact that the Dupin stories had been published fifteen years or so when *The Moonstone* appeared. But there is no need to seek in them for the original of Sergeant Cuff. He had his prototype in real life, and the whole nightgown incident was modelled, with some modifications, upon a famous case of the early 'sixties—the murder of little William Kent by his sixteen-year-old sister, Constance. Those who are interested in origins will find an excellent account of the "Road murder," as it is called, in Miss Tennyson Jesse's *Murder and its Motives,* or in Atkey's *Famous Trials of the Nineteenth Century,* and may compare the methods of Sergeant Cuff with those of the real Detective Whicher.

Wilkie Collins himself claimed that nearly all his plots were founded on fact; indeed, this was his invariable answer when the charge of improbability was preferred against him.

> " 'I wish,' he cries angrily to a friend, 'before people make such assertions, they would think what they are writing or talking about. I know of very few instances in which fiction exceeds the probability of reality. I'll tell you where I got many of my plots from. I was in Paris, wandering about the streets with Charles Dickens, amusing ourselves by looking into the shops. We came to an old book stall—half-shop and half-store—and I found some dilapidated volumes and records of French crime—a sort of French Newgate Calendar. I said to Dickens "Here is a prize!" So it turned out to be. In them I found some of my best plots.' " *

Not that Collins was altogether disingenuous in his claim never to have o'erstepped the modesty of nature. While each one of his astonishing contrivances and coincidences might, taken separately, find its parallel in real life, it remains true that in cramming a whole series of such improbabilities into the course of a single story he does frequently end by staggering all belief. But even so, he was a master craftsman, whom many modern mystery-mongers might imitate to their profit. He never wastes an incident; he never leaves a loose end; no incident, however trivial on the one hand or sensational on the other, is ever introduced for the mere sake of amusement or sensation. Take, for example, the great "sensation-scene" in *No Name,* where for half an hour Magdalen sits, with the bottle of laudanum in her hand, counting the passing ships. "If, in that time, an even number passed her—the sign given should be a sign to live. If the uneven number prevailed, the end should be—death." Here, you would say, is pure sensationalism; it is a situation invented deliberately to wring tears and anguish from the heart of the reader. But you would be wrong. That bottle of laudanum is brought in because it will

---

* Wybert Reeve: "Recollections of Wilkie Collins," *Chambers' Journal,* Vol IX., p. 458.

be wanted again, later on. In the next section of the story it is found in Magdalen's dressing-case, and this discovery, by leading her husband to suppose that she means to murder him, finally induces him to cut her out of his will, and so becomes one of the most important factors in the plot.

In *The Moonstone,* which of all his books comes nearest to being a detective-story in the modern sense, Collins uses with great effect the formula of the most unlikely person * and the unexpected means in conjunction. Opium is the means in this case—a drug with whose effects we are tolerably familiar to-day, but which in Collins's time was still something of an unknown quantity, de Quincey notwithstanding. In the opium of *The Moonstone* and the plastic surgery of *Checkmate* we have the distinguished forebears of a long succession of medical and scientific mysteries which stretches down to the present day.

During the 'seventies and early 'eighties the long novel of marvel and mystery held the field, slowly unrolling its labyrinthine complexity through its three ample volumes crammed with incident and leisurely drawn characters.†

SHERLOCK HOLMES AND HIS INFLUENCE

In 1887 *A Study in Scarlet* was flung like a bombshell into the field of detective fiction, to be followed within a few short and brilliant years by the marvellous series of Sherlock Holmes short stories. The effect was electric. Conan Doyle took up the Poe formula and galvanised it into life and popularity. He cut out the elaborate psychological introductions, or restated them in

---

* Franklin Blake—the actual, though unconscious thief. By an ingenious turn, this discovery does not end the story. The diamond is still missing, and a further chase leads to the really guilty party (Godfrey Ablewhite). The character of this gentleman is enough to betray his villainy to the modern reader, though it may have seemed less repulsive to the readers in the 'sixties. His motive, however, is made less obvious, although it quite honourably and fairly hinted at for the observant reader to guess.

† We must not leave this period without mentioning the stories of Anna Katharine Green, of which the long series begins with *The Leavenworth Case* in 1883, and extends right down to the present day. They are genuine detective-stories, often of considerable ingenuity, but marred by an uncritical sentimentality of style and treatment which makes them difficult reading for the modern student. They are, however, important by their volume and by their influence on other American writers.

crisp dialogue. He brought into prominence what Poe had only lightly touched upon—the deduction of staggering conclusions from trifling indications in the Dumas-Cooper-Gaboriau manner. He was sparkling, surprising, and short. It was the triumph of the epigram.

A comparison of the Sherlock Holmes tales with the Dupin tales shows clearly how much Doyle owed to Poe, and, at the same time, how greatly he modified Poe's style and formula. Read, for instance, the opening pages of "The Murders in the Rue Morgue," which introduce Dupin, and compare them with the first chapter of *A Study in Scarlet*. Or merely set side by side the two passages which follow and contrast the relations between Dupin and his chronicler on the one hand, and between Holmes and Watson on the other:

> "I was astonished, too, at the vast extent of his reading; and, above all, I felt my soul enkindled within me by the wild fervour, and the vivid freshness of his imagination. Seeking in Paris the objects I then sought, I felt that the society of such a man would be to me a treasure beyond price; and this feeling I frankly confided to him. It was at length arranged that we should live together . . . and as my worldly circumstances were somewhat less embarrassed than his own, I was permitted to be at the expense of renting, and furnishing in a style which suited the rather fantastic gloom of our common temper, a time-eaten and grotesque mansion . . . in a retired and desolate portion of the Faubourg Saint Germain . . . It was a freak of fancy in my friend (for what else shall I call it?) to be enamoured of the Night for her own sake; and into this *bizarrerie*, as into all his others, I quietly fell, giving myself up to his wild whims with a perfect abandon." *

> "An anomaly which often struck me in the character of my friend Sherlock Holmes was that, though in his methods of thought he was the neatest and most methodical of mankind, and although also he affected a certain quiet primness of dress, he was none the less in his personal habits one of the most untidy men that ever drove a fellow-lodger to distraction. Not that I am in the least conventional in that respect myself. The rough-and-tumble work in Afghanistan, coming on the top of a natural Bohemianism of dis-

---

* "The Murders in the Rue Morgue."

position, has made me rather more lax than befits a medical man. But with me there is a limit, and when I find a man who keeps his cigars in the coal-scuttle, his tobacco in the toe-end of a Persian slipper, and his unanswered correspondence transfixed by a jack-knife into the very centre of his wooden mantelpiece, then I begin to give myself virtuous airs. I have always held, too, that pistol-practice should distinctly be an open-air pastime; and when Holmes in one of his queer humours would sit in an arm-chair, with his hair-trigger and a hundred Boxer cartridges, and proceed to adorn the opposite wall with a patriotic V.R. done in bullet-pocks, I felt strongly that neither the atmosphere nor the appearance of our room was improved by it." *

See how the sturdy independence of Watson adds salt and savour to the eccentricities of Holmes, and how flavourless beside it is the hero-worshipping self-abnegation of Dupin's friend. See, too, how the concrete details of daily life in Baker Street lift the story out of the fantastic and give it a solid reality. The Baker Street ménage has just that touch of humorous commonplace which appeals to British readers.

Another pair of parallel passages will be found in "The Purloined Letter" and "The Naval Treaty." They show the two detectives in dramatic mood, surprising their friends by their solution of the mystery. In "The Adventure of the Priory School," also, a similar situation occurs, though Holmes is here shown in a grimmer vein, rebuking wickedness in high places.

Compare, also, the conversational styles of Holmes and Dupin, and the reasons for Holmes's popularity become clearer than ever. Holmes has enriched English literature with more than one memorable aphorism and turn of speech.

" 'You know my methods, Watson.'
" 'A long shot, Watson—a very long shot.'
" '—a little monograph on the hundred-and-fourteen varieties of tobacco-ash.'
" 'These are deep waters, Watson.'
" 'Excellent!' cried Mr. Acton.—'But very superficial,' said Holmes.
" 'Excellent!' I cried.—'Elementary,' said he.

---

* "The Musgrave Ritual."

" 'It is of the highest importance in the art of detection to be able to recognise out of a number of facts which are incidental and which vital.'

" 'You mentioned your name as if I should recognise it, but beyond the obvious fact that you are a bachelor, a solicitor, a Freemason and an asthmatic, I know nothing whatever about you.'

" 'Every problem becomes very childish when once it is explained to you.' "

Nor must we forget that delightful form of riposto which Father Ronald Knox has wittily christened the "Sherlockismus":

" 'I would call your attention to the curious incident of the dog in the night-time.'

" 'The dog did nothing in the night-time.'

" 'That was the curious incident.' "

So, with Sherlock Holmes, the ball—the original nucleus deposited by Edgar Allan Poe nearly forty years earlier—was at last set rolling. As it went, it swelled into a vast mass—it set off others —it became a spate—a torrent—an avalanche of mystery fiction. It is impossible to keep track of all the detective-stories produced to-day. Book upon book, magazine upon magazine pour out from the Press, crammed with murders, thefts, arsons, frauds, conspiracies, problems, puzzles, mysteries, thrills, maniacs, crooks, poisoners, forgers, garrotters, police, spies, secret-service men, detectives, until it seems that half the world must be engaged in setting riddles for the other half to solve.

THE SCIENTIFIC DETECTIVE

The boom began in the 'nineties, when the detective short story, till then rather neglected, strode suddenly to the front and made the pace rapidly under the ægis of Sherlock Holmes. Of particular interest is the long series which appeared under various titles from the pens of L. T. Meade and her collaborators. These struck out a line—not new, indeed, for, as we have seen, it is as old as Collins and Le Fanu, but important because it was paving the way for great developments in a scientific age—the medical mystery story. Mrs. Meade opened up this fruitful vein with *Stories from the Diary of a Doctor* in 1893,* and pursued it in various magazines almost without a break to *The Sorceress of the Strand* † in 1902. These tales range from mere records of queer cases to genuine detective-stories in which the solution has a scientific or medical foundation. During this long collaboration, the authors deal with such subjects as hypnotism, catalepsy (so-called—then a favourite disease among fiction-writers), somnambulism, lunacy, murder by the use of X-rays and hydrocyanic acid gas, and a variety of other medical and scientific discoveries and inventions.

More definitely in the Holmes tradition is the sound and excellent work of Arthur Morrison in the "Martin Hewitt" books. Various authors such as John Oxenham and Manville Fenn also tried their hands at the detective-story, before turning to specialise in other work. We get also many lively tales of adventure and roguery, with a strong thread of detective interest, as, for example, the "African Millionaire" series by Grant Allen.

Now in the great roar and rush of enthusiasm which greeted Sherlock Holmes, the detective-story became swept away on a single current of development. We observed, in discussing the Poe tales, that there were three types of story—the Intellectual ("Marie Rogêt"), the Sensational ("The Gold Bug"), and the Mixed ("Murders in the Rue Morgue"). "Sherlock Holmes" tales, as a rule, are of the mixed type. Holmes—I regret to say it—does not always play fair with the reader. He "picks up," or "pounces upon," a "minute object," and draws a brilliant deduction from it, but the reader, however brilliant, cannot himself anticipate that deduction because he is not told what the "small object" is. It is Watson's fault, of course—Holmes, indeed, remonstrated with him on at least one occasion about his unscientific methods of narration.

An outstanding master of this "surprise" method is Melville Davisson Post. His tales are so admirably written, and his ideas so ingenious, that we fail at first reading to realise how strictly

---

* In collaboration with "Clifford Halifax."

† In collaboration with Robert Eustace. In these stories the scientific basis was provided by Robert Eustace, and the actual writing done, for the most part, by L. T. Meade.

sensational they are in their method. Take, for instance, "An Act of God." from *Uncle Abner* (1911). In this tale, Uncle Abner uses the phonetic mis-spelling in a letter supposed to be written by a deaf mute to prove that the letter was not, in fact, written by him. If the text of the letter were placed before the reader, and he were given a chance to make his deduction for himself, the tale would be a true detective-story of the Intellectual type; but the writer keeps this clue to himself, and springs the detective's conclusions upon us like a bolt from the blue.

THE MODERN "FAIR-PLAY" METHOD

For many years, the newness of the genre and the immense prestige of Holmes blinded readers' eyes to these feats of legerdemain. Gradually, however, as the bedazzlement wore off, the public became more and more exacting. The uncritical are still catered for by the "thriller," in which nothing is explained, but connoisseurs have come, more and more, to call for a story which puts them on an equal footing with the detective himself, as regards all clues and discoveries.*

Seeing that the demand for equal opportunities is coupled today with an insistence on strict technical accuracy in the smallest details of the story, it is obvious that the job of writing detective-stories is by no means growing easier. The reader must be given every clue—but he must not be told, surely, all the detective's deductions, lest he should see the solution too far ahead. Worse still, supposing, even without the detective's help, he interprets all the clues accurately on his own account, what becomes of the surprise? How can we at the same time show the reader everything and yet legitimately obfuscate him as to its meaning?

Various devices are used to get over the difficulty. Frequently the detective, while apparently displaying his clues openly, will keep up his sleeve some bit of special knowledge which the reader does not possess. Thus, Thorndyke can cheerfully show you all his

---

* Yet even to-day the naughty tradition persists. In *The Crime at Diana's Pool*, for instance (1927), V. L. Whitechurch sins notably, twice over, in this respect, in the course of an otherwise excellent tale. But such crimes bring their own punishment, for the modern reader is quick to detect and resent unfairness, and a stern, though kindly letter of rebuke is presently despatched to the erring author!

finds. You will be none the wiser, unless you happen to have an intimate acquaintance with the fauna of local ponds; the effect of belladonna on rabbits; the physical and chemical properties of blood; optics; tropical diseases; metallurgy; hieroglyphics, and a few other trifles. Another method of misleading is to tell the reader what the detective has observed and deduced—but to make the observations and deductions turn out to be incorrect, thus leading up to a carefully manufactured surprise-packet in the last chapter.*

Some writers, like Mrs. Agatha Christie, still cling to the Watson formula. The story is told through the mouth, or at least through the eyes, of a Watson.† Others, like A. A. Milne in his *Red House Mystery*, adopt a mixed method. Mr. Milne begins by telling his tale from the position of a detached spectator; later on, we find that he has shifted round, and is telling it through the personality of Bill Beverley (a simple-minded but not unintelligent Watson); at another moment we find ourselves actually looking out through the eyes of Antony Gillingham, the detective himself.

IMPORTANCE OF THE VIEWPOINT

The skill of a modern detective novelist is largely shown by the play he makes with these various viewpoints.‡ Let us see how it is done in an acknowledged masterpiece of the genre. We will examine for the purpose a page of Mr. A. C. Bentley's *Trent's Last Case*. Viewpoint No. 1 is what we may call the Watson viewpoint; the detective's external actions only are seen by the reader. Viewpoint No. 2 is the middle viewpoint; we see what the detective

---

* C. E. Bentley: *Trent's Last Case;* Lord Gorell: *In the Night;* George Pleydell: *The Ware Case;* etc.

† An exceptional handling of the Watson theme is found in Agatha Christie's *Murder of Roger Ackroyd,* which is a *tour de force*. Some critics, as, for instance, Mr. W. H. Wright in his introduction to *The Great Detective Stories* (Scribner's, 1927), consider the solution illegitimate. I fancy, however, that this opinion merely represents a natural resentment at having been ingeniously bamboozled. All the necessary data are given. The reader ought to be able to guess the criminal, if he is sharp enough, and nobody can ask for more than this. It is, after all, the reader's job to keep his wits about him, and, like the perfect detective, to suspect *everybody*.

‡ For a most fascinating and illuminating discussion of this question of viewpoint in fiction, see Mr. Percy Lubbock: *The Craft of Fiction*.

sees, but are not told what he observes. Viewpoint No. 3 is that of close intimacy with the detective; we see all he sees, and are at once told his conclusions.

We begin from Viewpoint No. 2.

"Two bedroom doors faced him on the other side of the passage. He opened that which was immediately opposite, and entered a bedroom by no means austerely tidy. Some sticks and fishing-rods stood confusedly in one corner, a pile of books in another. The housemaid's hand had failed to give a look of order to the jumble of heterogeneous objects left on the dressing-table and on the mantel-shelf—pipes, penknives, pencils, keys, golf-balls, old letters, photographs, small boxes, tins, and bottles. Two fine etchings and some water-colour sketches hung on the walls; leaning against the end of the wardrobe, unhung, were a few framed engravings."

First Shift: Viewpoint No. 1.

"A row of shoes and boots were ranged beneath the window. Trent crossed the room and studied them intently; then he measured some of them with his tape, whistling very softly. This done, he sat on the side of the bed, and his eyes roamed gloomily about the room."

Here we observe Trent walking, studying, measuring, whistling, looking gloomy; but we do not know what was peculiar about the boots, nor what the measurements were. From our knowledge of Trent's character we may suppose that his conclusions are unfavourable to the amiable suspect, Marlowe, but we are not ourselves allowed to handle the material evidence.

Second Shift: Back to Viewpoint No. 2.

"The photographs on the mantel-shelf attracted him presently. He rose and examined one representing Marlowe and Manderson on horseback. Two others were views of famous peaks in the Alps. There was a faded print of three youths—one of them unmistakably his acquaintance of the haggard blue eyes [i.e. Marlowe]—clothed in tatterdemalion soldier's gear of the sixteenth century. Another was a portrait of a majestic old lady, slightly resembling Marlowe. Trent, mechanically taking a cigarette from an open box on the mantel-shelf, lit it and stared at the photographs."

Here, as at the opening of the paragraph, we are promoted to a more privileged position. We see all the evidence, and have an equal opportunity with Trent of singling out the significant detail—the fancy-costume portrait—and deducting from it that Marlowe was an active member of the O.U.D.S., and, by inference, capable of acting a part at a pinch.

Third Shift: Viewpoint No. 3.

"Next he turned his attention to a flat leathern case that lay by the cigarette-box. It opened easily. A small and light revolver, of beautiful workmanship, was disclosed, with a score or so of loose cartridges. On the stock were engraved the initials 'J. M.' . . .

"With the pistol in its case between them, Trent and the Inspector looked into each other's eyes for some moments. Trent was the first to speak. 'This mystery is all wrong,' he observed. 'It is insanity. The symptoms of mania are very marked. Let us see how we stand.' "

Throughout the rest of this scene we are taken into Trent's confidence. The revolver is described, we learn what Trent thinks about it from his own lips.

Thus, in a single page, the viewpoint is completely shifted three times, but so delicately that, unless we are looking for it, we do not notice the change.

In a later chapter, we get the final shift to a fourth viewpoint—that of complete mental identification with the detective:

"Mrs. Manderson had talked herself into a more emotional mood than she had yet shown to Trent. Her words flowed freely, and her voice had begun to ring and give play to a natural expressiveness that must hitherto have been dulled, he thought, by the shock and self-restraint of the past few days."

Here the words "had yet shown to Trent" clinch the identification of viewpoint. Throughout the book, we always, in fact, see Mrs. Manderson through Trent's emotions, and the whole second half of the story, when Trent has abandoned his own enquiries and is receiving the true explanation from Marlowe and Cupples, is told from Viewpoint No. 4.

The modern evolution in the direction of "fair play" * is to a great extent a revolution. It is a recoil from the Holmes influence and a turning back to *The Moonstone* and its contemporaries. There is no mystification about *The Moonstone*—no mystification of the reader, that is. With such scrupulous care has Collins laid the clues that the "ideal reasoner" might guess the entire outline of the story at the end of the first ten chapters of Betteredge's first narrative.†

ARTISTIC STATUS OF THE DETECTIVE-STORY

As the detective ceases to be impenetrable and infallible and becomes a man touched with the feeling of our infirmities, so the rigid technique of the art necessarily expands a little. In its severest form, the mystery-story is a pure analytical exercise, and, as such, may be a highly finished work of art, within its highly artificial limits. There is one respect, at least, in which the detective-story has an advantage over every other kind of novel. It possesses an Aristotelian perfection of beginning, middle, and end. A definite and single problem is set, worked out, and solved; its conclusion is not arbitrarily conditioned by marriage or death.‡ It

---

* It is needless to add that the detectives must be given fair play, too. Once they are embarked upon an investigation, no episode must ever be described which does not come within their cognisance. It is artistically shocking that the reader should be taken into the author's confidence behind the investigator's back. Thus, the reader's interest in *The Deductions of Colonel Gore* (Lynn Brock) is sensibly diminished by the fact of his knowing (as Gore does not) that it was Cecil Arndale who witnessed the scene between Mrs. Melhuish and Barrington near the beginning of the book. Those tales in which the action is frequently punctuated by eavesdropping of this kind on the reader's part belong to the merely Sensational class of detective-story, and rapidly decline into melodrama.

† Poe performed a similar feat in the case of *Barnaby Rudge,* of which he correctly prognosticated the whole development after reading the first serial part. Unhappily, he was not alive to perform the same office for *Edwin Drood!* Dickens came more and more to hanker after plot and mystery. His early efforts in this style are crude, and the mystery as a rule pretty transparent. In *Edwin Drood* he hoped that the "story would turn upon an interest suspended until the end," and the hope was only too thoroughly fulfilled. Undoubtedly his close friendship with Collins helped to influence him in the direction of mystery fiction; in the previous year (1867) he had pronounced *The Moonstone:* "Much better than anything he [Collins] has done."

‡ This should appeal to Mr. E. M. Forster, who is troubled by the irrational structure of the novel from this point of view. Unhappily, he has openly avowed himself "too priggish" to enjoy detective-stories. This is bad luck, indeed.

has the rounded (though limited) perfection of a triolet. The
farther it escapes from pure analysis, the more difficulty it has in
achieving artistic unity.

It does not, and by hypothesis never can, attain the loftiest level
of literary achievement. Though it deals with the most desperate
effects of rage, jealousy, and revenge, it rarely touches the heights
and depths of human passion. It presents us only with the *fait
accompli,* and looks upon death and mutilation with a dispassionate eye. It does not show us the inner workings of the murderer's
mind—it must not; for the identity of the murderer is hidden until the end of the book.* The victim is shown rather as a subject
for the dissecting-table than as a husband and father. A too violent
emotion flung into the glittering mechanism of the detective-story
jars the movement by disturbing its delicate balance. The most
successful writers are those who contrive to keep the story running from beginning to end upon the same emotional level, and
it is better to err in the direction of too little feeling than too
much. Here, the writer whose detective is a member of the official force has an advantage: from him a detached attitude is correct; he can suitably retain the impersonal attitude of the surgeon.
The sprightly amateur must not be sprightly all the time, lest at
some point we should be reminded that this is, after all, a question of somebody's being foully murdered, and that flippancy is
indecent. To make the transition from the detached to the human point of view is one of the writer's hardest tasks. It is especially hard when the murderer has been made human and sympathetic. A real person has then to be brought to the gallows, and
this must not be done too lightheartedly. Mr. G. K. Chesterton
deals with this problem by merely refusing to face it. His Father
Brown (who looks at sin and crime from the religious point of

---

* An almost unique example of the detective-story told from the point of view
of the hunted instead of the hunter is *Ashes to Ashes* by Isabel Ostrander. This
shows the clues being left by the murderer, who is then compelled to look on
while they are picked up, one after the other, by the detectives, despite all his
desperate efforts to cover them. It is a very excellent piece of work which, in the
hands of a writer of a little more distinction, might have been a powerful masterpiece. Isabel Ostrander, who also wrote under the name of Robert Orr Chipperfield
and other pseudonyms, was a particularly competent spinner of yarns. Her straightforward police-detective, McCarty, is always confounding the conclusions of Terhune
—a "scientific" private detective, who believes in modern psycho-analytical detective
apparatus.

view) retires from the problem before the arrest is reached. He is satisfied with a confession. The sordid details take place "off." Other authors permit sympathetic villains to commit suicide. Thus, Mr. Milne's Gillingham, whose attitude starts by being flippant and ends by being rather sentimental, warns Cayley of his approaching arrest, and Cayley shoots himself, leaving a written confession. Monsters of villainy can, of course, be brought to a bad end without compunction; but modern taste rejects monsters, therefore the modern detective-story is compelled to achieve a higher level of writing, and a more competent delineation of character. As the villain is allowed more good streaks in his composition, so the detective must achieve a tenderer human feeling beneath his frivolity or machine-like efficiency.

Love Interest

One fettering convention, from which detective fiction is only very slowly freeing itself, is that of the "love interest." Publishers and editors still labour under the delusion that all stories must have a nice young man and woman who have to be united in the last chapter. As a result, some of the finest detective-stories are marred by a conventional love-story, irrelevant to the action and perfunctorily worked in. The most harmless form of this disease is that taken, for example, in the works of Mr. Austin Freeman. His secondary characters fall in love with distressing regularity, and perform a number of conventional antics suitable to persons in their condition, but they do not interfere with the course of the story. You can skip the love-passages if you like, and nothing is lost. Far more blameworthy are the heroes who insist on fooling about after young women when they ought to be putting their minds on the job of detection. Just at the critical moment when the trap is set to catch the villain, the sleuth learns that his best girl has been spirited away. Heedlessly he drops everything, and rushes off to Chinatown or to the lonely house on the marshes or wherever it is, without even leaving a note to say where he is going. Here he is promptly sandbagged or entrapped or otherwise made a fool of, and the whole story is impeded and its logical development ruined.

The instances in which the love-story is an integral part of the plot are extremely rare. One very beautiful example occurs in *The Moonstone*. Here the entire plot hangs on the love of two women for Franklin Blake. Both Rachel Verinder and Rosanna Spearman know that he took the diamond, and the whole mystery arises from their efforts to shield him. Their conduct is, in both cases, completely natural and right, and the characters are so finely conceived as to be entirely convincing. E. C. Bentley, in *Trent's Last Case,* has dealt finely with the still harder problem of the detective in love. Trent's love for Mrs. Manderson is a legitimate part of the plot; while it does not prevent him from drawing the proper conclusion from the evidence before him, it does prevent him from acting upon his conclusions, and so prepares the way for the real explanation. Incidentally, the love-story is handled artistically and with persuasive emotion.

In *The House of the Arrow* and, still more strikingly, in *No Other Tiger,* A. E. W. Mason has written stories of strong detective interest which at the same time have the convincing psychological structure of the novel of character. The characters are presented as a novelist presents them—romantically, it is true, but without that stark insistence on classifying and explaining which turns the persons of the ordinary detective-story into a collection of museum exhibits.

Apart from such unusual instances as these, the less love in a detective-story, the better. *"L'amour au théâtre,"* says Racine, *"ne peut pas être en seconde place,"* and this holds good of detective fiction. A casual and perfunctory love-story is worse than no love-story at all, and, since the mystery must, by hypothesis, take the first place, the love is better left out.

Lynn Brock's *The Deductions of Colonel Gore* affords a curious illustration of this truth. Gore sets out, animated by an unselfish devotion to a woman, to recover some compromising letters for her, and, in so doing, becomes involved in unravelling an intricate murder plot. As the story goes on, the references to the beloved woman become chillier and more perfunctory; not only does the author seem to have lost interest, but so does Colonel Gore. At length the author notices this, and explains it in a paragraph:

"There were moments when Gore accused himself—or, rather, felt that he ought to accuse himself—of an undue coldbloodedness in these speculations of his. The business was a horrible business. One ought to have been decently shocked by it. One ought to have been horrified by the thought that three old friends were involved in such a business.

"But the truth was—and his apologies to himself for that truth became feebler and feebler—that the thing had now so caught hold of him that he had come to regard the actors in it as merely pieces of a puzzle baffling and engrossing to the verge of monomania."

There is the whole difficulty about allowing real human beings into a detective-story. At some point or other, either their emotions make hay of the detective interest, or the detective interest gets hold of them and makes their emotions look like pasteboard. It is, of course, a fact that we all adopt a detached attitude towards "a good murder" in the newspaper. Like Betteredge in *The Moonstone,* we get "detective fever," and forget the victim in the fun of tracking the criminal. For this reason, it is better not to pitch the emotional key too high at the start; the inevitable drop is thus made less jarring.

FUTURE DEVELOPMENTS: FASHIONS AND FORMULÆ

Just at present, therefore, the fashion in detective fiction is to have characters credible and lively; not conventional, but, on the other hand, not too profoundly studied—people who live more or less on the *Punch* level of emotion. A little more psychological complexity is allowed than formerly; the villain may not be a villain from every point of view; the heroine, if there is one, is not necessarily pure; the falsely accused innocent need not be a sympathetic character.* The automata—the embodied vices and virtues—the weeping fair-haired girl—the stupid but manly young man with the biceps—even the colossally evil scientist with the hypnotic eyes—are all disappearing from the intellectual branch of the art, to be replaced by figures having more in common with humanity.

---

* e.g. in J. J. Connington's *The Tragedy at Ravensthorpe,* where the agoraphobic Maurice is by no means an agreeable person to have about the house.

An interesting symptom of this tendency is the arrival of a number of books and stories which recast, under the guise of fiction, actual murder cases drawn from real life. Thus, Mrs. Belloc Lowndes and Mrs. Victor Rickard have both dealt with the Bravo Poisoning Mystery. Anthony Berkeley has retold the Maybrick case; Mr. E. H. W. Meyerstein has published a play based on the Seddon poisoning case, and Mr. Aldous Huxley, in "The Gioconda Smile," has reinterpreted in his own manner another famous case of recent years.*

We are now in a position to ask ourselves the favourite question of modern times: What next? Where is the detective-story going? Has it a future? Or will the present boom see the end of it?

THE MOST UNLIKELY PERSON

In early mystery fiction, the problem tends to be, *who* did the crime? At first, while readers were still unsophisticated, the formula of the Most Unlikely Person had a good run. But the reader soon learned to see through this. If there was a single person in the story who appeared to have no motive for the crime and who was allowed to amble through to the penultimate chapter free from any shadow of suspicion, that character became a marked man or woman. "I knew he must be guilty because nothing was said about him," said the cunning reader. Thus we come to a new axiom, laid down by Mr. G. K. Chesterton in a brilliant essay in the *New Statesman:* the real criminal must be suspected at least once in the course of the story. Once he is suspected, and then (apparently) cleared, he is made safe from future suspicion. This is the principle behind Mr. Wills Crofts' impregnable alibis, which are eventually broken down by painstaking enquiry. Probably the most baffling form of detective-story is still that in which suspicion is distributed equally among a number of candidates, one of whom turns out to be guilty. Other developments of the Most Unlikely Person formula make the guilty person a juror at

---

* *What Really Happened*, by Mrs. Belloc Lowndes; *Not Sufficient Evidence*, by Mrs. Victor Rickard; *The Wychford Poisoning Drama*, by the Author of *The Layton Court Mystery*; *Heddon*, by E. H. W. Meyerstein; *Mortal Coils*, by Aldous Huxley.

the inquest or trial; * the detective himself; † the counsel for the prosecution; ‡ and, as a supreme effort of unlikeliness, the actual narrator of the story.§ Finally, resort has been made to the double-cross, and the person originally suspected turns out to be the right person after all.‖

THE UNEXPECTED MEANS

There are signs, however, that the possibilities of the formula are becoming exhausted, and of late years much has been done in exploring the solution by the unexpected means. With recent discoveries in medical and chemical science, this field has become exceedingly fruitful, particularly in the provision of new methods of murder. It is fortunate for the mystery-monger that, whereas, up to the present, there is only one known way of getting born, there are endless ways of getting killed. Here is a brief selection of handy short cuts to the grave: Poisoned tooth-stoppings; licking poisoned stamps; shaving-brushes inoculated with dread diseases; poisoned boiled eggs (a bright thought); poison-gas; a cat with poisoned claws; poisoned mattresses; knives dropped through the ceiling; stabbing with a sharp icicle; electrocution by telephone; biting by plague-rats and typhoid-carrying lice; boiling lead in the ears (much more effective than cursed hebanon in a vial): air-bubbles injected into the arteries; explosion of a gigantic "Prince Rupert's drop"; frightening to death; hanging head-downwards; freezing to atoms in liquid air; hypodermic injections shot from air-guns; exposure, while insensible, to extreme cold; guns concealed in cameras; a thermometer which explodes a bomb when the temperature of the room reaches a certain height; and so forth.

The methods of disposing of inconvenient corpses are also varied and peculiar; burial under a false certificate obtained in a

* Robert Orr Chipperfield: *The Man in the Jury-Box.*
† Bernard Capes: *The Skeleton Key;* Gaston Leroux: *Mystère de la Chambre Jaune;* etc.
‡ G. K. Chesterton: "The Mirror of the Magistrate" (*Innocence of Father Brown*,.
§ Agatha Christie: *The Murder of Roger Ackroyd.*
‖ Father R. Knox: *The Viaduct Murder,* and others.

number of ways; substitution of one corpse for another (very common in fiction, though rare in real life); mummification; reduction to bone-dust; electro-plating; arson; "planting" (not in the church-yard, but on innocent parties)—a method first made famous by R. L. Stevenson.* Thus, of the three questions, "Who?" "How?" and "Why?" "How" is at present the one which offers most scope for surprise and ingenuity, and is capable of sustaining an entire book on its own, though a combination of all three naturally provides the best entertainment.†

The mystery-monger's principal difficulty is that of varying his surprises. "You know my methods, Watson," says the detective, and it is only too painfully true. The beauty of Watson was, of course, that after thirty years he still did not know Holmes's methods; but the average reader is sharper-witted. After reading half a dozen stories by one author, he is sufficiently advanced in Dupin's psychological method ‡ to see with the author's eyes. He knows that, when Mr. Austin Freeman drowns somebody in a pond full of water-snails, there will be something odd and localised about those snails; he knows that, when one of Mr. Wills Crofts's characters has a cast-iron alibi, the alibi will turn out to have holes in it; he knows that if Father Knox casts suspicion on a Papist, the Papist will turn out to be innocent; instead of detecting the murderer, he is engaged in detecting the writer. That is why he gets the impression that the writer's later books are seldom or never "up to" his earlier efforts. He has become married to the writer's muse, and marriage has destroyed the mystery.

There certainly does seem a possibility that the detective-story will some time come to an end, simply because the public will have learnt all the tricks. But it has probably many years to go yet, and in the meantime a new and less rigid formula will probably have developed, linking it more closely to the novel of manners

---

* *The Wrong Box.*

† Mr. Austin Freeman has specialised in a detective-story which rejects all three questions. He tells the story of the crime first, and relies for his interest on the pleasure afforded by following the ingenious methods of the investigator. *The Singing Bone* contains several tales of this type. Mr. Freeman has had few followers, and appears to have himself abandoned the formula, which is rather a pity.

‡ As outlined in "The Purloined Letter."

and separating it more widely from the novel of adventure. The
latter will, no doubt, last as long as humanity, and while crime
exists, the crime thriller will hold its place. It is, as always, the
higher type that is threatened with extinction.

At the time of writing (1928) the detective-story is profiting by
a reaction against novels of the static type. Mr. E. M. Forster is
indeed left murmuring regretfully, "Yes, ah! yes—the novel tells
a story"; but the majority of the public are rediscovering that
fact with cries of triumph. Sexual abnormalities are suffering a
slight slump at the moment; the novel of passion still holds the
first place, especially among women, but even women seem to be
growing out of the simple love-story. Probably the cheerful cyni-
cism of the detective-tale suits better with the spirit of the times
than the sentimentality which ends in wedding bells. For, make
no mistake about it, the detective-story is part of the literature of
escape, and not of expression. We read tales of domestic unhappiness because that is the kind of thing which happens to us; but
when these things gall too close to the sore, we fly to mystery
and adventure because they do not, as a rule, happen to us. "The
detective-story," says Philip Guedalla, "is the normal recreation
of noble minds." And it is remarkable how strong is the fascination of the higher type of detective-story for the intellectually-
minded, among writers as well as readers. The average detective-
novel to-day is extremely well written, and there are few good living
writers who have not tried their hand at it at one time or another.*

---

*Among men of letters distinguished in other lines who have turned their
attention to the detective-story may be mentioned A. E. W. Mason, Eden Phillpotts,
"Lynn Brock" (whose pseudonym protects the personality of a well-known writer),
Somerset Maugham, Rudyard Kipling, A. A. Milne, Father R. Knox, J. D. Beresford.

It is owing to the work of such men as these that the detective-novel reaches a
much higher artistic level in England than in any other country. At every turn the
quality of the writing and the attention to beauty of form and structure betray the
hand of the practised novelist.

The Professor and the Detective

(1929)

By Marjorie Nicolson

Of the hundreds of published articles and essays discussing the phenomenon of the detective story, a clear majority have concerned themselves, to the point of monotony, with expressions of wonder that so frankly un-serious a literary form has managed to attract as devoted readers so many men and women of superior intellectual attainment. The common weakness of such articles is that for the most part the writers have contented themselves with mere statement of the paradox, without attempting to assay the underlying reasons. A really thoughtful examination calculated to do simple justice to this interesting anomaly was long overdue when Marjorie Nicolson published in the Atlantic Monthly *for April 1929 the essay which follows. Miss Nicolson is the former dean of the department of English at Smith College, a past-national president of Phi Beta Kappa, and is presently associated with Columbia University in New York City.*

In generously granting permission to reprint her essay, Miss Nicolson writes: "I hope it may be possible for you to call the attention of your readers to the fact that this essay was published in 1929. The only part of the essay which I think is now seriously out-of-date is my statement that women do not write good detective stories. In 1929 Agatha Christie's The Murder of Roger Ackroyd *was well known, but as I indicated in the essay, it was written as a tour de force. In 1929 Dorothy Sayers was comparatively little known in America. Ngaio Marsh was still in her (literary) cradle. Other women like Mignon Eberhart and Leslie Ford were just beginning to appear on the horizon. As a matter of fact, so many of the best detective stories of the last decade have been written by women that my statement sounds either naïve or uncritical. Since these women are among my favorite mystery au-*

thors, I should not like readers to feel that I do not admire their works. Therefore if you can call the readers' attention to the fact, you will relieve my conscience and I won't feel that I have sold the ladies down the river!"

≈≈≈

THE DEADLY after-dinner pause had arrived. During the hour of the banquet itself, conversation had been general, if desultory; but in the drawing-room an awkward hush descended. The hostess surveyed with some alarm her tame lions, the most distinguished delegates to an international convocation of scholars. Nervously she threw into the arena for dissection the latest sensations in the world of books, the 'most provocative' of all provocatives, the 'most startling' of all exposés of human weakness. With weary courtesy the lions oped their mastic jaws; but it was only too obvious that the animals were lethargic. Desperately, she turned to the distinguished scholar at her right—a man whose name is known even to thousands who have never read his contributions.

'Tell me,' she begged, 'what do you think is the most significant book of recent years?'

'There you have me,' the great man declared with candor. 'I never can make up my mind between *The Bellamy Trial* and *The Murder of Roger Ackroyd*. Of course, I know there *are* people who would say that *Greene Murder Case,* but . . .'

His hostess gasped. But in another moment her horror had turned to amazement. Her lions forgot their tameness; the bodies thrown into the arena were no longer the lay figures by which they had been fooled so long. The odor of blood was in their nostrils. For an hour the struggle raged; and when at last the lions, gorged with prey, had departed to their cages, they left behind them a hostess who realized that her dinner had been a complete triumph, who had learned the most valuable of all lessons for her future entertainment of the academic guest: when all else fails, start your professors upon the detective story—if they have not already started themselves!

Throughout England and America to-day, you will find the same thing to be true. Lending libraries in college towns are hard put to it to keep up the supply; university librarians are forced to lay in a private stock 'for faculty only.' Let but two or three academics gather together, and the inevitable conversation ensues. At the meetings of learned societies this year, it will not be of the new physics or the new astronomy, of the new morality or the new psychology, that your specialists in these fields will be debating, but of footprints and thumb marks, of the possibility of poisoning by means of candles, of the chances of opening a locked door with a pair of tweezers and a piece of string! More heated the arguments, more violent the discussions, than ever were the contentions of mediæval schoolmen. And in time to come, when we shall have been gathered to our ancestors, you will find us, not in Paradise, but, like that little group of Milton's fallen angels in Hell, 'in discourse more sweet' than were ever hymns of rejoicing, sitting apart on some 'retir'd' hill, unaware of Pandemonium, unaware of Hades, while around us giants and demons tear up mountains and cast them into the sea, 'reasoning high' of clues and openings, of poisons and daggers, of tricks for disposing of unwanted bodies, of Dr. Thorndyke and of Colonel Gore.

I

That glib expositor of all mysteries, the pseudo-psychologist, has an explanation, of course. To the academic mind, he avers, detective stories constitute the 'literature of escape.' He goes even further: our lives, we hear, are barren and narrow; our college walls (not even modern American architecture can shake this metaphor) hem in a little unreal world, in which wander lost spirits, ghosts and shades as melancholy as any who ever haunted the tenebrous Styx, wailing—not, like those spirits, for a life they had lost—but for a life we have never had. Inhibited by our unnatural existence, we find 'release' in books of blood and thunder. Through tales of abduction and poisoning, shooting and stabbing, we are able to wallow for a moment in adventures we cannot share, to lose ourselves for an evening in a world of excitement, and return next day to our dry-as-dust lectures, refreshed by vicarious violence. Unworldly, unnatural academics, who would deny us our brief moment's respite! So, having explained us to his own satisfaction, having neatly docketed us in his capacious catalogue, the pseudo-psychologist passes on to fresher woods. Like an earlier gentleman, somewhat hasty in generalization, he does not stay for an answer.

Nor, I must confess, would we bother to give it to him, did he stay. For how can we explain to such as he that escape, in the sense in which he means it, is the last thing in the world the academic mind either requires or wishes? How can he know that, as a group, we are more free from 'suppressed desires,' 'inhibitions,' and 'complexes' than any other group in the world to-day? It is not from the life of the mind that we seek release, nor is it that we may flee from the bondage of academic walls that we revel in the literature of escape.

Yet, in a sense which he does not understand, the academic reader is turning to the detective story to-day seeking release. Consciously in eighty per cent of the cases, unconsciously in the other two tenths, he has reached the limit of his endurance of characteristically 'contemporary' literature. Contrary to the usual belief, the college professor to-day does keep up with recent literature. Gone is the bearded visionary who was a child in the affairs of the world, the pedant who boasted that he had read nothing published since 1660. There are few professors in the colleges of the arts who are not familiar with the 'latest' in drama, in fiction, in poetry. If the family budget will not cover the new books, there are the local book clubs; and, when all else fails, there are always the community bookshops, whose tables are surrounded by poverty-stricken academics, grimly reading the newest arrivals, standing now on one foot, now on the other, peering determinedly between uncut pages. Probably no other group except the professional book reviewers has, during the last ten years, waded through so many thousands of pages of psychological analysis. And now we are reaping the whirlwind.

Yes, the detective story does constitute escape; but it is escape not from life, but from literature. We grant willingly that we find in it release. Our 'revolt'—so mysteriously explained by the psychologists—is simple enough: we have revolted from an excessive subjectivity to welcome objectivity; from long-drawn-out dissections of emotion to straightforward appeal to intellect; from reiterated emphasis upon men and women as victims either of circumstances or of their glands to a suggestion that men and women may consciously plot and consciously plan; from the 'stream of consciousness' which threatens to engulf us in its Lethean monotony to analyses of purpose, controlled and directed by a thinking mind; from formlessness to form; from the sophomoric to the mature; most of all, from a smart and easy pessimism which interprets men and the universe in terms of unmoral purposelessness to a rebelief in a universe governed by cause and effect. All this we find in the detective story.

We are not alone in our revolt against the 'psychological novel,' but perhaps our cry for release is more passionate than that of any other group. As the new book lists appear in spring and autumn, as the brilliant new covers in violent hues bedeck the windows of the bookshops, as the publishers' blurbs grow necessarily more and more superlative, you may hear rising and swelling in protest the litany of the professors: 'From the *most profound and searching dissection of human emotions;* from the *poignant cry of a human soul;* from the *daring analysis of the springs of human action;* from the *wings of pain and ecstasy;* from the *brutal frankness of the seeker after truth;* from the *lyric passion of a youthful heart;* from the *biting and mordant wit of a satirist swifter than Swift;* from the *provocative demolishment of a fusty Victorianism;* from the *ruthless exposure of the shams and hypocrisies of the age*—Good Lord, deliver us!'

The chant is not ours alone; but assuredly our groans are deeper, our revolt more violent. For, to all whose daily contact is with college students, but most to those who profess to teach 'English,' the characteristic contemporary novel seems but the student theme, swelled to Gargantuan proportions. We wade yearly through pounds of paper liberally sprinkled with the pronoun 'I'; we have long ceased to expect complete sentences—and never even hope for complete thoughts; dots and dashes we accept as the only possible marks of punctuation. We read with a jaundiced eye dissections of human nature which their authors at least believe to be *profound* and *searching*. We listen to *lyric cries* and *passionate outbursts* until our ears are weary. We follow the *brutal destruction* and the *searching for truth* of young authors, automatically correcting their spelling as we do so. We suggest as delicately as possible—remembering always the sacred 'individuality' of these young people with which we must not interfere—that imitation of Mr. Mencken is not always the sincerest form of flattery. We labor all day with a generation which has always *reacted*—never been forced to *think* or *consider* or *judge*. Is it any wonder that, when the last paper has been corrected, the last reaction tabulated, we reach out a weary hand for books which will be as different as possible? Having labored all day with minds that are—and should be—those of sophomores, is there any reason why we should wish to spend our nights with literature that is sophomoric?

We revolt truly enough against subjectivity, because we are too used to promising young authors, who interpret their individual growing pains in terms of cosmic convulsions. We are clearly aware that adolescence will always emphasize the 'I'; will always find dissection of emotion more thrilling than analysis of intellect; will always fall victim to easy philosophies of pessimism and skepticism; will always prefer the formless, the vague, to the ordered, the defined; will always believe that it is facing the facts with candor and fearlessness—though, in reality, facts are so much less spectacular and so much less interesting than youth believes. But all this is the inevitable and natural feeling of adolescence. We whose business it is to teach the young accept it with tolerance, with sympathy—more frequently than the world believes, with humor. It is not strange, however, that we do not turn to-day for release to those children of a larger growth, the contemporary novelists, the 'bad boys' and 'smart girls' of literature. It is not mere chance that this decade is seeing a recrudescence of interest, on the part of thoughtful readers, in that most mature age of writing, the eighteenth century; that to-day Boswell and Johnson, Swift and Voltaire, are being read by constantly increasing numbers. These were men, not boys; their wit was intellectual, their method analytical; their appeal is constantly to the mind, never to the emotions.

It is likewise not mere coincidence that scholars, philosophers, economists, are creating a demand for detective stories unparalleled in the past; that the art which might otherwise have been expended upon literature is transforming the once-despised 'thriller' into what may easily become a new classic; that Oxford and Cambridge dons, a distinguished economist, a supposedly distinguished æsthetician (we have only his pseudonymous word for his identity), an historian, and a scientist should have set themselves to this new and entrancing craft. More than one well-known author, weary unto death of introspective and psychological literature, has turned with relief to this sole department of fiction in which it is still possible to tell a story. Gilbert Chesterton and Hilaire Belloc were pioneers; Lord Charnwood, A. A. Milne, and J. B. Priestley follow gladly after. It is, we granted earlier, escape; but the more one ponders, the more the question insistently thrusts itself forward: Is it not also return?

II

Certainly it is a return to the novel of plot and incident—that genre despised these many years by *littérateurs*. The appeal of the detective story lies in its action, its episodes. Gone are the pluperfect tenses of the psychical novel, the conditional modes; the present, the progressive, the definite past—these are the tenses of the novel of action. Character—so worshiped by the psychological novelists—troubles us little, though characters we have in abundance. Characters addicted to dependence upon the subconscious or upon the glands need not apply; men and women need all their conscious wits about them in the detective yarn. One brooding moment, one pluperfect tense, one conditional mode, may be fatal. We grant that our characters are largely puppets, and we are delighted once more to see the marionettes dance while a strong and adept hand pulls the strings cleverly. Our real interest is not in the puppets, but in the brain which designed them. Yet characters have emerged from the new detective form, in spite of their authors. The modern detective is as individual as Sherlock Holmes—though less and less often is he patterned after that famous sleuth. Our detective is made in our image and in that of the author; like ourselves, he can make mistakes; he

is no longer omniscient or ubiquitous. We are passing away from
the strong silent man who, after days of secret working, produces
a villain whom we could never have suspected. Sometimes, indeed, the detective is wrong until the last chapter; sometimes,
again, both he and we suspect the villain long before we can
prove his guilt, and our interest, like the detective's, is less in the
discovery than in the establishment of guilt. The nameless inspector of Scotland Yard has become, for instance, Inspector
French, who more than once is puzzled and confused by false
trails.

Often the detective is not a professional at all, or at least not
one connected with one of the central bureaus here or abroad.
There is Poirot, who is conveniently found upon the Blue Train
at the needed moment, who even was known to settle down in England for a time, growing cabbages, while he waited for murder
to be committed. There is Dr. Thorndyke, the medico-legal wiz-
ard, from whom we simple academics have learned most of the
natural science we know. There is the amateur Colonel Gore,
who began his career by a chance application for a golf secretary-
ship, and has now opened his own private inquiry office—a movement which his admirers greet with pleasure, as promising an indefinite number of cases for the future. There is our friend the
expert in poisons, who lives in his house around the corner from
the British Museum, whence he is summoned at dead of night by
the butler to a noble family and precipitated into a mystery he
does not choose to solve. There is even the psychological detective, keeping us up with the times. Yet, though we welcome the
technique of his creator, and call him master, many of the weary
academics are inclined to resent that upstart Philo Vance, whose
manners—like his footnotes—smack too much of the 'smart'
young novelists and students from whom we are escaping. With
all these characters, however, familiar though they are to us, the
interest of the reader lies never in what they are, but in what
they do. If they emerge as individuals, they emerge still from the
novel of action.

We have revolted also against contemporary realism, and in
these novels we return to an earlier manner. As every connoisseur
knows, the charm of the pure detective story lies in its utter un-

reality. This is a point the untrained reader does not comprehend. He wonders at our callousness, at our evident lack of sensitiveness; he cannot understand how we can wade eagerly through streams of blood, how we can pursue our man even to the gallows with the detachment of Dr. Thorndyke himself. He is tortured by visions of bloodstained rugs; he shudders at the smoking revolver, the knife still sticking in the wound. 'I dreamed all night of people lying in pools of blood,' declared my unsympathetic friend at breakfast this morning. 'How *can* you read those things and go to sleep at all?' And she will never believe me quite a human being again because I assured her that after five murders I can put out the light and sleep like a child until morning, the reason being that where she has seen, with horrible distinctness, an old man lying in a pool of his own blood, I had seen—a diagram. She brings to the thriller a mind accustomed to realism. But the essence of this new detective story lies in its complete unreality.

Hence, though we may read them also, we connoisseurs tend to disparage those novels of the Poe school, whose authors attempt to work upon the emotions; interesting they may be, but never in the purest style. No one of us ever believes that the murder actually occurred; no one of our best authors attempts to persuade us that it ever could occur. We come to the detective story with a sigh of relief—the one form of novel to-day which does not insist that we must lose ourselves to find ourselves; the one form of contemporary literature in which our cool impersonality need never fail. That, of course, is the great difference between detective literature and contemporary journalistic accounts of murders, in which we have no interest. Not for a moment can you fool us, either, with collections of *True Detective Stories,* or confessions of actual criminals. We seek our chamber of horrors with no adolescent or morbid desire to be shocked, startled, horrified. We handle the instruments of the crime with scientific detachment. It is for us an enthralling game, which must be played with skill and science, in which the pieces possess no more real personality than do the knights and bishops and pawns of chess, the kings and queens of bridge. Mediæval writers, to be sure, delighted in allegories of chess, in which the pieces took on moral or spiritual significance; but those who seek to read character and emotion into our pieces and our cards miss the essence of this most entrancing game.

Here perhaps we approach the real centre of the whole matter, which explains both our revolt and our return, and suggests the peculiar characteristic of this new style of writing. Your chess player will sit by the hour in frowning contemplation before a board set with pieces. Your true bridge player finds his real life when the cards are dealt and the contest of wits begins. Your crossword-puzzle expert, dictionary on knee, spends evening after evening in solitary occupation. In each case the expert, though kind enough in other relations of life, despises the amateur. So too the connoisseur of detective stories. We restrain ourselves with difficulty when the occasional reader seeks to dispute with us, to enter into conversations and debates sacred to the initiate. It is as if a body of specialists,—physicists, astronomers, and mathematicians,—met to discuss the Einstein theory, were to be forced, for politeness' sake, to talk about the concept of relativity with a bright youngster who labored under the popular delusion that Mr. Einstein has somehow reformed—or destroyed—the moral standard. We who are connoisseurs are profound and constant students of the new science, as regular in our practice of the art as the most passionate bridge or chess player. We 'keep up' as assiduously with the output as the physician, the scientist, the scholar, with learned journals. From ten to one at night is our favorite period for reading; the bedside table holds a varied assortment, drawn from rental collections or from the libraries of our wealthier colleagues.

Like the crossword puzzle, ours is a game which must be played alone; yet on the other hand, as in chess, the antagonists are really two, for the detective story is a battle royal between the author and the reader, and the great glory of the contemporary form is that we both accept it as such. How their eyes must twinkle—those creators of heroes and villains—as they set out their pieces before the game begins. They are the only authors, we must believe, who to-day find fun in writing. As in all other games, much depends upon the opening move, the significance of which each expert fully understands. We have our favorite open-

ings, to be sure, though we recognize all the traditional ones.
The familiar scene in the oak-paneled library, the white-haired
man sprawling upon his desk, two glasses beside him, the electric
light still burning—it is for us photographically real, though
never realistic. We know it as a type opening in our game of chess.
No detective quicker than we to be on the watch for clues: the
torn letter, the soiled blotter, the burned paper on the hearth,
the screen moved askew, particularly the book out of place on the
shelves—if our author is an expert, each of these has had its meaning to him, and must to us. Or there is that other familiar opening move—the body discovered in a place far from all human
haunts (this year tending to be fished up in a basket or packing
case from the depths of the sea). There is no limitation to the
number of places in which murder may be committed; the very
spot a real criminal would most surely avoid becomes for us a
glorious experiment. We have had more than one murder on a
golf links; no less than three of the season's favorites occur on
a train—a device more customary in the English carriages than
in American cars, though we still remember loyally *The Man in
Lower Ten.*

As the game proceeds, there are countless other signals which
we know and watch for. The move of your opponent and his discard are as important here as ever in bridge or chess. We learn
new moves and tricks at every game. We can distinguish with
deadly precision among tobaccos we have never seen; let but a
character casually be caught smoking an exotic cigarette in a yel-
lowish paper, and we have our eye upon him till the end. You
cannot fool us with the obvious tricks of a decade ago—and what
scorn we heap upon an amateur who attempts to write for us,
knowing far less of technique than we know ourselves. We are
aware that finger prints may be forged; we can tell you more accurately than many a scientist what will happen to your footprints
if you try to walk backward, if you are wearing borrowed shoes,
or if you insist on carrying through the garden the corpse of the
gentleman you have recently killed. We can tell you the exact
angle at which your body will hang if you commit suicide with
your silk stockings. We can detect with unerring precision
whether the body found by the railroad tracks is that of a man

killed by accident or murdered before the train passed. We can distinguish with more deadly accuracy than your hairdresser whether your hair is dyed, whether its wave is permanent or real.

Modern inventions are daily making our task more difficult. We have long been familiar with the dictaphone as a device for securing an alibi. We are not fooled by photographic evidence, which we know may have been faked. But the radio and the wireless, and particularly the airplane, give us pause. We used to know, as well as Bradshaw, the exact time of departure of every train in the British Isles, and the length of every journey in the United States. We know the location of every public airport in three countries; but the growing tendency toward private ownership of aircraft occasionally causes us trouble in our computations.

On the whole, we incline to deprecate the use of utopian devices on the part of our authors—the death ray, the drug which produces indefinite hypnosis, the fourth dimension. We dislike as a group the unfair use of amnesia and aphasia, just as we dislike the subconscious. Being the fairest-minded of all readers, we demand that our characters be given every chance, and we feel it is not 'cricket' if they are forced to work against undue psychological influence. We demand of our authors fair play; and for the most part we get it in full measure. Gone are the days of the identical twin, the long-lost brother from Australia. Gone for the most part is the trick ending—though over the last pages of *Roger Ackroyd* we divide into two passionate camps. My own party insists that that is not a trick ending in which every single thread has been put into our hands, every device has been a familiar one. Regretfully we acknowledge that, once used, that ending can never be employed again; nevertheless, the novel remains to us a classic, one of the few that ever completely fooled us.

And as we grow in knowledge and experience, it is becoming increasingly hard to fool us. It is seldom, indeed, that we do not know the identity of the murderer long before he is taken into custody. But if you think that such foreknowledge spoils the interest, you do not understand the new science. In that grimly contested battle of wits, it is inevitable that we should guess, unless the author is far more skilled than we. But once the decision is fairly certain in our minds, we have the added pleasure of watching the author's technique, of checking those passages in which he is trying to send us off the track. Just as he tries his best (and less than his best we will not have) to deceive us, so we do our best to catch him out. In this new game, both scrupulously observe the rules, but both of us know the rules so well that we take delight in reading each other's signals. The burden which the connoisseur is laying upon the writers of detective fiction to-day is a heavy one; but gallantly the best of them are accepting the challenge. This very interaction of specialized authors and readers in a new and international game is producing some of the cleverest technique in fiction to-day, and is developing in that fiction some remarkably interesting characteristics.

It is forcing upon the author a complete objectivity and impersonality in the handling of his material, which in the past has been peculiar to the highest art. I have suggested that this lack of subjectivity constitutes the chief appeal of the detective novel to its academic readers to-day. From the self-consciousness of youthful writers, who, having psychoanalyzed themselves, would seek to persuade us also of the astounding discovery that we are much like other men, we turn to breathe the purer air serene of complete impassivity, forced upon authors by the exigencies of the situation. One false step, and the enemy is ours. Let the author for a moment suggest a personal reaction, a sentimental affection for his character, and we have him on the hip. There is no group of readers so quick to catch a false cadence in an author's voice. And this requirement is having another effect upon technique. The author must weigh and balance all his characters; he cannot have a single unnecessary one; he cannot introduce a servant whom we will not scan sharply. The simplest action, the slightest gesture, is pregnant with meaning. He knows it, and so do we.

Very different, this insistence upon selection, from the all-inclusiveness of a *Ulysses*. The author is forced every moment to be alert, on guard; nothing can be left to chance, no unnecessary comments introduced. In this form of contemporary literature alone, ungoverned emotional reactions are fatal. Hence the pure detective story to-day is never—and what a relief!—a love story. If the love element is introduced at all,—the connoisseur prefers that it be omitted,—it must be distinctly subordinated, for to make your hero and your heroine sympathetic enough to permit their love story is at once to free them from the list of possible suspects. And in the pure detective story, as in that grimmest of legal theories, every man and woman is guilty until he has proved himself innocent. Our detective story has thus returned to-day to a welcome insistence that love between the sexes is not the only possible motif for fiction: jealousy, hatred, greed, anger, loyalty, friendship, parental affection—all these are our themes. No longer is the wellspring of man's conduct to be found only in the instinct of sex.

And, indeed, this change of emphasis is producing a curious effect upon the treatment of women in the detective novel. Men characters are always in the majority; the detective story, indeed, is primarily a man's novel. Many women dislike it heartily, or at best accept it as a device to while away hours on the train. And while we do all honor to the three or four women who have written surpassingly good detective stories of the purest type, we must grant candidly that the great bulk of our detective stories to-day are being written by men—again, perhaps, because of their escape from a school of fiction which is becoming too largely feminized. It is noticeable also that the woman characters in these contemporary stories are no longer inevitably sympathetic. More than once the victim is a woman; and even here, where our authors might become sentimental, we notice their impassivity. For in the great majority of cases the victim in a murder story is one who richly deserved to die. One or two authors have experimented with the woman detective, but for the most part with little success. Apart from minor characters, the two important rôles in the detective story for women are, alliteratively enough, victim and villainess. With the changing standards of sentimentality, there is no longer any assurance that a woman character is not the murderer. Time was when we could dismiss women with a wave of the hand; but all of us think of at least four contemporary heroines, three of them young and beautiful, who in the end turn out to be cold and calculating murderers. Inevitably, too, we recall the more subtle ending of *The Bellamy Trial*. Whatever may be the sentimental reaction of modern judges and juries in our courts of law, in the high tribunal of the detective story women are no longer sacred.

A high tribunal it is. Earlier, I suggested that our revolt was from a smart and easy pessimism, which interprets the universe in terms of relativity and purposelessness, our return to an older and more primitive conception of the cosmic order. Here lies, I believe, the really unique contribution of the detective story to contemporary ethics. With the engaging paradox of the old lady in *Punch,* who sought through shelves of psychological literature for 'a nice love story—without any sex,' we weary academics seek refreshment in a highly moral murder. Perhaps we are protesting against a conception of the universe as governed—if governed at all—by chance, by haphazard circumstance; against a theory which interprets the way of life as like the river in the 'Vision of Mirza,' the bridge of San Luis Rey; against a conception of men and women as purposeless, aimless, impotent; against a theory of the world as wandering, devoid of purpose and meaning, in unlimited space. In our detective stories we find with relief a return to an older ethics and metaphysics: an Hebraic insistence upon justice as the measure of all things—an eye for an eye, and a tooth for a tooth; a Greek feeling of inevitability, for man as the victim of circumstances and fate, to be sure, but a fate brought upon him by his own carelessness, his own ignorance, or his own choice; a Calvinistic insistence, if you will, upon destiny, but a Calvinistic belief also in the need for tense and constant activity on the part of man: last of all, a scientific insistence upon the inevitable operation of cause and effect. For never, in the just world of the detective story, does the murderer go undetected; never does justice fail in the end. No matter how charming, how lovable, the murderer, or how justifiable the killing, there is no escaping the implacable avenging Nemesis of our modern detective, Fury and Fate in one.

To be sure, we will not condemn our charming murderer to the gallows, for we are artists as well as moralists. We will allow the debonair, the charming rogue one final gallant moment—the sudden spurt of the match's flame as, for the last time, he lights his cigarette with that nonchalance we know so well. Do we not realize as well as he that that last cigarette is the one all well-trained murderers carry constantly for this purpose? We allow the murderess the reward of her cleverness—the last swift motion as the cyanide reaches her lips or the knife her heart. Yet the life must be spent for the life. Like the Greek dramatist, we excuse neither ignorance nor carelessness. No matter how great the personality, how masterful the mind, by one single slip he is hoist with his own petard. By fate or predestination,—what you will,— the murderer is from the beginning condemned to his end; his election is sealed. Not for a moment does our neo-Calvinistic justice permit him to go down to punishment without an intense struggle to escape the consequence of his act. But our science and our theology, our ethics and our metaphysics, are based upon a belief in implacable justice, in the orderly operation of cause and effect, in a universe governed by order, founded on eternal and immutable law.

III

Perhaps it is for this reason that the most persistent readers of detective literature to-day are the philosophers and the scientists who were bred under an older system of belief. It may be that their revolt from a changing universe, without standard and without order, is a return to a simpler causality under which they are more at home. They alone can tell. One thing more, however, I may add to our apologia. What effect this addiction to detective literature is having without the college world I cannot pretend to say; another must speak for its influence upon the life of the capitalist, the physician, the president-elect. But I dare challenge the academic critics to say that in the field of scholarship it is not making for a new vitality. After all, what essential difference is there between the technique of the detective tracking his quarry through Europe and that of the historian tracking his fact, the philosopher his idea, down the ages? Watch the behavior of your professor for but an hour, and you know him for what he is. Do his eyes sparkle, his cheeks flush, as he pursues his idea, forgetting his class, forgetting his audience, as he leaps from historical thumb mark to ethical footprint, from cigarette stub to empty glass? If so, he's the man for your money. In the long conversation which follows, though you begin with the quantum theory or the influence of Plato, you will end with Dr. Thorndyke or Hercule Poirot.

And if you come to compare the methods by which the scientist or the philosopher has reached his conclusions, you will find that they are merely those of his favorite detective. Only two methods are open to him, as to them. He may work by the Baconian method of Scotland Yard: he may laboriously and carefully accumulate all possible clues, passing over nothing as too insignificant, filling his little boxes and envelopes with all that comes his way, making no hypothesis, anticipating no conclusion, believing the man innocent until he can prove him guilty. Here he finds a single thread, there a grain of rice dropped in a drawing-room; here he measures a footprint, there he photographs a thumb mark. His loot finally collected, he of Scotland Yard will select the 'dominant clue,' and that he will follow with grim persistence until the end. Weary but victorious, he stands at last outside the prison to which he has condemned his idea, and listens to the passing bell. That is one method. But if he is of the opposite nature, he will follow the method of 'intuition,' upon which the detective bureaus of the country of Descartes have based their work. To him the torn cigarette and the discarded blotter are of little importance; he leaves such things for his indefatigable rivals of Scotland Yard. Tucked away behind the rose bushes in the garden maze, he devotes himself to thought. Having, like his great predecessor, thought away all else in the universe, nothing remains but the culprit. By strength of logic alone, he has reconstituted the universe, and in his proper place has set the villain of the piece.

Yes, those are the only two methods, both in scholarship and in the pursuit of criminals. For, after all, scholars are, in the end, only the detectives of thoughts. The canvas is vaster, the search more extensive; the 'case' takes, not a few weeks, but a lifetime. Yet, in the end, method and conclusion are the same. Evening after evening, throughout the length and breadth of the country, lights burn longer and longer in academic studies, and philosophers, scientists, historians, settle down with sighs of content to the latest and most lurid murder tale. Yet the professorial reader, pursuing with eager interest the exploits of Dr. Thorndyke or of Colonel Gore, is not, in the last analysis, escaping from his repressions; is not even consciously returning from the present to the past; but is merely carrying over to another medium the fun of the chase, the ardor of the pursuit, which makes his life a long and eager and active quest, from which he would not willingly accept release.

Masters of Mystery

(1931)

By H. Douglas Thomson

The gigantic strides made by the detective novel in England and America during the 1920's—together with the heightened critical interest on all sides—made the first full-length study of the form in the English language virtually inevitable. This was H. Douglas Thomson's Masters of Mystery: A Study of the Detective Story *(London: Collins, 1931). Mr. Thomson's work was not, to be sure, the first book-length treatment in any language: Frièdrich Depken's* Sherlock Holmes, Raffles, und Ihre Vorbilder: Ein Beitrag zur Entwicklungsgeschichte und Technik der Kriminalerzählung *(Heidelberg, 1914) and Régis Messac's ponderous and curious 698-page exegesis* Le "Detective Novel" et L'Influence de la Pensée Scientifique *(Paris, 1929) were both earlier at the post. In view, however, of the rather forbidding academism and esoteric content of these continental considerations, Thomson may fairly be termed the first major historian anywhere of the contemporary police romance as living literature. Withal that internal testimony suggests some portions of his work, too, may have been prepared with a scholastic purpose in mind, the modernity of his approach and his agreeable and accomplished discursive style set him some worlds apart from his formalistic French and German colleagues. His book reads as if he wrote it for his own enjoyment—which is as it should be. So far as can be ascertained, Mr. Thomson has never contributed fictionally to the genre of which he writes so well. The best evidence is that he is an English layman: like your present editor a detection "buff," or amateur of published crime. The selection printed here is taken from the opening chapter of* Masters of Mystery—*which work, incidentally, is an almost unobtainable collector's item on either side of the water today.*

IN ITS simplest form the detective story is a puzzle to be solved, the plot consisting in a logical deduction of the solution from *the existing data*. In this statement of the subject I am not unconscious of the implications of the language I have adopted. For I am insisting that the construction is essentially synthetic and scientific. Perhaps herein lies the detective story's attraction to E. M. Wrong's "highly educated" people, and also the failure of some of the cleverest detective stories when expressed through the media of the stage and the screen. Note that even in my italics I am vague; I do not say, for example, when the data begin to exist.

The detective story is, then, a problem; a dramatic problem, a "feather to tickle the intellect." The basic element is rational theorising. In "The Adventure of the Copper Beeches" Sherlock Holmes takes Dr. Watson to task for not confining himself to a bare record of the logical synthesis, "that severe reasoning from cause to effect."

> "If I claim full justice for my art, it is because it is an impersonal thing—a thing beyond myself. Crime is common. Logic is rare. Therefore, it is upon the logic rather than upon the crime that you should dwell. You have degraded what should have been a course of lectures into a series of tales."

The problem itself is of a curious and complex kind. Only at the beginning is it simple and defined. Thereafter it is a chameleon, changing colour as every page is turned. Our difficulties multiply; the problem is modified, then changed out of all knowing. Whereas we started with the simple question, Who killed So-and-So? we have now, in addition, to account for an alibi, or —more welcome labour, to find one. Every chapter brings in fresh information. We cannot say at such and such a place in the story, "Now that I have my data, I can sit back in my chair and argue it out as Descartes argued out his philosophical principles."

Suppose we take up for a moment the attitude of the disgruntled reader:—

"You rather presume on your cleverness, Mr. Author. You may steal a march on me, but is it by fair methods? You start by giving me a fact—the murder. You set me the problem of finding the murderer, but I must ask no questions. You tell me the victim

was found *in articulo mortis* with his left hand firmly grasping
the third waistcoat button; and that of two glasses of beer found
on the table one was left unfinished—a fact which proves the murdered man was neither a gentleman, nor a man of taste, as the
beer happened to be . . . (well, your own brand, plus commission). In ninety-nine cases out of a hundred these homely touches
will have nothing to do with your solution. When I am trying to
have a morbid interest in the corpse—its dimensions and attitude
—you whisk me off to fresh woods. You introduce me as fast as
you can to your *dramatis personæ*—as though I were royalty and
had so many handshakes to accomplish in so many seconds. Then
you seem to fasten with some injustice on one of this motley
crowd. In an insinuating way you ask: 'If he was not drinking
beer with the murdered man on the night of the murder, where
was he?' You seem to forget that there are some people who do
not prefer to account for their actions between ten and twelve
o'clock of a Friday night.

"Next you set me puzzling my wits why your blessed detective
has gone to Paris. You see I'm the actuality of the 'legal myth'—
the reasonable man. If your detective goes off to Paris without
a word to a soul—even to his accommodating landlady—well,
I'm bound to think the worst.

"You set me the problem of finding out the why, the how and
the wherefore of this murder. You won't for a minute let me go
the reasonable way about it. You are as evasive as a Hyde Park
orator. You only give me pinches of information, and slake my
curiosity by throwing me the golden apples of fresh problems
easier of solution, and for that reason more momentarily attractive. Sometimes these are connected with the main issue—but not
always. Small wonder then if towards the end you succeed in bam-
boozling me. But if I had my way. . . ."

And let us suppose the author deigns to reply:—

"But why should you? In the first place you assume that I am
setting *you* a problem. If you choose to identify yourself with
my detective, you are responsible for any displeasure you may
experience. At the very least, you cannot cavil at his methods or
mine. Your diatribe is neither here nor there. I do not tabulate
a series of theories (all founded on some fraction of fact) and

ask you to place them in a list of popularity and then write you a cheque for £1000. I have my own and very excellent formula for administering the short, sharp shock at the unexpected dénouement. You are being rather stupidly annoyed because you are not cleverer than you are—that is in being able to read my thoughts."

Obviously we can only have sufficient evidence when the problem is solved. The solving of the problem virtually means complete knowledge of its attendant circumstances. But once given that, there is no problem. Yet a little knowledge, though it may be dangerous, is often a very blissful state. We are thrown on our resources, now to hazard a guess, now to use our intuition, now to answer the author back in his own coin. You see, the problem is changing again. We begin to examine the author's technique: and here, as we shall see later, we have the slender aid of the canons of our Muse to restrain the author's diabolical legerdemain. We have now really two problems.

(1) How is the author in the habit of disposing of his problems?

(2) How can we apply this knowledge to the problem in hand?

In one sense the problem is thus not a problem at all, but a host of problems depending on knowledge not only proper to the mystery but also extraneous to it. In another sense it is not strictly a problem at all, but a piece of grand bluff. Even although we can spot the villain, we cannot know the steps. There are mercifully, however, degrees of probability which serve as a guide to the solution; and we do emphatically regard them as a satisfactory substitute. We scrap the intermediate steps and boast we are in at the kill.

*   *   *

Let us now turn our attention to the other principal element in the detective story, which has been labelled "the sensational element," but which, owing to the base connotation of that term, you may prefer to call the romantic or even the artistic element. Mental gymnastics are not sufficient to warrant the widespread popularity of our genre. Jaded business men or imaginative office boys are not so keen as all that on mind culture. The puzzle can be overdone, and it is fatal to deprive it of its trappings. Thus

The Baffle Book by Lassiter Wren and Randle McKay, and similar volumes, are only for the distracted host when the guests are proving troublesome. Herein the crime and the data are provided, and one has merely to take a pencil and "furiously to think"—or crib by looking at the end of the book (upside down). One ingenious firm of publishers, putting their shirts on human nature, tried out a scheme whereby they sealed up the latter half of their mystery stories, and undertook to refund the money for the book if the reader returned it to them with the seal intact. Such is the puzzle fever!

But we must have some more primitive attraction, to serve as an antithesis. This we find in the setting, which is painted at times with an imagination so indifferent to fact and possibility that it reduces the total result to a lurid chaos. In this respect the detective story has just outgrown the penny dreadful. Mountains do not divide Sherlock Holmes from Sexton Blake. But where the penny dreadful rushes in, our Muse is well advised to tread warily. Excitement may be had without the wholesale dissipation of anarchy, and romance without its toll of victims. Mr. Chesterton has boldly called the atmosphere of this setting "the poetry of modern life." It is unnecessary to dwell on its familiar effects— the dangers lurking in darkened alleys; the mystery of a large city at night; the secrets and the tragedies it harbours; the perpetual all but annihilation of law and order; the hero-detective as the saviour of society.

It is merely a recognition of dramatic values. Take first of all the character of the villain. Our writer of detective fiction is naïvely emphatic in his repetition of the fact that his detective's opponent is no "common crook." And so with a gay will he sets out to people the world with Calibans turned geniuses, whom a streak of madness debars from becoming the legislators of the world. It is not so much an attempt to make some begrudging allowance for evil—to which after all he is professionally indebted —that induces our author to depict these arch-fiends as art collectors, musicians and scientists. Rather he is for Art's sake a zealous *advocatus diaboli;* he is raising evil to an artistic plane.

Mr. F. Wills Crofts in a paragraph in *Inspector French and the Cheyne Mystery* pours scorn on these tales of the jeopardizing of civilisation; of gunpowder plots; of stolen plans; of the discovery of deadly poisons; of the "Napoleons of crime" sitting in their spiders' webs, spreading out their "vast tentacles"—the while they plan delirious dreams of harnessing world power. But so often do we stumble in the dark on lonely mansions which hold some diabolical secret, so often are we held close prisoners by their desperate denizens, and such relish do we take in our predicament, that we cannot—to be honest with ourselves—welcome Mr. Crofts's attitude. Surely the compelling reason for our delight is a sense of the dramatic, and the higher the stakes played for, the more is it intensified. Should, however, this explanation fail to satisfy the realist, we must be content to submit the criterion of *excitement* as a substitute. Excitement can only be rated by its degree. If the aim of the author is merely to arouse excitement, he is justified in choosing any means to achieve his object.

Similarly with the death of the villain. It is rightly felt bad artistry to pack him off to the gallows. Few murderers in the detective story are sentenced at the Old Bailey, and in only one story that I have read has there been a description of the execution. "Sapper" has confessed the difficulty which he experienced in getting rid of Carl Peterson for good and all. An arrest as the final event is tame; a reticent silence, implying that the Law is "taking its course," is unsatisfactory. The truth of the matter is that we expect the villain to make a "good end." He has been responsible for some share in our entertainment. Let him choose the manner of his death, and die "like a gentleman." The films have robbed him of one means of demise—the motor smash; and Melodrama dislikes the familiar. Let us have, then, just a suspicion of the Old Lyceum. Where is heard the "jingle of the bracelets," there must there also be the "fetid breath of almonds!"

After a moment's thought on this two-fold division of the problem and the setting, I am induced to make a further division on the same lines, but this time a division of the public that reads detective stories. Like all generalisations it is only a half-truth, but here it is for what it is worth. The average male reader reads the detective story for the problem, the female reader for the excitement of the setting. The man in the street loves a problem. There is always an excuse to solve it round the corner. Not that he is too practical of imagination to snap his fingers at suspense; but murders on paper do, as a rule, amuse rather than excite him. His is the enthusiasm of the cross-word fiend, as it were, spread out a bit.

Not so with Woman. "Is it worth while?" says Miss Emancipated, and in her earnestness stays not for any answer. Is there love? And we must confess there is more cupidity than Cupid. Is there fashionable controversy, religious, social or sexual? And we are shamed into admitting that the only kind of controversy she will be likely to find will be between an "impossible creature" and a stupid policeman on the properties of red sandstone. Not a triumphant emergence from the inquisition.

Well, we can be superior and blame the inquisition. One can blame Woman's proverbial illogicality, and say she has not the patience to argue out the problem. Personally, I often wonder which attitude is the more enjoyable, that of the active participator or that of the passive spectator—in view of the nature of the problem. As far as my own experience goes that peculiar property of woman, intuition, fails disastrously on the touchstone of detective fiction. Even her guesses are unusually wide of the mark—possibly because the mystery monger is too much of a rationalist to accept the myth!

But the most obvious reason for Woman's indifference to the intellectual fireworks is her delight in the emotional values. To every woman who prefers the problem there are at least four who prefer the shocker. Woman loves to be thrilled and to have her knees banging each against either like one of Mr. Frankau's heroines. The doubting Thomas I would advise to go to a cinema where a mystery film is being screened or to a theatre where a crook drama is being staged, and to listen if he has not the indecency to watch. Perhaps there is some other less stupid reason for these gasps and sudden twitchings. If there is, I congratulate these victims of hysteria, and envy their escorts.

*   *   *

It is time in parenthesis to say a few words about murder. I have been assuming all along that the proper subject of detection in literature is murder, as being the consummation of crime;

while all other forms, theft, blackmail, larceny, arson, abduction and the like should scarcely come within its province, as not meriting "the grand manner." This may appear heresy in view of the paucity of murders in the Sherlock Holmes tales; but, it should be remembered, we have here to deal with just these artistic and dramatic values to which reference has been made. From an æsthetic point of view, the theft of a Rajah's diamond remains a base act, on a par with the pilfering of a string of Ciro pearls. With murder it is different; we are on a higher plane. "The base element," wrote Schiller of murder, "disappears in the terrible." Where there is no murder, it almost seems like wasting the detective's valuable time.

Van Dine is reported in an interview to have said that he considered "murder" the strongest word in the English language. No other word was "so dramatic, so gripping, so compelling." For that reason he uses it in the title of each of his books!

On the subject of murder it is well to go back to De Quincey.

> "People," he says, "begin to see that something more goes to the composition of a fine murder than two blockheads to kill and be killed—a knife—a purse—and a dark lane. Design, grouping, light and shade, poetry, sentiment, are now deemed indispensable to attempts of this nature." And again:
>
> "The world in general are very bloody-minded; and all they want is a copious effusion of blood; gaudy display is enough for *them*. But the enlightened connoisseur is more refined in his taste."

Here, then, we have a beginning; and for the rest—*exit in mysterium*. We must have a murder and it must be well done. As enlightened connoisseurs the question, What constitutes a good murder? must give us pause. Obviously the more artistic a murder, the more artistic in one sense will be the detection of the murderer; for the artistry of a murder involves to some extent the immunity of the murderer from detection. Now, despite this correspondence of æsthetic values, the principles determining the murder perfect *per se,* and those determining the perfect murder of detective fiction are somewhat different, just as the latter differs, for example, from the ideal press murder.

In his rulings on the "principles" to which the man of sensibility looks in gauging the artistry of a murder, De Quincey gives us three heads, (1) the kind of person murdered; (2) the place where, and (3) the time when.

(1) As regards the first, he considers that the murdered man should not be a villain, and follows with the attractive corollary that he should not be a public man either. His former argument is this. If the murdered man be a villain it is just possible that he was himself contemplating murder when he was struck down. This robs the murder of all its pathos. Now the interest of the writer of detective fiction in the morality of the murdered man varies according to his purposes. For example, he may argue thus:—

"I shall be conventionally simple. I shall increase the reader's desire to have justice done by appealing to this preliminary pathos —parent of vengeful wrath. I shall, therefore, stress the unimpeachability of the victim's morals. The trick always works in the magazines."

Or he may argue thus: "A railway journey or a Saturday night are not the most fitting occasions for an indulgence in pathos. My reader is likely to have as little pity for my victim as I have myself—and I have none. Supposing on the contrary I renounce pathos, and make my murdered man a thorough scoundrel, what can I gain in this equation? Why, I shall simply float on motives. My characters will vie with each other to have the glory attached to them of ridding the world of a pest to society. I can also work out a happy ending, and incidentally collar the film rights."

Or he may argue in yet another way: "I shall trade on the old crux of morality and its semblance. I shall bestow the mythical ring of Gyges on the corpse. Thereby I shall cultivate my reader's righteous indignation, while flummoxing him as to the motive. Then, at my own pleasure, I shall turn the tables."

(2) Place where. Most writers have a preference for staging their murders in the library. It is dignified; it is homely. The corpse sits bolt upright at the desk, or sprawls over the blotting pad. The library incidentally opens on to a verandah. The folding windows are locked. A Virginia creeper climbs up the walls outside. Corpses have occasionally been stowed *submensa;* but such humour on the part of the murderer can only be regarded

as rather coarse. Cupboards form convenient receptacles, and bathrooms, had it not been for the French Revolution, would have had their points. A murder in a railway carriage leaves too much to chance, and the space is abominably confined.

The murder in a detective story should come unexpectedly; unexpectedly that is to those concerned. It should also be committed in the last place in the world you would expect it to be. Thus, a murder in the grotesque place has additional virtue. It surprises, it amuses, it takes us by storm.

Imagine a murder in a music shop, in Selfridge's bargain basement, in a parish hall, at the Grocers' Exhibition. After all the golf course takes some beating. It is an ideal depository. And what a joy to lay a corpse dead on the pin at the sixteenth. Some noble souls go through life with the fervent desire on their lips that when their day comes they may be taken away after a daisy down the fairway! Indeed, if the writers of detective fiction consulted the wishes of some of their victims, the golf course would be much more popular even than it is at present as the setting.

(3) As regards time when and other circumstances De Quincey has little to say. "The good sense of the practitioner has usually directed him to night and privacy"—a sentiment with which we are probably in agreement. In this category we must include also the means; the motive; the attendant circumstances; the presence or more likely the absence of witnesses—all the facts material to the unravelling of the plot. Naturally, the means and the motive are the most important. Miss Sayers has given us an attractive list of the "unexpected means"—"poisoned tooth-stoppings, shaving brushes inoculated with dread disease . . . poisoned boiled eggs . . . electrocution by telephone—hypodermic injections shot from air guns." But novelty's reign is usually short-lived, and the day of secret African poisons has passed. Of the motive it would be safe to premise that it should be (1) natural, and (2) adequate. It should spring from the primary and elemental emotions of jealousy, envy, fear, covetousness and the like, and the murderer should have some cause however slight for harbouring these passions. He should not, for example, commit murder for the fun of it, or from some trivial pique. Van Dine makes the following catalogue of primary motives for murder (1) murders

for profit; (2) murders for jealousy; (3) murders for revenge; (4) murders for ambition; (5) abnormal sex murders.

Well, we have made some progress. We have decided to have a murder. And let us have no beating about the bush, no subsequent disappearance or resuscitation of the corpse. That would be gross anticlimax. Father Ronald Knox should really have known better in *Footsteps at the Lock*. Further we shall probably agree with Macbeth—though we disregard his hypothesis—that

> " 'Twere well it were done quickly."

Mr. Bancroft's long and halting proem to the murder in the book version of *The Ware Case* tends to destroy our interest in it when it does come. Logically, the murder is the First Act, and the greatest economy can be used in the so-called "creation of atmosphere," for the reader is already keyed. Whoso considers the detective story beastly and morbid can put that in his pipe and smoke it. Notice how Mr. Chesterton goes to work in "The Three Tools of Death":—

> "But there came out of him a cry which was talked of afterwards as something unnatural and new. It was one of those shouts that are horribly distinct even when we cannot hear what is shouted. The word in the case was 'Murder.' But the engine driver swears he would have pulled up all the same if he had heard only the dreadful and definite accent, and not the word."

The unity of the plot should not be destroyed by a succession of murders. It is repulsive to the "enlightened connoisseur" to have to

> "Look on the tragic loading of this bed."

We may, indeed, grant the criminal a score of murders to his credit; the more the merrier, provided our evidence for them is mere hearsay. Even in a life of crime distance lends enchantment. But a repetition of murders within the scope of a single plot, as in Mr. Arthur B. Reeve's *The Exploits of Elaine* or Mr. Edgar Wallace's *The Green Archer*, is monotonously episodic. It is, as Mr. Darlington would say: too "bloomin' 'olesale."

*   *   *

We have discovered two ingredients in the detective story—the problem and the setting. We started the ball rolling by positing the perpetration of a satisfactory murder. We have now to fill in some of the details. Three main emotional elements are distinguishable in the detective story—the elements of excitement, of bewilderment, and of surprise. Of these the first is common, but in a variety of degrees, to all fiction. In the detective story it ought to be at white heat. The quick development of the plot, the interplay of the characters, the lurid background, the final solution of the mystery with the detective's triumphant Eureka, all contribute to this effect. The element of bewilderment is caused obviously by the nature of the problem. We cannot tell at once who the murderer is. Even if we claim to have intuitional powers, we shall experience some difficulty in finding a satisfactory motive for the murderer. This bewilderment of ours, be it added, is not always appeased and satisfied as the writer considers it ought to be. As regards the element of surprise the detective story may claim an advantage over fiction in general. Fiction, like government schemes, tends to work out according to plan; its conclusions are for the most part foreseen because they are the natural outcome of character and circumstance. In the detective story the important characters are not usually labelled, and the circumstances are shrouded in mystery, so that the unexpected is always happening. Unexpected, only in the sense that we have nothing to inform us of what is likely to happen next.

How is the plot evolved? Common sense will tell that it is bound to be a painstaking process, a putting together of a jig-saw puzzle, rather than the sudden spontaneity of the poet—the sublime unity of form and matter, and so forth. It is a cold, calculating business, cruelly selective—for the author has to choose between a number of roads all leading to the same place and of more or less equal length and gradient. And in this constructive process he has to be ever so circumspect or his edifice will begin to wobble, or—to change the figure—his cat will come tumbling out of the bag. Disparage, if you will, the limitations of his art, his meanderings in the labyrinth of the plot with the Minotaur of the Obvious, Sensationalism and his other enemies awaiting him at every corner.

Mr. John Buchan in *The Three Hostages* has suggested what must strike one as a singularly happy-go-lucky method for plot construction. The author takes a certain number of incongruous subjects—a Jew's harp, let us say for the sake of argument, a potato patch and a steam roller, and he then proceeds to establish a connection between them. A prolific writer of detective fiction naïvely admitted that his inspiration was due to his typewriter. So long as his fingers grasped the pen in the approved style his mind simply failed to function, but as soon as ever his fingers felt the keyboard, inspiration came to him simply oozing thousands of words. I have heard, too, of an author who constructed so mysterious a problem that (when the time came) he could not for the world solve it himself. Generally speaking it seems reasonable to suppose that the average detective story writer must start with one (supposedly) original idea which he proceeds to work up—this idea in eight cases out of ten being concerned with the actual perpetration of the crime. The process of detection will then be built up backwards. This is naturally a point which we shall have to discuss in greater detail in particular instances.

Be that as it may, the solution of the plot consisting virtually in the shifting of the relative position of the characters to each other in the light of the murder, it is the author's business to try to screen the criminal for as long as possible, and thus to contend with the reader's powers of identification by drawing before him a continual stream of red herrings. It is his business, for that is what his public expects of him. And what delight his public derives from its realisation now and again that they are red herrings! And what self-gratification in the boast, "You can't hoodwink me!" The author, recognising his public's perspicacity, can afford to be patronising and to give it some rope provided only he can deceive it over the final issue. But to the Red Herrings—specious and alluring—our writer must pay his court.

Let us take A, B, C, D, as four principal characters amongst whom our suspicions may be equally divided after the murder. The commonest procedure is what is known as double bluff or double-cross. A is made to attract our suspicions first; next B and C temporarily appear as potential criminals; then D, who has hitherto been eating his eggs and bacon, and been behaving in an exemplary fashion, is most foully incriminated. And when we imagine his guilt is all but confirmed, back we go to the laughing unsuspected A. This is a scheme to which most detective story writers have at some time or another a very strong leaning. Of course, even with four principals several variations are possible. A, as often as not the family lawyer, may caper genteelly in the foreground during the whole of the action while B, C and D are in turn made his scapegoats. Suspicion should be fairly evenly distributed. The more pigs in pokes that the author carries about with him the more fun for the reader. But when one or two characters get more than their proper share of suspicion—well, it becomes too patently obvious. When we speak of these suspects, it should be borne in mind that they may either be characters who are in a temporary disgrace to suit the author's purpose, or on the other hand those who for all their sheep's clothing do look unconscionably like wolves. So, if the author is as ingenious as Mrs. Agatha Christie, he can play a double game with the reader by establishing a subtle intercommunication between the sheep and the wolves travelling incognito to the forest and the fold.

I must say I have a special liking for those tales where one's field as a reader is to some extent determined and marked down. Supposing the circumstances make it necessary that the murder was committed by one staying in a certain house, one's attention is thus focused on a fixed number of people. This narrowing down of the possibles serves in a curious way to make the puzzle harder. You no longer try to reason on the assumption that anything is possible, but to choose out of a number of possibles the right solution.

It is with certain misgivings that I now proceed to attempt to summarise from the main trend of detective literature the phases of the action of the orthodox plot. The following structure is not intended to be in any way either a necessary or an exemplary one. It is only a typical one, and, from being typical, naturally a successful one.

(1) Murder most foul!

(2) Introduction of the characters. First suspects, these being either (*a*) the author's red herrings, or (*b*) those characters whom the reader suspects intuitively.

(3) The Inquest.

(4) Clues and False Trails. The investigation carried out by the police (or less often by a bombastic amateur) fails.

(5) Impasse.

(6) The detective "takes up the case;" his novel line of investigation.

(7) New Suspects; i.e. those characters whom the reader is supposed to conclude that the detective suspects. In reality, of course, the latter suspects somebody quite different.

(8) Dénouement. The detective's Eureka.

(9) Explanations.

The eleventh hour dénouement is the most satisfying. Mr. E. C. Bentley's *Trent's Last Case* shows with what effect the dénouement may be delayed. An explanation covering thirty or forty pages, either going over old ground or consisting of an archæological research into ancestral crooks and crimes, is intolerable anticlimax.

*   *   *

Criticism is at bottom a statement of personal feelings of appreciation or of censure. But it involves something more, and hereby criticism saves its face. Our feelings must be accounted for, attributed to certain elements in the work criticised. This is nothing else than the realisation of a code of rules to which the work under consideration must in general conform. Now it is a fair submission that the stricter the rules and the more stringently they are enforced, the higher will be the standard of play. If we admit this—as presumably we must—it will not be difficult to show that the detective story has a just claim to be a work of art.

To the methods of treatment in the detective story there seems no limit. The mystery may be left—if solved—yet unfinished, as in Mr. J. S. Fletcher's *The Mysterious Chinaman*. The detective may prove to be the criminal—a fashionable variation at the present time. Again the murder may turn out to be no murder at all, but a hoax. The story may even be told by the criminal, so that as far as the reader is concerned there is no mystery. An infinite number of variations is possible, yet I insist that there is, and must be in the better detective stories, this common adherence to a set of rules.

I do not wish to be saddled with the task of tabulating these rules. For when one embarks on this task, one is immediately aware of the distressing fact that one is merely emphasising a heap of truisms. This is due to the fact that we take up a detective story in a very definite frame of mind. Let me make myself a little clearer. When we read a detective story in which there is a murder, we expect to be told eventually who the murderer was, and how he murdered his victim. We expect that all the details of the evidence which did or did not puzzle us should be explained. We expect also a host of other things—that the murderer shall pay for his crime: that the detective's theory shall be the right one: that there shall be a detective, whatever those who consider *Edwin Drood* a first-class detective novel say to the contrary. And so on and so forth.

To put it in another way, the reader expects the writer to co-operate with him to some extent. This question has been aptly described as an "ethical" one. The average reader has a very definite idea that the author should play the game with him: and he is instantly up in arms if the canons of fairplay are violated. What he means by this is open to doubt. But probably, he means that the author has solved his problem in a way in which it was impossible for him to solve it. The whole process of detection is based on evidence. From the author's point of view the easiest procedure is to give the reader evidence, evidence and again evidence: for it is easier to deceive where there is a surfeit of it than where there is a scarcity. This also happens to fit in with the reader's way of thinking. But if the detective should calmly pocket a bullet that he found on the carpet without saying a word to a soul, and then calmly proceed to reconstruct the crime from this valuable clue, the irate reader feels bound to claim a penalty. For had he been there he might have found the clue himself. Similarly he feels that to keep the villain under lock and key—a relative from abroad, a rough diamond from the colonies, whose existence has barely been mentioned, then suddenly to bring him to light at the dénouement, is a piece of glaring insincerity. To abstain from recording vital evidence is a technical weakness. Vital evidence should be placed in the shop window.

The average reader is so far justified; but, before allowing him to have it all his own way, we should consider for a moment his *average* attitude of mind in reading a detective story. In the first place he is at liberty to, and invariably does, suspect every character in the book with possibly an exception or two. Allowing for this fact an impartial judge might on occasion describe the irate reader's plea for fair-play as an instance of sour grapes. Then again the reader is possibly familiar with the individual technique of the author he is reading. If he is reading Mr. Edgar Wallace, he probably sees through the attractive veneer of the villain. In Mr. A. E. W. Mason's yarns he is ready *chercher la femme,* and so forth. So you see the detective is handicapped in some ways. He has got to get the better of his creator. He has on occasion to lose his individuality without losing his identity.

It is just this discipline that justifies the consideration of the detective story as an independent genre. For without this restraint it merges into the other types of fiction, such as the adventure story, the spy story, and the picaresque novel, whose structure cannot be so clearly delineated. These other forms may bear at times the very strongest resemblance to the detective story. It can easily be seen that the "hunt" or "chase" theme is very much akin to the trapper-like pursuit of the detective. E. M. Wrong saw a close similarity between Mr. John Buchan's *The Thirty-Nine Steps* and *The Power House* and the orthodox detective story.

Again we may have the tale of the combat-to-the-death between Law and Anarchy, where the forces and objectives of the two camps are openly divulged. We note the same movements as in the sensational detective story: attack, pursuit and capture. Only the hares and the hounds regularly change sides.

Yet another kindred theme is where the Sword of Damocles is held over the hero for the greater part of the book. He learns by chance of an incriminating secret. A letter in the post asks him politely but firmly to mind his own business. He pays no attention to this, but is surprised to find a second warning, this time couched in language more succinct, under his porridge plate. Of course, he is too pig-headed not to disregard this too. Finally

comes the threat of immediate annihilation. Then things begin
to happen.

As a sop to the adventurous Adam this theme is frequently introduced into more or less orthodox detective stories. Sherlock
Holmes, you remember, after staging his comeback, had the very
devil of a time with the last of the Moriartyans. Hourly he stalked
in the shadow of death. But though the detective is from time
to time threatened with death, he has rarely, in the best circles,
to run the gauntlet of organised attempts at assassination. Father
Brown does not find bombs in his coal scuttle. In nine cases out
of ten, Poirot would be shocked if poisoned arrows were shot at
him through the skylight. E. M. Wrong thought that the reason
for this *motif* is that the criminal should give the detective a run
for his money. Rather it is that the criminal should give his reading fans a run for their money, for the sedentary life of the detective is not yet out of fashion.

*   *   *

There remains one question which had better be answered before we come to grips with our subject. Really, it is the conclusion
of our argument. What are we to regard as the true proportion
of reason and sensation? We shall see that, historically, the pen-
dulum swings fairly evenly in either direction. There have been
thrillers pure and simple; there have also been puzzles, possess-
ing as little sensational action as a novel of Trollope's. There
have also been hybrids, unfailingly attractive because of the compromise. But it was our view that the detective story must be first
and foremost a problem. The main ingredient must be logic. If
there is to be sensation—and we would not for worlds banish it
—it should *seem* rather incidental. All the same, there is quite
enough excitement in a problem without calling in the aid of
death, crape and flying squads. The logical detective story is the
finer form because it recognises a technique. The highbrow form
wins.

The Private Life of Sherlock Holmes

(1933)

By Vincent Starrett

*The affection of men of good will for Sherlock Holmes has ex-
pressed itself, in recent years, in a literature* sui generis: *half-
serious, half-humorous, often extravagant, based on the pleasant
make-believe that the king of sleuths was a man of flesh and blood.
As practiced by the Baker Street Irregulars of New York, shep-
herded by Christopher Morley, and affiliated or scion societies in
such world centers as London, Boston, Chicago, San Francisco,
Okinawa, and Akron, Ohio, this pursuit of the higher verities
has acquired the status of an original if minor biographical and
bibliographical science that may be called, for want of a better
term, Holmesiology. The studies and researches produced under
this devotional aegis are classified as Holmesiana or Sherlockiana,
or occasionally Watsoniana; the scriptures they interpret (known
in the Baker Street vernacular as The Sacred Writings) are the
narratives of John (or James) H. Watson, M.D., as transcribed for
publication by a certain Conan Doyle.*

*Already this harmless conceit has produced a good half-dozen
full-size volumes in England and America, not to mention an
infinite number of shorter publications. And word arrives at
press-time of the founding of a full-fledged journal, to provide
the faithful with their chosen fare at quarterly intervals.*

*How all this started has occasioned considerable conjecture,
which need not detain us here. The truth of the matter probably
is that the game belongs to no single individual, but to the unique
reality of Holmes himself. With all respect to such other selfless
toilers in the vineyard as Monsignor Ronald A. Knox, H. W. Bell,
S. C. Roberts, Mr. Morley, and Edgar W. Smith, the finest flowering if not necessarily the earliest beginning of Holmesian scholarship occurred in the series of fond, wise, and mellow essays by*

*Vincent Starrett which were collected between covers under the
irresistible title* The Private Life of Sherlock Holmes, (*New York:
Macmillan, 1933; London: Nicholson, 1934*). *In your editor's
opinion they will never be equalled, much less surpassed, for
sheer imaginative delight in their subject. Dealing explicitly with
Holmes and Watson, they contain at the same time much that
is implicit and valuable to know about the classical appeal of
the detective story as a whole.*

*Mr. Starrett is one of the few remaining American bookmen,
in the true sense of that word. Like Doyle before him, his association with Holmes seems likely to overshadow his other numerous and substantial achievements, which include a number of
enjoyable detective stories of his own and some beyond-the-
average thoughtful criticism of police fiction in general. The selection chosen to represent him (and Holmesiology) in the present
volume is the title essay from his book.*

It is, of course, notorious—we have Watson's word for it—that
Mr. Sherlock Holmes "loathed every form of society with his
whole Bohemian soul." The word *society* is poorly chosen. What
Watson—a careless writer—intended to convey was that *social
life* offended the Bohemian soul of his companion; in consequence
of which emotion he preferred to spend his time in Baker Street
when others might have gone to teas and parties: "buried among
his old books," as Watson says, "and alternating from week to
week between cocaine and ambition—the drowsiness of the drug
and the fierce energy of his own keen nature."

In time, it is true, the doctor weaned him from the drug—to
the detriment of romantic interest, whatever the benefit to
Holmes—but even then it is seldom that one finds the saturnine
detective accepting or turning down an invitation. He simply
didn't get them. No doubt there had been plenty of them in his
youth; but in the face of his consistent declinations—after an experience or two, perhaps, with bores—he would in time, of course,
be let alone. It is, one fancies, almost as great a nuisance to be

a detective as to be a doctor: there are always guests with problems to present.

The fact is, Watson too preferred the silences or the friendly arguments of Baker Street to any attraction London had to offer —a circumstance in which he is at one with his adoring readers. Each man preferred the company of the other, and was glad enough, no doubt, even to see a client leave the doorstep. Even, perhaps, Lestrade or Tobias Gregson. Even, perhaps, Inspector Stanley Hopkins; although for Hopkins Holmes had a considerable admiration, and on a cold night a prescription containing whisky.

To the casual student of the detective's cases it may appear that the rooms in Baker Street were always crowded. His first impression may be that of a bewildered client teetering on the rug; an arm-chair in which the detective is curled like a Mohammedan, smoking shag; a cane-backed chair or sofa containing Watson; and Mrs. Hudson entering to announce Lestrade—whose footstep is on the stair. In actuality, there were long hours of comradely communion between the occupants. Seldom indeed did anyone stay the night. And some of the happiest memories, surely, of the epic history are those of Holmes and Watson living their simple, private lives. Not Crusoe and his admirable Friday—one had almost said his goat—were more resolutely at home upon their island than Sherlock Holmes and Watson in their living-room. They passed there some of the most felicitous moments of their common life.

Not that they did not, on occasion, venture the Victorian whirl. There is ample record that Holmes, at least, was fond of opera— sufficiently so to hurry to Covent Garden, on a Wagner night, with no hope of arriving before the second act. This was after the successful culmination of the "Red Circle" adventure, and was possibly in the nature of a reward. Similarly, it will be remembered, after some weeks of severe work on the problem presented by Sir Henry Baskerville, the pair went off to hear the De Reszkes in *Les Huguenots*. Holmes had procured a box, and on the way they stopped at Marcini's for a little dinner. "Turning their thoughts into more pleasant channels," was the way in which Holmes described the De Reszke adventure. A musician himself, he would naturally turn to music for rest and surcease, after a desperate morning round with murderers. Not always was his own violin sufficient.

As early in their association as the celebrated *Study in Scarlet* the detective had dragged his companion off to Hallé's concert, after a triumphant morning of detection at Lauriston Gardens. Neruda was to play: "Her attack and her bowing are splendid," commented Sherlock Holmes. "What's that little thing of Chopin's she plays so magnificently?" If he really expected Watson to answer him, the suggestion is clear that the doctor also knew something about music. And luncheon, of course, immediately preceded Neruda. Both men, without being gluttons, were fond of eating, and frequently they posted off to some favourite London restaurant. After the hideous comedy of the "Dying Detective" it was to Simpson's they went for sustenance, however; not Marcini's. Possibly it seemed a better place to eat when food in quantity was what was needed. Holmes, it will be recalled, had been at that time fasting for several days.

*   *   *

St. James Hall was also a favourite sanctuary when it was possible for Holmes to interrupt his sleuthing. "And now, Doctor, we've done our work; it's time we had some play," one hears him cry to Watson, after a brilliant morning of deduction. "A sandwich and a cup of coffee; then off to violin land, where all is sweetness and delicacy and harmony, and there are no red-headed clients to vex us with their conundrums." The occasion of this pleasant interlude was the intermission, as it were, before the "crash" in the fantastic problem of Mr. Jabez Wilson. And all that afternoon, the doctor tells us, "he sat in the stalls, wrapped in the most perfect happiness, gently waving his long thin fingers in time to the music"—listening to Sarasate play the violin.

The picture galleries, too, it must be assumed, were browsing-spots attractive to the collaborators. No doubt they served as stopgaps in the long days of criminal investigation—when it was possible pleasantly to while away an hour while waiting for an appointment. A clue to this diversion is to be found in the early pages of the *Hound;* after the profitable discovery of the bearded

man, in Regent Street: "And now, Watson, it only remains for us
to find out by wire the identity of the cabman . . . and then
we will drop into one of the Bond Street picture-galleries and
fill in the time until we are due at the hotel." But the incident
was not, we may be sure, an isolated one. The mind turns easily
at such times to the familiar groove. Did they, one wonders, care
for Mr. Whistler? Or was "The Charge of the Scots Greys" more
to their British taste?

It is quite clear, at any rate, that the occasional social exercises
of the two were largely cultural. When they went forth from Baker
Street, it was upon a trail of evil import or to a place of decent
entertainment. Occasionally, to a Turkish bath; and very likely
—one suspects—now and again to Madame Tussaud's. On the
whole, however, they preferred to stay at home. Away from it,
the detective's temper was always uncertain, Watson tells us:
"Without his scrapbooks, his chemicals, and his homely untidi-
ness, he was an uncomfortable man."

From time to time they travelled on the continent, not always
on the business of a client; and several parts of rural England
knew them well. It was on one of these joint vacation jaunts that
they chanced upon the ugly business of the "Reigate Squires"—
when they were the guests of Colonel Hayter, down in Surrey;
and it was presumably a holiday adventure of a sort that furnished
them the instructive problem of the "Three Students"—a sort of
pendant to Holmes's laborious researches into early English char-
ters. Again, it was a vacation trip that took them—in 1897—to the
small cottage near Poldhu Bay, at the further extremity of the
Cornish peninsula, in which singular and sinister neighborhood
there befell that gruesome experience chronicled by Watson as
"The Devil's Foot." Once, it is certain, they went to Norway; but
if aught of criminal interest developed during the visit, it has yet
to be reported.

From these vacation trips—interrupted as they invariably were
by theft or murder—Holmes always returned to Baker Street refreshed. It was, however, only the thefts and murders that con-
soled him for the time thus spent away from Baker Street.

And it is at home, in Baker Street, that one likes best to think
of them—alone and puttering with their secret interests. Little

vignettes of perfect happiness, wreathed in tobacco smoke and London fog.

Of course they took in all the daily papers, and read them with a diligence almost incredible. Did the detective prop his journal against the breakfast sugar bowl? And did Watson, when he sat down at table, invariably thump his knee against the leg? For Watson, at any rate, there was usually a lecture. . . . After the return from Switzerland—by way of Lhassa—the papers rather disappointed Holmes. With Moriarty dead, London, from the point of view of the criminal expert, he said, had become a singularly uninteresting city. . . . "With that man in the field one's morning paper presented infinite possibilities. Often it was only the smallest trace, Watson, the faintest indication, and yet it was enough to tell me that the great malignant brain was there, as the gentlest tremors of the edges of the web remind one of the foul spider which lurks in the centre. Petty thefts, wanton assaults, purposeless outrage—to the man who held the clue all could be worked into one connected whole. To the scientific student of the higher criminal world no capital of Europe offered the advantages which London then possessed. But now—!"

One sees the pile of papers growing in a corner, mounting up toward the gasogene and pipe-rack, till in a fit of energy Holmes scissored them to fragments. That rid the room of papers, for the nonce, but presented the new problem of the clippings: there were probably thousands waiting to be pasted up. And then, another night, another burst of energy, and some hundreds would at length be docketed. Over the years the row of scrapbooks lengthened on the shelf. Cold winter evenings or rainy nights of autumn were likely to be dedicated to the pasting-up; sometimes to indexing what already had been pasted. A never-ending chore. When and if ever the British Museum shall acquire the scrapbooks of Mr. Sherlock Holmes one hopes to read the volume under V—a fascinating miscellany. The *Voyage* of the "Gloria Scott" is there, and a biography of *Victor Lynch* the forger. Also the case of *Vanderbilt* and the Yeggman—unchronicled by Watson—and somewhat concerning *Vittoria* the circus belle. *Vigor,* the Hammersmith Wonder, too; and *Vipers*—possibly *Vodka*—and a Draculian paper about *Vampires.* . . .

Holmes obviously had a system of his own. Most scrapbook makers would simply have listed *Lynch* and *lizard* under the letter L, letting it go at that. But the detective indexed his clippings to the last adjective and adverb.

*   *   *

The relationship between the collaborators was ideal, after the years had taught them to know each other. About his own share in the partnership Watson had no illusions; but he was not too servile. Some thousands of his readers, he must have known, would happily have traded places with him. His statement as to himself and Sherlock Holmes, candidly prefixed to the adventure of the "Creeping Man," is admirably lucid and not a little penetrating: "The relations between us," he asserts, "were peculiar. He was a man of habits, narrow and concentrated habits, and I had become one of them. As an institution I was like the violin, the shag tobacco, the old black pipe, the index books, and others perhaps less excusable. When it was a case of active work and a comrade was needed upon whose nerve he could place some reliance, my rôle was obvious. But apart from this I had uses. I was a whetstone for his mind, I stimulated him. He liked to think aloud in my presence. His remarks could hardly be said to be made to me—many of them would have been as appropriately addressed to his bedstead—but none the less, having formed the habit, it had become in some way helpful that I should register and interject. If I irritated him by a certain methodical slowness in my mentality, that irritation served only to make his own flame-like intuitions and impressions flash up the more vividly and swiftly. Such was my humble rôle in our alliance."

During the day, when no active occupation offered, Holmes smoked his pipe and meditated. With a case on hand, he also smoked and meditated. Sometimes—the picture is famous—he would sit for hours "curled up in the recesses of his shabby chair." Sometimes, in search of information, he "sat upon the floor like some strange Buddha, with crossed legs, the huge books all around him, and one open upon his knees." Obviously, the nature of the problem offered for his solution had an important bearing on his habits. Sometimes "a formidable array of bottles and test-tubes, with the pungent cleanly smell of hydrochloric acid" would tell the doctor—hastening in, himself, after a session with his patients —that he had spent his day in the chemical work which was so dear to him." Sometimes, horizontal upon a couch, wrapped in a purple gown—"a pipe-rack within his reach upon the right, and a pile of crumpled morning papers . . . near at hand"—the doctor would discover him in rapt examination of a hat which was for the moment an intellectual problem.

There is a curious glamour in the most trivial passages between the two, a sense of significance—of impending revelation—perhaps not always justified by the detective's disclosure. It is part of Watson's charm that he sets down everything. One would not have it otherwise. The little triumphs that are no part or parcel of the tale are his habitual prolegomena; they are our glimpses of that private life they lived together, when only the reader's eye might spy them out. . . .

"Sherlock Holmes," one genuinely thrills to hear, "had been bending for a long time over a low-power microscope. Now he straightened himself up and looked round at me in triumph. 'It is glue, Watson,' said he. 'Unquestionably it is glue. Have a look at these scattered objects in the field!' "

Actively engaged upon a malodorous bit of brewing, "his long, thin back curved over a chemical vessel" and his head sunk upon his chest, the detective looked to Watson "like a strange, lank bird, with dull grey plumage and a black top-knot." There is no need to illustrate the scene. But this would be, of course, upon a day when Holmes had put on his dressing-gown of grey, instead of the more familiar purple horror. On the whole, the picture that Watson has most vividly conveyed is that of Holmes recumbent—languid yet somehow rigid in his chair, wreathed in the vapours from his favourite pipe. The favourite pipe, of course, being subject always to change; since nothing, as Holmes himself remarked, has more individuality than a pipe, "save perhaps watches and bootlaces." For every mood in Baker Street there was a pipe. One sees him still as Watson saw and described him in that last of all the series of adventures. . . . "Holmes lay with his gaunt figure stretched in his deep chair, his pipe curling forth slow wreaths of acrid tobacco, while his eyelids drooped over his

eyes so lazily that he might almost have been asleep were it not
that at any halt or questionable passage of my narrative they half
lifted, and two grey eyes, as bright and keen as rapiers, transfixed
me with their searching glance."

One notes with interest that Holmes's eyes were grey. It is the
only record of their colour.

*　　*　　*

Occasionally, when the day was really fine, the friends walked
in the streets, savouring the singular sights and sounds of London.
Shop windows were of interest to them both, and passers-by absorbing. "The park"—some park or other—was close at hand, and
it is of record that they sometimes strolled there. Watson's account of one such episode is subdued. . . . "The first faint shoots
of green were breaking out upon the elms, and the sticky spear-
heads of the chestnuts were just beginning to burst into their five-
fold leaves. For two hours we rambled about together, in silence
for the most part, as befits two men who know each other intimately." But this diversion was not customary, since it encroached
on office hours. And on the afternoon described they missed a
client. "There had been a gentlemen asking for them."

"Holmes glanced reproachfully at me," confesses Watson." " 'So
much for afternoon walks!' said he."

The afternoons then were spent in running down their cases—
the detective's cases—not often strolling in the park. And for all
his love of Baker Street, it may be noted, during the active progress of a case Holmes was quite capable of hiding out. It is an
interesting revelation, frequently overlooked, that Watson makes
in his account of the adventure called "Black Peter." . . . "He
had at least five small refuges in different parts of London in
which he was able to change his personality." The reference is
tantalizing and obscure. The rooms of Mycroft Holmes, opposite
the Diogenes Club, would certainly be one of them; but it would
be satisfying to know the others. At such times—when he was operating in disguise—Holmes sometimes took the name of "Captain Basil," the better to deceive his casual assistants and to deceive and confound his unsuspecting enemies. It may be assumed

that in all of his five refuges he stored the materials of deception, as well as quantities of shag tobacco.

Not all of the detective's cases, though, drove him to his retreats or to his arm-chair. Sometimes for hours—once, certainly, for a whole day—he rambled about the living-room with knotted brows, his head upon his breast, charging and recharging his strongest pipe, and deaf to all of Watson's questionings. These were his bad days, when the trail was faint, and even Watson had failed him as a whetstone.

But it was to the papers that both invariably returned. The everlasting, never-ceasing papers. Edition after edition of them was delivered at the rooms, probably by the stout and puffing Mrs. Hudson, who would have them from the urchin at the door. Not only Holmes but Watson saturated himself with the unending chronicle of news; and they read it—it must be admitted—with a surprisingly reckless acceptance of its accuracy. In America, Holmes would have taken *none* of the papers in. In America, the papers are for the credulous Watsons.

It is at night one likes them best perhaps—the curious companions. And preferably with a beating rain outside. If Stanley Hopkins has dropped in from Scotland Yard, no matter; their simple hospitality is as hearty as it is restrained and masculine. They did not always save the whisky for Stanley Hopkins. Themselves, occasionally, good fellows, they tippled companionably. And usually in the early morning hours, after a trying day with thug or cracksman. Whisky-and-soda and a bit of lemon. And all the credit gone to Scotland Yard. Midnight or very early in the morning—the time of relaxation and revelation, while the "undying flame" leaps on the hearth. Holmes lifts out a glowing cinder with the tongs; lights the long pipe of sprightly disputation. "You see, Watson," he patiently begins, "it was all perfectly obvious from the first. . . ."

In the long evenings, too, Holmes played his fiddle. Doubtless his bowing was not comparable to Neruda's, but it was good enough for Watson. "Sometimes the chords were sonorous and melancholy. Occasionally they were fantastic and cheerful. Clearly they reflected the thoughts which possessed him, but whether the music aided those thoughts, or whether the playing was simply the result of a whim or fancy," was more than Watson could determine. And when some haunting strain had charmed and soothed the doctor—moved him to ask the name of the composer —as like as not it would be something by Sherlock Holmes.

* * *

Then, of an evening in the depths of February, one fancies Watson questing another tale. Permission, perhaps, to reveal an untold problem—one of the many hinted and then withheld. The truth, perhaps, about the atrocious conduct of Colonel Upwood, or the peculiar persecution of John Vincent Harden. It is understandable that some reticence must be observed with reference to the sudden death of Cardinal Tosca—an investigation carried out at the personal request of His Holiness, the Pope—and in that delicate matter arranged by Holmes for the reigning family of Holland; but surely the time must be at hand, thinks Watson, for the full disclosure of facts in the Tankerville Club Scandal. That often he spoke of these to Holmes, there can be no doubt at all. Having half promised his readers that he would some day tell them, his position may well have seemed to him embarrassing.

One sympathizes heartily with Watson. Too long has the world awaited the adventure of the Amateur Mendicant Society—which held a luxurious club in the lower vault of a furniture warehouse —and the little problem of the Grosvenor Square Furniture Van. The case of Wilson, the Notorious Canary-Trainer, too, is a whisper full of fascinating suggestion; and one would give much to read the long-suppressed adventure of the Tired Captain.

Holmes, we may be certain, listened to some urgent argument on evenings when the doctor decided to consider his reading public. Frequently he chided the narrator for his literary shortcomings, pretended that the tales were sad affairs; but when he came to write just two of them, himself, he changed his tune.

One can imagine them in whimsical discussion of the *ifs* of their achievements—the *what ifs,* as it were, conducted *post mortem* upon their cases. As for instance, after the rocket-throwing episode in the amusing case of Irene Adler. It is impossible to read the tale without a bit of wonderment: what if the ingenious rocket had missed fire? Would not the whole planned sequence have gone agley? But Watson, although he may have faltered, never actually blundered. Holmes knew the qualities of his assistant. No case was ever lost by Watson's failure. And his reward —all that he ever asked or cared for—was an approving word or nod from Holmes. Did not he get them both, outside the record? During those nights in Baker Street, perhaps? After the problem had been solved forever—after the reader had put down the book?

How many matters of absorbing interest must then have been revealed! By means most dexterously disingenuous, Holmes managed a glimpse of Godfrey Staunton's telegram; and on the first attempt. Yet he had seven different schemes, he told the doctor, if one had failed. What were the other six?

How many, many qustions must also have gone unanswered. Holmes was at times blood brother to the Sphinx. There is a bit of dialogue that is in nearly all the tales. "You have a clue?" asks Watson eagerly. The answer is immortal: "It is a capital mistake, my dear Watson, to theorize before one has the facts." If one were called upon to find in literature the best inscription for a tombstone, it would be Holmes's cautious apophthegm. Watson should bargain for it on his grave. For Holmes's tombstone— "Elementary!"

But there can be no grave for Sherlock Holmes or Watson. . . . Shall they not always live in Baker Street? Are they not there this instant, as one writes? . . . Outside, the hansoms rattle through the rain, and Moriarty plans his latest devilry. Within, the sea-coal flames upon the hearth, and Holmes and Watson take their well-won case. . . . So they still live for all that love them well: in a romantic chamber of the heart: in a nostalgic country of the mind: where it is always 1895.

Murder for Pleasure

(1941)

By Howard Haycraft

The first full-length American historical study devoted exclusively to police fiction was Murder for Pleasure: The Life and Times of the Detective Story (New York: Appleton, 1941; London: Davies, 1942), published in observance of the Centennial Year of the first detective story, Poe's "Murders in the Rue Morgue." By request of the publishers of the present volume, the chapter from this work devoted to Poe and his contributions, slightly condensed, is reprinted below.

I

TIPPECANOE (and Tyler, too) had triumphed at the polls, in an exciting spectacle of red fire and illuminated log cabins. Pigs annoyed visiting European celebrities in the streets of the largest cities. Respectable burghers nodded of an evening over the verses of Mr. Longfellow and the novels of Mr. Paulding and Mr. Simms. Their good wives scanned the pages of Godey's, The Gift, and The Token; the children had been put to sleep (rather readily, one imagines) with the indubitably instructive works of Peter Parley. "Society" danced polkas and Prince Albert waltzes, blew its nose on its fingers, and applauded with genteel kid gloves the rival pomposities of Edwin Forrest and Junius Booth. "Elegance" was the watchword of the day. Meanwhile, enterprising tradesmen turned handsome profits in Mineral Teeth, Pile Electuaries, Chinese Hair Eradicators, and Swedish Leeches. Still-new-fangled steam carriages jiggled and bounced adventurously between the more populous centers. The *Great Western* and her sister express packets (now only two weeks the crossing) brought all the news from abroad and the latest British romances for church-going publishers to pirate. In New York, Horace Greeley was busy founding his *Tribune*. In the White House, his term of office but a month old, William Henry Harrison lay already dying—carrying with him a struggling young author's hopes for political preferment. Mr. Brady was soon to open his Daguerrian Gallery. Mr. Morse had forsaken his fashionable portraits to tinker in seclusion with a queer contraption of keys and wires. And on the distant Illinois sod a lanky young giant was riding his first law circuits.

In short—America in 1841.

Philadelphia was a-tingle with the pleasurable sensations of a literary revival. Frankly commercial, often hopelessly lacking in taste, this renaissance nevertheless wore the face of popular and democratic revolt. The concept of "literature" for the few was giving way to the idea of "reading" for the many. Since the days of Ben Franklin, William Penn's city had been famous as a printing center. Now it was realizing its assets. The golden age of cheap magazine publishing was beginning, and Philadelphia was its American Athens. Here were printers and popular journals: the Carey and Lea firms, *Godey's, Atkinson's,* the *Gentleman's, Graham's, Alexander's,* the *Saturday Evening Post,* the *Dollar Newspaper*—among many. Here were editors: Burton, Godey, Graham, the Petersons, Mrs. Hale, the "Reverend" Griswold. Here were artists and engravers: Sully, Sartain, Darley, Neagle, and a host of lesser names. Here were writers of all descriptions: R. M. Bird, T. S. Arthur, Eliza Leslie, "Grace Greenwood," Willis Gaylord Clark, Captain Mayne Reid, George Lippard, "Judge" Conrad, Henry Beck Hirst, "Penn" Smith, Jane and Sumner Fairfield, Joseph and Alice Neal, Thomas Dunn English. And—like a stray cock-pheasant in a sedate domestic fowlyard—Edgar Allan Poe, age thirty-two; critic, poet, and story-teller, currently the guiding editor of *Graham's.*

Tragic Israfel was now at flood tide of success and happiness. The statement is relative and requires explanation. In return for his editorial duties at *Graham's,* Poe was receiving the startling salary of eight hundred dollars a year—more than he ever earned before or afterward. His child-wife, Virginia, was temporarily in good health, as was Poe himself. His salary enabled him for the first, and only, time to provide the necessities of life regularly, and even to add such luxuries as a harp and a tiny piano for Virginia. Faithful, harassed "Muddie" Clemm (Virginia's mother and Poe's foster-mother, surely one of the longest-suffering and noblest women in literary history) could smile for once as she went about her tasks as mater-familias of the little household. Her "Eddie's" bulging head was full of plans for a periodical of his own. Meanwhile, under his editorship *Graham's* became the world's first mass-circulation magazine, leaping in a few short months from a conventional five thousand readers to an unprecedented forty thousand. Poe's own writings were of a uniformly higher standard and greater number than at any other point in his career. The cream of them he contributed to *Graham's,* and they had a large share in its success. An inspiring if unmethodical editor, as well as the most imaginative and stimulating intellect of his time and place, Poe in his own works constantly pointed the way to new fields.

Crime had early claimed his attention. So had puzzles. In *Graham's* for April, 1841, he joined them together. The terrified dreamer of "The Tell-Tale Heart" and "The Fall of the House of Usher" met the analytic solver of cryptograms, the astute completer of *Barnaby Rudge,* on common soil. The result was a new type of tale.

It was a tale of crime, but it was also a tale of ratiocination. It had a brutal murder for its subject, but it had a paragon of crisp logic for its hero. It was "The Murders in the Rue Morgue."

It was the world's first detective story.

II

Puzzle stories, mystery stories, crime stories, and stories of deduction and analysis have existed since the earliest times—and the detective story is closely related to them all. Yet the detective story itself is purely a development of the modern age. Chronologically, it could not have been otherwise.

For the essential theme of the detective story is professional de-

tection of crime. This is its *raison d'être,* the distinguishing element that makes it a detective story and sets it apart from its "cousins" in the puzzle family. Clearly, there could be no detective
stories (and there were none) until there were *detectives.* This
did not occur until the nineteenth century.

Early civilizations had no police at all in the modern sense of
the word. Crime suppression (what there was of it) was a side
job of the military, with a little help from private guards. Both
relied on bludgeons rather than brains for the meager results they
achieved. Consequently, most felony went unpunished. When
malefactors grew too audacious, the handiest luckless suspect was
gibbeted, roasted, or garroted as an example; and authority was
perforce satisfied.

Such crude methods could be effective, of course, only as long
as entire nations lived under what to-day would be regarded as
martial law. As the complex way of life we call modern civilization gradually developed, the weakness as well as the brutality of
the system became increasingly apparent. Enlightened men began
to realize that only by methodical apprehension and just punishment of *actual* offenders could crime be adequately curbed and
controlled.

So torture slowly gave way to proof, ordeal to evidence, the
rack and the thumb-screw to the trained investigator.

And once the investigator had fully arrived, the detective *story*
followed, as a matter of course.

This would all seem to be sufficiently plain. Yet a curious misconception regarding the origin of detective fiction has gained
currency in recent years. The foundations of this error lie chiefly
in the presence of deductive and analytical tales in some of the
ancient literatures. This ancestral resemblance (at most) has mis-
led certain otherwise estimable writers, who really should know
better, into "discovering" detective stories in Herodotus and the
Bible and kindred sources. Fascinating as this game doubtless is,
the thoughtful reader can have but scant patience with so manifest a confusion of terms. For the deductive method is only one of
a number of elements that make up detection, and to mistake the
part for the whole is simply to be guilty of *non distributio medii.*
It would be quite as logical to maintain that the primitive pipings

of the Aegean shepherds were symphonies—because the modern symphony includes passages for reed instruments in its scores! As the symphony began with Haydn, so did the detective story begin with Poe. Like everything else in this world, both had precursors; but no useful purpose is served by trying to prove that either flourished before it did or could. The best and final word on the matter has been said by the English bibliophile George Bates: "The cause of Chaucer's silence on the subject of airplanes was because he had never seen one. You cannot write about police- men before policemen exist to be written of."

It is no more than fair to note, however, that the puzzle tales which have come down to us from the comparatively advanced Hellenic and Hebraic civilizations bear a closer *resemblance* to the present-day detective story than do the puzzle tales of any other age before modern times. This circumstance would seem to foreshadow the sharply parallel development of the detective story and the democratic processes, a fascinating subject in itself.

The first systematic experiments in professional crime-detection were naturally made in the largest centers of population, where the need was greatest. And so the early 1800's saw the growth of criminal investigation departments in the police systems of great metropolises, such as Paris and London. In Paris it was the Sûreté; in London, the Bow Street Runners, followed by Scotland Yard. The men who made up these organizations were the first "detec- tives," although the term itself was not used until some years later. (According to the Oxford Dictionary the earliest discovered appearance of the word *in print* occurred in 1843, but it was prob- ably in spoken circulation considerably before that date.)

Lurid "memoirs" of the Bow Street Runners had begun to ap- pear in England as early as 1827. And in 1829 the romantic "auto- biography" of François Eugène Vidocq, lately of the Sûreté, reached the Paris book-stalls. From about 1830, therefore, it was solely a question of time before the first avowedly fictional detec- tive story would be written. The only surprising circumstance is that it was written by an American, for American police meth- ods at the time were notoriously laggard. The explanation almost certainly rests in Poe's lifelong interest in France and the French: an admiration generously reciprocated by that people in later years. For, significantly, all Poe's detective tales are laid in Paris and display a remarkable knowledge of the city and its police system. Some chroniclers have gone so far as to suggest that Poe's "lost year," 1832, was spent in France; this, however, can not be accepted without more convincing proof than has yet been discovered. Other critics have ascribed the verisimilitude of the stories to close familiarity with Vidocq's *Mémoires*—which were also to serve Émile Gaboriau so faithfully a quarter of a century later. That Poe was thoroughly conversant with this work there can be no doubt. The extent of his indebtedness will be discussed later when the sources of his detective fiction are examined in detail.

A question of greater interest at the present point is the human paradox that led Poe—the avowed apostle of the morbid and grotesque—to forsake his tortured fantasies, even briefly, for the cool logic of the detective story.

Poe revealed his inner mind in his writings as have few authors in history. And what a mental chamber of terrors that mind was! Horror piles on horror in his early (and later) tales; blood, unnatural lust, madness, death—always death—fill his pages and the "haunted palace" of his brain. Why, then, this sea-change in mid-career, this brief return to temperate realms? Certain events in 1840 had conspired to this end. Poe's periodic jousts with his earthly demons are too well known to need description here. They had at least contributed to his dismissal from the editorship of William Burton's *Gentleman's Magazine*. This disappointment led to additional falls from grace and, eventually, to complete collapse and delirium. At length Poe awoke from the fever, weak but clearer than he had been in months and in a distinctly "morning after" frame of mind. At this opportune moment came prosy, kindly George Graham with his tender of a new editorship—provided the poet would make certain practical guaranties of behavior. A creature of extremes, Poe's reaction was swift and typical. He would accept Graham's offer and forswear the world of emotion for the sedater climes of reason.

All through Poe's fiction runs his hero—himself. In the earlier tales the hero is a tormented and guilt-driven wretch. Now, by a process of readily understandable rationalization, the puppet reflects the change in the master: he becomes the perfect reasoner, the embodiment of logic, the champion of mind over matter. Instead of bathing insanely in hideous crime, the new protagonist crisply hunts it down. He demonstrates his superiority over ordinary men by scornfully beating them at their own game; by solving with ease the problems which seem to them so baffling. In brief, he is—Auguste Dupin.

There is assuredly much to be said for Joseph Wood Krutch's brilliant over-simplification: "Poe invented the detective story that he might not go mad."

Men still read them for the same reason to-day.

III

Edgar Allan Poe wrote only three detective stories: "The Murders in the Rue Morgue," "The Mystery of Marie Rogêt," and "The Purloined Letter."

A fourth tale of Poe's, "The Gold Bug," is often carelessly miscalled a detective story. It is a fine story, a masterpiece of mystery and even of analysis—but it is not a detective story for the simple reason that every shred of the evidence on which Legrand's brilliant deductions are based is withheld from the reader until *after* the solution is disclosed. The same objection excludes still another Poe tale, "Thou Art the Man," which, in point of fact, comes much closer structurally to qualifying than "The Gold Bug." But here again it is the concealment of essential evidence— in this case the all-important factor of the bullet which passed *through* the horse—that rules the story out of court. Judged by any purely literary standards, "Thou Art the Man" is one of Poe's saddest débâcles, for reasons which have no place here; but as a startling prognostication of the mechanics of the present-day detective story it is far too little appreciated. In addition to the determinative point of evidence already referred to—surely the earliest bona-fide employment of the favorite physical-circumstantial clue —it is remarkable for the following "firsts," at least as applies to the modern tale of crime-cum-detection: the first complete if exceedingly awkward use of the least-likely-person theme; the first instance of the scattering of false clues by the real criminal; and the first extortion of confession by means of the psychological third degree (dependent, in turn, on two lesser devices making their earliest detective appearance, ventriloquism and the display of the corpse). A correspondent, who prefers to remain anonymous, declares: "My guess is that if Poe hadn't written the three great masterpieces, later-day critics would be doing handsprings over 'Thou Art the Man' as an amazing and trail-blazing tour de force." But for Poe's single slip in withholding the vitally conclusive point of evidence—coupled with the tale's unfortunate narrative style—this might still be the case. Detective story or not, it is worth the collateral attention of all serious students of the form equally with the more familiar yarn of Captain Kidd's cipher and the shiny scarabæus.

Before leaving this brief consideration of Poe's more incidental contributions, it is not without some chronological importance to note that virtually all his secondary ratiocinative efforts, including the two tales just mentioned and his analytical treatises on *Barnaby Rudge* and cryptography, were written during approximately the same years as were occupied by "The Rue Morgue," "Marie Rogêt," and "The Purloined Letter." Only the essay on Maelzel's Chess Player belongs to another, and earlier, period.

Poe's three detective tales proper are remarkable in many respects. Not their least extraordinary feature is the almost uncanny fashion in which these three early attempts, totalling only a few thousand words, established once and for all the mold and pattern for the thousands upon thousands of works of police fiction which have followed. The first tale exemplified, loosely, the *physical* type of the detective story. In the second, Poe reverted to the opposite extreme of the purely *mental*. Finding this (presumably) equally unsatisfactory, the artist in him led, unerringly, in the third story to the *balanced* type. Thus, swiftly, and in the brief compass of only three slight narratives, he foretold the entire evolution of the detective romance as a literary form. The types may be, and of course constantly are, varied and combined, but the essential outline remains unchanged to-day.

Equally prophetic and embracing were Poe's contributions to the internal structure of the genre. In the very first tale he proceeded to lay down the two great concepts upon which all fictional detection worth the name has been based: (1) That the solvability of a case varies in proportion to its outré character. (2) The famous dictum-by-inference (as best phrased by Dorothy Sayers) that "when you have eliminated all the impossibilities, then, whatever remains, however improbable, must be the truth," which has been relied on and often re-stated by all the better sleuths in the decades that have followed. As for the almost infinite minutiæ, time-hallowed to-day, which Poe created virtually with a single stroke of the pen, only a suggestive catalogue need be given. The transcendent and eccentric detective; the admiring and slightly stupid foil; the well-intentioned blundering and unimaginativeness of the official guardians of the law; the locked-room convention; the pointing finger of unjust suspicion; the solution by surprise; deduction by putting one's self in another's position; concealment by means of the ultra-obvious; the staged ruse to force the culprit's hand; even the expansive and condescending explanation when the chase is done: all these sprang full-panoplied from the buzzing brain and lofty brow of the Philadelphia editor. In fact, it is not too much to say—except, possibly, for the influence of latter-day science—that nothing really primary has been added either to the framework of the detective story or to its internals since Poe completed his trilogy. Manners, styles, specific devices may change—but the great principles remain where Poe laid them down and left them.

As Philip Van Doren Stern has well said: "Like printing, the detective story has been improved upon only in a mechanical way since it was first invented; as artistic products, Gutenberg's Bible and Poe's 'The Murders in the Rue Morgue' have never been surpassed."

IV

"The Murders in the Rue Morgue," chronologically the first of Poe's detective stories, was called in the original draft "The Murders in the Rue Trianon Bas," but happily the more "suggestive" title (to quote a contemporary writer) was substituted before publication. The circumstance must surely rank high among the magnificent afterthoughts of literature. (How the original manuscript was preserved by chance and rescued for posterity almost half a century after it was written is one of the fascinating and oft-told legends of American bibliophily, which, however, cannot occupy us here. It has been related in print by Dr. A. S. W. Rosenbach and others.) "The Rue Morgue" made three principal appearances in type in its author's lifetime. First, in *Graham's* for April, 1841. Second, as the only number of a still-born cheap-leaflet series of *The Prose Romances of Edgar A. Poe* (1843) which has become one of the greatest rarities of Americana-collecting: published at twelve and one-half cents, copies have sold in recent years for as much as twenty-five thousand dollars. And third, in the 1845 *Tales*, edited by Evert A. Duyckinck. It was also included, of course, in the "Griswold Edition" of the Collected Works, published in 1850. In addition to these American publications, at least three unauthorized French translations of the tale are known to have appeared in the 1840's.* In an era of international literary freebooting, Poe neither received nor expected any remuneration for them. It may be doubted, in fact, that the world's first detective story ever brought its author a penny in direct financial return—for Poe was the salaried editor of *Graham's* when "The Murders in the Rue Morgue" first appeared; the 1843 leaflet and the 1845 *Tales* alike were failures; † and Israfel was no more when the Griswold collection was issued. Ironically, in the years since Poe's death, the tale has been reprinted with a frequency which, under modern royalty and copyright engagements, would have netted the ill-fed poet a sizable fortune from this single effort; to say nothing of the untold millions which have accrued to his imitators and followers.

These reprints, however, have served to make the paragraphs of "The Murders in the Rue Morgue" thrice-familiar to every

---

* For an accurate account of this highly involved and usually misunderstood business, see C. P. Cambiaire, *The Influence of Edgar Allan Poe in France* (New York, G. E. Stechert & Co., 1927).

† It would indeed have made little difference to Poe in any immediate financial sense had they been successful. The terms between the author and his publishers virtually pass belief. There is preserved a singularly pathetic letter dated August 13, 1841, from Poe to the Messrs. Lea and Blanchard, proposing (unfruitfully) a volume of tales to include the recent "Rue Morgue," in which he says: "I should be glad to accept the terms you allowed me before—that is—you receive all profits, and allow me twenty copies for distribution to friends"!

school-boy. The story opens with a brilliant but to-day rather outmoded essay on the philosophy of analysis. At length the author introduces his hero, the eccentric and impoverished Chevalier, Dupin, and his anonymous companion and chronicler, the first of a thousand wondering Watsons. We join in their home-life, if their curious insistence on turning day into night may be designated by so domestic a term, and marvel dutifully with the narrator at Dupin's powers of deduction. Finally and belatedly, Plot raises its head. A hundred years of imitation have rendered the remainder of the story so much formula: the preliminary account of the crime; the visit to the scene; Dupin's satisfaction with what he finds, his companion's blank mystification; the methodical stupidity of the official police; the dénouement, arranged by the detective; the inevitable explanation.

Made trite by numberless repetitions, it is yet singularly satisfying.

The reasons why "The Murders in the Rue Morgue" is classified as belonging to the *physical* school of detective story writing may not at once be clear—for the proportions of plot and deduction seem roughly equal in the narrative. Reader, try a simple test for yourself. Without looking at the text, attempt to recall the story, which in all probability you haven't read since schooldays. What details stand out most vividly in your mind? The chances are ten to one you will form a mental picture of the murderous ape clutching his victim by the hair, or some related gory incident. Now, ask yourself: *by what train of reasoning* did the detective arrive at his solution? Unless you are a specialist, the same odds prevail that you will not be able to recall. In other words, the story is really dominated by sensational physical event —not by detection, excellently as Poe conceived it.

Poe's second detective story was distinctly a *roman à clef*. In July, 1841, a beautiful young girl named Mary Cecilia Rogers was murdered in New York under particularly involved and baffling circumstances. If contemporary accounts may be credited, the police bungled the investigation miserably. Poe was frankly contemptuous of their efforts, and more than hinted that he wrote "The Mystery of Marie Rogêt" to expose their ineptitude. For convenience he laid the scene in Paris and put his thoughts into the mouth of Dupin. The characters were only thinly disguised, however, and in all later publications the story has been printed with footnotes openly identifying the actors, streets, newspapers, and the like with their true American names. Unfortunately, the real crime was never solved (contrary to popular misconception), and we have no means of verifying the soundness of Poe's deductions. The story appeared in three instalments in *Snowden's Ladies' Companion* for November and December, 1842, and February, 1843, and was republished in the *Tales* (1845) and the posthumous Works (1850).*

This longest of Poe's three major excursions into detective literature is, unhappily, the least deserving of detailed attention. It might better be called an essay than a story. As an essay, it is an able if tedious exercise in reasoning. As a story, it scarcely exists. It has no lifeblood. The characters neither move nor speak. They are present only through second-hand newspaper accounts. A good three-quarters of the work is occupied with Dupin's (which is to say Poe's) reasoning from the evidence. Only a professional student of analytics or an inveterate devotee of criminology can read it with any degree of unfeigned interest. Applying our simple test again: practically no ordinary reader can relate from memory *either* the facts of the crime *or* the steps by which the detective reaches his rather qualified conclusion. This is the hallmark of the too involved, too dry, too *mental* detective story—and its confession of weakness.

We come now to the last, best, and most interesting historically and bibliographically of Poe's three detective stories.

As the 1840's marked the beginning of the magazine age, so, too, they denoted the crest of an earlier movement in the direction of popular literature: that now forgotten institution, the "gift book" or "literary annual." The gift annual was undeniably commercial and often pretentious, and largely for these reasons it has been slighted by purists. Yet between its gilded calf and

---

* The Mary Rogers legend has been retold by innumerable later writers, with varying degrees of success, and both the crime and Poe's analysis of it have been the subject of much and usually erroneous speculation. For a really scholarly and reliable account of the whole matter, the interested reader is referred to a study by William Kurtz Wimsatt, Jr., of Yale University: "Poe and the Mystery of Mary Rogers" (*Publications of the Modern Language Association*, March, 1941).

morocco covers appeared some of the best work (as well as some of the worst) of the leading writers and artists of the day. Its fees were generous for the times and had the further pleasant effect of coaxing magazine rates upwards to keep pace. And its format, paper, typography, and "embellishments" were in the main far above the era's drab standards of bookmaking.

The American gift annual was customarily published in the autumn months, in advance of the holiday season, and was dated for the *following* year. It is important to understand this circumstance, because one of the most baseless errors of contemporary bibliography has grown up around failure to remember it: the habit, even among eminent authorities, of assigning the initial publication of Poe's finest detective story to Britain rather than America.

Briefly, the history of the matter is this:

The apex of American gift-annual publishing, by common consent of connoisseurs, was reached in *The Gift: 1845*. The product of the Philadelphia house of Carey and Hart, this truly handsome volume numbered among its contributors of prose and poetry such luminaries of the era as Longfellow and Emerson (two poems each), Charles Fenno Hoffman, Mrs. Sigourney, N. P. Willis, Joseph C. Neal, H. T. Tuckerman, Mrs. Kirkland and Mrs. Ellet, C. P. Cranch, F. H. Hedge, and others of similar prominence. But, what is of greatest importance, between pages 41 and 61, *The Gift's* purchasers or recipients could devour (as they presumably chose to do) "The Purloined Letter," by Edgar A. Poe, no stranger to the buyers of Carey and Hart's gold-stamped yearly volumes.

The misapprehension alluded to has occurred because, at about the same time, solid British heads-of-household were perusing a sadly abbreviated version of the tale in that staunch parent of all penny-weeklies, *Chambers' Edinburgh Journal*, in its issue for November 30, 1844. This condensation was preceded by an explanatory paragraph so commonly—or wilfully—overlooked to-day as to warrant verbatim quotation here:

'THE GIFT'

THE GIFT is an American annual of great typographical excellence, and embellished with many beautiful engravings. It *contains an article* which, for several reasons, appears to us so remarkable, that we leave aside several effusions of our ordinary contributors to make room for *an abridgment of it.* [Italics supplied.] The writer, Mr. Edgar A. Poe, is evidently an acute observer of mental phenomena; and we have him to thank for one of the aptest illustrations which could well be conceived, of that curious play of two minds, in which one person, let us call him A., guesses what another, B., will do, judging that B. will adopt a particular line of policy to circumvent A. [Poe's "article" then follows, with its title in smaller type.]

Certainly this unequivocal language would seem to dispose for all time of the question of priority. Yet within the present decade a London private press has had the effrontery to reprint the *Chambers'* abridgment as a veritable reproduction of the "first publication" of the story—significantly *omitting* the introductory paragraph! (This precious bit of spuriosa even misquotes the source of its "find": ascribing the story to "Chambers' Edinburgh Magazine, November, 1844.") Still more puzzling is the passive support which has been given to the same fallacy by several first-rank American Poe-scholars, when a little obvious if tedious spadework to ascertain the publication date of *The Gift* would have removed any conceivable doubts left by the language of the *Chambers'* note. The qualified authorities having neglected this duty, it falls to the present writer to report that *The Gift: 1845* was "noticed" in at least one American magazine (the *Democratic Review*) as early as September, 1844; that on October 4, 1844, the New York *Tribune* honored it with a laudatory first-page review more than a column in length; and that its publication was chronicled in autumnal issues of virtually all the leading American periodicals, among them the *Knickerbocker, Peterson's, Graham's,* and *Godey's,* all published many weeks before the transatlantic readers of *Chambers'* were digesting their abridgment on November 30th. On the basis of these incontestable facts, it may now be stated for the first time beyond any reasonable doubt that the Philadelphia publication of "The Purloined Letter" preceded the Edinburgh condensation by approximately two months.

Bibliography aside, this third detective story of Poe's is far and away the most satisfying, structurally and aesthetically, of the

trio. It is simpler, shorter, more compact, more certain of itself
than the earlier two. Its quiet superiority appears from the moment it begins. Here is no delayed approach to the subject. A
few lines suffice to set the stage, and more plausibly, more naturally than before. Dupin and his companion sit in their book-
closet, *au troisiême* (as Poe wrote it), *No. 33, Rue Dunôt, Fau-
bourg St. Germain,* "enjoying the two-fold luxury of meditation
and a meerschaum." (How marvellously near is Baker Street!) Almost immediately Prefect G—— enters. The give-and-take of normal conversation replaces the stiff press-cuttings of the earlier tales
in revealing the essential facts of the problem. (That is, in the
American original. The *Chambers'* abridgment has been squeezed
almost as bloodless as "Marie Rogêt.") Dupin and the Prefect end
their colloquy and the latter goes his way. A month later he re-
turns. Dupin hands him the letter and revels in his open-mouthed
astonishment. Dupin's explanation to his bewildered comrade follows. A little too detailed, perhaps, for modern tastes ("a little
too self-evident"), it is nonetheless a true manual of detective
logic. The conclusion, moreover, has a mellow touch of humor
and humanity lacking in the previous stories. We discover a reluctant fondness for the originally glacial Chevalier as he thaws
to mortal vanity and malice for the first time.

To be completely fair, however, we must admit that the tale
contains also the one serious logical flaw committed by Poe in the
series. As a number of writers have pointed out, Dupin could not
possibly have seen at one and the same time (as he claimed he
did) *both* the seal and the address, that is to say both the front
and back, of the letter. Even apart from this, the minuteness of
his observations—seated as he was across the room, and peering
through green spectacles—bespeaks surely one of the most remarkable visions ever recorded!

Our test must serve once more. This time the odds favor the
author. Almost every one who has ever read the story can recall
something of both essential phases—detection and event. Almost
all readers remember Dupin's deduction that the letter was hidden by not being hidden at all (still a favorite gambit of the craft);
and his ruse of the staged street disturbance to acquire the docu-

ment (a plot-device directly appropriated by Conan Doyle half a century later in "A Scandal in Bohemia").

Here, at last, we have the *balanced* type—the detective story at its best.

V

Few American authors have undergone such minute inspection and dissection at the hands of scholarship as has Poe. Yet the literary scalpel-wielders have been strangely neglectful of the sources of his detective fiction. Aside from the obvious identifications of "Marie Rogêt," only a few minor "points" have been established. In Pauline Dubourg, the laundress of "The Murders in the Rue Morgue," Hervey Allen (that most readable of Poe biographers) has discovered the name of the maiden-proprietresses of the boarding-school which Poe attended during his boyhood stay in England. (But no one seems to have noted the further occurrence of a *Rue Dubourg* in the latter part of the tale: a repetition so foreign to Poe's usually meticulous workmanship as to suggest a concealed significance.) And some scholars contend that the episode of the escaped orang-outang in the same story grew out of a contemporary incident reported in American newspapers, while others believe that Poe drew on similar material in Scott's *Count Robert of Paris*. But one scans the academic journals in vain for light on so intriguing a problem—for example—as the origin of the first fictional detective's name. (Concerning Dupin's *person* there is no mystery. Unless all perception fails, he can be only Poe's mental self-portrait of the moment in French dress.)

How *did* Poe come to name his hero Dupin? The question may never be finally answered, but the author left at least one important clue when he described his Chevalier as "of an excellent, indeed of an illustrious family." For the name Dupin has in truth been a notable one in French history. The reader may, if he chooses, discover in the standard French encyclopedias no less than twelve prominent real-life Dupins dating from the fourteenth century to Poe's own years, including several of the presumptive ancestors of George Sand—born herself, a trifle dubiously perhaps, to the *nom*. Of this substantial number of eminent

flesh-and-blood bearers of the name, two were even more outstanding than the rest. Both were, suggestively, contemporaries of
Poe. Furthermore, they were brothers: André Marie Jean Jacques
(1783–1865) and François Charles Pierre (1784–1873). André, the
elder, was a statesman of ministerial rank who held the office of
Procureur-Général and other high governmental posts for the better part of a generation despite turbulent changes of party and
dynasty: a feat which called for no slight degree of political agility
—to employ the kindest phrase. As President of the Chamber of
Deputies from 1832 to 1840 he was at the pinnacle of his career
and consequently prominent in the native and foreign prints during the years immediately preceding Poe's creation of his fictional
hero. Besides, André Dupin was a prolific writer on a variety of
subjects: among them, French criminal procedure. Several of his
works were translated into English; one translation, in fact, was
published in Boston in 1839. That his name was familiar to Poe
can hardly be doubted. The younger brother (commonly called
Charles) was a noted mathematician and economist who also held
public office from time to time and was created a baron for his
services. His was an even more versatile pen than André's, and he
was known to the English-speaking world through numerous
translations covering a wide range of topics.

Almost inescapably these brief personal histories will have reminded the informed Poe-student of the Minister D——, the talented villain of "The Purloined Letter." D——, it will be recalled, was not only an accomplished and unscrupulous political
intriguant, but, as Poe made a special point of saying, a man-
of-letters as well—both "poet *and* mathematician." Moreover, he
possessed a brother who had also a "reputation in letters." The
parallel is by no means exact, and one would not wish to place
too much emphasis on what after all may have been only a coincidence. Yet, in the dual circumstances of Poe's appropriation
of the name and his adaptation of the characteristics of the real
brothers Dupin, the veriest psychological tyro will be quick to
scent a highly logical, if possibly unconscious, "transference." It
is, at the least, a fascinating subject for speculation. Perhaps some
scholar of the future will uncover more specific evidence: academic hoods have been awarded for contributions less notable.

Of Poe's indebtedness to Vidocq much has been written and more assumed. There can be no doubt that he was closely familiar with that worthy's exploits and memoirs, and that he drew on them for numerous details. But to identify Dupin, the ageless symbol of amateurism, with Vidocq, the professional—as some critics have done—is to commit a most uncritical error and to miss the whole point and purpose of Poe's ratiocinative stories. For throughout the tales Poe hammers ceaselessly to drive home his acutely personalized thesis of the superiority of the talented amateur mind—meaning, of course, his own. Nowhere is this more graphically brought out than in the patronizing words he places in Dupin's mouth near the conclusion of "The Rue Morgue." (This, incidentally, is Poe's sole reference to Vidocq in print.)

> The Parisian police [Dupin is made to say], so much extolled for their acumen, are cunning, but no more. Vidocq, for example, was a good guesser, and a persevering man. But, without educated thought, he erred continually by the very intensity of his investigations. He impaired his vision by holding the object too close. He might see, perhaps, one or two points with unusual clearness, but in so doing he, necessarily, lost sight of the matter as a whole. Thus there is such a thing as being too profound.

That the entire passage is a virtual *ad hoc* rendering of the quotation from Seneca which Poe later chose as the motto of "The Purloined Letter" (*Nil sapientiæ odiosius acumine nimio*) only shows how emphatic at all times was the distinction in his mind between amateur and professional, between Dupin and Vidocq.

If an identification must be made: a good deal of Vidocq (or of Poe's opinion of him) will be found in the unflattering portrait of the Prefect G—— in the tales. As for Dupin, he can clearly be no one but Poe—as Poe so obviously considered himself to be Dupin.*

---

* In a late issue of *The Pleasures of Publishing* (Columbia University Press, April 14, 1941) the eminent Poe scholar, Thomas Ollive Mabbott, is quoted as saying: "He [Dupin] is Poe—plus an eccentric French historian [named Dupin] I've recently run to earth, who turned day into night. I've been looking for such a character, found him last August."

VI

"The Purloined Letter" was Poe's last detective story, although he lived five more years, to the age of forty. Too many historians have argued carelessly that he dropped the genre because it failed to arouse sufficient interest. This is not supported by the facts. While it is true that much of Poe's work was relatively unappreciated in his lifetime, there is no reason to believe that his detective stories suffered more than his fantasies or his poetry. In point of fact, the weight of evidence clearly indicates the opposite situation. Poe not only complained several times in personal correspondence that the public seemed to prefer his ratiocinative tales to what he chose to consider his worthier efforts—he also frequently traded on their popularity in his dealings with editors and publishers. Further, two of the three stories were accounted important enough to be reprinted abroad, in an era when American literature was held in such low esteem that very little of it crossed the water. One of them, even, was the first of his tales to be translated into French, and appeared in no less than three separate versions in that language before his death. And at home, barely a decade after Poe died, young William Dean Howells thought it significant praise to assert of a nominee for President of the United States:

> The bent of his mind is mathematical and metaphysical, and he is therefore pleased with the absolute and logical method of Poe's tales and sketches, in which the problem of mystery is given, and wrought out into everyday facts by processes of cunning analysis. It is said that he suffers no year to pass without a perusal of this author.

Abraham Lincoln subsequently confirmed the statement, which appeared in his little known "campaign biography" by Howells in 1860 and has escaped later attention almost entirely. The instance is chiefly notable, of course, for its revelation of a little suspected affinity between two great Americans—utterly dissimilar save that they shared the same birth year, and that each died tragically before his time. And it serves to establish Lincoln as the first of the countless eminent men who have turned to the detective story for stimulation and solace: a circumstance which also seems, curiously, to have eluded previous mention. At its least, the incident is striking evidence how broadly and powerfully Poe's detective sorcery had captured the popular imagination.

The true reasons for Poe's desertion of the form he created are found in his own life. After 1845 the poet's circumstances, uncertain enough at any time, became increasingly distressing. Little Virginia died. His own end (as he must have suspected) was near. He wrote progressively less, and that little showed a pronounced return to his early morbidity. The last years were a nightmare of poverty, disease, drink, and delusion. In such waking dread there simply was no room for a "perfect reasoner."

The final, shameful curtain fell on the tragedy in October, 1849.

To-day Poe's position in literature is more than secure. He is universally recognized as one of the few poets of consummate genius America has produced, and its finest writer (if not, indeed, the inventor) of the short story. Yet, had he published nothing but the three Dupin tales, posterity would still award him an eminent and merited niche in Fame's corridors—as The Father of the Detective Story.

"Only a Detective Story"

(1944)

By Joseph Wood Krutch

Styles in criticism change as much as styles in the products evaluated. The early 1940's have witnessed a spontaneous and somewhat astonishing flood of published speculation about the detective story, for the most part by writers and in journals usually described by that most indefinite of adjectives, intellectual. Although these articles assume a wide variety of approaches, and reach a comparable number of conclusions, they meet on a common note of inquiry. Reduced to its simplest terms, this inquiry may be stated as: what makes people read detective stories? To say that the detective story is read for "escape" is, of course, no answer at all; for virtually anything that is written may be read as escape, by one man if not another. Why, then, of all the vast amount of published writing available, do so many readers choose police fiction for this purpose? Competent contemporary discussions of one phase or another of this problem have appeared over the signatures of such serious essayists as Louise Bogan, Jacques Barzun, H. R. Hays, Mary McCarthy, George Orwell. Somerset Maugham, and Bernard De Voto, among several. Lacking the space for all, your editor has chosen the present essay by Joseph Wood Krutch, from the Nation *for November 25, 1944, to represent the critical trend under discussion, as the most direct and succinct of the available statements. Mr. Krutch is a foremost American dramatic and literary critic and biographer, professor of English at Columbia University, and member of the editorial staff of the* Nation *for many years.*

THE DETECTIVE story, so I once assumed, was read only by weary statesmen on the one hand and by the barely literate on the other. Discreet inquiry among friends and acquaintances soon revealed, however, a very different state of affairs. It is read either aggressively or shamefacedly by nearly everyone, and it must be, at the present moment, the most popular of all literary forms. "Only a detective story" is now an apologetic and depreciatory phrase which has taken the place of that "only a novel" which once moved Jane Austen to unaccustomed indignation.

My own experience with the genre began with Nick Carter and the once almost equally famous, though now almost totally forgotten, Old King Brady. It continued through Sherlock Holmes and, I believe, the very first of the Mary Roberts Rinehart *opera*. But it stopped there. Philo Vance and Ellery Queen were only dimly familiar names, while Nero Wolfe was known chiefly because he was the creation of a friend and neighbor. Dorothy Sayers and Agatha Christie attained their eminence quite unbeknownst to me, and, so far as I was concerned, Erle Stanley Gardner wrote in vain (under two different names) his five or six novels per annum. During the past twelve months, however, I have read perhaps 150 volumes, among which were included most of the accepted classics as well as a reasonable number of the run-of-the-mill tales.

Even this, I realize, leaves me still a novice, and I dare speak only because so little, relatively, has been said about so astounding a phenomenon. Even those magazines and newspapers which review this sort of writing usually do so in a special department and thus emphasize the fact that detective stories constitute some realm entirely apart. Would it not, for a change, be interesting to encourage some discussion of the "detective story" in relation to something else, to treat it as a branch of fiction or as a department of literature, while maintaining some recognition of the fact that branches and departments are not wholly unconnected?

Many a best-selling novel of the sort commonly regarded as respectable is read from mixed motives. No small proportion of the recent readers of, say, *A Tree Grows in Brooklyn* and *Strange Fruit* read those books, in part at least, because they felt some compulsion to do so, some sense that it was a social obligation to be able to discuss what others were discussing. But no one feels any compulsion to read a detective story. Few discuss what they have read with their neighbors. These books are read for pure pleasure, and there is certainly some significance in that fact. Pleasure is, many would maintain, the only legitimate reason for reading any sort of belles-lettres, and it is, I would agree, at least a sounder motive than either the desire for "self-improvement" or an inability to resist social pressure.

Two arguments are sometimes advanced to prove that the detective story must be sub-literary: its authors are sometimes very prolific; and the stories themselves "follow a formula." But neither of these arguments will hold water. Copious productivity has often been one of the most striking characteristics of the great writers of fiction, and comparatively few of the outstanding detective-story writers can have written more than Balzac, Dickens, or Anthony Trollope. As for "following a formula," it would be more accurate to say that certain conventions tend to be followed, and it would certainly be pertinent to ask whether this fact is as damning as it is sometimes assumed to be. No inconsiderable part of the great literature of the world has been written within the limitations of an established tradition, and so written not because the authors lacked originality but because the acceptance of a tradition and with it of certain fixed themes and methods seems to release rather than stifle the effective working of the imagination. Perhaps instead of saying that the detective story follows a formula we should say that it has *form,* and perhaps we should go on from that to wonder whether this very fact may not be one of the reasons for its popularity at a time when the novel, always rather loose, so frequently has no shape at all.

Great popularity is not, to be sure, proof of literary excellence, but excellence does often attract great popularity. Moreover, works of art which are not good as a whole often owe their temporary vogue to some quality good in itself, and it is surely not impossible that the millions who read detective stories read them because of certain virtues more evident there than in most of the conventionally respectable novels. And it is for those virtues that I should like to see critics look, because I think it might be not only interesting but instructive to have them identified. They might even turn out to be virtues which the conventional novelist has failed to cultivate and for the lack of which his work has suffered.

To the sort of inquiry which I am proposing, the question of the extent to which detective-story writers do or do not exhibit certain of the virtues characteristic of the good novelist is quite irrelevant. No one could deny the broad statement that, in some general sense of the term, Dorothy Sayers writes very well indeed; but neither can anyone deny that certain of her almost equally popular rivals, write, in this sense, very badly. The fact that Miss Sayers is obviously a woman of cultivation and taste and that in her best work she draws character and creates atmosphere more successfully than do some quite respectable conventional novelists is of course all to Miss Sayers's credit. But since other popular detective-story writers get along very successfully without attempting anything of the sort, it is clear enough that the unique virtues of the genre are not these. Obviously the detective story has some characteristic appeal of its own.

The simple statement that men evidently love puzzles and violence has been repeated so often that it has come to seem almost meaningless, and the fact remains that if this supposedly "natural" taste is to be posited, one still wonders why one particular way of satisfying it should have developed at this particular time. Despite all that one can say about Poe and Wilkie Collins or even Conan Doyle, who is, of course, the true begetter of the modern manner, the contemporary detective story is rather different from anything written before. There are some hundreds of volumes every one of which is immediately recognizable as having been written within a very definite period, beginning, I should guess, about 1925, when the contemporary genre first defined itself.

A few months ago Louise Bogan, introducing the subject in the pages of the *Nation* for what may have been the first time in history, suggested the ingenious theory that the essential element was an element of dread which corresponds to a nameless sense of apprehension characteristic of men living in our insecure civilization. She suggested that this element might gradually detach itself and by so doing give rise to a new and terrible sort of fiction.

She implied, if I understand her aright, that Mr. Queen, to take an example, is really an unconscious Kafka or Kierkegaard *manqué*. But in actual fact apprehension is not by any means evoked in all detective stories. It is characteristic of some and serves to mark a sub-species, but the story in which the reader identifies himself with the detective rather than with either the criminal or his victim is at least equally common, and in such stories dread may often be entirely absent as one follows the sleuth in what is to him simply a matter of practicing his profession. If, for example, Mrs. Eberhart, Mr. Hammett, and Mr. Chandler frighten their readers, and if Mr. Gardner manages usually to combine two formulas by personally involving his lawyer-detective in dangerous adventures, many other of the most successful writers—S. S. Van Dine, Mr. Queen, Miss Sayers, Mrs. Christie, and Miss Allingham, for example—usually either employ dread as a very minor element in their effect or, by avoiding it completely, make the detective story one of the most detached and soothing of narratives.

Miss Bogan's suggestion remains interesting and provocative, but I doubt that her explanation is all-inclusive. There are, I suspect, simpler, less subtle reasons why thousands go to the detective story for some sort of satisfaction and relaxation which they find less often in more pretentious novels, and I am wondering if it does not commonly exhibit certain of the very elementary virtues of prose fiction which the serious novelist began utterly to despise just about the time that the detective-story writer stepped in to steal a large section of the reading public away from him. When Shakespeare wrote *Hamlet*, it was "only a play." When Jane Austen wrote *Emma* it was "only a novel." And while I am very far from suggesting that any of the detective stories which I have read are *Hamlets* or *Emmas*, I am suggesting that the fiction writer is in some ways better off and more successful when his public regards the reading of his works as a dubious self-indulgence than when the reading is regarded as a cultural duty.

Perhaps the "serious" novelist has tended to become, in some bad sense, too serious; perhaps, that is to say, he has tended to cultivate certain virtues and to pursue certain ends which, while laudable in themselves, are incompatible with the primary virtues of fiction or, if not quite that, have at least led him to be careless of, if not actually hostile to, these same primary virtues. We have grown accustomed to having reviewers say first of all that a novel is "important" or that it isn't, and to relegate, perhaps to the last paragraph, an expression of mild regret that some "important" novel or other is also structurally formless, stylistically inchoate, and pretty confusing as to intention. Even when such criticism is not made, the terms of praise are terms which do not necessarily imply excellence as fiction. Important novels are commonly described as "dealing with a serious problem," and as being, with rather monotonous regularity, "disturbing," "bitter," "uncompromising," "stark." But a novel can easily be—in fact it very often is—all these things without being readable and without furnishing any of the satisfactions which fiction, from the time of Homer through at least the great Victorians, was generally supposed to furnish.

The distinction is often made between what one "ought" to read and what one will enjoy reading. In connection with works of instruction and information, the distinction is one which is perfectly legitimate. But when it is employed also in connection with works of belles-lettres, it is preposterous in itself and an outward sign that those who permit themselves to employ it are also assuming some real distinction between what is important and what is interesting. But to the artist no such distinction ought to be possible. In art whatever is interesting is, artistically, important; and anything which seems important but not interesting is, artistically, not really important so far as that work of art is concerned. If it is important for some other artist, that artist will make it interesting, and it might be argued that a hopeless decline in the art of writing fiction began *when the novelist willingly acquiesced in a distinction between the important and the interesting.* I doubt that Homer or Chaucer or Shakespeare or Fielding or Balzac or Dickens ever permitted himself such an error.

Certainly it is one of which the detective-story writer is never guilty. He may often fail to be interesting, but he at least acknowledges that when he does so he is failing utterly and unredeemedly. And by acknowledging that fact he is driven to seek the elementary virtues of fiction as surely as the serious novelist who is concerned only to be "important" is led to neglect and despise them.

Two millenniums and a half ago Aristotle pointed out, first, that the "fable" is the most important element in a work of fiction, and, second, that the best fables are "unified," by which, as he explains, is meant that all the parts are inter-related in such a way that no part could be changed without changing all the others. And surely the popularity of the detective story is not un-connected with the fact that, whereas many serious novels are so far from exhibiting any such unity that they sometimes can hardly be said to have any fable at all, the detective story accepts the perfectly concatenated series of events as the *sine qua non* of a usable fable. Moreover, and partly as a consequence, the form of the detective story—that is, progress from the discovery of the corpse to the arrest of the criminal—insures that it shall have that self-determining beginning and that definite conclusion upon which also Aristotle insisted. In other words, the detective story is the one clearly defined modern genre of prose fiction impeccably classical in form.

Happy endings have of course come to seem to most people not only incompatible with "serious" fiction but also vulgar *per se*. But to those who hold this prejudice—in itself one of the most vulgar—it should be pointed out that detective stories commonly provide that particular sort of happy ending which is the most perfect of all and which may be described as "justice triumphant." Indeed, the detective story, alone of all the current forms of fiction—except, perhaps, the "Western"—generally tends to distribute what used to be called poetic justice even to minor characters, including those whose just deserts destine them to some middle state between success and failure. And if any attempt to insist that poetic justice must be administered in all fiction is to impose an almost intolerable burden, the fact remains that one source of the popularity of the detective story may be that in it poetic justice may be achieved without obvious artificiality or improbability. Dr. Johnson once observed as follows in commenting upon those who insisted on incorporating a demand for poetic justice among the "rules" of tragedy: "A play in which the wicked prosper, and the virtuous miscarry, may doubtless be good, because it is a just representation of the common events of human life, but since all reasonable beings naturally love justice, I cannot be easily persuaded that the observation of justice makes a play worse; or that, if other excellences are equal, the audience will not always rise better pleased from the final triumph of persecuted virtue."

It is not, I hope, necessary for me to add that I am not claiming for the detective story all possible virtues; I am not, as a matter of fact, actually claiming any except the very specific ones alluded to. Indeed, I am so far from urging all writers to write such stories or all readers to read nothing else that my remarks are really intended to be rather more about novels of a different sort than they are about the detective story itself. The serious novelist, it seems to me, is ill-advised either to rail against or remain indifferent to the vast popularity of what he is inclined to regard as a sub-literary genre. I am suggesting that he might be well-advised to consider whether it would be possible for him to incorporate into his own novels certain of the virtues which have won so many readers for works which, often enough, have no virtues except those which the "serious" novelist has come increasingly to scorn.

2

THE RULES OF

THE GAME

"Know the rules and when to break 'em," says the old adage. No one, so far as can be recalled, has been tempted to set down codes of behavior to govern the love story, the Western, or the historical novel. But surrounding the 'tec—even in its less rigid shapes— there is an element of sport, of contest between author and reader, not found in other fictional forms that has led inescapably to the propagation of canons of play.

Although it is the common failing of such codes that no two authorities can agree in all details, and further that virtually every precept laid down has been breached at some time by one or more detective stories accepted as great, three of the better known pronouncements are reproduced for the record in the section which follows.

For whatever it may be worth, your editor once experimented with reducing all the numerous obiter dicta *on this subject to two major commandments, with the following result:*

(1) The detective story must play fair.

(2) It must be readable.

Twenty Rules for Writing
Detective Stories

By S. S. Van Dine

◊◊◊

As the creator of Philo Vance, the late S. S. Van Dine (Willard Huntington Wright) requires no introduction here. His Credo for the genre, reproduced below, appeared first in the American Magazine *for September 1928 and was subsequently incorporated in the omnibus* Philo Vance Murder Cases (New York: Scribner's, 1936). *Stimulating as were his rules when they were first published, it is suggested that at least Nos. 3, 7, 16, and 19 would need to be liberalized or greatly modified to win any very wide acceptance today. The detective story does move!*

ℓℓℓ

THE DETECTIVE story is a kind of intellectual game. It is more— it is a sporting event. And for the writing of detective stories there are very definite laws—unwritten, perhaps, but none the less binding; and every respectable and self-respecting concocter of literary mysteries lives up to them. Herewith, then, is a sort of Credo, based partly on the practice of all the great writers of detective stories, and partly on the promptings of the honest author's inner conscience. To wit:

1. The reader must have equal opportunity with the detective for solving the mystery. All clues must be plainly stated and described.

2. No willful tricks or deceptions may be placed on the reader other than those played legitimately by the criminal on the detective himself.

3. There must be no love interest. The business in hand is to

189

bring a criminal to the bar of justice, not to bring a lovelorn couple to the hymeneal altar.

4. The detective himself, or one of the official investigators, should never turn out to be the culprit. This is bald trickery, on a par with offering some one a bright penny for a five-dollar gold piece. It's false pretenses.

5. The culprit must be determined by logical deductions—not by accident or coincidence or unmotivated confession. To solve a criminal problem in this latter fashion is like sending the reader on a deliberate wild-goose chase, and then telling him, after he has failed, that you had the object of his search up your sleeve all the time. Such an author is no better than a practical joker.

6. The detective novel must have a detective in it; and a detective is not a detective unless he detects. His function is to gather clues that will eventually lead to the person who did the dirty work in the first chapter; and if the detective does not reach his conclusions through an analysis of those clues, he has no more solved his problem than the schoolboy who gets his answer out of the back of the arithmetic.

7. There simply must be a corpse in a detective novel, and the deader the corpse the better. No lesser crime than murder will suffice. Three hundred pages is far too much pother for a crime other than murder. After all, the reader's trouble and expenditure of energy must be rewarded.

8. The problem of the crime must be solved by strictly naturalistic means. Such methods for learning the truth as slate-writing, ouija-boards, mind-reading, spiritualistic séances, crystal-gazing, and the like, are taboo. A reader has a chance when matching his wits with a rationalistic detective, but if he must compete with the world of spirits and go chasing about the fourth dimension of metaphysics, he is defeated *ab initio*.

9. There must be but one detective—that is, but one protagonist of deduction—one *deus ex machina*. To bring the minds of three or four, or sometimes a gang of detectives to bear on a problem, is not only to disperse the interest and break the direct thread of logic, but to take an unfair advantage of the reader. If there is more than one detective the reader doesn't know who his co-

deductor is. It's like making the reader run a race with a relay team.

10. The culprit must turn out to be a person who has played a more or less prominent part in the story—that is, a person with whom the reader is familiar and in whom he takes an interest.

11. A servant must not be chosen by the author as the culprit. This is begging a noble question. It is a too easy solution. The culprit must be a decidedly worth-while person—one that wouldn't ordinarily come under suspicion.

12. There must be but one culprit, no matter how many murders are committed. The culprit may, of course, have a minor helper or co-plotter; but the entire onus must rest on one pair of shoulders: the entire indignation of the reader must be permitted to concentrate on a single black nature.

13. Secret societies, camorras, mafias, *et al.*, have no place in a detective story. A fascinating and truly beautiful murder is irremediably spoiled by any such wholesale culpability. To be sure, the murderer in a detective novel should be given a sporting chance; but it is going too far to grant him a secret society to fall back on. No high-class, self-respecting murderer would want such odds.

14. The method of murder, and the means of detecting it, must be rational and scientific. That is to say, pseudo-science and purely imaginative and speculative devices are not to be tolerated in the *roman policier*. Once an author soars into the realm of fantasy, in the Jules Verne manner, he is outside the bounds of detective fiction, cavorting in the uncharted reaches of adventure.

15. The truth of the problem must at all times be apparent—provided the reader is shrewd enough to see it. By this I mean that if the reader, after learning the explanation for the crime, should reread the book, he would see that the solution had, in a sense, been staring him in the face—that all the clues really pointed to the culprit—and that, if he had been as clever as the detective, he could have solved the mystery himself without going on to the final chapter. That the clever reader does often thus solve the problem goes without saying.

16. A detective novel should contain no long descriptive pas-

sages, no literary dallying with side-issues, no subtly worked-out character analyses, no "atmospheric" preoccupations. Such matters have no vital place in a record of crime and deduction. They hold up the action, and introduce issues irrelevant to the main purpose, which is to state a problem, analyze it, and bring it to a successful conclusion. To be sure, there must be a sufficient descriptiveness and character delineation to give the novel verisimilitude.

17. A professional criminal must never be shouldered with the guilt of a crime in a detective story. Crimes by house-breakers and bandits are the province of the police departments—not of authors and brilliant amateur detectives. A really fascinating crime is one committed by a pillar of a church, or a spinster noted for her charities.

18. A crime in a detective story must never turn out to be an accident or a suicide. To end an odyssey of sleuthing with such an anti-climax is to hoodwink the trusting and kind-hearted reader.

19. The motives for all crimes in detective stories should be personal. International plottings and war politics belong in a different category of fiction—in secret-service tales, for instance. But a murder story must be kept *gemuetlich,* so to speak. It must reflect the reader's everyday experiences, and give him a certain outlet for his own repressed desires and emotions.

20. And (to give my Credo an even score of items) I herewith list a few of the devices which no self-respecting detective-story writer will now avail himself of. They have been employed too often, and are familiar to all true lovers of literary crime. To use them is a confession of the author's ineptitude and lack of originality. (*a*) Determining the identity of the culprit by comparing the butt of a cigarette left at the scene of the crime with the brand smoked by a suspect. (*b*) The bogus spiritualistic séance to frighten the culprit into giving himself away. (*c*) Forged fingerprints. (*d*) The dummy-figure alibi. (*e*) The dog that does not bark and thereby reveals the fact that the intruder is familiar. (*f*) The final pinning of the crime on a twin, or a relative who looks exactly like the suspected, but innocent, person. (*g*) The hypo-

dermic syringe and the knockout drops. (*h*) The commission of the murder in a locked room after the police have actually broken in. (*i*) The word-association test for guilt. (*j*) The cipher, or code letter, which is eventually unraveled by the sleuth.

A Detective Story Decalogue
By Ronald A. Knox

Monsignor Knox is a well-known English essayist and religious apologist and the author of several detective stories distinguished for their erudition and fair-play. His Ten Commandments of Detection with characteristic comments laid on, are reprinted from his Introduction to The Best [English] Detective Stories of 1928 *(London: Faber; New York: Liveright, 1929).*

I. *The criminal must be someone mentioned in the early part of the story, but must not be anyone whose thoughts the reader has been allowed to follow.*

The mysterious stranger who turns up from nowhere in particular, from a ship as often as not, whose existence the reader had no means of suspecting from the outset, spoils the play altogether. The second half of the rule is more difficult to state precisely, especially in view of some remarkable performances by Mrs. Christie. It would be more exact to say that the author must not imply an attitude of mystification in the character who turns out to be the criminal.

II. *All supernatural or preternatural agencies are ruled out as a matter of course.*

To solve a detective problem by such means would be like winning a race on the river by the use of a concealed motor-engine. And here I venture to think there is a limitation about Mr. Chesterton's Father Brown stories. He nearly always tries to put us off the scent by suggesting that the crime must have been done by magic; and we know that he is too good a sportsman to fall back upon such a solution. Consequently, although we seldom guess the answer to his riddles, we usually miss the thrill of having suspected the wrong person.

III. *Not more than one secret room or passage is allowable.*

I would add that a secret passage should not be brought in at all unless the action takes place in the kind of house where such devices might be expected. When I introduced one into a book myself, I was careful to point out beforehand that the house had belonged to Catholics in penal times. Mr. Milne's secret passage in *The Red House Mystery* is hardly fair; if a modern house were so equipped—and it would be villainously expensive—all the country-side would be quite certain to know about it.

IV. *No hitherto undiscovered poisons may be used, nor any appliance which will need a long scientific explanation at the end.*

There may be undiscovered poisons with quite unexpected re-actions on the human system, but they have not been discovered yet, and until they are they must not be utilized in fiction; it is not cricket. Nearly all the cases of Dr. Thorndyke, as recorded by Mr. Austin Freeman, have the minor medical blemish; you have to go through a long science lecture at the end of the story in order to understand how clever the mystery was.

V. *No Chinaman must figure in the story.*

Why this should be so I do not know, unless we can find a reason for it in our western habit of assuming that the Celestial is over-equipped in the matter of brains, and under-equipped in the matter of morals. I only offer it as a fact of observation that, if you are turning over the pages of a book and come across some mention of 'the slit-like eyes of Chin Loo', you had best put it down at once; it is bad. The only exception which occurs in my mind —there are probably others—is Lord Ernest Hamilton's *Four Tragedies of Memworth*.

VI. *No accident must ever help the detective, nor must he ever have an unaccountable intuition which proves to be right.*

That is perhaps too strongly stated; it is legitimate for the de-tective to have inspirations which he afterwards verifies, before he acts on them, by genuine investigation. And again, he will nat-urally have moments of clear vision, in which the bearings of the observations hitherto made will become suddenly evident to him. But he must not be allowed, for example, to look for the lost will in the works of the grandfather clock because an unaccount-able instinct tells him that that is the right place to search. He must look there because he realizes that that is where he would have hidden it himself if he had been in the criminal's place. And in general it should be observed that every detail of his thought-process, not merely the main outline of it, should be conscientiously audited when the explanation comes along at the end.

VII. *The detective must not himself commit the crime.*

This applies only where the author personally vouches for the statement that the detective *is* a detective; a criminal may legitimately dress up as a detective, as in *The Secret of Chimneys*, and delude the other actors in the story with forged references.

VIII. *The detective must not light on any clues which are not instantly produced for the inspection of the reader.*

Any writer can make a mystery by telling us that at this point the great Picklock Holes suddenly bent down and picked up from the ground an object which he refused to let his friend see. He whispers 'Ha!' and his face grows grave—all that is illegitimate mystery-making. The skill of the detective author consists in being able to produce his clues and flourish them defiantly in our faces: 'There!' he says, 'what do you make of that?' and we make nothing.

IX. *The stupid friend of the detective, the Watson, must not conceal any thoughts which pass through his mind; his intelligence must be slightly, but very slightly, below that of the average reader.*

This is a rule of perfection; it is not of the *esse* of the detective story to have a Watson at all. But if he does exist, he exists for the purpose of letting the reader have a sparring partner, as it were, against whom he can pit his brains. 'I may have been a fool,' he says to himself as he puts the book down, 'but at least I wasn't such a doddering fool as poor old Watson.'

X. *Twin brothers, and doubles generally, must not appear unless we have been duly prepared for them.*

The dodge is too easy, and the supposition too improbable. I would add as a rider, that no criminal should be credited with exceptional powers of disguise unless we have had fair warning that he or she was accustomed to making up for the stage. How admirably is this indicated, for example, in *Trent's Last Case!*

The Detection Club Oath

The Detection Club (commonly called the London Detection Club) was founded in 1928 by Anthony Berkeley, who promptly put the organization, thinly disguised, into his matchless tour de force The Poisoned Chocolates Case. *The first president (or Ruler) was G. K. Chesterton, who served from the inception of the club until his death in 1936. He was succeeded by E. C. Bentley, the author of* Trent's Last Case, *who still occupies the chair. Secretary of the club at this writing is the transplanted American, John Dickson Carr. The membership of the club is kept by charter relatively small, but includes the most distinguished names in British detective fiction. Election to membership is a coveted professional recognition. Dues are nominal, but the club maintains premises and a criminological library from the proceeds of occasional anthologies in which the members participate, with royalties accruing to the organization. Under the amusing lines of the initiation ritual reproduced below are some substantial hints of the society's elevated professional standards, thus bringing the matter within our purview.*

It is interesting to note that the Detection Club's recently organized American opposite number, Mystery Writers of America, Inc., has no comparable ritual or oath, but boasts of a suitably ungrammatical Latin motto of which the older organization may well be envious: Qui Fecit? *Or, in the vulgate: Whodunit?*

The Ruler shall say to the Candidate:
  M. N., is it your firm desire to become a Member of the Detection Club?
Then the Candidate shall answer in a loud voice:
  That is my desire.

197

Ruler:

Do you promise that your detectives shall well and truly detect the crimes presented to them, using those wits which it may please you to bestow upon them and not placing reliance on nor making use of Divine Revelation, Feminine Intuition, Mumbo-Jumbo, Jiggery-Pokery, Coincidence or the Act of God?

Candidate:

I do.

Ruler:

Do you solemnly swear never to conceal a vital clue from the reader?

Candidate:

I do.

Ruler:

Do you promise to observe a seemly moderation in the use of Gangs, Conspiracies, Death-Rays, Ghosts, Hypnotism, Trap-Doors, Chinamen, Super-Criminals and Lunatics; and utterly and for ever to forswear Mysterious Poisons unknown to Science?

Candidate:

I do.

Ruler:

Will you honour the King's English?

Candidate:

I will.

Then the Ruler shall ask:

M. N., is there anything you hold sacred?

Then the Candidate having named a Thing which he holds of peculiar sanctity the Ruler shall ask:

M. N., do you swear by (*here the Ruler shall name the Thing which the Candidate has declared to be his Peculiar Sanctity*) to observe faithfully all these promises which you have made, so long as you are a Member of the Club?

But if the Candidate is not able to name a Thing which he holds sacred, then the Ruler shall propose the Oath in this manner following:

M. N., do you as you hope to increase your Sales, swear to observe faithfully all these promises which you have made, so long as you are a Member of the Club?

Then the Candidate shall say:

All this I solemnly do swear. And I do furthermore promise and undertake to be loyal to the Club, neither purloining nor disclosing any plot or secret communicated to me before publication by any Member, whether under the influence of drink or otherwise.

Then shall the Ruler say to the Company:

If there be any Member present who objects to the Proposal let him or her so declare.

If there be an Objector, the Ruler shall appoint a time and place for the seemly discussion of the matter, and shall say to the Candidate, and to the Company:

Forasmuch as we are hungry and that there may be no unseemly wrangling amongst us, I invite you, M. N., to be our Guest to-night, and I hold you to the solemn promise which you have given as touching the theft or revelation of plots and secrets.

But if there be no Objector, then shall the Ruler say to the Members:

Do you then acclaim M. N. as a Member of our Club?

Then the Company's Crier, or the Member appointed thereto by the Secretary, shall lead the Company in such cries of approval as are within his compass or capacity. When the cries cease, whether for lack of breath or for any other cause, the Ruler shall make this declaration:

M. N., you are duly elected a Member of the Detection Club, and if you fail to keep your promise, may other writers anticipate your plots, may your publishers do you down in your contracts, may strangers sue you for libel, may your pages swarm with misprints and may your sales continually diminish. Amen.

Then the Candidate, and after him all the Members present, shall say:

Amen.

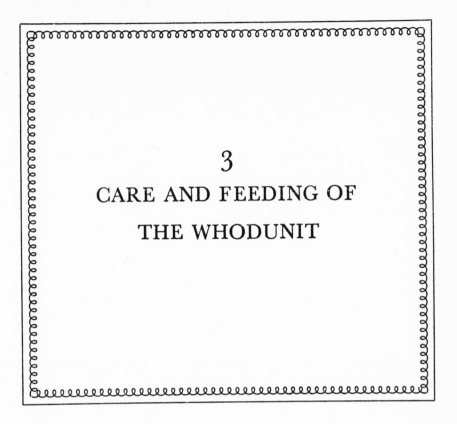

3
CARE AND FEEDING OF
THE WHODUNIT

In which leading writers, editors, and specialists discuss the craft of mystery fiction. Selections in this and succeeding sections which are not otherwise credited are original contributions, written especially for this volume.

The Case of the Early Beginning

By Erle Stanley Gardner

*The story of speed and movement—action, in short—has been a
characteristically American gift to modern detective fiction. Mr.
Gardner brings a fresh, authoritative, and important viewpoint to
bear on the true beginnings and nature of this vigorous "type,"
which has become the preferred reading of so many devotees on
both sides of the ocean. As a foremost alumnus of the hard-fisted
school which originated this variety of crime fiction, the creator
of Perry Mason and Douglas Selby will be heard with respect on
his chosen subject.*

THE ACTION type of mystery story made its first bow in the American woodpulp magazines. Every so often someone will make the statement that it originated with Dashiell Hammett in a book entitled *The Maltese Falcon,* published in 1930. (Actually, Hammett himself had published two previous detective stories in book form: *Red Harvest* and *The Dain Curse,* both issued in 1929.) But by the time the action mystery story first appeared in books it was old stuff.

It is hard to tell who originally started the vogue. I think it was around 1923 or 1924 that Hammett's first detective stories began to appear in magazine form. At least as early as 1922 Carroll John Daly had published a story entitled "The False Burton Combs" in *Black Mask* magazine. That story featured Race Williams, who was, perhaps, the forerunner of all the hard-boiled detective characters. At that time, George Sutton was editor of *Black Mask.* I believe that Sutton published the first detective story Carroll John Daly ever wrote, the first detective story Dashiell Hammett ever wrote, and the first detective story I ever wrote.

(At that time, 1923, I was writing under the name of Charles M. Green.)

Shortly afterwards, Phil Cody became editor of *Black Mask*, and had an associate editor named Harry North. Cody had a keen appreciation of literature and of the detective story, and under his regime the new action type of detective story took a long stride forward. But I doubt if even Phil Cody appreciated the full extent to which this type of story was destined to change the reading habits of mystery fans. He did, however, confide to me that he used Daly, Hammett, and Gardner as the backbone of the magazine and intended to continue to do so.

Then, commencing with the November 1926 issue, Captain Joseph T. Shaw became editor of *Black Mask*. Shaw quickly appreciated the importance of the type of stories that the magazine had been running and made a conscious effort to feature them as a distinct literary departure from the older school of writing.

Carroll John Daly published his first detective book (*The White Circle*) in 1926, some three years before Hammett brought out *Red Harvest* and four years before *The Maltese Falcon* made its appearance in book form. The late William Lyon Phelps was one of the few book reviewers who appreciated the rugged virility of Daly's work. The old maestro delved into woodpulps as well as books and had an especial fondness for mystery stories. I think he probably knew fully as much about them as any book reviewer. I remember that about a year before his death I discussed with him the first beginnings of the new type of detective story, and was interested to find out that he had been watching Daly's work for years and was fully familiar with the part Daly had played in developing the new type.

Understand, there is a great difference between *type* and *style*. After the success of *The Maltese Falcon*, many writers began to imitate Hammett's *style*, which was distinct and original with him. I think of all the early pulp writers who contributed to the new format of the detective story, the word "genius" was more nearly applicable to Hammett than to any of the rest. Unfortunately, however, because Hammett's manner was so widely imitated, it became the habit for the reviewers to refer to "the Hammett School" as embracing the *type* of story as well as the *style*. This has caused some confusion. Daly did as much, or more, than any other author to develop the *type*.

Just by way of illustration, let's consider a few of Daly's openings. These are the first paragraphs of some of his early stories. Here's one: *"I dropped to one knee and fired twice."* Here's another: *"I didn't like his face and I told him so."*

And here's a third: *"The dead girl lay in the gutter. She was not a pretty sight. Someone had stuck a knife in her chest and turned it around."*

Daly started his stories with action and told them in terms of action. The readers liked them. In fact, I remember Harry North telling me that when he put Race Williams on the cover, the magazine sales jumped fifteen per cent.

It was right around this time that Hammett started his "Continental Operative" stories in *Black Mask*. They were told in terms of action, but not quite as vivid, or perhaps one might say as lurid, an action as those of Daly. But they were told objectively, and there was about them that peculiar attitude of aloofness and detachment which is so characteristic of the Hammett *style*.

My own stories during this period largely featured the adventures of one Ed Jenkins, a so called "Phantom Crook," as well as a Western character named Black Barr and a juggler detective who used a billiard cue cane to pop out the teeth of the villains in the last paragraph.

In those days the doctrine of "playing fair with the reader" was in its infancy. I remember writing a long letter to the editor complaining that readers of the early classical detective stories couldn't be expected to compete with the detective because they didn't know that there had been a shower just before midnight in a certain section of London until after the detective casually mentioned it, etc., etc., and insisting that a story *could* be told in which all of the clues were actually placed in the hands of the reader.

Personally, I think it is a mistake to confuse the so called "hardboiled" type of detective story with the action type of detective story. For very apparent reasons, the hard-boiled story is almost invariably told in the format of the action story; but the action story is not necessarily the hard-boiled story. In fact, there is some evidence indicating that the so-called hard-boiled story may be losing in popularity while the action detective story is gaining in popularity.

Perhaps one reason for this is that there is, after all, an inherent improbability in most of the hard-boiled stories. The hero is usually captured by the big, bad villains, given a shot of morphine, awakens in an isolated house with a huge gorilla sitting in the room, methodically chewing gum. The hero asks questions, makes wisecracks, and from time to time the gorilla calmly gets up, walks over to the bed and beats up on the hero. After that, three or four other villains come in and start exercising. The hero is beaten into unconsciousness two or three times, but eventually manages to slug his way into the clear. Thereafter the only evidence of his beatings is shown by the increased tempo with which he dashes around making love to complaisant women and killing villains.

A short time ago I was discussing the hard-boiled story with a citizen who had quite apparently been around a good deal. He told me he simply couldn't read the things. I asked him why not. He looked at me with a mournful expression. "Have you," he asked, "ever been beaten up?—I mean really and truly beaten up."

I muttered something about my boxing days and remembered a couple of particularly nasty fights. . . .

He shook his head, "I mean *really* beaten up."

I confessed that I hadn't been.

He had. Three gangsters had really gone to work on him. He was a pretty tough individual, but it was three months before he could carry on. Every time he read of a beaten-up hero going on the make with a hot number, he shuddered and tossed the book aside.

But one thing is certain. Regardless of the type of story or the style in which it is told, it is now pretty well established that it isn't cricket for the detective to peer into a dark corner, pick up something "which I couldn't see" and casually drop it into his pocket. It is also interesting to note that many of the clues these days are clues of action. In other words, the detective doesn't find a broken cuff link or a fragment of curved glass at the scene of the crime. Instead, one of the characters *does* something that turns out to be the significant clue.

All of this, in turn, is having a rather interesting effect on reader psychology. The modern detective novel has to be logical. It is usually fast moving. It has about it an air of authenticity and generally is getting to be more true to life. As a result, some of the readers of detective stories are not only getting pretty smart when it comes to picking out the guilty party in the book, but they're becoming pretty good detectives in real life.

In 1943 when I was sent to the Bahamas by the New York *Journal-American* to cover the famous DeMarigny murder trial at Nassau, I received many letters from readers who were eagerly following my account of the trial. Some of these letters and the accompanying suggestions were of course merely obvious guesses, but a surprisingly large number contained practical suggestions which would have done credit to any detective in the history of crime fiction.

All of which goes a long way toward supporting a theory I have held for some time that, taken by and large, the readers of the modern detective stories are a pretty shrewd lot, and the more that detective stories become logical in treatment and development, the more the mystery story fans—or addicts if you will—are developing their powers of deductive reasoning.

Gaudy Night

By Dorothy L. Sayers

ᚖᚖᚖ

Mr. Gardner has told us valuably of the origins and growth of an important American type-contribution to the detective story. Now comes Miss Sayers with a self-searching account of the creation and development of the most widely known of contemporary English detective characters, Lord Peter Wimsey, and—by inference—of a school of police fiction as indigenously British as the action story is American. Her essay, which has not been previously published in America, appeared as a chapter in Titles to Fame, *edited by Denys K. Roberts (London: Nelson, 1937). The title of the essay is of course taken from Miss Sayers' novel of the same name.*

ᚑᚑᚑ

WHEN IN a light-hearted manner I set out, fifteen years ago, to write the first "Lord Peter" book, it was with the avowed intention of producing something "less like a conventional detective story and more like a novel." Re-reading *Whose Body?* at this distance of time I observe, with regret, that it is conventional to the last degree, and no more like a novel than I to Hercules. This is not really surprising, because one cannot write a novel unless one has something to say about life, and I had nothing to say about it, because I knew nothing. However, the book eventually (with what labour, O Prince, what pain) found a publisher, and that in spite of what an Oxford coach of mine used to call "lamentable lacunae" in the plot, due to technical ignorance. I doubt very much whether, if *Gaudy Night* had been written in 1922, it would ever have seen the light. The detective story of that period enjoyed a pretty poor reputation, and was not expected to contain anything that could be mistaken for "serious reading."

G. K. Chesterton had, indeed, succeeded in making it the vehicle of a reasoned philosophy; but then, he was an acknowledged genius, renowned for fantastical paradox, and a philosophical detective story was just one more paradox to his credit.

The ordinary beginner had to proceed with caution and to acquire technical facility in the process. During the next ten years the technique of detective fiction did improve out of all knowledge in the hands of a number of brilliant writers, and we all became a great deal more careful about our facts. Some of us, from time to time, even indulged in a little "good writing" here and there, and were encouraged by finding it well received. We also took occasion to preach at every opportunity that if the detective story was to live and develop it *must* get back to where it began in the hands of Collins and Le Fanu, and become once more a novel of manners instead of a pure crossword puzzle. My own voice was raised very loudly to proclaim this doctrine, because I still meant *my* books to develop along those lines at all costs, and it does no harm to let one's theory act as herald to one's practice. Some people did not agree with us. Mr. Willard Huntington Wright (Van Dine) still believes, for example, that every vestige of humanity should be ruthlessly expunged from the detective novel; but I am sure he is wrong and we are right. It is not only that the reader gets tired after a time of a literature without bowels; in the end the writer gets tired of it too, and that is fatal.

Taking it all in all, I think it is true that each successive book of mine worked gradually nearer to the sort of thing I had in view. *The Documents in the Case,* which is a serious "criticism of life" so far as it goes, took a jump forward rather out of its due time; *The Five Red Herrings* was a cast back towards the "time-table" puzzle-problem. *Strong Poison,* to which I shall have to return later, rather timidly introduced the "love-element" into the Peter Wimsey story. I think the first real attempt at fusing the two kinds of novel was made in *Murder Must Advertise,* in which, for the first time, the criticism of life was not relegated to incidental observations and character sketches, but was actually part of the plot, as it ought to be. It was not quite successful; the idea of symbolically opposing two cardboard worlds—that of the advertiser and the drug-taker—was all right; and it was suitable that Peter, who stands for reality, should never appear in either except disguised; but the working-out was a little too melodramatic, and the handling rather uneven. *The Nine Tailors* was a shot at combining detection with poetic romance, and was, I think, pretty nearly right, except that Peter himself remained, as it were, extraneous to the story and untouched by its spiritual conflicts. This was correct practice for a detective hero, but not for the hero of a novel of manners. At this point you will begin to suspect that Peter was fast becoming a major problem to his inconsiderate creator, and so indeed he was.

It is amazing how recklessly one embarks upon adventures of the most hideous toil and difficulty, and that with one's eyes wide open. I had from the outset, of course, envisaged for Peter a prolonged and triumphal career, going on through book after book amid the plaudits of adoring multitudes. It is true that his setting forth did not cause as great a stir as I had expected, and that the adoring multitudes were represented by a small, though faithful, band of adherents. But time would, I hoped, bring the public into a better frame of mind, and I plugged confidently on, putting my puppet through all his tricks and exhibiting him in a number of elegant attitudes. But I had not properly realized— and this shows how far I was from understanding what it was I was trying to do with the detective novel—that any character that remains static except for a repertory of tricks and attitudes is bound to become a monstrous weariness to his maker in the course of nine or ten volumes. Let me confess that when I undertook *Strong Poison* it was with the infanticidal intention of doing away with Peter; that is, of marrying him off and getting rid of him—for a lingering instinct of self-preservation, and the deterrent object-lesson of Mr. Holmes's rather scrambling return from the Reichenbach Falls, prevented me from actually killing and burying the nuisance.

Two things stood in the way of my fell purpose. First, in accordance with the general contradictoriness of things, just when I had decided that I could not do with Peter for a single moment more, the multitudes began, though rather sparsely and belatedly, to roll up and hang hopefully about along the route, uttering agreeable cheers and convinced that the show was billed to continue. Some of them even did a little mild adoring, and I was quite pathetically grateful to them and disposed to give Peter a little longer run. But what really stayed my hand was something still more unexpected, and in a sense more creditable. I could not marry Peter off to the young woman he had (in the conventional Perseus manner) rescued from death and infamy, because I could find no form of words in which she could accept him without loss of self-respect. I had landed my two chief puppets in a situation where, according to all the conventional rules of detective fiction, they should have had nothing to do but fall into one another's arms; but they would not do it, and that for a very good reason. When I looked at the situation I saw that it was in every respect false and degrading; and the puppets had somehow got just so much flesh and blood in them that I could not force them to accept it without shocking myself.

So there were only two things to do: one was to leave the thing there, with the problem unresolved; the other, far more delicate and dangerous, was to take Peter away and perform a major operation on him. If the story was to go on, Peter had got to become a complete human being, with a past and a future, with a consistent family and social history, with a complicated psychology and even the rudiments of a religious outlook. And all this would have to be squared somehow or other with such random attributes as I had bestowed upon him over a series of years in accordance with the requirements of various detective plots.

The thing seemed difficult, but not impossible. When I came to examine the patient, he showed the embryonic buds of a character of sorts. Even at the beginning he had not been the complete silly ass: he had only played the silly ass, which was not the same thing. He had had shell-shock and a vaguely embittered love affair; he had a mother and a friend and a sketchy sort of brother and sister; he had literary and musical tastes, and a few well-defined opinions and feelings; and a little tidying-up of dates and places would put his worldly affairs into order. The prognosis seemed fairly favorable; so I laid him out firmly on the operating-table and chipped away at his internal mechanism through three longish books. At the end of the process he was five years older than he was in *Strong Poison,* and twelve years older than he was when he started. If, during the period, he had altered and mellowed a little, I felt I could reasonably point out that most human beings were altered and mellowed by age. One of the first results of the operation was an indignant letter from a female reader of *Gaudy Night* asking, What had happened to Peter? he had lost all his elfin charm. I replied that any man who retained elfin charm at the age of forty-five should be put in a lethal chamber. Indeed, Peter escaped that lethal chamber by inches.

But I was still no further along with the problem of Harriet. She had been a human being from the start, and I had humanized Peter for her benefit; but the situation between them had become still more impossible on that account. Formerly, she could not marry him to live on gratitude; now, he had advanced to a point where he could not possibly want her to do anything of the kind. Her inferiority complex was making her steadily more brutal to him and his newly developed psychology was making him steadily more sensitive to her inhibitions. Clearly, they could not go on like this; and time was passing with alarming rapidity, at this rate they would be grey-headed before they were reconciled. At all costs, some device must be found for putting Harriet back on a footing of equality with her lover. It was clear that it would be of great help to her to receive a proposal from another, and entirely disinterested man; but this, by itself, was not enough.

About this time I was playing with the idea of a "straight" novel, about an Oxford woman graduate who found, in middle life, and after a reasonably satisfactory experience of marriage and motherhood, that her real vocation and full emotional fulfilment were to be found in the creative life of the intellect. While investigating the possibilities of this subject, I was asked to go to Oxford and propose the toast of the University at my College Gaudy dinner. I had to ask myself exactly what it was for which one had to thank a university education, and came to the conclusion that it was, before everything, that habit of intellectual integrity which is at once the foundation and the result of scholarship.

Having delivered myself of these sentiments in a speech, the substance of which (stripped of its post-prandial rhetoric) was later embodied in an article in the official organ of the Oxford Society, I discovered that in Oxford I had the solution to all my three problems at once. On the intellectual platform, alone of all others, Harriet could stand free and equal with Peter, since in that sphere she had never been false to her own standards. By choosing a plot that should exhibit intellectual integrity as the one great permanent value in an emotionally unstable world I should be saying the thing that, in a confused way, I had been wanting to say all my life. Finally, I should have found a universal theme which could be made integral both to the detective plot and to the "love-interest" which I had, somehow or other, to unite with it.

The more I looked at the idea, the more I liked it. It had a further advantage in its setting. Books had been written before about the women's colleges, but usually by dissatisfied young persons recently down from Oxford, and concerned only to deride her external futilities and absurdities without understanding of or sympathy for her inner values. Possibly it is easier to realize those values after twenty years of reflection in other surroundings. I did not suppose that many people would be interested in academic women or academic values, but since there was something I wanted to say about them, that was good enough.

The plot itself gave me little trouble. Murder—the first crime that suggests itself to the detective novelist—must be excluded. Murder meant publicity and the police, and I wanted to keep my action within the control of the Senior Common Room. There was one crime which could readily be dealt with by academic authorities, and which they would be particularly anxious to screen from publicity, and that was the crime of disseminating obscene libels, and committing malicious damage. It was the kind of crime which the world in general would be ready enough to connect with a community of celibate women, and which, for that very reason, would automatically place all the members of the college staff under the suspicion both of each other and of the reader. And it was not too outrageously melodramatic: murder is rare, though not unknown, in college life; mischief-making in a minor way is less uncommon and has a much more plausible air.

Next, it was necessary for my theme that the malice should be the product, not of intellect starved of emotion, but of emotion uncontrolled by intellect. And to knit the plot tight it must be more than this: it must be emotion revenging itself upon the intellect for some injury wrought by the intellect upon the emotions. What harm could intellectual women do, in virtue of their intellect, to an emotional woman? I imagined the case of a woman who, in her academic capacity, was obliged to expose a crime of intellectual dishonesty committed by a man (somebody's husband, father, lover, brother), and so deprive him of his academic status and, consequently, of his livelihood. I placed this suggestion before an academic friend, asking whether the situation were possible. The reply was, "It is not only possible; it happened." In fact, when I came to look into details, the real case was so like my imagination that I had to make some alterations in my plot so as to avoid a dangerously close resemblance to fact. This weakened probability a little, but not in such a way as to affect the course of the story.

The actual mechanics of the plot presented problems. A college of the size and importance I had in mind may contain two hundred people, not counting some thirty of the resident domestic staff and the daily cleaning women. Also, a college is a large, rambling place into any part of which anybody may penetrate at all hours of the day. At night it is, or is supposed to be, securely locked against outsiders; but every building in it possesses at least one open door, and both students and dons may parade the corridors and gardens unquestioned whenever it seems good to them. Obviously, one could not cope with a couple of hundred suspects within the college, not to say the entire university and city of Oxford without the walls. By various devices I endeavoured to eliminate (a) the majority of the students, (b) the majority of the scouts, and (c) all persons who could only have access in the daytime; leaving myself with the Senior Common Room, a few students, a few scouts, and a rascally ex-porter to carry the brunt of suspicion. Among these persons I placed my culprit, the exasperated widow of the dishonest scholar. I engaged a kindly and competent architect to design me a feasible college, so that I should not tie myself up in my own geography, and I obtained the courteous permission of the Master of Balliol to erect that college upon the Balliol playing-fields off Jowett Walk.

All this part of the business was the commonplace mechanics of the detective-novelist's job. The new and exciting thing was to bring the love-problem into line with the detective-problem, so that the same key should unlock both at once. I had Harriet, feeling herself for the first time on equal ground with Peter, seeing in the attractions of the intellectual life a means of freeing herself from the emotional obsession he produced in her, and yet seeing (as she supposed) that the celibate intellectual life rendered one liable to insanity in its ugliest form. I had Peter, seeing the truth from the start and perfectly conscious that he had only to leave her under her misapprehension to establish his emotional ascendancy over her. The temptation to take advantage of her mistake had to present itself to him in some form or other. That he should consider abandoning the investigation and leaving the upshot in doubt was too crude. It would be enough if, while she was still hesitating, he was tempted to use his physical charm to precipitate an emotional surrender from which there could be no subsequent return. I presented him with three opportunities for betrayal: once when Harriet exposes her own weakness in a sentimental moment on the river; again, when in the Botanical Gardens he warns her against letting emotions interfere with judgment; and finally, when she throws herself into his arms under the shock of finding the mischief-maker's malice turned against herself. In the meantime, I had made Harriet's surrender easier by letting her see Peter's weaknesses instead of (as hitherto) his strength: his jealous irritation at the misdeeds of a prodigal nephew; his personal vanities, his carefully concealed sentimentalities, his resentment of his own small stature and its compensating outbursts of childish exhibitionism; the mere helplessness of physical fatigue and so forth; and had further enhanced his attractions by making somebody else fall in love with him. I had also, to my great delight, succeeded in working into the book my original idea of a proposal from another man, in the imbecile episode where Mr. Pomfret avows his undergraduate passion in the grim presence of the Proctor. Thus, the train was laid for the overthrow of Harriet's defences if Peter chose to fire it.

This was where the theme of intellectual integrity came in. Peter's honesty of mind had to tell him that if Harriet accepted him under any sort of misapprehension, or through any insincerity on his part, they would be plunged into a situation even more false and intolerable than that from which they started. She must come to him as a free agent, if she came at all, and must realize that she was independent of him before she could bring him her dependence as a willing gift. At all costs, and even at the risk of losing her altogether, he must prevent her from committing

> the greatest treason:
> To do the right deed for the wrong reason,

and (through the machinery of the detective plot) show her the final baseness of which love was capable before he could ask her to risk the adventure with him.

The book is thus seen to be very tightly constructed, the plot and the theme being actually one thing, namely, that the same intellectual honesty that is essential to scholarship is essential also to the conduct of life. This proposition is fully discussed in the long conversation in the Senior Common Room between Peter and the dons. By one of those curious ironies which provide so wholesome a check to the vanity of authors, *Gaudy Night* had been loudly condemned by some critics for lack of construction. It would be truer to say that it is the only book I have ever written which has any construction at all, beyond a purely artificial plot-construction. Some of the blame is undoubtedly mine for not having made the construction more explicit (though I thought I was laying its articulations bare with an openness verging on indecency). I really think, however, that the construction was obscured by the conviction, still lingering in many people's minds, that a detective plot cannot bear any relation to a universal theme.

In the sixties of the last century there was still no divorce between plot and theme. *Man and Wife* is a mystery story built on the theme of the unequal marriage laws of the Three Kingdoms; and that theme provides the mainspring of the plot. It is only of recent years that we have had detective stories composed entirely of plot, without theme, or with the theme a mere incidental embroidery. We have even had stories divorced from their settings; bodies are discovered (for instance) in churches, theatres, railway stations, ships, aeroplanes, and so forth, which might just as well have been discovered anywhere else, the setting being put in only for picturesqueness and forming no *integral* part either of theme or plot. To make an artistic unity it is, I feel, essential that the plot should derive from the setting, and that both should form part of the theme. From this point of view, *Gaudy Night* does, I think, stand reasonably well up to the test; the setting is a women's college; the plot derives from, and develops through, episodes that could not have occurred in any other place; and the theme is the relation of scholarship to life. I am sure the book is constructed on the right lines, though I am naturally conscious of innumerable defects in the working.

I admit that when I had completed my monster, I felt some of the uneasiness of Count Frankenstein under the same circumstances. Some of my friends were dubious: they admitted that they had been led up the garden path, like Harriet, by the psychological red-herring, and had quite properly suspected the celibates and been surprised by the final anagnorisis; they added, with sincere politeness, that this was an "important" piece of work, but what (they asked) would the public make of it? Male readers would probably not be interested in a bunch of middle-aged academic women, and would find Harriet unattractive. I rather agreed with them, but thought there was one chance in a million that the thing might come off. In any case, I knew it was useless to try and write with a view to what the public might like: the only thing one can do is to write what one wants to write and hope for the best. I deposited the bulky manuscript on my publisher's desk, telling him that if it didn't strike lucky it would be a sensational flop. He smiled cheerfully, and said he would take the risk. I said I was afraid it was rather long. He, being an adept in turning necessity to glorious gain, said that in that case we could advertise it as the first detective story to be published at 8s 6d. He then read it (a thing which not every publisher will do for his author) and comforted me with an expensive and expansive telegram predicting success. We wrote him down an incurable optimist.

Oddly enough, he was right, and the book sold. The "male reader" confounded prophecy by not merely displaying interest in academic women, but by producing a strong "pro-Harriet" party, which asserted, in the teeth of those female readers who complained of Peter's throwing himself away on Harriet, that Harriet, on the contrary, was completely thrown away on Peter. In America, opinion was divided: Boston in the east was wholly favourable; with every succeeding meridian the accusations of "culture" became more numerous and embittered, and the lament over the absence of bloodshed more shrill; wrath reached howling-point in the voice of an anonymous gentleman in the Middle West, who wrote to me with regrettable familiarity, "You have done for yourself this time, Dot." The American sales, however, contradicted this ancestral voice prophesying doom.

I was once challenged, in a circle of writers, to account for the sales of *Gaudy Night*. I had not the honesty to say that I thought it sold because it was a good book. I do think it sold because it was a sincere book upon a subject about which I really had something to say. I think, too, it sold because it dealt in a knowledge-able way with the daily life of a little-known section of the community. Readers seem to like books which tell them how other people live—any people, advertisers, bell-ringers, women dons, butchers, bakers or candlestick-makers—so long as the detail is full and accurate and the object of the work is not overt propaganda. Finally, of course, there was Peter, who, escaping annihilation and surviving a drastic surgical operation, has lived to see himself surnamed "the Incomparable."

I should like to be frank about Peter. It is not always wise to take one's puppets to pieces and display the mechanism, because, with the present vogue for the sub-conscious, it is often supposed that anything done consciously must be done insincerely. But that is a blasphemy against the intellect. A character will not stand square on its legs without conscious carpentry any more than a table will; I would not put anything I valued on a table that had dreamily evolved itself from the sub-conscious. I know quite well how Peter was put together, and how his love-affair was put to-gether; but the fact of my knowledge does not make the construc-tion in the wrong sense artificial. There is more truth in the accusation, frequently made, that Peter is a "wish-fulfilment"; that is, there would be more truth in it if those who make it were in a position to understand my wishes in the matter. There are two ways of creating a fictitious character: one, the more superficial perhaps, is to take observed behaviour and try to deduce from it the motives from which it springs. The other is to take some passing mood of one's own mind and say to one's self, If this fleeting mood were to become a dominant attitude of mind, what would my behaviour be under given circumstances? Putting aside the accidental attributes that an amateur detective must possess to get through his work without too much outside help—such, for example, as money, leisure, physical endurance, and the tricks of this or that trade—the essential Peter is seen to be the familiar figure of the interpretative artist, the romantic soul at war with the realistic brain. Harriet, with her lively and inquisitive mind and her soul grounded upon reality, is his complement—the creative artist; her make-up is more stable than his, and far more capable of self-dependence. On the surface he is a comedian; his dislocation is at the centre: she is tragic externally, for all her dissatisfactions are patent, but she has the central unity which he has not. In the novel *Busman's Honeymoon* Harriet says "I've hated almost everything that ever happened to me, but I knew all the time it was just things that were wrong, not everything." Peter replies, "With me it's always been the other way round. I can enjoy practically everything that comes along—while it's happening. Only I have to keep on doing things, because if I once stop, it all seems a lot of rot." They are the two moods of the artistic spirit, separated and shown as dominant in two distinct personalities. Their only hope of repose is in union, though even then (as Miss De Vine says in *Gaudy Night*) "it can only be the repose of a very delicate balance." In that sense Peter—or rather, the Peter-Harriet combination—does represent the wish-fulfilment of the artist; though when people use that phrase I do not suppose that is what they mean by it.

It is difficult to make these explanations without appearing to take Peter too solemnly. I am comforted by the reflection that his readers are far more solemn about him than I am. I have received letters saying, "I absolutely refuse to go and see Peter and Har-

riet portrayed upon the stage, for fear of having my ideals shattered." The robust author, having preserved her ideals unscathed
through three grinding weeks of rehearsal and several months of
the play's run, can, under these circumstances, only marvel at a
sensitiveness so exaggerated, and gnash her teeth over the loss of
royalties.

I am often asked, "Will Peter's career end with his marriage?"
Alas! I can now see no end to Peter this side of the grave. The Incomparable Peter is more fatally than ever Peter the Ineluctable.
Formerly a periodic visitation, he has become a permanent resident in the house of my mind. His affairs are more real to me than
my own; his domestic responsibilities haunt my waking hours,
and I find myself bringing all my actions and opinions to the
bar of his silent criticism. He darkens the future, so that I cannot now contrive an episode in his career without considering how
it will affect him and his in ten years' time, and have to write
every book with wary eye to the next book but two. He is surrounded by a gang of friends and relations, who all have to be
fitted into the story somehow; I discover with alarm that his children are coming tumbling into the world before I have time to
chronicle these events, and I am distracted and confused by the
friendly letters of readers, giving him and Harriet the best advice
upon child-welfare. He sprawls over the past like an octopus. The
faces of his former loves—Barbara, the moonlight princess, and
the red-haired Viennese singer ("music is his line"), and Natalie
with her Gibson-girl figure and pompadour hair who taught him
his *métier d'amant* so many years ago, the lady (was she a Pole
or a Spaniard?) who lived in the Avenue Kléber and made "des
histoires" with her maid, and the Italian who involved him in a
ridiculous duel in Corsica—peep nodding and smiling out of the
curtains of Peter's marriage-bed and threaten to reappear in his
life. The course of English history is disturbed by the antics of
dead-and-gone Wimseys, who leap from its waters like so many
salmon in the mating season. My friends have become infected
with my own madness; they wrestle valiantly with dates and genealogical trees and armorial bearings; they assist me to write spoof
pamphlets about eighteenth century Wimseys, adorned with plausible excerpts from Evelyn and Bubb Dodington and Horace Wal-

pole; they embellish these fantasies with family portraits and contemporary views of Bredon Hall; they accept the existence of a poetical Wimsey who was a friend of Sir Philip Sidney, and meekly sit down to set his songs to music, while the local chemist prepares ink from an Elizabethan recipe wherewith I may forge the original manuscripts in a fair secretary hand. We discover Wimsey ciphers embedded in the plays of Shakespeare, and retrieve Wimsey common-place books from remote corners of Australia; we sally forth in a team to foist these discoveries upon bewildered literary societies in respectable universities. I cannot imagine where all this is going to end; it is all very well to Peter to be a comedian, but he must have inherited that trait from somebody, and I occasionally wonder whether the comedian in one or other of us is not getting a little out of hand. At any rate, the whole thing is a warning against inventing characters whose existence has to be prolonged through a long series of books:

Et certes est-ce bien un grief labeur que d'excogiter cent contes drolatiques?

The Simple Art of Murder
By Raymond Chandler

There are readers who can enjoy virtually any variety of detective story so long as it is sufficiently well done in its kind. There are sterner souls—and in the democracies such is their inalienable right—who hold to likes and dislikes for specific types approaching the violent. As one of the most aware, articulate, and literarily gifted of American detective novelists—the creator of Philip Marlowe and author of such purposeful narratives as The Big Sleep *and* Farewell My Lovely—*Raymond Chandler is admirably qualified to wield the cudgels for what he terms "realistic mystery fiction" and against those he considers its traducers. His essay appeared originally in the* Atlantic Monthly *for December 1944; the version presented here was specially revised by Mr. Chandler for this publication.*

FICTION IN any form has always intended to be realistic. Old-fashioned novels which now seem stilted and artificial to the point of burlesque did not appear that way to the people who first read them. Writers like Fielding and Smollett could seem realistic in the modern sense because they dealt largely with uninhibited characters, many of whom were about two jumps ahead of the police, but Jane Austen's chronicles of highly inhibited people against a background of rural gentility seem real enough psychologically. There is plenty of that kind of social and emotional hypocrisy around today. Add to it a liberal dose of intellectual pretentiousness and you get the tone of the book page in your daily paper and the earnest and fatuous atmosphere breathed by discussion groups in little clubs. These are the people who make best-sellers, which are promotional jobs based on a sort of indirect snob-appeal, carefully escorted by the trained seals of the critical fraternity, and lovingly tended and watered by certain much too powerful pressure groups whose business is selling books, although they would like you to think they are fostering culture. Just get a little behind in your payments and you will find out how idealistic they are.

The detective story for a variety of reasons can seldom be promoted. It is usually about murder and hence lacks the element of uplift. Murder, which is a frustration of the individual and hence a frustration of the race, may, and in fact has, a good deal of sociological implication. But it has been going on too long for it to be news. If the mystery novel is at all realistic (which it very seldom is) it is written in a certain spirit of detachment; otherwise nobody but a psychopath would want to write it or read it. The murder novel has also a depressing way of minding its own business, solving its own problems and answering its own questions. There is nothing left to discuss, except whether it was well enough written to be good fiction, and the people who make up the half-million sales wouldn't know that anyway. The detection of quality in writing is difficult enough even for those who make a career of the job, without paying too much attention to the matter of advance sales.

The detective story (perhaps I had better call it that, since the English formula still dominates the trade) has to find its public by a slow process of distillation. That it does do this, and holds on thereafter with such tenacity, is a fact; the reasons for it are a study for more patient minds than mine. Nor is it any part of my thesis to maintain that it is a vital and significant form of art. There are no vital and significant forms of art; there is only art, and precious little of that. The growth of populations has in no way increased the amount; it has merely increased the adeptness with which substitutes can be produced and packaged.

Yet the detective story, even in its most conventional form, is difficult to write well. Good specimens of the art are much rarer than good serious novels. Rather second-rate items outlast most of the high velocity fiction, and a great many that should never have been born simply refuse to die at all. They are as durable as the statues in public parks and just about that dull. This is very annoying to people of what is called discernment. They do not like it that penetrating and important works of fiction of a few years back stand on their special shelf in the library marked "Best-Sellers of Yesteryear," and nobody goes near them but an occasional shortsighted customer who bends down, peers briefly and hurries away; while old ladies jostle each other at the mystery shelf to grab off some item of the same vintage with a title like *The Triple Petunia Murder Case,* or *Inspector Pinchbottle to the Rescue.* They do not like it that "really important books" get dusty on the reprint counter, while *Death Wears Yellow Garters* is put out in editions of fifty or one hundred thousand copies on the news-stands of the country, and is obviously not there just to say goodbye.

To tell you the truth, I do not like it very much myself. In my less stilted moments I too write detective stories, and all this immortality makes just a little too much competition. Even Einstein couldn't get very far if three hundred treatises of the higher physics were published every year, and several thousand others in some form or other were hanging around in excellent condition, and being read too. Hemingway says somewhere that the good writer competes only with the dead. The good detective story writer (there must after all be a few) competes not only with all the unburied dead but with all the hosts of the living as well. And on almost equal terms; for it is one of the qualities of this kind of writing that the thing that makes people read it never goes out of style. The hero's tie may be a little off the mode and the good gray inspector may arrive in a dogcart instead of a streamlined sedan with siren screaming, but what he does when he gets there is the same old futzing around with timetables and bits of charred paper and who trampled the jolly old flowering arbutus under the library window.

I have, however, a less sordid interest in the matter. It seems to me that production of detective stories on so large a scale, and by writers whose immediate reward is small and whose need of critical praise is almost nil, would not be possible at all if the job took any talent. In that sense the raised eyebrow of the critic and the shoddy merchandizing of the publisher are perfectly logical. The average detective story is probably no worse than the average novel, but you never see the average novel. It doesn't get published. The average—or only slightly above average—detective story does. Not only is it published but it is sold in small quantities to rental libraries, and it is read. There are even a few optimists who buy it at the full retail price of two dollars, because it looks so fresh and new, and there is a picture of a corpse on the cover. And the strange thing is that this average, more than middling dull, pooped-out piece of utterly unreal and mechanical fiction is not terribly different from what are called the masterpieces of the art. It drags on a little more slowly, the dialogue is a little grayer, the cardboard out of which the characters are cut is a shade thinner, and the cheating is a little more obvious; but it is the same kind of book. Whereas the good novel is not at all the same kind of book as the bad novel. It is about entirely different things. But the good detective story and the bad detective story are about exactly the same things, and they are about them in very much the same way. There are reasons for this too, and reasons for the reasons; there always are.

I suppose the principal dilemma of the traditional or classic or straight-deductive or logic—and—deduction novel of detection is that for any approach to perfection it demands a combination of qualities not found in the same mind. The cool-headed constructionist does not also come across with lively characters, sharp dialogue, a sense of pace and an acute use of observed detail. The grim logician has as much atmosphere as a drawing-board. The scientific sleuth has a nice new shiny laboratory, but I'm sorry I can't remember the face. The fellow who can write you a vivid and colorful prose simply won't be bothered with the coolie labor of breaking down unbreakable alibis. The master of rare knowledge is living psychologically in the age of the hoop skirt. If you know all you should know about ceramics and Egyptian needlework, you don't know anything at all about the police. If you know that platinum won't melt under about 2800 degrees F. by itself, but will melt at the glance of a pair of deep blue eyes when put close to a bar of lead, then you don't know how men make love in the twentieth century. And if you know enough about the elegant flânerie of the pre-war French Riviera to lay your story in that locale, you don't know that a couple of capsules of barbital small enough to be swallowed will not only not kill a man—they will not even put him to sleep, if he fights against them.

Every detective story writer makes mistakes, and none will ever know as much as he should. Conan Doyle made mistakes which completely invalidated some of his stories, but he was a pioneer, and Sherlock Holmes after all is mostly an attitude and a few dozen lines of unforgettable dialogue. It is the ladies and gentlemen of what Mr. Howard Haycraft (in his book *Murder for Pleasure*) calls the Golden Age of detective fiction that really get me down. This age is not remote. For Mr. Haycraft's purpose it starts after the first World War and lasts up to about 1930. For all practical purposes it is still here. Two-thirds or three-quarters of all the detective stories published still adhere to the formula the giants of this era created, perfected, polished and sold to the world as problems in logic and deduction. These are stern words, but be not alarmed. They are only words. Let us glance at one of the glories of the literature, an acknowledged masterpiece of the art of fooling the reader without cheating him. It is called *The Red House Mystery*, was written by A. A. Milne, and has been named by Alexander Woollcott (rather a fast man with a superlative) "one of the three best mystery stories of all time." Words of that size are not spoken lightly. The book was published in 1922, but is quite timeless, and might as easily have been published in July 1939, or, with a few slight changes, last week. It ran thirteen editions and seems to have been in print, in the original format, for about sixteen years. That happens to few books of any kind. It is an agreeable book, light, amusing in the *Punch* style, written with a deceptive smoothness that is not as easy as it looks.

It concerns Mark Ablett's impersonation of his brother Robert, as a hoax on his friends. Mark is the owner of the Red House, a typical laburnum-and-lodge-gate English country house, and he has a secretary who encourages him and abets him in this impersonation, because the secretary is going to murder him, if he pulls it off. Nobody around the Red House has ever seen Robert, fifteen years absent in Australia, known to them by repute as a no-good. A letter from Robert is talked about, but never shown. It announces his arrival, and Mark hints it will not be a pleasant occasion. One afternoon, then, the supposed Robert arrives, identifies himself to a couple of servants, is shown into the study, and Mark (according to testimony at the inquest) goes in after him. Robert is then found dead on the floor with a bullet hole in his face, and of course Mark has vanished into thin air. Arrive the police, suspect Mark must be the murderer, remove the debris and proceed with the investigation, and in due course, with the inquest.

Milne is aware of one very difficult hurdle and tries as well as he can to get over it. Since the secretary is going to murder Mark once he has established himself as Robert, the impersonation has to continue on and fool the police. Since, also, everybody around the Red House knows Mark intimately, disguise is necessary. This is achieved by shaving off Mark's beard, roughening his hands ("not the hands of a manicured gentlemen"—testimony) and the use of a gruff voice and rough manner. But this is not enough. The cops are going to have the body and the clothes on it and whatever is in the pockets. Therefore none of this must suggest Mark. Milne therefore works like a switch engine to put over the motivation that Mark is such a thoroughly conceited performer that he dresses the part down to the socks and underwear (from all of which the secretary has removed the maker's labels), like a ham blacking himself all over to play Othello. If the reader will buy this (and the sales record shows he must have) Milne figures he is solid. Yet, however light in texture the story may be, it is offered as a problem of logic and deduction. If it is not that, it is nothing at all. There is nothing else for it to be. If the situation is false, you cannot even accept it as a light novel, for there is no story for the light novel to be about. If the problem does not contain the elements of truth and plausibility, it is no problem; if the logic is an illusion, there is nothing to deduce. If the impersonation is impossible once the reader is told the conditions it must fulfill, then the whole thing is a fraud. Not a deliberate fraud, because Milne would not have written the story if he had known what he was up against. He is up against a number of deadly things, none of which he even considers. Nor, apparently, does the casual reader, who wants to like the story, hence takes it at its face value. But the reader is not called upon to know the facts of life; it is the author who is the expert in the case. Here is what this author ignores:

1. The coroner holds formal jury inquest on a body for which no competent legal identification is offered. A coroner, usually in a big city, will sometimes hold inquest on a body that *cannot* be identified, if the record of such an inquest has or may have a value (fire, disaster, evidence of murder, etc.). No such reason exists here, and there is no one to identify the body. A couple of witnesses said the man said he was Robert Ablett. This is mere presumption, and has weight only if nothing conflicts with it. Identification is a condition precedent to an inquest. Even in death a man has a right to his own identity. The coroner will, wherever humanly possible, enforce that right. To neglect it would be a violation of his office.

2. Since Mark Ablett, missing and suspected of the murder, cannot defend himself, all evidence of his movements before and after the murder is vital (as also whether he has money to run away on); yet all such evidence is given by the man closest to the murder, and is without corroboration. It is automatically suspect until proved true.

3. The police find by direct investigation that Robert Ablett was not well thought of in his native village. Somebody there must have known him. No such person was brought to the inquest. (The story couldn't stand it.)

4. The police know there is an element of threat in Robert's supposed visit, and that it is connected with the murder must be obvious to them. Yet they make no attempt to check Robert in Australia, or find out what character he had there, or what associates, or even if he actually came to England, and with whom. (If they had, they would have found out he had been dead three years.)

5. The police surgeon examines the body with a recently shaved beard (exposing unweathered skin), artificially roughened hands, yet the body of a wealthy, soft-living man, long resident in a cool climate. Robert was a rough individual and had lived fifteen years in Australia. That is the surgeon's information. It is impossible he would have noticed nothing to conflict with it.

6. The clothes are nameless, empty, and have had the labels

removed. Yet the man wearing them asserted an identity. The presumption that he was not what he said he was is overpowering. Nothing whatever is done about this peculiar circumstance. It is never even mentioned as being peculiar.

7. A man is missing, a well-known local man, and a body in the morgue closely resembles him. It is impossible that the police should not at once eliminate the chance that the missing man *is* the dead man. Nothing would be easier than to prove it. Not even to think of it is incredible. It makes idiots of the police, so that a brash amateur may startle the world with a fake solution.

The detective in the case is an insouciant gent named Antony Gillingham, a nice lad with a cheery eye, a cozy little flat in London, and that airy manner. He is not making any money on the assignment, but is always available when the local gendarmerie loses its notebook. The English police seem to endure him with their customary stoicism; but I shudder to think of what the boys down at the Homicide Bureau in my city would do to him.

There are less plausible examples of the art than this. In *Trent's Last Case* (often called "the perfect detective story") you have to accept the premise that a giant of international finance, whose lightest frown makes Wall Street quiver like a chihuahua, will plot his own death so as to hang his secretary, and that the secretary when pinched will maintain an aristocratic silence; the old Etonian in him maybe. I have known relatively few international financiers, but I rather think the author of this novel has (if possible) known fewer. There is one by Freeman Wills Crofts (the soundest builder of them all when he doesn't get too fancy) wherein a murderer by the aid of makeup, split second timing, and some very sweet evasive action, impersonates the man he has just killed and thereby gets him alive and distant from the place of the crime. There is one of Dorothy Sayers' in which a man is murdered alone at night in his house by a mechanically released weight which works because he always turns the radio on at just such a moment, always stands in just such a position in front of it, and always bends over just so far. A couple of inches either way and the customers would get a rain check. This is what is vulgarly known as having God sit in your lap; a murderer who needs that much help from Providence must be in the wrong business. And there is a scheme of Agatha Christie's featuring M. Hercule Poirot, that ingenius Belgian who talks in a literal translation of school-boy French, wherein, by duly messing around with his "little gray cells," M. Poirot decides that nobody on a certain through sleeper could have done the murder alone, therefore everybody did it together, breaking the process down into a series of simple operations, like assembling an egg-beater. This is the type that is guaranteed to knock the keenest mind for a loop. Only a halfwit could guess it.

There are much better plots by these same writers and by others of their school. There may be one somewhere that would really stand up under close scrutiny. It would be fun to read it, even if I did have to go back to page 47 and refresh my memory about exactly what time the second gardener potted the prize-winning tearose begonia. There is nothing new about these stories and nothing old. The ones I mentioned are all English only because the authorities (such as they are) seem to feel the English writers had an edge in this dreary routine, and that the Americans, (even the creator of Philo Vance—probably the most asinine character in detective fiction) only made the Junior Varsity.

This, the classic detective story, has learned nothing and forgotten nothing. It is the story you will find almost any week in the big shiny magazines, handsomely illustrated, and paying due deference to virginal love and the right kind of luxury goods. Perhaps the tempo has become a trifle faster, and the dialogue a little more glib. There are more frozen daiquiris and stingers ordered, and fewer glasses of crusty old port; more clothes by *Vogue,* and décors by the *House Beautiful,* more chic, but not more truth. We spend more time in Miami hotels and Cape Cod summer colonies and go not so often down by the old gray sundial in the Elizabethan garden. But fundamentally it is the same careful grouping of suspects, the same utterly incomprehensible trick of how somebody stabbed Mrs. Pottington Postlethwaite III with the solid platinum poignard just as she flatted on the top note of the Bell Song from *Lakmé* in the presence of fifteen ill-assorted guests; the same ingenue in fur-trimmed pajamas screaming in the night to make the company pop in and out of doors and ball up the timetable; the same moody silence next day as they sit around sipping Singapore slings and sneering at each other, while the flat-feet crawl to and fro under the Persian rugs, with their derby hats on.

Personally I like the English style better. It is not quite so brittle, and the people as a rule, just wear clothes and drink drinks. There is more sense of background, as if Cheesecake Manor really existed all around and not just the part the camera sees; there are more long walks over the Downs and the characters don't all try to behave as if they had just been tested by MGM. The English may not always be the best writers in the world, but they are incomparably the best dull writers.

There is a very simple statement to be made about all these stories: they do not really come off intellectually as problems, and they do not come off artistically as fiction. They are too contrived, and too little aware of what goes on in the world. They try to be honest, but honesty is an art. The poor writer is dishonest without knowing it, and the fairly good one can be dishonest because he doesn't know what to be honest about. He thinks a complicated murder scheme which baffles the lazy reader, who won't be bothered itemizing the details, will also baffle the police, whose business is with details. The boys with their feet on the desks know that the easiest murder case in the world to break is the one somebody tried to get very cute with; the one that really bothers them is the murder somebody only thought of two minutes before he pulled it off. But if the writers of this fiction wrote about the kind of murders that happen, they would also have to write about the authentic flavor of life as it is lived. And since they cannot do that, they pretend that what they do is what should be done. Which is begging the question—and the best of them know it.

In her introduction to the first *Omnibus of Crime,* Dorothy Sayers wrote: "It (the detective story) does not, and by hypothesis never can, attain the loftiest level of literary achievement." And she suggested somewhere else that this is because it is a "literature of escape" and not "a literature of expression." I do not know what the loftiest level of literary achievement is: neither did Aeschylus or Shakespeare; neither does Miss Sayers. Other things being equal, which they never are, a more powerful theme will provoke a more powerful performance. Yet some very dull books have been written about God, and some very fine ones about how to make a living and stay fairly honest. It is always a matter of who writes the stuff, and what he has in him to write it with. As for literature of expression and literature of escape, this is critics' jargon, a use of abstract words as if they had absolute meanings. Everything written with vitality expresses that vitality; there are no dull subjects, only dull minds. All men who read escape from something else into what lies behind the printed page; the quality of the dream may be argued, but its release has become a functional necessity. All men must escape at times from the deadly rhythm of their private thoughts. It is part of the process of life among thinking beings. It is one of the things that distinguish them from the three-toed sloth; he apparently—one can never be quite sure—is perfectly content hanging upside down on a branch, and not even reading Walter Lippman. I hold no particular brief for the detective story as the ideal escape. I merely say that *all* reading for pleasure is escape, whether it be Greek, mathematics, astronomy, Benedetto Croce, or *The Diary of the Forgotten Man*. To say otherwise is to be an intellectual snob, and a juvenile at the art of living.

I do not think such considerations moved Miss Dorothy Sayers to her essay in critical futility.

I think what was really gnawing at her mind was the slow realization that her kind of detective story was an arid formula which could not even satisfy its own implications. It was second-grade literature because it was not about the things that could make first-grade literature. If it started out to be about real people (and she could write about them—her minor characters show that), they must very soon do unreal things in order to form the artificial pattern required by the plot. When they did unreal things, they ceased to be real themselves. They became puppets and cardboard lovers and papier mâché villains and detectives of exquisite and impossible gentility. The only kind of writer who could be happy with these properties was the one who did not know what reality was. Dorothy Sayers' own stories show that she was annoyed by this triteness; the weakest element in them is the part that makes them detective stories, the strongest the part which could be removed without touching the "problem of logic and deduction." Yet she could not or would not give her characters their heads and let them make their own mystery. It took a much simpler and more direct mind than hers to do that.

In the *Long Week-End,* which is a drastically competent account of English life and manners in the decade following the first World War, Robert Graves and Alan Hodge gave some attention to the detective story. They were just as traditionally English as the ornaments of the Golden Age, and they wrote of the time in which these writers were almost as well-known as any writers in the world. Their books in one form or another sold into the millions, and in a dozen languages. These were the people who fixed the form and established the rules and founded the famous Detection Club, which is a Parnassus of English writers of mystery. Its roster includes practically every important writer of detective fiction since Conan Doyle. But Graves and Hodge decided that during this whole period only one first-class writer had written detective stories at all. An American, Dashiell Hammett. Traditional or not, Graves and Hodge were not fuddy-duddy connoisseurs of the second rate; they could see what went on in the world and that the detective story of their time didn't; and they were aware that writers who have the vision and the ability to produce real fiction do not produce unreal fiction.

How original a writer Hammett really was, it isn't easy to decide now, even if it mattered. He was one of a group, the only one who achieved critical recognition, but not the only one who wrote or tried to write realistic mystery fiction. All literary movements are like this; some one individual is picked out to represent the whole movement; he is usually the culmination of the movement. Hammett was the ace performer, but there is nothing in his work that is not implicit in the early novels and short stories of Hemingway. Yet for all I know, Hemingway may have learned something from Hammett, as well as from writers like Dreiser, Ring Lardner, Carl Sandburg, Sherwood Anderson and himself. A rather revolutionary debunking of both the language and material of fiction had been going on for some time. It probably started in poetry; almost everything does. You can take it clear back to Walt Whitman, if you like. But Hammett applied it to the detective story, and this, because of its heavy crust of English gentility and American pseudo-gentility, was pretty hard to get moving. I doubt that Hammett had any deliberate artistic aims whatever; he was trying to make a living by writing something he had first hand information about. He made some of it up; all writers do; but it had a basis in fact; it was made up out of real things. The only reality the English detection writers knew was the conversational accent of Surbiton and Bognor Regis. If they wrote about dukes and Venetian vases, they knew no more about them out of their own experience than the well-heeled Hollywood character knows about the French Modernists that hang in his Bel-Air château or the semi-antique Chippendale-cum-cobbler's bench that he uses for a coffee table. Hammett took murder out of the Venetian vase and dropped it into the alley; it doesn't have to stay there forever, but it was a good idea to begin by getting as far as possible from Emily Post's idea of how a well-bred debutante gnaws a chicken wing. He wrote at first (and almost to the end) for people with a sharp, aggressive attitude to life. They were not afraid of the seamy side of things; they lived there. Violence did not dismay them; it was right down their street.

Hammett gave murder back to the kind of people that commit it for reasons, not just to provide a corpse; and with the means at hand, not with hand-wrought duelling pistols, curare, and tropical fish. He put these people down on paper as they are, and he made them talk and think in the language they customarily used for these purposes. He had style, but his audience didn't know it, because it was in a language not supposed to be capable of such refinements. They thought they were getting a good meaty melodrama written in the kind of lingo they imagined they spoke themselves. It was, in a sense, but it was much more. All language begins with speech, and the speech of common men at that, but when it develops to the point of becoming a literary medium it only looks like speech. Hammett's style at its worst was almost as formalized as a page of Marius the Epicurean; at its best it could say almost anything. I believe this style, which does not belong to Hammett or to anybody, but is the American language (and not even exclusively that any more), can say things he did not know how to say or feel the need of saying. In his hands it had no overtones, left no echo, evoked no image beyond a distant hill. He is said to have lacked heart, yet the story he thought most of himself is the record of a man's devotion to a friend. He was spare, frugal, hardboiled, but he did over and over again what only the best writers can ever do at all. He wrote scenes that seemed never to have been written before.

With all this he did not wreck the formal detective story. Nobody can; production demands a form that can be produced. Realism takes too much talent, too much knowledge, too much awareness. Hammett may have loosened it up a little here, and sharpened it a little there. Certainly all but the stupidest and most meretricious writers are more conscious of their artificiality than they used to be. And he demonstrated that the detective story can be important writing. *The Maltese Falcon* may or may not be a work of genius, but an art which is capable of it is not "by hypothesis" incapable of anything. Once a detective story can be as good as this, only the pedants will deny that it *could* be even better. Hammett did something else, he made the detective story fun to write, not an exhausting concatenation of insignificant clues. Without him there might not have been a regional mystery as clever as Percival Wilde's *Inquest,* or an ironic study as able as Raymond Postgate's *Verdict of Twelve,* or a savage piece of intellectual double-talk like Kenneth Fearing's *The Dagger of the Mind,* or a tragi-comic idealization of the murderer as in Donald Henderson's *Mr. Bowling Buys a Newspaper,* or even a gay and intriguing Hollywoodian gambol like Richard Sale's *Lazarus No. 7.*

The realistic style is easy to abuse: from haste, from lack of awareness, from inability to bridge the chasm that lies between what a writer would like to be able to say and what he actually knows how to say. It is easy to fake; brutality is not strength, flipness is not wit, edge-of-the-chair writing can be as boring as flat writing; dalliance with promiscuous blondes can be very dull stuff when described by goaty young men with no other purpose in mind than to describe dalliance with promiscuous blondes. There has been so much of this sort of thing that if a character in a detective story says, "Yeah," the author is automatically a Hammett imitator.

And there are still quite a few people around who say that Hammett did not write detective stories at all, merely hard-boiled chronicles of mean streets with a perfunctory mystery element dropped in like the olive in a martini. These are the flustered old ladies—of both sexes (or no sex) and almost all ages—who like their murders scented with magnolia blossoms and do not care to be reminded that murder is an act of infinite cruelty, even if the perpetrators sometimes look like playboys or college professors or nice motherly women with softly graying hair. There are also a few badly-scared champions of the formal or the classic mystery who think no story is a detective story which does not pose a formal and exact problem and arrange the clues around it with neat labels on them. Such would point out, for example, that in reading *The Maltese Falcon* no one concerns himself with who killed Spade's partner, Archer (which is the only formal problem of the story) because the reader is kept thinking about something else. Yet in *The Glass Key* the reader is constantly reminded that the question is who killed Taylor Henry, and exactly the same effect is obtained; an effect of movement, intrigue, cross-purposes and the gradual elucidation of character, which is all the detective story has any right to be about anyway. The rest is spillikins in the parlor.

But all this (and Hammett too) is for me not quite enough. The realist in murder writes of a world in which gangsters can rule nations and almost rule cities, in which hotels and apartment houses and celebrated restaurants are owned by men who made their money out of brothels, in which a screen star can be the finger-man for a mob, and the nice man down the hall is a boss of the numbers racket; a world where a judge with a cellar full of bootleg liquor can send a man to jail for having a pint in his pocket, where the mayor of your town may have condoned murder as an instrument of money-making, where no man can walk down a dark street in safety because law and order are things we talk about but refrain from practising; a world where you may witness a hold-up in broad daylight and see who did it, but you will fade quickly back into the crowd rather than tell anyone, because the hold-up men may have friends with long guns, or the police may not like your testimony, and in any case the shyster for the defense will be allowed to abuse and vilify you in open court, before a jury of selected morons, without any but the most perfunctory interference from a political judge.

It is not a very fragrant world, but it is the world you live in, and certain writers with tough minds and a cool spirit of detachment can make very interesting and even amusing patterns out of it. It is not funny that a man should be killed, but it is sometimes funny that he should be killed for so little, and that his death should be the coin of what we call civilization. All this still is not quite enough.

In everything that can be called art there is a quality of redemption. It may be pure tragedy, if it is high tragedy, and it may be pity and irony, and it may be the raucous laughter of the strong man. But down these mean streets a man must go who is not himself mean, who is neither tarnished nor afraid. The detective in this kind of story must be such a man. He is the hero, he is everything. He must be a complete man and a common man and yet an unusual man. He must be, to use a rather weathered phrase, a man of honor, by instinct, by inevitability, without thought of it, and certainly without saying it. He must be the best man in his world and a good enough man for any world. I do not care much about his private life; he is neither a eunuch nor a satyr; I think he might seduce a duchess and I am quite sure he would not spoil a virgin; if he is a man of honor in one thing, he is that in all things. He is a relatively poor man, or he would not be a detective at all. He is a common man or he could not go among common people. He has a sense of character, or he would not know his job. He will take no man's money dishonestly and no man's insolence without a due and dispassionate revenge. He is a lonely man and his pride is that you will treat him as a proud man or be very sorry you ever saw him. He talks as the man of his age talks, that is, with rude wit, a lively sense of the grotesque, a disgust for sham, and a contempt for pettiness. The story is his adventure in search of a hidden truth, and it would be no adventure if it did not happen to a man fit for adventure. He has a range of awareness that startles you, but it belongs to him by right, because it belongs to the world he lives in.

If there were enough like him, I think the world would be a very safe place to live in, and yet not too dull to be worth living in.

Murder Makes Merry
By Craig Rice

One of the few contemporary writers of detective fiction who has been able, successfully and consistently, to wed humor to homicide, mirth to murder, is the American novelist Craig Rice, known to a wide audience for the fast-moving John J. Malone and Helene and Jake Justus mysteries and such classics of cachinnatory crime as Home Sweet Homicide *and* The Thursday Turkey Murders. *At the invitation of your editor, Mrs. Rice takes the platform to reveal —in characteristically informal fashion—some of her innermost thoughts on this delicate problem.*

THE GIRL was young, and incredibly lovely; with honey-colored hair falling to her shoulders; odd-shaped, almost greenish eyes framed in lashes long enough to use for water-color brushes, and a scarlet, sulky, beautiful mouth. She appeared at her best in a close-fitting white bathing suit that showed her tanned, slender legs to advantage. She was heiress to several million dollars, and a number of disgruntled wives suspected her (and rightly) of turning her charms, full-blast, on their husbands.

By disposition, she was something of a—well, let's say that she barked, wagged her tail, and chased cats. Everyone hated her, save the various men who were madly in love with her and couldn't make the faintest impression on her Heart-of-Stone.

You know, by this time, that inevitably she is murdered in at least chapter three. Brutally murdered. Everyone in the cast suspects somebody else, and the reader suspects everybody. The crime is eventually solved by a blithe and light-hearted young couple, or a hardboiled dick who gets beaten to a pulp at least five times, or a pair of whimsical elderly spinsters.

In the course of the story, naturally, a charming old snowy-haired gentleman, (a retired professor of Romance Languages) stumbles on an important clue, and gets his venerable head bashed in. The handsome young man with Hollywood ambitions, who turns out to have been the victim's secret husband (and therefore a prime suspect) is found under an ancient grey stone culvert, with his throat cut. And at last, after the sleuth in the case has narrowly escaped a horrible death, it developes that the murderer was dear old Aunt Martha, who'd tenderly tended the victim since early childhood. A case, no doubt, of frustration, poor soul, or of an illegitimate son in Patagonia who would inherit the several millions.*

Some reviewer (and quite possibly myself) is sure to say, "Funniest book I've read in years!"

Which sounds a little like, "Ain't laffed so much since gramps fell in the well!"

Murder is not mirthful, and there is nothing comic about a corpse. Ask any squad car dick, or special prosecutor, or medical examiner. Or, any murderer, if you're lucky enough to know one. You'll be told that there is seldom, if ever, a really hilarious homicide.

In his preface to *The Chicago Murders*, Sewell Peaslee Wright says: ". . . murder is the ultimate sin; the most abominable crime." He also adds that ". . . murder is a horrid word."

Encountered in real life (perhaps in this case one should say, "real death") murder is, at its worst, frightful and, at its best, sordid. The victim himself objects to it, in many cases violently. He leaves behind friends and/or relatives who mourn for him, whose future lives may very well be ruined by this single act of violence—for there are very few in this world who do not leave someone to mourn. The police, the coroner, the D.A.'s office—all the authorities have a mess on their hands, and I *do* mean a mess. And, to be truthful, it is very seldom that the murderer is happy about it, either.

Yet the public continues to demand—and get—humor with its homicides, and mirth with its mysteries.

That's a fact every writer knows. Shakespeare knew it, and used

---

* *Looking these pages over, there appears to be a good plot for a murder mystery. If no one else uses it first, I'll write it myself!*—C.R.

it to good account. Poe knew it (though frankly, I've had very few real belly-laughs from Jupiter's wise-cracks in *The Gold Bug*). Conan Doyle knew it, and there are chuckles all through the pages of the immortal Sherlock. It's been known for centuries, but I'm darned if I'll go digging through all the reference books in the Public Library for instances to quote, just in order to give the impression that I'm a scholar.

The producers of B pictures know it. And too often come up with a Quaint Comic Character who is far, far more horrible than the Monster.

Smart criminal lawyers know it, and so do newspaper reporters. The tragic and horrible real-life murder becomes a comedy in the courtroom. You don't believe me? Go to any murder trial, and count the laughs.

Something very learned should be said at this point about comic relief. . . . I'd rather quote an instance.

A certain murder trial I covered as a reporter was one of the grimmest and most harrowing I've ever seen or read about. The defendant, a middle-aged woman, was being tried as accessory before the fact. The man who had already confessed to the actual murder was a tragic, tubercular little hobo. The victim—the woman's lover—had been a thoroughly objectionable character who, some years before, had figured prominently in a murder trial almost as gruesome as this one.

Most of the defense was based on the character of the victim (the defense lawyer was nobody's fool) and the fact that he had driven the defendant temporarily insane by his abnormal behavior. Every now and then the details reached a point where the judge would order all female spectators to leave the courtroom. (He didn't bother about female reporters, in fact he didn't admit that such a phenomenon existed. Addressing the press table, he invariably said "Gentlemen . . .")

You get the impression, I trust, that this trial was no laughing matter. Then came the day when the poor little man who claimed to have fired the shot was brought from the penitentiary where he was starting a life term, and placed on the witness stand.

This was the high spot of the trial. Everyone was as tense as an overtuned harp.

Murderer or not, no one could help feeling a pang of sympathy for him. About five foot three, weighing about a hundred pounds, with a pale, frightened face, and dressed in the cheap suit of clothes the warden had provided for him, he began telling his version of the actual killing.

Does this seem to you, so far, an occasion for mirth?

It didn't seem so to the spectators, the judge and the jury. As the story unfolded, you not only could have heard a pin drop in the courtroom, you could have heard the echo. In fact, if a pin *had* dropped, chances are everybody present would have fainted.

Then came the questions everybody had been waiting to hear:

"What did you do then?"

"I aimed the gun and shot him dead."

Something almost like a sigh of relief went through the crowded room.

"And then what happened?"

The poor little guy looked surprised at the question, but he answered it, truthfully.

"He fell down."

It took fifteen minutes to restore order in the court.

Reading that incident in cold black and white print, does it convulse you with laughter?

Naturally not. But coming at that moment, those three words, "He fell down," topped anything ever spoken by Jack Benny or Bob Hope. It was several minutes before the judge could start calling for order, because he had to straighten out his own face first.

It was simply that the situation had reached a point where everybody had to laugh, scream, or go crazy. That, perhaps, helps to explain why humor and homicide go hand in hand.

(Note: I am *not* going to delve into the psychology of the mystery novel reader at this point. I'm not nosey. If *you* want to delve into your psychology, go to it and good luck to you. But what you come up with is none of my business.)

But what makes a mystery novel funny?

(Note #2: I am *not* going to go all-out literary at this point and discuss What is Humor. Other writers have done it, and better than I ever could. To me, humor is anything that makes somebody laugh, somewhere and sometime.)

There is the device of peppering an otherwise plain-and-honest mystery story with so many brilliant wisecracks that every now and then the reader doesn't know if he is reading about murder or listening to Fred Allen. That, for the writer, is the easy method, providing he is smart enough to think up the wisecracks, or knows a lot of witty friends and carries a notebook.

There is the device of larding an otherwise heavy story with a couple of quaint bucolic characters who go around stumbling and bumbling and getting in everybody's way, and, at intervals, emitting gems of earthy philosophy until you can't see the plot for the platitudes.

Then there is the situation of the humorously bungling policeman. This is sure-fire stuff. Practically everyone in this vale of tears and jeers has, at some time in his life, been scared by and/or mad at a policeman. Therefore, to make a fool of a cop is all that the mystery novel detective has to do to make himself a hero. (I know, I promised to lay off the psychology stuff. I just tossed this in for free. *You* take it up from there.)

The cop, regardless of rank, is the fall guy. He's the sand in the crank case, the worm in the apple, and the flea in the eye of the amateur or professional detective who finally brings the killer to justice.

(This makes for good reading, but not for realism. If you've ever known any policemen, you'll know right away what I mean. Whether he's a uniformed guy pounding a beat, or head of a big city homicide bureau, he's probably smart, fast-moving, quick-thinking, and honest. Oh sure, there are exceptions, but not many. You may read all the mystery novels published, and chuckle over the way the police are shown up to be a bunch of dopey-joes, but—if somebody kidnaps your child, or steals your car, or shoots your butler, what do you do? You call a cop. Chances are he brings back your child, finds your stolen car, and gets you another butler.)

There is the situation of the innocent bystander who has (1) incriminating papers, (2) stolen property, (3) a corpse he has to dispose of in a hurry. Naturally he has a *terrible* time, and everything goes wrong.

There is the combining of fabulous, wonderful, and incredible characters who cook, paint pictures, keep pet mice, collect woodcarvings, or indulge in such mild hobbies as kleptomania or dipsomania. If the writer gets enough of such characters into one story, the reader will ultimately get so confused that he won't even care who committed the crime. In a case like this, it's a pretty safe bet that the author didn't care either.

And we mustn't forget the situation of the frightened young female alone in a dark and dreary house where a murder was committed twenty-two years before. This is one of the best of the available situations. She's rented the house, you understand, because she's tired, run-down, overworked—she's going mad, *mad*, MAD, listening to those adding machines all day and going home every night to her lonely little room, with her memories of the man she loved and left for the noblest and most spiritual reasons. The man who will, ultimately, meet her—by a curious coincidence—in that dark and dreary house. A dusty old corpse, in which neither of them has the slightest personal interest, lies between them on the hand-hewn floor.

It's been many years since they met. They have much to talk about. But first, they have to remove the corpse—a tiresome and unpleasant task. They mutter sweet nothings to each other as they drag him out to the old boneyard, which providentially came with the house. She knows that he left her to marry the other girl. But he explains to her—it was simply that the other girl had money. Unfortunately, he had been forced to leave her, due to her incurable habit of nibbling on phosphorent matches, which made her glow in the dark.

Having disposed of the rather tiresome corpse, by the simple process of burying it, they return to the gloomy old mansion. A curious light appears in the windows. Instead of hailing the nearest taxi and driving off to South Bend, this couple explores the house. What do they find? You guess. His first wife, brutally murdered, and stuffed into the grand piano which was out of tune anyway.

At this point, there enters that unbeatable vaudeville team of the shrewd detective and the comic cop.

You finish the story. I can't stand it any longer. I'll tip you off to the ending, though. The gal and the guy turn out to be innocent, and are last seen heading for the nearest marriage license bureau.

Please don't ask me what makes a mystery novel funny. If I knew the formula, I'd mimeograph it, sell it to mystery novel writers, and become the richest woman on earth without doing a lick of work. And wouldn't that be a wonderful way to make a living!

*   *   *

P.S.: No Bibliography included. I can't list *all* the good examples of Humor-in-Homicide, and I have enough enemies already.

Trojan Horse Opera

By Anthony Boucher

An outstanding technical development in the field of crime-mystery-detective fiction during the years of World War II was the flowering of the spy story (modern variety) and its near-relative the novel of suspense. The circumstances and directions of this interesting trend are discussed here by one of the most thoughtful practicing American students of the detective novel. Mr. Boucher is widely known as the author of such diverting whodunits as The Case of the Seven of Calvary *and* The Case of the Baker Street Irregulars; *for the closely-knit "locked-room" stories signed by H. H. Holmes; as a radio writer; and for his valuable and discursive "Department of Criminal Investigation" in the* San Francisco Chronicle, *which in 1946 was awarded the first annual "Edgar" given by Mystery Writers of America Inc., for the best detective story criticism of the previous year.*

THAT GROUP of novels which publishers and librarians bracket as "mysteries" has always been a mixed lot. A "mystery" may be a problem in deduction, a study in criminal psychology, a farce, or a love story. And stories of espionage (and their close relatives, the novels of pure suspense) have always been lumped in as a small part of this heterogeneous collection.

No longer, however, are they a small part. During the war years, the mystery has thrown wide open its gates to the Trojan horse.

I have reviewed mystery novels for the *San Francisco Chronicle* for over three years. Well over one-fourth of those novels have had espionage and/or sabotage as a major element of the plot. At periods the proportion has run as high as a third or even a half of books received.

If the spy story were still what it used to be, this state of affairs would be a major calamity. Only ten years ago, a mystery of any serious literary pretensions might belong to any of the other sub-divisions, but certainly not to the espionage category. Spy stuff meant Oppenheim and Le Queux or at best Van Wyck Mason (without the F.).

At last Ambler came; and from his *Background to Danger* (1937, originally *Uncommon Danger*) we may date the transfiguration of the spy story (though perhaps that transfiguration really began, in another medium, in the film melodramas of Alfred Hitchcock). Ambler showed that human characterization, good prose, political intelligence, and above all a meticulously detailed realism, far from getting in the way of intricate spy adventures, can strengthen them and raise them to a new plane.

Several post-Ambler factors combined to maintain the new high level of espionage. One was the success, outside of the strict mystery market, of such writers as Ethel Vance, Helen MacInnes, and Manning Coles.

Another was the political awareness developed in England after Munich, which led almost every top-flight mystery writer to save the Empire from Fascism by the intervention of his star detective. Margery Allingham's *Traitor's Purse,* Nicholas Blake's *The Smiler with the Knife,* Michael Innes' *The Secret Vanguard* brought to international espionage a literacy and dexterity hitherto lavished on purely private murder. Perhaps the most surprising of these war-time conversions was that of Peter Cheyney, hitherto a mediocre imitator of Hammett, who developed, in such novels as *Dark Duet,* an astonishing ability to make fictional espionage sound as immediate and convincing as the best factual report on the agents of the late Admiral Canaris.

The American spy novel lagged behind the British. One principal cause is readily evident. What brought the British spy story to life was the realization that espionage isn't an exotic diversion involving deftly draped damsels with Lynn Fontanne laughs lolling luringly on the private yacht of the Prince of Ruritania, but a practical commercial pursuit which might penetrate any ordinary humdrum life—particularly yours. It is largely the this-could-happen-to-*me* feeling that gives the new spy novel its impact.

And we in America, up till Pearl Harbor, knew damned well it couldn't happen to us, don't be silly, so why write about it?

But the past three years have closed the gap between British and American endeavors, with David Keith, Richard Lockridge, Helen McCloy, Kenneth Millar, Darwin Teilhet, Robert Terrall, and Mitchell Wilson (to name only a handful) utilizing all the best devices of the new school with the American setting to add immediacy.

Even in other languages, the spy story seems to be booming. Norway offered us a superlative example in Axel Kielland's *Shape of Danger;* Manuel Peyrou and Diego Keltiber write of the Fascist infiltration in South America; and France offers espionage as diverse as the shoddy colportage of Valentin Mandelstamm and the beauty and reality of Joseph Kessel's *Army of Shadows.*

The spy novel, in short, stands now where the strict detective story stood in the late 'twenties. An old-established hack form, it is at last coming into its own under the leadership of a group of writers who know that humor, understanding, humanity, and good prose are not amiss in any form.

Like the mystery novel, the spy story is a literary microcosm. It includes the leisurely literary novel (Michael Innes), the grim hard-boiled school (Peter Cheyney, Charles L. Leonard), the social comedy of manners (Ngaio Marsh), the light adventure farce (Oliver Weld Bayard), and so on down to the purest romantic trash, wherein Cinderella foils the Nazis to get her Prince.

That this flowering of the spy story should come in war time is understandable enough. But why this war should produce such results where the last emphatically did not (perhaps the only satisfactory spy fiction from World War I is Maugham's *Ashenden*— published ten years after the war) is harder to explain.

One reason—perhaps the principal—is the coincidence of the war with a certain stage in the development of mystery fiction. The detective story made its first appeal through the ingenuity of its plot and the eccentricities of its detective. By now all plot-ingenuities seem to have been exhausted (though such rare masters as Carr and Queen can still produce them regularly), and one detective has become painfully like another.

The reading public, satiated with these factors, has come to demand more and more a heightening of the element of pure suspense. For certain minds there can be sufficient suspense to carry them through 80,000 words in the unraveling of a perfect puzzle; but even such minds can find no such satisfaction in the average mystery of today. Like MacLeish's Hamlet, they know the answers —all the answers. It is the question that they want to know; and that question must be something urgent, vital—a matter of life and death to the protagonist, not merely a pretty puzzle.

As that master of suspense, Alfred Hitchcock, says in the introduction to his recent anthology of *Suspense Stories:*

> This difference [between the pure suspense story and the element of suspense necessary to all narration] lies in the fact that Suspense is here accompanied by Danger—danger mysterious and unknown, if possible. Or, if the danger is known—then as inexorable or as insurmountable peril as may be imagined.

Obviously such inexorable and insurmountable peril can most readily be achieved within the framework of an espionage story. In a private murder, your hero is pitted only against a single antagonist, however sinister; in a story of criminal warfare, only against a limited gang. But the protagonist who is a spy, counter-spy, or Underground agent must face the combined forces of an entire nation or Axis of nations. His enemies are unknown; the parish priest or the Fuller brush man is equally apt to be his deadly destroyer.

A few writers have developed the suspense aspect of the mystery story without recourse to international implications. Notably Elisabeth Sanxay Holding and Cornell Woolrich (and/or William Irish) have achieved effects of suspenseful terror which any spy practitioner might envy. The trend is undoubtedly growing—its influence appears in such relatively "straight" detective writers as Anthony Gilbert. Now that the end of the war has made the spy story nominally less topical (I have, for instance, had stories about *Nach Niederlage* German activities rejected as "not entertainment"; whereas the activities of wartime Nazis apparently were entertaining in the extreme), there will doubtless be much further development of this privately motivated suspense story. But where the spy writer found the reader already prepared to shudder at the menace presented, only a writer as skilful as a Holding or a Woolrich can attain the same effect with a freshly-created, small-scale situation.

What the future of the spy story is may be debated. It is at least likely that readers, as well as reviewers, are fed up with the intrusion of the spy element into the routine detective story—the sort of thing in which the munitions magnate, apparently murdered by one of his heirs for good oldfashioned profit, was really assassinated by the secretary who had one German grandmother and is therefore obviously a Nazi agent. (For a fine variation, see Mrs. Christie's *The Patriotic Murders.*)

More and more, in peace time, the spy story proper will probably be subordinated to the private suspense story. Already, for instance, Mitchell Wilson has abandoned espionage to write, in *None So Blind,* what he calls a straight novel, but what is simply an application of the mystery-suspense technique to a situation of purely personal emotions.

The books that still treat directly of spies will probably move further and further away from the whodunit, subordinating the mystery-detection-surprise element (rarely too strong in them) to study of character, the mechanics of intrigue, and pure suspense. Michael Hardt's *A Stranger and Afraid* and Katherine Roberts' *Private Report* have already exemplified what is not so much a spy novel as a novel which happens to have a spy as protagonist.

Whatever its future, the new spy novel seems to be second only to the personal narrative as the characteristic fresh development in letters of World War II; and it has shown possibilities as the most effectively pamphleteering form of popular fiction. One can already envisage the future Ph.D. dissertations on *The Espionage Novel of the 1940's, with special reference to* . . .

For one generation's meat is the next generation's kitchen midden; and those future literary archeologists may find the new spy novel by no means the least enlightening of our remains.

Afternote: I seem to have discussed exclusively the spy novel, with almost no reference to espionage in the mystery short story. The omission is of no consequence. All that needs to be said about the spy short has been said superlatively well by Vincent Starrett in his anthology *World's Great Spy Stories* (Forum, 1944).

Dagger of the Mind
By James Sandoe

That the roads to mystery are many and varied has been more than hinted at in this chapter. In the selection just preceding, Mr. Boucher has ably analyzed the nature and relationships of the spy story and what we call the suspense or pursuit story. Close kin to the latter, but less external, more interior in its workings, is the modern tale of terror, often termed the "psychological thriller" (with what accuracy Mr. Sandoe will determine). One of the most fascinating mutations of the crime-detective novel in recent years— and one of its most promising avenues for the future—this new, yet old, addition to the genre is examined by Mr. Sandoe in a brilliant and penetrating piece of contemporary scholarship. A member of the bibliography and English faculties at the University of Colorado, James Sandoe has won increasing respect in recent years as a critic and chronicler of modern literature, with special attention to crime and police fiction. The selection which represents him here was originally delivered as an invitation lecture in the Modern Arts Series sponsored by Poetry Magazine *and was subsequently reprinted, in the present condensation, in that journal for June 1946.*

I

I MAY AS WELL confess at the outset that through the course of my remarks I am going to pay very little attention to the philological distinction between the word "terror" and the word "horror." There is a perfectly clear distinction between them: terror is intense fear or dread and horror is the same fear or dread mingled with repugnance or loathing. Horror is the more complex emotion and, presumably, the more overwhelming. And, unlike fear, it is an emotion that cannot be felt persistently. Fear's keen knife may cut and cut insatiably; it is a delicate torture at its most refined, and never more agonizing than when we invent it in our minds for use upon ourselves. Horror may recur but it cannot be sustained; it dulls the senses. And very few writers have attempted successfully to sustain horror without relief. It is too anesthetic. For my purposes here, horror and terror, while not synonymous are good companions and any attempt to do without either or devote ourselves to one makes for distinctions refined beyond use.

The varieties of literary experience are nearly infinite. The subjects about which books may be written are incredibly numerous and the treatment of any one subject is staggeringly diverse. Even within a relatively small range diversity is often very great. One speaks of the detective story as if it were a plain enough fact. But within the detective story there is exceedingly various company and the detective story, after all, has one exceedingly important physical limitation. It must pose a question (whodunit?) and it must answer that question. It may do so as plainly as a jigsaw puzzle or it may deck its puzzle out in the most infinite furbelows of character and atmosphere and setting. Its variety is great, but its variety is of decoration rather than of structure—and this is so even when it stands on its head and tells the story of a murderer rather than the story of his detection.

The horror story ranges more freely because horror imposes no structure but rather an emotion, a feeling. And there is no retreat, however sheltered, to which horror may not penetrate. We find it in the newspapers, called tragedy. A child crushed by a truck or dismembered by a madman. The most placid and contented of households obliterated at Sunday dinner by a falling airplane. Horror "has no limit nor is circumscribed within one place."

A good many writers, from Coleridge to Edmund Wilson, have tried to discover the reason why men engage in what Dorothy Sayers calls "the art of self-tormenting" by reading horror stories. Their explanations are all valid in some degree. But none seems sufficient to explain the cause or the effect of the diversity of horrors which literature contains.

II

Perhaps the first sort of tale which the phrase "horror story" brings to mind is the story of the supernatural. Stories of witchcraft, of evil fairies, of vampires and werewolves, of ghosts and all the array of the kingdom of evil to the Prince of Darkness himself. These are all ancient conceptions and most of them were serving writers and readers admirably some centuries ago. Christopher Marlowe transformed a wandering German legend into a play whose ultimate physical horror was the palpable rending of Faustus by a host of demons; but its most horrible lines are still the infinitely despairing confession of Mephistopheles. He has been goaded by Faustus' skeptical curiosity to tell him something of the nature of Hell:

> *F.* How comes it then that thou art out of hell?
> *M.* Why, this is Hell, nor am I out of it.
>   Think'st thou that I, who saw the face of God
>   Am not tormented with ten thousand hells
>   In being deprived of everlasting bliss?

The torture of Mephistopheles is a torment of the mind, more racking than torment of his body.

The story of the supernatural, despite our pride in skepticism, has by no means vanished from the earth. We can still find a very genuine pleasure in horror when, lending ourselves to an author's wiles, we settle down to read a tale of the impossible.

Unfortunately, however, the old formulae lack novelty. The first ghost we meet, and the first vampire, are far more terrifying than the second and the third. The whole machinery of ghosts and poltergeists is nearly bound to be fascinating when one meets it first. But, this first acquaintance over, the novelty vanishes and it is only a very skillful artist or juggler who can make the now familiar impossibilities immediate. Custom "makes it an easiness" in us.

Only a very few of the writers who have conjured up supernatural horrors can, in the end, be relied upon to horrify us at all. And of them the older masters, while we may bow in theory to their enterprise, seem often more laborious than effective. Of the acknowledged masters of the more conventional story of the supernatural, I find few as steadily palatable as M. R. James, the Cambridge don who found horrid, possessive creatures in cloistered studies, in Canon Alberic's scrapbook, in an old mezzotint. Part of James' lingering effectiveness lies, I think, in the half-jocular mode of his tale-telling. The stories of Sheridan Le Fanu, the master he acknowledged, are only rarely as satisfying. And this, I think, is because they are wordy. Le Fanu is usually laboring meticulously toward a discovery we have made for ourselves before in other pages. And when his characters suffer blankly through ten thousand words at the end of which they come, thunderstruck, upon a vampire, the reader—already acquainted with vampires—will have written them off as blockheads for their delay.

Still, among Le Fanu's tales there are a few which seem perennially capable of shocking us *(Madam Crowl's Ghost, Mr. Justice Harbottle* are two) and from the history of the tale of terror a good many more have been plucked by anthologists of varying tastes. In every collection are a few stories capable of affecting all but the most obdurate reader. And for this reason I do not believe we can allow Edmund Wilson's contention that the ghost story is "an obsolete form . . . killed by the electric light," capable of flourishing only during the era of candle light and merely surviving the hot glare of gas light. Here, as elsewhere, Mr. Wilson's insistence is more arbitrary than thoughtful. The electric light has been turned on, without question; but like the radio it can be turned off.

Still, I was for a time inclined to agree with Julius Fast who, in presenting his collection of fantastic stories, *Out of This World,* observed that he had omitted all ghost stories "because long ago the last original ghost plot was hashed to death along with vampires and werewolves. . . . We can use them to scare children but all too often their only response in an adult audience is half-amused tolerance."

But *Out of This World* disproves this very contention. Its first story is John Collier's *Evening Primrose,* a haunting and very nasty little ghost story indeed. To be sure, Collier never calls them ghosts. And he sets his tale in the bustling coziness of a huge department store—sets it there after closing hours, from dusk to dawn, and peoples it with a hierarchy of bloodless, transparent creatures that once were men but who are certainly now ghosts in what is unquestionably a new ghost story and a lingeringly horrid one.

Writers themselves have seemed to feel the limitations of the old machinery. Late in the nineteenth century and with the earlier stirrings of the science of psychology, writers began to forego the palpable and horrid creatures of ancient legend for the impalpable monsters which are the products of the mind.

For horror, as we have said, is by no means confined to supernatural creatures, solid or impalpable. Horror, especially physical horror, is a part of a great many novels which have nothing to do with fantasy, and during the past year we have seen pictorial evidence of physical horror on a scale so tremendous that it cannot be grasped. Indeed, I wonder whether any of the older horrors—mere vampires and warlocks—can remain horrible in the flash of the atomic bomb. And I wonder even more whether the thoughtful reader can find imaginary terrors—these witches and demons—half as shocking as he could before he saw the pictures of Belsen and Dachau. For of all the horrors, the most horrifying still is the most obvious one of all, the most evident, the most widespread—the horror of man's inhumanity to man.

III

My concern here, though, is the innocently calculated horror of the storyteller, especially with what is known as the "psychological horror story" or the "psychological thriller." According to Anthony Boucher, the "psychological thriller" is primarily a gleam in a publisher's eye.

Publishers love detective stories because they have a basement of sales. That is the blessing and the curse of the detective story as an article of merchandise. Rental libraries are so many and their readers so hungry that almost any detective story, good or bad, will sell automatically at least fifteen hundred copies, whereas a straight novel, even a good one, may sell as few as two hundred.

But if mysteries in their original editions have a basement of sales, they have a ceiling of sales as well. Mysteries comprise about a fourth of all the fiction published in this country; but it is a rare mystery that sells more than, say, fifteen thousand copies. The public is enormously fond of mystery stories but it rents or borrows them; it doesn't buy them. This is true, I have no doubt, because of some lingering feeling that they are not absolutely respectable, and partly from the easy view that when you've read one, when you've discovered the name of the murderer, the story is finished forever, and need never be looked at again.

Now a publisher with a promising manuscript—a manuscript, say, like Margaret Millar's *The Iron Gates*—will naturally hesitate to call it a detective story and so, almost infallibly, limit its sales. Random House called *The Iron Gates* "a psychological novel" and from the evidences of its advertising, must have sold a good many more copies than would have been sold without such merchandising.

But if the "psychological thriller" is a publisher's device, it is also a phrase that appears to have a meaning of some sort for critics and readers as well. Psychology is the science which explores the mind. A thriller, in its broadest sense, is any tale bent on describing and transmitting excitement. Some sort of definition might be hammered out from this pair, but it would describe astonishingly few of the many novels which have been called "psychological thrillers." The phrase is imposing, it makes a show of being scientific and hence serious, and it is fashionable. It is as fashionable as the phrase "Gothick tale" was a hundred years ago. Now the "psychological thriller" is the contemporary manifestation of the Gothic tale, and they are both much more accurately, if less impressively, described simply as tales of terror.

The psychological thriller need not be regarded as a kind of special development of the detective story. But it tends to be regarded so just the same. And I am willing enough to seize this as a convenience. Certainly, within the range of the detective story there is more than enough matter for discussion.

In a sense every detective story must, at least in theory, be a psychological novel because it must, at the last, explain why one man's mind was bent away from the horror or the fear of killing long enough to commit murder in spite of the great personal and social barriers against it. And rarely one finds a detective story which manages an analysis of motive in a manner more than merely perfunctory.

The first step from the conventional detective story toward a psychological thriller might be the sort of step which Freeman Wills

Crofts took when he first forsook the dry time-table sort of tale for which he is best known, to write his story as the murderer knew it. Nobody is normally less concerned with fine-spun analysis of criminal motives than Mr. Crofts. His particular genius is the meticulous piecing together of a literary jigsaw. This was true of his first novel, *The Cask,* in 1920, and has been true of most of its successors. All of his energies are bent toward discovering the identity and the means of the criminal; and when the flaw in the time-table has been discovered the criminal's alibi is broken and there is little time left to explore the motive for his murder. Mr. Crofts tacks on any one of the acceptable, standard brands—fear, revenge, gain—and lets it go at that.

But Crofts has written another sort of detective story. The sort which Howard Haycraft calls the "inverted" detective story, the story of a crime told before its solution. (When Dostoievski wrote *Crime and Punishment,* critics were content to call it a novel, but since the advent of the detective story, a naggingly various form, critical terminology has become much more meticulous.)

In *Willful and Premeditated,* Crofts set himself to tell first the account of the slow growth of the idea of murder in the mind of Charles Swinburn, his preparations and his success and his failure to escape detection. Here Crofts began with motive and here, for once, detection is as much compressed as motive had been in his earlier novels. Financial trouble, an ill-advised passion for a disagreeable female, sympathy for his workmen in the plant and irritation at his useless, rich, suspicious uncle combine to suggest murder and to make it breed. The novel is meticulously cumulative and thoroughly absorbing. Absorbing most of all because we share in the struggle which goes on within the mind of the wretched protagonist.

Thus Freeman Wills Crofts has written the tale of detection at its most dryly calculated and has taken a first step toward the psychological thriller as it explores the mind of a murderer. Of course he was by no means the first to do so. The struggle is nearly as old as man and its chroniclers have been multitudinous:

> Art thou not, fatal vision, sensible
> To feeling as to sight? or art thou but
> A dagger of the mind, a false creation,
> Proceeding from the heat-oppressed brain?

The Thane of Cawdor strides gigantically and piteously among the company.

Even among contemporary detective story writers, Crofts was by no means the first to deal at length with the mind of the murderer; nor is he the most considerable, if we recall only Francis Iles and Richard Hull among the others.

Lately, though, there has been an increasing tendency on the part of writers to explore more morbid states of the murderous mind. From relatively simple aberration they venture into conditions of mind still further from the norm, into the twisting ways of psychopathology.

A very striking example of this is Patrick Hamilton's tale of a schizophrenic, *Hangover Square; or, The Man With Two Minds.* This is the unhappy history of George Bone, caught by his own inanition, snarled hopelessly in his dull passion for a selfish, useless, beautiful little slut, and dragged down by his own goaded madness. George's two minds are the mind of the tongueless and loutish lover, and the other, the schizophrenic mind in revolt which has two perfectly clear objectives: to kill Netta and to go to the childish memory of a haven at Maidenhead. He goes there at last, having killed Netta and her most obnoxious lover and then finds that Maidenhead is no Nirvana. So, his two minds satisfied at last that they cannot find satisfaction, he turns on the gas.

Patrick Hamilton tells his story subjectively. We see Earl's Court (Hangover Square) through one or the other of George's two minds. Hamilton has ventured from the cool objectivity of the psychiatrist's study inside the mind of his patient. And in the fullest, most genuine sense of the term this is a psychological thriller, an anatomy of madness. But when the last page has been turned it is still, as well, the story of Hangover Square and its vicious, idle coterie of parasites—the company the wretched George has fallen into, the company to which he has been chained by his love and hate for Netta.

Hangover Square is far more genuinely a psychological thriller than a good many other novels which have been given the name. One other sort, in particular, has been given the name and a good deal of admiring attention recently. This other sort may be said to operate on the eat-your-cake-and-have-it-too plan. Its most spectacular exponent is Mrs. Margaret Millar who began a few years ago writing detective stories in which the sleuth was a psychiatrist, and who more recently has written two novels, both very highly praised, which attempt to combine the fascination of a clinical history with the charms of a detective story and its last minute surprise.

In *Wall of Eyes,* Mrs. Millar concerns herself with an oddly sorted household dominated by a blind and vindictive younger sister who holds her power by holding the family purse-strings. To be sure, this presumed an unsympathetic limpness on the part of her victims—the father, drained by his wife; the housekeeper-sister; the simple, hulking brother; the young and sensitive pianist—but Mrs. Millar's skill mitigated this in part. The blind tyrant is murdered and the ultimate object of the tale is the object of any detective story: to uncover the murderer.

But the method of the narrative is to present the tale through the perceptions of its characters and obviously, if she is to keep her murderer a secret, Mrs. Millar must at the same time lose her richest opportunity for exploring the murderer's mind. She must so sharply select his thoughts that she presents him piecemeal until, after all, it appears that what we have had is not a psychological study but some exceedingly adept sleight-of-hand. We have been in the fairly improbable position of sharing a murderer's mind fully, except for what after all must be occupying most of it—the matter of murder itself.

Mrs. Millar's latest novel, *The Iron Gates,* uses the same technique. Once more she is dealing with an uneasily ingrown family. At first the narrative is directed chiefly through the consciousness of Lucille Morrow, second wife of a distinguished gynecologist whose first wife has been hacked to death some years earlier while returning from an evening at her successor's house. The author establishes very deftly the pride of the second Mrs. Morrow in her possession of her husband, marks easily her humorous tyranny over him and the enmity felt toward her by her two stepchildren. And then, suddenly, after a ragged stranger's visit to deliver a box, Lucille disappears. Later she is found, raving. The second part of the novel describes her short stay behind the iron gates—the protecting gates—of Penwood asylum. But the gates are not impregnable, and Lucille's overwhelming fear that she will be murdered (why she fears we do not know; we share her fear but not its source) drives her to suicide. The third part of the novel is the unraveling, the diagnosis of madness and of murder's motive. Once more Mrs. Millar's concern has been to observe the workings of the terrified mind. But she has insisted, as well, upon hiding the causes of the terror so that she can surprise us at the last. And because of this, it would be a good deal more accurate to call her novel not a psychological novel but a tale of terror. For as a psychological study it is, by its own limitations, necessarily superficial.

Mrs. Millar is one of several younger writers who have given a new and various life to that sort of tale of terror which was for so long bogged in the celebrated Had-I-But-Known morass. The shrinking heroine of *The Mysteries of Udolpho* uttered that unfashionable phrase in spirit if not in fact. And a century and a half of shrinking heroines have echoed it, especially since the building of *The Circular Staircase,* with resounding silliness.

Occasionally there is a writer—like Lenore Glen Offord—who can make sense of the old formula by the simple application of taste and good sense. Her *Skeleton Key* is an excellent example of a self-respecting tale in the old tradition. And before her emotion became as overblown as her later settings, Mabel Seeley was a memorable writer of this sort. More exotic variations have been performed by Dorothy B. Hughes whose best novels—*The Blackbirder, The Delicate Ape*—are superlatively skillful tales of pursuit and escape; by Elisabeth Sanxay Holding in her stories of half-understood horrors viewed in a nightmare of uncertainties. The list might be extended by many names but this is enough to suggest the variety and the rich promise of the form.

All of these writers are concerned, if very differently, with the tale of terror; but their methods are nearly as diverse as their capacities. Cornell Woolrich is in some ways the most superb and garish literary juggler of the lot and his special capacity has been to perform a series of variations on what will be remembered as the puzzle of the vanishing lady.

You will recall the story of the girl and her mother who arrived in Paris one afternoon during the year of the Exposition, went to a crowded hotel and were assigned to different rooms, whereupon the mother vanished as completely as if she had never existed while all the world seemed bent upon denying to the frantic girl that she had ever existed.

The theme is common property and its variations nearly as many as those of the equally celebrated puzzle of the locked room. The essence of this sort of tale is the discovery of the inexplicable within the circle of the ordinary. One of Cornell Woolrich's most facile variations was the one he called *Phantom Lady* and published under the name of William Irish.

Woolrich has sought and found terror not where one has been led to expect it—in the graveyard at midnight, in the deserted-haunted house—but in the streets of the city. He shows fear stalking the subway and walking along Broadway, fear all the more striking for making its way boldly through crowds in the light of day.

But while his skill in contriving variations is staggering, his stories are inclined in retrospect to seem more than a little absurd. To seem, that is, as staged as they are. Woolrich has a facility for catching the reader's attention with a striking situation and then bustling him from shock to shock with a kind of numbing swiftness. The mere facility is apparent only after the last page has been turned and then if one is so unwise as to glance back, the tale itself vanishes into incredibility, very much as Eurydice vanished when Orpheus forsook his vow and turned to look at her before she crossed the threshold of Hell.

And very much the same thing is true of a good many of the tales of espionage that have been published in such quantity during the last five years. The spy story had languished in the doldrums for a good many years when Eric Ambler gave it a fresh wind. The spy story flourishes on his account—and on the more obvious account of war—but its really successful practitioners are still very few.

Eric Ambler took over the form in a sad state of disrepair. Buchan had forsaken it, largely, and the heavy dominance of E. Phillips Oppenheim had grown excessively tedious. Ambler took the spy story by the scruff of its well-washed neck, whipped the monocle out of its astonished eye and pushed it down among people, away from the world of diplomatic mummies. One of his earliest novels, *Epitaph for a Spy,* has as its hero a most unheroic young Czech teacher of languages on vacation in a small Mediterranean fishing village. He is not sleek and polished and experienced, but diffident and frightened and bewildered; as a man without a country, as a stranger among unconcerned and unsympathetic foreign laws, he must become, however unwillingly, a catspaw for the police as they reach for the real spy. The real spy, once discovered, is equally unheroic and his epitaph is a shabby little phrase and a very revealing one: "He needed the money." Maugham's *Ashenden* knew this twenty years before, but he was unique.

Ambler brought to the spy story, with this new realism, a literacy that nobody had bothered to expend on it for years. He brought as well a political awareness before it was fashionable, and I trust that he will maintain it in his later novels when that now fashionable awareness has faded away as it seems already to be fading.

Equally unheroic is the almost anonymous protagonist (he is called only D.) of Graham Greene's novel, *The Confidential Agent,* which as far surpasses Eric Ambler's admirable tales in skill and in depth as Ambler's tales surpass the laborious scintillation of Oppenheim. *The Confidential Agent* is a study of fear and defeat. It is not Greene's best novel but it is a fine and a sensitive one. Its protagonist, D., has been a professor of Romance languages in a Spanish university; he is a scholar of some renown and we see him, landing in England from his war-torn country, on a mission for the Loyalists. He is middle-aged and he has suffered, with a people, such racking agonies, physical and spiritual, that he has only one emotion left —fear. "One of the things which danger does to you after a time is—well, to kill emotion. I don't think I shall ever feel anything again except fear."

His duty in England is to buy coal. "If Lord Benditch chose to sell his coal at a price they were able to pay, they could go on for years; if not, the war might be over before the spring." He is a lonely man in a hostile world. "Danger was part of him. It wasn't like your overcoat you sometimes left behind; it was your skin. You died with it; only corruption stripped it from you. The person you trusted was yourself."

He can trust no one, depend upon no one but himself. Therefore he has no faith in the whimsical if friendly gesture of the peer's loud daughter. And he manages only after a series of agonizing doubts to believe in the honesty of a hotel slavey to whom he trusts

his papers out of necessity. When he has found her faithful, his enemies among his friends push her out of a window and he is alone
again.

On its physical plane, the action in *The Confidential Agent* is as
rapid and as brutal as it is in Ambler's *Journey into Fear*. Where
Greene's novel surpasses Ambler's is in its brooding speculation and
in its intellectual analysis of fear, in its remorseless exploration of
human selfishness, and in D.'s bleak mistrust of man and of himself.
D.'s story, for all that he has found a limited faith at the last and is
no longer quite alone, is a profoundly depressing exploration of
man's insensitivity, of man's brutality and greed and preoccupation
with himself.

With all this, it is more hopeful than an earlier and a more ambitious novel which I should like to use as my text of the ultimate
horror. We have come a considerable distance away from the ghosts
and the goblins, the things that go bump in the night. The devil in
the bottle is a futile and comic little monster when the magazine
beside it shows the bodies piled high at Belsen and the impassive
face of the young monster who tortured them.

But I see a horror even beyond this intentional sadism. It is the
unintentional sadism of the passive, the horrifying spectacle not of
slaughtered innocents but of preoccupied innocence. And this is a
horror ruthlessly observed in Graham Greene's appalling novel,
Brighton Rock.

Brighton Rock is the story of Pinkie, the Kid, the precocious head
of a gang at Brighton. Its plot is an assembly of violence. The gang
kills a reporter who was involved with a rival gang in the murder of
their own former leader. When a member of his own gang threatens
to turn informer through fear, Pinkie shoves him over a rickety
banister and breaks his neck. Pinkie himself dies hideously, his face
splashed with vitriol and his body broken from a fall over a cliff.

But the physical violence, terrible as it is, is only the shadow of
the violence within the boy's twisted mind. It is a mind ruled by
fear: by the fear of sinking back into the slum he remembers with
loathing, by the fear of women, and his loathing of what those same
slums have taught him of sex, by fear of being caught and hanged.
In spite of his loathing, he marries a blindly adoring little waitress
to shut her mouth because she is able to witness against him. She

sees nothing of his motive and scrapes up a dream from the penny romances, a dream of which he is the hero. In her access of happiness she says, "Life's not so bad." "Don't you believe it," he answers, "I'll tell you what it is. It's jail, it's not knowing where to get some money. Worms and cataract, cancer. . . . It's dying slowly."

And at the end, racked by his death but proud and hopeful because she is carrying his child, she walks back to her shabby room to play the record he has made for her on Brighton pier, her gift from him. And so, Greene says as the novel concludes, "She walked rapidly in the June sunlight toward the worst horror of all." For we have heard him as he made the record, his frantic, bitter virginity crying out desperately. And the message she will hear is his agonized cry against her, "God damn you, you little bitch, why can't you go back home forever and let me be?"

Pinkie's mind is as vicious as the little razor blade he can fit under his thumbnail to slash his enemies. Greene shows it to us in a hundred different aspects and against the flyblown grubby setting of raucous piers and grand hotels and shallow, selfish people bent on mindless fun and games. He shows Pinkie's mind taking a malicious delight in friendly farewells as he escorts the craven Spicer to the racetrack where he expects Spicer to be cut to death; and he shows Pinkie's mind, shocked and hurt, when his body bleeds from slashes dealt out impartially to the lamb and his shepherd by the rival gang; he shows Pinkie's mind writhing in torment at the drink and at the flesh he must meet in his race away from fear. But behind Pinkie's mind are the place and the people who have twisted it.

And there is a kind of compassion for Pinkie in the view of the larger greed, the enormous, inanimate selfishness of society which has spawned this mad little mind. For there is something even more horrible in the viciousness of inanition than in the calculated viciousness of the man who sets out to do wrong, taking pleasure in it. The real villain of *Brighton Rock* is not Pinkie, nasty as he is, but mankind which has let him become so.

Once more, set the gnarled imaginings of the writer of ghost stories against the gnarled realities of our society, and the real, the ultimate horror is always the horror of man's inhumanity to man.

Clues

By Marie F. Rodell

Whether the writing of whodunits—or, for that matter, any kind of writing—can ever be successfully taught is a moot question. Nonetheless, in a form as technically exacting as mystery fiction, an understanding of the basic problems of craftsmanship can be helpful to the beginner. The most useful handbook on the subject to date is Marie F. Rodell's Mystery Fiction: Theory & Technique *(New York:Duell, Sloan & Pearce, 1943). Presently editor of Duell, Sloan & Pearce's "Bloodhound Mysteries," Mrs. Rodell was previously associated with the house of Morrow, has written* Grim Grow the Lilacs *and other whodunits under the pen-name of Marion Randolph, and has lectured on the theory and practice of mystery fiction at New York University. The chapter on clues, reprinted here from her book by special permission, will be no less engrossing to the mystery addict as a conducted behind-the-scenes tour than to the neophyte writer for its practical hints.*

CLUES ARE the traces of guilt which the murderer leaves behind him. Whether they are tangible, material things, like a button torn off at the scene of the crime; or personal traces like footprints or fingerprints; or whether they are intangible habit patterns or character traits, they are the signposts leading detective and reader in the right—or sometimes wrong—direction.

A clue is seldom in itself a proof of guilt. It is the deductions which the detective makes from it which are significant; it is because of these deductions, and where they lead him, that eventually that button may prove the murderer's undoing.

A good clue, then, is one which does in fact point in the right direction, but which seems at first to point in the wrong direction, to mean something other than it does, or to point nowhere at all.

The tangible clues are those actual objects the forgetful murderer leaves behind him, and any other things which can be detected by any of the senses. A scent of a particular perfume, a tune whistled at a significant moment, a strange taste to a bit of food, or something odd about the texture of a cloth or leather—these may all be clues. Only one thing is required of them: that they be such that they can adequately be described in words. The reader sees, hears, tastes, smells or feels these clues only as they are described to him. A whiff of perfume must be characterized if it is to mean anything to the reader, who cannot smell it from the page: it may be pungent, or sickeningly sweet; it may be rose or jasmine or carnation; or, more subtly, it may evoke certain reactions in the detective, which are always the same whenever he smells that particular perfume. In that case, the reader recognizes the recurrence of the clue by the way in which it affects the detective, not by the aroma of the clue itself.

A tune or bit of music can of course be represented on a page in music note form, and most people, even if they cannot read music, will recognize the familiarity of the pattern on the page. But unless one of the characters in the book has a definite reason for putting the notes on paper, this is an unsatisfactory solution. Music, like perfume, can be characterized either by its qualities— its tempo, its pitch, its key, its mood—or by the effect it has on the character hearing it.

In either case, of course, if the clue is not to be elusive in itself, a definite label can be attached. The perfume is recognized as Chanel Number 5, or the tune is an old French folk song.

Something more may be deduced from such clues, however. Perfume is a personal thing; the same woman does not wear light, flower-bouquet scents, and perfumes heavy with chypre or musk. A man with a basso profundo cannot convincingly sing an air written for a soprano—in the proper key, that is.

So too with the clues depending on taste and touch. The actual qualities may be described—salty, sweet, bitter, sour, burnt; or rough, smooth, silky, uneven, bristly—or the reaction to taste and touch may be given.

If the tangible clue is to be used as a factor of mystification in itself—if it is to be a clue whose function is not immediately apparent—great care must be given the description of it. A bit of metal, a splinter of wood, a scrap of cloth, a sliver of glass or a fragment of stone must be accurately described to the reader, as the detective sees and feels it; its color, shape, weight, condition of wear and, when possible, the way in which it has become a fragment—by breaking, by cutting, by burning, by tearing, etc. If the detective does not know what the function of the scrap may be, the reader then has as great an opportunity to deduce it for himself as has the detective. It goes without saying, however, that no important clue of this nature must have a function so obscure or unusual that the average reader knows little more about it after it is explained than before. If the function of the scrap is unusual, then ample provision must be made for a description of that function under some other guise, so that the reader may spot it.

Thus, if the sliver of glass is from a shattered light bulb, if the bit of metal is the tip of a carving knife, if the splinter of wood comes from an umbrella shaft, and the fragment of stone from a statuette, the reader may be expected to have sufficient knowledge to deduce the function of the scrap for himself. But if the metal is the screw from a highly technical machine, the reader cannot be expected to recognize it—unless the machine is elsewhere in the book described to the reader. In the same way, if the music clue had been presented in notes, and its significance lay in the fact that it came from a Mozart sonata, the average reader would not be able to deduce the significant factor for himself.

The clues which the murderer leaves behind him in the nature of fingerprints, footprints, blood stains, sweat or saliva stains, indications of height or weight, bits of hair or skin or nail, are, on the contrary, clues whose significance the reader cannot be expected to deduce for himself. Such clues are subject to analysis and classification in the police laboratory, and it is the findings which the technician makes, and which of course must be reported to the reader, on which reader and detective will base their conclusion. The over-elaborate use of such clues is apt to turn the mystery into a spectator sport; the ultra-scientific detective has his reader at such a great disadvantage, that the reader can only wonder and admire, without participating, for a large part of the story.

All such tangible clues may be significant in still another way, however. Their absence or their displacement may be more significant than their character. The classic expression of this is, of course, in the famous words of Sherlock Holmes:

"I would call your attention to the curious incident of the dog in the night-time."

"The dog did nothing in the night-time."

"That was the curious incident."

Thus, to transpose this into other terms, the lack of footprints in an area of soft ground around the victim who had met his death by stabbing would be as important a clue as footprints would be, and much more baffling. If the footprints were there, they would be a clue to the identity of the murderer; if the footprints were not there, they would be a clue to the method by which the crime was committed, and therefore, by extension, to the character of the murderer and his identity.

We have already spoken of the reversed clothing in *The Chinese Orange Mystery,* which is an example of a clue by misplacement or disarrangement. A commonplace object might become a clue if it were out of place; a thimble in the breadbox or a loaf of bread in the clothes basket might constitute a clue, not because either thimble or bread had been used as an active means of murder, but because their displacement indicated something out of the ordinary.

Anything may serve as a clue which suits the purpose of the author, provided, as we have said, that its description and function can be made plain to the reader. But certain clues have been used so often and have grown so commonplace that the reader will greet them with a groan. The cigarette butt and handkerchief are the two prime offenders here. But if a new and fresh way can be found of treating them, they are still permissible. Lawrence G. Blochman has shown, for instance, in *See You At The Morgue,* how the trite handkerchief can be given a new function. It is neither the ownership of the handkerchief nor fingerprints on it which constitute the decisive nature of the clue, but the traces of sweat from the murderer's hands. Mr. Blochman, keeping abreast of the times, used here one of the newer discoveries of the scientific laboratory: that sweat and saliva follow the same groupings as blood. It is by an analysis of the sweat on the handkerchief, and not by the handkerchief itself, that the criminal is caught.

The bizarre clue, the exact opposite of the trite clue, is a potential source of delight and bafflement to the reader, but it must be handled with care. Erle Stanley Gardner is perhaps the greatest master of this technique; he has used even so apparently unpromising a thing as the length of a canary's claws (*The Case Of The Canary's Claws*); but the neophyte along this path must be careful to follow Mr. Gardner's footsteps not only in the oddness of his clues, but also in the careful logic which explains them and gives them a function in the solution as important as their oddness warrants.

If such bizarre clues come to an author easily, he should by all means use them, and should capitalize on their oddity by making them extremely important to the course of the story. A truly bizarre and baffling clue used only incidentally in a story is wasteful both of material and effect. But the author whose mind does not run to this sort of thing should not spend his time straining after it; the bizarre clue is one potential element of originality and mystification, but it is far from being the only one; and time and effort spent seeking it had better be applied to more basic elements of the story.

The intangible clues become more and more important in mystery fiction as murderers realize that fingerprints are dangerous and that science can unravel the secrets of even the most unpromising physical clues. Moreover, from the writer's point of view, the tangible clue grows less and less effective as science progresses, for if the laboratory unaided can deduce from a man's pockets where he has lived and what work he has done, too little is left to exercise the deductive capacities of both fictional detective and reader.

Consequently, the intangible or character clue gains in importance. Such clues may be divided roughly into two classifications: those revealing basic character traits, and those having to do with behavior patterns.

Clues to the basic character traits are clues to motive—to the temperamental likelihood or tendency to kill, and to the specific motive involved in the killing. Thus, a detective observing a man kick a dog, slap a child and beat his wife, may deduce that the man has definite sadistic tendencies, and that murder might well be possible to him; while a character who faints at the sight of blood is not apt to have bashed in grandma's head with a blunt instrument. These clues lead from suspect to crime, while the tangible clues lead in general from crime to suspect (though a bloodstain on the coat of a suspect would certainly be a physical clue leading from suspect to crime).

Such broad general traits as sadism or squeamishness do not present any very subtle problem either to detective or author. But the character clues which indicate the suspect's probable attitude toward the victim can be more complex. A man who is jealous of his wife will be more apt to kill her lover than a man indifferent to his wife's behavior; a man who tries to arrange other people's lives for them is more likely to kill out of a rationalized conviction that he is doing good, than one who minds his own business. It is from the actions and words of such suspects, and their behavior toward other characters in the story, that the detective and the reader deduce the probability of motive in the suspect.

The behavior pattern clues can be fun to work with, but they are tricky to present convincingly to a reader. Not so long ago, the New York police included with their description of a man wanted for bank robbery two facts: that he habitually tilted his hat to the right (he preferred his left profile) and that in moments of abstraction, he always took the coins from his pocket and jingled them in his hands. Careful observation of the criminal had shown the police that the man was unable to stop either of these habits, although he knew that he had them. He could not always remember to put his hat on straight, nor to leave the coins in his pocket alone.

Such behavior patterns are difficult to present in mystery fiction, for they put the author in danger of giving the reader a sense of let-down. The reader expects that the criminal will commit as nearly perfect a crime as possible, and that his behavior thereafter will be always purposefully and alertly on guard against observation. If the criminal is caught in the end because he forgets at some moment to be alert, praise for the solution of the mystery cannot fairly go to detective or reader: the solution has depended on a weakness of the murderer's, not on a talent of the detective's.

But such clues can be used to advantage. In the non-formula mystery, particularly the mystery written from the murderer's point of view, such an unconscious behavior pattern can be a very effective means of suspense; reader and murderer struggle through the book to subdue the habit, but a sense of doom hangs over the effort: sooner or later habit will reassert itself.

The effective use of such clues in the regular mystery will depend on their absence or the substitutes for them which the murderer provides. He knows that he must stop tilting his hat to the right; that means that every time he puts it on, he must stop and think for an infinitesimal second—and the reader and the dectice can note that hesitation. Or perhaps he will make doubly sure and go without a hat altogether, though the weather and the occasion demand it. The absence of hat, in that case, might be significant. He is too long accustomed to doing something inconsequential with his hands when he is thinking to be able to hold them still; perhaps he substitutes fiddling with a watchchain. Perhaps he is careful always to put his coins in a coin purse, so they will not be available if his fingers go after them unconsciously; in this case, his hands will go automatically to his pockets before he can remember. Perhaps, more elaborately, he invents a little trap for himself; puts a pin just inside the pocket, which will prick his hand and remind him the habit is dangerous. If the detective observes him prick his finger in such fashion once, he may think nothing of it; but if he sees him do it two or three times, he may wonder why the man does not simply remove the pin.

A great variety of such behavior patterns are available for use by the mystery author, and present a field for novelty which has been little explored. The woman who always gets her lipstick on her teeth might be forced to go without to stop the habit; the man who habitually pulls on the lobe of his ear might have to invent an apparently plausible and temporary reason for it—a shaving cut which requires a bandage, which he may logically touch from time to time, to see if it is in place, and which will remind him not to pull on the ear. The man who always twirls his mustache will shave it off, but he will probably find himself plucking at his upper lip. There are as many variations possible as there are habits.

But the writer's chief problem with clues is apt to be less their nature than the manner of their presentation. If a clue leads directly and unequivocally to the suspect, there is no room left for mystification.

We have already included in this chapter two ways of concealing the significance of a clue: concealing its function, or nature; and distorting or misplacing it. But these are devices of the murderer's, not of the author's.

The author's devices for concealing the significance of a clue are three. He may use the old conjuring technique, and immediately after presentation of the clue introduce a bit of action so exciting and important that the reader forgets all about the casual mention of the clue that went just before. The author is, in other words, distracting the reader's attention at the important moment, as the pretty girl on the other side of the stage distracts the audience's attention from the magician's hands.

Secondly, the author may bury the clue among a number of equally casual things which have no great significance. The inventories of the victim's pockets often hide clues in this fashion: something in a pocket which belongs in a pocket, with the change purse and handkerchief and wallet and keys, is actually significant where these are not. This specific example of hiding is not a very good one, because it has been used too often: readers are accustomed to scanning the inventory with an eagle eye for the significant clue. The same is true of the contents of a purse which spills open accidentally, or of the bottles and jars in a medicine chest, or the papers in a desk. Just the description of a room may do it: among the couches, chairs, tables, bric-a-brac and pictures there may be one small item of importance. Perhaps it is only a small picture of a cat, and the inhabitant of the room has a phobia against cats; perhaps it is a bit of dust under the bed, and the inhabitant is a fanatic housekeeper.

This type of concealment is most effective if used in conjunction with the third method, which is concealing by timing. In this method, the clue and its application are separated by fifty or a hundred pages; put together, the two are significant, but if the reader has forgotten the first one, the second one will mean nothing to him. Thus, in the example given above, if the bit of dust is observed on page five, and the character's passion for cleanliness is shown on pages forty and seventy, what has gone between may make the reader forget that there ever was a bit of dust. Carter Dickson has used this method brilliantly in *The White Priory Murders* with the murder weapon itself.

The Locked-Room Lecture
By *John Dickson Carr*

The "locked-room" puzzle is at once the most fascinating and difficult of detective story themes. Its greatest exponent, indisputably of the present day, possibly of all time, is John Dickson Carr, the brilliant American-born English writer who also signs himself as Carter Dickson. His famous "locked-room lecture," delivered by harrumphing Dr. Gideon Fell in the novel known in England as The Hollow Man *(London: Hamilton, 1935) and in the United States as* The Three Coffins *(New York: Harper, 1935), still stands as the classic exposition of the subject in all its aspects. The chapter which includes the lecture is reproduced here in full, exactly as it appeared in the book. If it moves the reader to hunt out a copy of the original novel for reading or re-reading—what's wrong with that?*

THE COFFEE was on the table, the wine-bottles were empty, cigars lighted. Hadley, Pettis, Rampole, and Dr. Fell sat round the glow of a red-shaded table lamp in the vast, dusky dining-room at Pettis's hotel. They had stayed on beyond most, and only a few people remained at other tables in that lazy, replete hour of a winter afternoon when the fire is most comfortable and snowflakes begin to sift past the windows. Under the dark gleam of armour and armorial bearings, Dr. Fell looked more than ever like a feudal baron. He glanced with contempt at the demi-tasse, which he seemed in danger of swallowing cup and all. He made an expansive, settling gesture with his cigar. He cleared his throat.

"I will now lecture," announced the doctor, with amiable firmness, "on the general mechanics and development of that situation which is known in detective fiction as the 'hermetically sealed chamber.' "

Hadley groaned. "Some other time," he suggested. "We don't want to hear any lecture after this excellent lunch, and especially when there's work to be done. Now, as I was saying a moment ago—"

"I will now lecture," said Dr. Fell, inexorably, "on the general mechanics and development of the situation which is known in detective fiction as the 'hermetically sealed chamber.' Harrumph. All those opposing can skip this chapter. Harrumph. To begin with, gentlemen! Having been improving my mind with sensational fiction for the last forty years, I can say—"

"But, if you're going to analyze impossible situations," interrupted Pettis, "why discuss detective fiction?"

"Because," said the doctor, frankly, "we're in a detective story, and we don't fool the reader by pretending we're not. Let's not invent elaborate excuses to drag in a discussion of detective stories. Let's candidly glory in the noblest pursuits possible to characters in a book.

"But to continue: In discussing 'em, gentlemen, I am not going to start an argument by attempting to lay down rules. I mean to speak solely of personal tastes and preferences. We can tamper with Kipling thus: 'There are nine and sixty ways to construct a murder maze, and every single one of them is right.' Now, if I said that to me every single one of them was equally interesting, then I should be—to put the matter as civilly as possible—a cock-eyed liar. But that is not the point. When I say that a story about a hermetically sealed chamber is more interesting than anything else in detective fiction, that's merely a prejudice. I like my murders to be frequent, gory, and grotesque. I like some vividness of colour and imagination flashing out of my plot, since I cannot find a story enthralling solely on the grounds that it sounds as though it might really have happened. All these things, I admit, are happy, cheerful, rational prejudices, and entail no criticism of more tepid (or more able) work.

"But this point must be made, because a few people who do not like the slightly lurid insist on treating their preferences as rules. They use, as a stamp of condemnation, the word 'improbable.' And thereby they gull the unwary into their own belief that 'improbable' simply means 'bad.'

"Now, it seems reasonable to point out that the word improbable is the very last which should ever be used to curse detective fiction in any case. A great part of our liking for detective fiction is *based* on a liking for improbability. When A is murdered, and B and C are under strong suspicion, it is improbable that the innocent-looking D can be guilty. But he is. If G has a perfect alibi, sworn to at every point by every other letter in the alphabet, it is improbable that G can have committed the crime. But he has. When the detective picks up a fleck of coal dust at the sea-shore, it is improbable that such an insignificant thing can have any importance. But it will. In short, you come to a point where the word improbable grows meaningless as a jeer. There can be no such thing as any probability until the end of the story. And then, if you wish the murder to be fastened on an unlikely person (as some of us old fogies do), you can hardly complain because he acted from motives less likely or necessarily less apparent than those of the person first suspected.

"When the cry of 'This-sort-of-thing-wouldn't-happen!' goes up, when you complain about half-faced fiends and hooded phantoms and blond hypnotic sirens, you are merely saying, 'I don't like this sort of story.' That's fair enough. If you do not like it, you are howlingly right to say so. But when you twist this matter of taste into a rule for judging the merit or even the probability of the story, you are merely saying, 'This series of events couldn't happen, because I shouldn't enjoy it if it did.'

"What would seem to be the truth of the matter? We might test it out by taking the hermetically sealed chamber as an example, because this situation has been under a hotter fire than any other on the grounds of being unconvincing.

"Most people, I am delighted to say, are fond of the locked room. But—here's the damned rub—even its friends are often dubious. I cheerfully admit that *I* frequently am. So, for the moment, we'll all side together on this score and see what we can discover. Why are we dubious when we hear the explanation of the locked room? Not in the least because we are incredulous, but simply because in some vague way we are *disappointed*. And from that feeling it is only natural to take an unfair step farther, and call the whole business incredible or impossible or flatly ridiculous.

"Precisely, in short," boomed Dr. Fell, pointing his cigar, "what O'Rourke was telling us today about illusions that are performed *in real life*. Lord! gents, what chance has a story got when we even jeer at real occurrences? The very fact that they do happen, and that the illusionist gets away with it, seems to make the deception worse. When it occurs in a detective story, we call it incredible. When it happens in real life, and we are forced to credit it, we merely call the explanation disappointing. And the secret of both disappointments is the same—we expect too much.

"You see, the effect is so magical that we somehow expect the cause to be magical also. When we see that it isn't wizardry, we call it tomfoolery. Which is hardly fair play. The last thing we should complain about with regard to the murderer is his erratic conduct. The whole test is, *can* the thing be done? If so, the question of whether it *would* be done does not enter into it. A man escapes from a locked room—well? Since apparently he has violated the laws of nature for our entertainment, then heaven knows he is entitled to violate the laws of Probable Behaviour! If a man offers to stand on his head, we can hardly make the stipulation that he must keep his feet on the ground while he does it. Bear that in mind, gents, when you judge. Call the result uninteresting, if you like, or anything else that is a matter of personal taste. But be very careful about making the nonsensical statement that it is improbable or far fetched."

"All right, all right," said Hadley, shifting in his chair. "I don't feel very strongly on the matter myself. But if you insist on lecturing—apparently with some application to this case—?"

"Yes."

"Then why take the hermetically sealed room? You yourself said that Grimaud's murder wasn't our biggest problem. The main puzzle is the business of a man shot in the middle of an empty street. . . ."

"Oh, that?" said Dr. Fell, with such a contemptuous wave of his hand that Hadley stared at him. "That part of it? I knew the explanation of that as soon as I heard the church bells.—Tut, tut, such language! I'm quite serious. It's the escape from the room that bothers me. And, to see if we can't get a lead, I am going to outline roughly some of the various means of committing murders in locked rooms, under separate classifications. This crime belongs under one of them. It's got to! No matter how wide the variation may be, it's *only* a variation of a few central methods.

"H'mf! Ha! Now, here is your box with one door, one window, and solid walls. In discussing ways of escaping when both door and window are sealed, I shall not mention the low (and nowadays very rare) trick of having a secret passage to a locked room. This so puts a story beyond the pale that a self-respecting author scarcely needs even to mention that there is no such thing. We don't need to discuss minor variations of this outrage: the panel which is only large enough to admit a hand; or the plugged hole in the ceiling through which a knife is dropped, the plug replaced undetectably, and the floor of the attic above sprayed with dust so that no one seems to have walked there. This is only the same foul in miniature. The principle remains the same whether the secret opening is as small as a thimble or as big as a barn door. . . . As to legitimate classification, you might jot some of these down, Mr. Pettis. . . ."

"Right," said Pettis, who was grinning. "Go on."

"First! There is the crime committed in a hermetically sealed room which really is hermetically sealed, and from which no murderer has escaped because no murderer was actually in the room. Explanations:

"1. It is not murder, but a series of coincidences ending in an accident which looks like murder. At an earlier time, before the room was locked, there has been a robbery, an attack, a wound, or a breaking of furniture which suggests a murder struggle. Later the victim is either accidentally killed or stunned in a locked room, and all these incidents are assumed to have taken place at the same time. In this case the means of death is usually a crack on the head—presumably by a bludgeon, but really from some piece of furniture. It may be from the corner of a table or the sharp edge of a chair, but the most popular object is an iron fender. The murderous fender, by the way, has been killing people in a way that looks like murder ever since Sherlock Holmes' adventure with the Crooked Man. The most thoroughly satisfying solution of this type of plot, which includes a murderer, is in Gaston Leroux's *The Mystery of the Yellow Room*—the best detective tale ever written.

"2. It is murder, but the victim is impelled to kill himself or crash into an accidental death. This may be the effect of a haunted room, by suggestion, or more usually by a gas introduced from outside the room. This gas or poison makes the victim go berserk, smash up the room as though there had been a struggle, and die of a knife-slash inflicted on himself. In other variations he drives the spike of the chandelier through his head, is hanged on a loop of wire, or even strangles himself with his own hands.

"3. It is murder, by a mechanical device already planted in the room, and hidden undetectably in some innocent-looking piece of furniture. It may be a trap set by somebody long dead, and work either automatically or be set anew by the modern killer. It may be some fresh quirk of devilry from present-day science. We have, for instance, the gun-mechanism concealed in the telephone receiver, which fires a bullet into the victim's head as he lifts the receiver. We have the pistol with a string to the trigger, which is pulled by the expansion of water as it freezes. We have the clock that fires a bullet when you wind it; and (clocks being popular) we have the ingenious grandfather clock which sets ringing a hideously clanging bell on its top, so that when you reach up to shut off the din your own touch releases a blade that slashes open your stomach. We have the weight that swings down from the ceiling, and the weight that crashes out on your skull from the high back of a chair. There is the bed that exhales a deadly gas when your body warms it, the poisoned needle that leaves no trace, the—

"You see," said Dr. Fell, stabbing out with his cigar at each point, "when we become involved with these mechanical devices we are rather in the sphere of the general 'impossible situation' than the narrower one of the locked room. It would be possible to go on forever, even on mechanical devices for electrocuting people. A cord in front of a row of pictures is electrified. A chessboard is electrified. Even a glove is electrified. There is death in every article of furniture, including a tea-urn. But these things seem to have no present application, so we go on to:

"4. It is suicide, which is intended to look like murder. A man stabs himself with an icicle; the icicle melts; and, no weapon being found in the locked room, murder is presumed. A man shoots himself with a gun fastened on the end of an elastic—the gun, as he releases it, being carried up out of sight into the chimney. Variations of this trick (not locked-room affairs) have been the pistol with a string attached to a weight, which is whisked over a parapet of a bridge into the water after the shot; and, in the same style, the pistol jerked out of a window into a snowdrift.

"5. It is a murder which derives its problem from illusion and impersonation. Thus: the victim, still thought to be alive, is already lying murdered inside a room, of which the door is under observation. The murderer, either dressed as his victim or mistaken from behind for the victim, hurries in at the door. He whirls round, gets rid of his disguise, and instantly comes out of the room *as himself*. The illusion is that he has merely passed the other man in coming out. In any event, he has an alibi; since, when the body is discovered later, the murder is presumed to have taken place some time after the impersonated 'victim' entered the room.

"6. It is a murder which, although committed by somebody outside the room at the time, nevertheless seems to have been committed by somebody who must have been inside.

"In explaining this," said Dr. Fell, breaking off, "I will classify this type of murder under the general name of the Long-Distance or Icicle Crime, since it is usually a variation of that principle. I've spoken of icicles; you understand what I mean. The door is locked, the window too small to admit a murderer; yet the victim has apparently been stabbed from inside the room and the weapon is missing. Well, the icicle has been fired as a bullet from outside—we will not discuss whether this is practical, any more than we have discussed the mysterious gases previously mentioned —and it melts without a trace. I believe Anna Katharine Green was the first to use this trick in detective fiction, in a novel called *Initials Only*.

"(By the way, she was responsible for starting a number of traditions. In her first detective novel, over fifty years ago, she founded the legend of the murderous secretary killing his employer, and I think present-day statistics would prove that the secretary is still the commonest murderer in fiction. Butlers have long gone out of fashion; the invalid in the wheel-chair is too suspect; and the placid middle-aged spinster has long ago given up homicidal mania in order to become a detective. Doctors, too, are better behaved nowadays, unless, of course, they grow eminent and turn into Mad Scientists. Lawyers, while they remain persistently crooked, are only in some cases actively dangerous. But cycles return! Edgar Allan Poe, eighty years ago, blew the gaff by calling his murderer Goodfellow; and the most popular modern mystery-writer does precisely the same thing by calling his arch-villain Goodman. Meanwhile, those secretaries are still the most dangerous people to have about the house.)

"To continue with regard to the icicle: Its actual use has been attributed to the Medici, and in one of the admirable Fleming Stone stories an epigram of Martial is quoted to show that it had its deadly origin in Rome in the first century A.D. Well, it has been fired, thrown, or shot from a crossbow as in one adventure of Hamilton Cleek (that magnificent character of the *Forty Faces*). Variants of the same theme, a soluble missile, have been rock-salt bullets and even bullets made of frozen blood.

"But it illustrates what I mean in crimes committed inside a room by somebody who was outside. There are other methods. The victim may be stabbed by a thin swordstick blade, passed between the twinings of a summer-house and withdrawn; or he may be stabbed with a blade so thin that he does not know he is hurt at all, and walks into another room before he suddenly collapses in death. Or he is lured into looking out of a window inaccessible from below; yet from above our old friend ice smashes down on his head, leaving him with a smashed skull but no weapon because the weapon has melted.

"Under this heading (although it might equally well go under head number 3) we might list murders committed by means of poisonous snakes or insects. Snakes can be concealed not only in chests and safes, but also deftly hidden in flower-pots, books, chandeliers, and walking-sticks. I even remember one cheerful little item in which the amber stem of a pipe, grotesquely carven as a scorpion, comes to life a real scorpion as the victim is about to put it into his mouth. But for the greatest long-range murder ever committed in a locked room, gents, I commend you to one of the most brilliant short detective stories in the history of detective fiction. (In fact, it shares the honours for supreme untouchable top-notch excellence with Thomas Burke's, *The Hands of Mr. Ottermole,* Chesterton's, *The Man in the Passage,* and Jacques Futrelle's, *The Problem of Cell 13.*) This is Melville Davisson Post's, *The Doomdorf Mystery*—and the long-range assassin is the sun. The sun strikes through the window of the locked room, makes a burning-glass of a bottle of Doomdorf's own raw white wood-alcohol liquor on the table, and ignites through it the percussion cap of a gun hanging on the wall: so that the breast of the hated one is blown open as he lies in his bed. Then, again, we have . . .

"Steady! Harrumph. Ha. I'd better not meander; I'll round off this classification with the final heading:

"7. This is a murder depending on an effect exactly the reverse of number 5. That is, the victim is presumed to be dead long before he actually is. The victim lies asleep (drugged but unharmed) in a locked room. Knockings on the door fail to rouse him. The murderer starts a foul-play scare; forces the door; gets in ahead and kills by stabbing or throat-cutting, while suggesting to other watchers that they have seen something they have not seen. The honour of inventing this device belongs to Israel Zangwill, and it has since been used in many forms. It has been done (usually by stabbing) on a ship, in a ruined house, in a conservatory, in an attic, and even in the open air —where the victim has first stumbled and stunned himself before the assassin bends over him. So—"

"Steady! Wait a minute!" interposed Hadley, pounding on the table for attention. Dr. Fell, the muscles of whose eloquence were oiling up in a satisfactory way, turned agreeably and beamed on him. Hadley went on: "This may be all very well. You've dealt with all the locked-room situations—"

"All of them?" snorted Dr. Fell, opening his eyes wide. "Of course I haven't. That doesn't even deal comprehensively with the methods under that particular classification; it's only a rough off-hand outline; but I'll let it stand. I was going to speak of the other classification: the various means of hocussing doors and windows so that they can be locked on the inside. H'mf! Hah! So, gentle-men, I continue—"

"Not yet you don't," said the superintendent, doggedly. "I'll argue the thing on your own grounds. You say we can get a lead from stating the various ways in which the stunt has been worked. You've stated seven points; but, applied to *this* case, each one must be ruled out according to your own classification-head. You head the whole list, 'No murderer escaped from the room because no murderer was ever actually in it at the time of the crime.' Out goes everything! The one thing we definitely do know, unless we presume Mills and Dumont to be liars, is that the murderer really was in the room! What about that?"

Pettis was sitting forward, his bald head gleaming by the glow of the red-shaded lamp as he bent over an envelope. He was making neat notes with a neat gold pencil. Now he raised his prominent eyes, which seemed more prominent and rather frog-like as he studied Dr. Fell.

"Er—yes," he said, with a short cough. "But that point number 5 is suggestive, I should think. Illusion! What if Mills and Mrs. Dumont really didn't see somebody go in that door; that they were hoaxed somehow or that the whole thing was an illusion like a magic-lantern?"

"Illusion me foot," said Hadley. "Sorry! I thought of that, too. I hammered Mills about it last night, and I had another word or two with him this morning. Whatever else the murderer was, he wasn't an illusion and he did go in that door. He was solid enough to cast a shadow and make the hall vibrate when he walked. He was solid enough to talk and slam a door. You agree with that, Fell?"

The doctor nodded disconsolately. He drew in absent puffs on his dead cigar.

"Oh yes, I agree to that. He was solid enough, and he did go in."

"And even," Hadley pursued, while Pettis summoned the waiter to get more coffee, "granting what we know is untrue. Even grant-ing a magic-lantern shadow did all that, a magic-lantern shadow didn't kill Grimaud. It was a solid pistol in a solid hand. And for the rest of the points, Lord knows Grimaud didn't get shot by a mechanical device. What's more, he didn't shoot himself—

and have the gun whisk up the chimney like the one in your example. In the first place, a man can't shoot himself from some feet away. And in the second place, the gun can't whisk up the chimney and sail across the roofs to Cagliostro Street, shoot Fley, and tumble down with its work finished. Blast it, Fell, my conversation is getting like yours! It's too much exposure to your habits of thought. I'm expecting a call from the office any minute, and I want to get back to sanity. What's the matter with you?"

Dr. Fell, his little eyes opened wide, was staring at the lamp, and his fist came down slowly on the table.

"Chimney!" he said. "Chimney! Wow! I wonder if—? Lord! Hadley, what an ass I've been!"

"What about the chimney?" asked the superintendent. "We've proved the murderer couldn't have got out like that: getting up the chimney."

"Yes, of course; but I didn't mean that. I begin to get a glimmer, even if it may be a glimmer of moonshine. I must have another look at that chimney."

Pettis chuckled, tapping the gold pencil on his notes. "Anyhow," he suggested, "you may as well round out this discussion. I agree with the superintendent about one thing. You might do better to outline ways of tampering with doors, windows, or chimneys."

"Chimneys, I regret to say," Dr. Fell pursued, his gusto returning as his abstraction left him, "chimneys, I regret to say, are not favoured as a means of escape in detective fiction—except, of course, for secret passages. There they are supreme. There is the hollow chimney with the secret room behind; the back of the fireplace opening like a curtain; the fireplace that swings out; even the room under the hearthstone. Moreover, all kinds of things can be dropped *down* chimneys, chiefly poisonous things. But the murderer who makes his escape by climbing up is very rare. Besides being next to impossible, it is a much grimier business than monkeying with doors or windows. Of the two chief classifications, doors and windows, the door is by far the more popular, and we may list thus a few means of tampering with it so that it seems to be locked on the inside:

"1. Tampering with the key which is still in the lock. This was the favourite old-fashioned method, but its variations are too well-known nowadays for anybody to use it seriously. The stem of the key can be gripped and turned with pliers from outside; we did this ourselves to *open* the door of Grimaud's study. One practical little mechanism consists of a thin metal bar about two inches long, to which is attached a length of stout string. Before leaving the room, this bar is thrust into the hole at the head of the key, one end under and one end over, so that it acts as a lever; the string is dropped down and run under the door to the outside. The door is closed from outside. You have only to pull on the string, and the lever turns the lock; you then shake or pull out the loose bar by means of the string, and, when it drops, draw it under the door to you. There are various applications of this same principle, all entailing the use of string.

"2. Simply removing the hinges of the door without disturbing lock or bolt. This is a neat trick, known to most schoolboys when they want to burgle a locked cupboard; but of course the hinges must be on the outside of the door.

"3. Tampering with the bolt. String again: this time with a mechanism of pins and darning-needles, by which the bolt is shot from the outside by leverage of a pin stuck on the inside of the door, and the string is worked through the keyhole. Philo Vance, to whom my hat is lifted, has shown us this best application of the stunt. There are simpler, but not so effective, variations using one piece of string. A 'tomfool' knot, which a sharp jerk will straighten out, is looped in one end of a long piece of cord. This loop is passed round the knob of the bolt, down, and under the door. The door is then closed, and, by drawing the string along to the left or right, the bolt is shot. A jerk releases the knot from the knob, and the string drawn out. Ellery Queen has shown us still another method, entailing the use of the dead man himself—but a bald statement of this, taken out of its context, would sound so wild as to be unfair to that brilliant gentleman.

"4. Tampering with a falling bar or latch. This usually consists in propping something under the latch, which can be pulled away after the door is closed from the outside, and let the bar drop. The best method by far is by the use of the ever-helpful ice, a cube of which is propped under the latch; and, when it melts,

the latch falls. There is one case in which the mere slam of the
door suffices to drop the bar inside.

"5. An illusion, simple but effective. The murderer, after committing his crime, has locked the door from the outside and
kept the key. It is assumed, however, that the key is still in the
lock on the inside. The murderer, who is first to raise a scare
and find the body, smashes the upper glass panel of the door,
puts his hand through with the key concealed in it, and 'finds'
the key in the lock inside, by which he opens the door. This
device has also been used with the breaking of a panel out of
an ordinary wooden door.

"There are miscellaneous methods, such as locking a door from
the outside and returning the key to the room by means of string
again, but you can see for yourselves that in this case none of
them can have any application. We found the door locked on the
inside. Well, there are many ways by which it could have been
done—but it was *not* done, because Mills was watching the door
the whole time. This room was only locked in a technical sense.
It was watched, and that shoots us all to blazes."

"I don't like to drag in famous platitudes," said Pettis, his forehead wrinkled, "but it would seem pretty sound to say exclude
the impossible and whatever remains, however improbable, must
be the truth. You've excluded the door; I presume you also exclude the chimney?"

"I do," grunted Dr. Fell.

"Then we come back in a circle to the window, don't we?"
demanded Hadley. "You've gone on and on about ways that obviously couldn't have been used. But in this catalogue of sensationalism you've omitted all mention of the only means of exit the
murderer *could* have used. . . ."

"Because it wasn't a locked window, don't you see?" cried Dr.
Fell. "I can tell you several brands of funny business with windows if they're only locked. It can be traced down from the earliest dummy nail-heads to the latest hocus-pocus with steel shutters. You can smash a window, carefully turn its catch to lock
it, and then, when you leave, simply replace the whole pane with
a new pane of glass and putty it round; so that the new pane looks
like the original and the window is locked inside. But this win-

dow wasn't locked or even closed—it was only inaccessible."

"I seem to have read somewhere of human flies . . ." Pettis suggested.

Dr. Fell shook his head. "We won't debate whether a human fly can walk on a sheer smooth wall. Since I've cheerfully accepted so much, I might believe that if the fly had any place to light. That is, he would have to start from somewhere and end somewhere. But he didn't; not on the roof, not on the ground below. . . ." Dr. Fell hammered his fists against his temples. "However, if you want a suggestion or two in that respect, I will tell you—"

He stopped, raising his head. At the end of the quiet, now deserted dining-room a line of windows showed pale light now flickering with snow. A figure had darted in silhouette against them, hesitating, peering from side to side, and then hurrying down towards them. Hadley uttered a muffled exclamation as they saw it was Mangan. Mangan was pale.

"Not something else?" asked Hadley, as coolly as he could. He pushed back his chair. "Not something else about coats changing colour or—"

"No," said Mangan. He stood by the table, drawing his breath in gasps. "But you'd better get over there. Something's happened to Drayman; apopleptic stroke or something like that. No, he's not dead or anything. But he's in a bad way. He was trying to get in touch with you when he had the stroke. . . . He keeps talking wildly about somebody in his room, and fireworks, and chimneys."

Command Performance

By Lee Wright

Lee Wright has been editor, since its inception, of Simon & Schuster's "Inner Sanctum Mystery" department, an imprint that has come increasingly to stand for catholicity of taste and healthy iconoclasm in the mystery field. Her present article makes a typically original contribution to current thinking about the writing and publishing of whodunits. Did you, reader, ever stop to think that you are responsible for the kind of mysteries authors write and publishers print?

THERE IS nothing revolutionary in the theory of supply and demand. And yet it has not occurred to a number of mystery critics —both amateur and professional—that supply and demand also operate in the field of fictional homicide.

The kind of mysteries that are published at any given time faithfully reflects the kind of mysteries most people want to read at that time.

For the past ten years a great many wistful articles have been written by lovers of the detective story, deploring the non-essential elements that have insinuated themselves into this art form. The intrusion of Love, Humor, Politics, Sociology fills them with loathing. Give us The Great Detective in his pure form, they plead. Give us the Puzzle, the Clues, the Deductions, the Solution—unadorned. Give us, in other words, Sherlock Holmes.

They are living in the past, in an era when people lined up in queues outside newsstands in gaslit London to get their new copy of *Strand Magazine,* an era when the detective story was new and young, as vigorous as any healthy baby. And as attractive. So attractive, in fact, that it was the readers themselves who made

Conan Doyle continue with his great detective even after he had killed off Holmes in what can only be called a burst of unjustifiable savagery. He was forced to bring him back to life—a veritable Lazarus.

But there came time for the infant to grow up—when for most people this pure puzzle form of the mystery story was not quite enough. Perhaps they began to be curious about how a great detective would act when faced with such trivial, but horribly real, crises as human beings who would not stay in appointed places, trains that would not be caught on time, telephones that went out of order, hansom cabs that would not wait conveniently on corners—in fact, all the monstrous calamities of real life.

In answer to this growing demand, which was inarticulate—but effective in bookstores—things began to happen. In England, E. C. Bentley created a great detective and made him operate in a setting that was a reasonable facsimile of life. Philip Trent not only had an immediate success, but he has survived as a great detective practically from this one outstanding performance in *Trent's Last Case*. At any rate, he set the style for much that followed in England, and a very fine style it was.

It is significant that the attitude of the readers in England, their respect for this art form, their willingness not only to read these books but to be *seen* reading them, influenced many fine English writers to contribute to the literature. G. K. Chesterton gained prestige when he created Father Brown. He had proved himself a master at other literary forms, and he proved himself again a master at this one. The English public has never wavered in its admiration and respect for the mystery story, and, as a result, the English product has maintained a consistently high standard. The editors and publishers responsible, the writers themselves, react instinctively to the audience they are supplying with books. They do not have to apologize for Father Knox when he writes a mystery story. They can bring the fact out as an added feather in his cap.

In America the record has been a very different one. A certain meritricious snobbishness early crept in to the mystery field. This was probably inevitable in a society that was just beginning, deprecatingly, to produce its own art forms, that sat endlessly and willingly at the feet of lecturers purveying culture. Sinclair Lewis' Babbitt might read a Penny Dreadful overnight on a train trip, but he was taught not to keep a copy of it on his library table.

As a result of this artificial and phony culture, the mystery story in America suffered a long and dreary eclipse. Since readers thought of mystery stories as being sensational, unliterary, and shabby, most of them became so. The supply, as usual, followed the demand. Fine novelists didn't dream of trying their hand at such writing. And if they had, they would have insisted upon using pen names.

Fortunately, after too many decades, several things happened that had an effect on American reading opinion. The first, and probably the most powerful, was the news that Woodrow Wilson, that incontestably high-minded and intellectual idealist, was not only an avid reader of mystery stories, but also was perfectly willing to admit it handsomely. Then, along came S. S. Van Dine, whose books, through a combination of expert craftsmanship from the writer and brilliant exploitation from the publisher, became fashionable. One began to see a great many obviously respectable and reasonably cultivated people openly carrying around copies of Van Dine's novels. This same era produced the first books of Dashiell Hammet, who made the most profound impression on the mystery story technically (as had Bentley in England), but Van Dine's work certainly created much more of a social splash.

At any rate, once again the demand created the supply. Almost at once the literary quality of the mystery story in America went up, and in the past ten years has reached an artistic and competent level.

At the same time a new and important influence on public opinion was exercised through the medium of motion pictures. Alfred Hitchcock was the first to prove that a Pearl White serial was not necessarily the only way one could represent an exciting mystery story on the screen. It is largely through his work, and the work of other fine directors and producers who came after him, that the mystery novel of suspense is today the most widely read of all types of mystery fiction.

There are still, of course, the few diehards who want to keep the mystery story in its original, rigidly-restricted form. They are like a great many other people who yearn for the good old days economically and socially as well as literarily. The present disappoints them, and the future appalls them, because they want to live in the past.

And it is still true in America, of course, that mystery readers are set apart—in a patronizing, though kindly way—from readers of all other types of books, in the same way that one is indulgent to the crossword puzzle fan or the ardent quiz-program listener. This attitude—in other words, the demand—still operates very powerfully in the creation and promotion of the supply. The manner in which mystery stories are reviewed in magazines and newspapers reflects the attitude. The manner in which mystery stories are distributed—mostly by rentals instead of direct consumer purchases—reflects this attitude. The too-great volume of hastily written and automatically published mysteries reflects this attitude. Recent polls indicate that although most readers are now ready to admit that they enjoy mystery stories, they are not yet ready to grant that such novels are "worthwhile," appropriate for addition to a library—in other words, not to be purchased at prices equal to those of other novels.

Obviously, these are all obstacles in the path of the successful sale of any mystery story no matter what its literary quality. More and more, publishers get around the obstacle instead of trying to jump over it, by entirely artificial means. By omitting the category "mystery" from the jacket of the book itself and from their advertising, by charging for it more than they charge for a mystery, they have managed to make best-sellers out of a number of mystery novels. The classic example, of course, is *Rebecca* by Daphne DuMaurier. This is a mystery novel, well-written, with a superstructure of characterization, romance, and emotional overtones, which do not make it any less a mystery story. Interesting to speculate its fate had it been published as one.

However, it is an encouraging sign that these books should be so successful no matter how published. The methods are artificial, but the result proves that the demand is there and that more and more readers want and respect this kind of story. That demand will grow and eventually will sweep away the artificial devices.

When that day comes—when the mystery story is accepted as a completely responsible member of the fiction family—instead of the attractive, but irresponsible, stepchild it now is—when that happens, the demand for the best will create the appropriate supply. Then, John Steinbeck, Sinclair Lewis, Ernest Hemingway will occasionally turn their talents to the mystery story. It is even possible that they will write one as good as the classic few that have enriched our literature since Edgar Allan Poe first solved "The Murders in the Rue Morgue."

Mystery Midwife: The Crime Editor's Job

By Isabelle Taylor

As editor of Doubleday & Company's "Crime Club," Mrs. Taylor is responsible for the largest mystery output under one imprint in the United States: forty-eight new crimes a year. (The denominator is four books per month, not one for each state of the Union.) Her fully documented article describing the trials, joys, and multiple responsibilities of the mystery editor's job will come as a revelation to those readers who conceive of that individual's function as limited to reading and accepting "masterpieces."

As THE scope of the mystery story has widened, the job of an editor who publishes mysteries has become more involved and much more complex. In the days when detective stories followed the Sherlock Holmes pattern exclusively, an editor checked for correct plot resolution and proper Scotland Yard procedure in the investigation of crime. Now it is a very different task, and an increasingly fascinating one. An editor must be a combination of foster-mother, father-confessor, and *accoucheur*—which is a neat trick if you can do it!

I remember the season when almost every author wrote asking if he shouldn't do a spy story. Obviously a writer who combines humor with homicide would be ill-advised to branch into a field with which he was not familiar; the same thing was true of people who handled the family-conflict stories. A reputation made by several excellent books based on the psychological study of murder would fall flat on its face if a creaky who-stole-the-formula yarn issued from the same pen. So—the answer to most of these queries was "No." A year or two later several writers turned out very good yarns, in their accustomed style, but working in the sabotage at home, and the enemy within our gates, theme. It was a matter of adjusting individual styles to current themes and public interest.

Once a manuscript is in, and the decision has been made to publish it, an editor goes to work on checking every detail for accuracy, credibility, and taste. And here is where a large reference library, a good memory, and a "feel" for the market is necessary. Some beautiful howlers undoubtedly get by even the most careful copy-reader, but an endeavor is made to avoid them. We heard from several irate fans when a young girl was permitted to visit her fiancé in the death-house, wearing a blue wool dress when she entered, and a green silk when she left fifteen minutes later. Relationships, ages, time factors, and details of geography are comparatively easy to bring into line. But police procedure, legalities governing wills, divorces, admission of evidence, types of punishment vary in all the forty-eight states. Sometimes I sigh for the simplicity of Scotland Yard. Then I wouldn't have to remember that there is no capital punishment in Michigan, that California executes by the gas-chamber, Maryland by hanging, and New York by the electric chair. You can't wait for the coroner to view the body in New York, because there is no such person, he's a medical examiner, and there are some states where a doctor or a butcher are excluded from jury duty. In the case of a writer producing a first mystery story, a wise editor will inquire how carefully he has checked on the police and legal procedure for the locality where the story is laid.

There is also the question of libel, and good taste. A victim may be bashed over the head with a bottle of a nationally-advertised soft drink, but he can't be poisoned by drinking from that bottle because a lethal dose has been previously introduced into the liquid—not when the advertisements make much of the fact that you are served the drink untouched by human hands from the time it leaves the factory until it is opened in your presence. Jokes may be made about public figures, but when they verge on the too-personal the public verdict is "we are not amused."

Characters in a mystery story do not operate in a vacuum, and the editor must have a weather eye out to catch errors or omissions in the background fill-in. During the war, long drives in an automobile, huge family dinners with a couple of sides of beef, and an unaccounted-for number of young civilian men, had to be gently but firmly removed. If a story is definitely placed in a certain year, in a certain locality, every effort must be made to create verisimilitude in details, because the plot itself is usually enough of a strain on one's imagination. In fairness to mystery writers one has to admit that they are much more careful with these details than a great many novelists. Perhaps the training in plot construction has made them methodical about sweeping up or lopping off the various bits and pieces of window dressing that don't belong.

The title of a mystery is something to be considered gravely, almost with prayer. Some titles are naturals, the book couldn't be called anything else. Others are the best of a bad bargain, and represent a compromise in the author's mind between what he would like, and what would be a grand title but have no connection with the story. Occasionally a manuscript will have a very apt title, and be well along toward appearance on the bookstalls, but the editor opens *Publishers' Weekly* and sees another mystery with the exact same title announced for publication next week! So there is a hasty re-titling that must be caught all along the line—jacket, title-page, running-heads, advertisements, catalogue, etc. A title should be fitted to the type of book it labels. A punning, or wisecracking title, doesn't belong on a straightforward story. It's wasted, and may attract readers who will feel sold down the river when they don't get what they want and expect. You as a reader may not be aware of how you react to titles, but watch yourself the next time you select a story from a long shelf of mysteries. The one that strikes you as offering the type of entertainment you want may represent agonized hours on the part of the author and the editor to make it sound just right. The war added the necessity for extra care, in order to avoid anything that might give the impression that the book was a non-fiction war report.

From titles the next step is jackets. Here again, the style of the jacket should carry on the general style of the story. A hard-boiled number gets nowhere when plastered with an illustrative drawing of a sweet old lady peering down a dark stairwell, *although* such a scene may be lifted from the yarn itself. A leisurely English novel of detection and deduction is badly advertised by a modernistic design poster jacket. It is eminently desirable to have the artist who is doing the jacket read the manuscript before he starts to work. Then one gets a true marriage of mood and pace between the novel and the wrapper. When an author writes to me, after receiving bound copies of his book, to say that the jacket is perfect and please thank the art department for it, I am content. Then I know a reader who has selected the book because the jacket appealed to him will be satisfied and entertained.

A mystery story to the author who has just finished it and sent it off to his publisher is naturally a favored and indulged only child. (If its own creator doesn't so regard it, it isn't very well prepared to meet the wide, wide world.) But to the editor who receives it, it is a very welcome member of a family, each of whom must be cared for, dressed in its best, and presented at the proper time and in the proper company to make the best impression. Scheduling a large list of mysteries can resemble a jig-saw puzzle, put and take, and a juggling act all at the same time.

When several mysteries appear in the same month (my own schedule calls for four) one must be careful to provide for a wide range of tastes. Consequently a fast-moving fairly tough story is put on the same date with what Will Cuppy calls a "soft-boiled" one. Two chess puzzles together would be bad business, so we pair each one of these with a spy-adventure type, or a modern Robin Hood yarn. It would not be fair to authors producing first books to line three of them up in one month, so we salt them through a list into spots where the fact that they *are* new is an added attraction, not a wholesale green entry feature. Four English stories a month wouldn't be any smarter than four Hollywood settings, and sameness in the house-party, snowbound hunting lodge, or marooned sailing party frame is to be avoided.

Publishing mysteries has, I believe, fewer occupational hazards than other forms of presenting printed matter to the public. Authors who turn out the murder or adventure book are less temperamental, more professional about meeting deadlines and accepting editorial suggestions than writers who fancy themselves as producers of "lit'rature." Most whodunit-ers know and accept certain commercial truths, even though they don't like them any more than the publisher does. For instance, a mystery story has only four to six months active life, unless it is a world-beater, or unique in its content or topical appeal. The percentage of published mysteries sold to lending libraries runs, by various estimates, from seventy-five to ninety. This means that for every copy sold to the lending library the author gets one royalty (and the publisher sells one copy), and the readers may run as high as forty or fifty on that one copy. A mystery which is being widely discussed and merits excellent reviews *sells* to only a fraction of the market it reaches. This isn't fair to anybody concerned but to date there has been no workable answer to the problem.

Few mystery writers are personally vain; they know that publicity about their habits, their taste in cereal, and even their love lives has no effect on the readers of their books, and that the only angle on their own background that carries any weight is whether or not they know what they are talking about when they write. A person familiar with life in a small college town can imbue a story with the gentle malice, the bull sessions, and the faculty intrigue that abound in such a setting, and nobody gives a damn whether she's married to an English professor or got straight A's when she graduated at fifteen. Ownership of a sailboat by an author is only important when a story concerns sailing and the writer obviously knows his jib from his galley.

There is more co-operation and less competition between mystery story writers than is the case with most creative artists. Perhaps this is occasioned by the fact that enormous success in one publishing season by a mystery doesn't at all decrease the popularity of the other good books published at the same time. Booksellers may speak of "this year's big historical novel" or "the leading non-fiction title on such-and-such a phase of international relations" but everybody in the game knows that there is always room for any number of good mysteries. The sale of each one should, and usually does, help the sale of the others.

In addition to what is called the "trade sale" of a book, meaning those copies which are sold to dealers and booksellers for re-sale at the full retail price, there are other channels of distribution which the editor must explore for his foster-children. Second serial is the term applied to publication of the book in newspapers or magazines after book publication. Not all mysteries lend themselves to this use because they may be too long to cut properly for condensed versions, they may be strong meat for a family newspaper, or the general subject matter may be considered by a magazine as too dated.

There are book clubs specializing in the mystery and detective story. These usually offer three or four full-length books in one volume a few months after original publication. The major book clubs have been known to use super-duper mystery tales for their monthly selection. Each club has its own preferences and taboos, with which the editor should be familiar. Stories with a fairly lurid sex tangle obviously can't be submitted to a club which has a large circulation for family use, and the ultra-literate tour de force wouldn't get far in a club that does most of its advertising in the tabloids.

The twenty-five cent paperbound books have made available to readers a vast number of excellent books at a popular price, and on the other side of the picture they have opened up a new and potentially large source of revenue to the writers of mysteries. Because the original trade life of a mystery is short, this new field of distribution may go far toward equalizing the profits derived from a well-constructed, carefully thought-out story for which, up to recent years, the author did not usually receive adequate compensation. It is quite true that a second rate story isn't going to go into a cheap reprint, but the first class stories will, so that large numbers of new readers will become familiar with authors' names, and enlarge the market for new books by their favorites.

As an editor of mystery stories, my profound hope is that writers have as much fun writing them as I have editing them. Then everybody in this game of whodunit will be satisfied.

Hollywoodunit

By Richard Mealand

Mr. Mealand, for many years story editor of Paramount Pictures, and a former magazine fiction editor, is currently the conductor of a department, "Books Into Pictures," in Publishers' Weekly, *trade journal of American book publishing. His lively and enlightening article on whodunits on the screen answers many questions readers have asked about the greatest of all American mysteries—Hollywood.*

IT'S QUITE all right for the mystery writer to make a fool of me in a book. If he's cleverer than I, then I am like the gypsy in *For Whom the Bell Tolls* who, upon first examining a watch, cried out in admiration, "What a com-plic-ca-tion!" But if he's not as clever as I, that's quite all right, too, for then I have him, poor thing, at my mercy, so to speak; I can be arrogant, superior; I can yawn at his pages, cut him down to size, toss him away—and enjoy my victory over him. He can say that the butler did the murder, or the chief of detectives did it, or charming little Candace ("friends called her Candy") did it, or the quiet librarian did it, or Jim did it to shield Mary, or Count Xerxes did it because Solange had got him under her skin, or Luther he done it because he didn't know no better, or the author himself did it, or even I did it, I the reader! He can say anything he pleases in a book, put the blame anywhere, solve the mystery in a word or in three chapters of explanation, write it all in jive talk, put in crossword puzzles or Egyptian hieroglyphics, play symphonies with colored wine glasses, cut his victims into long strips of human bacon, paint a room with blood, kill a woman by taking away her sugar ration stamps. What the hell. Anything goes—in a book.

But Hollywood would never approve. In mysteries Hollywood asks for form, construction, certain well-defined patterns, order, truth, justice, character. Above all, Hollywood wants to do, in mysteries, either one of two things: scare the living daylights out of the audiences, or roll 'em in the aisles. (Incidentally, I have never actually seen anyone ever roll in the aisles from a picture, and I am wondering if Hollywood doesn't sometimes exaggerate, just a little, perhaps.)

Hollywood is choosey about murder. Because of the Hays code, crime must be properly punished, evil cannot prevail at the end, gruesomeness and horror must not be presented too boldly or disgustingly to the eye, sexual crime may be implied but never stated in visual terms. Motherhood may not be defiled, religion must not be ridiculed. The murderer may not cut a woman's breasts off, and if he's a ripper, the exact nature of the slicing must not be told nor shown. The corpse, too, must remain singularly unmutilated. A little blood from the mouth, perhaps, or a dark stain on the clothing over the heart, but no exposed intestines, no headless bodies or bodiless heads, no widely distributed limbs or parts. A clean stab, a straight shot, a strong quick strangulation—that's the ticket. Poison in moderation, but no vomiting, please. No ugly convulsions. (And did you know that if a character in a film ever swallows any indigestible object, such as a diamond ring, he can never get it back, because audience imagination can conceive of only two ways of retrieving it, and both of them are taboo on the screen?)

Hollywood's taboos, self imposed by the motion picture industry, are for the protection of the great, literal minded, highly suggestible mass of the people to whom murder is murder and not a mental exercise. The motion picture differs from the book in this respect: the former, to the majority of people, is life; the latter, to a comparatively small minority, is a diversion and an escape. This may appear to be a paradox, for most of us regard the movies as an escape. But to the moviegoer, what he sees on the screen he takes for fact, relative to the nature of the picture; for, in his view, flesh-and-blood people are going through the motions.

For this reason, the "whodunit"—in which the author deliberately misleads the reader by concealing the murderous character of the villain—is generally poor fare for the screen. The people who act in pictures are selected for their roles because of the precise character impressions which they convey to audiences. For instance, the moment you see Walter Pidgeon in a film you know immediately that he could not do a mean or petty thing. He is noble. Greer Garson is noble. And no audience would want either of them to stand on their heads, pick their noses, steal from a blind man, or murder somebody without good and sufficient reason. Once you assemble the cast of a murder film, the audience must know instinctively who is good and who is bad, who plays second fiddle and who brings up the rear. Films which falsely label the characters of their actors are usually doomed to failure; the audience is tricked in its judgment of human nature, and audiences don't like trickery—unless it's funny.

There have been unfair mystery films, but they haven't made much money. Possibly the only exception was *Suspicion,* adapted from Francis Iles' famous book, *Before the Fact,* in which Cary Grant came dangerously close to turning into a first class heel. Alfred Hitchcock made the picture, and he knew that, if he had stuck to the book, his audiences would have walked out in a body at the end. So he "treated" the book for pictures, removing the unbearable suspicion from Cary's character in the last reel; the guy was not really a potential murderer, it only looked that way for a while to pretty Joan Fontaine. And the result, considered critically, was a somewhat puzzling picture, not entirely convincing, even though it did sell tickets. It almost, but finally didn't, trick the audience. They could still feel that Cary Grant was, as he seemed to be, a fine man.

Hitchcock's earlier success as the creator of a certain type of mystery film can be attributed to two things: the novelty and variety of his imagination in the sustaining of suspense, and the willingness of his audiences to accept his illogical sequences as logical because he entertained them so well. With one or two exceptions, Hitchcock's mysteries simply didn't make sense. His plots were full of holes and loose ends, characters appeared pointlessly and never reappeared, sub-plots emerged and were forgotten. In fact, if he hadn't the rare gift of holding the "hero line" and the "menace line" in exactly parallel positions along a track of constantly mounting apprehension, he would have been lost in a wilderness of ridiculous beginnings without endings. In *Rebecca,* of course, he worked from a soundly constructed book. Being Hitchcock, he couldn't go wrong there. And in his other later pictures he has abandoned his early carefree technique and settled down to solid scripts.

Other successful mystery films have been those in which the emphasis has been placed not on the working out of an intricate plot—which is often the sole interest in many book mysteries—but on the charm, amusing qualities, or superior deadly cleverness of the detective. I defy any of you to recall one single plot of any of the *Thin Man* pictures, in which Myrna Loy and William Powell appeared (and are appearing again). Actually the crime was negligible except that it offered a temporary menace to the happy, albeit bibulous, life of Mr. and Mrs. Nick Charles and dog, Asta. *The Saint* films were entertaining, not because they had particularly good stories, but because you liked to watch George Sanders successfully elude his enemies. *Sherlock Holmes* has been interesting on the screen because of Sherlock Holmes and Watson, not because the plots have any intellectual stimulus or are memorable. In other words, it's character that counts in pictures, which is probably why John Dickson Carr (or Carter Dickson), good though he is in books, has never scaled the Hollywood ramparts with any of his carefully plotted but somewhat lifeless stories. And the same goes for scores of other mystery writers who are more concerned with puzzles than with people.

The sex crime in films has only recently come into favor, but the results have been so salutary at the box office that writers have been influenced away from the straight whodunit into the more difficult field of the so-called psychological murder drama. Such films as *Double Indemnity, The Lodger, Laura, The Suspect, The Woman in the Window* (the Hays office spoiled that one) and others, have made such a hit with audiences that readers of mysteries are no longer content with the formula murder story. Five minutes of real horror in *Night Must Fall* can do more to make the confirmed mystery reader a cynic and a skeptic about his reading matter than a whole year's supply of *Mystery Story Magazine* can do. What's more, the best of Hollywood's mysteries are so good that writers have felt the temptation of big movie offers and have raised the character quality of their work to an appreciable and widening extent. Ten years ago the mystery story writer, except in the classical field, would have been lucky to have earned as much as a thousand or two from one title. Today, if he's good, he can make a fortune from one of his books. The nearer he gets to the novel, and the farther from the whodunit, the better are his chances to clean up in one stroke. Hollywood, the stage, and the radio are all after him, boosting his status from the cent-a-word class into the dollar or even five-dollar-a-word category. But he has to create character, and he has to be convincing. The plot is only incidental.

Gaslight, Experiment Perilous, The Letter, Ladies in Retirement, The Uninvited are the best fairly recent examples of mystery films which have abandoned the old purely horror aspects in which Hollywood formerly dressed its mysteries. The monster motif, the clawed hand reaching out from the concealed panel, the creaking door, the choked-off scream—all the familiar trappings of the scary film have been repeated so often on the screen that, like songs on the Hit Parade, they have quickly lost their power to entertain. When Bob Hope appeared in *The Cat and the Canary* and *The Ghost Breakers* he knocked the old fashioned horror story into a cocked hat; the result was bound to be such japery as *Arsenic and Old Lace.* Now, when audiences go to see Boris Karloff, they go with bags of peanuts and come out full of peanuts instead of chewed finger nails. The real horror now lies elsewhere—in psychological exposition of fear and subtle hate and slow death. As audiences grow increasingly blasé, the screen draws nearer to the truth.

Oddly enough, the film producer, ranging over the whole mystery story market in his search for new thrills for his voracious audiences, has been instrumental in bringing a number of hitherto obscure writers into great popularity in the book world. Dashiell Hammett had only a small following before the movies took him up in *The Maltese Falcon.* Raymond Chandler had written five or six books and was getting nowhere when Hollywood suddenly discovered *The Big Sleep* and *Farewell My Lovely,* and signed him up. Now even his least successful book, *The Lady in the*

Lake is going to be produced. Cleve Adams, Cornell Woolrich (William Irish), Vera Caspary, Dorothy B. Hughes, and half a dozen others have lately become Important because the films have brought them out from under their bushels. Even old Wilkie Collins is being dusted off and rediscovered by the studios, much to the delight of the anthology boys on Publishers' Row.

The Murder Mystery, in fact, has attained at last the stature of the novel, and, in pictures, the budget of the super-colossal epic. And now, if you'll excuse me, I'll go back to Lizzie Borden and try, once again, to come to some conclusion about her. If they ever try to put *her* on the screen, in the person of some Hollywood glamour girl, so help me, I'll murder the producer . . .

There's Murder in the Air

By Ken Crossen

*A founder and first executive vice-president of Mystery Writers
of America, Inc. (the American counterpart of the London Detection Club), Ken Crossen is a mystery writer, editor, critic, radio
director, and producer. He writes with authority and from personal knowledge of the problems of mystery at the microphone.*

EVERY DAY, 365 days a year, four and one-half * mystery and detective stories are broadcast to the American radio audience. According to those efficient organizations which make a business of
informing sponsors how many people listen to their programs,
the average radio mystery show will have more than five million
sets tuned in on it, with an average of two listeners per set. To
accomplish this task, advertisers and networks spend approximately $62,000 per week, or three and a quarter million dollars
annually, exclusive of radio time.

Of the thirty-one shows currently on the air, twelve star detectives who originally appeared in books, and two shows specialize
in adaptations of the "best" of the published mysteries, yet readers of those books would be hard put to recognize their favorites
after the face-lifting routine of radio. Certainly, the Perry Mason
fan, after hearing that show over CBS, will dig feverishly through
his Erle Stanley Gardner books to find the source of this ether
mutation. Similarly, Hammett worshippers have been known to
brood for days after hearing *The Thin Man* on the air, and then
to forswear mysteries for Spengler.

---

* This figure is based on the week of November 18, 1945, when there were 31
mystery shows on the air on the major networks, all of them contracted for 13 weeks
or longer.

Mystery writers, publishers and readers have all become rather pleased with themselves in the past few years because they've consigned concealed rooms, unknown poisons, and other lazy devices of the early mystery to limbo. Radio, however, proceeds at its made pace, blissfully unaware of progress. In fact, this ignorance is one of the mainstays of the writer and producer of radio mystery shows. Granting each mystery broadcast one murder for each performance, there are 1,612 such murders committed annually. Of these, 800 are by gun, and 800 by poison, with the remaining twelve accomplished through methods dreamed up in the fertile mind of a radio hack. The less said about the last, the better.

Death by shooting, on the air, is manufactured with meticulous attention to how it will sound; the gun shot, the hacking cough of a man shot through the large intestine, the fall of the body. But there the care comes to an end. Radio thinks nothing of guns that leave no powder marks when fired at close range, serial numbers that mysteriously vanish, revolvers with the firing power of rifles. One script on *The Falcon* had the murderer fire at a woman from a distance of a few feet, with a Police Positive. The bullet struck a small Pekingese dog which she held in her arms, killing the animal, but the only injury to the woman was being knocked unconscious. The bullet, apparently bouncing against the tough hide of the Peke, did not leave a mark on her.

Poison, in the realm of radio, means only one thing—prussic acid. Victims are fed prussic acid in pill, liquid, or any other form that seems convenient, and the only identification is the odor. Therefore, 799 times a year, a radio detective will sniff audibly into a microphone and mutter something about bitter almonds.

With the exception of five or six shows, the regular police are always the fatuous morons that they were in books thirty years ago. Radio networks which object to a script suggesting police brutality are perfectly content for the guardians of the law to score .65 I.Q. It is seldom that the police ever think of fingerprinting a suspect; if they do they bungle it; and they obviously view all criminology with suspicion. The chief and only clue on a recent major mystery show was the absence of a bullet hole in the shirt of a man who had a bullet hole in his chest—all of which the police had overlooked. The detective discovered this when he viewed the corpse, still fully clothed, in the morgue.

With few exceptions, the mystery novels of thirty years ago were pretty sorry affairs, deservedly called "shockers" or "thrillers." But in the past twenty-five years, mystery writing has made significant strides toward literary dignity and maturity of form. The same cannot be said for radio. The quality of mystery drama in radio has all the puerility of a bad Edgar Wallace, and, many times, all the confusion of a Harry Stephen Keeler.

Undoubtedly, a strong factor in the poor quality of mystery shows is the censorship enforced by networks. Network officials apparently are under the impression that the American public, despite the publication of newspapers, millions of copies of mystery and detective magazines, and millions of copies of mystery novels, has a virginal innocence so far as murder and mayhem are concerned. A radio mystery show has more don'ts per square inch than a home for wayward girls. These rules not only concern methods of murder and morals, but such common practices as drinking and gambling. Shows have been known to be thrown out because a policeman struck a criminal. This censorship springs, of course, from a morbid fear that someone will become angry and refuse to buy a product. About the only group which can be insulted on the air is the Java Man.

Hand in hand with the censor, goes the problem of the professional genius among the networks and agencies. Raised by hand, and trained by making mountains out of molehills, these men work their way up the aerial until they are put in charge of productions. Somewhere along the way, they grow antennae which take the place of judgment in other fields. One such man, in charge of all production for a large network, throws out lines in mystery shows because his "mother wouldn't understand it." All shows over that network, therefore, are beamed for his mother—which seems to be carrying the "cult of Mom" too far.

The top shows, if you judge by rating, that statistical god of those who rule the airwaves, or by the appraisal of the radio professionals, undoubtedly excel in production; that is, direction, engineering skill and sound technics. But the stories themselves are too often on a par with those published in horror pulp magazines following World War I. Sex and sadism, often presented coyly for the sake of the censor, constitute the motif, and the level of presentation is not far above those magazines which were so heartily and justifiably condemned.

No analysis of radio mysteries, even one as brief as this, would be complete without mentioning two programs that occasionally afford a glimpse of the quality that is possible in the air mystery drama. *Suspense* and *Mystery Theatre,* although their batting averages have not been high, have presented many dramatizations of mystery novels and short stories that were to the average radio mystery what Norman Corwin is to *Portia Faces Life.* Certainly in such dramatizations as *Cocaine* by Cornell Woolrich, *The Big Sleep* by Raymond Chandler, and *Home Sweet Homicide* by Craig Rice, they have proved that radio can do an artistic job when it chooses to treat mysteries seriously. Unfortunately, *Mystery Theatre* has always been slightly marred by billing its announcer as a mystery expert whereas he is merely an AFRA actor speaking lines written by an agency man who believes the third degree to be an honor given by the Masonic Lodge.

All of this adds up to one glaring conclusion concerning radio mystery shows: they stand now, despite a huge following and millions of dollars for the budget, where mystery novels stood thirty years ago. Since they have maintained good listener ratings, and successfully sell products, advertising agencies and sponsors have not been impelled to consider the writing and presentation of mysteries as a specialized business which cannot be turned over to radio hacks and directors whose only qualification is a knowledge of the mechanics of a stop watch.

Some day a pioneering sponsor will make the daring plunge into quality performances of better mystery stories, and sell so many razor blades, jars of shaving soap, or gallons of wine, that every other mystery show sponsor will follow suit—the one move which they always make by instinct.

Until then, what happens to murder on the radio is—murder.

4
THE LIGHTER SIDE
OF CRIME

Watson Was a Woman
By Rex Stout

The now-famous travesty on Holmesiological scholarship which follows was first delivered by the bearded creator of Nero Wolfe and Archie Goodwin before a dinner meeting of the Baker Street Irregulars in New York on January 31, 1941—a date that lives in infamy for all the faithful. Even after the passage of years, Mr. Stout attends the annual festivities of this august and nominally peace-loving society only when accompanied by a personal bodyguard.

GASOGENE: Tantalus: Buttons: Irregulars:

You will forgive me for refusing to join your commemorative toast, "The Second Mrs. Watson," when you learn it was a matter of conscience. I could not bring myself to connive at the perpetuation of a hoax. Not only was there never a second Mrs. Watson; there was not even a first Mrs. Watson. Furthermore, there was no Doctor Watson.

Please keep your chairs.

Like all true disciples, I have always recurrently dipped into the Sacred Writings (called by the vulgar the Sherlock Holmes stories) for refreshment; but not long ago I reread them from beginning to end, and I was struck by a singular fact that reminded me of the dog in the night. The singular fact about the dog in the night, as we all know, was that it didn't bark; and the singular fact about Holmes in the night is that he is never seen going to bed. The writer of the tales, the Watson person, describes over and over again, in detail, all the other minutiæ of that famous household—suppers, breakfasts, arrangement of furniture, rainy evenings at home—but not once are we shown either Holmes or

Watson going to bed. I wondered, why not? Why such unnatural
and obdurate restraint, nay, concealment, regarding one of the
pleasantest episodes of the daily routine?

I got suspicious.

The uglier possibilities that occurred to me, as that Holmes
had false teeth or that Watson wore a toupee, I rejected as preposterous. They were much too obvious, and shall I say unsinister.
But the game was afoot, and I sought the trail, in the only field
available to me, the Sacred Writings themselves. And right at the
very start, on page 9 of *A Study in Scarlet,* I found this:

> . . . It was rare for him to be up after ten at night, and he had
> invariably breakfasted and gone out before I rose in the morning.

I was indescribably shocked. How had so patent a clue escaped
so many millions of readers through the years? That was, that
could only be, a woman speaking of a man. Read it over. The true
authentic speech of a wife telling of her husband's—but wait. I
was not indulging in idle speculation, but seeking evidence to
establish a fact. It was unquestionably a woman speaking of a
man, yes, but whether a wife of a husband, or a mistress of a
lover, . . . I admit I blushed. I blushed for Sherlock Holmes, and
I closed the book. But the fire of curiosity was raging in me, and
soon I opened again to the same page, and there in the second
paragraph I saw:

> The reader may set me down as a hopeless busybody, when I
> confess how much this man stimulated my curiosity, and how often
> I endeavored to break through the reticence which he showed on all
> that concerned himself.

You bet she did. She would. Poor Holmes! She doesn't even
bother to employ one of the stock euphemisms, such as, "I wanted
to understand him better," or, "I wanted to share things with
him." She proclaims it with brutal directness, "I endeavored to
break through the reticence." I shuddered, and for the first time
in my life felt that Sherlock Holmes was not a god, but human
—human by his suffering. Also, from that one page I regarded
the question of the Watson person's sex as settled for good. Indubitably she was a female, but wife or mistress? I went on. Two
pages later I found:

. . . his powers upon the violin . . . at my request he has played me some of Mendelssohn's *Lieder* . . ."

Imagine a man asking another man to play him some of Mendelssohn's *Lieder* on a violin!

And on the next page:

. . . I rose somewhat earlier than usual, and found that Sherlock Holmes had not yet finished his breakfast . . . my place had not been laid nor my coffee prepared. With . . . petulance . . . I rang the bell and gave a curt intimation that I was ready. Then I picked up a magazine from the table and attempted to while away the time with it, while my companion munched silently at his toast.

That is a terrible picture, and you know and I know how bitterly realistic it is. Change the diction, and it is practically a love story by Ring Lardner. That Sherlock Holmes, like other men, had breakfasts like that is a hard pill for a true disciple to swallow, but we must face the facts. The chief thing to note of this excerpt is that it not only reinforces the conviction that Watson was a lady—that is to say, a woman—but also it bolsters our hope that Holmes did not through all those years live in sin. A man does not munch silently at his toast when breakfasting with his mistress; or, if he does, it won't be long until he gets a new one. But Holmes stuck to her—or she to him—for over a quarter of a century. Here are a few quotations from the later years:

. . . Sherlock Holmes was standing smiling at me. . . . I rose to my feet, stared at him for some seconds in utter amazement, and then it appears that I must have fainted. . . ."
—"The Adventure of the Empty House," page 4.

I believe that I am one of the most long-suffering of mortals.
—"The Tragedy of Birlstone," page 1.

The relations between us in those latter days were peculiar. He was a man of habits, narrow and concentrated habits, and I had become one of them. As an institution I was like the violin, the shag tobacco, the old black pipe, the index books, and others perhaps less excusable.
—"The Adventure of the Creeping Man," page 1.

And we have been expected to believe that a man wrote those things! The frank and unconcerned admission that she fainted at sight of Holmes after an absence! "I am one of the most long-suffering of mortals"—the oldest uxorial cliché in the world; Aeschylus used it; no doubt cave-men gnashed their teeth at it! And the familiar pathetic plaint, "As an institution I was like the old black pipe!"

Yes, uxorial, for surely she was wife. And the old black pipe itself provides us with a clincher on that point. This comes from page 16 of *The Hound of the Baskervilles:*

> . . . did not return to Baker Street until evening. It was nearly nine o'clock when I found myself in the sitting-room once more.
>
> My first impression as I opened the door was that a fire had broken out, for the room was so filled with smoke that the light of the lamp upon the table was blurred by it. As I entered, however, my fears were set at rest, for it was the acrid fumes of strong coarse tobacco which took me by the throat and set me coughing. Through the haze I had a vague vision of Holmes in his dressing-gown coiled up in an armchair with his black clay pipe between his lips. Several rolls of paper lay around him.
>
> "Caught cold, Watson?" said he.
>
> "No, it's this poisonous atmosphere."
>
> "I suppose it *is* pretty thick, now that you mention it."
>
> "Thick! It is intolerable!"
>
> "Open the window, then!"

I say husband and wife. Could anyone alive doubt it after reading that painful banal scene? Is there any need to pile on the evidence?

For a last-ditch skeptic there is more evidence, much more. The efforts to break Holmes of the cocaine habit, mentioned in various places in the Sacred Writings, display a typical reformist wife in action, especially the final gloating over her success. A more complicated, but no less conclusive, piece of evidence is the strange, the astounding recital of Holmes's famous disappearance, in "The Final Problem;" and the reasons given therefore in a later tale, "The Adventure of the Empty House." It is incredible that this monstrous deception was not long ago exposed.

Holmes and Watson had together wandered up the valley of the Rhone, branched off at Leuk, made their way over the Gemmi Pass, and gone on, by way of Interlaken, to Meiringen. Near that village, as they were walking along a narrow trail high above a tremendous abyss, Watson was maneuvered back to the hotel by a fake message. Learning that the message was a fake, she (he) flew back to their trail, and found that Holmes was gone. No Holmes. All that was left of him was a polite and regretful note of farewell, there on a rock with his cigarette case for a paper-weight, saying that Professor Moriarty had arrived and was about to push him into the abyss.

That in itself was rather corny. But go on to "The Adventure of the Empty House." Three years have passed. Sherlock Holmes has suddenly and unexpectedly reappeared in London, causing the Watson person to collapse in a faint. His explanation of his long absence is fantastic. He says that he had grappled with Professor Moriarty on the narrow trail and tossed him into the chasm; that, in order to deal at better advantage with the dangerous Sebastian Moran, he had decided to make it appear that he too had toppled over the cliff; that, so as to leave no returning footprints on the narrow trail, he had attempted to scale the upper cliff, and, while he was doing so, Sebastian Moran himself had appeared up above and thrown rocks at him; that by herculean efforts he had eluded Moran and escaped over the mountains; that for three years he had wandered around Persia and Tibet and France, communicating with no one but his brother Mycroft, so that Sebastian Moran would think he was dead. *Though by his own account Moran knew, must have known, that he had got away!*

That is what Watson says that Holmes told her (him). It is simply gibberish, below the level even of a village half-wit. It is impossible to suppose that Sherlock Holmes ever dreamed of imposing on any sane person with an explanation like that; it is impossible to believe that he would insult his own intelligence by offering such an explanation even to an idiot. I deny that he ever did. I believe that all he said, after Watson recovered from the faint, was this, "My dear, I am willing to try it again," for he was a courteous man. And it was Watson, who, attempting to cook up an explanation, made such a terrible hash of it.

Then who was this person whose nom de plume was "Doctor Watson"? Where did she come from? What was she like? What was her name before she snared Holmes?

Let us see what we can do about the name, by methods that Holmes himself might have used. It was Watson who wrote the immortal tales, therefore if she left a record of her name anywhere it must have been in the tales themselves. But what we are looking for is not her characteristics or the facts of her life, but her *name,* that is to say, her *title;* so obviously the place to look is in the *titles* of the tales.

There are sixty of the tales all told. The first step is to set them down in chronological order, and number them from 1 to 60. Now, which shall we take first? Evidently the reason why Watson was at such pains to conceal her name in this clutter of titles was to *mystify* us, so the number to start with should be the most *mystical* number, namely seven. And to make it doubly sure, we shall make it seven times seven, which is 49. Very well. The 49th tale is "The Adventure of the Illustrious Client." We of course discard the first four words, "The Adventure of the," which are repeated in most of the titles. Result: "ILLUSTRIOUS CLIENT."

The next most significant thing about Watson is her (his) constant effort to convince us that those things happened exactly as she (he) tells them; that they are on the *square.* Good. The first square of an integer is the integer 4. We take the title of the 4th tale and get "RED-HEADED LEAGUE."

We proceed to elimination. Of all the factors that contribute to an ordinary man's success, which one did Holmes invariably exclude, or eliminate? Luck. In crap-shooting, what are the lucky numbers? Seven and eleven. But we have already used 7, which eliminates it, so there is nothing left but 11. The 11th tale is about the "ENGINEER'S THUMB."

Next, what was Holmes's age at the time he moved to Baker Street? Twenty-seven. The 27th tale is the adventure of the "NORWOOD BUILDER." And what was Watson's age? Twenty-six. The 26th tale is the adventure of the "EMPTY HOUSE." But there is no need to belabor the obvious. Just as it is a simple matter to decipher the code of the Dancing Men when Holmes

has once put you on the right track, so can you, for yourself, make
the additional required selections now that I have explained the
method. And you will inevitably get what I got:

Illustrious Client
Red-Headed League
Engineer's Thumb
Norwood Builder
Empty House

Wisteria Lodge
Abbey Grange
Twisted Lip
Study in Scarlet
Orange Pips
Noble Bachelor

And, acrostically simple, the initial letters read down, the carefully hidden secret is ours. Her name was Irene Watson.

But not so fast. Is there any way of checking that? Of discovering her name by any other method, say *a priori?* We can try and
see. A woman wrote the stories about Sherlock Holmes, that has
been demonstrated; and that woman was his wife. Does there appear, anywhere in the stories, a woman whom Holmes fell for?
Whom he really cottoned to? Indeed there does. "A Scandal in
Bohemia" opens like this:

To Sherlock Holmes she is always *the* woman. . . . In his eyes
she eclipses and predominates the whole of her sex.

And what was the name of *the* woman? Irene!

But, you say, not Irene Watson, but Irene Adler. Certainly.
Watson's whole purpose, from beginning to end, was to confuse
and bewilder us regarding her identity. So note that name well.
Adler. What is an adler, or, as it is commonly spelled, addler?
An addler is one who, or that which, addles. Befuddles. Confuses.
I admit I admire that stroke; it is worthy of Holmes himself.
In the very act of deceiving and confusing us, she has the audacity
to employ a name that brazenly announces her purpose!

An amusing corroborative detail about this Irene of "Scandal
in Bohemia"—*the* woman to Holmes according to the narrator of

the tales—is that Holmes was present at her wedding at the Church of St. Monica in the Edgeware Road. It is related that he was there as a witness, but that is pure poppycock. Holmes himself says, "I was half-dragged up to the altar, and before I knew where I was I found myself mumbling responses. . . ." Those are not the words of an indifferent witness, but of a reluctant, ensnared, bulldozed man—in short, a bridegroom. And in all the 1323 pages of the Sacred Writings, that is the only wedding we ever see—the only one, so far as we are told, that Holmes ever graced with his presence.

All this is very sketchy. I admit it. I am now collecting material for a fuller treatment of the subject, a complete demonstration of the evidence and the inevitable conclusion. It will fill two volumes, the second of which will consist of certain speculations regarding various concrete results of that long-continued and—I fear, alas—none-too-happy union. For instance, what of the parentage of Lord Peter Wimsey, who was born, I believe, around the turn of the century—about the time of the publication of "The Adventure of the Second Stain"? That will bear looking into.

Don't Guess, Let Me Tell You
By Ogden Nash

Ogden Nash is a widely known American humorous poet and satirist. Not the least of his achievements is his feat of attaching the telling label "Had-I-But-Known" to a school of mystery writing about which the less said the more chivalrous. The selection below is from a collection of Mr. Nash's verse entitled The Face is Familiar *(Boston: Little, Brown, 1940).*

PERSONALLY, I don't care whether a detective-story writer was educated in night school or day school.
So long as he doesn't belong to the H.I.B.K. school,
The H.I.B.K. being a device to which too many detective-story writers are prone;
Namely, the Had I But Known.
Sometimes it is the Had I But Known what grim secret lurked behind that smiling exterior, I would never have set foot within the door;
Sometimes the Had I But Known then what I know now, I could have saved at least three lives by revealing to the Inspector the conversation I heard through that fortuitous hole in the floor.
Had I But Known narrators are the ones who hear a stealthy creak at midnight in the tower where the body lies and, instead of locking their door or arousing the drowsy policeman posted outside their room, sneak off by themselves to the tower and suddenly they hear a breath exhaled behind them,

And they have no time to scream, they know nothing else till the
men from the D.A.'s office come in next morning and
find them.

Had I But Known-ers are quick to assume the prerogatives of
the Deity,

For they will suppress evidence that doesn't suit their theories
with appalling spontaneity,

And when the killer is finally trapped into a confession by some
elaborate device of the Had I But Known-ers some hundred pages later than if they hadn't held their knowledge
aloof,

Why, they say, Why, Inspector, I knew all along it was he, but I
couldn't tell you, you would have laughed at me unless
I had absolute proof.

Would you like for your library a nice detective story which I
am sorry to say I didn't rent but owns?

I wouldn't have bought it had I but known it was impregnated
with Had I But Knowns.

The late American humorist Christopher Ward (1868–1943) was the author of the following parody, which appeared in the Saturday Review of Literature *for November 2, 1929, at the height of the S. S. Van Dine-Philo Vance vogue.*

The Pink Murder Case

By S. S. Veendam

Author of the "Green," "Canary," "Mauve," and "Beige Murder Cases"

CHAPTER I

THE HOUSE ON THE MARSH

(Tuesday, February 22, 1732; 1 A. M.)

AMONG ALL the vari-colored murder cases from which Philo Pants has derived his reputation and I my income during the last few years, certainly there was none more horrifying, nor, in its. outcome, more astounding than the Pink one.

My friend Pants was, as I have often written, a young social aristocrat with carefully chiselled features, especially a fine, hand-engraved, aquamarine nose. His conversation was the most completely satisfying I have ever known. No one ever felt the need of a second dose.

He was a close friend of Barker,* the District Attorney, who entrusted to him the most interesting murder cases, much to my profit, since thus the murderer was given time to kill a whole book-full of people, † which is really necessary nowadays to keep

---

* George A. ("Gabby") Barker was the most efficient District Attorney of that name New York ever had. After retirement from office, he became a private citizen.

† The Blue Murder Case (Scribblers, 1929; $2.50).

The Cardinal Murder Case (Scribblers, 1927; $2.50).

the reader's interest. So it was that the frightful Pink holocaust was made possible. Pants had been for several days immersed in a Coptic translation of Schizzenheimer's "Nuovi Studi de la Physiologie des Heisshundes." He could not read Coptic, but was trying to decide which was the right side up of the fascinating volume, when Barker came in.

"A new murder for you, Pants," said Barker gloomily.

"Oh, I say, don't y' know, eh what?" drawled Pants. "How dashed amusin'. Most intriguin' and all that sort of thing. I could bear to hear about the bally homicide, old bean, don't y' know."

Barker frowned, glowered, and gritted his teeth. Pants's parts of speech always had this effect on him.

"It's a Pink case this time," he grumbled. "They're bad enough plain, but when they come in colors they're devilish. Some day a Scotch plaid will turn up and finish me."

"Who's the jolly old victim of the distressin' crime? My flutterin' heart's anguished to know."

Barker tore his hair and spat through his teeth grudgingly. "Alonzo Pink," he said, with biting sarcasm.

"I say, y' know, you don't say so," drawled Pants. "Old pal of mine. Spent last evenin' with him, discussin' terra cotta ornamentation of renaissance patisseries and all that. Dead, eh? Amusin' predicament, eh what?"

"Know any other Pinks?" asked Barker in a rage.

"Whole dashed lot, Citronella and Palooka, sisters, Hercules, brother, contemp'ry offspring of heredit-ry sire, old Paresis Pink, bally old blighter."

"Come along, then," gargled Barker furiously.

CHAPTER II

Shrieks in the Night

(Tuesday, December 25, 1929; 3 A. M.)

The Pink mansion stood on Broadway three blocks south of the Battery, a gloomy pile, embowered in funereal yews and gaunt weeping willows. A foreboding of woe came over me as we neared its ghastly portal.

Snoot, the butler, admitted us. A man of more sinister aspect I have never seen. He had but one eye on each side of his nose and his mouth was practically horizontal. In a sepulchral voice, he told us he had found Alonzo dead in his bedroom, shot through the head, and that all the doors and windows were locked on the inside. A Colt .32 lay by his side. Then he took us to the chamber of death.

"Oh, I say, my word!" drawled Pants. "How dashed amusin'!"

"What?" barked Barker.

"Don't notice anything funny, eh? Of course, you wouldn't. Why, man, the jolly old corpse is standin' on its head."

And so it was, but only the quick eye of Philo Pants had marked the fact.

"Now," drawled Pants, "we'll interview the caressin' family."

Citronella Pink met us in the library. She was gently but firmly dressed in a jade green bathing suit, a brown bowler, and white spats. She was a beautiful woman, but something about her made me think of either Lucrezia Borgia or Lizzie Borden or both.

"Ever do any shootin', Citronella?" drawled Pants.

"Lots," she said nonchalantly, whipping out a Colt .32.

"Ever shoot Alonzo?"

"Don't you wish you knew?" she said teasingly. "Ask Herc, he knows."

We found Hercules and his sister, Palooka, in the garage. They were shooting at each other with .32 Colts, but, as he had a harelip and St. Vitus's dance and she was cockeyed, neither had hit the other. Pants turned to Barker.

"Think I'll take on this amusin' pair after dinner," he drawled. "Give the servants jolly old once over now."

The entire staff was paraded for inspection. They all looked like jailbirds, and it was, indeed, found that they all were. Suspicion having thus been satisfactorily distributed, Pants dismissed Barker. "Run along, old fruit," he drawled. "I'll carry on with silly old Veendam."

CHAPTER III

GHOULS AND VAMPIRES

(Thursday, April 1, 1066; 4 A.M.)

At 9:30 the next morning Pants, in purple velvet pajamas, was sipping his cognac as he idly turned the leaves of an illuminated copy of Teufelsdrockh's "Ichweissnicht Wassolles Bedeutendass Ichsotraurigbin," when our phone rang.

"Barker speaking," said an agitated voice. "Pink case again. Palooka and Hercules found dead in rooms. Doors and windows all locked inside. Colt .32 by side each. Come at once. Mother."

"How deuced annoyin'," drawled Pants. "Must go around to jolly old slaughter-house again."

We met Barker there. "Undoubtedly an inside job," said he, "though it probably started outside. Ku-Klux, I think, with a dash of Mafia and a sprinkling of Paprika. By their fingerprints I've identified Snoot as the late Belle Boyd, the Beautiful Rebel Spy, and the parlor maid as Jesse James."

Pants looked at him with pained surprise. "Listen, Barker," he said earnestly. "There's something terrible going on here. Can't you feel it? In this lonely old mansion—poor thing!—polluted with a miasma of corrupt and rotting ambitions, black hatreds, hideous impulses, rheumatism, catarrh, coughs, colds, and indigestion—in this loathly mansion three bozos have been bumped off. Deuced amusin', eh what? Must have little old parley-voo with Citronella. Roll along, old egg. Toodle-oo and all that sort of thing."

Gasping with rage, Barker left Philo Pants, the master-mind, to pursue his inquiries.

CHAPTER IV

RED DARRELL'S REVENGE

(St. Valentine's Day, 1444, 5 A.M.)

At 9:30 the following morning Barker again appeared at our apartment. He was accompanied by Detective Bogan * and two

---

* Thomas Aquinas Bogan was first on the scene of the murders of Elwell and

policemen. Pants greeted the party with his usual charming insouciance.

"Ah, bobbies, what? Why the parade?"

"New development in the Pink case," said Barker in a tone of forbearance. "Citronella dead as per former plans and specifications."

"Pinks all wiped out, eh?" drawled Pants brightly. "No more cannon-fodder, crime wave will subside."

"Wait a bit," hissed Barker. "I've been studying this case and I've reached certain conclusions. First, these victims were all found dead in locked rooms, shot through heads with .32 calibre bullets and—mark this hitherto disregarded fact—a .32 Colt was found by the side of each! Do you see what that means? I didn't until Bogan told me. It was in each and every case—*suicide*." His voice sunk to a whisper as he pronounced the unexpected and dreadful word.

"Very well," he went on. " 'Why?' I asked Bogan. He answered like a flash—'Bughouse.' A logical working hypothesis, I said to myself. 'Why bughouse?' I asked Bogan. He answered in two words. But before I tell you what they were let me ask you a few questions. Who was with Alonzo Pink the evening before he shot himself? Who questioned Hercules and Palooka the day before their fatal night? Who 'parley-vooed' with Citronella before she shuffled off? The answer is in the two words of the astute Bogan —*Philo Pants!*

"It was you, Pants. Your blithering blah, your musical-comedy English accent drove these people mad, made them fly for relief to self-destruction. You are their murderer. And you, Veendam, were not only his wretched accomplice in this case, but your books, disseminating his words, have sowed the seeds of madness in many homes. Arrest these men!"

As the cops stepped forward, Philo Pants lightly laughed and, unscrewing the tip of his aquamarine nose, took from a cavity within two pellets.

"Catch, old dear," he drawled, as he tossed one to me. "Sorry

---

Arnold Rothstein and in the Dorothy Arnold disappearance case. He is now raising turtle-doves in Hoboken.

to disappoint, old fruit," he said to Barker. "It's dashed distressin', but must say toodle-oo and all that sort of thing."

Then together we swallowed the pellets and in a moment we both lay dead upon the floor.

"As usual," said Barker resignedly, "cyanide of potassium."

Murder at $2.50 a Crime

By Stephen Leacock

The beloved Canadian humorist Stephen Leacock (1869–1944) was a lifelong devotee of detective stories and wrote and lectured frequently on the subject. The selection below is from his Here Are My Lectures and Stories *(New York: Dodd, Mead, 1937; London: Lane, 1938).*

I PROPOSE tonight, ladies and gentlemen, to deal with murder. There are only two subjects that appeal nowadays to the general public, murder and sex; and, for people of culture, sex-murder. Leaving out sex for the minute—if you can—I propose tonight to talk about murder as carried on openly and daily at two dollars and fifty cents a crime.

For me, I admit right away that if I'm going to pay two dollars and fifty cents for a book I want to make sure that there's going to be at least *one* murder in it. I always take a look at the book first to see if there's a chapter headed "Finding of the Body." And I know that everything is all right when it says, *The body was that of an elderly gentleman, well dressed but upside down.* Always, you notice, an "elderly gentleman." What they have against us, I don't know. But you see, if it said that the body was that of a woman—that's a tragedy. The body was that of a child! —that's a horror. But *the body was that of an elderly gentleman* —oh, pshaw! that's all right. Anyway he's had his life—he's had a good time (It says he's well dressed.)—probably been out on a hoot. (He's found upside down.) That's all right! He's worth more dead than alive.

·   ·   ·   ·   ·   ·   ·   ·   ·   ·

But as a matter of fact, from reading so many of these stories I get to be such an expert that I don't have to wait for the finding of the body. I can tell just by a glance at the beginning of the book who's going to *be* the body. For example, if the scene is laid on this side of the water, say in New York, look for an opening paragraph that runs about like this:

Mr. Phineas Q. Cactus sat in his downtown office in the drowsy hour of a Saturday afternoon. He was alone. Work was done for the day. The clerks were gone. The building, save for the janitor, who lived in the basement, was empty.

Notice that, *save for the janitor.* Be sure to save him. We're going to need him later on, to accuse him of the murder.

As he sat thus, gazing in a sort of reverie at the papers on the desk in front of him, his chin resting on his hand, his eyes closed and slumber stole upon him.

Of course! To go to sleep like that in a downtown deserted office is a crazy thing to do in New York—let alone Chicago. Every intelligent reader knows that Mr. Cactus is going to get a crack on the cocoanut. He's the body.

.   .   .   .

But if you don't mind my saying so, they get a better setting for this kind of thing in England than they do with us. You need an old country to get a proper atmosphere around murder. The best murders (always of elderly gentlemen) are done in the country at some old country seat—any wealthy elderly gentleman has a seat—called by such a name as the Priory, or the Doggery, or the Chase—that sort of thing.

Try this for example:

Sir Charles Althorpe sat alone in his library at Althorpe Chase. It was late at night. The fire had burned low in the grate. Through the heavily curtained windows no sound came from outside. Save for the maids, who slept in a distant wing, and save for the butler, whose pantry was under the stairs, the Chase, at this time of the year, was empty. As Sir Charles sat thus in his arm-chair, his head gradually sank upon his chest and he dozed off into slumber.

Foolish man! Doesn't he know that to doze off into slumber in an isolated country house, with the maids in a distant wing, is little short of madness? But do you notice—Sir Charles! He's a baronet. That's the touch to give class to it. And do you notice that we have *saved* the butler, just as we did the janitor? Of course he didn't really kill Sir Charles, but the local police always arrest the butler. And anyway, he'd been seen sharpening a knife on his pants in his pantry and saying, "I'll do for the old Devil yet."

. . . .

So there is the story away to a good start—Sir Charles's Body found next morning by a "terrified" maid—all maids are terrified—who "could scarcely give an intelligent account of what she saw"—they never can. Then the local police (Inspector Higginbottom of the Hopshire Constabulary) are called in and announce themselves "baffled." Every time the reader hears that the local police are called in he smiles an indulgent smile and knows they are just there to be baffled.

. . . .

At this point of the story enters the Great Detective, specially sent by or through Scotland Yard. That's another high class touch—Scotland Yard. It's not a Yard, and it's not in Scotland. Knowing it only from detective fictions I imagine it is a sort of club somewhere near the Thames in London. You meet the Prime Minister and the Archbishop of Canterbury going in and out all the time—but so strictly incognito that you don't know that it is them, I mean that they are it. And apparently even "royalty" is found "closeted" with heads at the yard—"royalty" being in English a kind of hush-word for things too high up to talk about.

Well, anyway, the Yard sends down the Great Detective, either as an official or as an outsider to whom the Yard appeal when utterly stuck; and he comes down to the Chase, looking for clues.

Here comes in a little technical difficulty in the narration of the story. We want to show what a wonderful man the Great Detective is, and yet he can't be made to tell the story himself. He's too silent—and too strong. So the method used nowadays is to have a sort of shadow along with him, a companion, a sort of Poor Nut, full of admiration but short on brains. Ever since

Conan Doyle started this plan with Sherlock and Watson, all the
others have copied it. So the story is told by this secondary person. Taken at his own face value he certainly is a Poor Nut.
Witness the way in which his brain breaks down utterly and is
set going again by the Great Detective. The scene occurs when the
Great Detective begins to observe all the things around the place
that were overlooked by Inspector Higginbottom.

*"But how," I exclaimed, "how in the name of all that is in-
comprehensible, are you able to aver that the criminal wore rubbers?"*

My friend smiled quietly.

*"You observe," he said, "that patch of fresh mud about ten feet
square in front of the door of the house. If you would look, you
will see that it has been freshly walked over by a man with rubbers on."*

*I looked. The marks of the rubbers were there plain enough—
at least a dozen of them.*

*"What a fool I was!" I exclaimed. "But at least tell me how
you were able to know the length of the criminal's foot?"*

My friend smiled again, his same inscrutable smile.

*"By measuring the print of the rubber," he answered quietly,
"and then subtracting from it the thickness of the material multiplied by two."*

"Multiplied by two!" I exclaimed. "Why by two?"

"For the toe and the heel."

*"Idiot that I am," I cried, "it all seems so plain when you ex-
plain it."*

In other words, the Poor Nut makes an admirable narrator.
However much fogged the reader may get, he has at least the comfort of knowing that the Nut is far more fogged than he is. Indeed, the Nut may be said, in a way, to personify the ideal reader,
that is to say the stupidest—the reader who is most completely
bamboozled with the mystery, and yet intensely interested.

Such a reader has the support of knowing that the police are
entirely "baffled"—that's always the word for them; that the public are "mystified"; that the authorities are "alarmed"; the newspapers "in the dark"; and the Poor Nut, altogether up a tree. On
those terms, the reader can enjoy his own ignorance to the full.

Before the Great Detective gets to work, or rather while he is getting to work, the next thing is to give him *character, individuality.* It's no use to say that he "doesn't in the least look like a detective." Of course not. No detective ever does. But the point is not what he doesn't look like, but what he does look like.

Well, for one thing, though its pretty stale, he can be made extremely thin, in fact, "cadaverous." Why a cadaverous man can solve a mystery better than a fat man it is hard to say; presumably, the thinner a man is, the more acute is his mind. At any rate, the old school of writers preferred to have their detectives lean. This incidentally gave the detective a face "like a hawk," the writer not realizing that a hawk is one of the stupidest of animals. A detective with a face like an orang-outang would beat it all to bits.

Indeed, the Great Detective's face becomes even more important than his body. Here there is absolute unanimity. His face has to be "inscrutable." Look at it though you will, you can never read it. Contrast it, for example, with the face of Inspector Higginbottom, of the local police force. Here is a face that can look "surprised," or "relieved," or, with great ease, "completely baffled."

But the face of the Great Detective knows of no such changes. No wonder the Poor Nut is completely mystified. From the face of the great man you can't tell whether the cart in which they are driving jolts him or whether the food at the Inn gives him indigestion.

To the Great Detective's face there used to be added the old-time expedient of not allowing him either to eat or drink. And when it was added that during this same period of about eight days the sleuth never slept, the reader could realize in what fine shape his brain would be for working out his "inexorable chain of logic."

But nowadays this is changed. The Great Detective not only eats, but he eats well. Often he is presented as a connoisseur in food. Thus:

"Stop a bit." Thus speaks the Great Detective to the Poor Nut and Inspector Higginbottom, whom he is dragging round with him as usual. "We have half an hour before the train leaves Paddington. Let us have some dinner. I know an Italian restaurant

near here where they serve frogs' legs à la Marengo better than anywhere else in London."

A few minutes later we were seated at one of the tables of a dingy little eating place whose sign board with the words "Restauranto Italiano" led me to the deduction that it was an Italian restaurant. I was amazed to observe that my friend was evidently well known in the place, while his order for "three glasses of Chianti with two drops of vermicelli in each," called for an obsequious bow from the appreciative padrone. I realized that this amazing man knew as much of the finesse of Italian wines as he did of playing the saxophone.

We may go further. In many up-to-date cases the detective not only gets plenty to eat but a liberal allowance of strong drink. One generous British author of today is never tired of handing out to the Great Detective and his friends what he calls a "stiff whiskey and soda." At all moments of crisis they get one.

For example, when they find the body of Sir Charles Althorpe, late owner of Althorpe Chase, a terrible sight, lying on the floor of the library, what do they do? They reach at once to the sideboard and pour themselves out a "stiff whiskey and soda." It certainly is a great method.

But in the main we may say that all this stuff about eating and drinking has lost its importance. The Great Detective has to be made exceptional by some other method.

And here is where his music comes in. It transpires—not at once but in the first pause in the story—that this great man not only can solve a crime, but has the most extraordinary aptitude for music, especially for dreamy music of the most difficult kind. As soon as he is left in the Inn room with the Poor Nut, out comes his saxophone and he tunes it up.

"What were you playing?" I asked, as my friend at last folded his beloved instrument into its case.

"Beethoven's Sonata in Q," he answered modestly.

"Good Heavens!" I exclaimed.

.   .   .   .

Up to this point the story, any detective story, has been a howling success. The body has been found; they're all baffled and full of whiskey and soda, and everything's fine! But the only trouble is how to go on with it! You can't! There's no way to make crime really interesting except at the start; it's a pity they have to go on, that they can't just stay baffled and full, and call it a day.

But now begin the mistakes and the literary fallacies that spoil a crime story. At this point in comes the heroine—the heroine!—who has no real place in a murder story but is just a left-over remnant of the love story. In she comes, Margaret Althorpe, wild and all dishevelled. No wonder she's wild! Who wouldn't be? And dishevelled—oh, yes, the best writers always dishevel them up like that. In she comes, almost fainting! What do they do, Inspector Higginbottom and the Great Detective? They shoot a "stiff whiskey and soda" into her—and hit one themselves at the same time.

.   .   .   .

And with that, you see, the story drifts off sideways so as to work up a love-interest in the heroine, who has no business in it at all. Making a heroine used to be an easy thing in earlier books when the reading public was small. The author just imagined the kind of girl that he liked himself and let it go at that. Walter Scott, for example, liked them small—size three—"sylph-like" was the term used; in fact the heroine was just a "slip of a girl"—the slippier the better.

But Margaret Althorpe has to please everybody at once. So the description of her runs like this:

Margaret Althorpe was neither short nor tall.

—That means that she looked pretty tall standing up but when she sat down she was sawed off.

. . . *Her complexion neither dark nor fair, and her religion was neither Protestant nor Roman Catholic. She was not a prohibitionist but never took more than a couple of gins at a time. Her motto was, "No, boys, that's all I can hold."*

That at least is about the spirit of the description. But even at that, description of what is called her "person" is not sufficient by itself. There is the question of her "temperament" as well. Unless a heroine has "temperament" she can't get by; and temperament consists in undergoing a great many physiological changes

in a minimum of time. Here, for example, are the physiological
variations undergone by the heroine of a book I read the other
day, in what appeared to be a space of seventeen minutes:

A new gladness ran through her.

.   .   .   .

A thrill coursed through her (presumably in the opposite direction).

.   .   .   .

Something woke up within her that had been dead.

.   .   .   .

A great yearning welled up within her.

.   .   .   .

*Something seemed to go out from her that was not of her nor
to her.*

.   .   .   .

Everything sank within her.

That last means, I think, that something had come unhooked.

.   .   .   .

But, you see, by this turn the novel has reached what the diplo-
mats call an *impasse,* and plainer people simply a *cul de sac* or a
ne plus ultra. It can't get on. They arrested the butler. He didn't
do it. Apparently nobody did it.

In other words all detective stories reach a point where the
reader gets impatient and says to himself: "Come now; *somebody* murdered Sir Charles! Out with it." And the writer has no
answer. All the old attempts at an answer suitable for literary
purposes have been worn thin. There used to be a simple and
easy solution of a crime mystery by finding that the murder was
done by a "tramp." In the old Victorian days the unhappy creature called a tramp had no rights that the white man had to respect, either in fiction or out of it. They'd hang a tramp as un-

concernedly as they'd catch a butterfly. And if he belonged to the class called a "villainous-looking tramp" he registered as A.1., and his execution (indicated but not described) was part of the happy ending, along with Margaret Althorpe's marriage to the Poor Nut as a by-product on the side—not of course to the Great Detective. Marriage is not for him. He passes on to the next mystery, in which "royalty" itself is deeply concerned.

.   .   .   .

But all the tramp stuff is out of date. With a hundred million people "on the dole" and on "relief," we daren't set them to work at murder. We have to get another solution.

Here is one, used for generations but still going fairly strong. The murderer is found; oh, yes, he's found all right and confesses his guilt, *but* it is only too plain that his physical condition is such that he must soon "go before a higher tribunal." And that doesn't mean the supreme court.

It seems that at the moment when the Great Detective and Inspector Higginbottom have seized him he has developed a "hacking cough." This is one of those terrible maladies known only in fiction—like "brain fever" and a "broken heart," for which all medicine is in vain. Indeed in this case, as the man starts to make his confession, he can hardly talk for hacks.

"Well," said Garth, looking round at the little group of police officers, "the game is up—hack! hack!—and I may as well make a clean breast of it—hack, hack, hack."

Any trained reader when he hears these hacks knows exactly what they are to lead up to. The criminal, robust though he seemed only a chapter ago when he jumped through a three-story window after throttling Sub-Inspector Juggins half to death, is a dying man. He has got one of those terrible diseases known to fiction as a "mortal complaint." It wouldn't do to give it an exact name, or somebody might get busy and cure it. The symptoms are a hacking cough and a great mildness of manner, an absence of all profanity, and a tendency to call everybody "you gentlemen." Those things spell finis.

In fact, all that is needed now is for the Great Detective himself to say, *"Gentlemen"* (They are all gentlemen at this stage of the story.), *"a higher conviction than any earthly law has, et cetera, et cetera."* With that, the curtain is dropped, and it is understood that the criminal made his exit the same night.

That's better, decidedly better. And yet, lacking in cheerfulness, somehow.

In fact this solution has something a little cowardly about it. It doesn't face the music.

One more of these futile solutions may be offered. Here's the way it is done.

The Great Detective stood looking about him, quietly shaking his head. His eye rested a moment on the prostrate body of Sub-Inspector Bradshaw, then turned to scrutinize the neat hole drilled in the glass of the window.

"I see it all now," he murmured. *"I should have guessed it sooner. There is no doubt whose work this is."*

"Who is it?" I asked.

"Blue Edward," he announced quietly.

"Blue Edward!" I exclaimed.

"Blue Edward," he repeated.

"Blue Edward!" I reiterated, *"but who then is Blue Edward?"*

This, of course, is the very question that the reader is wanting to ask. Who on earth is Blue Edward? The question is answered at once by the Great Detective himself.

"The fact that you have never heard of Blue Edward merely shows the world that you have lived in. As a matter of fact, Blue Edward is the terror of four continents. We have traced him to Shanghai, only to find him in Madagascar. It was he who organized the terrible robbery at Irkutsk in which ten mujiks were blown up with a bottle of Epsom salts.

"It was Blue Edward who for years held the whole of Philadelphia in abject terror, and kept Oshkosh, Wisconsin, on the jump for even longer. At the head of a gang of criminals that ramifies all over the known globe, equipped with a scientific education that enables him to read and write and use a typewriter with the greatest ease, Blue Edward has practically held the police of the world at bay for years.

"I suspected his hand in this from the start. From the very outset, certain evidences pointed to the work of Blue Edward."

After which all the police inspectors and spectators keep shaking their heads and murmuring, "Blue Edward, Blue Edward," until the reader is sufficiently impressed.

.   .   .   .

The fact is that the writer *can't* end the story, not if it is sufficiently complicated in the beginning. No possible ending satisfies the case. Not even the glad news that the heroine sank into the Poor Nut's arms, never to leave them again, can relieve the situation. Not even the knowledge that they erected a handsome memorial to Sir Charles, or that the Great Detective played the saxophone for a week can quite compensate us.

Everything Under Control

By Richard Armour

One of the better known young American poets, Richard Armour has demonstrated a special facility for topical verse. His poem below appeared in the Saturday Review of Literature *for October 18, 1941.*

THE PUBLICATION of mystery novels will be strictly controlled in Italy, because they are considered harmful to the minds of fascist youth.—*News Item.*

> In the land of Mussolini
>   They are viewing with alarm:
> The authorities are spleeny
>   When they think how great the harm
>
> To the dormant cerebrations
>   Of impressionable youths,
> Should the ratiocinations
>   Of detective-story sleuths
>
> Interfere, despite hoodwinking
>   Of the best fascistic kind,
> And evoke a little thinking
>   In the regimented mind.

The Whistling Corpse
By Ben Hecht

Parody has long been recognized as one of the sharpest of all forms of criticism. If the proponents of a certain variety of over-ripe mystery fiction, usually associated with the American women's magazines, can hold up their heads after reading this scathing lampoon of their kind they are a hardy crew indeed. Like Ogden Nash, Mr. Hecht suggests by implication that the sorority concerned had better mind their mannerisms and curtail their clichés —or else! (A view shared by a wide and growing section of the mystery-reading public.) Ben Hecht is a renowned American wit and man-of-letters. His satire appeared in Ellery Queen's Mystery Magazine *for September 1945.*

(AUTHOR'S NOTE: I am indebted to the writers of mystery books for many hours of diversion. In part payment of this debt I offer them this Chapter One, gratis and unencumbered, to use as a beginning for any of their subsequent works.)

Dedication

To Maybell, Gladys, Hortense, Marianne, Mathilda, Tinee, Ginger, Ethyl, Gussykins, Helena, Chickie, Bernice, Fifi, Dorothea, Gugu, Greta, My Wife and Mom, without whose love and tender understanding and jolly evenings at Grapes End this book would never have been written.

Author's Note

(The characters in this book bear no resmblance to anyone living or dead with the exception of course, of Colonel Sparks and the charming Eulalia. I have used their red barn as a scene for two of

the murders but Marroway Hall is entirely fictional and, as everyone knows, there is no such state in the U.S.A. as Bonita.)

CHAPTER ONE

I SHALL never forget the bright summer afternoon when poor
Stuffy found the green button under Grandma Marnoy's knitting
bag—on the lawn out there, a stone's throw from Indian Creek
that bisects the rolling Marpleton grounds where Toppet, Ruby
and I used to play pirate and chase butterflies. I have often wondered what would have happened if Stuffy had given me the button instead of swallowing it. For one thing, Consuela Marston
would never have met the man with the pick ax and I would
never, of course, have gone to that dreadful carnival which was
the beginning of everything.

Had I known, of course, even after the button, what seems so
obvious to us all now—I mean, about Uncle Massie's love for that
curious creature during his mining days in Texas when he
founded the great Micheljohn fortune—I might have prevented
some of the disasters which for a time threatened to wipe out the
descendants of Nathaniel Colby. But poor Madelaine had always
misunderstood Percival Massie's reasons for selling the great coffee
warehouses that had been in the family—even before Jebby was
born.

Percival loved Madelaine—in his own way, of course—arrogant,
thin lipped and even sneeringly. But it *was* love as we all were
to discover when the green button came home to roost and poor
Stuffy was no more. That afternoon of the autopsy still brings
a chill into my bones. Poor Stuffy! How can I ever blot out the
memory of his bewildered face when the dead rose up and
whistled at him—that whistle that changed Marroway Hall into a
charnel house!

The events are still too fresh in my mind for me to write without a shudder as I recall that summer afternoon when Loppy and
Coppy, Grandma Marnoy's favorite twins, arrived on the 3:18
at Maskincott, in answer to her imperial summons. Marroway
Hall was never so festive as on that moment when these two ill-
fated youngsters came laughing down the baronial staircase that
led from Cousin Marshall's secret laboratory—as we were to find

out—straight into the old Colonial living room that had once been a fort—the fort where the British had massacred the last of the Green Mountain boys on that Sunday hundreds of years ago before Bonita had yet become a state.

As children we used to be proud of the bloodstains over the mantelpiece which neither old Jebby nor any of the staff was allowed to efface. Little did we think that those bloodstains would someday become the clue that would put a rope around the necks of three people we all loved.

But, to return to the Green Button and poor Stuffy's untimely gourmandizing, I knew, of course, on that afternoon that Jennifer and Siegfried Mersmer had left two sons at the time of their tragic death in the south of France, although Delmar had disappeared when he was twelve and Happy (as we called him) had inherited the entire Marvin fortune, including the great stables of Marvingrovia. Word of Delmar's marriage to the ill-fated Agatha had been brought to us much later by Uncle Mooney when he returned with faithful Jebby after settling his affairs in the Transvaal. It was much too late for any of us to do anything, and I'm afraid we did just that—nothing. We all knew, of course, that the young wife had died in childbirth and that the twins Loppy and Coppy belonged to a previous marriage. But none of us—with the exception, of course, of the dead man who whistled through those awful nights—had any inkling of Uncle Morehead's last will and testament. But I am getting ahead of my story a wee bit.

It all really begins with the finding of the green button. We were all sitting on the veranda, the Countess Marsley, Spike Hummer, catcher for the Giants, and Uncle Murchison's two nephews —Milton and the irrepressible Pliny. And Grandma Marnoy was knitting away, laughing and agile despite her hundred and two years. And poor ill-fated Cousin Mullineaux was poring over his famous stamp collection. We sat sipping those adorable juleps that only old Jebby knew how to make and listening to Joel, the wittiest and yet cruellest man I have ever known, describe his recent trip to Charlestown.

I detected a curious tightening of Aunt Molby's eyelids as Joel talked and, despite the languorous mood of that moment, I felt a number of undercurrents. Jerry's hatred of the lovely Marianne and Uncle Milford's twenty years of silent rage against the woman who had left him for that impecunious art student—poor Jon Mungo whose lovely portrait of Senorita X hangs before me even now as I write—these were some of the undercurrents. There were others that I was to learn of later.

But we were all gay and frightfully witty as we sat there, listening to the chatter of the twins and watching Stuffy playing pirate on the lawn by himself. Suddenly something green flashed in the Bonita sun. I remember hearing a sharp intake of breath behind me, as if someone were stifling a gasp of terror. And then the flash of green was gone. The green button had disappeared down Stuffy's throat.

I turned, wondering who had gasped, and looked into the blazing eyes of Cousin Maynard—lank, easy going Maynard with his patrician nose and the ne'er-do-well droop to his sensual mouth. A knowing chuckle came from Grandma Marnoy's esoteric face! And then we were all chatting gayly again. All but Madelaine.

Poor Loppy! Maynard's love for her is something that still brings a glow to me as I recall him whittling that first boomerang—the one we found later at the bottom of Indian Creek, covered with her blood. It lies before me on my desk as I write, together with the green button, the cross-bow, the little torn laundry list, the pile of empty envelopes, and the old-fashioned fireless cooker that were all to open our eyes before that awful summer in Bonita was over.

I have always had a distaste for family reunions—and despite my interest in Grandma Marnoy's declaration that she had decided to change her will, I felt bored. Which may explain why I was the first to leave the veranda and why it was I, of all people, who first saw the daintily shod pair of feet dangling over the baronial staircase. For a moment I was too overcome to scream! A woman, still beautiful, still voluptuous, hanging in our ancient living room! I stared in horror at the lovely dead face now contorted in agony. And I had barely time to realize that this dangling corpse was whistling—whistling an old French-Canadian nursery song—*Arouet, ma' jollie Arouet*—before the room turned black and I felt myself plunging into an abyss.

Oh, England! Full of Sin

By Robert J. Casey

Although "Bob" Casey is best known to the American reading public as journalist, traveler, and war correspondent, he also has a respectable collection of mystery thrillers to his credit. He is additionally an omnivorous reader of other people's whodunits, as this lively survey of the curious tribal mores of the British school (from Scribner's Magazine *for April 1937) will testify.*

THE ENGLISH are a strange people who murder their grandmothers (named Lady Pamela) in hermetically sealed rooms. They pursue a cozy communal existence in one-roomed houses called The Library. They have no calendar; everything happens on a single date—a fortnight come Michaelmas. They live in a constant fog, surrounded by blighters, toffs, and outlanders who say "Waal" and "I reckon." They play a bit of golf so that corpses can be found on the thirteenth green. Occasionally they vary this and go hunting on the downs or the moors—two benighted localities where life is short and generally sinful.

One is told that in other times the English were divided into three classes: upper, middle, and lower. But readers of English detective stories know all that has been done away with. Through the leveling influence of crime, everybody in England is now like everybody else, with mystery in his soul, a past on his conscience, and rubber heels on his feet—rubber heels that leave a peculiar imprint in peculiar mud especially designed to receive peculiar heelprints in Devonshire or Sussex or Shropshire.

Lady Pamela is never what she seems. Even when she plays her favorite rôle as a corpse, there is something suspicious about her

343

until the climax of all that is good in English life is reached—Chapter XXXI (copyright, Hodder & Stoughton). The butler is a missing heir or jewel thief, or perhaps only a wandering minstrel from Australia who cherishes a secret sorrow. The second maid is the child of Sir Roger Branksome by a former marriage or by no marriage at all. She is gray-haired and silent and inscrutable, or young and wistful and frightened by the memory of other murders that she saw done when she was in the service of the Duke of Wuffenbaugh—the night the candles about Lady Whosit's coffin set fire to the great hall. (That was twenty years ago a fortnight come Michaelmas.)

Marriage exists as a legal institution in England—the old family lawyer mentions that when all the relatives assemble, after the current murder, for the reading of the will. But in the tired eyes of the detectives, who warn everybody that anything they say may be used in evidence against them, such conventions count for little. The visitors at English country houses are uniformly folks who can't or won't tell where they were last night between the third rubber of bridge and the time the shot was fired—say five A.M. For that matter, they are very shy about talking of themselves at all. Most of the young women have been at Brighton out of season, and the young men who don't care who knows when they were at Brighton or with whom are against cross-examination on principle. They are afraid that somebody might find out about that business in The City when Tancred's Ltd. failed and old Sir Oswald shot himself without respect for the familiar tradition of the locked room.

It is perhaps fortunate for this interesting commonwealth that the population is about evenly divided between murderers, victims, and detectives—this gives everybody an even break. One might think that so definite a classification would reduce life on the Island to a strict routine through which the average citizen would wander benighted, from birth to the coroner's inquest, without variety of occupation or hope for advancement. But that is not true, because nobody can tell by looking at these three classes of English gentlefolk just which one is which. Life can never be staid or humdrum in a community where a detective may turn out to be a murderer or a corpse, or, stranger still, a detective.

Each time the chauffeur loses his way in the rain (the windscreen wipers working like fury against the thickening veil of beaded gray); each time the pale-faced man in evening dress with a patch over his right eye admits one to the silent company of men and women clustered about the dying fire in the library; each time these things happen there is a new thrill. They are always happening, of course, but their charm is unending.

The reason novelty springs eternal in such commonplace occurrences (which every Englishman has experienced thousands of times, exclusive of reprints) is that the scene and characters remain the same, but the lines and motivation are always different. One never knows, as he stands by the fireplace and checks up on the oddly assorted company into which circumstance has thrust him, whether he is scheduled to be the long-lost heir or, much to his own surprise, an inspector from Scotland Yard, or merely another victim for the old four-poster bed—the old four-poster bed in the north wing which has claimed so many wet visitors since old Malcolm got his throat cut there in the early hunting season of 1894. One doesn't ask, of course. If one is truly English, one doesn't forget himself even to notice that the host with the patch on his eye has a Spanish poniard sticking out of his back some four and a half inches.

Trained on the playing fields of Eton, one doesn't so much as lift an eyebrow when the tall, icy blonde at the end of the divan adjusts her pearls and discloses three bullet holes (Lee-Enfield service rifle, caliber .30). It wouldn't be cricket to observe that the ormolu clock has just struck thirteen or that somewhere beyond the shadowy bend in the black oak staircase a mad woman is screaming. In England, one doesn't call the cops until there is real need for them. One just doesn't, that's all.

When one comes in out of the wet and claims the hospitality of a host with a knife sticking out of his back, one knows what to expect and how to act. That is part of one's heritage as an Englishman. One explains that he can go no farther because the windscreen wiper isn't working properly and that he is sorry to cause inconvenience. Then he offers cigarettes to such of the assemblage as happen to be alive and thoughtfully watches the steam rising from his sodden boots. It is permitted him under the rules of etiquette to observe out of the corner of his eye some of the people who glare at him balefully through the dizzy reflections of the fire—the hard-faced young man in the aviator's costume, the suave graybeard beside the icy blonde (one knows him instantly for a retired colonel recently arrived from India), the beautiful ingénue who tries to smile as she tears her lace handkerchief to shreds with pale, nervous hands, the apoplectic draper from Manchester, the Malay servant with the mark of the kris across his villainous jaw—one notes them all and files them away in his retentive memory, aware that he will see them all again—in the dock. Then one carries on.

These jolly evenings in England, almost as much of a national institution as cricket, have, it is true, been criticized. Since the War no conventions of conduct, amusement, or social relationship have survived in quite their original form. Some of the younger generation prefer to have their murders done in night clubs or among the sprightly Chinese of Whitechapel. But one who knows the stability of English thought, the inflexibility of English ideals, the deep-rooted love of England for the things that time has proved worthwhile, must realize that the finding of mysterious houses on rainy nights will never lose its popularity.

One may feel that he has met all of the patch-eyed host's friends before, as indeed he has, on other bad nights when the windscreen wiper failed to work and the spark plugs got wet. But he is always cheered by the thought that he never can tell in advance what the current purpose of the conclave may be. Perhaps Old Patch-eye (Doctor Zingara Pachi, as he is sometimes called) may be plotting the overthrow of Downing Street or the spread of anthrax through shaving brushes; perhaps he has called the clan to write confessions of murder, arson, or misdemeanor on the backs of £50,000 notes; perhaps he is merely breeding monsters in his basement. The uncertainty of it all is what gives English country life its zest.

When one is tempted to be bored on discovering the same old faces in the same old library, he is permitted to cast a second glance about the company and try to settle in his own mind which one will turn out to be Superintendent Muggs of Scotland Yard. One stares moodily into the fireplace and remembers that Superintendent Muggs is one of the Big Five, perhaps all of the Big Five. Normally he can be found raising prize fowl somewhere around Wembley or pottering about among his roses at Ealing Broadway. On any one of his numerous vacations he can be found salmon fishing in some locality where the murders occur most unexpectedly and in the greatest numbers. On such a night as this, however, he is certain to be the five fellows whose spark plugs got wet just ahead of yours.

Unless you die before you wake, you'll find out all about it in the morning. You'll look through your window on a dew-pearled countryside where the greenery steps down through the lace of the yew trees toward the sunny opalescence of the distant sea. And you'll observe Superintendent Muggs gratefully accepting his prisoner from the hands of Horace, the second groom, who was wise enough to know who was guilty before the murder was committed.

Of course, in the meantime, the criminal may have confessed. Confession is a habit of English murderers—a habit that makes them *sui generis* and wins for them the love of countries where lawbreakers are less thoughtful. There can be no perfect crime in England so long as English killers remain true to the traditions of their craft and tell all any time the detectives find themselves all muddled up with footprints, fingerprints, suicide notes, and drippings from umbrellas.

It must not be supposed that all of the big detectives in England are Superintendent Muggs of the Big Five. Scotland Yard, for the most part, is composed of bright young men trained to listen to explanations of how the crime was committed. They are skilled in advancing theories. Since the days of the late Sherlock Holmes they have been able to distinguish the difference between heat and cold and the quick and the dead. With the years, they have cultivated an abiding calm that makes their decisions on such subjects important. But they never relinquish their English citizenship or their English prerogative of committing an occasional murder themselves or letting themselves be found cold and stiff in the customary locked room.

Your real detective is quite likely to be a doctor—an ancient specialist in tonsillectomy—who is interested in finding out why

some people kill other people. Or he may be a barrister, or a play-
wright, or Sir Henry himself, or perhaps the vicar. One great
English detective was, in fact, a retired French detective, so you
see how difficult it is to judge, how useless to guess. In a country
where your physician may turn out to be a secret agent for the
Polynesian Poi League and your chemist may one day stand revealed as the King of Sweden, such things cease to matter.

In point of fact it is no great task to be a detective in England.
For, to be explicit, no true British murderer ever ended his work
with the provision of a cadaver. Always he leaves those little marks
of his individuality which make the crime worth eight shillings
between hard covers. If he is an amateur, he may leave only a
set of fingerprints—his own and quite a lot of those of his friends
and relatives. If he is skillful but in a hurry, he may leave only
meager exhibits of Devonshire mud and stubs of rare old Gold
Flyke cigarettes.

In well-contrived murders, he leaves his hat, ladder marks under the window, buttons on the floor of the sealed room, railroad-
ticket stubs, samples of his hair, army discharge papers, fingernail
clippings, footprints, handprints, Bertillon measurements, and
letters from his mother. In the United States, criminals don't do
that, and the percentage of escapes is correspondingly higher. In
England, it is customary to ask some innocent bystander to assume sponsorship for the exhibits, but when he fails to cooperate,
the guilty man or woman is duly notified, and there's an end to it.

Apparently there are no law courts in England, because the
murderers all commit suicide in picturesque fashion as soon as
the evidence is completed. This simplification of the legal procedure alone saved Great Britain countless pounds during the
recent depression, although it had the effect of putting numerous
magistrates and barristers out of work.

English railway-station employees are the greatest memory experts in the world. They are given close competition for this distinction by the taxicab drivers, inasmuch as either of them can
remember the age, weight, complexion, dress, and distinguishing marks of anybody who checked his aunt's body on the up
goods train from Kings Cross a fortnight come Michaelmas. However, the birthday-honors list favors the engine drivers, guards,

and station attendants who can remember not only the shipper of the clinical material, but the punch marks in his ticket from Twiddergglellyn (pronounced Chumley), Wales. This gift has been invaluable to the police who, after interviewing them, have only to consult the roster of people with missing aunts in Twiddergglellyn and thus arrive at a rough idea of what is going on.

Off duty, the taxi drivers live in places called pubs which are opposite other places called the mews. These pubs have historic significance, particularly in London. There they were once the haunt of five Hindus freshly arrived in search of the idol's eye. In those colorful days people were sometimes killed in pubs and tossed into the river, later to be identified by laundry marks and restored to families who had friends or business acquaintances in Baker Street. Now, aside from their function as resting places for taxi-driving experts in mnemonics, they serve no useful purpose, save as an occasional rendezvous for the Big Ben Listeners' Club, whose members always hear Big Ben strike just as the innocent suspect comes out of the fog with blood on his shoes.

London life, of necessity, differs in setting if not in tempo from that of the country. The city itself is a gray and mysterious place whose streets have not been mapped since Doctor Jekyll and Mr. Hyde. Its dank lanes, around the corner from the pub and mews, have never been plumbed, its thick fogs are filled with lost pedestrians, lorries, trams, hansom cabs, and screams.

Living in London has been amazingly simplified since the concentration of populace which began some time before the War. In the days when avenging angels from Utah were wandering about, painting cabalistic signs on doors, they had a lot of trouble. There were so many people who lived in houses, and consequently so many doors. London must have had quite an area in those days. The patient Hindus who came looking for moonstones trotted for hundreds of miles over rough cobbles without getting a glimpse of it, and presumably had to be relieved by fresh batches of Hindus working in relays. Even at the turn of the century, a policeman's lot was not a happy one because so many families occupied individual houses or flats, or bed sitting rooms—a habit due no doubt to British reserve, which is cultivated on the playing fields of Eton.

Now, however, things are different. If a murder is committed on the embankment or in the hermetically sealed room, or in the pantry or vestry of the Dean of St. Paul's, Scotland Yard has an easy task. The whole population is immediately questioned—after first being warned that anything the populace says may be used in evidence against it. And this is simple because everybody lives in the Adelphi apartments in Maida Vale. Of course, there are a few exceptions. All doctors live in Harley Street. All barristers live in Lincoln's Inn. All Italians live in Soho.

Aside from the several million citizens whose names are over the doorbells, several unidentified but interesting people inhabit the Adelphi. There is the old man who plays the *Moonlight Sonata* on the violin every morning at two o'clock. His name has not yet been learned because nobody wishes to intrude on his privacy. It seems more than likely that he is a murderer and a very good one. He couldn't very well be the corpse.

Then there is the woman in black who comes in through the windows of the bed sitting room at midnight when the gale is howling outside and the fire is crackling cozily in the grate. You are sitting in front of the fire with a good book and a mug of mulled sack—you a handsome bachelor who cannot imagine why somebody took three shots at you with arrows dipped in henbane tonight as you were leaving your office in the Admiralty. You feel a draft on the back of your neck and you turn around just in time to see this voluptuous blonde (cloaked in black velvet with a collar of astrakhan) float into the room from behind the curtains. Sometimes she is clutching a gun, sometimes her heart. There is a wild look in her eyes. She is biting her lips. She is trembling—exhausted—desperate. And there is a little something about her that reminds you of wind in the heather. (That is a little more difficult to explain than the lady's presence in your apartment, but wind in the heather is what she reminds you of.) So, even if she hasn't a gun, you arise with a full supply of that reserve which you acquired on the playing fields of Eton, and you say: "Stupid of me not to have heard you ring. Please sit down and let me chase Jasper [or Ali or Ganeshi Lal] for another cup of sack. . . . Or perhaps you would prefer a noggin of gin?"

After you have met the woman in black, night after night—

always under the most decorous circumstances, however unconventional they may seem to the lift operator—you perform these rites almost automatically. But you never tire of the situation. You never think of turning the hounds loose on the authors who have been chasing this girl through the stormy night for the last three decades. After all, one must do something with one's evenings. You take the whole business as a matter of course, and the young woman dries herself on her own specially embroidered guest towel and lolls about kittenlike in your great big overstuffed pyjamas. She comes, in time, to trust you—as who wouldn't?

Tomorrow morning you will find out that she is somebody —Little Lotus Flower from the East India Docks, or Queen Marie, or the Lady That's Known as Lou. But whatever happens, you know that she isn't going to be a murderess—at any rate she never has been up to now. She has taken the better part. She is the lovely voice that one will hear forever in the sighing of the wind, the beautiful face that one will see eternally in the fire. She is the reason Adelphi tenants learned to sleep with their windows open—especially windows leading to fire escapes.

Considering the tremendous number of crimes occurring in London, the longevity of its citizens is remarkable. It is impossible from this distance (say 3000 miles) to conduct an adequate research into the causes, but a study of reports may give us a clue. People have to stay alive because of the unsettled conditions of the graveyards and the overproduction of cadavers. Such corpses as do find their way into graves are always dug up in a day or two. The London Underground could have been sunk five times over through the exhumation processes of the detective-story writers. Other products of violent crime are not buried at all, but are checked at Waterloo or Victoria stations until called for—making for congestion at these points that is truly deplorable.

It is difficult to die in England, no matter who breaks into your apartment with pistols, deadly gases, poisoned darts, Mills bombs, or copies of *The London Times*. In fact, the published records contain no mention of a death from natural causes since the demise of Wilkie Collins, and there seems to be some doubt about him. Apparently if you don't get murdered, you live forever.

Murders and Motives

By E. V. Lucas

Edward Verrall Lucas (1868–1938) was one of the most finished present-day English practitioners of that gentle and well-nigh lost art, the familiar essay. The amusing fancy printed here is from his A Fronded Isle and Other Essays *(London: Methuen, 1927; New York: Doubleday, 1928).*

WE WERE talking about the woful condition of country-house parties when the weather is bad and conversation flags. For if it has been too wet for golf, how can a man relate the misadventures that beset him at the fifth hole or his triumphs at the seventh? Bridge, of course, is useful between meals, but at meals there can be serious silences, particularly among those whose luck is out.

'Let me tell you,' said little Mrs. ffolliott, 'of a scheme that I invented. You may all have it if you like. It's perfect. Last year we had a party in Scotland and it rained all the time, as one might have expected. Indeed, as I did expect, and that is why I took such pains to make it a success.'

She paused to give someone the opportunity of saying earnestly, 'Do tell us.'

As a matter of fact we all said it.

Little Mrs. ffolliott composed herself happily to hold the floor.

'Just before leaving for Scotland,' she said, 'I went to the book-sellers' and asked what was the very latest detective novel. They showed me several old ones. "No," I said, "I don't mean these; I have read these. I want one that was published yesterday or won't be published till to-morrow—absolutely new;" and at last they found one. It was not to be on sale till two days later, but

352

they let me have a dozen copies. I remember the title and the author perfectly, although it was last year: *The Mystery of Grewsam Grange*, by Avery Cross Traylor.'

'I've read that,' said half a dozen voices at once.

'Of course you have,' said Mrs. ffolliott, 'but the point is that no one had read it then.'

'Isn't that the story,' asked the bishop, 'in which the murderer turns out to be the maiden aunt?'

'That's the one!' we exclaimed.

'It seemed to me,' said the bishop, 'highly improbable: more than improbable, unfair. There was no motive, and a motive there must be. My theory is that murderers should be murderers, whereas this estimable lady would never have hurt a fly. I doubt if it is playing the game to make the guilty person a fundamentally innocuous one like that, just to put readers off the scent.'

'True,' said Mrs. ffolliott, who was getting a little restive under this interruption, 'but if readers weren't put off the scent there would be very little in my scheme, and that's why *The Mystery of Grewsam Grange* was so useful. You see, this is what I did: I had those twelve copies cut up into chapters, and each chapter separately bound and lettered; and, having discovered that none of my guests had read the book—except one meek little man, and I swore him to secrecy—I distributed Chapter I on the day of their arrival, with injunctions that it was to be read before dinner. Read; no skipping. What was the result? As they all had the same absorbing topic of conversation, dinner was one long and successful clash or harmony of theories as to the probable course of events.'

Mrs. ffolliott paused for praise and got it.

'When they went to bed,' she continued, 'they found Chapter II in their rooms. And so on through the week; the sections were carefully distributed. I kept them myself under lock and key, and such was the excitement that I had to hide the key for fear of theft. The man who had read the story in London was so pestered for private information that he arranged for a telegram to be sent to himself and left. Everybody joined in; even Percy, who has never been known to read anything but *The Times*. But,' added little Mrs. ffolliott, 'it's astonishing how, when you come to detective stories, the dullest men, City men, shooting men, even hunting men, can display literary taste.'

A murmur of doubt, led by the bishop, ran round the company.

'Well, at any rate,' Mrs. ffolliott amended, 'curiosity concerning the printed word.'

'Better,' said the bishop approvingly.

'You never heard such a rattle as we used to have at lunch and dinner,' Mrs. ffolliott resumed; 'and I don't know what the servants would have thought if they had not known about it, for there was nothing but murders and motives all the time. But as a matter of fact the butler was playing too, for it seems that my maid gave him one of the extra copies.'

'Did many of your guests guess the guilty party?' the bishop inquired.

'Oh, yes; two or three. But only, I think, out of perversity. They agreed with you,' said little Mrs. ffolliott, 'that to make it the maiden aunt was not quite the thing.'

'Indeed no,' said the bishop, 'most reprehensible.'

'I was sorry for the little man who had to leave,' Mrs. ffolliott went on. 'The perfect way, of course, would be to get one of the swell authors to write one a special story—Conan Doyle or Austin Freeman or J. W. Crofts or Edgar Wallace or Father Knox or Mrs. Christie—and then there would be no possible chance of anyone knowing the end. But only a millionaire could do that.'

'No need to buy the work completely,' I suggested. 'You could acquire merely the country-house rights.'

'I didn't know there were such things,' said Mrs. ffolliott.

'Nor I,' I replied; 'but I don't see why there shouldn't be. It would be an additional source of income for necessitous novelists.'

The bishop rose. 'I am afraid I must be going,' he said. 'Of course you all know the earliest form of detective story? No? You will find it in the Apocrypha—the story of Susanna and the Elders; its hero, Daniel, was the first detective.'

Murder on Parnassus

By Pierre Véry

In his native France, M. Véry is considered second only to Georges Simenon among detective story writers (though, unlike Simenon's, none of his police romances has yet been translated into English). His delightful and typically Gallic commentary on the craft which follows appeared in the Parisian topical weekly Marianne *and was subsequently reprinted in translation in* Living Age *for April 1935.*

'Pupil Lacroix, tell me what you know about Mlle Stangerson's secret.'

'Mlle Stangerson's secret? Well . . . that is, the secret of Mlle Stangerson . . .'

'I see you don't know the first thing about it. Never mind. Quote the famous sentence Rouletabille heard in the Élysée gardens beside the wall that borders the Avenue Marigny.'

'. . . .'

'I see that you have not opened your Gaston Leroux. You will copy the following sentence thirty times: *"Le presbytère n'a rien perdu de son charme ni le jardin de son éclat."* You may sit down.'

'Pupil Mercier, what do you know about Mlle Stangerson's secret?'

'Sir, Mlle Stangerson secretly married a certain John Russell in Philadelphia. He was none other than the sinister bandit Ballmeyer, alias Detective Frédéric Larsan, also known as Big Fred, and she bore him a son, who was first called Joseph Joséphin and then Joseph Rouletabille.'

'Very good. What was the first material clue that Joseph Rouletabille discovered in the *Chambre Jaune?*'

355

'A woman's blond hair, sir.'

'Thank you.'

'Pupil Jozont, name Sherlock Holmes's most mortal enemy.'

'Professor Moriarty.'

'What was the date of the murder of the widow Lerouge in the *Affaire Lerouge* written by Gaboriau?'

'March 4, 1862.'

'Thank you. Pupil Gharantec, tell me about Isidore Bautrelet.'

'Isidore Bautrelet, the schoolboy in the adventure of the *Aiguille creuse,* was Arsène Lupin's formidable adversary. He knew that the corpse found on the cliff . . .'

This scene takes place in a French lycée about 2935. Criminal literature, which was incorporated in the school curriculum about 2500, has little by little taken precedence over all other forms of literature, which have become discredited and forgotten. Edgar Allan Poe, Edgar Wallace, and certain highly specialized authors who wrote at the beginning of the twentieth century have become classics, whom the pupils study from the time they are twelve or thirteen years old until they graduate.

II

It begins early in the morning with dictation: 'At exactly six o'clock, as he had announced, Herlock Sholmès, wearing a pair of trousers that were too short and a coat that was too narrow, both of which he had borrowed from an innkeeper . . .'

An exercise in grammar follows: 'The policeman took the old judge by the arm and squeezed him energetically . . .'

Then comes a translation. 'Open your *Meurtre de Roger Ackroyd* at page 269, chapter 23: Poirot's little party—from "and now, said Caroline, rising, that child is coming upstairs to lie down," until, "what is it? I asked." '

And so it goes until noon. At home the children ask their parents strange questions. 'Mother,' says the eldest girl at the table, fencing with her beefsteak, 'suppose that you want to poison father.'

'Yes,' says the mother.

'You have nothing but arsenic at your disposal.'

'Very well.'

'What food would you put the poison into so that father could not tell by the taste?'

The father looks up and waits for the answer.

'Well,' says the mother, 'I think that good strong coffee would do the trick.'

'Good Lord, no,' the father cries, 'that wouldn't do at all, my dear. I could tell right away. If I were you, I'd wait until the cold weather came because then I get my attacks of acidity and take malt. Well, you put your arsenic in my malt . . .'

The pupils return to school. The professor draws figures and numbers on the blackboard. This is the geometry class. 'Given a closed space in the form of an isosceles triangle, ABC, and another closed space Z in the form of a hexagon MNOPQR. Find . . .'

And a physics class. 'If you have a safe covered with armored plate x millimetres thick and a blow-torch whose power is b, find the time necessary to make around the lock a circular aperture having a diameter of . . .'

At last the recreation period. The pupils form groups and chat while they walk around the courtyard. 'Say, you! How do you say in English *pas une âme?*'

'I think it's "nobody." Why?'

'I need it for my lesson. The professor gave us some *Gallet décédé* to translate: *Pas une âme pour égayer le decor et renseigner le voyageur, etc.*'

Another pupil asks, 'Who did you say was the criminal in the last induction and logic problem?'

'Why, the school inspector, of course.'

'Oh, no, he isn't the criminal. It's the detective. The cigarette butt shows that.'

'Not at all,' says a third. 'The whole trick depends on the alibi. In the beginning the victim was working hand in glove with the murderer.'

In a hangar a group are standing around a physical education instructor. 'The exercise consists in climbing up to a window two yards above the ground without leaving any traces. Since the wall is stuccoed, the exercise is done in four beats. The first position, rise on the toes, hands on hips, chest back . . .'

We are again in the classroom. Philosophy is the subject. 'Gentlemen, the emotions in *Arsène Lupin* . . .'

Latin class: 'I give you the old proverb, *Is fecit cui prodest* . . .'

Zoölogy class: 'Gentlemen, "hotel rat" means . . .'

Literature class: 'Gentlemen, the triangle in literature is represented by three main characters—the victim, the murderer, and the detective. We have as many as thirty-two dramatic situations . . .'

Evening at home: 'Mother, imagine that you have killed your lover with a sickle.'

'Very well.'

'You want to escape justice. In what store would you buy your clothes? Would you wear a wig? Would you leave Paris on foot, on a bicycle, in a taxi, and by which door. Would you take a train? If so, at what station, and what would your destination be?'

'Father, imagine a corridor that has seven doors. A millionaire is sleeping in the last room. His door and his window are locked from within. His secretary is on watch in the next room. How would you go about entering the millionaire's room, murdering him, robbing him, and getting away without leaving any clues?'

The father meditates for a moment and makes a gesture of annoyance. 'That's childish, my boy. That's the old problem of the enclosed space. There are a lot of solutions. Theoretically, I can use the inexplicable-gallery trick, or I can have recourse to the funereal-odor system. Or, better yet—but what do you want me to tell you? I knew my enclosed space by heart once upon a time, but it's been so long since I've looked at a book. Go ask your big brother . . .'

III

The children sweat blood over these problems. Wearily they drag their schoolbooks filled with such repulsive titles as *L'Étrange mort de Sir Jeroboam Backdrive, Triple assassinat rue Sébastien-Bottin, L'Affaire des oreillers rouges*.

Mortal, stifling boredom emanates from these schoolbooks, from these texts that have become colder than the corpses they deal with since they have been made into a school subject to be dissected and discussed. Long ago schoolboys stopped reading adventure stories for the pleasure of it. They have stopped dreaming of themselves as gangsters and gentlemen robbers. They read forbidden books and delight in a bizarre, vanguard literature in which revolutionary authors resolutely break the old formulæ and compose strange works that they call tragedies and that are generally written in Alexandrine verse.

Extravagant and sentimental conflicts are depicted. The vanguard authors have invented a new triangle—the husband, the wife, and the lover. A Spanish prince asks himself whether his prime loyalty belongs to his father or to his mistress. An old man drily watches a fratricidal war between his three sons and their brothers-in-law, and there is the story of an incestuous queen burning with passion for her chaste son-in-law. Young people also enjoy those short narratives in irregular verse called fables, which describe animals—the fox, the stork, the little rabbit, the ant, and the grasshopper.

Of course, the professors scorn such frivolous works, but in small chapels, in secret meetings, it is whispered that these despised 'tragedies,' which are so disconcerting by their extreme novelty, may some day become classics.

5
CRITICS' CORNER

In which professional critics and reviewers hold the floor.

The Life of Riley

By Isaac Anderson

For more years than they can remember, a goodly number of American whodunit devotees have been looking to the painstaking and eminently fair reviews by Isaac Anderson in the New York Times Book Review *to tell them which mysteries to read and which to pass by. Mr. Anderson, long a member of the* Times *staff, here looks back on his career of crime (reviewing) with affection and gentle satire.*

THIS MAN Riley may well have been a reviewer of detective stories with nothing to do all day and every day but to read about the fascinating subject of murder. That would explain why his name has become a symbol of the happy life. Imagine him opening the latest thriller, not yet on sale at the bookstores, and gloating over the gory details set forth in its pages. Presently the corpse is discovered. It may be that of the white-haired old financier and philanthropist slumped over the desk in his library with the hilt of an oriental dagger protruding from his back. Or it may be that of a nameless vagabond done to death with a blunt instrument and left lying at the bottom of the old stone quarry. It may even be that of a beautiful young woman who was on the morrow to have married the heir to a dukedom. In any case it is a corpse, and the story is well under way.

Enter the detective. Perhaps he is a derby-hatted, cigar-smoking member of the Homicide Squad, followed by a retinue consisting of the bored Medical Examiner and the equally bored photographers and finger-print men. If there is a brash young reporter lurking in the background or, more likely, pushing his way to the front, keep your eye on him. He is going to beat the police to the solution of the crime, thereby earning a fat bonus from his publisher and establishing himself as the ace of aces among crime reporters.

Sometimes a private investigator appears on the scene, called in either because the family of the victim has no faith in the police or because there is some deep, dark secret in the past which must at all costs be prevented from coming to light. The first step taken by this private eye, as he is sometimes called, is in the direction of the nearest supply of liquor. He has learned by long experience that his brain functions best when he is stewed to the gills or when he has a hangover, and he makes it a point to be in top form all of the time. The official police, who are not permitted to drink while on duty, are jealous of this man and do all they can to impede his efforts and to rob him of all credit when his work is successful. The private dick is not dismayed. He can be as tough as anybody else, and tougher. His ability to absorb punishment is exceeded only by his ability to dish it out.

Riley's favorite detective is the brilliant amateur. There is a guy who knows all the answers. He has no official standing whatever, but that doesn't matter. The police are compelled to respect him because of his vast knowledge of everything under the sun from Egyptian hieroglyphics to the batting averages of the Brooklyn Dodgers. He listens patiently while Inspector Whoozis demonstrates beyond the possibility of a doubt that the butler bumped off the old gentleman in the library. He admits cheerfully that the butler had ample opportunity, that he had access to the lethal weapon and that he had good reason to hate his employer. But the brilliant amateur knows that the butler did not do the killing. Butlers don't do such things. It would be contrary to all the conventions of detective fiction. The brilliant amateur knows that the only person who could have done the foul deed is the person who has a perfectly sound alibi and who hasn't the shadow of a motive, so far as anyone knows. What is more, the brilliant amateur proves it. How does he do it? That is a secret not to be disclosed until the last chapter, and not always then.

The one thing common to all detective heroes, as distinguished from the bunglers who muddle things up for them, is that they

always get their man—or woman or child. And this brings us to
the subject of clues, those jigsaw pieces which the reader tries,
usually in vain, to fit together for himself before the author announces the solution in the last chapter. Now the more difficult
a puzzle is the better the addict likes it, and the author of a detective story tries to make it as difficult as he can without violating
the cardinal principle of his craft, which is that all clues, like the
incriminating letter in Poe's tale of "The Purloined Letter,"
must be in plain sight for those who have the eyes to see. He
does this in part by providing more puzzle pieces than there are
places to put them, in part by so placing the vital clues that they
blend with their surroundings in such a way that only the eye
of his superlatively perceptive hero is able to distinguish the real
clues from the phony ones and to recognize them for what they
are.

It is astonishing how many authors there are who are able to
bamboozle their readers in this way. Even Riley, who has read
and reviewed thousands of mysteries, is frequently fooled, perhaps quite as frequently as anyone else. Indeed, he is disappointed
when he is able to guess the solution too early, for a mystery
which can be guessed is no mystery at all.

As Riley reads book after book in his chosen field, he notes,
perhaps with alarm, perhaps with perverse satisfaction, that the
language employed is nothing like that of the dime novel detective stories of his boyhood days—"Old Cap Collier," "Old Sleuth"
and the rest. There wasn't a "hell" or a "damn" in a carload of
those forbidden books. The detectives in the stories of our day
have bigger and worse expletives than these, and they speak freely
of things which Old Cap Collier would have blushed to mention.
"Hell" and "damn" are mere conversational small change, just
as they are in what used to be called polite society. Ah well! Times
change, and what the— I mean, what are you going to do about it?

But Riley, who occasionally reads so-called "straight" novels
just to see how the other half lives, knows that their language is
no better than that of the whodunits, while the plots, in his opinion, are far worse. They deal far too often with love, which may
be evanescent, while murder, on the other hand, is as permanent
as anything can be. A man or woman in love may fall out of love,

but a corpse remains a corpse for all time. The writer who deals with murder has one character who is going to stay put, no matter what the others may do.

This, then, is the kind of literature we mystery reviewers are privileged to read. No doubt there are some carping critics who will question my use of the word "literature" in this connection, but if the detective story is not literature, what is it? It is not always great literature, I grant you, but how many of the thousands of books published every year deserve to be called great? Or literature? How many characters in modern fiction will be remembered as long as Sherlock Holmes, for example? Call it what you will, this is the sort of stuff we read and like. If we didn't like it we couldn't go on reviewing it year after year without becoming victims to mental indigestion.

Best of all—and this is where we have it all over the general reader who must buy, borrow or steal his whodunits—we are paid for reading them. Not enough to put us in the higher income brackets, it is true, but look at the fun we have.

Battle of the Sexes: The Judge and His Wife
Look at Mysteries

By "Judge Lynch"

Pseudonymous "Judge Lynch" is chief critic of whodunits for the Saturday Review of Literature *and is the principal originator of the succinct tabular form of mystery review featured by that publication and widely copied elsewhere. A journalist and publisher, the "Judge" has been reviewing mystery fiction for various American magazines and newspapers since the early 1920's. He discusses here a hitherto neglected aspect of the subject—the differences between the genders in mystery preferences and appreciation.*

THE FOLLOWING is written in self-defence.

Whenever the Judge takes home a batch of new mystery stories, he is greeted with small feminine cries of delight and calls of "Gimme! Gimme!" So he gimmes, keeping out one for his own evening stint. There was a time when he would have selected *any* one, but he has long since learned that the longest, most leisurely, stodgiest English mystery is the one for him to choose—until the commotion subsides. Otherwise, he could not dodge the books that are quite likely to hurtle across the room accompanied by angry shrieks. Even when the initial disturbance is past and the Judge's wife settles down with a story that appears to meet her requirements, the Judge is not yet in the Safety Zone. He can never tell when the book will be closed with a snap, a scornful voice will say, "Pooh! What nasty people! Who cares about what they do or what happens to them!" And then—wham!

This has gone on long enough.

So the Judge has decided to set down, for his bodily safety and peace of mind, just what—he thinks—it is that women like, and what they don't like, in mystery stories. He knows full well that women have always read mystery stories and that more women are reading them today than ever before. He has learned, somewhat to his surprise, that their tastes differ from men's in various ways, so that it is unwise to make sweeping assertions about the goodness or badness of any given mystery story. Obviously, we cannot label mystery stories "For Men Only" and "For Woman Only." You can't cut the distinction that clear. Indeed, the Judge has found that most men like most mystery stories that most women like—-but most women don't like *some* mysteries that most men like—not by a long shot. Let's get the whole thing clear, if possible, and, since clarity begins at home, here goes. . . .

"The people must be nice." Not nice in the prissy or Sunday-school sense, but, in the main, the kind of people that could be in your circle of friends or that you wouldn't mind adding to your acquaintances, the kind of people that you're really concerned about as the story unrolls. They don't necessarily have to be paragons of virtue, but they must be interesting and believable. Detectives (male) who drink six quarts of Bourbon before breakfast and indulge in boudoir badinage with a bevy of blondes are out. Likewise, the detective (female) who weighs three hundred pounds, laps up likker, smokes cigars, and swears like a trooper. Women don't like their own sex tough—in mystery stories. They like Mrs. Latham, although they are a bit derisive over her endless pursuit of Col. Primrose; they enjoy Pamela North, except that some of them think poor Pam has borne the brunt of too many last-chapter nick-of-time rescues; they approve of Miss Marple and Miss Silver—but do not agree with the Judge that Hildegarde Withers is about the only bearable spinster sleuth in the field. They would love to see Craig Rice do something more with Mrs. Bill Smith (née Marion Carstairs) and the kids who made *Home Sweet Homicide* so delightful—but most of them don't give too many hoots about Jake and Helen Justus and lawyer Malone. (The Judge disagrees.)

They like "psychological" mysteries. In such stories they will even tolerate nasty people—Doris Miles Disney's *Dark Road* for instance; but they like them better when a leaven of likeability leavens the lurid lump as in Margaret Millar's *The Iron Gates* or Elisabeth Sanxay Holding's *The Innocent Mrs. Duff.*

By and large they like stories with an American background and characters better than they do the English variety. They admire Sherlock Holmes, perhaps more for atmosphere than for plot, and they like Father Brown much better. For Joshua Clunk they have small regard and they only tolerate Reggie Fortune. Oddly enough, they rather like Arthur Crook, perhaps because he is unobtrusive and doesn't interfere with character development. They laugh at "The Saint." The bull-dog British brand of deliberate deduction, as exemplified by Inspector French and Dr. Priestley, positively infuriates them. Peter Wimsey used to be one of their favorites—but not the Wimsey of *Gaudy Night.*

Give them good characters and a sound plot and they don't care much about the background—so long as it isn't the underworld. Gangsters and their molls leave them cold, as do the dese-dem-and-dose guys who talk out of the corners of their mouths. Imperious "Little Caesar" is dead and turned to clay so far as they're concerned. They like the tinkle of tea cups or highball glasses in a Westchester garden with a fresh corpse behind the rose bush much more than the staccato rattle of gangland tommy guns. Physical brutality in mystery stories is not much to their liking. Psychological torture is O.K. Physical ditto—no. A character can be scared to death and they like it, but when Mike Shayne or some similarly indestructible sleuth takes a six hour slugging from a bunch of hoods, they turn the pages rapidly until he swings agilely into action a few hours later—when they don't believe it. Nor does the Judge.

Women don't like "puzzle" mysteries *per se.* The puzzle is important but only if the people in it are the kind you care about. There is a John Rhode bump on the Judge's head right now and the last vestiges of a Freeman Wills Crofts bruise on his chest. Stories with a scientific background or that depend on chemical formulae or the like for their elucidation are frequently used as door-stops.

But, mind you, women are regular devils when it comes to plots. Much, oh much more persnickety than men. They are not content to finish a story and let it lie. No, if they feel that they have been deliberately fooled somewhere, they'll go back, and back and back until they find the place where the author put one over on them, or dragged a particularly odoriferous herring (how they hate 'em) across the trail, and if they locate the tiniest crevice in the plot structure—are they mad! Women are much more attentive to details than men, too. A Southern character who says "you-all" to a gathering of less than two auditors has run up the storm signals in the Judge's Chambers, and the immaculate housewife with an apartment full of antiques who loaned her home to a girl friend with a penchant for throwing moderately wild parties just didn't make the grade at all.

Women like their mystery stories as neat as their hair-dos. When the story concludes, they want no loose ends. They want every clue and every character present and accounted for. Being dabsters for detail they rarely forget a person or a clue and they are much annoyed if the lad or lass who crossed the detective's trail in the middle of the story with every appearance of an important part in the plot is suddenly chucked aside—as sometimes happens—and is among those missing when the cards are all in and recapitulations are in order. Likewise the deceptively dangled clue that is introduced with much fanfare and that is still hanging high at the finish.

Women like plenty of suspense—nerve-harrowing suspense at the expense of biff-bang action in many cases—and they like that suspense to rise and rise to a *sforzando* finish. They are annoyed by stories that ascend to Everest heights of excitement and then, at the end, go bleh! In that they are not unlike most men readers, but a terminal let-down affects them more. They don't, as a rule, like mass-murders. One "good" murder is generally enough for them, although they will tolerate two and possibly three. But holocausts like Dashiell Hammett's *Red Harvest* or *The Dain Curse,* to name two favorites of the grisly Judge, set them squirming. On the other hand, women like Hammett's *Thin Man* and *Maltese Falcon* and the various masterpieces of Raymond Chandler. They like them in spite of their general dislike for "tough guy" opera—because they are keenly appreciative of brilliant writing and superb characterization.

Women do not agree with the late S. S. Van Dine that the ugly head of love should never be raised in a mystery story. They like stories that have a well-defined but moderate "love interest," although they draw a thin line of distinction between "mystery stories" and the emotional crime-novels of the much admired Mignon Eberhart. And, as they object to love interest overshadowing the grim business of murder and its detection, so do they scorn the story in which the characters are smart-alecky and greet each new deed of violence with a wise-crack. They like humor, of course, but the story that overbalances murder with mirth offends their sense of propriety and is promptly dubbed "silly!" Then, too, their sense of the fitness of things is frequently disturbed by stupid cops, or dense detectives (professional) who are scornfully kicked around by a brilliant amateur. As realists they know that such things ain't. As noted before they like Sherlock Holmes, especially *The Hound of the Baskervilles,* and fogs and moors and London of the gaslight era, and they are very fond of Dr. Watson—in the *books.* But they hate and despise the ridiculous chuckleheaded blusterer of the film perversion. Again—"Silly!"

They like a whiff of the "supernatural," now and then, as in the frozen horror of Dorothy Macardle's *The Uninvited* or, to a lesser degree, in Vera Caspary's *Laura* with its "return from the dead." Such John Carter-Dickson-Carr stories as *The Burning Court* chill them delightfully, but it takes all the bluff antics of H. M. and Dr. Fell to interest many of them in this expert practitioner's "puzzle" stories. Interesting, too, how they goggle over ghost stories, when you know that if they ever saw a ghost they'd shy a shoe at it and go off to sleep again without a tremor.

For masterworks in the allied field of espionage and intrigue stories they have a grudging admiration. The Judge has never been able to raise any feminine raves about Eric Ambler's *A Coffin for Dimitrios* or the magnificent exploits of Tommy Hambledon in the Manning Coles novels. Perhaps it's because these books have so little love-interest and so few "nice people."

Yes, "they must be nice people." To the Judge's knowledge, that has always been a feminine criterion for mystery stories. The first mystery story the Judge read, at the age of eleven, was given to him by a woman. His mother. It was a paper-bound copy of *The Leavenworth Case* by Anna Katharine Greene, and it helped to make the dismal desquamation of a scarlet-fever convalescent more bearable. It wasn't a new book, not by many a year, and the Judge's mother knew it by heart. One of the reasons why she gave it to him was that she thought Inspector (or was it Mr.?) Gryce was "such a very nice person."

How to Read a Whodunit

By Will Cuppy

Will Cuppy is by vocation reviewer of mystery and adventure fiction for the New York Herald Tribune Weekly Book Review *and other publications, and by avocation the author of such inimitable humorous works as* How To Be a Hermit, How To Tell Your Friends From the Apes, *and* How To Become Extinct. *(His current "work in progress" is known as* The Decline and Fall of Everything. *He combines vocation and avocation in this unorthodox guide for mystery addicts from* Mystery Book Magazine *for January 1946.*

AND HOW do you like the title of this article? You don't, eh? Why, a man once wrote a whole book called "How to Read a Book" and everybody loved the title. I consider mine an improvement.

That book, by the way, sold like wildfire and the man was instantly classed as one of the great thinkers of all time. Thousands of grateful customers give the tome credit for their present mental state, such as it is.

I didn't read it myself. It came too late to help me, as I had already read a book.

Now that I look again, there's more sense in my title than appears at first glance. At least, it gives me a chance to deny the silly idea that reading a whodunit requires a lot of special equipment, such as a thorough knowledge of plain and fancy detecting, proper handling of clues and goodness knows what—a view that actually keeps some people from tackling mysteries at all. They're afraid they won't make the grade.

The fact is, it's easy. You just listen to me and you, too, can read a whodunit.

No kidding, one of our higher-priced critics recently stated in his column that he couldn't undertake to peruse a mystery some publisher had sent him, since he was not a fan and was not acquainted with the rules. He wouldn't be able to tell whether it was any good or not.

He then proceeded to evaluate a volume dealing, as near as I could make out, with the fields of politics, economics and the state of the world in general from the ground up and far into the future. He had read that one without a moment's hesitation. How he did so I have no means of knowing. He didn't say.

I must admit that there are some desperate puzzlers, devotees of what they call the real-for-sure detective tale, who carry around with them a set of rules originally designed by Tom, Dick and Harry for the authors of such works—and pretty foolish some of the regulations are, too. If the addict finds that one of them has been broken, he yells that the story is awful. He doesn't like it.

Well, that's one way to read a book. These particular persons, however, appear to be a dwindling species and may soon become extinct from lack of material to feed upon. Most of their favorite authors have died off and they aren't feeling so well themselves.

How, then, should one read a whodunit? If I'm so smart, what is my advice on the subject?

My first suggestion would be to operate exactly as you would with any other form of light printed matter bound in the form of a book or magazine, without any laws of the Medes and Persians in your mind, which probably has enough to handle without that.

What, you just begin at the first page, then go to the second and so forth until you've had enough? That's right. And if you like the stuff you're lucky. If not, toss the volume out the window.

Jumping around in the book, of course, is allowable as a preliminary in the case of customers who simply have to do that before they buy or rent a whodunit. They have to know how it looks in the middle and whether it sounds right at various other points. They can tell in one minute whether or not the whole will appeal to them. This is a frequently rewarding habit to which I myself am somewhat given.

For instance, if you open to Page 30 and find three or four

jerks pointing guns at one another in various stages of sadistic glee, you drop it with a mild curse and try another whodunit and hope for better luck.

In a word, if whatever page you open proves beyond the shadow of a doubt that the author should be in an institution and that the publisher should be hanged, read no more in that one. Thus you are spared hours of agony and two bucks. So much for jumping around. One might almost say, look before you leap into a whodunit.

But no peeking into the last chapter to see who shot the philandering delicatessen man in his place of business! Anyhow, that's what most people would tell you. That is supposed to be farthest south in moral turpitude, the equivalent of cheating at solitaire and the very hallmark of a low and despicable nature.

Is it that bad, really? Let us realize that some people simply cannot wait two hours to see whether or not Grandma, bedridden for ages and supposedly unable to sit up for her gruel, committed the series of dastardly crimes which held the village in the grip of terror for so long.

Of course Grandma is guilty as hell, as the reader ought to know without peeking. I knew it the instant I laid eyes on her and heard that she hadn't taken a step these twenty years or more. She's been getting up at night, disguising herself and shooting folks almost at random, then beating it back to bed in time to fool the family, a battery of trained nurses and two generations of local cops.

Most of us can let such a story run its natural course, aware that we'll know all the details in the end. Peekers are different, that's all, and what I say is, why not let them alone? What harm do they do you and me? Besides, they probably can't help it. The Cuppy Plan gives them a break, but I'm not saying that I'd trust any of them with my watch, if I had one.

Which brings us to the rather more vital problem of fast or slow reading. There again I'd leave it up to the individual, with the suggestion that perhaps those who take their time are more likely to understand what goes on in the book and that it must be more fun to know, if only vaguely, what you are reading about.

There are persons who tear through a mystery in half an hour at most, sometimes much less, then start a new one. They may be prodigies of some kind, but I notice that they hate to be cross-questioned on the details of the will and such matters. When cornered, they try to change the subject or grow sulky and silent.

What they get out of their lightning activities I can't say, but I can guess. On the other hand, some people practically form each syllable with their lips and seem to be little the wiser.

As for those who consume whodunits with the radio on full blast and a blissful smile on their maps, no comment. Since this form of pleasure does not come under the head of reading, it falls outside the scope of this article. I pass these happy ones by with my blessing. Live and let live is my motto.

I have never rightly understood all this talk about reading mysteries in bed, but they say it's wonderful. I don't know whether it is supposed to put you to sleep, or keep you awake, or what. Oh, well, it's none of my business what people do at that time of night.

Four Mystery Reviews

It is every reviewer's dream that he will recognize genius and penetrate pretentiousness—and his nightmare that he won't. How have mystery critics fared with some of the classics of the past?

Absence of comment is sometimes comment in itself. Edgar Allan Poe's first two detective tales ("The Murders in the Rue Morgue" and "The Mystery of Marie Rogêt") made their first appearances in magazines, and it is therefore not too surprising that no contemporary criticism of them seems to exist. But Poe's third and greatest Dupin story, "The Purloined Letter," was included in the pre-dated "annual," The Gift: 1845, a handsome presentation volume which received a detailed though unsigned review on the first page of young Mr. Greeley's newly-founded New York Tribune *for October 4, 1844. Occupying more than a column over-all, this chatty critique complimented the publishers at length on the "elegance" of their offering to the holiday purchaser, praised the illustrations in detail, reprinted poems by Emerson and Longfellow, in full, and found room to speak glowingly of a half-dozen or more of the prose contributors by name —but mentioned proud Israfel and his tale of the ingeniously concealed epistle not at all! Almost needless to say, no other prose selection in the volume survives or is read today.*

In short, the sole approach to a contemporary "review" of "The Purloined Letter" which your editor has seen is the brief introductory note (found on page 170 of the present volume) accompanying the abridged reprinting of the tale in Chambers' Edinburgh Journal *for November 30, 1844.*

A similar critical vacuum surrounds the first Sherlock Holmes story by Arthur Conan Doyle, A Study in Scarlet, *which—according to Dorothy Sayers—"was flung like a bombshell into the field of detective fiction" when it appeared as the featured story in* Beeton's Christmas Annual *late in 1887. If Miss Sayers is correct, this must surely be one of the earliest instances on record of a*

377

delayed-action bomb; for diligent search by your editor over a period of years has failed to unearth anything nearer to a bona fide review than this one-line (possibly pre-publication) "notice" accorded Beeton's *by the English booktrade journal, the* Publishers' Circular, *for December 6, 1887: ". . . the leading fiction [i.e. Doyle's tale] . . . is vigorously written and possesses much sensational interest."*

So much for comment by omission. Of the four representative reviews selected for reproduction below, the Athenaeum's *evaluation in 1868 of Wilkie Collins' immortal* Moonstone *does not fare too badly, all things considered, on the score of prescience— though the anonymous reviewer does not always select for his admiration the same qualities esteemed by modern readers of the novel. . . . The same journal's consideration in 1890 of Doyle's second Holmes novel,* The Sign of Four, *is chiefly memorable, aside from its unique prose style, for the entire omission of reference to the central character and the astounding prophecy in the last sentence. . . . In several respects the American* Bookman's *staid and eminently respectable 1913 review of E. C. Bentley's* Trent's Last Case *might almost have appeared in this week's book supplement. Yet (allowing for the manifest advantages of hindsight) the opening statement does seem a little odd, when one recalls that this is the novel which later historians have credited with changing the whole course of the detective romance by its introduction of "character." Nor does the reviewer, writing at a time when the great number of detective stories were virtually unreadable (if you don't believe it, go back and try some), seem unduly cognizant of the superior literary qualities, the humor and naturalism, that have enabled Bentley's masterpiece to survive the years.*

The final and only signed review, Dashiell Hammett *on S. S. Van Dine's* The Benson Murder Case, *is in many ways the most remarkable of the four. In recent years it has become somewhat the fashion (often unjustly) to scorn Van Dine and all his works. But it should be remembered that when Hammett loosed his shattering shaft in 1927, Van Dine was by way of becoming the high priest and Philo Vance the patron saint of "intellectual" detective story fanciers—and Ogden Nash's famous dictum concerning the latter individual's need for a kick in the "pance" was still some years away; while Hammett (not yet the author of* The Maltese Falcon *or any published book) was known only to readers of the pulp magazine* Black Mask. . . . *The weakness in Hammett's argument, of course, is that in insisting on the yardstick of literal realism, he denies to Van Dine the artistic license so necessary for acceptance of his (Hammett's) own superb hardboiled but equally unrealistic detective romances. For a delightful comparison of the private investigator in fiction and in fact (a subject too long neglected) read John Bartlow Martin's "Peekaboo Pennington, Private Eye" in* Harper's *for May 1946. (See also Hammett's own "From the Memoirs of a Private Detective" in the present volume.)*

Now the reviews.

I. THE MOONSTONE

(From the *Athenaeum*, London, July 25, 1868)

WHEN PERSONS are in a state of ravenous hunger they are eager only for food, and utterly ignore all delicate distinctions of cookery; it is only when this savage state has been somewhat allayed that they are capable of discerning and appreciating the genius of the *chef*. Those readers who have followed the fortunes of the mysterious Moonstone for many weeks, as it has appeared in tantalizing portions, will of course throw themselves headlong upon the latter portion of the third volume, now that the end is really come,* and devour it without rest or pause; to take any deliberate breathing-time is quite out of the question, and we promise them a surprise that will find the most experienced novel-reader unprepared. The unravelment of the puzzle is a satisfactory reward for all the interest out of which they have been beguiled. When, however, they have read to the end, we recommend them

---

* This refers to the fact that *The Moonstone* appeared serially in Dickens' weekly *All the Year Round*, beginning in January 1868 and ending in August; thus the 3-decker book edition, published in July, anticipated the completion of serialization by some weeks. Information by courtesy of David Randall, the Scribner Bookstore, New York.—ED.

to read the book over again from the beginning, and they will see, what on a first perusal they were too engrossed to observe, the carefully elaborate workmanship, and the wonderful construction of the story; the admirable manner in which every circumstance and incident is fitted together, and the skill with which the secret is kept to the last; so that even when all seems to have been discovered there is a final light thrown upon people and things which give them a significance they had not before. The "epilogue" of *The Moonstone* is beautiful. It redeems the somewhat sordid detective element, by a strain of solemn and pathetic human interest. Few will read of the final destiny of *The Moonstone* without feeling the tears rise in their eyes as they catch the last glimpse of the three men, who have sacrificed their caste in the service of their God, when the vast crowd of worshippers opens for them, as they embrace each other and separate to begin their lonely and never-ending pilgrimage of expiation. The deepest emotion is certainly reserved to the last.

As to the various characters of the romance, they are secondary to the circumstances. The hero and heroine do not come out very distinctly, though we are quite willing to take them upon testimony. Ezra Jennings, the doctor's assistant, is the one personage who makes himself felt by the reader. The slight sketch of his history, left purposely without details, the beautiful and noble nature developed in spite of calumny, loneliness, and the pain of a deadly malady, is drawn with a firm and masterly hand; it has an aspect of reality which none of the other personages possess, though we fancy we should recognize old Betteredge if we were to meet him, even without a copy of *Robinson Crusoe* in his hand! We wish some means could have been found to save Rosanna Spearman. The cloud that hangs over her horrible death might have been lifted by a true artist, and she might have been allowed to live and recover her right mind, under the tender influence of her friend, "Limping Lucy." Mr. Godfrey Ablewhite, the distinguished philanthropist and his lady worshippers, as seen by the light thrown on him by his ardent admirer, Miss Clack, is very cleverly managed; the reader suspects him, like Sergeant Cuff and Mr. Bruff; but the reader is destined to be quite as much taken by surprise as they were.

II. THE SIGN OF FOUR

(From the *Athenaeum,* London, December 6, 1890)

A detective story is usually lively reading, but we cannot pretend to think that *The Sign of Four* is up to the level of the writer's best work. It is a curious medley, and full of horrors; and surely those who play at hide and seek with the fatal treasure are a curious company. The wooden-legged convict and his fiendish misshapen little mate, the ghastly twins, the genial prizefighters, the detectives wise and foolish, and the gentle girl whose lover tells the tale, twist in and out together in a mazy dance, culminating in that mad and terrible rush down the river which ends the mystery and the treasure. Dr. Doyle's admirers will read the little volume through eagerly enough, but they will hardly care to take it up again.

III. TRENT'S LAST CASE

(From the *Bookman,* New York, May, 1913)

Although he just fails of making Philip Trent a personality, Mr. E. C. Bentley, in *The Woman in Black,** has constructed a detective story of unusual originality and ingenuity. An American multi-millionaire, a power in the world's finance, is murdered on his estate on the south coast of England. Half a dozen persons are presented to the reader as possible objects of suspicion—the dead man's young wife, the "Woman in Black," his American secretary, his English secretary, an elderly Englishman with whom he has had a violent quarrel, his butler, and a French maid. Trent, a painter, who on several previous occasions has shown decided talent in solving criminal mysteries, is sent to the scene of the crime by a great London newspaper. There is the inevitable foil in the person of Inspector Murch, of the official police, whose years of experience in the practical service of Scotland Yard avail him but little when pitted against the superior imagination of the brilliant amateur. Trent finds the key to a greater part of the mystery in

---

* Title of the first American publication of *Trent's Last Case;* subsequent American editions have employed the original English title.—Ed.

a pair of worn patent leather shoes that had belonged to the dead American multi-millionaire, and in certain finger prints. But the story of the affair that he writes out but does not send to his newspaper lacks accuracy in one or two important points, the explanation that seems to cover everything when the book has run less than two-thirds its course is not quite complete, and it is not until the final chapter is reached that the reader is in possession of the full account of the events surrounding the death of Sigsbee Manderson. In his use of Americanisms, Mr. Bentley is rather better than most English writers, which is not saying a great deal.

IV. THE BENSON MURDER CASE

(Review by Dashiell Hammett in the *Saturday Review of Literature,* New York, January 15, 1927)

Alvin Benson is found sitting in a wicker chair in his living room, a book still in his hand, his legs crossed, and his body comfortably relaxed in a life-like position. He is dead. A bullet from an Army model Colt .45 automatic pistol, held some six feet away when the trigger was pulled, has passed completely through his head. That his position should have been so slightly disturbed by the impact of such a bullet at such a range is preposterous, but the phenomenon hasn't anything to do with the plot, so don't, as I did, waste time trying to figure it out. The murderer's identity becomes obvious quite early in the story. The authorities, no matter how stupid the author chose to make them, would have cleared up the mystery promptly if they had been allowed to follow the most rudimentary police routine. But then what would there have been for the gifted Vance to do?

This Philo Vance is in the Sherlock Holmes tradition and his conversational manner is that of a high-school girl who has been studying the foreign words and phrases in the back of her dictionary. He is a bore when he discusses art and philosophy, but when he switches to criminal psychology he is delightful. There is a theory that any one who talks enough on any subject must, if only by chance, finally say something not altogether incorrect. Vance disproves this theory: he manages always, and usually ridiculously, to be wrong. His exposition of the technique employed by a gentleman shooting another gentleman who sits six feet in front of him deserves a place in a *How to be a detective by mail* course.

To supply this genius with a field for his operations the author has to treat his policemen abominably. He doesn't let them ask any questions that aren't wholly irrelevant. They can't make inquiries of any one who might know anything. They aren't permitted to take any steps toward learning whether the dead man was robbed. Their fingerprint experts are excluded from the scene of the crime. When information concerning a mysterious box of jewelry accidentally bobs up everybody resolutely ignores it, since it would have led to a solution before the three-hundredth page.

Mr. Van Dine doesn't deprive his officials of every liberty, however: he generously lets them compete with Vance now and then in the expression of idiocies. Thus Heath, a police detective-sergeant, says that any pistol of less than .44 calibre is too small to stop a man, and the district attorney, Markham, displays an amazed disinclination to admit that a confession could actually be false. This Markham is an outrageously naïve person: the most credible statement in the tale is to the effect that Markham served only one term in this office. The book is written in the little-did-he-realize style.

The Ethics of the Mystery Novel

By Anthony Boucher

*Some of the most original and provocative American criticism—
as distinguished from reviewing—of crime and mystery literature
has been appearing in recent years over the signature of Anthony
Boucher, detective novelist and crime specialist for the* San Francisco Chronicle. *The selection by Mr. Boucher which follows,
however, was published in* Tricolor *(the American edition of* La
France Libre) *for October 1944. Whether or not the reader agrees
with Mr. Boucher in all respects (it is possible, for example, to
argue that the best answer to reactionary propaganda in the whodunit is not necessarily counter-propaganda, but the absence of
special pleading) he must grant that here is forthright criticism
in the higher meaning of the word and with—literally—a venge-
ance.*

THE PHRASE, "the ethics of the mystery novel," is a commonplace
of mystery writers' shop talk and always means one thing: the
fair-play technique by which the author scrupulously presents all
relevant facts and enables the reader (at least in theory) to solve
the problem as readily as the detective.

This piece is not, however, a consideration of the fairness of
Roger Ackroyd or the legitimate use of the insane murderer. Its
title means that it will try to sketch the ethical problems and attitudes present in the contemporary whodunit.

"Ethics?" you say. "In the mystery novel?" But why not? It is
all but impossible for any writer above the hack level (and many
mystery novelists are far above it) to write about people and problems without implying some set of values, some ethical standard.

And the mystery novel, dealing as it must with crime and punishment (and now so often with political ideology) can never effect quite so complete an escape from realities as the hammock romance or the western.

Mystery novels, particularly since the burgeoning of the pocket-size reprints, reach an audience running at least into the hundreds of thousands. Any ethical tendencies detectable in such a field surely deserve examination.

Back in the 'thirties there was occasional concern from the Left about the mystery novel. The very form of the whodunit, with its asserted glorification of the police (cossacks to you), was denounced as essentially fascistic. The argument hardly needed an answer; if any had been needed, it came in Italy and Germany in the fascist ban on the corrupt and democratic mystery novel.

A more plausible interpretation of the political meaning of the mystery novel in general is that of Howard Haycraft, who has often maintained, notably in his invaluable history *Murder for Pleasure,* the thesis that the very essence of the whodunit is democratic, that its interest depends upon a concept of absolute justice, a detective resolved to find the murderer and not (as a Gestapo or NKVD man might prefer) a frameable enemy of the State, and that the mystery can flourish only in a democracy—a thesis borne out by geographic and historical fact.

But if the mystery as a form is democratic, what political opinions find expression within that form? Marie Rodell, in her essential textbook *Mystery Fiction: Theory & Technique,* lays down the rule that "As escape literature, the mystery is not designed to preach a message, correct an evil, or advocate a Utopia. Controversies on such questions as these are among the things the reader is trying to escape from," and goes on to insist that the mystery writer cannot use "highly controversial material."

This is a somewhat misleading statement of the situation. The body of mysteries, to be sure, has not been "controversial"; it has simply assumed, without controversy, the most conservative attitude toward the status quo. In most mysteries up to recent years, you could safely assume that a labor organizer was a racketeer, that a Communist had a bomb in his pocket, that a Negro was either sinister or comedy relief, that the British caste system was inviolate and a Good Thing, and that imperialism was the glory of the Anglo-Saxon race, on either side of the Atlantic.

This attitude is no longer invariable. In *The Brass Chills,* Hugh Pentecost presented a Communist who was intelligent and a man of good will. In *Judas Incorporated,* Kurt Steel combined a first-rate mystery with a solidly pro-union labor novel, probably achieving, through its greater readability, more propaganda value than a half-dozen proletarian epics. In *Johnny on the Spot,* Amen Dell wrote a story that was as quietly and uncontroversially pro-labor as any earlier mystery had ever been labor-baiting.

The mystery has, of course always dealt largely with the moneyed and overmoneyed classes, and some reflection of their attitudes was inevitable. But the past decade has tended, in the words of Raymond Chandler, "to get murder away from the upper classes, the week-end house party and the vicar's rose-garden, and back to the people who are really good at it"; and even the writers who cling to the wealthy are beginning to assume a slightly more critical attitude toward them.

This same trend away from the upper classes has made the racial question in the mystery more acute. The common man may be no more anti-semitic or anti-Negro than the wealthy, but he is more pungent in his expression of his dislikes. Such writers as Chandler have legitimately recorded this pungency; lesser fry have seemed almost to revel in it—even to take for granted that the reader concurs, as in H. W. Roden's *You Only Hang Once,* which presents an intelligent, educated, supposedly likeable hero whose sole word for Jew is yid. It is true of the mystery, as of most popular fiction, that a sympathetic protagonist is of necessity white and a gentile. Oddly, it is quite permissible for him to be a Catholic, though one writer whose detective is a nun reports that his novels have often been rejected for reprints because of their "controversial" nature.

This double pattern of legitimate recording and wilful wallowing exists also, particularly in the hard-boiled school, in regard to sex. The mystery novel as originally developed, especially in England, was so sexless as to bear little relation to life or crime. The inevitable reaction has torn down the barriers until (again *pace* Rodell on Tabus) there are few sexual manifestations which have not been at least suggested in murder novels. At times (one thinks of Georges Simenon or of Matthew Head's *The Smell of Money*) these suggestions have been novelistically valid and powerful; at other times (libel laws advise no mention of names) they have approached the pornographic.

The sexual ethic of the whodunit as a whole (aside from the fast-and-loose school in which characters leap in and out of bed with singular ease and innocence) might be described simply as a recognition of the sexual mores of our times, particularly as motivating factors in crime.

Except, of course, for the slick female hammock novel, in which sex (under the trade name of love) and avarice (disguised as ambition and the American way) are the sole motivating forces of all characters. The blithe amorality of the people of Jonathan Latimer or Richard Shattuck seems clean and refreshing beside the smug hypocrisy of the Cinderella heroine who lies, cheats, steals (and usually gets herself almost—but never quite—killed) to protect the stalwart hero, not because she is convinced of his innocence, but because she must save him from the gallows for the altar, guilty or not.

The moral attitude of the mystery novel toward murder is predominantly, as one might imagine, that of Coolidge's minister toward sin. But a sympathetic murderer occasionally goes scot free, or more frequently is allowed to contrive his own exit. The killing of a murderer, even when the element of self-defense is scarcely present, is generally condoned; private, rather than public justice is frequently invoked in the dénouement. Exact statistics are lacking, but one might estimate that at least two murderers meet death at their own hands, or those of other characters, for every one that goes to the chair, gallows, or gas chamber.

Inevitably, private execution is common in the spy novel. A few writers, notably Graham Greene and Dorothy B. Hughes, have shown a concern for the moral effect of necessary killing upon a man inherently *bonae voluntatis*. More make the killing of the enemy either a grim but perfunctory business matter (an attitude excellently exploited by Peter Cheyney) or more frequently just good clean fun. The grounds need not be sufficient for rational judgment; let a man (today) once be suspected of being a Nazi and he is fair game for any sympathetic character.

As dangerous a tendency as is visible in the field at present is this of the spy novel to plant the most elemental racial suspicion and enmity. In the run of the mill spy story, you can know at once that any character with a guttural accent or a Prussian haircut is, by logical progression, therefore a Nazi, therefore also the murderer; therefore also a legitimate private target. Which is a specimen of the very reasoning which, according to Mr. Haycraft, makes the mystery novel impossible in any totalitarian country.

(Curious parallel: If a character says *l* for *r,* you know he is supposed to be Japanese, though the opposite confusion is the linguistic fact.)

The spy novel has been growing in popularity (at least among writers and publishers) since 1939 until for the past year spy stories have made up more than a third of the books which I have read as a mystery reviewer. Inevitably the spy novel must, in a time like this, be a propaganda novel; one cannot write of a duel between American and Axis agents with the romantic and forgetful impartiality of a novelist writing about the Blue and the Gray.

Many spy novels reduce this propaganda to its simplest terms, offering a black and white picture of Good men *vs* Huns which sounds like the 1917 vintage or even more like Cowboys *vs* Indians. But the best of the current spy stories probe deeper. They are aware that this is not simply a war against Germans and Japs, but a battle against Fascism. And they realize that a fascist is not necessarily an enemy alien.

Ethel Vance in *Escape,* Michael Hardt in *A Stranger and Afraid,* Katharine Roberts in her Belgian novels, and various others have successfully portrayed the conflict of fascism and humanity in Europe. Mark Saxton in *The Year of August,* John August in *Advance Agent,* and most surprisingly Leslie Charteris in *The Saint Steps In* have depicted the perils of that purely American fascism whose slogan will be, inescapably, "No isms but Americanism."

This is perhaps the field in which the propaganda value of the mystery may be most beneficial. The average reader does not need

to be told to hate the enemy, but he may need occasional promptings as to who the enemy is; and *The Saint Steps In* may, in its
picaresque way, open eyes that have not read *Under Cover*.

There is other propaganda present in the mystery. There is
Dennis Wheatley's *Faked Passports* which explains that Goering is
a gentleman and that one could easily do business with the Prussian generals. There is Helen MacInnes' *While Still We Live*,
which defends the Polish aristocracy by minimizing the importance of idealogical differences and implying that democracy is
only one of many tenable political attitudes.

There is Cleve F. Adams' *Up Jumps the Devil,* a stalwart white
Nordic novel which has only contempt for what the author consistently terms kikes, wops, spigs, and niggers, and only scorn for
the war effort. The private detective here solves the case by guessing at a suspect, kidnaping him, and having him tortured by a gangster until he confesses. When an F. B. I. man objects to these
Gestapo-like methods, the private eye ringingly proclaims, "An
American Gestapo is what we goddamned well need!"

These three books are hardly typical of the field. The mystery
novel is a microcosm; and almost every type, taste or trend can
be found therein that exists in fiction as a whole. But to gen-
eralize as far as is safe, it can be said that there is little danger in
the growing popularity of the whodunit.

As opposed to the reader of the so-called "general" fiction, the
mystery fan will be indoctrinated with a slightly more reactionary view on labor and race relations (though the influence of the
liberal left is slowly increasing), but a much sharper awareness
of the possible growth of American fascism; a slightly more carefree attitude toward sex, but a much sterner sense of justice and
retribution.

And if liberals are impatient (as some may well be) with the
mystery's slow emergence from conservatism, they have two possible courses of action: to write to mystery editors (who do read
such mail) praising liberal books and damning the devils which
jump up; or themselves to write mystery novels which will present
the liberal viewpoint, not dogmatically, but easily and taken-for-
granted. And thereby brighten the days of at least one reviewer.

Who Cares Who Killed Roger Ackroyd?

By Edmund Wilson

At the height of the literary season 1944–45, the eminent American critic and novelist Edmund Wilson published in the New Yorker *(of which he is chief literary critic) a now-famous series of three leading articles sharply critical of modern detective stories and their readers. The outcries of the faithful touched off by this circumstance surpassed even the storm that greeted the English critic Howard Spring (who shares Mr. Wilson's disapproval of the genre) when, a few years ago, he reviewed a detective novel and disclosed the murderer, method, and motive.*

Since (we must face facts) there are some people who unhappily don't like detective stories, and since freedom and representation are our watchwords, Mr. Wilson is made welcome to the present pages as an honored guest, a visitor from another and sadder world. In the further interest of hospitality, the second of his articles—in which he has the advantage of rebuttal and restatement of his position—has been chosen for reprinting, in order to present his missionary message in the fairest possible light. (His third article, a re-examination of the Sherlock Holmes saga, is less directly pertinent to the main discussion.) The present selection appeared in the New Yorker *for January 20, 1945. It is reprinted by permission of Mr. Wilson and the* New Yorker. *Copyright 1945 The F-R. Publishing Corporation. . . . Without further comment, Mr. Wilson.*

THREE MONTHS ago I wrote in these pages—in the issue of October 14th—an article on some recent detective stories. I had not read any fiction of this kind since the days of Sherlock Holmes, and, since I constantly heard animated discussions of the merits of the mystery writers, I was curious to see what it was like today. The specimens I read I found disappointing, and I made some rather derogatory remarks on my impression of the genre in general. To my surprise, this brought me letters of protest in a volume and of a passionate earnestness which had hardly been elicited even by my occasional criticisms of the Soviet Union. Of the thirty-nine letters that have reached me, only seven approve my strictures. The writers of almost all the others seem deeply offended and shocked, and they all say almost exactly the same thing: that I had simply not read the right novels and that I would surely have a different opinion if I would only try this or that author recommended by the correspondent. In many of these letters there was a note of asperity, and one lady went so far as to declare that she would never read this department again unless I was prepared to reconsider my position. In the meantime, furthermore, a number of other writers have published articles defending the detective story: Jacques Barzun, Joseph Wood Krutch,* Raymond Chandler,* and Somerset Maugham have all had something to say on the subject—nor has the umbrageous Bernard DeVoto failed to raise his voice.

Overwhelmed by so much insistence, I at last wrote my correspondents that I would try to correct any injustice by undertaking to read some of the authors that had received the most recommendations and taking the whole matter up again. The preferences of these readers, however, when I had a tabulation of them made, turned out to be extremely divergent. They ranged over fifty-two writers and sixty-seven books, most of which got only one or two votes each. The only writers who got as many as five or over were Dorothy L. Sayers, Margery Allingham, Ngaio Marsh, Michael Innes, Raymond Chandler, and the author who writes under the names of Carter Dickson and John Dickson Carr.

The writer that my correspondents were most nearly unanimous in putting at the top was Miss Dorothy L. Sayers, who was pressed upon me by eighteen people, and the book of hers that eight of them were sure I could not fail to enjoy was a story called *The Nine Tailors*. Well, I set out to read *The Nine Tailors* in the hope of tasting some novel excitement, and I must confess that

---

* Found elsewhere in this volume.—ED.

it seems to me one of the dullest books I have ever encountered
in any field. The first part of it is all about bell-ringing as it is
practised in English churches and contains a lot of information
of the kind that you might expect to find in an encyclopedia article on campanology. I skipped a good deal of this, and found
myself skipping, also, a large section of the conversations between
conventional English village characters: "Oh, here's Hinkins with
the aspidistras. People may say what they like about aspidistras,
but they do go on all the year round and make a background,"
etc. There was also a dreadful conventional English nobleman
of the casual and debonair kind, with the embarrassing name of
Lord Peter Wimsey, and, though he was the focal character in the
novel, being Miss Dorothy Sayers' version of the inevitable Sherlock Holmes detective, I had to skip a good deal of him, too. In
the meantime, I was losing the story, which had not got a firm
grip on my attention, but I went back and picked it up and stead-
fastly pushed through to the end, and there I discovered that the
whole point was that if a man was shut up in a belfry while a
heavy peal of chimes was being rung, the vibrations of the bells
might kill him. Not a bad idea for a murder, and Conan Doyle
would have known how to dramatize it in an entertaining tale
of thirty pages, but Miss Sayers had not hesitated to pad it out
to a book of three hundred and thirty, contriving one of those
stock cock-and-bull stories about a woman who commits bigamy
without knowing it and larding the whole thing with details of
church architecture, bits of quaint lore from books about bell
ringing, and the awful whimsical patter of Lord Peter.

I had often heard people say that Dorothy Sayers wrote well,
and I felt that my correspondents had been playing her as their
literary ace. But, really, she does not write very well: it is simply
that she is more consciously literary than most of the other detective-story writers and that she thus attracts attention in a field
which is mostly on a sub-literary level. In any serious department
of fiction, her writing would not appear to have any distinction
at all. Yet, commonplace in this respect though she is, she gives
an impression of brilliant talent if we put her beside Miss Ngaio
Marsh, whose *Overture to Death* was also suggested by several
correspondents. Mr. DeVoto has put himself on record as believ-

ing that Miss Marsh, as well as Miss Sayers and Miss Margery Allingham, writes her novels in "excellent prose," and this throws for me a good deal of light on Mr. DeVoto's opinions as a critic. I hadn't quite realized before, in spite of his own rather messy style, that he was totally insensitive to writing. It would be impossible, I should think, for anyone with the faintest feeling for words to describe the unappetizing sawdust which Miss Marsh has poured into her pages as "excellent prose" or as prose at all except in the sense that distinguishes prose from verse. And here again the book is mostly padding. There is the notion that you could commit a murder by rigging up a gun in a piano, so that the victim will shoot himself when he presses down the pedal, but this is embedded in the dialogue and doings of a lot of faked-up English county people who are even more tedious than those of *The Nine Tailors.*

The enthusiastic reader of detective stories will indignantly object at this point that I am reading for the wrong things: that I ought not to be expecting good writing, characterization, human interest, or even atmosphere. He is right, of course, though I was not fully aware of it till I attempted *Flowers for the Judge,* considered by connoisseurs one of the best books of one of the masters of this school, Miss Margery Allingham. I looked forward to this novel especially because it was read by a member of my family, an expert of immense experience, and reported upon very favorably, before I had got to it myself. But when I did, I found it completely unreadable. The story and the writing alike showed a surface so wooden and dead that I could not keep my mind on the page. How can you care who committed a murder which has never really been made to take place, because the writer hasn't any ability of even the most ordinary kind to make you see it or feel it? How can you probe the possibilities of guilt among characters who all seem alike because they are all simply names on the page? It was then that I understood that a true connoisseur of this fiction is able to suspend the demands of his imagination and literary taste and take the thing as an intellectual problem. But how you arrive at that state of mind is what I do not understand.

In the light of this revelation, I feel that it is probably irrelevant to mention that I enjoyed *The Burning Court,* by John Dickson

Carr, more than the novels of any of these ladies. There is a tinge of black magic which gives it a little of the interest of a horror story, and the author has a virtuosity at playing with alternative hypotheses which makes this element of detective fiction more amusing than it usually is.

I want, however, to take up certain points made by the writers of the above-mentioned articles.

Mr. Barzun informs the non-expert that the detective novel is a kind of game in which the reader of a given story, in order to play properly his hand, should be familiar with all the devices that have already been used in other stories. These devices, it seems, are now barred: the reader must challenge the writer to solve his problem in some novel way, and the writer puts it up to the reader to guess the new solution. This may be true, but I shall never qualify. I would rather play Twenty Questions, which at least does not involve the consumption of hundreds of ill-written books.

A point made by three of these writers, Mr. Maugham, Mr. De-Voto, and Mr. Krutch, is that the novel has become so philosophical, so psychological, and so symbolic that the public have had to take to the detective story as the only department of fiction where pure story-telling still survives.

This seems to me to involve two fallacies. On the one hand, it is surely not true that "the serious novelists of today"—to quote Mr. Maugham's assertion—"have often," in contrast to the novelists of the past, "little or no story to tell," that "they have allowed themselves to be persuaded that to tell a story is a negligible form of art." Joyce and Proust and Mann—who, I suppose, must be accounted the heaviest going—have all their peculiar modern ways of boring and playing tricks on the reader. But how about Richardson and Sterne? How about the dreadful bogs and obstacles that one has to get over in Scott? the interpolated essays in Hugo? the leaking tap of Thackeray's reflections on life, in which the story is always trickling away? Now, all these top novelists of the present time do certainly have stories to tell and they have organized their books with an intensity which has been relatively rare in the novel and which, to my mind, more than makes up for the occasional viscosity of their narrative.

On the other hand, it seems to me—for reasons that I have suggested in my complaints above—perfectly fantastic to say that the average detective novel is an example of good story-telling. The gift for telling stories is uncommon, like other artistic gifts, and the only one of this group of writers—the writers my correspondents have praised—who seems to me to possess it to any degree is Mr. Raymond Chandler. His *Farewell, My Lovely* is the only one of these books that I have read all of and read with enjoyment. But Chandler, though in his recent article he seems to claim Hammett as his father, does not really belong to this school of the old-fashioned detective novel. What he writes is a novel of adventure which has less in common with Hammett than with Alfred Hitchcock and Graham Greene—the modern spy story which has substituted the jitters of the Gestapo and the G.P.U. for the luxury world of E. Phillips Oppenheim. It is not simply a question here of a puzzle which has been put together but of a malaise conveyed to the reader, the horror of a hidden conspiracy which is continually turning up in the most varied and unlikely forms. To write such a novel successfully you must be able to invent character and incident and to generate atmosphere, and all this Mr. Chandler can do, though he is a long way below Graham Greene. It is only when I get to the end that I feel my old crime-story depression descending upon me again—because here again, as is so often the case, the explanation of the mysteries, when it comes, is neither interesting nor plausible enough. It fails to justify the excitement produced by the picturesque and sinister happenings, and I cannot help feeling cheated.

My experience with this second batch of novels has, therefore, been even more disillusioning than my experience with the first, and my final conclusion is that the reading of detective stories is simply a kind of vice that, for silliness and minor harmfulness, ranks somewhere between crossword puzzles and smoking. This conclusion seems borne out by the violence of the letters I have been receiving. Detective-story readers feel guilty, they are habitually on the defensive, and all their talk about "well-written" mysteries is simply an excuse for their vice, like the reasons that the alcoholic can always produce for a drink. One of the letters I have had shows the addict in his frankest and most shameless phase.

This lady begins by trying, like the others, to give me some guidance in picking out the better grade of stories, but as she proceeds, she goes all to pieces. She says that she has read hundreds of detective stories, but "it is surprising how few I would recommend to another. However, a poor detective story is better than none at all. Try again. With a little better luck, you'll find one you admire and enjoy. Then you, too, may be

A MYSTERY FIEND."

This letter has made my blood run cold: so the opium smoker tells the novice not to mind if the first pipe makes him sick; and I fall back for reassurance on the valiant little band of readers who sympathize with my views on the subject. One of these tells me that I have underestimated both the badness of the detective stories themselves and the lax mental habits of those who enjoy them. The worst of it is, he says, that the true addict, half the time, never even finds out who has committed the murder. The addict reads not to find anything out but merely to get the mild stimulation of the succession of unexpected incidents and of the suspense itself of *looking forward* to learning a sensational secret. That this secret is nothing at all and does not really account for the incidents does not matter to such a reader. He has learned from his long indulgence how to connive with the author in cheating: he does not pay any real attention when the disappointing dénouement occurs, he does not think back and check the events, he simply closes the book and starts another. This theory is confirmed by my own sensations in reading such a novel as, say, Rex Stout's *The Red Box*. I read to the end of the story to find out what was in the box, but from the moment when I came to realize that the box was only a bait and that there was nothing astonishing in it, I did not bother with the plot any more but dropped the book, after I had finished it, without ever making much effort to figure out what all the fuss had been about.

To detective-story addicts, then, I say: Please do not write me any more letters telling me that I have not read the right books. And to the seven correspondents who are with me and who in some cases have thanked me for helping them to liberate themselves from a habit which they recognized as wasteful of time and degrading to the intelligence but into which they had been bullied by convention and the portentously invoked examples of Woodrow Wilson and André Gide—to these staunch and pure spirits I say: Friends, we represent a minority, but Literature is on our side. With so many fine books to be read, so much to be studied and known, there is no need to bore ourselves with this rubbish. And with the paper shortage pressing on all publication and many first-rate writers forced out of print, we shall do well to discourage the squandering of this paper which might be put to better use.

The Detective Story—Why?

By Nicholas Blake

Nicholas Blake is best known to American readers as a foremost "new generation" English detective story writer, the author of such fine novels as The Beast Must Die, *and for his poetry published under his birth-name, C. Day Lewis. He has also written from time to time outstanding criticism of the detection genre, chiefly for the* Spectator. *It is to be hoped that his novels and criticism, both apparently interrupted by the war, will be soon resumed. The selection which follows is excerpted from Mr. Blake's introduction to the English edition of the present editor's* Murder For Pleasure: The Life and Times of the Detective Story *(London: Davies, 1942); which will explain certain otherwise perplexing references.*

I DO not mean, by this, to ask why the detective story came into existence when it did. That question has been answered succinctly, if negatively, by Mr. Haycraft—"Clearly, there could be no detective stories . . . until there were detectives. This did not occur until the nineteenth century." A negative answer, because it merely re-defines the question: after all, there were no railway systems, either, until the nineteenth century, but their creation did not produce any considerable body of literature about engine-drivers.

Nor do I intend to discuss at length the subsidiary though fascinating problem, "Why do we write detective stories?" Many solutions, all of them correct, will suggest themselves to the reader. Because we want to make money. Because the drug addict (and nearly every detection-writer is an omnivorous reader of crime fiction) always wants to introduce other people to the habit. Because artists have a notorious *nostalgie de la boue,* and our own hygienic, a-moral age offers very little honest mud to revel in except the pleasures of imaginary murder. Democratic civilisation does not encourage us to indulge our instinct for cruelty: the quite different attitude of the dictatorships towards this, as well as their different conception of justice, legal evidence and legal proof, must—as Mr. Haycraft points out—account for the Nazis' banning of all imported detective-fiction and characterising it as "pure liberalism" designed to "stuff the heads of German readers with foreign ideas": a people whose blood-lust was sublimated by reading and writing fiction murders would certainly have less zest for murdering real Poles.

An agreeable monograph might indeed be written on The First Plunge Into Detective Writing. Gone, alas, are the good old days when "without an idea in his head and with no previous knowledge of crime or criminals, Leblanc [creator of the great Arsène Lupin] took up his pen, and his impudent hero sprang into spontaneous being." So expert and exacting is the detection-fan today that the detective novelist must possess a good working knowledge of police procedure, law and forensic medicine if he is to escape severe letters from the public pointing out his errors: (how many plots, I wonder, have been complicated by the writer's need to skirt round some obstacle raised by his technical ignorance?) From what dark incentive, by what devious and secret psychological passages have detective writers—timid and law-abiding persons for the most part, who faint at the sight of blood and tremble when the eye of a policeman is turned upon them—first set out upon the sinister paths of crime-fiction?

The question is enthralling. But it must here be subsumed under my general question: "The Detective Story—Why?" Why, I mean, has the detective story attained such remarkable popularity, rising—as Mr. Haycraft tells us—from a ratio of twelve in 1914 to ninety-seven in 1925 and two hundred and seventeen in 1939, and holding its own even against that most insidious and degraded of mental recreations, the cross-word puzzle?

We may imagine some James Frazer of the year 2042 discoursing on "The Detective Novel—the Folk-Myth of the Twentieth Century." He will, I fancy, connect the rise of crime fiction with the decline of religion at the end of the Victorian era. The sense of guilt, psychologists tell us, is deeply rooted in man and one of the mainsprings of his actions. Just as, in the primitive tribe, the idiot or the scapegoat is venerated and the murderer wreathed with flowers, because he has taken upon himself the guilt of the community, so in more civilised times one function of religion is to take the burden of guilt off the individual's shoulders through the agency of some Divine or apotheosised Being. When a religion has lost its hold upon men's hearts, they must have some other outlet for the sense of guilt.

This, our anthropologist of the year 2042 may argue, was provided for us by crime-fiction. He will call attention to the pattern of the detective-novel, as highly formalised as that of a religious ritual, with its initial necessary sin (the murder), its victim, its high priest (the criminal) who must in turn be destroyed by a yet higher power (the detective). He will conjecture—and rightly —that the devotee identified himself both with the detective and the murderer, representing the light and the dark sides of his own nature. He will note a significant parallel between the formalised dénouement of the detective novel and the Christian concept of the Day of Judgment when, with a flourish of trumpets, the mystery is made plain and the goats are separated from the sheep.

Nor is this all. The figure of the detective himself will be exhaustively analysed. Our anthropologist, having studied Mr. Haycraft's work, will have been informed that many readers of crime fiction remembered the name of the detective but not of the book or its author. Sherlock Holmes, Peter Wimsey, Hercule Poirot were evidently figures of supernatural importance to the reader: and to the writer, for their creators bodied them out with a loving veneration which suggested that the Father Imago was at work. The detective is, indeed—to change the metaphor—the Fairy Godmother of the twentieth century folk-myth, his magic capabilities only modified to the requirements of a would-be scientific and rational generation. It will be noted, too, that these semidivine figures fell into two categories. On the one hand was the more primitive, the anthropomorphised type—Holmes and Wimsey its most celebrated examples—in which human frailty and eccentricity, together with superhuman powers of perception, are carried to a supralogical conclusion. On the other hand there was the so-to-speak modernist detective—generally a policeman rather than an amateur—a figure stripped of human attributes, an instrument of pure reason and justice, the Logos of the detective world.

Such may well be, in brief, the theory advanced by posterity to account for the extraordinary hold which the detective novel possessed on the twentieth-century mind. It would be difficult, at any rate, to explain the popularity of a so fantastic offshoot of literature without reference to some fundamental instinct in mankind.

But the general lines of such an inquiry have not been sufficiently adumbrated if they do not include the minor curiosity of class-bias in crime fiction. It is an established fact that the detective-novel proper is read almost exclusively by the upper and professional classes. The so-called "lower-middle" and "working" classes tend to read "bloods," thrillers. Now this is not simply a matter of literary standards, though the modern thriller is generally much below the detective story in spohistication and style. When we compare these two kinds of crime fiction, we cannot fail to notice that, whereas in the detective novel the criminal is almost invariably a squalid creature of irremediably flagitious tendencies, the criminal of the thriller is often its hero and nearly always a romantic figure.

This is, of course, as Mr. Haycraft has pointed out, a natural development of the Robin Hood myth. The detective story's clientele are relatively prosperous persons, who have a stake in the social system and must, therefore, even in fantasy, see the ultimate triumph of their particular social values ensured. It is significant that even the "thrillers" most popular with the ruling classes usually represent their hero as being on the side of law and order—the bourgeois conception of law and order, of course (that unspeakable public school bully and neurotic exhibitionist, Bulldog Drummond, is a case in point), or as a reformed criminal (e.g. Father Brown's right hand man); or, like Arsène Lupin, he starts as a criminal character but, after a number of anti-social adventures, gradually goes over to the other side. Not so with the lower ranks of democratic society. Having little or no stake in the system, they prefer such anarchistic heroes, from Robin Hood down to the tommy-gun gangster, who have held to ransom the prosperous and law-abiding. To such readers the policeman is not the protective figure he appears to your politician, your stockbroker, your rural dean: for them his aura is menacing, his baton an offensive weapon rather than a defensive symbol: and therefore the *roman policier* does not give them much of a kick.

The guilt-motive perhaps operates here too. On the whole, the working classes have less time and incentive than the relatively leisured to worry about their consciences. In so far as their lives are less rich, the taking of life (the detective story's almost invariable subject) will seem to them less significant and horrifying. They themselves sometimes kill for passion; seldom, unlike their more fortunately placed brethren, for gain. The general sense of guilt (which is the reverse or seamy side of social responsibility), the specific moral problems which tease the more prosperous classes, affect them less nearly. So, for them, the detective novel —the fantasy-representation of guilt—must have a shallower appeal.

It is the element of fantasy in detective fiction—or rather, the juxtaposition of fantasy with reality—that gives the genre its identity. Mr. Haycraft mentions Carolyn Wells' dictum that "the detective novel must *seem* real in the same sense that fairy tales *seem* real to children." By implication, this statement defines very accurately the boundaries of the detective novel. The fairy tale does not reach its greatest heights when—as in the Irish fairy stories—fantasy is piled on fantasy, but by a judicious blending of the possible with the impossible. Similarly, in crime fiction, if we set down unrealistic characters in fantastic situations, we cross the frontier into the domain of the pure "shocker." If on the other hand both our action and our characters are realistic, we produce fiction of the Francis Iles' type which, as Mr. Haycraft rightly points out, does not come within the strict canon of the detective story.

The detective novelist, then, is left with two alternatives. He can put unreal characters into realistic situations, or he can put realistic characters into fantastic situations. The former method produces the classical *roman policier,* of which Freeman Wills Crofts is perhaps the most able living exponent, where the crime and the police investigation are conducted on strictly realistic lines, and the element of fantasy necessary to the detection novel is achieved by making the characters simple ciphers—formalised simulacra of men and women, that have no life outside the plot they serve. To call this type of novel "mere puzzles" and decry it for its "un-lifelike" characters is to misunderstand the whole paradox of the detective story.

The second alternative, which has produced the at present most fashionable kind of crime fiction, is to place "real" characters in unreal, fantastic, or at least improbable situations. This school of writing covers a wide range. At one extreme we find such books as John Dickson Carr's, where the plot possesses the mad logic and extravagance of a dream, while the *dramatis personae* are roughed in with just enough solidity to stand out against the macabre and whirling background: (Carr's Dr. Fell, incidentally, may be coupled with Rex Stout's Nero Wolfe as the most notable old-style or anthropomorphic detective in contemporary fiction—wayward, masterful, infallible). At the other extreme we get the work of such writers as Ngaio Marsh. Her Inspector Alleyn, like Michael Innes' detective, is gentlemanly, unobtrusive and almost provocatively normal. Her characters have real body, but derive nothing from textbooks on morbid psychology. Where the characters are ordinary people and the plot is neither *outré* nor melodramatic, one might suppose that the element of paradox necessary to the detective story would be missing. But murder is in itself such an abnormal thing that its mere presence among a number of nice, respectable, civilised characters will be paradox enough.

It is reasonable to suppose that this—the "novel of manners," as Mr. Haycraft calls it—will remain a predominant type of detective fiction for some time to come. Certainly we can be sure that the general raising of the literary level in the genre has come to stay. Fresher observation, more careful, realistic handling of character and situation are demanded today, and the general level of detective writing is thus improved. But something has been lost in the process. The high fantasy of the old masters cannot now be achieved. No detective novelist today could allow his hero to exclaim, in a moment of strong excitement, "Hold! Have you some mucilage?"

Another interesting line of development is in the detective himself. For some years, the sleuth has been undergoing modification—a toning down from the Sherlock Holmes to the Roderick Alleyn type. Even when, as with Peter Wimsey, his pedigree, family background, hobbies and tastes are diligently documented, he has become a much less far-fetched personality. If this process continues, we may expect in the future a school of detectives without personality at all. I myself rather fancy the idea of a detective who shall be as undistinguished as a piece of blotting paper, absorbing the reactions of his subjects; a shallow mirror, in which we see reflected every feature of the crime; a pure camera-eye. Professor Thorndyke and Dr. Priestley are precursors to this anonymous type. Inspector Maigret is its highest development up to date.

At first sight Maigret, the most formidable embodiment in crime fiction of the "stern, unhurrying chase" of Justice, might seem also the best model for the ambitious writer today. But his influence may well be disruptive of the detective novel as we know it. It is not simply that Simenon breaks the rules, by allowing Maigret to keep so much of his detection-processes under his hat. The real trouble is Simenon's deep and unerring sense of evil, which in practise runs counter to the basic principle of the detective story—that evil must, both for myth-making and entertainment, be volatised by a certain measure of fantasy. In the Maigret stories, evil hangs over everything, as heavy, as concentrated, as real as a black fog. It is a raw wine, which must burst the old bottles. You may remember that remarkable story in which the criminal is so fascinated by Maigret that he cannot keep away from him: he is like a moth dashing itself again and again into a passive flame. Now this exemplifies a proved psychological truth. As the Greek tragedians knew, crime carries within itself the seed of retribution; some fatal flaw (or saving grace) in human nature impels a wrong-doer to betray himself: that is why even the most painstaking and cold-blooded murderer is apt to leave a glaring clue behind, or talk too much one evening in the public bar.

This is all very right and proper in real life. But the traditional pattern of the detective novel would be disintegrated if writers emphasised the fact that the criminal does, unconsciously, hunt himself down. The fictional detective's occupation would indeed be gone. Perhaps this is the direction we are to move in. Perhaps the detective story, as we know it, will be supplanted by the crime novel. If so, future generations will look back on Simenon and Iles as the fathers of the new genre. It should be some time though, in any event, before we cease to read murder for pleasure.

Leaves from the Editors' Notebook
By Ellery Queen

Criticism is not limited to reviews and discussion: it may be historical and factual as well. Some of the finest scholarship of the latter type in the detection field has been appearing for the last few years in the lively and learned introductory notes to the stories published in Ellery Queen's Mystery Magazine. *At the invitation of your editor, the Messrs. Queen have personally selected seven of these "critical commentaries"—a veritable treasure trove of mystery miscellany—for reproduction in the present volume. As almost everyone knows, Ellery Queen (who surely requires no identification as one of the most outstanding and versatile figures in the American detective story) is really two men—Frederic Dannay and Manfred B. Lee.*

Leaf Number One: *The Detective Story, 1845–1861*

THE FIRST book of detective stories published on this planet was Edgar Allan Poe's *Tales*, which appeared in 1845 and contained the great Dupin trilogy. Incredible as it may seem today, Poe's experiments in fictional ratiocination fell on deaf ears: they were not popular with contemporary readers and they failed to impress contemporary writers. For consider: in the seventeen years that followed the first edition of Poe's *Tales*, not a single book was published in the United States that contained a detective story!

In the eighteenth year A.P. (After Poe)—in 1863—two books finally appeared to crack the long silence. One was *Strange Stories of a Detective: or, Curiosities of Crime*, by "a retired member of the detective police," brought out by Dick & Fitzgerald of New York; the other was *The Amber Gods and Other Stories*, by Harriet Prescott (Spofford), issued by Ticknor and Fields of Boston, and containing one detective story called "In a Cellar." Two years later, in 1865, Dick & Fitzgerald published *Leaves from the Note-Book of a New York Detective: The Private Record of J. B.,* written by a Dr. John B. Williams, and containing no less than 22 exploits of detective James Brampton. This book has barely survived the years—have you ever even heard of sleuth James Brampton?

Three volumes in 20 years! Indeed, it may be said that the detective story was born with Poe and almost died with him.

In London the seed of Poe's noble experiment took firmer root, sprouted, and bore more abundant fruit. Jolted by the appearance in 1850 of four police articles in *Household Words,* a magazine edited by Charles Dickens, English writers heard the knock of Opportunity on their door; for nearly half a century (1850–1890), they spewed forth a spate of detective "reminiscences." As John Carter has pointed out, most of these so-called real-life "diaries" were thinly disguised fiction, written by anonymous and pseudonymous hacks of the day. Immensely popular and literally read to death, these "revelations" vanished into limbo: less than half a hundred different titles remain with us. The survivors include the work of "Waters" (Thomas Russell), Andrew Forrester, Jr., Charles Martel (Thomas Delf), Alfred Hughes, and a few others. Rare today and extremely desirable for historical and collectival reasons, they are nevertheless a purple patch on the *corpus detectivus.*

But during the fifties and sixties in the United States there was no corresponding flood of pseudo "memoirs." Over here the "revelations" were to come later—in our lush Dime Novel Era; the first Dime Novel detective, Old Sleuth, did not appear until 1872. From 1845 to 1862 the American detective story lapsed (to coin a word) into biblivion. In all those seventeen years not a single book of detective stories achieved the immortality of cloth, wrappers, or pictorial boards. Occasionally, however, detective short stories appeared in the many "household" magazines which flourished so romantically in this period. For example, find and read "The Garnet Ring" by M. Lindsay, in Ballou's *Dollar Monthly Magazine,* issue of May 1861. And only after you have thus "rediscovered" the past, gone back into those vaunted "good old days," will you realize fully how superb in technique, how rich in imagination, are the offerings of our Hammetts, our Carrs, our Chestertons, our Christies, our Sayerses, in these "the good new days."

Poe, the Great Father of us all, died in 1849. Had he lived long enough to stumble on one of these "household" horrors, he would have wept melancholy tears. But if in some celestial cottage Poe has been following the careers of Uncle Abner, Father Brown, Sam Spade, Dr. Gideon Fell, and all the others we take too much for granted, he will not regret having invented what is now the most fabulous literary form in the history of man's eternal search for *les mots justes*.

Leaf Number Two: *B-Change, Rich and Strange*

You've probably seen movie adventures of the Falcon "based on the character created by Michael Arlen." (Some of the screenplays were written by our old friends, Stuart Palmer and Craig Rice.) As a matter of fact, Michael Arlen wrote only one short story about the Falcon. Thus, from short stories long sagas grow . . .

One curious point: It is rare indeed for any story, long or short, to come off the Hollywood assembly line without suffering a B-change, rich and strange. Michael Arlen's "Gay Falcon" proved no exception to the cinematic rule. In the original version, Gay Falcon is a hardboiled, sardonic detective—not the man, as Mr. Arlen tells us, "who would have succeeded in politics, where charm of manner is said to be an advantage." In the movie "adaptations," Gay Falcon emerges, picture after picture, as a charming and romantic rogue! Oh, well, life is real, life is earnest . . .

Leaf Number Three: *Literary Digest*

H. Douglas Thomson, the eminent English detective-story critic, once wrote that "the short story has been developed and fostered by modern conditions, by the general acceleration of our lives . . . with the result that storytelling, like the after-dinner speaker, is adjured in the name of Providence to be brief."

The pressure of outside forces to shorten stories is curiously illustrated among certain American magazines. A new literary form has been widely popularized—the so-called one-shot, or Complete-Novel-in-One-Issue. From personal experience your Editors know how a 100,000-word Ellery Queen novel can be cut down to 50,000 words; how the 50,000-word version can be given an even stronger dose of sodium dinitrophenol, reducing the original full-length novel to the skin-and-bones of a 25,000-word novelette. If we agree that the Law-of-Diminishing-Returns is not the proverbial immovable body and further, that the Law-of-Approaching-Zero-as-a-Limit is not an irresistible force, there is no logical reason to disbelieve that a 25,000-word novelette can't be cut in half once more, thus transforming a full-blooded novel to an anemic short story. From that point the condensation to a short-short is merely another cut-throating by that fearsome weapon, the blue pencil.

Leaf Number Four: *The Quality of Greatness*

The ultimate test of a great story is merely this: How long does it remain in your memory? You may forget the names of the characters, or where you first read the story, or even the title and author's name: those are the superficial details. But if, years and years later, you still have a vivid recollection of the original impact; if the significance of the story, its point, or its subtle overtone, still sticks in a pigeon-hole of your mind, then surely the story has the quality of greatness.

Leaf Number Five: *Literary Unity*

Roughly speaking, there are 1000 different books of detective-crime short stories. These 1000 volumes are divided, like ancient Gaul, into three parts. About one-third are mixed and general collections in which some of, most of, or all the stories in each book concern crime and detection, but not about the same central character. About one-half of the 1000 volumes contain stories wholly unrelated in plot but all revolving, within each book, around the same protagonist—like Reggie Fortune, Arsène Lupin, Craig Kennedy, and Dr. Thorndyke. The remaining volumes—

approximately one-sixth of the total 1000—consist of the smaller subdivisions, including the books of pseudo-real life "memoirs," secret service shorts, parodies and pastiches, anthologies, and so on.

In the first two parts of modern Gore—five-sixths of all the detective-crime shorts ever published in book form—the degree of unity as between the two groups varies. For example, among the mixed and general collections the only unity in each separate book lies in the fact that all the stories are written by the same author and are therefore stamped with a consistent, uniform style. Occasionally, it is true, the author ties up the stories by using the Scheherazade method (one person relating all the tales), or the Decameron approach (various people telling the stories); but these and similar devices add only a superficial unification at best.

In the second group, the degree of unity is considerably higher. While in each volume the individual stories are completely different from each other in plot, the presence of a dominating and continuing central character (like Father Brown, Max Carrados, or The Old Man in the Corner) binds the heterogeneous stories into a more cohesive and symmetrical pattern. But rarely, in a book of detective-crime short stories, does one find a creative unity greater than that implied by the stock titles—*The Adventures of Sam Spade,* or *The Memoirs of Sherlock Holmes,* or *The Case-Book of Jimmie Lavender.*

That is one of the reasons why Agatha Christie's latest series of Hercule Poirot short stories has a special and unusual appeal. It offers a unity of theme that, unlike the mathematical dictum, is larger than the sum total of the individual parts. Mrs. Christie's literary motif was positively inspired. True, it was made feasible only because the given name of her famous detective is Hercule; but that fortuitous circumstance in no way lessens the brilliance of her basic idea. Isn't Hercule Poirot (Agatha Christie must have asked herself) a modern Hercules? Why not, then, write a saga of modern Herculean labors in which Hercule Poirot emulates his legendary namesake? And so, Poirot, before retiring from active practice (we hope not!), decides to accept only twelve more cases—the Twelve Modern Labors of Hercules.

Each story stems from an ancient Herculean theme, but the

symbolism is completely modernized and detectivized. Thus, in the first "labor" Poirot captures the lion of Nemea—in the modern sense, a kidnaped Pekinese; in the sixth "labor" Poirot deals with the iron-beaked birds of Stymphalus—the modern blackmailers; in the eighth "labor" Poirot tames the wild horses of Diomedes—the modern drug peddlers; and so on.

If you want an exciting refresher-course in mythology, we recommend Agatha Christie's brilliantly conceived *Modern Labors of Hercules.*

Leaf Number Six: *'Tec Trademarks*

In the field of the detective story comparatively few writers have capitalized on the advertising advantages and identification value of a pictorial trademark; and of the few attempts made, nearly all have failed to achieve their objective—"the shock of recognition." For example: most of Edgar Wallace's books show somewhere—on the dust wrapper, on the cover, or on the verso of the half-title—a red circle (black, when inside the book) with a holograph signature of Wallace slashed across the bottom; but how many of you associate this trademark with Wallace, or even remember it at all? In the early days of Ellery Queen, we sported a small line-cut, usually placed in the lower right-hand corner of the dust jacket: a drawing of two playing cards (Queens of Diamonds) with a detectival dagger transfixing both at the top; but this piece of juvenilia was quickly abandoned; it didn't "take" and we were glad of it. . . . By all odds the most successful 'tec trademark is the cartoon figure and rakish halo that represent none other than Simon Templar, The Saint. This seemingly child-ish picture has charm and sophistication, and effectively identifies the modern Robin Hood of fictional felony created by Leslie Charteris. Indeed, it is surprising in view of the catchy success of Charteris's gay little figure that imitative cartoons did not multiply rabbitly among other crimeteers . . . The hallmark of a partially unfurled umbrella would point to quite a few fictional ferrets—Edgar Wallace's Mr. J. G. Reeder and Eric Ambler's Dr. Jan Czissar, among others; but in all likelihood you

would not think of them. The homely, humble bumbershoot
seems exclusively the property of Gilbert K. Chesterton's Father
Brown, although no serious attempt has been made by Chesterton's publishers to exploit such a fixed idea . . . If you came
upon the likeness of a tweedy deerstalker, you wouldn't need two
guesses. The device of a deerstalker means only one detective—
Sherlock Holmes. And yet it can be said that for once a 'tec trade-

mark oversold itself, became *too* successful. For
the deerstalker (like the magnifying glass) has
acquired a universal significance: it has come to
identify all detectives in general even more than
Holmes in particular. The criminological cha-
peau illustrated was drawn by the greatest of all
Sherlockian artists, the late Frederic Dorr Steele; it is one of a
group of Holmesian hats that Mr. Steele sketched especially for
your Editors' anthology, *The Misadventures of Sherlock Holmes*
(1944) . . . It is not generally known that Stuart Palmer, creator
of Hildegarde Withers, also has his armorial bearings, so to speak.
It is a personal symbol of which only his intimates are aware. Mr.
Palmer signs all his letters to your Editors with a more-or-less hastily scrawled "Stu," but when the mood is upon him, he sometimes adds a little pen-and-ink insignia—a cute Disney-like creature with a sad eye and an air of pathetic loneliness. There are
two poses—plain and fancy—as the drawings below reveal. The
source of Stu's personal trademark is easy to trace: it stems from
his first great success, *The Penguin Pool Murder,* published by
Brentano's in 1931. This book was snapped up by Katharine
Brown, then East Coast story editor for RKO, as a vehicle for the
late Edna May Oliver. (The same Katharine Brown, by the

way, who later scooped all
her competitors when she
snapped up *Gone With the
Wind.*) Edna May Oliver—
and wasn't she grand as
Hildy?—was teamed with
Jimmy Gleason as Inspector

Piper, another happy casting choice. Later, because of Miss Oliver's fading health, the role of Hildy was assigned to Helen Brod-

erick, and then to Zasu Pitts. The trained penguin who appeared in the first picture was named Oscar, and apparently he won an eternal niche in Stu's affections. Stu recalls how Oscar, who had a tendency to faint under the glare of Klieg lights—temperamental little actor, that Oscar!—finally had to be given a stand-in. No, we're not kidding—this is on the level! The stand-in was a duck, so help us! The name of the duck is not recorded—could it have been the great Donald himself, incognito, sort of playing the Caliph of Bagdad in true Hollywood style? There are other amusing anecdotes of Stuart Palmer's life among the *Aptenodytes forsteri:* for example, when Stu was last in London the keeper of the penguins at Regent's Park gave Stu the key to the Zoo, and Stu (obviously the patron saint of the penguins) spent afternoons sketching, photographing, and playing games with the big Emperors—doing everything, as Stu says, but sitting on an egg, a sedentary service seductively suggested by the rotary come-hither of one lady penguin's flipperlike wing.

Leaf Number Seven: *Detectives' Names*

More random speculations on the 1000 books of detective-crime short stories published since Poe's tall *Tales:* a few thoughts on nomenclature, with particular reference to namesakes:

In a field so comparatively limited, the duplication of a detective's surname is naturally rare. There is only one Holmes, one Fortune, one Thorndyke. When a newcomer faces the problem of christening a new detective character, he usually avoids the well-known and famous surnames. It would be odd indeed if a second Hewitt came upon the modern scene, or a second Carrados, or a second Zaleski. And since there is almost an infinite variety of names to choose from, even the lesser-known patronymics are seldom used by more than one writer.

The exceptions to the rule are few but fascinating. For example: there are two short-story detectives named—and this is not a common name by any means—Chetwynd. One is Dr. Chetwynd in Mrs. L. T. Meade's and Robert Eustace's scarce book, *The Sanctuary Club;* the other is Dennis Chetwynd, chronicled by Henry J. Fidler. There are, allowing for a nationalistic difference in spelling, only two Becks—M. McDonnell Bodkin's Paul Beck, the Rule of Thumb Detective, and William LeQueux's Monsieur Raoul Becq, *ex-sous-chef* of the Sûreté Générale of Paris. There are two sleuths named Barnes, three baptized Bell, and two who bear the family name of Treadgold.

Even the names of Brown, Jones, and Smith have hardly been overworked in books of detective shorts. There is only one Brown —Chesterton's immortal and doubly unique Father Brown. There are only two Joneses, excluding parody names of Holmes—Samuel Hopkins Adams's Average Jones and Bennet Copplestone's "Cholmondeley Jones." And of that most ubiquitous (but no less honored) of all names, Smith, there are only three—R.T.M. Scott's Aurelius Smith, James B. Hendryx's Black John Smith, and Edgar Wallace's antidetective, Anthony Smith.

6

DETECTIVE FICTION

vs.

REAL LIFE

From the Memoirs of a Private Detective
By Dashiell Hammett

Dashiell Hammett is one of the few living detective story writers to whom the word great may be applied without fear of serious contradiction. As the writer who symbolizes the American "hard-boiled" school in the public mind (whether or not he was the sole founder of that school) he has influenced and changed the detective story more radically than any other single author since Doyle. One of the reasons for the force and validity of The Maltese Falcon, The Glass Key, *and the "Continental Op" stories is found in Hammett's own eight years' experience as a Pinkerton detective. Here are his reminiscences of those years, as he told them in the old Mencken-Nathan* Smart Set *for March 1923—just about the time (see Erle Stanley Gardner in this volume) that he was beginning to publish his first detective fiction in* Black Mask *magazine.*

1

WISHING TO get some information from members of the W.C.T.U. in an Oregon city, I introduced myself as the secretary of the Butte Civic Purity League. One of them read me a long discourse on the erotic effects of cigarettes upon young girls. Subsequent experiments proved this trip worthless.

2

A man whom I was shadowing went out into the country for a walk one Sunday afternoon and lost his bearings completely. I had to direct him back to the city.

3

House burglary is probably the poorest paid trade in the world; I have never known anyone to make a living at it. But for that matter few criminals of any class are self-supporting unless they toil at something legitimate between times. Most of them, however, live on their women.

4

I know an operative who while looking for pickpockets at the Havre de Grace race track had his wallet stolen. He later became an official in an Eastern detective agency.

5

Three times I have been mistaken for a Prohibition agent, but never had any trouble clearing myself.

6

Taking a prisoner from a ranch near Gilt Edge, Mont., to Lewistown one night, my machine broke down and we had to sit there until daylight. The prisoner, who stoutly affirmed his innocence, was clothed only in overalls and shirt. After shivering all night on the front seat his morale was low, and I had no difficulty in getting a complete confession from him while walking to the nearest ranch early the following morning.

7

Of all the men embezzling from their employers with whom I have had contact, I can't remember a dozen who smoked, drank, or had any of the vices in which bonding companies are so interested.

8

I was once falsely accused of perjury and had to perjure myself to escape arrest.

9

A detective agency official in San Francisco once substituted "truthful" for "voracious" in one of my reports on the ground that the client might not understand the latter. A few days later in another report "simulate" became "quicken" for the same reason.

10

Of all the nationalities haled into the criminal courts, the Greek is the most difficult to convict. He simply denies everything, no matter how conclusive the proof may be; and nothing so impresses a jury as a bare statement of fact, regardless of the fact's inherent improbability or obvious absurdity in the face of overwhelming contrary evidence.

11

I know a man who will forge the impressions of any set of fingers in the world for $50.

12

I have never known a man capable of turning out first-rate work in a trade, a profession or an art, who was a professional criminal.

13

I know a detective who once attempted to disguise himself thoroughly. The first policeman he met took him into custody.

14

I know a deputy sheriff in Montana who, approaching the cabin of a homesteader for whose arrest he had a warrant, was confronted by the homesteader with a rifle in his hands. The deputy sheriff drew his revolver and tried to shoot over the homesteader's head to frighten him. The range was long and a strong wind was blowing. The bullet knocked the rifle from the homesteader's hands.

As time went by the deputy sheriff came to accept as the truth the reputation for expertness that this incident gave him, and he not only let his friends enter him in a shooting contest, but wagered everything he owned upon his skill. When the contest was held he missed the target completely with all six shots.

15

Once in Seattle the wife of a fugitive swindler offered to sell me a photograph of her husband for $15. I knew where I could get one free, so I didn't buy it.

16

I was once engaged to discharge a woman's housekeeper.

17

The slang in use among criminals is for the most part a conscious, artificial growth, designed more to confuse outsiders than for any other purpose, but sometimes it is singularly expressive; for instance, *two-time loser*—one who has been convicted twice; and the older *gone to read and write*—found it advisable to go away for a while.

18

Pocket-picking is the easiest to master of all the criminal trades. Anyone who is not crippled can become an adept in a day.

19

In 1917, in Washington, D.C., I met a young woman who did not remark that my work must be very interesting.

20

Even where the criminal makes no attempts to efface the prints of his fingers, but leaves them all over the scene of the crime, the chances are about one in ten of finding a print that is sufficiently clear to be of any value.

21

The chief of police of a Southern city once gave me a description of a man, complete even to a mole on his neck, but neglected to mention that he had only one arm.

22

I know a forger who left his wife because she had learned to smoke cigarettes while he was serving a term in prison.

23

Second only to "Dr. Jekyll and Mr. Hyde" is "Raffles" in the affections of the daily press. The phrase "gentleman crook" is used on the slightest provocation. A composite portrait of the gentry upon whom the newspapers have bestowed this title would show a laudanum-drinker, with a large rhinestone horseshoe aglow in the soiled bosom of his shirt below a bow tie, leering at his victim, and saying: "Now don't get scared, lady, I ain't gonna crack you on the bean. I ain't a rough neck!"

24

The cleverest and most uniformly successful detective I have ever known is extremely myopic.

25

Going from the larger cities out into the remote rural communities, one finds a steadily decreasing percentage of crimes that have to do with money and a proportionate increase in the frequency of sex as a criminal motive.

26

While trying to peer into the upper story of a roadhouse in northern California one night—and the man I was looking for was in Seattle at the time—part of the porch roof crumbled under me and I fell, spraining an ankle. The proprietor of the roadhouse gave me water to bathe it in.

27

The chief difference between the exceptionally knotty problem confronting the detective of fiction and that facing a real detective is that in the former there is usually a paucity of clues, and in the latter altogether too many.

28

I know a man who once stole a Ferris-wheel.

29

That the law-breaker is invariably soon or late apprehended is probably the least challenged of extant myths. And yet the files of every detective bureau bulge with the records of unsolved mysteries and uncaught criminals.

Inquest on Detective Stories

By R. Philmore

R. Philmore is a pseudonymous English detective story writer whose novels are well regarded in his native land, though for some reason they are too little known in America. In Part I of this original and fascinating "Inquest," Mr. Philmore poses the medical means employed in each of five famous detective novels and Dr. John Yudkin, English medical specialist, renders scientific verdict on their real-life plausibility. In Part II, Mr. Philmore, alone, tests the motives of a number of fictional crimes for psychological validity. This selection appeared in two installments in the English magazine Discovery *for April and September 1938.*

I

THE INCREASE in detective literature has forced writers to look for odder and odder methods of killing their victims. But they have not only to be odd: they must be plausible. Some of them make us ask a lot of questions of our medical friends. Here are five fairly recent examples of complicated killing—which have each been submitted for Dr. Yudkin's opinion.

LORD PETER'S BICYCLE PUMP

First of all there is Dorothy Sayers' *Unnatural Death.* In this story we suspect that a woman has killed a number of people; she had motive enough, and opportunity—only, unfortunately, their deaths were all put down to heart failure. Lord Peter Wimsey discovers the secret. The murderer injected an air-bubble into an artery, and stopped the circulation. Here is Lord Peter's own description of the method of death (in conversation with a doctor).

"Look here, the body's a pumping-engine, isn't it? The jolly old heart pumps the blood round the arteries and back through the veins and so on, doesn't it? That's what keeps things working, what? Round and home again in two minutes—that sort of thing?"

"Certainly."

"Little valve to let the blood out; 'nother little valve to let it in—just like an internal combustion engine, which it is?"

"Of course."

"And s'posin' that stops?"

"You die."

"Yes. Now, look here. S'posin' you take a good big hypodermic, empty, and dig it into one of the big arteries and push the handle—what would happen? What would happen, doctor? You'd be pumpin' a big air-bubble into your engine feed, wouldn't you? What would become of your circulation, then?"

"It would stop it. . . ."

". . . the air-bubble, doctor—in a main artery—say the femoral or the big vein in the bend of the elbow—that would stop the circulation, wouldn't it? How soon?"

"Why, at once. The heart would stop beating."

"And then?"

"You would die."

"With what symptoms?"

"None to speak of. Just a gasp or two. The lungs would make a desperate effort to keep things going. Then you'd stop. Like heart failure. It would *be* heart failure."

Now, if one consults medical opinion, one finds some doubts thrown on the efficacy of this method. Here is the report I had:

(J. Y.) "The presence of air in the blood may cause death in either of two ways. It may lodge in the blood vessels supplying the brain, causing death in coma by cutting off the blood supply to some vital part. Or it may embarrass the action of the heart, causing heart failure, by creating a froth in the chambers of the heart with which the heart cannot deal. The entry of air into the circulation occurs most commonly in operations on the neck. It may occur, too, during an attempt to inject air into the chest (pneumothorax) when the needle inadvertently enters a vein.

"In practice, however, death does not commonly occur in these cases. So it is difficult to say whether injection of air into a vein by means of a syringe will cause death. It would be unlikely with a hypodermic syringe, which rarely holds more than 2–3 c.c. It would be more likely—even probable—with larger quantities, say 20 c.c. or more, but I think one could never be certain that the method would work in any particular instance.

" (Incidentally, it is difficult to inject into an artery. It would almost certainly have to be a vein.)"

References

BOYD. *Text-book of Pathology.*
ROMANIS and MITCHINER. *Science and Practice of Surgery.*

The idea is extremely ingenious—but, in fact, it looks as though the murderer could make certain of killing the victim only by connecting a bicycle pump with the vein.

ARSENIC AS A FOOD

In another of her books Miss Sayers has a much more plausible method. *Strong Poison,* the novel which introduces Harriet Vane —probably the most successful character in detective fiction—has a murder by arsenic poisoning. The victim shared an omelette with the murderer: he died, the murderer survived. Lord Peter established that the murderer had built up an immunity from arsenic. Here is his own (again characteristic) description, together with a medical report.

"Some fellow . . . found that, whereas liquid arsenic was dealt with by the kidneys and was uncommonly bad for the system, solid arsenic could be given day by day, a little bigger dose each time, so that in time the doings—what an old lady I knew in Norfolk called 'the tubes'—got used to it and could push it along without taking any notice of it, so to speak. I read a book some-where which said it was all done by leucocytes—those jolly little white corpuscles, don't you know—which sort of got round the stuff and bustled it along so that it couldn't do any harm. At all events, the point is that if you go on taking solid arsenic for a good long time—say a year or so—you establish a what-not, an immunity, and can take six or seven grains at a time without so much as a touch of indi-jaggers. . . . Well, it occurred to me, don't you see, old horse, that if you'd had the bright idea to im-munize yourself first, you could easily have shared a jolly old arsenical omelette with a friend. It would kill him and it wouldn't hurt you."

(J. Y.) "Solid arsenic (As_2O_3), unlike soluble arsenic com-pounds, produces well-marked tolerance if taken in small doses over a long period. It appears that the tolerance (Lord Peter's 'immunity') is due to the fact that the lining cells of the intestine become more resistant and consequently less arsensic is absorbed. I think therefore that it would be quite possible on these lines to eliminate one's friend by sharing an arsenic omelette with him."

References

DOUTHWAITE. *Hale-White's Materia Medica.*
CLARK. *Applied Pharmacology.*
JOACHIMOGLU. *Archiv für experimentelle Pathologie und Pharma-kologie.* 79, 419.

HANNASYDE AND THE TOOTHPASTE

One of the wittiest of detective writers, Georgette Heyer, had an ingenious poisoning device in her book: *Behold Here's Poison.* An unpleasant head of a family is found to have been poisoned with nicotine; several relatives with motives had, it appeared, op-portunities of poisoning various foods, drinks and medicines which he had taken, but, since nothing of these remained for analysis, the suspicions of Superintendent Hannasyde were pretty widely spread. Shortly afterwards an odd, but by no means well-hated, sister of the victim also died of the same poison. She, how-ever, left an unfinished tube of toothpaste; it was discovered that this had also been used by her brother.

Here are Hannasyde's words, followed by the medical com-ment:

"The nicotine did not pass through the stomach. It was ab-sorbed through the tissues of the mouth. This is the analyst's re-port which I've been waiting for. The medium through which your aunt was poisoned was a tube of toothpaste. . . . The poison was in all probability injected . . . by means of a hypodermic syringe, inserted into the bottom end of the tube, and driven up a little way through the paste. The paste at the bottom of the tube is untainted, and it is obvious that the paste at the top end must also have been free from poison."

(J. Y.) "On the whole, the absorptive powers of the 'tissues of the mouth' are not great, as witness the fact that many gargles and mouth washes contain substances which would cause severe symptoms if swallowed. But it has been shown recently that certain drugs are quite readily absorbed in the mouth: in particular, it was found that one drop of nicotine placed on the tongue or throat of a cat killed it within a few minutes. Since as little as two or three drops of nicotine when swallowed will kill a man very rapidly, it is quite possible that a toxic dose would be absorbed from, say, toothpaste in the mouth. In view, however, of its very strong tobacco-like taste and smell, one would have to imagine that the composition of the paste was such as to mask these properties of nicotine."

References

HEFFTER. *Handbuch der experimentellen Pharmakologie.* II, 2.
MACHT. *Journal of the American Medical Association.* 110, 409.

H. M. NEARLY BAFFLED

The most amusing of detectives, Sir Henry Merrivale, has one of his best cases in *Red Widow Murders.* Here Carter Dickson gives us a locked, and supposedly deadly room, in which a man sits to kill a family superstition. The door is watched by several people, the windows are barred on the inside; yet he dies. The post mortem shows that he had been poisoned by curare—which, of course, is harmless if swallowed; to be lethal it must be injected into the blood by way of some cut in the skin. No one could have reached the victim, to inflict such a cut. The problem stumped H. M. for some time; but at last he discovered that the victim had had a gum lanced that day, and had received from the

murderer a flask containing whiskey and (so he was told) a drug
to stop the pain. The flask contained curare. The murderer had
to run a risk in taking away the flask when the body was discovered; but for some time no one thought of looking for a flask,
since no one was concerned with what he had swallowed. This
is how H. M. describes the manner of death:

"I steered myself wrong from the first; I insisted to myself and
everybody else that the curare could never have been swallowed,
because it wouldn't have hurt Bender. . . . But what I didn't
realize, and what nobody else looked for, was a small puncture
in the gum, toward the wisdom teeth, probably, where the gum
is so apt to get infected—a puncture made the afternoon of his
death. Blood-stream! Of course it poured right into the blood-
stream, and killed him quicker than any injection. We look all
over his body, and find absolutely no wound by which you could
shove in the poison; but how are we ever to spot a little thing
like a lanced gum?"

(J. Y.) "Theoretically, it is certainly possible to die when certain poisons, innocuous when swallowed, are absorbed into the
blood through a cut. I cannot say how likely it is for someone to
have such an amount of curare—an extraordinarily bitter substance—in his mouth that he might be able to absorb the two or
three grains which would be needed to kill him."

INSPECTOR POOLE'S MIXTURE

Finally, there is Henry Wade. In his *No Friendly Drop* we have
the sudden death of a Lord, one of those county figures whom
Wade handles so sympathetically. The murder is a complicated
one; it depends, after the manner of *The Mysterious Affair at
Styles,* on a combination of substances; but in this case they are
not mixed until they reach the body of the victim. He has taken
chloral tablets (containing a non-lethal dose of di-dial) for neu-
ralgia. Then the murderer puts hyoscine in his morning cup of
tea. Inspector Poole hears the verdict of the police analyst:

"I found di-dial scattered throughout practically the whole of
the digestive tract. . . . In all I estimate there must have been

between two and three grains, certainly not more. I should not regard that as, in itself, a lethal dose, especially to a subject who had been taking it for some little time. But there was also present a second poisonous substance, of a different genus but having a somewhat similar hypnotic effect—scolopamine, more generally known, perhaps, as hyoscine. . . . There's not much of this stuff, either, perhaps one forty-eighth of a grain, nearly all in the stomach—nothing like a toxic dose. And that is the interesting part of this case. Here you have two poisonous substances present in the body, neither of them in sufficient quantity to be toxic, but combined—deadly."

(J. Y.) "Certain combinations of drugs are much more potent than their individual properties would lead one to expect. Such synergic or potentiating effects are, for example, seen with chloral and morphine. However, I have not been able to find a definite statement of the synergic effect of hyoscine and dial. Of course, the number of known drugs with an hypnotic action is enormous and the possibilities of combining any two of them is little short of infinite. But hyoscine is a common drug and so are the barbiturates like dial, and I feel that if they had any marked synergic action, I should have come across a reference to it. But what seems important is that I cannot find a reference to a case in which a combination of two such drugs, each in less than the toxic dose, have actually caused death. I feel here too that if the possibility existed, it would be important enough to be included in the standard works on pharmacology and toxicology."

References

CUSHNY. *Text-book of Pharmacology.*
MEYER und GOTTLIEB. *Experimentelle Pharmakologie.*

In this case (as in the artery injection) we have no definite denial that the suggested method could kill its man: but we have a distinct note of doubt. All these five murderers sailed near the wind; all were lucky, in varying degrees, to kill their victims. But they took the risk, and their creators are plausible.

II

Most of the famous murders in real life that one remembers have been committed for greed or lust or jealousy. Most of the murders that one does not remember were committed for similar motives, so the statistics tell us. It is perhaps surprising, at first sight, that these motives have not usually been the most successful in the hands of writers of detective stories.

The writers of serious fiction have stuck to these motives when they introduced murder. Some of the best writers have described Dostoievsky's *Brothers Karamazov* as "almost the best detective story ever written," as well as probably the greatest novel. Here the murderer is actuated by greed. So is Raskolnikov in *Crime and Punishment;* and his greed is for a comparatively small amount of money, too. The heroine of *The Idiot* is murdered by a jealous lover.

Disadvantages of Standard Motives

But the use of these motives has certain very definite disadvantages for the detective writer. As a rule greed, lust and jealousy are pretty obvious things, and it is difficult for the writer to conceal his murderer, if that murderer is powerfully actuated by one of them. Either we know the murderer all along, or, when we are told his name, we don't believe it. The serious novelist is concerned to examine the working of a man's mind and the pattern of his motives until they make murder inevitable. The detective writer cannot prove this inevitability without telling us early on in the book who the subject is.

Some good attempts have been made. The great classic, *Mysterious Affair at Styles,* is an example of murder for greed. Here Agatha Christie manages by extraordinarily clever juggling with clues and devices to hide the lack of clear murderous intent in her main villain. She has tried to do the same thing again, quite often. Perhaps her greatest success in this medium was in *Peril at End House,* where she contrived to create a murderer who, we felt at the end, was probably good for anything: but here the motive was more than greed, it had elements of jealousy and revenge. Here, again, any doubts we may have felt during our next-morning reflection as to the psychological state of the murderer were dispelled by the brilliance of the central detective device.

Murder for greed appears in *Have His Carcase*—perhaps the best-worked-out of the books of Dorothy Sayers, and one of the better balanced of them in so far as the powerful influence of Harriet Vane is there to restrain Lord Peter Wimsey, to whom she had not yet surrendered—and in *Hamlet Revenge!*, that splendidly written book by Michael Innes. But in both these cases there is more to it than sheer greed. In the first-named the murderer is concerned to prevent the loss of something he had counted on; in the second the author almost convinces us that his murderer was ready to commit his crimes for the excitement.

JEALOUSY AND LUST

It is, of course, difficult to make a clear distinction between jealousy and lust as motives for murder, since one is not often present without the other. A number of serious writers have tried to build up a condition in which a character murders for this reason. They have not found it easy. Shakespeare's *Othello* is spoilt for many of us by the unconvincing gullibility of its hero. Moravia's *The Wheel Turns* is a recent splendid failure in this direction. Detective writers have found it even more difficult. Philip McDonald, in *Rope to Spare,* has contrived an atmosphere so intense that we are prepared to believe in his murderer at the end; but our belief scarcely survives reflection. Ellery Queen's masterpiece, *Halfway House,* is so ingeniously contrived, and the final solution so neatly thrust on us, that we overlook the fact that we have not been given much chance to study the murderer and feel his pulse. *The Cask,* which is often erroneously regarded as Freeman Wills Crofts's greatest book, has a convincing enough murderer. But he is so convincing that he is the only possible suspect, and the interest of the reader lies, not in detecting him, but in uncovering the ingenious tricks by which he has laid suspicion on his rival. (Incidentally, it ought to be stated that the charm of Crofts lies very largely in his style: it is so unpretentious and so naturalistic that most of us not only enjoy reading it: we patronize the writer, saying that he does very well without any literary gifts.)

Academic Motives

Several writers have tried to escape from the difficulty of handling the greed or lust-jealousy motive by inventing somewhat remote motives for their murderers. We have had several murders for altruistic motives. The master of this type is Anthony Berkeley, whose wit and graces are sufficient to make up for shakiness of motive and, sometimes, lack of straight detection. In *Second Shot* he gives us a brilliant essay in this kind of thing. In *Jumping Jenny* he does it again—except that here he adopts the supremely cunning device of pretending to reveal his murderer at the time of the murder. (This is done with one of the most effective colons in literature.) In *Trial and Error* he makes most of us believe that he is doing it again. Ellery Queen has a precious nearly altruistic murder in *Spanish Cape:* here the sheer grandeur of the main device is so powerful that we are too grateful to pick holes in the character of the murderer. Nicholas Blake, in *A Question of Proof,* writes so brilliantly that he almost convinces us that a man could murder for sheer hate; but it would not be wise for a lesser artist to try to copy him.

Revenge

Murder for revenge is usually pretty effective in detective fiction. Here the convincing note is usually provided by making the victim so odious that, as we read, we all want to kill him; so that, when someone in fact does the trick for us, we don't stop to question whether our murderous feelings could in life have been translated into action. Everyone hates a blackmailer; everyone sympathizes with the amiable murderers in Austin Freeman's *Mr. Pottermack's Oversight* and Georgette Heyer's *Behold Here's Poison*—two fascinating books. Here, of course, there is the additional motive of stopping the blackmailer from blackmailing. Sheer revenge seems a perfectly adequate motive for the murderer in Nicholas Blake's *The Beast Must Die,* because we all hate motoring murderers. Similarly, the world's horror at kidnapping was capitalized by Agatha Christie in her delightful *Murder on the Orient Express*—a book which, if it is not her best detective story, is certainly Poirot's best and most charming appearance. But, to my mind, the best exploitation of this kind of motive appears in Carter Dickson's *Plague Court Murders,* which must be put on a list of the dozen best detective stories ever written. Here the motive is revenge, so to speak, for something which has not yet been done—the murder of the murderer. The "atmosphere" is slightly bogus: but it works. Of course, H. M. is so much the best detective that, once having invented him, his creator could get away with almost any plot. In fact he doesn't try to. Incidentally, the method of killing employed in this book is unusual and ingenious: the victim is shot with pellets of rock-salt to give the impression that he was stabbed. I must remember to consult my friend Dr. Yudkin as to its feasibility.

UNCONVINCING MOTIVES

Some writers—a good many of them eminent ones—have been thrown back on what seem to me quite inadequate and unconvincing motives for murder. After all, murder is an unusual activity. We can imagine a professional revolutionary or a neurotic gangster killing without much thought; but when a normal citizen murders in these days it is usually under some terrific compulsion (even though the compulsion may not be evident to the casual observer, and no novelist, not even so humble a craftsman as the detective writer, can be a casual observer). I can't believe in Dorothy Sayers's murderer in *Busman's Honeymoon.* Both the gain and the chances of gain were so small for any but a most abnormal murderer: and this one gives precious little hint of abnormality. (But then, the chief detective interest in this book is not so much in who did the murder as in what Lord Peter and Lady Peter were up to in that bedroom.) Much as I enjoy Philip MacDonald's writing, I can't accept most of his alleged motives for murder. I don't believe that his film favourite in *The Crime Conductor* would kill a man who had a slight control over his actions, nor that his eminent statesman in *The Rasp* would kill another eminent statesman because he was slightly more eminent. I have to confess that my admired Agatha Christie sometimes tries to bamboozle me into accepting an unreal motive for murder. I refuse to believe that her famous actor in *Three-Act Tragedy* would commit a murder merely as a rehearsal for another murder (which in itself was scarcely believable). Nicholas Blake's *Thou Shell of Death* is an exciting and brilliantly written affair: but the very skill with which the writer builds up the semi-heroic figure of his hero makes me refuse to consider him as the despicable murderer he is finally revealed to be. I seldom believe in the motives supplied for his murders by S. S. Van Dine; I could be induced to believe, for instance, that some human beings might try to run through a whole household, but certainly not the alleged culprit in the *Greene Murder Case*. And, while on the whole I must choose Ellery Queen as my favourite detective writer, I am afraid I raise my eyebrows at some of his motives. I am not convinced that anyone would murder so widely for revenge and petty gain as did his villain in *The Egyptian Cross Mystery,* nor that his unpretentious little criminal in *The Chinese Orange Mystery* would kill a complete stranger for such doubtful gain.

MURDER BECAUSE OF THE PAST

On the whole the safest line to take is to make your murderer afraid of exposure. We can believe that most men, if they have done something really guilty, will kill to hide its coming to light. Perhaps we believe it too easily; it may be because everyone has a shame or a streak of guilt in him, so that threat of revelation strikes a responsive chord. (Murder for gain doesn't do this. How many of us hate the rich profiteers we know strongly enough to dream of killing them?) And there is an advantage for the writer in this kind of motive, since he has two mysteries to hang over us: who did the murder? what was there in his past? Most of the very best murders in detective fiction have been committed for this reason. I suppose the best judges will without undue anger allow me to mark Dickson Carr's *Arabian Nights' Murder* as the best detective story ever written. Here the motive (though containing elements of revenge) is chiefly to hide the fact that a family has been disgraced by an unfortunate liaison: and we are shown enough of the murderer to believe he had it in him. In *House of the Arrow* and *Murder of Roger Ackroyd* there is the same motive, fear of exposure of blackmailing; and, although neither A. E. W. Mason nor Agatha Christie keeps to the strict known rules, few would regard these two books as other than masterpieces. In *Cards on the Table,* an even better Agatha Christie book, we have a murder committed for fear of exposure of another murder. In that extraordinarily exciting work, *Give Me Death,* Isobel Briggs Myers makes an American commit murder to prevent his negroid ancestry being exposed, and Philip MacDonald's best book, *The Noose,* is that in which his murderer has the best motive—fear of being exposed as a coward and a cheat —so that here the combination of MacDonald's style and characterization with a really convincing motive makes one of the books we must all put on our favourite shelf.

The Lawyer Looks at Detective Fiction
By John Barker Waite

The real-life legal validity of fictional police procedure has long been a moot subject. Here is a valuable case-study of the problem by qualified authority. Professor Waite, long a member of the law faculty of the University of Michigan, is also well known as the author of several standard works on jurisprudence and as a contributor to both legal and general magazines. His present article, prepared in collaboration with Miles W. Kimball, appeared in the American Bookman for August 1929.

Valid as are the points established by Professor Waite, it is no more than fair to point out that his article expresses essentially a specialist's viewpoint. While a small if usually vocal number of lay devotees of detective fiction insist on rigid fidelity to real life in all respects, the large majority of readers are content if their mystery fare measures up to the dictum of the late, well-loved Carolyn Wells: the detective story must seem real to the reader in the same sense that fairy tales seem real to children. Nonetheless, careful craftsmen have long known that judicious deference to the actualities is of first importance in achieving this needed "sense of verisimilitude." No detective story ever suffered from a little extra effort by the author in this respect.

IT IS an easy matter to convict a murderer—in books! The writer of mystery stories has only to set his dauntless detective spinning analyses and collecting evidence, and the culprit is inevitably led repining to the death cell.

The chief reason justice is so much better served in fiction than in reality is that the mythical detective enjoys enormous advantages over actual investigators. The storybook hero can get his man by all manner of devices prohibited in real life—from breaking-and-entering to conniving with United States postal officials to rob the mails. Detective novels are few in which the protagonist does not accomplish some brilliant stroke in flagrant violation of the law. Furthermore, when it comes to trying the prisoner on the strength of the evidence the usual detective collects to support his brilliant hypotheses, what looks so invulnerable in print would make him a laughing-stock if introduced in an actual court of justice.

Not, of course, that it would be unreal to write about arrests which did not result in convictions. Police reports tabulate a large proportion of criminal homicides as "cleared by arrest" when nothing has happened but the arrest of a suspect charged with a particular crime. He may be in no danger of conviction. Often the arrest has been made for no better reason than that the police want to still a clamorous and embarrassing press. On the great majority of such occasions the available evidence is wholly inadequate to convince a trial jury or even to gain a hearing of the state's case. Detective fiction, in this regard, is most life-like: where it departs from reality is in the author's naïve assurance that the suspect was actually and in due form convicted.

Mr. J. S. Fletcher, who is himself a lawyer, must have realized the inherent weakness of his case in *The Strange Case of Mr. Henry Marchmont,* for he does not assert that the accused was ultimately punished, but merely that he was arrested and led away protesting. And good reason he had to protest!

It will be recalled that in this tale Marchmont had been shot in the back while ascending the stairs in his own home, and that coincidentally with his death, bank notes to the amount of one hundred thousand dollars were stolen from an upstairs room. No less than six persons had strong reason to desire Marchmont's death:

John Landsdale.... *Whose real identity Marchmont had discovered and was threatening to reveal, to the ruin of a business coup Landsdale was about to execute.*

Vandelius	{	*Who with Landsdale was interested in the deal.*
Granch and Garner	{	*Who also stood to profit if the negotiations were successful, and who were in sore need of money.*
Simpson	{	*Marchmont's clerk, to whom would go a fifty-thousand-dollar legacy upon Marchmont's death.*
Cora Sanderthwaite	{	*Half-mad enemy of Landsdale, who might have committed the murder in the belief that Marchmont was Landsdale.*

Each of these six persons had had opportunity to fire the fatal shot. Moreover, all of them except Vandelius could be proved to have been at the scene of the murder at about the time the tragedy occurred. Considering all the evidence described in the book, the most plausibly guilty was Garner. It is true that after he had been plunged to his death from the rotten bridge in his attempt to escape pursuers, a letter was found on his person which attempted to divert suspicion to Vandelius and Cora Sanderthwaite; in it Garner admitted the theft of a few gold coins but denied guilt of the murder, declaring he had seen Cora outside the Marchmont home at the time of the crime, and that he had observed Vandelius leaving the house immediately afterward.

This letter, however, would not have been admitted as evidence against either Vandelius or Cora by any court of law in England or America. Neither as a matter of strict law nor of common sense could such a document be properly used: it was a self-serving declaration by a man who had every reason to direct suspicion away from himself. Whereas his letter was self-incriminatory of larceny, such an admission might have been made solely to lend verisimilitude to his denial of the major crime. It is even possible that he mistook Cora and Vandelius; it happens frequently that an honest witness admits his own error of identification when forced by cross-examination into an analysis of the situation. It is for such reasons that our constitutions give every man on trial for crime the right to demand confrontation by the witnesses against him. There is no question that the letter would have been kept out.

There was, indeed, nothing at all to negative Garner's probable guilt. Any fairly intelligent police officer would have charged him with the crime.

As to Vandelius there was no evidence at all, save the fact that his visiting card was on the card-tray in Marchmont's living room. And yet, out of all these possibilities, and with the imposing array of facts against Garner, it was Vandelius who was arrested as the murderer! The case against him consisted almost entirely of speculations as to how he *might* have committed the crime. Mr. Fletcher showed his acquaintance with realities in ending his story with the mere fact of Vandelius's arrest. In real life, Vandelius would have been freed at once. No English or American examining magistrate will even hold a suspect for trial simply because he *could* have committed a crime, without any evidence that he *did* commit it—especially when there is cogent evidence that another person is more likely to have done it. Had Vandelius by some chance been put on trial, no jury would have convicted; or, had the unprecedented happened, the Appellate Court would have reversed the conviction for lack of evidence. It was only a few months ago that the Illinois Supreme Court reversed a conviction of the notorious Shelton brothers * with the statement that "a conviction of crime cannot rest upon probabilities alone, but the proof must be sufficient to remove all reasonable doubt that the defendant, and not somebody else, committed the crime, and it is not incumbent on the defendant to prove who did commit it."

In *The Room with the Tassels,* Carolyn Wells is not so careful as Mr. Fletcher. She goes further and states that her suspect was arrested "and received his just deserts." If by this statement Miss Wells means to imply that John Tracy was convicted of murder, she is somewhat in error. There is no evidence presented that Tracy committed the murders. True, he might have done so, but it is ridiculous to suppose that he was guilty merely because no other person was proved guilty. It is well-settled law that the state

---

* People v. O'Hara, Illinois, 1928, 163 N. E. 804.

must prove affirmatively; the accused is under no obligation to prove himself innocent; innocence is presumed until the contrary is demonstrated beyond all reasonable doubt.

The confession of Rudolph Braye that he hired Tracy to commit the crime would be excluded from any Anglo-American court as unreliable, hearsay evidence. This is not a mere legal technicality operating to the defeat of justice: the point is that the detectives' plausible theories of guilt are in no way facts proving guilt. No actual court will convict a defendant solely on another man's guesses. The Tracy case, had it been real, would have been another murder "cleared by arrest," but with no subsequent conviction.

The real trial of the Reverend Mr. Avery * for the murder of Sarah Cornell instances what actually happens in such cases. Avery had reason to desire Sarah's death. She had left in her bag a note suggesting that "if she should be missing," he could explain it. And the killing was under such circumstances that he could have committed it. Avery insisted that he was miles away from the scene at the time of the crime, but he had not a single witness to corroborate him. The state, on the other hand, asserted as positively that Avery was present and that his alibi was wholly fictive. Like Avery, the state had no witnesses to prove his presence. Although the general public was convinced of Avery's guilt, the jury, hearing no affirmative proof of guilt, was constrained to bring in a verdict of acquittal.

It is trite law not only that every fact adduced as circumstantial evidence must be affirmatively demonstrated and that the facts as a whole must be consistent with the defendant's guilt, but also that the circumstances pointing to his guilt *must be inconsistent with the guilt of anyone else.*

In *The Greene Murder Case,* therefore, Mr. Van Dine's thoughtfulness in allowing Ada to commit suicide saved the District Attorney considerable embarrassment. Ada could not possibly have been convicted on the irritating Mr. Vance's belief in her guilt. An acquittal would have been inevitable, much to the chagrin of the doughty sergeant and the harassed District Attor-

---

* Edmund Pearson: *Murder at Smutty Nose.*

ney, whose lawful functions, as a matter of common knowledge, really have nothing to do with detective work.

Perhaps the known facts in that case—which, as known facts, were surprisingly few—were consistent with Ada's guilt. She *might* have concocted all the improbabilities of which Vance accused her, but it is incredible that an American jury would have *believed* that she did. Further, all the known facts consistent with Ada's guilt point with equal logic to Sibella's guilt. Vance's theories are wholly *a priori*.

This by no means exhausts the detective stories in which evidence against the alleged murderer is entirely too sketchy and fantastic to gain a conviction outside the covers of a book. In a vast number of such fictions the authors seem more intent upon dramatic "surprise endings" than upon logical construction of legal evidence. And if the detective of fiction enjoys an altogether unnatural latitude in the matter of making arrests merely on his own theorizing, so is he allowed startlingly illegal *modi operandi*.

The charming young assistant District Attorney in Earl Derr Biggers's tale, *Behind That Curtain,* uses a technique unavailable to officials in the flesh. When Grace Lane suddenly disappears and the police are at a loss, Miss Morrow casually observes, "Grace Lane was an old friend of Mrs. Tupper-Brock, which may mean that Grace Lane will write to her from wherever she is hiding. I am going to make immediate arrangements with the postal authorities. Mrs. Tupper-Brock's mail will reach her through my office from now on." Mr. Biggers naïvely permits the postal officials to enter into this impossible agreement! Even a mere man, Hercule Poirot, in Agatha Christie's *The Mystery of the Blue Train,* accomplishes much the same feat.

Every school boy should know that such a conception is totally absurd—not only as a matter of formal law, but even as an extralegal practice. The prosecuting attorney of a populous county notorious for its crime, where social safety demands the use of every available weapon and where certain co-operative informalities of legal procedure might seem justifiable, has averred that such arrangements as Mr. Biggers and Miss Christie describe are absolutely unheard of. The only means by which the police can secure a piece of mail is by a warrant accurately describing the specific letter in question. It is inconceivable that the postal authorities would regularly deliver a suspect's mail to the prosecutor's office.

Another advantage accruing to fictive detectives and denied the actual police is the absence of restriction in securing evidence. This, however, does not necessarily redound to the discredit of the authors of such stories, since in many cases the heroes are amateur rather than official investigators. A legal limitation which in a score of American jurisdictions restricts the activity of detectives in government employ does not hamper those who are not so employed. Hence, if the investigator in the story is, like Sherlock Holmes, or Philo Vance, or Charlie Chan (acting unofficially and out of his jurisdiction) a mere private citizen, he may legitimately do much that would be futile as well as illegal if attempted by a government operative.

Because this limitation exists in some states and not in others, a detective story may be basically inaccurate if laid in one setting, while quite real if the action transpires in a different state, or in England, where police-detectives have much greater freedom in the methods by which they may obtain evidence. For instance, H. C. Bailey's short tale of "The Little House" would have been fantastic had the locale been Chicago or Detroit instead of London. It will be remembered that in this yarn a neighbor's denial that a kitten had entered her premises struck amateur detective, Reggie Fortune, as being so peculiar that he and a police officer disguised themselves as water inspectors and searched the neighbor's house. The criminal evidence they found during this visit could never have been introduced in most American courts, and there is some reason to believe that even in England this visit of the "inspectors" would have been held actually unlawful because "unreasonable." In any event, the eventualities would have proved disastrous to the state's case in the majority of jurisdictions in this country; when the defendants were formally charged, preceding the trial, their attorney would have moved the court for an order suppressing all evidence secured either through the visit of the pseudo-inspectors *or by means of any later activities under a search warrant.* And the order would have been granted.

The explanation is brief. Practically all of our constitutions declare that the persons, houses, papers and possessions of the people shall be secure against "unreasonable" search and seizure. The Supreme Court has said that search of a private house can never be reasonable unless made under the authority of a properly issued search warrant describing the place to be searched and the thing sought, or in connection with an actual arrest therein. Moreover, an unreasonable search does not necessitate force; it may be made by stealth, or through deceit. On this theory of the courts, therefore, the visit of Fortune and the police officer was an unreasonable search. Granting the premise that it was unreasonable because made without a warrant, it was undeniably a search.

The judicial reasoning is that if a police officer can *use* evidence of crime secured by unreasonable search, he will make such searches in his zeal to secure convicting evidence. The courts fear that even risk of legal consequences to himself will not deter him; hence, they have removed the incentive to unreasonable searches by refusing to recognize evidence secured thereby. Long ago the Supreme Court laid down the dictum that to make effective the constitutional guarantee against unreasonable search, it was incumbent on the courts to prohibit society from utilizing any evidence so obtained. The state courts, in the beginning, were inclined to disagree; they followed the older precedent that although the searcher himself might be liable to punishment, nevertheless, the criminal could not gain by the searcher's over-zeal. But of recent years a certain fear of their own police has led many state courts to adopt the Federal rule. In these particular states, therefore, society could have availed nothing from what the "water inspectors" learned. And, as the later-secured search warrant was issued on the strength of this unreasonably secured information, it, too, was illegal and the search which it purported to authorize was also unreasonable.

Now, had Reggie Fortune gone alone on his visit of inspection, or had he taken with him another amateur as assistant, instead of an official police investigator, the evidence might have been used even in our own courts. The search, obviously, would not have been more reasonable, but the rule of exclusion applies only to evidence unreasonably secured by government agents. Fiction detectives who dispense with active official police co-operation are therefore an asset to the author in this respect. They remove, at least, a large part of the risk of writing bad law.

Likewise is an author fortunate in his freedom to elect where the crime shall be committed. Had Mr. A. E. W. Mason not set *The House of the Arrow* in France, detective Hanaud's foresight and effort would have proved quite futile. All his proof, one remembers, came from what he learned by secret and unauthorized search of the suspect's house. Had the law of his country necessitated his having a search warrant to make that evidence usable, it is more than probable that he would have found no evidence to be used, since, as it later developed, the private secretary to the *Commissaire* of Police was a member of the gang and was shrewd enough to have all incriminating evidence removed after Hanaud's request for a warrant. Hence, this entire story hinges upon the legality of the detective's unauthorized search; that the book is accurate is due to the fact that its locale is France, rather than America.

In *The Fellowship of the Frog*, Mr. Edgar Wallace, the author, allows the police to use a detectaphone for purposes of overhearing the conversation of persons under suspicion. Real policemen are not permitted facilitation of their objective by such means, in United States courts. The decision of the Supreme Court in the case of the notorious Olmstead conspiracy has laid the seal of official disapproval on such techniques.

The Olmstead organization was engaged in large-scale bootlegging. Olmstead, with a dozen or so associates, had put up a capital of twenty thousand dollars, and he and his colleagues were grossing over two million dollars annually. They operated a fleet of boats, including two sea-going vessels, had innumerable automobiles and trucks, owned an underground cache outside the city and various storage stations within the municipal limits, and employed a horde of scouts, salesmen, drivers, boatmen, clerks, telephone operators, bookkeepers and attorneys. The organization was as close an approach to the Fellowship of the Frog as reality is likely to come.

Efforts of the police to break up this ring consistently failed.

An occasional minion of the trust was picked up now and then, assessed his small fine and allowed his freedom. But the big frogs remained elusive. In time, however, the police got wind of who the chiefs were. By means of tapping telephone wires, running from the headquarters of the gang to the homes of four of the leaders, the police were able to secure over seven hundred type-written pages of memoranda recording incriminating conversations. It is to be noted that the officers did not trespass on the suspects' property in obtaining this information. The headquarters wires were tapped in the basement of the office building in which the organization was housed, and the connections with the private 'phones of the gang leaders were made from the street.

Olmstead and his fellow malefactors were indicted on the evidence secured through the wire-tapping and through subsequent searches made under warrants. The evidence obtained under the warrants, however, was suppressed on the ground that the warrants had not described with sufficient exactness the incriminating evidence which the police discovered. This left the state with nothing but the evidence secured through "listening in" on the telephone conversations.

The Olmstead attorneys then moved that this evidence be suppressed on the ground that it had been obtained by "unreasonable search." The trial court, however, denied this petition, and the Olmstead leaders were convicted. The case was, of course, appealed, and it finally came to the Supreme Court, where the significant question to be answered was concerned with the legality of this evidence.

Five of the justices agreed that its use was proper, four decided against it. The conviction stood affirmed. It is of interest, nevertheless, to note that the majority of the justices, in passing favorably on the question, did not so much as suggest that the police had acted "reasonably": they merely took the rather technical position that "listening in" without trespass on the suspects' property was not a "search" within the meaning of the Constitution. Some of the minority insisted that tapping wires and listening to criminals' or suspected criminals' private conversations is a violation of the law, is a search, and is—even under such circumstances as obtained in the Olmstead case—unreasonable. Some of the justices believed that whether or not there was a technical search in this case, the evidence should have been suppressed because th police had acted illegally. But all, apparently, would have agreed that, had the officers entered Olmstead's house and installed a detectaphone, as Inspector Elk did in fighting the Fellowship of the Frog, any incriminating evidence thus obtained could not have been used against the defendants.

It might be a happy facilitation of the police task in repressing crime if we could invest our real detectives with these privileges which detectives in fiction enjoy. But desirable privilege and power presuppose discretion, and real detectives are not endowed with discretion by mere alteration of the law. Perhaps Hanaud with his high ideals and delicacy of feeling could be entrusted with power; perhaps Poirot, and Philo Vance, complacent and irritating though he is, have the tact and intelligence essential to high privilege. But what of Sergeant Heath, of Gregson of Scotland Yard, and all the other dogged folk of detective fiction? What of the average police officer in real life?

In any event, when one considers the inequality of facilities between fiction and reality, it is not surprising that fiction is successful where reality frequently fails.

The Crux of a Murder: Disposal of the Body
By F. Sherwood Taylor

ᚥᚥᚥ

This pleasantly grim and realistic examination of a problem close to the hearts of murderers appeared in the Spectator *for April 9, 1937. . . . Suggested exercise in practical criticism: let the reader apply Mr. Taylor's method and logic to the problem in Lord Dunsany's much-acclaimed short story, "The Two Bottles of Relish," beloved of anthologists.*

ᶅᶅᶅ

WHEN DORIAN GRAY murdered Basil Hallward, he knew at once that the disposal of the corpse in the locked room was no task for his exquisite fingers. Fortunately he knew a secret about the man of science, Alan Campbell, which was so discreditable that the latter consented to destroy the corpse. Said he,

"Is there a fire in the room upstairs?"

"Yes, there is a gas-fire with asbestos."

"I shall have to go home and get some things from the laboratory."

(Dorian Gray would have none of this and sent his valet.)

"After ten minutes a knock came to the door, and the servant entered carrying a large mahogany chest of chemicals, with a long coil of steel and platinum wire and two rather curiously shaped iron clamps."

After five hours of work Campbell completed his task.

"As soon as Campbell had left he went upstairs. There was a horrible smell of nitric acid in the room. But the thing which had been sitting at the table was gone."

Since the days when I believed *The Picture of Dorian Gray* to be the high-water mark of English fiction, I have wondered how Campbell did it. Nitric acid is an admirable agent: a mouse boiled

447

in it for a few minutes is converted into a transparent pale-yellow solution. But how did Alan get enough nitric acid to boil Basil? And what did he do with the coils and the curiously-shaped clamps?

The problem of the murderer who has been imprudent enough to find himself burdened with a corpse, whose existence is proof of his crime, is one which has presented itself to many writers of the detective-novels which enjoy such deserved popularity today. It may be stated—a little crudely—thus. It is required to resolve about 120 lbs. of protein, fat and bone into matter unrecognisable as having formed part of a human body. There are, moreover, at least three essential conditions. The operation is to be performed single-handed, without attracting attention, and within a few days.

It is doubtful whether the problem has ever been solved in practice. Looked at as a chemical operation, it involves the conversion of protein, fat and bone—calcium phosphate—into an unorganised condition. It is best that the final product should be gas or liquid, which will become utterly lost in the air or the sewer respectively. The simplest means of destruction is fire, used with some success by Landru; but, unless very powerful and large fires, as of a steam-boiler, are available, it is very difficult to complete the combustion, and the smell of burning is such as to lead to detection. The four or five pounds of ash which are left contain far more phosphates than that from any wood or coal; and, as Landru found, metal objects, dentures, &c., may survive the fire. The extraordinary criminal Herman Webster Mudgett, *alias* H. H. Holmes, who equipped a "castle" in Sixty-third and Wallace Streets, Chicago, for the purpose of murder, had a private crematorium of a most efficient type. Such luxuries are not a fair solution of the murderer's problem. Given a crematorium or heated furnace-chamber, cremation followed by dissolving of the ashes in hydrochloric acid and the flushing of the liquid down the drains, would be admirable practice; always provided that fragments of gold and porcelain from dentures were strained off and later dropped into the sea from a Channel steamer.

Caustic alkalis and strong acids will do the work as well as fire, and without the tell-tale odour of burning. Strong acids are difficult to manipulate, because it is hard to obtain any vessel at once proof against their corrosion, capable of being heated and large enough to contain a body. The use of alkalis is simpler, and in 1897 the Chicago sausage-maker Luetgert nearly solved the problem. He bought 750 lbs. of caustic potash, much used for making soft-soap—and imprudently enough caused an employee to break it up. He put the potash and his murdered wife in a vat, used for colouring sausages, and blew in steam from a boiler. The strong solution of caustic potash dissolved the whole body, except the bones, to a brown liquid. The bones he broke up and burned in the steam-boiler's furnace. But, like most murderers, he failed in matters of detail. He did not conceal his unusual actions from the night-watchman and did not empty the vat. In it were found a few recognisable human bones and two tell-tale rings; the ashes from the furnace also contained recognisable fragments of human bone. In France an attempt was recently made to destroy a body by immersion in sulphuric acid. It failed because the action of the acid, if unheated, is slow and partial.

Having said so much, I cannot decline the inevitable challenge to solve the problem myself for the benefit of future weavers of the fiction of crime. Here, then, is my solution. If I ever decided to take to murder, I would prefer to use my professional powers of synthesising poisons which would baffle the very moderate resources of the analyst, rather than to attempt the revolting butcher's work of destroying a body. But if destruction there must be, I ask for a reasonably small cadaver, and a house with a gas-copper, and main drainage. I need a minimum of forty-eight hours undisturbed. I also suppose myself to have a complete indifference to corpses, acquired, let us say, by years in the post-mortem room.

As soon as I have committed the murder, I lay the corpse in the bath. I at once drive in my own car to London or a neighbouring town. I buy at an oil-and-colour merchants a 1 cwt. drum of flake caustic soda. From my chemical retailers I buy a piece of wire gauze, some rubber tubing, and four Winchester quarts of nitric acid. The purchase excites no attention, as I am known as a chemist. I also purchase a whetstone, a very large casserole and some string. I ligature the limbs, each in two places, to prevent effusion of much blood and, leaving the corpse in the bath with cold water running, I sever the limbs between the ligatures, with a sharp knife and a hacksaw. I eviscerate the trunk and cut it into four pieces. I also split the skull. The blood is so diluted by running water that no deposit is made. Meanwhile I have put half the caustic soda in the copper and just covered it with water. The heat of solution causes the liquid to boil. I light the gas under the copper, and introduce the limbs one by one. As soon as the flesh of each limb has dissolved, I remove the larger bones with tongs, wash them and break them into fragments.

Meanwhile I have half filled the casserole with concentrated nitric acid and heated it on a gas-ring set up in a fireplace. I add the bone fragments one at a time to the hot nitric acid, whereupon they rapidly dissolve, the fumes passing up the chimney with the hot air. As each lot of acid becomes exhausted, I pour it down the toilet, after diluting it in a slop-pail with 30 times its bulk of water, so making it too dilute to attack the pipes. When dissolving the jawbone I take care to collect the gold tooth-fillings and put them in my waistcoat-pocket. Finally I dissolve my over-all and the victim's clothes in the hot caustic soda solution. The liquid left in the copper I ladle down the drains, running the taps all the while. Any residue of small bones, buttons, &c., left in the copper—the wire gauze has its uses here—is dissolved in the casserole of nitric acid. The copper, sink, bath and casserole are carefully washed, and the rooms cleaned up. I now cook myself a hearty meal in the kitchen and have a good hot bath, so accounting for the disturbed state of the rooms.

The empty drum of caustic soda, the acid bottles and the casserole are taken in the car to my laboratory, where there are many others of the same kind. Here I dissolve the gold tooth fillings in *aqua regia,* grind the porcelain false teeth in an iron mortar and dissolve them in hydrofluoric acid in a leaden dish. The body is now converted into liquid and gaseous matter and is wholly unrecognisable. *Quod erat faciendum.*

But the process is not really to be recommended. Something would go wrong somewhere, for a new chemical technique can rarely be learned by less than two or three attempts. With the exception of the virtuosi, such as Landru and H. H. Holmes, few of us commit enough murders to become adepts in the art of concealing them. Perhaps it is just as well.

7
PUTTING CRIME ON
THE SHELF

For bibliophiles, bibliographers, and—readers.

Collecting Detective Fiction
By John Carter

John Carter is best known to the transatlantic reading public as the distinguished co-author, with Graham Pollard, of An Enquiry Into the Nature of Certain Nineteenth Century Pamphlets, *an innocently titled volume which, nevertheless, exploded in 1934 one of the most devastating literary bombshells of all time—the exposure of the Thomas J. Wise forgeries. Vincent Starrett has called the book "one of the great detective stories of the world." Manifestly, Mr. Carter was qualified by experience and inclination to become the first important bibliographer of the detective story itself. The present selection was first published as a chapter in* New Paths in Book-Collecting, *edited by Mr. Carter (London: Constable, 1934) and was subsequently reissued in its own right as* Collecting Detective Fiction *(London: Constable; New York: Scribner's, 1938). Despite the passage of years, this pioneer work has yet to be superseded as a whole, though later and specialized information has modified some of its findings: it is still the "bible" of the collector of detective fiction. . . . During World War II, Mr. Carter directed the general division of the British Information Services in New York; he has now returned to England as director of the London branch of the American publishing house of Scribner. An Englishman, he should not be confused with the American journalist and detective story writer John Carter, who writes variously as "Jay Franklin" and "Diplomat."*

INTRODUCTION

THE DETECTIVE story shows every sign of having come to stay. As a literary form it is not yet 100 years old, and there have not been wanting during its most recent heyday (which is still going on) certain crabbed persons to prophesy that such a boom must end in a slump, with the implied, or sometimes explicit, rider that the sooner this happens the better for the republic of letters. But even if the output of detective stories stopped to-morrow, the vogue has been long enough and prolific enough for the production of a body of literature which the Taines and Saintsburys of the future will not be able to ignore, even should they wish. In point of fact, there is no reason why they should wish. For quite apart from the distinguished authors scattered up and down its history, it is notorious that the detective story is the favourite reading of statesmen, of dons in our older universities, and in fact of all that is most intellectual in the reading public. The late Lord Rosebery possessed a first edition of *The Memoirs of Sherlock Holmes,* and Mr. Philip Guedalla has been credited with the observation that "the detective story is the normal recreation of noble minds." The Provost of Eton is an acknowledged authority on this, as on so many other subjects; Mr. Desmond MacCarthy is a prominent Holmesian scholar; and the Secretary to the Syndics of the Cambridge University Press is responsible for the standard life of Doctor Watson.*

If we err, therefore, in our liking for detective stories, we err with Plato.

But if we are pleased to take them reasonably seriously, our first consideration must be to distinguish the detective story proper from the various types of literature which are its first cousins on one side or the other. This may not be essential to the reader, but the collector, even one with ample shelf room, will probably find himself, amongst such a wealth of kindred material compelled to reserve his energies and space for the genuine article only. On the one hand, then, he will avoid criminology; any records of actual facts. This principle need not, of course,

---

Note.—The binding of all books referred to must be understood to be cloth, unless otherwise stated. Where particulars are given of any book which I have not examined personally I have indicated the fact (after the manner of the illustrious Hain) by attaching a double asterisk. Dates, etc., in such cases must therefore be understood to derive from the standard reference books or other authorities.

* S. C. Roberts, *Doctor Watson* (Faber, 1931). The first part of this had previously appeared in *Life and Letters.*

exclude fiction based on fact, like Poe's "The Mystery of Marie Rogêt" or Wilkie Collins' *The Moonstone*. The former, as is well known, was constructed from the newspaper accounts of an investigation then actually proceeding in New York, and the paper which published Poe's story did not dare, for very good reason, to take it as far as his conclusion. It is said * that, years later, the confession of the persons he indicated confirmed the accuracy of his solution. As for *The Moonstone,* several incidents and the detective himself—the immortal Sergeant Cuff—were lifted from the sensational Constance Kent case, which had taken place a few years earlier.† Nor need fiction masquerading as fact be barred. Some of the many volumes which appeared in London from the 'fifties onwards, purporting to be reminiscences, may actually have been genuine; but the authors of most of them were literary hacks, and it is probably safe to label the whole class of "Revelations" and "Experiences" and "Diaries" of "Real Detectives" and "Ex-detectives" as fiction, at any rate as far down as 1890.

At the other end of the scale the line is often much more difficult to draw. Many uncritical people, if suddenly asked to name a modern writer of detective stories, would offer Edgar Wallace; but actually Wallace wrote very few detective stories proper.‡ If we decide, as surely we must, that a detective story within the meaning of the act must be mainly occupied with detection and must contain a proper detective (whether amateur or professional), it is clear that mystery stories, crime stories, spy stories, shockers, even Secret Service stories, will have to be excluded unless any particular example can show some authentic detective strain. We may choose to admit to our collection *The Four Just Men* § or *Raffles* ‖ or *The Thirty Nine Steps,*¶ but it must be realised (unless we are prepared for their logical results—to the

---

* Sayers, *Detection, Mystery and Horror* (Gollancz, 1928) p. 18.

† Famous Trials Series. *The Trial of Constance Kent* (Hodge, 1931).

‡ Exceptions are *Room* 13 (John Long, 1924) and *The Clue of the Silver Key* (Hodder & Stoughton, 1930).

§ By Edgar Wallace (The Tallis Press, 1905). The book was published without the concluding chapter and a prize of £500 was offered for the correct solution. The competition slip comes at the end of the book.

‖ E. W. Hornung, *The Amateur Cracksman* (Methuen, 1898).

¶ By John Buchan (Edinburgh: Blackwood, 1915).

tune of several thousand volumes) that they are there as a matter of grace and not of right.

Considering that all the historical and literary criticism of the detective story is the product of so short a period, the subject is singularly fortunate in the commentators it has attracted. The specialists * in the exegesis and chronology of the *Sherlock Holmes* cycle are perhaps rather advanced for the layman, who often finds the higher criticism wearisome, to whatever it is applied; but if Mr. H. W. Bell's thoroughness † is terrifying, others besides Conan Doyle enthusiasts enjoy Father Ronald Knox's erudite virtuosity.‡

Of workers in the field as a whole four names stand out. The late E. M. Wrong, Fellow of Magdalen College, Oxford, and a distinguished historian, introduced his selection of *Crime and Detection* in the *World's Classics* series § with an essay, analytical, philosophical and historical, which remains the best thing yet written on the subject. Willard Huntington Wright, who is probably better known by his pen name of S. S. Van Dine, introduced a bulkier anthology ‖ in the following year with an excellently balanced survey, which has for our present purpose this advantage over Wrong's that it is packed with detail. In 1928 Miss Dorothy Sayers,¶ in a similar rôle, proved herself as distinguished a critic and historian as she is a creative artist. And in 1931 Mr. H. Douglas Thomson produced, in a work whose title †† belies its merits, the first full-length study of the detective story.

Although there have been other, mostly critical, contributions

---

* *E.g.*, T. S. Blakeney, *Sherlock Holmes, Fact or Fiction?* (Murray, 1932); Vincent Starrett, *The Private Life of Sherlock Holmes* (New York: Macmillan, 1933); *Baker Street Studies*, edited by H. W. Bell (Constable, 1934). *Cf.* also Roberts' book.

† *Sherlock Holmes and Doctor Watson* (Constable, 1932).

‡ "Studies in the Literature of Sherlock Holmes" in *Essays in Satire* (Sheed & Ward, 1928). This had previously appeared in *The Blue Book* and in *Blackfriars*.

§ No. 301 (Oxford University Press, 1926). As with all volumes in this series, late issues are usually betrayed by the inserted advertisements listing subsequently published titles.

‖ *The Great Detective Stories* (New York: Scribner's, 1927).

¶ *Great Short Stories of Mystery, Detection and Horror* (Gollancz, 1928). In her introduction to the Second Series (1931) Miss Sayers discusses the present and future, rather than the past.

†† *Masters of Mystery* (Collins, 1931).

from such writers as G. K. Chesterton,* Father Knox,† and Vernon Rendall,‡ those four authors are our main authorities § for the general history and development of the detective story.

THE MAIN OUTLINE

I. THE POE-WILKIE COLLINS-GABORIAU PERIOD

The main outline is familiar enough. There have been attempts, it is true, to establish Herodotus, Sophocles and the authors of certain books of the Apocrypha as early exponents of the detective story; but these are hardly justified; and though we today may account it strange that there were no true examples of the form before 1840, it is usually and rightly held that it originated with Edgar Allan Poe. Poe's three great stories ‖ touched a level of excellence very remarkable in view of their incunabular position and one to which no other writer attained for twenty-five years, even if (as some doubt) they have ever been equalled.¶ Poe may have tired of his brilliant creation, or (and the lack of immediate successors in his own country makes this more likely) perhaps public response was lukewarm. At any rate it was not until Charles Dickens' interest in the recently created police detective force in London †† had been communicated by him to

---

* See *The Defendant* (Brimley Johnson, 1901); also his Preface to W. S. Masterman's *The Wrong Letter* (Methuen, 1926).

† *E.g.* his introduction to *The Best Detective Stories of* 1928 (Faber, 1929).

‡ *London Nights of Belsize* (Lane, 1917).

§ None of them are pedantically concerned with the dates of the original editions, as the collector must naturally be, and he will do well to check all dates given. The first attack on the subject from a bibliographical and collecting angle with which I am familiar is an article by Mr. E. A. Osborn in *The Bookman* of February, 1932, and to that pioneer effort I take this opportunity of making a bow.

‖ "The Murders in the Rue Morgue," "The Mystery of Marie Rogêt" and "The Purloined Letter." "Thou Art the Man," although an inferior example, should not be ignored (as it usually is), but "The Gold Bug" is not a true detective story at all.

¶ They are analysed in full by Thomson (*op. cit.*, pp. 75–85), following Sayers (*op. cit.*, pp. 17–18).

†† Sir Robert Peel's creation of the police force dates from 1928, but it was only in 1845 that the germ of the Criminal Investigation Department (1876) was born. In that year Sir James Graham detailed twelve police officers for exclusive plain clothes detective work. Dickens was the first writer to recognise their importance, and he devoted four articles in *Household Words* (July—September, 1850) to a description of their work. "It is significant," writes Mr. Osborn, "that it is after that period that the spate of detective reminiscences and pseudo-reminiscences appears," and to these we shall return later.

Wilkie Collins, that we come to the next landmark. In 1868, however, appeared *The Moonstone,** which Mr. T. S. Eliot † has called "the first, the longest and the best of modern detective stories." Mr. Eliot is inaccurate in his first adjective, a little rash perhaps in his second,‡ but unlikely to meet with much disagreement over his third. If Poe created the short detective story, Wilkie Collins is the undisputed father of the full-length variety, and it remained in the ascendant for higher class work until the arrival of Sherlock Holmes.

Meanwhile a star had arisen across the English Channel, and the novels of Emile Gaboriau § took France by storm. *L'Affaire Lerouge ** was published in *Le Pays* in 1866 and Gaboriau produced a number of equally famous successors ‖ to it before his death in 1873. He was followed by Fortuné de Boisgobey, whose novels, always full of dramatic incident, sometimes degenerate into mere sensational police stories; but at his infrequent best he was not unworthy of his acknowledged master.¶ The influence of these two was more productive abroad than at home. There are few †† French detective stories of any note between Boisgobey's death in 1891 and the appearance of another pair of contemporaneous masters, MM. Leroux and Leblanc, about fifteen years

---

* Three vols., Tinsley, 1868. (See Sadleir, *Excursions in Victorian Bibliography*, p. 142.)

† Introduction to the *World's Classics* edition, first issued in 1928 (No. 316). Mr. Eliot emphasises Dickens' influences on Wilkie Collins at this time, and there is little doubt that in the unfinished *Edwin Drood*, 1870, we have lost what might well have been a masterpiece of full length detection.

‡ Several other three-deckers must run it pretty close; such as *Is He the Man?*, by W. Clark Russell (Tinsley, 1876), or *The Wrong Road*, by Major Arthur Griffiths (Edinburgh: Blackwood, 1888); while *Le Crime de l'Opéra ** by Fortuné de Boisgobey (Paris, 1880), runs to "over four hundred pages of microscopic type" (Thomson, *op. cit.*, p. 111).

§ It is not impossible that Gaboriau was familiar with Baudelaire's translation of Poe's *Tales*, which had appeared in Paris in 1856 and 1857. If so, it was very suitable that America should reciprocate so much more promptly than England with translations of Gaboriau.

‖ *Le Dossier* 113,** 1867; *Le Crime d'Orcival,** 1868; *Monsieur Lecoq,** 1869, etc.

¶ His best known works are *L'Homme sans Nom,** 1872; *Le Forçat Colonel,** 1872; *Le Crime de l'Opéra,** 1880; and *Le Crime de l'Omnibus* (Paris: Dentu, 1881). In one story, *The Old Age of Lecoq,** he does honour to his master, Gaboriau, by borrowing his detective.

†† Mention may be made, however, of *Three Exploits of M. Parent*, from the French of Jules Lermina (Osgood, McIlvaine, 1894), and *The Meudon Mystery*, by Jules Mary Vizetelly, 1888).

later. Translations of Gaboriau and Boisgobey did not appear in
London until the 1880's, but once launched in Vizetelly's cheap
red-wrappered editions they sold in very large numbers, and their
illustration of French police methods has had considerable influence in the development of what we regard to-day as the Crofts
school of writers.* But, as one finds, unexpectedly, in the case of
other of Vizetelly's continental importations, England waited on
the United States; translations of Gaboriau had appeared in Boston and New York years before his fellow countryman introduced
them to London.† They stimulated a public interest which rapidly evoked response in the form of native products, and though
their influence on the celebrated Pinkerton series ‡ was probably
no greater than that exerted by the numerous volumes of fictional
memoirs which had pervaded the English bookstalls since 1855,
it is plainly apparent in the work of Anna Katharine Green,
whose vogue, beginning in earnest with *The Leavenworth Case* §
in 1878, remained the dominant feature of the American scene
for several decades.|| Lawrence L. Lynch (Mrs. Murdoch van

* Of Lecoq, Thomson says (*op. cit.*, p. 98): "Here is Inspector French's prototype."
† Startlingly prompt was *The Steel Safe, or The Stains and Splendours of New
York Life (Adapted from E. Gaboriau's Le Dossier No. 113)*, by H. L. Jr. (New York:
De Witt, 1868 **). After this came others: *File 113*,** from Estes and Lauriat, of
Boston, in 1875 (London: Vizetelly, 1883 **); *The Mystery of Orcival*,** ditto, 1871
(London: Vizetelly, 1885); *The Widow Lerouge*,** from Osgood, of Boston, 1873
(London: Vizetelly, 1885 **); and Boisgobey's *The Golden Tress*,** Claxton,
Remington and Haffelfinger, Philadelphia, 1875 (London: Vizetelly, 1887 **).
‡ The first of these, as far as I can find, was *The Expressman and the Detective*,
by Allan Pinkerton (Chicago: W. B. Keen, Cooke & Co., 1874), and by 1883 more
than a dozen *soi-disants* selections from the case book of the famous agency had
appeared. Between 1875 (*The Detective and the Somnambulist*) and 1876 (*The
Model Town and the Detectives*) publication seems to have been taken over by
G. W. Carleton & Co., of New York, but all the volumes are illustrated with engravings and embellished as to their covers with a vignette in gilt of a fierce and rather
oriental looking eye, accompanied by the firm's slogan, "We Never Sleep."
There was also a later series, issued monthly from March, 1887, onwards, by
Laird & Lee, of Chicago. This was called *The Frank Pinkerton Detective Series*, and
included such titles as *Dyke Darrel the Railroad Detective*,** $5000 Reward,** and
Jim Cummings or the Great Adams Express Robbery. The bindings of these are
more elaborate, but omit the firm's trade mark.
§ New York, Putnam. Three editions were published in London in 1884, of which
Strahan's is probably the earliest, the British Museum copy having been received
on May 2nd. The reception date of the Ward, Lock edition is August 8th, of the
Routledge edition October 13th (both pictorial wrappers).
|| W. H. Wright (*op. cit.*, p. 15) selects for mention from her long list *Hand and
Ring*, (New York: Putnam, 1883), *Behind Closed Doors* (ditto, 1888, cloth or
wrappers); *The Filigree Ball* (Indianapolis: Bobbs-Merrill, 1903); *The House of the*

Deventer) was a fairly prolific runner-up,* but although subsequent American writers were by no means idle, they contributed †
little of importance to the development of the genre until comparatively recent years.

II. THE SHERLOCK HOLMES PERIOD

In 1887 two remarkable events occurred, which make this year
perhaps the most memorable in the whole history of detective fiction. The first was the sensational success of *The Mystery of a
Hansom Cab,* by Fergus W. Hume. Published in Melbourne,
Australia, the first edition of 5,000 copies was sold out in a week
and others followed in quick succession; the publisher, Frederick
Trischler, migrated with the book to London; the first London
edition ‡ of 25,000 copies, issued over the imprint of the Hansom
Cab Publishing Company, was exhausted in three days; and when
the author died,§ in 1932, over half a million copies in all had
been sold. No other detective story before or since can have
touched such sale records,‖ and it is not surprising that by the
historians as well as by the public Hume is to-day regarded as a
one-book man. In fact, he wrote over a hundred other books, of
which about half were detective stories,¶ and if he is now not

Whispering Pines ** (New York: Putnam, 1910); and *The Step on the Stair* **
(New York: Dodd, 1923).

* *Shadowed by Three* ** (Chicago: Donnelley, Gassette & Loyd, 1879); *Madeline
Payne* ** (Chicago: A. T. Loyd & Co., 1884); *The Diamond Coterie* ** and *Dangerous Ground* (ditto, both 1885), etc., etc. Ward, Lock & Routledge were busy with
sixpenny editions in London from 1884 onwards, and the former became her authorised publishers in the 'nineties, re-issuing the early titles and publishing new
ones in superbly pictorial cloth at half-a-crown each.

† Mention should perhaps be made of Julian Hawthorne's books, *e.g.*, *Section 558*
(New York: Cassell, 1888); *Another's Crime* (ditto, 1888).

‡ These details are drawn from a sixteen-page pamphlet advertising the book
which Trischler issued shortly after it had appeared in London. No copy of the first
London edition has so far been discovered: that in the British Museum is of the
250th thousand; and the earliest I have examined is a copy of the 100th thousand,
the cover of which was reproduced in Mr. Osborn's *Bookman* article. All these early
editions are in black and white pictorial wrappers.

§ It was stated at this time that Hume had originally sold the MS. outright for
£50.

‖ In 1888 the book achieved the distinction of a full length parody—*The Mystery
of a Wheel-Barrow or Gaboriau Gaborooed,* by W. Humer Ferguson (Walter Scott,
1888, pictorial wrappers).

¶ The most important to the collector are *The Piccadilly Puzzle* (F. V. White,
1889, cloth or wrappers); *The Gentleman Who Vanished* (F. V. White, 1890, pictorial

much read, his position in any historical survey is a significant one.

The other event of the year is unquestionably the more important. "In 1887," writes Miss Sayers (*op. cit.,* p. 28), *"A Study in Scarlet* was flung like a bombshell into the field of detective fiction, to be followed within a few short and brilliant years by the marvellous series of Sherlock Holmes short stories. The effect was electric. Conan Doyle took up the Poe formula and galvanised it into life and popularity." Sherlock Holmes quickly reached, and has never lost, a position in the detective world which no other and abler practitioners have ever approached. It may be that we read these stories now less for their purely detective interest (always considerable) than for their masterly character drawing; it is true that the more fanatical tend to regard Watson as almost more important than Holmes, just as there are always some who attribute Socrates' quality to Plato or Johnson's to Boswell; * but it is as impossible to exaggerate Holmes' pre-eminent influence over the next generation of detectives as it is to recreate that golden age when the public stood in queues at the bookstall for the new issue of *The Strand Magazine.* Conan Doyle has been a favourite with collectors for some years now, and as he has his own bibliographer † the details of his books need not detain us. The resounding success of Holmes was the signal for a great increase in activity among detective story writers, and the last decade of the nineteenth century was favoured with a good deal of excellent work. *The Wrong Box,* by R. L. Stevenson and Lloyd Osborne ‡ and *The Black Box Murder* ** by [Maarten Maartens],§ both published in 1889, showed serious authors tackling the medium, and in 1894 Arthur Morrison introduced in Martin

---

wrappers); *The Black Carnation* (Gale & Polden [1892], pictorial wrappers); *The Chinese Jar* (Sampson Low, 1893, pictorial boards); *A Midnight Mystery* (Gale & Polden [1894], pictorial wrappers); *The Lone Inn* (Jarrold, 1894); *The Lady from Nowhere* (Chatto & Windus, 1900).

* Holmes himself said "I am lost without my Boswell."

† The late Captain Harold Locke's *Bibliography* was published in 1928 (Tunbridge Wells: D. Webster).

‡ Longmans, Green. The first issue has the headings of the Contents page and the first page of text in the same type (Prideaux, 1918, p. 71).

§ Remington published this, according to *The English Catalogue.* There is no copy in the British Museum and I have failed to discover one in several years' search.

Hewitt * the most considerable of Holmes' immediate successors. The work of L. T. Meade and Clifford Halifax proved that the combination of a novelist and a doctor could be a fruitful one, and the two series of *Stories from the Diary of a Doctor* † marked the advance of scientific detection towards its most famous exponent, Doctor Thorndyke. M. P. Shiel's Prince Zaleski ‡ has many of the immortal Dupin's characteristics, and his talents are not unworthy of his prototype; but Mr. Shiel's books in collaboration with Louis Tracy § are not up to the standards of either author working alone. Tracy has a number of good books to his credit,‖ but his principal detective, Furneaux, was eclipsed by the rising stars of the new century.

In 1904, Arnold Bennett showed, in *The Grand Babylon Hotel*,¶ that he could write an adventure-detective story as well as anybody; but he wrote no more. In 1907, however, Dr. R. Austin Freeman published through the obscure firm of Collingwood a book which marks a new level in scientific detection. *The Red Thumb Mark* †† introduced Doctor Thorndyke, whom Wrong considered "the greatest detective now in business," and it was only the first of a long series. *John Thorndyke's Cases* (Chatto & Windus, 1909) followed, and in *The Singing Bone* (Hodder & Stoughton, 1912) Dr. Freeman achieved one of his greatest tri-

---

* *Martin Hewitt, Investigator* (Ward, Lock & Bowden, Ltd., 1894; the cloth blue, red or green); *Chronicles of Martin Hewitt* (ditto, 1895); *The Adventures of Martin Hewitt* (Ward Lock & Co., Ltd., 1896). *The Dorrington Deed Box* (ditto, 1897) records the exploits of the detective who gives his name to the title.

† Newnes, 1894; and Bliss, Sands & Foster, 1896.

‡ John Lane, 1895, No. VII. of the *Keynote Series*. The bright purple cloth is almost always faded.

§ These appeared over the pen name of "Gordon Holmes." *The Arncliffe Puzzle* (Werner Laurie, 1906); *A Mysterious Disappearance* (New York: A. Wessels Company, 1906); *The Late Tenant* (Cassell, 1907); *By Force of Circumstances*, which probably appeared in U.S.A. prior to the issue of the English edition (Mills & Boon, March 10th, 1910). Mr. John Gawsworth, in *Ten Contemporaries* (1931), pp. 194–5, states that Mr. Shiel repudiates any connection with the first two titles: in this case, Tracy must presumably have been using the alias alone before the collaboration began.

‖ *E.g., The Strange Disappearance of Lady Delia* (Pearson, 1901); *The Silent House* (Eveleigh Nash, 1911); *The Case of Mortimer Fenley* (Cassell, 1915).

¶ Chatto & Windus, 1904.

†† This was issued simultaneously in cloth and in wrappers, in each case black and ornamented with a red thumb print. Both forms are very scarce indeed.

umphs with a series of stories in which the reader is first shown the crime being committed and afterwards accompanies Thorndyke in his solution. To waive the advantages of suspense and surprise is a severe test for any detective author, but in the event these are among Freeman's best stories.*

Baroness Orczy's *The Old Man in the Corner* (Greening, 1908) is an early and persuasive example of the intuitive school of detectives, which has become better known through the work of G. K. Chesterton's Roman Catholic Priest, Father Brown; † and, more lately, by H. C. Bailey's series of books describing the exploits of Reginald Fortune,‡ whose conversational powers prevent some people from estimating his talent as dispassionately as they otherwise might. Ernest Bramah's Max Carrados,§ being blind, is to some extent inevitably intuitive, but his methods in general are as ruthlessly logical as the purist could wish.

With A. E. W. Mason's Hanaud in 1910 we return to a really great policeman, after a period in which the amateur or the private agent had been practically in possession of the field. *At the Villa Rose* ‖ was followed by *The House of the Arrow* and *The Prisoner in the Opal,*¶ but their author has other fish to fry and we have not had as many of Hanaud's cases as could be wished.

In 1913 what may be called the Sherlock Holmes period comes to an end; and it ends with a book which can hold its own with

---

* Other early and scarce titles are *The Mystery of 31 New Inn* (Hodder & Stoughton, 1912); *A Silent Witness* (ditto, 1914); *The Eye of Osiris* (ditto, 1911: first in brown cloth with Egyptian style decoration and lettering, later issue in plain brown); *The Great Portrait Mystery* (ditto, 1918). Most of the later Thorndyke books are, naturally, easier to come by, but the first editions are not always easy to distinguish, owing to Messrs. Hodder & Stoughton's exasperating antipathy to dating their publications.

† *The Innocence of Father Brown* (Cassell, 1911); *The Wisdom* (ditto, 1914), etc. Mr. Chesterton later devoted his attention to the illustrations, for Mr. Hilaire Belloc, of a special kind of burlesque detective story which, being *sui generis,* is appropriately known as the *Chester-Belloc.*

‡ *Call Mr. Fortune* (Methuen, 1920); *Mr. Fortune's Practice* (ditto, 1923); *Mr. Fortune's Trials* (ditto, 1926), etc.

§ *Max Carrados* (Methuen, 1914); *The Eyes of Max Carrados* (Grant Richards, 1923); *Max Carrados Mysteries* (Hodder & Stoughton, 1927).

‖ Hodder & Stoughton, 1910. The first binding is light blue cloth; later issues of the book were put out in buff, and also in maroon with vertical buff stripes, with the edges cut down.

¶ Hodder & Stoughton (1924) and ditto (1929) respectively.

any detective story ever written—E. C. Bentley's *Trent's Last Case* (Nelson, 1913). Trent's few other cases, published later, were perhaps disappointing, but his last is sufficient for his immortality.

III. THE MODERNS IN ENGLAND

The European War put an effective stop to the production of detective fiction, but its revival was signalised in 1920 by the appearance of *The Cask*,* by Freeman Wills Crofts; a book not only of very remarkable quality but one which has profoundly influenced the modern detective story as a whole. Mr. Crofts combined the elaboration of Gaboriau with an integrity of method which set an altogether new standard for the many police detectives who have followed Inspector French. The amount of patient work French gets through is often too much for the reader who wants entertainment rather than intellectual exercise, but it gives an effect of realism which is an indispensable quality; and in practice his scrupulous care for details, especially of time, produces remarkable results, so that one critic has observed that any character in a Crofts novel who has an absolutely impregnable alibi becomes *ipso facto* an object of immediate suspicion to the reader. *The Cask* did not reach a second edition until 1921, and the first, a small one, is extremely scarce. *The Ponson Case,* which seems to be even scarcer, appeared in 1921, and *The Pit Prop Syndicate* in the following year; and although French was then joined by a number of distinguished rivals, he has continued to add workmanlike cases to his record.

The years from 1920 onwards introduce one by one names which are now household words in detective fiction. Nineteen-twenty, Agatha Christie (*The Mysterious Affair at Styles,* New York, Lane **); 1921, Eden Phillpotts (*The Grey Room,* New York, Macmillan) †; 1922, A. A. Milne (*The Red House Mystery,* Methuen);

---

* This and all Mr. Crofts' subsequent books down to 1933 were published by Collins. The collector should be on his guard against occasional secondary bindings of light blue cloth lettered in black, instead of the dark blue lettered in red which seems to have been standard from *The Pit Prop Syndicate,* 1922 down to *Inspector French and the Starvel Tragedy,* 1927. The cloth of the first two books, mentioned above, is red.

† Mr. Phillpotts has also written under the pen name of "Harrington Hext"— *e.g., The Thing at Their Heels* (Thornton Butterworth, 1923), and it should be

1923, Dorothy Sayers (*Whose Body?*, New York, Boni & Liveright) and G. D. H. Cole (*The Brooklyn Murders*, Collins); 1924, Philip MacDonald (*The Rasp*, Collins) and Lynn Brock (*The Deductions of Colonel Gore*, Collins); 1925, Anthony Berkeley (*The Layton Court Mystery*, Jenkins: published anonymously), Ronald Knox (*The Viaduct Murder*, Methuen); 1926, Henry Wade (*The Verdict of You All*, Constable); and so on, down to the present day. The later books by these authors are too well known to need listing here; and as for others, the output of more recent years has been so enormous, the general level of quality is so high, and the very various enthusiasms of the cognoscenti are so intemperate, that a selection would be as rash as it would be impractical.

IV. FRANCE AND AMERICA SINCE 1895

Of detective writers outside England since the Holmesian renaissance, there are two Frenchmen * who must be considered—Leblanc and Leroux; and something will be said about them in the final section of this essay. There are also a large number of Americans. It is true that for a time America tended to lag behind England in the achievements and originality of method of her fictional detectives—what a poor figure Arthur Reeve's Craig Kennedy cuts, for instance, beside Doctor Thorndyke; but there have been plenty of good stories written by such authors as Melville Davisson Post, Mary Roberts Rinehart, John T. McIntyre and Isabel Ostrander (alias Robert Orr Chipperfield), and it is unfortunate that it is impossible to provide adequate bibliographical details here. But the difficulty of getting the books from across the Atlantic has been an insuperable obstruction, and the collector will have to wait for a prophet from their own country, or do his investigating for himself. Mr. W. H. Wright treats them, as is fitting, more fully than our other authorities, and his information provides an excellent groundwork.

As for the moderns: Hammett, Van Dine, Ellery Queen, Frances

noted that other detective stories of his were first published in U.S.A.—*e.g.*, *The Red Redmaynes* (New York: Macmillan, 1922). The collector is referred to the *Bibliography* by Percival Hinton, published in 1931 (Birmingham: Greville Worthington).
* No attempt will be made here to deal with the Germans and other Continental writers. For a brief survey the reader is referred to W. H. Wright (*op. cit.*, pp. 29–32).

Noyes Hart and the rest; their names and works are as familiar
as those of their English colleagues and it is equally unnecessary
to insult the enthusiast by recapitulation.

SOME LESS KNOWN NAMES

The foregoing brief summary of the history of the detective
story covers no ground unfamiliar to even the casual student of
the subject, and it now remains to fill in a few of the gaps which
the authorities have left unbridged. The literary critic and the
historian rightly jump from one peak to another when they are
describing their explorations to readers largely ignorant of the
ground. But the collector is not only as much interested in the
out-of-the-way books of all periods as in the familiar titles; he is
also particularly curious about the early specimens of an afterwards popular and well-known literary form. There may be fifty
detective stories published this year better than the best published
in, say, 1860, but the interest of the latter lies, and very properly,
in the fact that it represents a period in the history of the type
about which the average collector is unlikely to know anything
at all. *"Vixere fortes ante Agamemnona,"* says Wrong, "but we
have forgotten them, and tend to think of the pre-Holmes detectives as of the pre-Shakespearian drama; to call them precursors
only." This is true enough; and there are plenty of unregarded
post-Holmes detectives, too, to attract the curious eye of the collector.

It was remarked above that police detection in England followed, at some distance, the disestablishment of the Bow Street
Runners; * and although fictional reminiscences of the latter force
are very rare,† and not for our purpose very important, the large
output of similar productions by, or purporting to be by, detectives and ex-detectives was a notable feature of those "dark

---

* Griffiths (*Mysteries of Police and Crime,* 1898, Vol. 1, p. 129) says that "the old
Bow Street Runner either retired from business or set up what we should now call
private enquiry offices."

† One example will suffice: *Richmond, or Scenes in the Life of a Bow Street
Officer. Drawn up from his Private Memoranda* (Colburn, 3 vols., 1827, boards).
The book was apparently no great success, for the original sheets were furnished
with cancel titles in 1845 by A. K. Newman and re-issued in maroon zebra-striped
cloth.

ages," the 1850's and 1860's. These collections mostly appeared in the form of "yellow backs" and they continued to find a public right down to the end of the century, but their complete omission from the history books is amply accounted for by their extraordinary rarity to-day—due mainly, of course, to this perishable and ephemeral format. Nevertheless, to skip gaily from Poe to *The Moonstone* is to ignore a large school of writers, whose influence and early date promote them to a position of importance usually, it is true, disproportionate to the actual quality of their work.

The most prolific author of this school was William Russell, who wrote under the name of "Waters." His best work was contained in the two series of *Recollections of a Detective Police Officer* (J. & C. Brown, 1856, and W. Kent, 1859), and the general character of the style is typified by the caption to the elegant frontispiece of the first volume *—"The game is up, my good Mr. Gates, I arrest you for felony"—and by the quotation from Denman on the title page. This reads: "Police or Peace Officers are the lifeguards of the sleeping realm, without whom chambers would not be safe, nor the strong law of more potency than a bulrush." This book is also a good example of the bibliographical puzzles presented by the whole class, and indeed by yellow-backs in general. In the first issue, the title page is dated, the preface runs on to p. vii, and p. [viii] carries the *Contents;* for the second, signature [A] was reprinted, there is no date on the title, the preface is compressed to end on p. vi, p. [vii] taking the *Contents* and p. [viii] being blank; the title of the third issue is identical with that of the second, but by printing the frontispiece on a separate single leaf instead of on [A]2 and removing the *Contents* to the verso of the title, signature [A] is now reduced to two leaves only. All three issues appeared in yellow picture boards at the price of eighteen pence.

The same author's *Experiences of a French Detective Officer* "adapted from the MSS. of Theodore Duhamel" (Clarke [1861], Parlour Library, No. 234, pictorial boards or cloth) contains an

---

* A German translation of this volume appeared in 1857—*Erinnerungen eines Criminal-Polizisten von Waters* (Leipzig: Kollman, printed wrappers); and a French translation by Victor Perceval—*Mémoires d'un Policeman* (Paris: Degorge-Cadot [1868?], printed wrappers)—which does not give Waters' name anywhere. Both these translations appeared in series of a similar character to the yellow back original.

Introduction explaining "The Difference between English and French Detectives," which indeed a perusal of the text shows to have been badly needed; and among his other books are *Experiences of a Real Detective* by Inspector F. (Ward & Lock, 1862, Shilling Volume Library, printed wrappers); *The Autobiography of An English Detective* (two volumes, Maxwell, 1863, maroon cloth); *Undiscovered Crimes* (Ward & Lock, 1862, decorated wrappers); *Mrs. Waldegrave's Will and other Tales* (Ward, Lock & Tyler, Parlour Library Sixpenny Series, No. 14, pictorial wrappers [? 1870]); *A Skeleton in Every House* (Clarke [1860] Parlour Library, No. 222, pictorial boards or cloth). The tradition of Waters, Charles Martel,* Andrew Forrester, Jr.† and others of similar type ‡ was carried on by a host of later writers, few of whom stand out with any considerable run of titles. An exception is James Mc-Govan, who produced a series of five extremely popular collections during the 'seventies and 'eighties.§ William Henderson, also a Scotsman, prefaced a similar volume in 1889 || with a statement that "most of the so-called 'Experiences of Detective Officers' have had no foundation in fact." Inspector Moser,¶ in *Stories from Scotland Yard* (Routledge, 1890) also insists that his tales "are all founded upon actual facts," and this tendency seems to have increased during the 'nineties.

---

* *The Detective's Note Book* (Ward & Lock, 1860); *The Diary of an Ex-Detective* (ditto, 1860). The real name of the author, or "editor," was Thomas Delf.

† *Revelations of a Private Detective* (Ward & Lock, 1863); *Secret Service or Recollections of a City Detective* (ditto, 1864); *The Female Detective* (ditto, 1864).

‡ Examples are *The Experiences of a Barrister* (J. & C. Brown, 1856); *Curiosities of Crime in Edinburgh*, by James McLevy (Edinburgh: Nimmo, 1861); *The Irish Police Officer*, by Robert Curtis (Ward & Lock, 1861); *Tom Fox or the Revelations of a Detective* (Vickers, 1860); *The Autobiography of a French Detective from 1828–1858*, by M. Canler, Ancien Chef du Service de Sûreté (Ward & Lock, 1862). There was even a contribution from the anonymous syndicate responsible for the *Anonyma* series (see Mr. Sadleir's essay, p. 159), entitled *The Revelations of a Lady Detective* (Vickers, 1864). Clarke's re-issue of this [1884] is attributed in the British Museum catalogue to W. S. Hayward, almost certainly incorrectly. All these books were issued in pictorial boards.

§ The first of these, *Brought to Bay, or Experiences of a City Detective* (Edinburgh and Glasgow: Menzies, pictorial boards), was published in 1878, ran through five editions in eighteen months, and had reached its fifteenth by 1890.

|| *Clues, or Leaves from a Chief Constable's Note Book* (Edinburgh: Oliphant, Anderson & Ferrier, 1889, pictorial boards).

¶ Moser afterwards conducted a paper called *The Modern Detective*, which began in 1898.

In fact, towards the end of the century the "below stairs" school of detective fiction gradually split into two branches, as its chief vehicle, the yellow-back, became obsolete. On the one side it turned to fact; * on the other it joined up with that huge stream of "bloods" which had run so strongly all through the Victorian period. Hogarth House, sponsors of *Jack Harkaway* and many other heroic figures, ran a department of their *Gem Pocket Library* which offered detective stories of "128 pages of new and original text, illustrated, in coloured wrappers" at twopence a volume. *The People's Pocket Story Books* were only threepence each, and the series contained many of the early exploits of the celebrated *Nick Carter,* a detective who later gave his name to a weekly magazine and ran *Sexton Blake* † close for the blue ribbon of the popular priced field. Nor was the Aldine Publishing Company left behind: in May, 1899, the titles in its series of Detective Tales (twopence each) had reached 256, and it numbered on its staff Detectives Thrash and Pulcher, Harry Hunter the Bootblack Detective, and Daisy Bell, the Pavement Detective.

Turning to the more literary type of detective story, we find, as is natural, that fewer names have been overlooked by the historians, anyway before 1890, when the success of Holmes began seriously to affect output. *The Disappearance of Jeremiah Redworth* by Mrs. J. H. Riddell, shows some interesting features for its early date (Routledge, [1878], pictorial wrappers), but it is much inferior to *Fort Minster, M.P., A Westminster Mystery* by Sir Edward J. Reed (Bristol, Arrowsmith, 1885, printed wrappers), in which the detective, Strange, gives a very capable performance. There are, moreover, in *Almack the Detective,* by E. H. Cragg ([The London Literary Society, 1886]), some remarkably early applications of scientific processes to detection, including deductions from blood corpuscles and microscopic photographs of the corpse's eyes, showing a blurred reflection of the murderer's face. H. F. Wood's *The Passenger from Scotland Yard* and *The Englishman of the Rue*

---

* In such books as *Masterpieces of Crime,* by A. van Dam (Eden, Remington & Co., 1892, printed boards).

† Sexton Blake is the eponymous hero of what became a large syndicate of detective authors. The significance of the cycle is discussed by Miss Sayers (*op. cit.,* p. 16)

Cain * deserve to be noticed, as also does *The Queen Anne's Gate Mystery* † by Richard Arkwright, if only for its modern-sounding title. "Dick Donovan" (Joyce Emmerson Muddock) is a much more considerable figure. Cast often in the form of the Waters-Martel "Reminiscences," his numerous books show a high level of competence, and they were extremely successful. *The Man-Hunter* (1888), *Caught at Last* (1889), *Tracked and Taken* (1890) were all published by Chatto & Windus, simultaneously in picture boards and in cloth. *The Man from Manchester* (1890) is a full-length novel, but in *Link by Link* (1893) Donovan returned to short stories.‡ Milton Danvers produced a number of rather sensational stories during the 'nineties, published in pictorial boards or wrappers by Diprose & Bateman,§ and the work of such detectives as John Pym ‖ and Michael Dred,¶ though derivative, is by no means contemptible. Max Pemberton †† and B. L. Farjeon ‡‡ both turned momentarily from other fields to the detective story, and Milne's *Express Series* included some examples §§ good enough to make one wish it had had a longer life.

The work of Richard Marsh is more interesting, and in *The Datchet Diamonds,*‖ ‖ *The Crime and the Criminal* ¶¶ and other books his touch is as effective in detection as it is in that remarkable horror-story, *The Beetle,* on which his fame to-day is based. Headon

---

* Both published by Chatto & Windus; the second in 1889, the first in February, 1888, of which I have only seen the second edition, published in September of the same year. This is a full-blooded yellow-back in style, though the basic colour is in fact white.

† Two vols. F. V. White, 1889.

‡ Other books by Donovan are: *A Detective's Triumph*, 1891, picture boards; *Dark Deeds*, 1895; *The Mystery of Jamaica Terrace*, 1896; *The Records of Vincent Trill*, 1899—all published by Chatto & Windus.

§ *E.g., The Doctor's Crime, or Simply Horrible* (1891).

‖ *The Investigations of John Pym*, by David Christie Murray (F. V. White, 1895).

¶ *Michael Dred, Detective*, by Marie Connor Leighton and Robert Leighton (Grant Richards, 1899).

†† *Jewel Mysteries I Have Known* (Ward, Lock & Bowden, 1893).

‡‡ *Samuel Boyd of Catchpole Square* (Hutchinson, 1899), etc.

§§ *The Rome Express*, by Major Arthur Griffiths (1896); *The Ivory Queen*, by Norman Hurst (1899). In each case the first issue is scarlet cloth, g.t., later issues in picture boards.

‖ ‖ Ward, Lock & Co. (1898). It is possible that the issue of this book in (*a*) red cloth, uncut, and (*b*) picture boards, cloth back, cut edges, were simultaneous; but if there is any priority the usual practice of Ward, Lock ·at this time argues in favour of (*a*).

¶¶ Ward, Lock & Co. (1897).

Hill, too, ill deserves his oblivion: *Clues from a Detective's Camera* (Bristol, Arrowsmith, [1893], printed wrappers) and *Zambra the Detective* (Chatto & Windus, 1894) were followed by a number of other competently written stories.*

There are innumerable lesser names, and it must suffice here to pick out half a dozen or so for mention. George R. Sims is chiefly remembered for *The Dagonet Ballads*, but he also wrote two detective books, *The Case of George Candlemas* (Chatto & Windus, 1899, pictorial wrappers) and *Dorcas Dene, Detective* (F. V. White, 1897, issued simultaneously in pictorial wrappers and in cloth). M. McDonnell Bodkin, Q.C., was responsible for *Paul Beck, the Rule of Thumb Detective*,† and also for another lady detective, Dora Myrl.‡ G. W. Appleton,§ E. W. Hornung, the creator of Raffles,|| Burford Delannoy,¶ A. C. Fox Davies,†† the authority on heraldry, Jacques Futrelle,‡‡ Major Griffiths, Arthur W. Marchmont §§ all contributed work of merit; and one author, T. W. Hanshew, earns a niche apart as having written several detective novels || || in the style of Amanda McKittrick Ros, with results which have to be read to be believed. Finally, a tribute must be paid to a remarkable and inexplicably neglected book, *Thrilling Stories of the Railway* (Pearson, 1912, pictorial wrappers) by Victor L. White-

---

* *E.g., Guilty Gold* (Pearson, 1896); *Tracked Down* (Pearson, 1902); *Her Grace at Bay* (Cassell, 1906); *Links in the Chain* (Long, 1909); *The Comlyn Alibi* (Ward, Lock, 1916).

† Pearson, 1898. This was followed by *The Quests* and *The Capture of Paul Beck*, published by Fisher Unwin in 1908 and 1909 respectively.

‡ Chatto & Windus (1900). Lady detectives are uncommon and, on the whole, undistinguished. Other examples are found in Wilkie Collins' *No Name* (three vols., Sampson Low, 1862) and *The Law and the Lady* (three vols., Chatto & Windus, 1875); Baroness Orczy's *Lady Molly of Scotland Yard* (Cassell, 1910); and a curious American work, *Clarice Dyke the Female Detective,* of which I have only seen the re-issue of 1883. Some others are listed by Miss Sayers (*op. cit.,* p. 15).

§ *François the Valet* (Pearson, 1899); *The Silent Passenger* (Long, 1906).

|| *The Shadow of the Rope* (Chatto & Windus, 1902).

¶ *The Margate Murder Mystery* (Ward, Lock, 1902).

†† *The Dangerville Inheritance* and *The Mauleverer Murders,* both published by Lane in 1907.

‡‡ *The Thinking Machine* (Chapman & Hall, 1907); *The Professor on the Case* (Nelson, 1909); *The Master Hand* (Hodder & Stoughton, 1914).

§§ *A Millionaire Girl* (Cassell, 1908); *The Eagrave Square Mystery* (Hodder & Stoughton, 1912).

|| || *The Mallison Mystery* (Ward, Lock, 1903); *The Man of the Forty Faces* (Cassell, 1910).

church, who has recently come into his own with *Shot on the Downs* * and other detective stories.

RARITIES AND POINTS

It remains finally to consider two aspects of the subject which are particularly pertinent to the actual collecting of the detective fiction: bibliographical points and relative scarcities; and in the present immature stage of this branch of collecting activity such remarks as can be offered must necessarily be tentative in character.

There is, of course, no need to emphasise the rarity of some of the more important material. The collector will be fortunate if he can secure the corner-stones—Poe's *Tales,*† *The Moonstone, A Study in Scarlet,*‡ *The Leavenworth Case, The Mystery of a Hansom Cab, The Red Thumb Mark, The Cask* and so on—without a very considerable expenditure of patience; and the first three will cost him money into the bargain. As with other forms of collecting, it will be found that the first book of any author is nearly always hard to come by, and the perishable format in which so many of the most covetable detective items first appeared ensures them a permanent standard of scarcity in any sort of decent condition. The yellow-backs, for instance, are practically impossible in fine original state and extremely uncommon even re-bound; the same applies to the first English editions of Gaboriau (Boisgobey is comparatively common), and here the situation is complicated further by the difficulty of establishing the dates of the first Vizetelly editions with any certainty. Reprints are often undifferentiated except (in some cases) by date, and the information supplied by *The English Catalogue* is vague. All the early Humes and Donovans are conspicuously scarce; the Martin Hewitt books are not common,

---

* Fisher Unwin, 1927.

† For the bibliographical details, see *The Bibliography of Edgar Allan Poe,* by Charles Heartman and Kenneth Rede (Metuchen, New Jersey, 1932).

‡ This first appeared in *Beeton's Christmas Annual* for 1887, and although it is the principal item in the issue it is accompanied by several other stories. The first book edition was published by Ward, Lock in 1888 (wrappers). Both forms are very rare. *The Sign of the Four,* the second Holmes story, first appeared in *Lippincott's Magazine* (February 1890) and afterwards in book form as *The Sign of Four* from Spencer Blackett in 1890. Of the other Holmes books, *The Adventures* (Newnes, 1892) is commonly found in very poor state, while *The Return* (Newnes, 1905) is actually rarer than either *The Adventures* or *The Memoirs* (Newnes, 1894).

and the early Thorndykes worse. Most of the obscurer books are probably so difficult to find only because up to now there has not been much demand for them.

The first English editions of Leroux and Leblanc are both scarce and bibliographically complicated. Leroux' *The Mystery of the Yellow Room* was issued as No. 54 of the *Daily Mail Sixpenny Novels* series, with illustrations by Cyrus Cuneo, in [1908]; in the following year a slightly different translation appeared in solid book form from Edward Arnold. Whether the *Daily Mail* edition has points connected with its wrappers or advertisements I do not know; * but it is more than likely, if we may judge from the sequel story, *The Perfume of the Lady in Black*. This was No. 72 of the same series, [1909], and the first issue has yellow ornamental wrappers with a picture by R. Savage in the front centre, printed in blue, while the list of the series on [a]1 verso (facing the half-title) concludes with No. 71. The second issue has a rose-coloured front wrapper with a striking picture of the Lady, in black and white, and the series list goes down to No. 79. As with the parallel cases of many Arrowsmith books of the 'eighties and 'nineties, there are probably further issues, only distinguishable in the same way.

Leblanc is equally difficult. The first Arsène Lupin volume to appear in England was *The Seven of Hearts* (Cassel, 1908) † and beyond its rarity it is not remarkable. The next, however, *Arsène Lupin versus Holmlock Shears* (Grant Richards, 1909) † had originally been entitled *The Fair-Haired Lady,* from the longest story in the book, and at least two copies exist in this suppressed state. The maroon and black bindings are identical except for the lettering, and the same inserted catalogue (Spring, 1908) occurs in both, but for the amended form the prelims [A⁴] were reprinted. The same book was afterwards published under still another title, *The Arrest of Arsène Lupin* (Eveleigh Nash, 1911). Then of 813, *A New Arsène Lupin Adventure,* the first English edition † was published

---

* The only perfect copies I have ever seen had what I take to be the correct advertisements—the list of the series stopping at No. 53.

† It is possible that these were preceded by American editions, though the U.S.A. copyright notices, which in each case give the previous year's date, may of course refer only to serial or magazine publication.

by Mills & Boon in 1910, and usually contains a thirty-two-page inserted catalogue of the same date; but the re-issue of the same sheets in 1913 bears no obvious indication of its status. It has, however, a small panel "Price 6/-" at the foot of the pictorial front cover; * the prelims, [A⁴] have been reprinted, omitting the date; the advertisements on the outside leaves of the first and last signatures differ; and the 1910 catalogue is usually replaced by a 1913 one of the same size.†

CONCLUSION

These observations are based on the experience of only three or four years' serious attention to the collecting of detective fiction, and they are offered, therefore, with proper diffidence. Further attention, and the growth of public demand for the books, will no doubt bring to light many more bibliographical points, and will also probably modify any estimates of relative scarcity. I myself have had the greatest difficulty in running down copies of many *desiderata,* whether among those mentioned in this essay or among the many for which no space could be found here. And although the obscurer authors naturally give the most trouble, it is surprising how elusive several well-known titles by well-known authors have proved to be.

The evolution of a form of literature which is so much a part of our daily life as the detective story is a study as fascinating as it is deserving of serious attention, and from a collector's point of view it has a host of attractive features. The general outline, and the most important books, are fairly well known, but there are infinite opportunities for exploration among the obscurer authors and large tracts of practically virgin country. Detective stories have appeared in every kind of physical form from the full-dress three-volume novel down to the *Detective Supplement* of *The Union Jack,* and the prevalence of boarded or wrapped ephemera among the less literary, and therefore socially and historically more interesting strata, supplies the keenest collector with quarry worthy of his steel.

---

* The original issue had, as a matter of fact, been published at the same price.
† Other early first English editions of this author are *The Crystal Stopper* (1913) and *The Teeth of the Tiger* (1915), both published by Hurst and Blackett.

Finally, pioneer collecting of this kind has one very practical attraction to offer to its devotees. If it is stimulating to be ahead of the historian and the bibliographer, it is satisfactory to all of us, and a *sine qua non* to many of us, to be ahead of the market. In the few instances where the collector of detective fiction as such crosses the path of author collectors—as for instance with Poe, Wilkie Collins and, to a less extent, Conan Doyle—he will, of course, find the prices already up; but over practically all the rest of the field he will find that though these books will cost him time, trouble and sometimes disappointment, they will not make much demand on his purse.

The Detective Short Story: The First Hundred Years

By Ellery Queen

In addition to his other numerous and notable accomplishments, Ellery Queen is the owner of the most complete library of detective short stories in existence and is widely recognized as the foremost authority on that subject. Parenthetically, it may be doubted if any other writer of detective fiction has demonstrated a comparable devotion to his craft and all its lore. The selection which follows is a 1946 revision of the introductory essay to Queen's definitive Centennial anthology, 101 Years' Entertainment: The Great Detective Stories, 1841–1941 *(Boston: Little, Brown, 1941). Here, historically and analytically, is all the general reader will wish to know about the detective short story. The more specialized reader who may wish to pursue the subject bibliographically is referred, without question, to the sole and ultimate authority: Queen's full-size volume* The Detective Short Story: A Bibliography *(Boston: Little, Brown, 1942).*

I. *Prenatal Note*

THE FIRST violent crime of literature was a murder, complete with victim, criminal, motive, and—inferentially—weapon; for although Chapter 4 of Genesis merely remarks: "Cain rose up against Abel his brother, and slew him," we may assume the instrument to have been a forked-stick plow, or a primitive hoe, since it came to pass "when they were in the field," and Cain, as everyone knows, was "a tiller of the ground."

This historic fratricide nevertheless cannot be said to have initi-

476

ated the literature of detection for the profound reason that the case lacked the essential element—a detective. And while the bloody corpse of history swarms with homicides and inferior crimes, and literature has fattened on the pleasant details, the simple fact is that the detective story had to wait upon the detective, and the detective—as we know him today—did not make his début on the human scene until A.D. 1829, when Sir Robert Peel created the first official police force in London. After all, literature follows man like a dog, and in this connection man has lagged badly.

A round dozen years after the first bobby, the young editor of a Philadelphia magazine, *Graham's*, while pondering the problems of circulation, wrote a new kind of tale and inserted it—we may suppose with the twin-barreled anxiety of author and editor—into one of his issues. Mark well the date—April, 1841—for upon this date the first detective story the world had ever known was thrust before its astonished nose.

Many editors since have found that Edgar Allan Poe, in this as in peculiarly literary matters, was a gentleman of prescience. For detective stories have saved many a bashful journal from oblivion, and to say that they have given joy and surcease to multitudinous millions for three long generations would be merely to repeat a point grown dull with repetition.

II. *The First Hundred Years*

Modern readers tend to think of "detective stories" as novels, and admittedly the novels are numberless. But the original, the "legitimate," form was the short story. The detective novel is a short story inflated by characterization and description and romantic nonsense, too often for purposes of padding, and adds only one innovation to the short-story form: the byplot, or red herring, which when badly used serves only to irritate when it is meant to confuse. Poe published the world's first detective short story in 1841, but what is generally considered the world's first detective novel—Gaboriau's *L'Affaire Lerouge*—did not appear in *Le Pays* until 1866, twenty-five years after "The Murders in the Rue Morgue."

Notwithstanding the pristine purity of the short form, there has been a deplorable tendency among many prominent authors of detective fiction to avoid it. Whether this is because in the 20th Century the publication of detective short stories has proved commercially unprofitable or for some less worthy reason, the fact remains that no short story exists at the time of this writing which involves Detectives Charlie Chan (Earl Derr Biggers), Nero Wolfe (Rex Stout), Nick Charles (Dashiell Hammett), Perry Mason (Erle Stanley Gardner), or Philo Vance (S. S. Van Dine).

For that matter there are other, equally important, detectives of fiction whose short-story exploits are so few as to escape all but the keenest-eyed enthusiast. John Rhode's Dr. Priestley appears in only two short stories, "The Elusive Bullet" and "The Vanishing Diamond." A. E. W. Mason's Hanaud appears in only one, "The Affair at the Semiramis Hotel"; Anthony Berkeley's Roger Sheringham in four, "The Avenging Chance," "White Butterfly," "The Wrong Jar," and "Mr. Bearstowe Says" (the last in *Ellery Queen's Mystery Magazine,* issue of July, 1945); John Dickson Carr's Dr. Fell in four, "The Wrong Problem," "The Proverbial Murder," "The Locked Room," and "A Guest in the House"; Anthony Abbot's Thatcher Colt in two, "About the Disappearance of Agatha King" and "About the Perfect Crime of Mr. Digberry"; and David Frome's Mr. Pinkerton in one, "Policeman's Cape."

But if the aforementioned worthies have been remiss, certainly others have not; and *101 Years' Entertainment* is dedicated to those others. The stories in *101 Years' Entertainment* are not necessarily "the best"; perfection is a matter of individual judgment, and it would be presumptuous of us to attempt to canonize for posterity our betters.

But we *can* paint a whole picture of what the First Hundred Years have brought forth by reprinting stories old, derivative, not so old, recent, and new; representative stories; interesting stories; unusual stories; the classic greats as well as tales which to the average reader—indeed, to many an expert—are unknown. For we have kept an eye cocked for that four-leaf clover which is the object of all who browse in the green pastures of literary research—the "discovery," the story overlooked by other anthologists. Of such we have been fortunate to detect a surprising number; and they are here, in *101 Years' Entertainment,* for your delight. Most readers know "The Purloined Letter" of Poe, "The Absent-Minded Coterie" of Robert Barr, and "The Cyprian Bees" of Anthony Wynne; but how many know Inspector Barraclough and "The Pink Edge," or that fascinating female Gwynn Leith in "The Mackenzie Case" of Viola Brothers Shore, or "The Two Bottles of Relish," by Lord Dunsany, in which an astounding deduction is made by a gentleman named Linley—a deduction which, if it were the only one he ever made (as happens to be the case), would give him automatic citizenship in the Eternal City of the élite?

For the rest, we give you joy of Doyle's incomparable Sherlock Holmes; that hero of your boyhood, Nick Carter; that most durable of Sherlockian imitators, Arthur Morrison's Martin Hewitt; scholarly Dr. Thorndyke of R. Austin Freeman; that humble little genius of the cloth, Father Brown, invented by the master of paradox, Gilbert K. Chesterton; Melville Davisson Post's stalwart, religious, early-American Uncle Abner; Ernest Bramah's blind sleuth, Max Carrados; Agatha Christie's conceited and delightful exponent of the little gray cells, M. Hercule Poirot; H. C. Bailey's mourning, moaning, indefatigable Mr. Fortune; Dorothy L. Sayers's dilettante Lord Peter Wimsey; and E. C. Bentley's Philip Trent of *Trent's Last Case* renown.

Nor will you take less joy in these less advertised but no less brilliant lights: M. P. Shiel's Prince Zaleski; Samuel Hopkins Adams's Average Jones; Ronald A. Knox's Miles Bredon; Margery Allingham's Albert Campion; Dashiell Hammett's Sam Spade; Pulitzer-Prizewinner T. S. Stribling's Professor Poggioli; Carter Dickson's Colonel March—among many others known and unknown to the connoisseur of the detective short story.

III. *Sources and Classifications*

What have the First Hundred Years of the detective-crime short story produced? Let us examine the record.

The two principal sources of the detective-crime short story for student and lay reader are: periodicals and books. On the number of such tales published in magazines and newspapers since 1841, no statistics are available; but certainly their total must run into astronomical figures. All slick-paper popular magazines at one time or another publish detective-crime stories; and among the so-called "pulps" of America and England there have been hundreds of parti-colored publications dedicated vigorously to this brand of fiction. See your nearest kiosk.

As a rule, the best magazine stories eventually achieve book publication. This natural winnowing process has been a boon to enthusiasts, who may read in one volume the grist of scores of scattered and heterogeneous periodicals. Of course, not all the worthy stories find a home between hard covers; magazines do yield nuggets of gold if only one digs hard and deep enough. We unearthed Dashiell Hammett's "A Man Called Spade" in *American Magazine,* Miss Shore's "The Mackenzie Case" in a long-deceased magazine named *Mystery League,* T. S. Stribling's "The Resurrection of Chin Lee" in that admirable pulp, *Adventure,* Octavus Roy Cohen's "The Mystery of the Missing Wash" in *Saturday Evening Post,* and Pearl S. Buck's "Ransom" in *Cosmopolitan.* But these are exceptions. The point to bear in mind is that, for convenience and quality, books remain the chief source of the detective-crime short story.

The volumes in which such tales have been collected may be divided into seven groups: (a) The short stories of "pure" detection; (b) books containing tales of mixed types; (c) books of crook short stories; (d) parodies and pastiches of Sherlock Holmes; (e) pseudo-real life tales; (f) secret service stories; and (g) anthologies.

IV. *The Short Story of "Pure" Detection*

Considering the virulence of the literary bug and its affinity for all manner of hosts, the first century since Poe has produced a remarkably small number of books of detective short stories. One reason for this we have already mentioned: even detective-story writers must live, and such books do not sell. It is interesting in this connection to note the extremes to which some authors (or their publishers) have resorted to keep from their innocent patrons, in whom this prejudice against volumes of short stories generally persists, the fact that a given book *is* a book of short stories. The favorite device is to disguise the book as a novel. This feat of publishing magic is achieved by editorial and typographic legerdemain —dividing the book into "chapters" instead of candidly separate stories. Such business psychology no doubt dictated the interior format of, among many others, Robert Barr's *The Triumphs of Eugène Valmont* (1906), Jacques Futrelle's *The Thinking Machine on the Case* (1908), Baroness Orczy's *The Old Man in the Corner* (1909), T. W. Hanshew's *Cleek, the Man of the Forty Faces* (1910), Melville Davisson Post's *The Nameless Thing* (1912), and Herbert Jenkins's *Malcolm Sage, Detective* (1921).

The last word in this bibliodeception is illustrated by M. Mc-Donnell Bodkin's *Young Beck*, a very scarce book published in 1911 by T. Fisher Unwin of London. Typographically, this book was also set up to look like a novel; not only was it divided into chapters, with individual chapter-titles, but it was also divided into parts—Part I, Part II, and Part III. The truth is, however, the book consists of twelve separate and distinct short stories, each composed of two chapters, and with no inter-relationship of plot. The height of the deception was reached in the eighth story: the first half of this story is the last "chapter" of Part II, and the second half of the story is the first "chapter" of Part III!

If the number of books of detective short stories of all types is surprisingly small, the number of those of the "pure" detection type is amazingly so. Only 347 known titles of this type exist, breaking down into three classifications: (1) 305 about male detectives, like Sherlock Holmes, Father Brown, Mr. Fortune; (2) 35 about female detectives—from C. L. Pirkis's Loveday Brooke (1894) and George R. Sims's Dorcas Dene (1897) to the more modern Mme. Storey (1926) of Hulbert Footner, Mignon Eberhart's Susan Dare (1934), and the Coles' Mrs. Warrender (1939); and (3) 7 about boy detectives. Five of these last concern the adventures in detection of young P. J. Davenant written by Lord Frederic Hamilton; the other two are *The Adventures of Detective Barney* by Harvey J. O'Higgins and *Bang! Bang!* by George Ade, about Eddie Parks, the Newsboy Detective.

Of the 347 volumes of stories of "pure" detection, 56 are the work of only 5 authors! These fertile scriveners are Dick Donovan (believe it or not, once an immensely popular writer—his real name was Joyce Emmerson Muddock); Gilbert K. Chesterton, who created not only Father Brown but also Horne Fisher, Mr. Pond, and Gabriel Gale; Arthur B. Reeve, creator of Craig Kennedy and Constance Dunlap; Agatha Christie; and H. C. Bailey. This leaves a mere 291 books of "pure" detective short stories written by all the rest of mankind since 1841! And many of these 291 volumes are so scarce today as to be virtually unobtainable—such rarities as Headon Hill's *Zambra the Detective* (1894); David Christie Murray's *The Investigations of John Pym* (1895); H. Frankish's *Dr. Cunliffe, Investigator* (1902); Duncan Dallas's *Paul Richards, Detective* (1908); Victor Whitechurch's *Thrilling Stories of the Railway* (1912), about Thorpe Hazell, detective; Cecil Henry Bullivant's *Garnett Bell, Detective* (1920); Scott Campbell's paperbacks about Detective Felix Boyd; and numerous others.

V. *The Books of "Mixed Types"*

To add to the labors of the research worker, many books exist whose stories are not exclusively devoted to the adventures of a single detective. In such collections of stories a tale of "pure" detection may be smothered under a haystack of straight mystery stories, or stories of crime-*sans*-detection. Such a heterogeneous volume is Anna Katharine Green's *Masterpieces of Mystery* (1913) —surely the publisher's title, which he regretted, for six years later it was reissued under the new title *Room Number 3.* J. S. Fletcher is the author of many such: *The Secret of the Barbican* (1924), *The Malachite Jar* (1930), etc. Prolific as he was, Fletcher produced only two volumes of stories of "pure" detection: *The Adventures of Archer Dawe, Sleuth-Hound* (1909) and *Paul Campenhaye: Specialist in Criminology* (1918). The books of William LeQueux often concern a single central character (as *In Secret,* 1920; *Bleke the Butler,* 1923; and others) but the tales are nonetheless of the mixed type—some detection, some mystery, some crime, and some out-and-out adventure.*

There are 350 titles in this "mixed-type" group. It should be noted that this figure does not include all the E. Phillips Oppen-

---

* The most important exception is LeQueux's *Mysteries of a Great City* (1919) which are the reminiscences of M. Raoul Becq, *ex-sous-chef* of the Sûreté Générale of Paris, consistently tales of "pure" detection.

heim's books of short stories, which alone number 38. Most of these are not properly books of detection or crime, being of the adventure-spy-international-intrigue school. Oddly enough, for all his literary virility Oppenheim has fathered few books of "pure" detection: such works as *The Hon. Algernon Knox, Detective* (1920); *Nicholas Goade, Detective* (1927); and *Slane's Long Shots* (1930) are almost lost in the crowd.

Even more exasperating to the bibliophilous Nimrod (and, by the identical token, upon discovery more satisfying) is the occasional publication of a volume of short stories by an author distinguished in a field of writing other than detection-crime. Here the ardent explorer may be pardoned if his foot slips, for who would normally associate W. W. Jacobs with detective tales, or Aldous Huxley, or Ben Hecht, or W. Somerset Maugham? Yet these literary respectables are merely a few who have composed stories of detection-crime. Jacobs has at least two in his *The Lady of the Barge* (1902). Huxley has one, the unforgettable "The Gioconda Smile," in *Mortal Coils* (1922). Ben Hecht succumbed to the virus in his book, *The Champion From Far Away* (1931); he is also the author of a detective story, "The Mystery of the Fabulous Laundryman," included with three other murder stories in *Actor's Blood* (1936). And W. Somerset Maugham has a story called "Footprints in the Jungle," in *Ah King* (1933), which any self-respecting hunter must include in his bag.

Other celebrities of letters who have strayed from their customary habitat into the enchanted land are Owen Johnson in his volume, *Murder in Any Degree* (1913), one story in which, "One Hundred in the Dark," is especially notable; Stacy Aumonier in *Miss Bracegirdle and Others* (1923), which contains at least one superb tale, "Miss Bracegirdle Does Her Duty"; Wilbur Daniel Steele in *The Man Who Saw Through Heaven* (1927) and *Tower of Sand* (1929), containing respectively those brilliant stories, "Blue Murder" and "Footfalls"; Arnold Bennett in *The Night Visitor* (1931), with its unusual tale, "Murder"; and Christopher Morley whose detective, Dove Dulcet, is to be found in three stories in *Tales From a Rolltop Desk* (1921). Famous literary figures who also "stooped to conquer" include Nathaniel Hawthorne, Charles Dickens (we recommend "Hunted Down"), Thomas Hardy, Mark

Twain (particularly "The Stolen White Elephant"), Robert Louis Stevenson, Anton Chekhov, and Rudyard Kipling.

From the obscure dossier of authors not usually linked with mystery and crime writings, we have reprinted in *101 Years' Entertainment* tales by these other illustrious culprits: Irvin S. Cobb, Thomas Burke, F. Tennyson Jesse, Hugh Walpole, and Pearl S. Buck. There are one or two further surprises. Mary Roberts Rinehart has written many mystery stories, but who would dream of Tish as a sleuth? Yet the ineffable Tish is here in all her blithesome glory! As is Florian Slappey, that dark harlequin of Birmingham, in a comic-detective story by Octavus Roy Cohen (whose fat, gold-toothpick-wielding Jim Hanvey might have done a more workmanlike detecting job than Florian, but surely would not have executed it with such rapierlike élan).

VI. *The Crooks*

The names Raffles and Arsène Lupin are so universally familiar that one would think the bound literature of crooks-in-short-stories to be a vast continent for exploration. Curiously enough, there are a mere 100 different book titles—in one hundred years! These sing the roguish escapades of E. W. Hornung's Raffles; Maurice Leblanc's Arsène Lupin; and Leslie Charteris's Simon Templar, alias the Saint—to mention the best-known. They also include certain lesser luminaries who nevertheless have shed a scoundrelly fame: Frederick Irving Anderson's The Infallible Godahl; Bruce Graeme's Blackshirt; Frank Heller's Mr. Philip Collin; Harry Stephen Keeler's DeLancey, King of Thieves; Frank L. Packard's Jimmie Dale, alias the Gray Seal; E. Phillips Oppenheim's Michael Sayers; Bertram Atkey's Smiler Bunn; Peter Cheyney's Alonzo Mac-Tavish; Rupert Hughes's Dirk Memling; Herman Landon's Elusive Picaroon, Martin Dale; May Edginton's Napoleon Prince; and Sax Rohmer's Séverac Bablon. And you, O student, might do worse than to investigate the assorted sculduggeries of this obscure trio: Barry Pain's Constantine Dix (1905), A. C. Fox-Davies's Sir John Kynnersley (1908), and Edgar Wallace's Anthony Newton . . . What—have we neglected Grant Allen's Colonel Clay? Inexcusable omission! For surely you recall—if you are old enough—that engaging rapscallion. The Colonel beat Raffles to it by two years!

But come. Surely the ladies have amassed sufficient loot to merit inclusion in books of short stories? They have, and their small number is no reflection on their burglarious daring. These lovely creatures of sin include: Mrs. Raffles (1905), who stalks through the book of short stories of that name by John Kendrick Bangs, and who never tackled a "job" for less than millions; of course, this is parody typically Bangsian. Then there are Frederick Irving Anderson's *The Notorious Sophie Lang* (1925) who lives in that single volume of stories and, more recently, has been resurrected in motion pictures; Edgar Wallace's *Four Square Jane* (1929); and Roy Vickers's *The Exploits of Fidelity Dove* (1935).

VII. *Parodies and Pastiches of Holmes*

A parody is a burlesque imitating some serious work; a pastiche is usually a serious imitation in the exact manner of the original author. Only the illustrious call forth such passionate homage; and in the literature of detection who is more illustrious, as a character and a catholic institution, than Sherlock Holmes?

The parodies of Holmes far exceed the pastiches, which are rare. John Kendrick Bangs did lusty work in Sherlockian parody. Stories of this type may be found in these Bangs volumes: *The Pursuit of the House-Boat* (1897), *The Dreamers: a Club* (1899), *The Enchanted Type-Writer* (1899), and *Potted Fiction* (1908). In 1903 Bangs wrote a series of Holmes parodies for newspapers which he called "Shylock Homes: His Posthumous Memoirs"; these were never assembled between boards; and in 1906, trifling with genetics, he created Raffles Holmes, the "son" of Sherlock Holmes and the "grandson" of A. J. Raffles, whose merry exploits were assembled under the title *R. Holmes & Co.*

Robert Barr wrote about Sherlaw Kombs in his story, "The Great Pegram Mystery" (from the book *The Face and the Mask*, 1895)— Barr, you will recall, was the creator of Eugène Valmont who, alas, has been parodied by no one. Bret Harte came up with Hemlock Jones in "The Stolen Cigar Case" (from *Condensed Novels, 2nd Series*, 1902). Maurice Leblanc, Gallically testing the commercial possibilities of a marriage of immovable detection and irresistible thievery, composed "Holmlock Shears Arrives Too Late," which comes from the volume *The Exploits of Arsène Lupin* (1907), in which Lupin and Holmes clashed and—this was courteous of Leblanc—wound up in a pretty stalemate. Stephen Leacock, refusing to tamper with the master's Doyle-given name and calling him simply The Great Detective, parodied Holmes in "Maddened by Mystery: or, The Defective Detective," which you will find in Mr. Leacock's *Nonsense Novels* (1911). O. Henry labored to conceive Shamrock Jolnes—an appealing abortion!—in the tales "The Sleuths" and "The Adventures of Shamrock Jolnes," to be found in the otherwise respectable *Sixes and Sevens* (1911). But for sheer stupendous imagination we have always bowed in admiration before the appellative genius of R. C. Lehmann, who gave us *The Adventures of Picklock Holes* (1901).

The pastiche, whose intent is serious, and the fashioning of which requires immense knowledge, discrimination, and courage, is necessarily a rare literary form. The best pastiche of Sherlock Holmes is Vincent Starrett's *The Unique Hamlet* (1920). William O. Fuller's *A Night With Sherlock Holmes* (1929) also merits your respectful attention. Other parodies and imitations include Carolyn Wells's "The Adventure of the Clothes-Line"; A. B. Cox's (Anthony Berkeley's) "Holmes and the Dasher"; Stuart Palmer's "The Adventure of the Remarkable Worm"; Sir James M. Barrie's "The Adventure of the Two Collaborators"; Mark Twain's *A Double-Barrelled Detective Story;* Logan Clendening's "The Case of the Missing Patriarchs"; August Derleth's "The Adventure of the Norcross Riddle" (about Solar Pons)—all to be found, with a complete history of the Holmesian take-off, among the 33 stories that make up our Sherlockian anthology, *The Misadventures of Sherlock Holmes* (1944).

VIII. *Pseudo-Real Life Stories*

Between 1856 and 1890 detective-crime literature suffered an epidemic of "realism." People became interested in crimes that actually happened and detectives who existed in three-dimensional form; so a gout of books gushed forth from the presses, professing to be the memoirs of this police officer or that, many of which were fiction concocted by professional writers; and fact and fiction were so jumbled that today it is difficult to differentiate one from the other. It is hardly necessary to add that most of these "diaries," "reminiscences," "memoirs," and "revelations" of supposedly real-life policemen were purest balderdash, and consequently few of them survive; in their original paperback state they are rare.

The survivors include the work of "Waters" (William Russell) —*Recollections of a Detective Police-Officer* (1856 and 1859); Charles Martel's (Thomas Delf) *The Detective's Note-Book* (1860); Lieut.-Col. H. R. Addison's *Diary of a Judge* (1860); James M'Levy's *Curiosities of Crime in Edinburgh* (1861); M. Canler's *Autobiography of a French Detective* (1863); Andrew Forrester Jr.'s *The Revelations of a Private Detective* (1863); Alfred Hughes's *Leaves from the Note-Book of a Chief of Police* (1864); James M'Govan's *Brought to Bay* (1878); William Henderson's *Clues, or Leaves from a Chief Constable's Note Book* (1889); Inspector Maurice Moser's *Stories from Scotland Yard* (1890, in collaboration with Charles F. Rideal).

The editors know of 40 different titles in this group, although at the present writing, and after continuous bloodhound trailing, possess copies of only 22.*

You are not to confuse the above-mentioned group with Allan Pinkerton's legitimate memoirs in *Thirty Years a Detective* (1884) and Arthur Train's (creator of Mr. Tutt) in *True Stories of Crime* (1908), among many others, including the famous Major Arthur Griffiths's *Mysteries of Police and Crime* (1898) and even *Mémoires de Vidocq* (1828–1829). These are the true constellations, and do not come within our orbit, which is thick with the planetary bodies of fiction.

IX. *Secret Service Stories*

Among the 1000-odd books which represent the entire publishing output of detective-crime short stories in the first one hundred

---

* Exclusive of "pseudo-real life" books, the Ellery Queen library of detective-crime short story volumes is at this writing 90% complete. But for research purposes connected with *101 Years' Entertainment* we had access to most of the volumes missing from the Queen collection, thanks chiefly to E. T. (Ned) Guymon Jr. of San Diego, California, who possesses the largest library of mystery fiction (in total number of volumes) in the world.

years, only a handful, surprisingly enough, are devoted exclusively to the machinations of secret service agents. Of course many of the demi-detectives created by E. Phillips Oppenheim, William LeQueux, and Sax Rohmer flirt constantly with international intrigue, but few of their books deal wholly with diplomatic sculduggery; and occasionally one of the great manhunters of fiction takes a fling at counter-espionage—Sherlock Holmes, for example, in "The Adventure of the Bruce-Partington Plans" and "His Last Bow"—but these are random shots in otherwise stately, if not affairs-of-stately, careers.

Perhaps the finest of all English books of secret service stories is W. Somerset Maugham's *Ashenden, or the British Agent* (1928). Here the emphasis is not on plot, in the usual blood-and-thunder sense; Maugham is too crafty a craftsman to subordinate the higher virtues of compelling realism and depth of characterization to tricks and counter-tricks. Much closer, however, to the conventional conception of secret agents are the exploits of William Dawson in *The Lost Naval Papers* (1917), by Bennet Copplestone; *The Adventures of Heine* (1919), by Edgar Wallace; and the secret service tales in Valentine Williams's *The Knife Behind the Curtain* (1930). Even the English boy-detective has taken a whack at the insidious and sinister spy—witness the two books about P.J., the Secret Service Boy (1922–1923), by Lord Frederic Hamilton; P.J. is, of course, young Philip John Davenant. And if memory serves, Headon Hill's Sebastian Zambra saves Britain from a fate worse than death in one of the stories that make up *Cabinet Secrets* (1893). Thus, from Ashenden to Zambra . . .

In America, the secret service sleuths include George Bronson-Howard's Yorke Norroy in *Norroy, Diplomatic Agent* (1907), *Slaves of the Lamp* (1917), and *The Black Book* (1920)—Norroy derives from the Graustarkian school of diplomatic detectives; Clarence Herbert New's Lord Trevor (an American despite his title) in *The Unseen Hand* (1918); R. T. M. Scott's *Secret Service Smith* (1923), first name Aurelius; and Melville Davisson Post's *Walker of the Secret Service* (1924). There are others, on both sides of the Atlantic, but not enough to fill a five-foot shelf.

X. *Anthologies*

It goes without saying that where joy is truly precious, it begs to be communicated; and so it is not wonderful that detective-story anthologies should spring up and multiply like unregimented rabbits. The number of anthologies is relatively high—135 known volumes, and at least half a dozen more in preparation (being edited by Lee Wright, Howard Haycraft, ourselves, and others).

The earliest legitimate anthology was published by Chapman & Hall in London in 1895. It was called *The Long Arm & Other Detective Stories;* Mary E. Wilkins (Freeman) contributed "The Long Arm" and George Ira Brett (later known as Oswald Crawfurd), Roy Tellet, and Professor Brander Matthews contributed the "Others." This pioneer work was followed (circa 1897) by the paperback *Diprose's Annuals* which technically are anthologies because they contain some mystery-crime short stories by a variety of authors. The first American anthology did not appear until 1906: Vol. I (called *Detective Stories*) in the 3-volume set entitled *Great Short Stories,* edited by William Patten. Perhaps the first specialized anthology was *Twenty-Five Tales of the Railway* (Newnes, 1909), stories of crime, adventure, and detectives, but all on railway themes. A great many of the 135 known anthologies were published in England only; because of the war they are now virtually impossible to procure.

It is not remarkable that detective-story writers themselves should be prominent among the anthologists. For one thing, the writer in this field who has made his mark is generally infected with a pride of profession and an irresistible desire to build a better anthology —"a truly *definitive* job, you know!"—than anyone living or dead. For another, it is the only certain method of immortalizing one of one's own stories. At any rate, we have had numerous professional anthologists, among them Carolyn Wells, S. S. Van Dine, Vincent Starrett, Dorothy L. Sayers, Ronald A. Knox (with H. Harrington), Dashiell Hammett (more strictly a supernatural anthology), E. C. Bentley, E. Phillips Oppenheim, Raymond Postgate, John Rhode, Peter Cheyney, Anthony Boucher, and (work in progress) John Dickson Carr.

The value of the anthology to both student and lay reader is threefold: (a) It often contains short stories which never saw book publication and are taken directly from periodicals and original manuscripts. (b) It keeps alive the best work of the older authors, whose books have been long out of print and would not therefore be available to present-day readers. (It can be said with exact truth that characters like The Old Man in the Corner and Eugène Valmont owe their continued existence wholly to anthologists.) And (c) it memorializes the best stories of modern authors.

XI. *Apology and Good Wishes*

So there are the statistics of the First Hundred Years of the detective-crime short story. In *101 Years' Entertainment* we have tried to range over as wide a terrain of places, authors, subjects, famous characters, and "discoveries" as possible in commemoration of the centennial event; but of course space limitations have forced us to be cruelly selective, and there are many excellent detectives and samples of their investigations which have had to be omitted. Perhaps a short auxiliary list of authors and titles would, to some degree, make up for these enforced omissions. We especially commend to your attention (if you can find the books!) the following:

Edwin Balmer's and William MacHarg's *The Achievements of Luther Trant* (1910); Trant was the first detective to employ the then-newfangled science of psychology as a method of crime-detection—including the first use in fiction of the "lie-detector," although Craig Kennedy (of Arthur B. Reeve) ran Trant a close second as a scientific psychologist. Francis Lynde's *Scientific Sprague* (1912). Hesketh Prichard's *November Joe* (1913), the only backwoods detective on record, a sort of detecting Leatherstocking. Octavus Roy Cohen's *Jim Hanvey, Detective* (1923). Basil Thomson's *Mr. Pepper, Investigator* (1925), a *rara avis* indeed: the comic detective. Edgar Wallace's *The Orator* (1928), about Chief Inspector O. Rater, a little-known Wallace character and yet, next to Mr. J. G. Reeder, Wallace's best sleuth. Nicholas Olde's *The Incredible Adventures of Rowland Hern* (1928). Harvey J. O'Higgins's *Detective Duff Unravels It* (1929), literature's first approach to a psychoanalytical detective. Percival Wilde's *Rogues In Clover*

(1929), about Bill Parmelee, who specializes in card and gambling mysteries. Henry Wade's *Policeman's Lot* (1933), about Inspector Poole, very Scotland Yard. Kenneth Livingston's *The Dodd Cases* (1934), about Cedric Dodd, a physician-detective. And C. Daly King's *The Curious Mr. Tarrant* (1935), a collection of eight stories and one of the most imaginative books of detective short stories to appear in the last decade.

So here's to crime, to detection—and to the Second Hundred Years!

Readers' Guide to Crime

By James Sandoe *

So much for the professional book-collector and the specialist. For less exacting readers who like to fill their library shelves with tried favorites for fireside rumination, unmindful of edition, condition, or purely historical significance, the list which follows by an outstanding contemporary scholar of The Blood (though compiled originally for college library use) will be a veritable boon.

Your editor owns to three principal reasons for printing Mr. Sandoe's Honor Roll of Crime Fiction: (1) its sound modernity and refreshing iconoclasm both in selection and annotation; (2) the fact that it represents the judgment of not one but several informed and discriminating minds; and (3) the fun of talking back to Mr. Sandoe and his collaborators—an opportunity I know (let's drop the third person for awhile) many fellow addicts will envy, for in no precinct of modern letters are preferences and antipathies more personal or strongly held.

With Mr. Sandoe's main selection of authors, few readers, I believe, will quarrel seriously, nor will many important omissions of individual writers be found (though the absences of R. A. J. Walling, Edgar Wallace, Phoebe Atwood Taylor and her alter ego *Alice Tilton, and Patrick Quentin and his other self Jonathan Stagge, are disturbing and difficult to comprehend). My own disagreements are chiefly with some of the titles chosen. For example, I cannot understand how so perceptive a group of critics could name Raymond Chandler's* The High Window *to the exclusion of his* Farewell My Lovely *(1940), to my mind the finest single performance in the mannered hardboiled division since Hammett. Likewise, I side with those readers who find Eric Ambler's* Journey Into Fear *(1940) preferable to his more highly polished and publicized* Coffin for Dimitrios, *if only for the reason that the peril in the former is*

* Assistant Professor of Bibliography and English Literature, in charge of Order Division, University of Colorado Libraries.

*genuine because inescapable; in the latter, synthetic. I am moved
to a protest of some violence by the choice of Dorothy Hughes' comparatively routine* The Fallen Sparrow, *when the selectors might
have named her first novel* The So Blue Marble *(1940), an unforgettable experience in contemporary sensation fiction. I find, in fact,
a hitherto unsuspected predilection for early efforts: I would include Rex Stout's* Fer de Lance *(1934), the Lockridges'* The Norths
Meet Murder *(1940),* Timothy Fuller's Harvard Has a Homicide
(1936), H. C. Bailey's early Joshua Clunk story The Red Castle
Mystery *(1932), Georgette Heyer's* Merely Murder *(1935), Hilda
Lawrence's* Blood Upon the Snow *(1944), and E. H. Clements'* Let
Him Die *(1939)—all first or early novels—in place of the later (and
in my opinion inferior) titles selected by Mr. Sandoe and his colleagues to represent these authors. . . . I am grateful for the opportunity to amend publicly an earlier judgment of my own with
regard to that highly important Anglo-American writer John Dickson Carr under his two signatures. In a list published some years
ago I chose* The Arabian Nights Murder *to represent Carr and*
The Plague Court Murders *to stand for Carter Dickson. After
careful, and possibly maturer, re-reading I beg to change my vote
to* The Crooked Hinge *(1938) by Carr as imaginatively outstanding
among Dr. Fell's many superlative performances and* The Judas
Window *(1938) by Dickson (included in the Sandoe list) as the
most brilliant of Sir Henry Merrivale's deductive achievements.*

*As Mr. Sandoe has no doubt discovered, the penalty of the un-
restricted bibliography which admits "borderliners" of any kind
to the sacred premises (as contrasted with the limited or "classic"
list) is that once the gates are open it is almost impossible to check
the flood. If* Rogue Male *is included here, why not Ethel Vance's*
Escape *(1939); not to mention Philip MacDonald's fine and too-
little-known pursuit-classic of the same title, published in 1932? If
Graham Greene's suspenseful "entertainments" belong, what about
Helen MacInnes'* Above Suspicion *(1941)? If there is room for*
A Bullet in the Ballet, *why leave out Elliot Paul's comparably
hilarious* Mysterious Micky Finn *(1939) and its vinous progeny?
If the merely historical* Achievements of Luther Trant *is admissi-
ble, how exclude Frederick Irving Anderson's rich and rewarding*
Book of Murder *(1930), or even his early Godahl and Sophie Lang*

crook adventures? If the supernatural overtones of He Arrived at
Dusk *are legitimized, for our purposes, by the novel's strain of
sleuthing, why not stretch the point only a little farther to admit
Henry James'* The Turn of the Screw (*1898*) *and Dorothy Macardle's* The Uninvited (*1942*)? *If Raoul Whitfield comes within the
canon, how deny entry to James M.* Cain with his The Postman
Always Rings Twice (*1934*) *and* Double Indemnity (*1943*)? *And
why, in heaven's name, omit for any reason Daphne Du Maurier's*
Rebecca (*1938*), *one of the indisputable mystery classics of this generation for all that it was accepted by the Philistines as a "novel"?*

*These are details. Mr. Sandoe's list, or so it seems to me, has also
one generic shortcoming: a tendency to minimize the American
medium-to-hard-boiled school of crime writing which, while admittedly beginning to pay the penalty for careless craftsmanship
and excess, has nevertheless done so much to re-vitalize and sustain
the form in the last decade-and-a-half. To remedy this vitamin de-
ficiency, I would salt the list with a few novels of the type and range
of, say, David Dodge's* Death and Taxes (*1941*), *Hugh Pentecost's*
Cancelled in Red (*1939*), *Cleve Adams'* Sabotage (*1940*), *Robert
George Dean's* Murder by Marriage (*1940*), *and/or the reader's
own favorites from the works of such familiars of the "private eye"
as Whitman Chambers, George Harmon Coxe, John Spain, H. C.
Grafton, H. W. Roden, Brett Halliday, and Dana Chambers.*

*In the non-tough or general category, some further authors and
volumes I think might be profitably added to so broadly based a
shelf-list as enjoyable and above-the-average representatives of their
several styles are—strictly at random and as they come to mind:
Clemence Dane and Helen Simpson's* Re-Enter Sir John (*1932*),
Richard Keverne's The Man in the Red Hat (*1930*), *Bernard Capes'*
The Skeleton Key (*1919*), *Katherine Woods'* Murder in a Walled
Town (*1934*), *David Keith's* A Matter of Iodine (*1940*), *Virginia
Perdue's* He Fell Down Dead (*1943*) *or* Alarum and Excursion
(*1944*), *Patrick Quentin's* A Puzzle for Fools (*1936*), *Elizabeth
Dean's* Murder Is a Collector's Item (*1939*), *J. H. Wallis'* Once Off
Guard ("The Woman in the Window") (*1942*), *Theodora Du Bois'*
Death Wears a White Coat (*1938*), *Dorothy Cameron Disney's* The
Balcony (*1940*), *Doris Miles Disney's* Compound for Death (*1943*),
Richard Marsh's The Beetle (*1915*), *Lord Charnwood's* Tracks in

the Snow (*1906*), *of more than historical interest, Valentine Williams'* The Portcullis Room (*1934*), *Margaret Millar's* The Iron Gates (*1945*), *Allan Bosworth's* Full Crash Dive (*1942*), *Anthony Rolls'* A Clerical Error (*1932*), *Virgil Markham's* Death in the Dusk (*1928*), *Vera Caspary's* Laura (*1943*), *E. C. Bentley's* Trent's Own Case (*1936*), *C. H. B. Kitchin's* Death of My Aunt (*1930*), *P. W. Wilson's* Bride's Castle (*1944*), *R. C. Woodthorpe's* Rope for a Convict (*1940*), *Baynard Kendrick's* The Odor of Violets (*1941*), *Samuel Rogers'* Don't Look Behind You! (*1944*), *Phoebe Atwood Taylor's* The Cape Cod Mystery (*1931*), *Alice Tilton's* The Cut Direct (*1938*), *Edgar Wallace's* The Murder Book of J. G. Reeder (*1926*), *R. A. J. Walling's* The Fatal Five Minutes (*1932*), *Jonathan Stagge's* The Stars Spell Death (*1939*), *James Norman's* Murder Chop Chop (*1942*), *Victor Luhrs'* The Longbow Murder (*1941*), *a curiosity, Henry Wade's* The Duke of York's Steps (*1929*), *Rosemary Kutak's* Darkness of Slumber (*1944*), *A. R. Hilliard's* Justice Be Damned (*1941*), *Eden Phillpotts'* The Grey Room (*1921*), *Anne Hocking's* Deadly Is the Evil Tongue (*1940*), *William Gillette's* The Astounding Crime in Torrington Road (*1927*), *and two anthologies for connoisseurs compiled by the membership of the Detection Club of London,* The Floating Admiral (*1932*) *and* Ask a Policeman (*1933*).

But now—at long last!—Mr. Sandoe.

For TWENTY-FIVE years now critics have been defending the detective story as a form against an opposition which, twenty-five years ago, was not very determined and which is now little more than a voiceless superstition. "All professors read detective stories" is a new truism which observation bears out astonishingly. But however many professors read detective stories, few if any university libraries possess any systematic collection of detective fiction.

Public libraries, gauged to meet popular taste, usually have large collections; but even these are not commonly designed to stand except accidentally and temporarily as an historical view of the form. Too, detective stories in public libraries, worn and re-bound and cracked and patched, eventually wear out and few libraries have budgets large enough to replace older detective stories (even the best of them) and keep up with the spate of new ones, good and bad, which must be bought to placate readers. Rental library collections change with each season's new books. Only in a few private collections, not accessible to the general public and not generally accessible to the student, can any systematic survey of the history of the detective story at its best be found.

Now the astonishing bulk of the form (recently one of every four new works of fiction) alone will ultimately necessitate attention, even from that anomaly, the inimical professor, if he is to be a complete scholar. And it is not the bulk of the form nor its wide popularity, but its vigor, its ingenuity and—latterly—its literacy, its curiosity, its deeper interest in character which have won it serious attention and respect as a portion of literature.

With some notion in mind of pointing out a responsibility of university libraries to collect detective stories, I drew up a preliminary list of "tecs" from two earlier and designedly limited bibliographies by Howard Haycraft.* This new list, observing sundry omissions and many additions, was designed to sketch the form's history, but even more to gather its excellencies and its varieties in puzzling, literacy, and vigor. This revised list, submitted to a number of critics, writers, editors, and readers, was subjected to their scrutiny and their often vigorous exclamation, demanding omission or addition. Thus corrected the list was published, under the title "The Detective Story and Academe," in the *Wilson Library Bulletin* for April 1944, where it aroused some interest and comment. It has now been further revised (through 1945) and corrected by the compiler at the suggestion of the editor of the present volume. Bibliographical details have been held to a minimum in the list. Many of the titles it notes are out of print in the original editions but nearly all are pretty easily obtainable at second hand, or—for the private library—in the several series of paperback reprints.

---

* "From Poe to Hammett; a Foundation List of Detective Fiction," in *Wilson Library Bulletin*, February 1938, p. 371–77, and "A Detective Story Bookshelf," Chapter XIV in his *Murder for Pleasure: The Life and Times of the Detective Story*, 1941.

ANTHOLOGIES

Boucher, Anthony, pseud. (White, William A. P.) ed. *Great American Detective Stories* (1945) a fresh and admirable selection, with stimulating notes.

Haworth, Peter, ed. *Before Scotland Yard: Classic Tales of Roguery and Detection, Ranging from the Apochrypha to Charles Dickens* (1927). Vincent Starrett points this out as "an excellent anthology of incunabula."

Queen, Ellery, pseud. (Dannay, Frederic and Lee, Manfred) ed. *101 Years' Entertainment: The Great Detective Stories, 1841–1941*. The best, most comprehensive collection. Starrett would add "all the Queen anthologies as they appear." These include *Challenge to the Reader* (1938) in which twenty-four famous detectives appear with their names altered, the challenge being to identify the detective from his manner and the story's; *Sporting Blood: The Great Sports Detective Stories* (1942), *The Female of the Species: The Great Women Detectives and Criminals* (1943), *The Misadventures of Sherlock Holmes* (1944), and *Rogues' Gallery: The Great Criminals of Modern Fiction* (1945). With these should certainly be noted *Ellery Queen's Mystery Magazine* which, since its first issue in 1941, has distinguished itself for the unusual diversity and quality of its stories, old and new.

Rhode, John, pseud. (Street, Cecil John Charles) ed. *Detection Medley* (London, 1939) stories and articles by members of The Detection Club. A selection from this excellent collection was published in this country as *Line-Up* (1940).

Sayers, Dorothy L., ed. *The Omnibus of Crime* (1929), *The Second Omnibus of Crime* (1932), *The Third Omnibus of Crime* (1935). Each is a mixture of tales of detection and stories of unconfined mystery and horror. The introduction to the first omnibus is a brilliant and concise introduction to the form, equalled only by Miss Sayers' introduction to still another anthology, *Tales of Detection* (London, 1936).

Starrett, Vincent, ed. *World's Great Spy Stories* (1944). The first American collection of the sort, urbanely annotated.

Five other anthologies may be noted briefly: *Sleuths,* ed. by Kenneth MacGowan (1931), *World's Best Detective Stories,* ed. by. Eugene Thwing (1929) a very uneven collection in ten small volumes but containing much not easily accessible elsewhere; *Great Detective Stories* (1927) ed. by Willard Huntington Wright (S. S. Van Dine) with a sound introduction; *Crime and Detection* (1926) with an introduction by E. M. Wrong; and *Fourteen Great Detective Stories,* ed. by Vincent Starrett (1928).

NOVELS AND TALES

Allingham, Margery. *Death of a Ghost* (1934) and *Flowers for the Judge* (1936). Miss Allingham's stories are of such quality that nearly all of her later novels are mentioned. Her earlier tales (before *Police at the Funeral,* 1931), although they present the same detective, Albert Campion, are farcical thrillers rather than tales of detection.

Ambler, Eric. *A Coffin for Dimitrios* (1939) although Anthony Boucher and Helen E. Haines would have four of Ambler's novels in the omnibus volume *Intrigue* (1943).

Ashby, R. C. *He Arrived at Dusk* (1933) an extraordinary tale of terror.

Bailey, H. C. *Meet Mr. Fortune* (1942) contains a biographical note about Dr. Reginald, a novel (*The Bishop's Crime*) and twelve short stories from earlier collections. In *Orphan Ann* (1941) appears Bailey's other detective, that pious fraud, Joshua Clunk.

Balmer, Edwin and MacHarg, William. The *Achievements of Luther Trant* (1910) was submitted with warm insistence by Lillian de la Torre and Vincent Starrett. Their historical interest is unquestionable but, unquestionably, the stories have faded with the years.

Beeding, Francis, pseud. (Palmer, John Leslie and Saunders, Hilary St. George) is best known for a series of pretty footling tales of intrigue; but he is author as well of a few detective novels, one of which, *Death Walks in Eastrepps* (1931) is in the considered opinion of Vincent Starrett, "one of the ten greatest detective novels."

Bell, Josephine, *Murder in Hospital* (1937) or *From Natural Causes* (1939) two among several fine novels by a writer still not published in this country.

Bellairs, George. *Death of a Busybody* (1934) by a humorously observant new English writer.

Bennett, Arnold. *The Grand Babylon Hotel* (1902). An extravaganza, "borderline detection but an interesting specimen," says Starrett.

Bentley, E. C. *Trent's Last Case* (1913) to which Boucher and Starrett would add Bentley's short stories, *Trent Intervenes* (1938).

Berkeley, Anthony, pseud. (Cox, Anthony Berkeley). *The Poisoned Chocolates Case* (1929) characteristically dry and acrid, and *Trial and Error* (1937) with its unexpected sympathy.

Biggers, Earl Derr. *The Chinese Parrot* (1926). Detective: Charlie Chan.

Blake, Nicholas, pseud. (Day Lewis, Cecil). *The Beast Must Die* (1938).

Boucher, Anthony, pseud. (White, William A.P.) *The Case of the Seven of Calvary* (1937) an unusually good first novel with a university setting, or *The Case of the Baker Street Irregulars* (1940) a cheerful Sherlockian frolic.

Boutell, Anita. *Death Has a Past* (1939).

Bowers, Dorothy. *Fear and Miss Betony* (1942).

Bramah, Ernest, pseud. (Smith, Ernest Bramah). *Max Carrados* (London, 1914) or *The Eyes of Max Carrados* (1924). Carrados has been followed by many blind detectives but none is his equal.

Brahms, Caryl, pseud. (Abrahams, Doris Caroline) and Simon, A. J. *A Bullet in the Ballet* (1938) a burlesque for balletomanes.

Branson, H. C. *The Pricking Thumb* (1943) or *The Case of the Giant Killer* (1944) both quietly skilful.

Brock, Lynn, pseud. (McAllister, Alister). *The Kink* (1927) or *The Stoat* (London, 1940) both long, sedate, intricate, and absorbing.

Buchan, John. *The 39 Steps* (1915) primarily a tale of pursuit but with a tidy mystery.

Cannan, Joanna. *Death at "The Dog"* (1941).

Carpenter, Margaret. *Experiment Perilous* (1943).

Carr, John Dickson. *The Burning Court* (1937) although Ellery Queen objects that it is "not really in the genre" and Anthony Boucher sets it among "borderline" novels. *The Three Coffins* (1935) is the most learned of Carr's many "locked room" puzzles expounded by Dr. Gideon Fell. Lillian de la Torre argues warmly for *The Murder of Sir Edmund Godfrey* (1936) Carr's brilliant and careful treatment of a great English case.

Chandler, Raymond. *The Big Sleep* (1939) and *The High Window* (1942) respectively in and beyond the Hammett tradition.

Chesterton, G. K. *The Father Brown Omnibus* (1945) gathers all of the stories about that engaging and penetrating priest.

Cheyney, Peter. *Dark Duet* (1943) is the first and much the best of an increasingly trying series of counter-espionage tales.

Christie, Agatha. *The Murder of Roger Ackroyd* (1926) probably the most disputed of detective stories for its startling use of a famous cliché; *The ABC Murders* (1936), *Murder in Retrospect* (1942). The critics agree pretty generally on all but the last although a good many others by Mrs. Christie were suggested as well. Several critics spoke restively of Poirot's too familiar "little grey cells."

Clason, Clyde B. *The Man from Tibet* (1938). This and other cases of Theocritus Lucius Westborough are noted with surprisingly frequent approval.

Clements, E. H. *Perhaps a Little Danger* (1942). Miss Haines observes that "this may not be strictly within the canon, but it is admissible and delightful."

Cole, G. D. H. and Margaret. *Death in the Quarry* (1934) is certainly one of the best among the Coles' many and very unequal novels.

Coles, Manning, pseud. (Manning, Adelaide and Coles, Cyril). *Drink to Yesterday* and *A Toast to Tomorrow* (1941) both spy stories, the first in a fairly grim, realistic tone; the second, its sequel, in more characteristic and conventional vein.

Collins, Wilkie. *The Moonstone* (1868). In his introduction to the World's Classics (Oxford University Press) edition of this, T. S. Eliot calls it, more strikingly than accurately, "the first, the longest, and the best of modern English detective novels"; the warmth informing his judgment will be contested by few.

Connington, J. J. pseud. (Stewart, Alfred Walter). *The Sweepstake Murders* (1932) one among many, all meticulous, scrupulous, unspectacular, sound.

Cores, Lucy. *Painted for the Kill* (1943), a sound and witty first novel.

Crofts, Freeman Wills. *The Cask* (1920) and *Wilful and Premeditated* (1934). The first is an excellent sample of Crofts' painstaking "time-table" tales whose climax is the meticulous destruction of a false alibi; the latter is a sound example of the "inverted" detective story which recounts the flowering of a crime before it concerns itself with detection.

Cunningham, A. B. *The Strange Death of Manny Square* (1941) is one of a sound series of tales observantly and compassionately set in the southern hill country.

Daly, Elizabeth. *Murders in Volume 2* (1941) or *Arrow Pointing Nowhere* (1944) quietly brilliant, reserved and ingenious.

De la Torre, Lillian, pseud. (McCue, Lillian de la Torre Bueno). *Elizabeth Is Missing* (1945) reconstruction of an 18th century mystery by the author of a series of engaging Boswellian detective pastiches.

Dickens, Charles. *The Mystery of Edwin Drood* (1870) ed. by Vincent Starrett (1941). Starrett's is the first scholarly edition of the text of Dickens' unfinished novel; its introduction is a fine summary of the various theories about its proper conclusion.

Dickson, Carter, pseud. (Carr, John Dickson). *The Red Widow Murders* (1935) and *The Judas Window* (1938) "locked room" puzzles unlocked ebulliently by Sir Henry Merrivale.

Doyle, Sir Arthur Conan. *The Complete Sherlock Holmes* (1936) to which may be added with profit *The Private Life of Sherlock Holmes* (1933) by Vincent Starrett and, as guide to the intricate conjectures of Holmesians, *Baker Street Inventory: A Sherlockian Bibliography* (1945) compiled by Edgar W. Smith and supplemented quarterly in the new *Baker Street Journal*.

Duke, Winifred. *Skin for Skin* (1935) based on the murder of Julia Wallace.

Eberhart, Mignon G. *Fair Warning* (1936). Several critics, sharing Ogden Nash's dislike for the "Had-I-But-Known" school of feminine hysterics, argue for Mrs. Eberhart's omission; others point rather to her earlier tales—especially *The Patient in Room 18*—starring Nurse Keate.

Fair, A. A., pseud. (Gardner, Erle Stanley). *The Bigger They Come* (1939) first and funniest in a lusty series.

Falkner, John Meade. *The Nebuly Coat* (London, 1903) anticipates many of the qualities of Russell Thorndike's *The Slype* (1927) and both of these cathedral tales deserve wider acquaintance.

Fletcher, J. S. *The Middle Temple Murder* (1918) is, I think, listed from habit rather than merit. Fletcher's later novels are pretty generally condemned, but Miss Haines is one of the advocates of the "early stories, about 1915 to 1925."

Ford, Leslie, pseud. (Brown, Zenith). *The Simple Way of Poison* (1937) whose romantic heroine, Grace Latham, has been the target of some irritated comment.

Freeman, R. Austin, *Dr. Thorndyke's Omnibus* (1932) collected the five volumes of short stories published in this country, most notably the "inverted" tales in *The Singing Bone* (1912), and *Dr. Thorndyke's Crime File* containing a biographical introduction, Freeman's essay on "The Art of the Detective Story," "5A King's Bench Walk," an essay by the editor, P. M. Stone, and three novels: *The Eye of Osiris* (1911); *The Mystery of Angelina Frood* (1924) which is, incidentally, an answer to certain solutions of Dickens' novel; and *Mr. Pottermack's Oversight* (1930) an "inverted" tale.

Frome, David, pseud. (Brown, Zenith). *The Man from Scotland Yard* (1932) one of several novels about Mr. Pinkerton which are noted with pleasure.

Forester, C. S. *Payment Deferred* (1926) a lean story of murder with a finale as malicious as Francis Iles' for *Malice Aforethought* (1931).

Fuller, Timothy. *Reunion with Murder* (1941).

Gaboriau, Emile. *Monsieur Lecoq* (1869) and *L'Affaire Lerouge* (1866) although Ellery Queen, bowing to the historical importance of the tales, points out that they are "tough reading in these streamlined days."

Gardner, Erle Stanley. *The Case of the Counterfeit Eye* (1935). Gardner's tales are nearly equal although recently Perry Mason has become appallingly sententious.

Gilbert, Anthony, pseud. (Malleson, Lucy Beatrice). *Mystery in the Woodshed* (1942) although it shows too little of ripe Mr. Crook.

Greene, Anna Katharine. *The Leavenworth Case* (1878). Ellery Queen suggests omission, waiving "historical value in favor of readability." The historical importance of the novel is argued in S. S. Van Dine's introduction to the edition of 1934.

Greene, Graham. *The Confidential Agent* (1939) one of several sorrowfully savage "entertainments" by a fine novelist.

Greene, Ward. *Death in the Deep South* (1936) a novel based on the Leo Frank case of 1915.

Grey, A. F., pseud. (Neal, Adeline Phyllis). *Momentary Stoppage* (London, 1942). A delicately humorous tale set richly in a Paris *pension*.

Gruber, Frank. Considerable disagreement as to whether Gruber ought to be admitted. His *French Key* (1939) was twice proposed. Anthony Boucher preferred his pseudonymous *Last Doorbell* (1941) by "John K. Vedder."

Hammett, Dashiell. *The Complete Dashiell Hammett* (1942) contains his five novels but should be supplemented by the curious retrieved "pulp" novelette, *Blood Money* (1943) and Ellery Queen's three collections of Hammett's short stories: *The Adventures of Sam Spade* (1944); *The Continental Op* (1945); and *The Return of the Continental Op* (1945).

Hare, Cyril, pseud. (Clark, Alfred Alexander Gordon). *Tragedy at Law* (1943).

Hart, Frances Noyes. *The Bellamy Trial* (1927), reported in the courtroom.

Head, Matthew, pseud. (Canaday, John). *The Smell of Money* (1943) a fresh and immediate first novel.

Heard, H. F. (otherwise Gerald Heard). *A Taste for Honey* (1941) widely praised as a tale for connoisseurs.

Heyer, Georgette. *Envious Casca* (1941).

Hilton, James. *Was it Murder?* was published first as *Murder at School* (1933) by "Glen Trevor." Starrett calls it "unusual, very well written . . . a first rate story." Hilton's own opinion of it is low.

Holding, Elisabeth Sanxay. *Lady Killer* (1942) or *The Obstinate Murderer* (1938).

Holmes, H. H. pseud. (White, William A. P.) *Rocket to the Morgue* (1942) sound "locked room" puzzling set down among the interesting tribe of "scientifiction" writers.

Homes, Geoffrey, pseud. (Mainwaring, Daniel). *The Doctor Died at Dusk* (1936).

Hornung, E. W. *A Thief in the Night* (1905). Rogue stories about Raffles, the amateur cracksman; a necessary obverse of the detective story.

Household, Geoffrey. *Rogue Male* (1939) an absorbing and skilful story of pursuer and pursued. Deems Taylor marks it among the most memorable.

Hughes, Dorothy B. *The Fallen Sparrow* (1942) or *The Delicate Ape* (1944) tales of espionage and terror.

Hull, Richard, pseud. (Sampson, Richard Henry). *The Murder of My Aunt* (1935) a brilliantly unpleasant "inverted" tale.

Huxley, Elspeth. *Murder at Government House* (1937) better than the better known *Murder on Safari* (1938).

Iles, Francis, pseud. (Cox, Anthony Berkeley). *Before the Fact* (1932) filmed by Alfred Hitchcock as *Suspicion* (1941) with a softened (readers said soft-headed) finale.

Innes, Michael, pseud. (Stewart, John Innes Mackintosh). *Lament for a Maker* (1938) or *Hamlet, Revenge!* (1937) ingenious and erudite.

Jarrett, Cora. *Night over Fitch's Pond* (1933) a "borderline" novel.

Jepson, Selwyn. *Keep Murder Quiet* (1941).

Johns, Veronica Parker. *The Singing Widow* (1941). Anthony Boucher proposes this with surprising warmth, observing that it "has a plot of such strongly intertwined horror that Tourneur would have leaped at the chance to write it."

Johnson, W. Bolingbroke, pseud. (Bishop, Morris). *The Widening Stain* (1942) was written with arched eyebrows and of a university library.

Keene, Faraday, pseud. *Pattern in Black and Red* (1934).

King, Rufus. *Valcour Meets Murder* (1932) or the improvisation, *Profile of a Murder* (1935).

Knox, Ronald A. *The Viaduct Murder* (1926) dry and satirically ingenious.

Latimer, Jonathan. *The Lady in the Morgue* (1936). Sample of the rye-soaked, zany-cum-sex school.

Lawrence, Hilda. *A Time to Die* (1945) delicately incisive.

Leblanc, Maurice. *Les Huit Coups de l'Horloge* (Paris, ca.1922) translated as *The Eight Strokes of the Clock* (1922) a series of connected short stories presenting Arsène Lupin, "gentleman-cambrioleur," in the character of detective. But Ellery Queen insists that the novels about Lupin are too little read and recommends, in order, *813* (1910), *The Crystal Stopper* (*Le Bouchon de Cristal*, 1912), and *The Teeth of the Tiger* (*Les Dents du Tigre*, 1914).

Lee, Gypsy Rose. *The G String Murders* (1941) arouses wild dissension among the critics, half of them damning it out of hand, half defending it for its richly reeking background.

Lees, Hannah, pseud. (and Bachmann, Lawrence). *Death in the Doll's House* (1943).

Leroux, Gaston. *The Mystery of the Yellow Room* (1908). Craig Rice writes: "I would have no doubts regarding the inclusion of Leroux. *The Mystery of the Yellow Room* . . . with all its faults, remains the most fascinating locked-room puzzle of all time." Some readers will regard this as too generous a tribute.

Lockridge, Frances and Richard. *Murder out of Turn* (1941) second of the adventures of Mr. and Mrs. North.

Lorac, E. C. R., pseud. (Rivett, Edith Caroline). *Death of an Author* (1937) is only one of many warmingly competent tales.

Lowndes, Marie (Belloc). *The Lodger* (1913) but three diverse critics damn this as "vastly overrated."

McCloy, Helen. *Cue for Murder* (1942) excellent puzzling, or *The Goblin Market* (1943) a thriller presenting Dr. Basil Willing pseudonymously.

MacDonald, Philip. *Warrant for X* (1938) far better than Anthony Gethryn's first, cluttered, unfair and usually cited case, *The Rasp* (1924).

McGuire, Paul. *A Funeral in Eden* (1938) or *Enter Three Witches* (1940) both brilliant, mordant and sensitive.

Marsh, Ngaio. *Overture to Death* (1939) or *Death in a White Tie* (1938). Most critics added *Colour Scheme* (1943) despite its almost incidental interest in crime or detection.

Mason, A. E. W. *The House of the Arrow* (1924) and/or *At the Villa Rose* (1910). Commentators disagree violently as to which is good, but all agree that *one* of them is great.

Maugham, W. Somerset. *Ashenden: or, The British Agent* (1924) six unconventionally realistic tales of espionage. All are contained in the omnibus *East and West* (1934).

Milne, A. A. *The Red House Mystery* (1922) appears on lists rather habitually; its refreshment is largely dissipated and its artifices more trying with time.

Mitchell, Gladys. *When Last I Died* (1942) is fine, slowly cumulative in effect and rewarding. It is also, mysteriously, the only one of Miss Mitchell's many novels to have been published in this country for a good many years. Alternates: *Laurels Are Poison* (London, 1942), *Sunset over Soho* (London, 1943), *The Rising of the Moon* (London, 1945).

Morrison, Arthur. *Martin Hewitt: Investigator* (1894). Of the short stories of Jacques Futrelle, a fairly typical contemporary, only *The Problem of Cell 13* (1907) retains much of its original novelty; but Morrison's less striking short stories have stood the passage of time well.

Offord, Lenore Glen. *Skeleton Key* (1943) a refreshingly intelligent and humorous variant of the HIBK-school, or Mrs. Offord's quieter, richer *Glass Mask* (1944).

Oppenheim, E. Philips. Several critics insisted that *The Great Impersonation* (1920) must be admitted if Eric Ambler's tales were. A re-reading of the Oppenheim extravaganza leaves their insistence mysterious.

Page, Marco, pseud. (Kurnitz, Harry). *Fast Company* (1938).

Palmer, Stuart. *The Puzzle of the Blue Banderilla* (1937). A case for Hildegarde Withers.

Patrick, Q., pseud. (Webb, Richard Wilson). *The Grindle Nightmare* (1935) is among the "twelve best detective stories" in Anthony Boucher's estimation. Ralph Partridge (Raymond Postgate?), writing in the *New Statesman and Nation* prefers *S.S. Murder* (1933). Q. Patrick is a pseudonym used first by Mr. Webb and Martha Mott Kelley, then by Mr. Webb alone, and at present by him and Hugh Callingham Wheeler. (They also write as "Patrick Quentin" and "Jonathan Stagge.") Both of the novels cited appear to be solo performances by the constant Mr. Webb.

Poe, Edgar Allan. "The Murders in the Rue Morgue" (1841) the first detective story; "The Mystery of Marie Rogêt" (1842); and "The Purloined Letter" (1844) with the two contested tales, "The Gold Bug" (1843) and "Thou Art the Man" (1844) are reprinted in *Monsieur Dupin* (1904). The last tale is curiously absent from the otherwise sound edition of Poe's short stories edited by Killis Campbell (1927).

Post, Melville Davisson. *The Strange Schemes of Randolph Mason* (1896) are "dated" but significant; more memorable are the fine tales about *Uncle Abner* (1918).

Postgate, Raymond. *Verdict of Twelve* (1940) or *Somebody at the Door* (1943).

Queen, Ellery, pseud. *The Chinese Orange Mystery* (1934) or "Barnaby Ross's" *Tragedy of X* as samples of Queen's puzzling at its most ingenious, with the still surprising *Calamity Town* (1942) for its substance and texture as well as its puzzle.

Rawson, Clayton. *Death from a Top Hat* (1938) first and most striking of the Merlini novels.

Rhode, John, pseud. The consensus finds Rhode dull but two critics present a minority report for his *Murders in Praed Street* (1928).

Rice, Craig. *Trial by Fury* (1941) or *Home Sweet Homicide* (1944).

Rinehart, Mary Roberts. *The Door* (1930) is one of a distinguished series, but two critics argue convincingly for her first book, *The Circular Staircase* (1908). Mrs. Rinehart founded the HIBK-school.

Sale, Richard. *Lazarus #7* (1942) is a competent sample of the sensation and sex school although he may be surpassed by James Hadley Chase (*No Orchids for Miss Blandish,* tough stuff at its nadir).

Sayers, Dorothy L. Here ensues wild disorder, no two critics agreeing which of her fine novels shall be preferred. The innocent intrusion of Harriet Vane into the life of Lord Peter Wimsey (in *Strong Poison*) and her extensive self-probings before she marries him, make many readers howl with rage. The latest of Miss Sayers' novels, *Busman's Honeymoon* (1937) is significantly absent from all lists. In spite of their protests against Miss Vane, *Strong Poison* (1930) is listed oftenest and after it *The Nine Tailors* (1934) and *Have His Carcase* (1932) second of the novels involving the Vane. The only solution would appear to be purchase of all of the novels. The epistolary *Documents in the Case* (1930) written in collaboration with "Robert Eustace" (Eustace Barton) is admirable in itself and unique for Lord Peter's absence, and *Gaudy Night* (1936) notable to the university book buyer for its academic background.

Seeley, Mabel. *The Listening House* (1938) is a terrifying reply to those who object to the HIBK-school.

Shearing, Joseph, pseud. (Long, Gabrielle Margaret Vere Campbell). *Blanche Fury* (1939) in the estimation of Dr. Margery Bailey of Stanford University, "is nearly worthy to rank with *Wuthering Heights*," and *The Crime of Laura Sarelle* (1941) a sound second.

Simenon, Georges. *Maigret Keeps a Rendezvous* (1941) contains *The Sailors' Rendezvous (Au Rendez-vous des Terre-Neuvas)* and *The Saint-Fiacre Affair (L'Affaire Saint-Fiacre); Maigret to the Rescue* (1941) contains *The Flemish Shop (Chez les Flammands)* and *The Guinguette by the Seine (La Guinguette à Deux Sous).* Maigret's audience is relatively small but intensely and compellingly vocal. Readers used to more conventional detective stories are advised to read something about the author before reading the novelettes. See, for instance, John Peale Bishop's "Georges Simenon" in *The New Republic,* March 10, 1941 or Raymond Mortimer's "Simenon" in *The New Statesman and Nation,* March 10, 1942.

Starrett, Vincent. *Midnight and Percy Jones* (1936).

Steel, Kurt, pseud. (Kagey, Rudolph). *Judas, Incorporated* (1939) one of a number of generally sound tales about Hank Heyer, private investigator.

Steeves, Harrison. *Good Night, Sheriff* (1941).

Stevenson, Robert Louis and Osbourne, Lloyd. *The Wrecker* (1891) was designed as a *roman policier* by its authors but has generally been denied admittance to the genre by critics. Here submitted for reconsideration as a splendid piece of storytelling, soundly mysterious.

Stout, Rex. *The Red Box* (1937), *Too Many Cooks* (1938). Nearly all of Archie Goodwin's accounts of Nero Wolfe's cases are suggested.

Strange, John Stephen, pseud. (Tillett, Dorothy Stockbridge). *Look Your Last* (1943).

Stribling, T. S. *Clues of the Caribbees* (1929) short stories, curiously little known.

Talbot, Hake, pseud. (Nelms, Henning). *Rim of the Pit* (1944) the second novel by a newcomer in the demanding tradition of Melville Davisson Post and John Dickson Carr.

Upfield, Arthur W. *Murder Down Under* (1943; published in Australia, 1937, as *Mr. Jelly's Business*) is slow-moving but meticulous and richly set.

Vandercook, John W. *Murder in Trinidad* (1933).

Van Dine, S. S., pseud. (Wright, Willard Huntington). *The Bishop Murder Case* (1929) is oftenest preferred although there is much sympathy with Ogden Nash's insistence that "Philo Vance needs a kick in the pance" for his abominably obtrusive erudition.

White, Ethel Lina. *The Wheel Spins* (1936) is a happy exception among the tryingly inefficient tales of terror by Miss White. It was adapted by Alfred Hitchcock as *The Lady Vanishes* (1938).

Whitfield, Raoul. *Death in a Bowl* (1931). Whitfield is an unjustly forgotten contemporary of Dashiell Hammett.

Wilde, Percival. *Inquest* (1940).

Wilson, Mitchell. *Footsteps Behind Her* (1941) an excellently sustained chase if, like most tales of pursuit, Eurydicean in retrospect.

Woolrich, Cornell. *The Bride Wore Black* (1940) or, under his pseudonym of William Irish, *Phantom Lady* (1942) tales of rushing terror.

8
WATCHMAN, WHAT OF THE NIGHT?

The Passing of the Detective in Literature

THE DETECTIVE in literature is hardly more than fifty years old, but already he is passing into decay. He has enjoyed extraordinary popularity, and may even claim to be the only person equally beloved by statesmen and by errand boys. His old achievements enthral as ever. But he makes no new conquests. So far as he survives at all, he has been compelled to curb his energies within the compass of the magazines, and instead of contending forces marshalled in regular order on the board, presents now the bare problem: "White to play, and mate in three moves."

It is curious to note the shifts to which the novelist has been put in the attempt to clothe his detective with a garment of disinterestedness. And the reason lies on the surface. Arrange the persons of the drama as you will, the detective will always emerge as the hero. The crime is comparatively a small detail, and, so it be not too revolting in character, almost any infringement of the law will do. The criminal cannot ordinarily attract much sympathy or play a very large part.

Thus it will be seen that the detective has to be a personage of peculiar type. He must be officially deputed to detect this particular crime, yet romance demands that he shall not work merely for money. Standing outside the police force and usually hostile to it, he must be able to command its services for investigations beneath his dignity. If an amateur, he must bear no antagonism to the criminal, yet his connection with the affair must be sufficiently close to lend him authority to act. Above all, if he is to command interest, it is essential that he should possess the "flair," the subtle sense which reveals to him the trend of little indications. Unless his possession of this sense be emphasised, the deductive method will appear arbitrary guesswork, and it is on this rock that many modern attempts at mystery-weaving go to pieces. For the weak point of the deductive system is that every indication found is capable of bearing a dozen different interpretations. The ideal detective of romance pieces details together as a thought-reader divines things from the pressure of a hand. He detects not by virtue of simple powers of observation, but by a trained intuition amounting almost to second sight. It is this which lent him his grand air and brought him to greatness. It is this which is working his decay.

It was inevitable, perhaps, that the prestige of the detective should fade in proportion as the business of detecting crime assumed a more specialised character. For alas! modern scientific methods have overtaken him, and he has fallen hopelessly behind the times. He who was accustomed to issue terse commands to muddled members of the force is now ignorant of the very A B C of criminal investigation. He who smiled at professional ignorance must now bear to find his own amateur little ways the scorn of amused experts. It is hard, for he certainly led the way in creating the modern detective force before whose unerring eyes the secrets of sinful Europe lie unfolded. At the epoch when he came into being, no efficient police existed. In France, the highest quality aimed at was the kind of blood-hound tenacity of identification illustrated in *Les Miserables.* In England, there was the good-natured shrewdness of Inspector Bucket in *Bleak House,* but there was no science of investigation, no regular course of training, no system. And the detective of fiction easily triumphed. He triumphed in France more decisively on account of the astounding manœuvres permitted to the Juge d'Instruction under the French law. But he did very well in England, even under the more sportsmanlike system of judge and jury which he was bound to respect.

And it is modern education, the relentless adaptation of means to an end, which has prepared his downfall. The regular force has taken its revenge, and the lordly person who used to throw them his secrets, at whose feet they sat in awe, is beaten by the very weapons he first taught them to use.

From henceforth he retires to limbo with the dodo and the District Railway's trains. He carries with him the regret of a civilised world.

The foregoing selection appeared in the Academy *(London) for December 30, 1905.*

A Sober Word on the Detective Story

By *Harrison R. Steeves*

With his literate, sensitive novel Good Night, Sheriff *Harrison R. Steeves made a single but important contribution to detective fiction. Published in 1941, the book has been frequently named on lists of "best" police stories compiled since that date. He also made a single, thoughtful contribution to the critical literature of the subject in the present essay, which appeared in* Harper's Magazine *for April 1941. For many years a professor of English at Columbia University, Mr. Steeves carries on the tradition of the men and women of academic distinction on both sides of the water who have interested themselves purposefully in the genre.*

There is both room and need in detective story criticism for the kind of trained dissection and diagnosis Mr. Steeves performs in the present essay; and he puts his finger accurately if painfully on many of the ills the modern police novel is heir to. Much of what he says cannot, and should not, be shrugged off. Yet the judicious reader, encountering the pessimism of his final paragraphs may wish to recall that similar and no-less-logical prophecies of doom have been uttered for—as we have seen in the preceding selection—a good forty years and possibly longer.

I READ detective stories. I read them and I enjoy a good one. I can tolerate a mediocre one. I am strong-minded enough to put down —or to throw down—a poor one; and there are countless such. And I have read enough of them to wonder why they interest me; for I have little actual respect for the art. I cheerfully concede that I peruse ten quite worthless books for every reasonably good one; and at that I try to pick my writers. At least I keep a black-list of the duds. It saves time and expense.

For run-of-the-mill readers this confession of corrupt taste might be an innocent one, or at least an excusable one. But I am an accredited apostle of culture; for I am a college professor, and a professor of literature at that. That's quite another thing, isn't it?

Or is it? So far as I know, my occasional wallow has never affected my interest in or my judgment of "respectable" literature. "Lear," "Lycidas," *The Portrait of a Lady, Growth of the Soil*—all these work the same powerful magic as ever—in spite of my having discussed them for years with undergraduates. No, I think I've not been soiled, nor my intelligence reproached. And for the waste of hours in a confessedly idle pursuit, of course some hours were meant to be wasted. I'm neither sorry nor humble about it; nor am I proud.

I am intellectually interested, however, in my tolerance; and I should like to account for it in some reasonable way, and with a less glib explanation than "escape," which explains nothing. In the first place, escape must be from a stupid or depressing scheme of life into an imagined world more roomy or more roseate. But the professorial job is for me neither stupid nor depressing. I like an occasional change from it, to be sure, but I can get that in many and various ways. In the second place, escape must be, or should be, to desirable latitudes in the world of fancy; and the doings and interests of detectives, amateur or professional, would be my last notion of an agreeable way of life. If I actually sought escape on one of the lower planes of literary interest, I ought to be attracted by the "Westerns"; for as a scene the West is for me (an anchored Easterner) a breathless emotional glory. But a story set in that scene I find invariably as arid as its physical background.

No, escape has little to do with the matter. I cheerfully admit the "escape" motive in the crotchet that divides my interest with the detective story—books on strange and out-of-the-way corners of the world. Tibet, Greenland, the Australian wilds, desert China, the reaches of the Amazon—they and their denizens perennially fascinate me, and I know why. It is because they are the farthest extreme from the seemingly tame and ordered life that civilization has wished upon me. But the detective story doesn't interest me in that way at all. I have no feeling whatever toward detectives as a class; it takes an extremely good crime (not necessarily a sensational one) to draw me beyond the column-head of the daily paper; and I have only an academic interest in the genesis and psychology of the inordinate social aggressions.

I can tell you the state of mind in which I read detective stories, but I am not sure that that answers the question why I read them. They seem an unforgivable waste of time when my mental energy is high. When it hangs in a loose loop they can interest me. After dinner, at the end of two or three days of scarcely remitted work, when conversation is an effort and company a tax, they have their use. They go well in an armchair, with tobacco sufficient, and preferably with one's feet well elevated. Of course the final fifty pages should be read in pajamas. They are the best preparative in the world (except perhaps the story portions of the Bible) for thoughtless, unburdened sleep. For me, then, detective stories are a narcotic, mildly stimulative, to be taken as a rule when productive energy is low and discrimination more or less deliberately put aside. I can read them also in vacation intervals when idleness is virtue.

But if the mood in which I can read them is one of conditioned irresponsibility, I must nevertheless, as a "professional" reader, so to speak, allow my critical judgment and my self-respect their day in court. I am not sure, however, that defense is necessary for readers who have no reputation at stake and who take their detective yarns without qualms. And I am seriously interested in what detective stories give them.

When I speak of detective stories, of course I mean detective stories; not melodramatic crime stories nor clap-trap mysteries nor international spy stories with the thin thread of a sinister plot running uncertainly through them; nor miracle stories, not even when the miracle can be substantiated in the pharmacopoeia or the purlieus of the criminal courts. I mean stories in which a respectable problem of identity is presented to a respectable intelligence with, by preference, of course a modicum of literary intelligence in the writing and, if one is lucky, even a touch of literary grace above the mere needful trickery of the performance. Such stories have had good readers. We are told that bishops and Supreme Court justices have shared the weakness for them. That doesn't sanctify the weakness or give it more than a fictitious dignity, but it helps to make it critically intelligible.

Curiously enough, the taste for detective fiction (like that for chess and for great claret) seems to be all but exclusively masculine. To the best of my memory I have never met a woman who turned to it recurrently for sensation, escape, solace, amusement, or drug. Apparently there is something in the type that is foreign to women's minds or to their sympathies. Or perhaps their common sense revolts from its transparencies. Yet women are great readers of fiction, and possibly by mental constitution better readers of the novel than men. And women probably digest much of their usable philosophy in the very assimilable form of fiction; for a deserving novel demands some thought upon aspects of conduct and social responsibility that are not centered in one's own experience.

But fiction for women seems to require a distinct and significant animat'•.g idea. That is true, I think, even on the lower levels of wishful romanticism. There may lie the reason why the run of men —I don't of necessity mean cultivated readers—have to have their own kind of fiction—not that they are too busy or too tired to do "serious" reading, but that action, physical or mental, presented to them in relatively simple and static terms, has more appeal than subtler questions of ways of living presented through serious though fictitious cases. Men read the detective story largely for the reason that it does not have to be taken seriously. Probably women decline it for exactly the same reason.

Yet women write them! That doesn't alter the fact that (within the area of my own knowledge) women don't as a rule read them. And if there is any explanation to be made of their writing them, and sometimes writing them extremely well, I am inclined to put it down to the simple fact that in any kind of good-humored trickery any clever and thoroughly intent woman can put it over any man, any time.

II

The absence of seriousness in the detective story is apparent first of all in the nonchalance, or even the sardonic humor, of the attitude it takes toward crime, and in its habitual compromise with retributive justice through the hundred and one expedients which will save from the gallows the perpetrator of an offense which has any colorable sanction. This indifference to moral intention, however, seems to me a small matter. A literary *divertissement* can, as Lamb pointed out, dispense with moral consistency.

There is a sense, however, in which detective fiction is more culpably unserious; and that is in its almost unvarying failure to evoke the emotional atmosphere of the situation that surrounds a considered crime from the birth of motive to the last heavy moments of expiation. And that failure is noteworthy because it is artistic failure. Of course the rules of the form prescribe that the animus of the detective's search be intellectual, not moral and not sentimental; yet the fact remains that most of these stories seem to flourish in an emotional vacuum, and that fact would seem at the very outset to come perilously close to barring them from the realm of art.

But why, you ask, do we need to drag art into the discussion of an essentially artless form? That question itself begs another question. *Is* detective fiction necessarily artless? My guess is that the early writers of it—Brockden Brown, Poe, Wilkie Collins—did not believe so, for their stories have emotive force. And the embroidery that has been expended upon recent stories of the type at least shows a sense of this insufficiency, though with less happy because less integral effects. The widely expressed contempt for the type is not altogether "high-hat." It must come from knowing readers who expect a few of the vitamins which good art should afford. And once in a while, once in a long, long while, the detective story provides them. There are, I insist, a few actually classic detective stories—at least a dozen or a score. They are not artless. Still more importantly, they are not inartistic; and an inartistic work is simply one which fails to realize the proved potentialities of its form.

Possibly it is a corollary to the last remark that a work of art must accept also the limitations of its form—if that form is clearly defined. We don't look for Matthew Arnold's "high seriousness" in the *Ingoldsby Legends;* nor can we normally expect great revelation within the prescribed confines of the genre we are considering. Yet the mystery tale can be good art, at least in those respects which are elemental for any work of fiction. We should be allowed to breathe the real air of real places, feel the charm or the pressure of a distinct local life, hear the stir and play of agreeable con-

versation, and savor the everyday emotions. Above all, we can ask
that the story be inhabited by convincing human beings, doing
things that human beings do. Indeed I know of no first-class detective story in which the exigencies of a special complication are
not managed with all-round literary competency—and with the
air of social truth.

So far as the detective story is deficient in these clear requirements of good art it is deficient in fundamentals. And that de-
ficiency in organic or "functional" art is intensified for the good
reader's consciousness by an increasingly disturbing use of every
sort of irrelevant and trivial appliqué art—glitter, gratuitous flippancy, meaningless wit, and conventional beautification. This is
no depreciation of decorative purpose, but merely a reminder that
art must be *in* a work, and not *on* it. Much, needless to say, of this
æsthetic frivolity must be blamed upon commercialism. In a "sellers' market," the economists tell us, the goods produced are likely
to cheapen. Even the author of *The Middle Temple Murder* and
the authoress of *The Murder of Roger Ackroyd* have at times fallen
victims to their own industry.

I doubt that the particular principles of this art, however, are as
tightly formulated as some of its sponsors would have us believe. I
have in mind at least three pronouncements—*ex cathedra*—which
tell us what a detective story can and cannot be. And I have seen
almost all these principles profitably ignored. In E. C. Bentley's
Trent's Last Case three points of the law are violated: the detective is defeated in his inquiry (which we are told should never
be); the effective clues to the criminal are not plainly planted, or
rather not at all (and that, it is said, is sheer dishonesty); and there
is no readable motive for the crime, though there is a triumphantly
reasonable explanation—after the fact. But in spite of these presumed irregularities (and despite the fact that the story belongs to
the past generation) I have never followed a plot with more urgent
interest, and never been more utterly delighted with the brisk travel
of incident, with the clear picture of a credible society, and with
the deftness and the logic of the conclusion. That is as it should
be: the critics cannot tell the writers the rules of the game, for all
rules in art (as the best critics themselves have told us) were made
to be broken. And in a form so wholly dependent as the detective

story upon ingenuity and surprise the bout between the writer and the reader must be catch-as-catch-can.

It is still a step or two to the determination of what goes to the making of a good detective story. I am convinced, however, that it is all but impossible to offer any confident judgment upon that question; for while baseball-fans and Dadaists and Muggletonians have firm collective convictions, the detective-story readers are not only many but formidably varied. All discussion of preferences is ultimately reduced to the question of what one likes because he looks for it, and there are many types within the type, as well as authors, to choose from. So any statement of preferences that I can offer must be invidious. I might add to the three or four works that I have mentioned in passing, Anthony Berkeley's *Trial and Error,* Margery Allingham's *Flowers for the Judge,* Percival Wilde's *Inquest,* Frances Noyes Hart's *Hide in the Dark,* Dorothy Sayers' *Nine Tailors,* and perhaps—with a conscious bow to tradition— Conan Doyle's *The Sign of Four.* I have named books, not authors, for I have read some pretty unsatisfactory stories by most of these writers. And my omission of Dashiell Hammett, S. S. Van Dine, H. C. Bailey, Michael Innes, and a dozen others has no particular point, because I simply refuse to stand behind my preferences as a selection of the "ten best." They are not; they are stories that I like, and I know why I like them. The most erudite fan I know refuses to share all these likings and rates highly things that I have thought stupid or affected or weakly put together.

All of the stories I have mentioned except Doyle's, and—yes— Fletcher's *Middle Temple Murder,* are definitely more than well-made detective yarns. There is some breath of humanity, some charm, some wisdom of the world, even a quaint rarity of situation in *Trial and Error,* that proves the writer's possession of the literary sense. Beyond that, they are all literately and competently written. If there is no formula for success in those very general considerations, there is at least a refuge for the reader's self-esteem.

III

Yet if it seems impossible to find a common denominator for the preferences of detective-story readers, the question still persists:

Why do you and I read these things? Why, particularly, when we know the formula so well, and when the studied variations upon the inevitable theme only attest the limitations of the theme itself? We know they are agreeable rot, in the main. If they may be proficiently written, they are usually not. We seem, like the patient two outside the gates of Heaven in Dunsany's play, to reach toward that slow-motion shower of empty beer bottles in the agonizing hope that one, by unthinkable good luck, may be a full one.

Perhaps the first reason for the acceptableness of the detective story is its relative brevity. No distinctive literary type outside the drama is more definitely cut to length. A rapid reader can read a detective story in a three-hour sitting, a slow one, in six hours—two evenings at home. A man can undertake that much without the feeling that he has a contract on his hands. But if half his diversion after business hours is found outside the four walls of his house, he might count the number of nights it would take to get to the 786th and final page of the novel over which his wife has been gasping admiration. On the other hand, the detective story is not too short. The story magazine is well enough for short sessions, but too sketchy, too scattered, for the four-hour stretch before bedtime.

Then there is its tonic cheerfulness. Detective fiction is in reality a standing defiance of crime, social disorder, and all the varieties of calculated bad luck that may befall good people. In the end everything comes right. There is nothing in art—even in the lowest forms—more unswervingly optimistic, and nothing more steadily moral, at least in its acceptance of moral principles, though the Olympian-right-mindedness of the writer may traffic strangely with those principles when an agreeable offender confronts them. This optimism and this morality, however, organic as they are, are in no sense critical or philosophic. They are casually and naturally accepted, as unexacting readers accept most simple views of life. On the whole, the detective story and the "crime story" appeal to quite different readers. The two types may cross, but the true detective fan is impatient or disgusted if too much is made of the morbid sensations of crime and crime-hunting. Multiple murders he inclines to regard as excessive; and for the noise and sweat of mere gangster and police activity he feels a respectable contempt.

The good detective stories are not as a rule morbid. They focus in murder; but it is not the nature of the crime that intrigues us —except in relation to the solution. I doubt whether we need rationalize the almost exclusive concern with murder. Murder is after all the cardinal crime. Petty larceny would never do; and when grand larceny, arson, or conspiracy is used it is only as a setting for a good workmanlike murder. Kidnapping has had its place in the grosser sort, but again as occasion for murder. Rape is for fairly obvious reasons "out."

But there does seem to be a reason for the ubiquity of the murder theme. Murder is irrevocable and irremediable. It may have extenuations or justifications; it may even command active sympathy; but its hard finality places the offender beyond the power of compromise with the social temper or the usage of the law. Sympathy can be vindicated only in the facile equity of a lenient conclusion. Yet, I repeat, the incidents and the character of the murder are not matters of leading interest; a detective story is a story of detection.

But most of all, in the nature of things, the sustained vogue of detective fiction is dependent upon the type of challenge presented in the actual treatment of the unvarying problem. The prevailing view is that it is a challenge to the wits that holds us—patent as the challenge may be. It is a game, a pleasantly and harmlessly agreeable game of solitaire in which human beings take the place of pasteboards or pieces and the problems are problems of human activity.

But is that imagined challenge to the intellect any more than imaginary? Does the detection story really rank with the "intellectual diversions"? For the majority of readers I am inclined to think not. I deeply doubt whether the process of deduction, as it is commonly called (though goodness knows the larger processes of detection are inductive) is followed with the conscience that one brings to chess, or even to contract bridge. We like to imagine the scrupulous "fan" ticking off point after point of evidence, matching character against character as the most promising suspect, carrying throughout the narrative a complete picture of the interrelations of events and characters, always on his caution of course against that final turn of the trick which will both defeat and dazzle the unwary. When Poe and Conan Doyle flourished, the reader did reason ahead—but in a straight line of well-oriented items of evidence which were carefully marked as the distinctive and necessary ones. Conan Doyle followed Poe's predilection for lucidity, deliberately "planting" the clue, though he might suspend the brilliant act of reason that gave it its value.

To-day that is all greatly changed. The elaboration of devices and expedients that attends the development of all arts (of all genres, if you don't like "arts"), and still more the vast extension and diversification in the mechanics of actual scientific detection, have quite naturally made the sowing of clues and the analysis of them a much more complicated business. And the cultivation of the reader in that immensely extended technic has forced the writer more and more into the practice of bafflement of a confusing and sometimes even an oppressive sort. When *A Study in Scarlet* was written, in 1887, there was no Bertillon system, no finger-printing; there were no radio cars, no such battery of lethal devices, either mechanical or chemical. But more important than that, there was no widely organized system of police intelligence, no comparable procedure in "forensic" science, and above all, no education of the criminal in the evasion of any or all of the methods of scientific detection. Holmes's instant reconstruction of the leading features of both crime and criminal in *A Study in Scarlet* would strike our contemporaries as flashy and precipitate, and his tactics in the apprehension of the criminal would simply be laughed at. But the problem itself reposes in simple evidence simply handled.

To-day the writer of the detective story multiplies clues, multiplies suspects within an eligible *dramatis personæ* of at least four or five characters, offers a choice of solutions which is finally determined on the principle of the *reductio ad absurdum,* and frequently employs comprehensive time and place arrangements which require diagramming rather than arguing. Indeed, I have reached the conviction that the detective-story writer should be obliged by statute to supply all requisite maps, house plans, working diagrams, and time schedules, and if the characters are many (and particularly if they have no clearly defined personalities) he should furnish also a descriptive *dramatis personæ*. Stories so intricately contrived can be interesting—witness Ngaio Marsh's *Death in a White Tie* and John Rhode's *Death Pays a Dividend*—but it takes very good writing as well as elaborate routine to make them so.

But in stories of this type—and they are, after all, far the greater part of our modern mystery stories—complication of matter and method go far to defeat themselves. The casual reader tends to accept the fact that the author can, and will, fool him, keeps the maze of events loosely in his mind, and nonchalantly looks back over the path of cause and effect (if it is at all clear) after he has reached its end. The use of the mind hasn't much place in that experience. And it might be noted that the fascinating cases in the history of actual crime are not of the ingenious order. The Crippen case, the Becker case, the Hauptmann case all depended, at least in the retrospect, upon the assiduous working up of a few small but critical items of evidence. Possibly the proof of the supposition that it is not the unraveling of a confused problem that holds us is found in the fact that the substitutes for the detective story in the form of crime "problem" books and "exercises" in detection have had no consistent success.

IV

No, I am sure the "good" reader is in the minority—and a small minority at that. For the greater number of us the case is different, and not so complimentary to the quality of our mental interests. Possibly we can get at the reality through a pertinent analogy.

Men like machinery, any product of skill and imagination that puts power into visible and continuous use. They like it at rest, but so much more in motion, because then it is living the kind of life that machines were meant to live. Dynamos, steam shovels, streamlined locomotives and marine engines are all success stories. The least technically informed of us men can hardly pass a battery of compressed air drills or a road-making machine in operation without a qualm of resentment that it is only adolescents and loafers who are permitted really to enjoy, for an hour on end, the working of a big and slick invention. It is not in the least necessary that we understand the mechanics of the thing; it is just a magnificent eye-filler. For a man the motor under the hood of his car is an object of delight if not of affection; for a woman it is only a mystery, and therefore troublesome and perhaps terrifying. All she wishes to know about it is that it is nasty and oily and hot and refractory,

and that the only person who can deal with such a thing properly
is another mystery in overalls. For a man the power-house across
the hill is a monument of beautiful efficiency and quiet energy.
For a woman it is an eyesore, and the source of the smoke that con-
taminates the week's wash.

Under all the inaccuracy of this generalization there is an undeniable psychological truth. And it fits the detective story as it fits
the world of invention. We have the glowing sense of the mind in
action. But the mechanism of the mind is not presented by the
writer or perceived by the reader psychologically, for the matter of
the story is altogether concrete, and there is no particular concern
for the relation between idea and behavior. The story of mental
action has replaced the somewhat effete story of physical action—
Rob Roy and *Treasure Island*—which also seemed to interest men
more than women. By the same token murder, the almost unvary-
ingly standard subject matter, while it is felt by women as unpleasant to the touch, is accepted by the less fastidious minds of men
simply as the raw material for the mental machine to work upon.
That is why men like it, and why at least a score of men read it
for every woman.

And that vicarious and fanciful spectator's pride that we men feel
in the scientific and (we choose to think it) the male mind at
work, almost demands that the owner of that mind be a male. Even
the women writers seem to concede this. Agatha Christie has departed from the precept in this respect, but she flatters us by giving to her pleasant motherly detective (who is not a professional)
a sedentary and intuitive shrewdness, accompanied by modest de-
nials of any special capacity beyond observation and common-sense.
And she has been presented to us, if I remember rightly, only in
short stories, episodes that demand no sustained or highly sys-
tematized application to detective routine. The basic equipment
of the story detective still remains what the male, by character, nur-
ture, and opportunity, seems able to supply. Practically every writer
of detective fiction recognizes that the anchorage of his story is a
precise imaginative mind in a masculine personality of some
uniqueness.

Here again the very determinants of interest in the type have
tended to decadence. The uniqueness of Sherlock Holmes lay not

in his mannerisms, his patronage of the adoring Watson, his cocaine, or any other trifling attachments of the person, but in his impressive consistency with himself and the part he had to play. He
was the detective fully in character. But the heritage of mannerism
has fallen heavily upon more up-to-date writers, and the search for
distinction has given us a flock of personalities who are unique in
quite a different way. I am bored by the airs and the parade, the
ostentatious savoir, of the Reginald Fortunes, the Philo Vances;
equally by the intrusive unpersonableness of Mr. Pinkerton and
Joshua Clunk. Ellery Queen, Monsieur Poirot, Lord Peter Wimsey,
I can stand very well, though I am not greatly entertained by what
is adventitious in their characters, their velvet lives, or their esoteric
tastes. But occasionally I find myself fervently wishing that the
favorites of detective fiction would die quick but quiet deaths, or
that they might, in the saga style, breed clever sons and daughters
to take their places. Bentley's singularly good story, *Trent's Last
Case,* has as principal a perfectly normal and politely bred human
being, and until an unhappy year or two ago there was no reason to
think he would ever reappear in fiction.

This brings us to a final consideration—that the detective story
does not occupy so isolated a niche in literary art that it can dispense with what is known as "good writing." The besetting pain
of the informed reader's experience is that there are so many of
them (and how can he avoid them?) that are scandalously badly
written, even down to the plainest requisites of grammar and syn-
tax. There are fewer, but far too many, pretentiously over-written.
And that failure to respect the "nothing too much" is peculiarly
disturbing in detective fiction because its essential treatment is factual. That remains true no matter how dramatic the appeal of the
factual may be.

But the future? No one who has followed the history of the arts
has failed to be struck with the stench of a thoroughly extinct vogue.
The æsthetic record is full of those painful revelations that what
was thought to be good taste or tolerable taste is really bad taste.
The mystery type is still holding up surprisingly well, but it will
inevitably belong some day amongst the curiosa: the Gothics, the
sporting novels, the penny dreadfuls. For it is, like them, a freak, a
specialty. Perhaps even now the knowing ones, sensing its precari-

ous state, are accumulating first editions and queer rarities.

I should like to see the detective story renew its youth and flourish —at least for my lifetime. But I painfully suspect that it has been acquiring years as men acquire them, that what it has gained during its prime in spread, in cleverness, in diversification, in actual (though not consistent) power to stimulate the mind, has been gained as men's experience and aptitudes are gained, at the price of hardened arteries and cellular disintegration and exhaustion of physical resources. The signs of decadence seem unmistakable— excessive ingenuity, dissonant cleverness, an infectious flippancy and indifference to moral scruple; above all, a failure of humane interest in those disorders of the soul that underlie desperate acts and give them literary substance.

Yet the type has shown extraordinary stamina. It has lived powerfully in spite of the æsthetic and the ethical doubts about it and the ridicule of those who take their literature seriously. If it has fallen into infirmity the doctors may still keep it going for a long time to come. But when it is time for it to die we must be content to part from it as we do from the pleasantly aged, and shed no restless tears beside its bier.

The Case of the Corpse in the Blind Alley
By Philip Van Doren Stern

There is, so wise men have said, no surer sign of maturity than self-criticism. The literally tremendous increase, on both sides of the ocean, in the writing and publishing of crime-mystery-detective fiction in the 1920's and 1930's brought in its wake trends and developments that called for the kind of sober re-examination and plain speaking contained in the present selection, which first appeared in the Virginia Quarterly Review *for Spring 1941. Even those who believe—as does your editor—that Mr. Stern has overestimated both the villainy and the influence of the reactionary "professional" detective story reader will presumably agree that more of his reasoned and healthy pessimism in contemporary mystery criticism would be a good thing for all concerned. Philip Van Doren Stern is well known in the American literary scene as novelist, biographer, editor, and publisher. Under a pen name he has written at least one detective story of his own.*

THIS YEAR is the one hundredth anniversary of the birth of the detective story. No academic convocations are likely to be held to celebrate it, nor will any great body of commemorative literature be written for the occasion. Yet the detective story is a much discussed field of writing; it is of great importance to our publishing and printing industries; and the circumstances of its birth were respectable enough to warrant academic attention.

Edgar Allan Poe was its originator; the first of his stories to show how a killing could be solved by pure ratiocination—"The Murders in the Rue Morgue"—appeared just a century ago in the April, 1841 issue of *Graham's Magazine*, a Philadelphia periodical of some literary standing in its day. Poe, of course, was not the first to write

527

about murder. He had been preceded by hundreds of authors from the recorder of the Biblical story of Cain and Abel to Thomas De Quincey, who published the second part of his essay "On Murder Considered as One of the Fine Arts" only two years before "The Murders in the Rue Morgue" was printed. Nor was Poe the first to make use of deduction as literary material. Ancient writers in a dozen different lands had done that. But Poe was the first to write the detective story as we know it today. He added the puzzle element to the tale of murder; he gave us our first real detective—the brilliant and eccentric Dupin; and he was the originator of the Dr. Watson method of presenting a story through an observer who tells how the sleuth went about solving the case. Poe's rigidly logical structure has continued almost unchanged; his philosophical asides are imitated to this day; his atmospheric effects have defied successful imitation. Like printing, the detective story has been improved upon only in a mechanical way since it was first invented; as artistic products, Gutenberg's Bible and Poe's "The Murders in the Rue Morgue" have never been surpassed.

In fact, it may be said that whatever artistic possibilities the detective story had were realized at its birth. Certainly its modern descendants are a poor lot. Nearly three hundred book-length mysteries—using the word "mystery" as a generic term for all crime fiction to include the detective story, the murder story *sans* detection, and the horror story—were published in 1940, but most of them were as artless as radio soap-opera and quite as tiresome. Their writers forgot that murder implies the existence of a murderer; they ignored the fact that killing is still a serious business, accompanied in real life by very real emotions and fraught with genuine danger and fear. Our mystery stories are long on gore and short on good red blood; they are bedside stories for tired adults, intended to put their readers to sleep from sheer boredom.

The fact that so many of them are written, published, bought, and eagerly read simply proves that the genre has astounding vitality, for it survives a flood of bad writing, a drought of ideas, and the deadly attrition caused by endless imitation and counterimitation.

There are critics, of course, who maintain that the detective story has nothing to do with literature, that it is simply an intellectual puzzle intended to amuse the reader by enabling him to dwell for a few hours on solving an imaginary murder and so escape a real world in which actual death daily becomes more imminent. But this is to take the shallowest possible view of what is necessarily a literary form; were the detective story only a puzzle there would be no need to make it into a book complete with characters, background, and some attempt at good writing. The purely puzzle element could be covered in a few hundred words. What is wrong with the detective story of today is that it lacks literary value. It must go beyond simple arithmetic to a higher field of æsthetic endeavor or it is worth nothing at all.

There is nothing inherent in the mystery story that limits it as literature. Its central core is almost always premeditated murder (stories dealing with lesser crimes are never completely successful), and premeditated murder is one of the greatest themes in all literature: witness such works as *Electra, Hamlet,* and *Crime and Punishment.* If it is true that the average mystery story makes little attempt to deal with the great drama of life and death, that is because it is an average mystery story, written by a hack. There is no reason why a tale concerning itself with the most soul-racking deed a human being can undertake should be a silly, mechanically contrived affair. The writer of murder mysteries holds high cards in his hand; if he does not know how to play them, that does not lessen their value.

Murder is a subject of universal interest; the study of it offers most people their only experience with the emotion of terror; and it carries with it the suspense and excitement of gambling for high stakes, for the man who kills sets himself against all society and risks his own life on being clever enough to outwit even his cleverest fellow men. The reader can at will put himself either in the place of the murderer or his pursuers and take part in the most thrilling of all sports—the man hunt—as quarry or hunter.

It must be noted at this point that murder per se is likely to be a more interesting and potentially richer subject than the mere detection of it. A writer can be more eloquent about death than he can about details of evidence or alibis. The reader instinctively senses this, and as a result, the circulation of detective stories is confined to a much smaller circle than is the reading of tales of murder. No detective story published in this century has come near achieving the wide popularity of a straightforward murder novel like Daphne du Maurier's *Rebecca*. And very few tales of detection have the perennial vitality of Mrs. Belloc-Lowndes's superb murder story, *The Lodger*.

There is a timelessness, too, about the pure tale of murder or horror that is lacking in nearly all detective stories, even the best of them. To the modern reader who is honest with himself and not overawed by reputation, the Sherlock Holmes detective stories, great as they are, are beginning to take on a slightly antiquated flavor. Poe's tales of ratiocination are period pieces in many respects, but their artistry saves them from seeming dated. They also have the advantage of using only the simplest of means. Nothing makes a detective story appear outmoded so much as the employment of elaborate scientific methods which the progress of science soon renders obsolete. Fingerprinting and chemical analysis have sent hundreds of our older detective stories into the discard.

Simplicity of means, valid characters, and distinguished writing are the qualities that best enable crime fiction to defy the ravages of time. In that respect it will be seen that the mystery story does not differ from other forms of literature.

II

Some element, not too well understood, seems to be at work to damage both the sales and literary value of the mystery story. It has been charged that book-trade customs and reviewing methods which confine mysteries in a classification that is too rigid are responsible for their not reaching a wider audience. This, however, is not enough of an explanation, for other kinds of books sometimes reach the best-seller lists despite all the obstacles placed in their way by their own publishers. No detective story has become enormously popular in our time—the sales even of such record-breakers as the S. S. Van Dine books and Dashiell Hammett's *The Thin Man* are insignificant compared with the sales of non-detective best sellers, or with Miss du Maurier's tremendously successful story of murder.

The common belief that detective stories are enormously popular is simply not true; they are popular as a type, but no one of them is read widely. A brief investigation into the methods of book distribution will shed some light on this curious circumstance.

First of all, mysteries are not sold in any great quantity directly to the public; probably as much as eighty-five per cent of all copies circulated reach their readers through rental libraries which buy the books and lease them out for a few pennies a day. Consequently, relatively few copies of any one title will serve a great many readers. This practice is at once the blessing and the curse of writing or publishing mysteries. The rental library system insures a minimum sale of about fifteen hundred copies for almost any mystery; it also places a top limit of about thirty-five hundred copies for even the best ones. Thus there can be little chance of loss—but also little chance of great gain. Only a few well established authors can expect to see their books sell beyond the thirty-five hundred figure— and even then not far beyond that figure. So if you have ever wondered why publishers charge two dollars for a short, cheaply made mystery story, you will now understand that you are not supposed to buy the book. The publisher is simply trying to get some return from the rental libraries. Under our present system of distribution two dollars is actually a very low price for a mystery story; the publisher knows he is not selling a book but is indirectly leasing out reading privileges.

But one must go beyond book-trade customs to find out why mystery stories rank so low in public esteem and as literature. Not even the unprofitable rental system will explain the stalemate, although it must be admitted that the prospect of earning only a few hundred dollars by writing a full-length book discourages many good authors from entering the field, especially since they cannot even hope for serious critical attention as a result.

Investigation of the whole situation surrounding the writing, publishing, selling, and reviewing of mysteries, reveals one little-noticed fact: the mystery story is at a standstill because it is being written for a purely professional audience.

Around each one of the many rental libraries scattered across the country is a small but determined group of readers—most of them men—who devour almost every mystery story published. They take their daily dose of murder with the frenzied enthusiasm of a drug addict. They know all the tricks; they have followed all the detectives, erudite, dumb, exotically Oriental, depressingly home-spun; they are familiar with all the ways a human being can be put to death; they are better acquainted with the homicide laws than a Leibowitz or a Darrow; there is nothing new to them under the sun, and they complain continually that mysteries get worse and worse. Yet Heaven help the writer who tries to give them any-thing but the old familiar brand!

There is no use wasting time deploring the miserable lot of these devotees who spend their lives so vicariously and so futilely. The root of their devotion can probably be traced to an unhappy child-hood, business worries, or a maladjusted sex life rather than to a genuine interest in any kind of literature. Unfortunately, these regular patrons of the rental libraries are the determining factor in making success or failure for any mystery writer's work. They are the ones who first read a new author's work; their approval induces the rental library clerks trying to extend the possible market, to recommend the story to those who are not mystery fans; their disap-proval causes the new book to be shelved quietly.

Since this small group holds so much power it is obvious that publishers cater to its tastes. Writers are encouraged to repeat old formulas, since there is nothing which is more of an anathema to a drug addict than a change of narcotics. The mystery story goes round and round but it never goes forward. Originality is stifled and orthodoxy reigns supreme.

All kinds of extraneous novelties have been injected into the basic pattern of the mystery story to lend it some freshness: cooking recipes, learned dissertations on campanology, and much second-rate humor have been utilized to give the reader what is known in merchandising as "plus value." But these subsidiary devices are simply evidence of a decadence that is now far advanced. No such trivial means can rescue the mystery story from the sterility that comes from long inbreeding.

III

The great need of the mystery story today is not novelty of ap-paratus but novelty of approach. The whole genre needs overhauling, a return to first principles, a realization that murder has to do with human emotion and deserves serious treatment. Mystery story writers need to know more about life and less about death—more about the way people think and feel and act, and less about how they die.

The mystery story is concerned with murder and its detection and nothing else. Yet the reactions of its characters count most. The mind of the murderer, the intellect of the detective, the quirks of behavior of the minor characters give it interest. It must always treat its main subject with respect; Keystone cops and wisecracking detectives are out of place in the presence of a corpse, and it cannot be pleaded that police handling of an actual killing often has its low-comedy aspects. An artist cannot take his material from life and reproduce it stenographically—he must select and heighten. When he makes murder the central theme of his story he needs to utilize those aspects of murder which make their greatest appeal to the reader. Humor or erudition are only adventitiously connected with his theme; his major concern is with death and horror and the unknown, with fear and uncertainty, and finally with solution, consummation, catharsis.

There is a simple test which can be used to judge a mystery story. Put yourself in the place of the murderer. Then ask whether you would go about killing a man in the way indicated in the story under consideration. Would you put bacteria-infected cheese mites in the Stilton the butler is about to serve to the gentleman you want to slay? Would you transmit your instructions tattooed in ideographs on the posterior of a Chinese orphan? Of course you would not, and thus you immediately know the story is trash. Would you, as a potential murderer, undertake the exceedingly dangerous business of killing with a lighthearted whimsical attitude when you know a slip so slight as leaving a fingerprint can send you to your own death? The shadow of the noose is already falling on you when you contemplate an act of murder; the hideous whine of high-voltage current beats on your eardrums when you begin your plotting!

In real life, if you are determined to put some one out of the way, you will go about your work with a deadly earnestness that transcends every other interest. You will want to use straightforward methods, not devious ones. Even if you possess only animal cunning you will soon realize that the best way to kill is to kill simply and quickly. The man who uses a stout club on a dark street has ten thousand chances of escape compared with the too clever slayer who employs a rare poison distilled from the stings of Tibetan honey bees, if for no better reason than that there are at least ten thousand people who have ready access to a stick of wood compared with those who can obtain an exotic poison. Too much intelligence is a limiting factor that may lead to identification. When you are risking your own life the anonymity that comes from imitating mankind's widespread stupidity can be remarkably useful.

When you put yourself in the murderer's place you will see, too, that you do not want to involve yourself in any elaborate alibi, especially in one that necessitates the use of undependable mechanisms. Phonograph records that reproduce your voice while you are away somewhere busily engaged in murder; string-and-pin devices that enable you to lock the door to the room containing a dead man who appears to have committed suicide; spring-discharged pistols, automatic poisoned needles, and deadly tropical insects— all have an awkward way of refusing to function smoothly at the critical moment. You will not want to trust your own life to such unsure instruments, for you will be acutely aware of the fact that the arm of the law is long and its grip deadly. The stout stick in the dark street is as good a way of killing as any and not likely to fail. Nor will it be suspected that you were out lurking for your victim if you use plain horse sense in arranging your murder. It will be noted, also, that real murderers seldom depend on unusual means or elaborate alibis. But then, real murderers have real lives to risk so they naturally tend to be careful of them.

Mystery story writers have much to learn from life. They can learn that their characters are most convincing when they act like human beings and not like clever automatons; they can learn that men have all sorts of odd motives for murder, and that they kill more often for obscure and sometimes apparently trivial reasons— which are nevertheless deeply rooted in sound psychology—than they do for the possession of a trio of valuable postage stamps or the right to inherit a lordly title. Mystery story authors may even discover the one elementary fact underlying the writing of all fiction

—that unless the reader is made to care about the characters in a book he is utterly indifferent to their fates. As a corollary to this they may find out that when fifty people are all equally suspected of having committed a murder the reader is bored at the prospect of having to see forty-nine of them eliminated before he can close the book with a sigh of relief. They should be made to realize, too, that when the culprit turns out to be a character so obscure that his own unimportance in the story has concealed him from view, the reader has a right to feel angry. The murderer cannot be so meanly subordinated. He is, after all, the prime mover of the story. Without him there can be no plot, no action, no suspense. He needs to be a major figure, clever, desperate, and strong, for the man hunt is interesting only when the quarry is worthy of the chase.

In addition to emphasis on character the mystery story has need of that quality with which Poe endowed it at birth—atmosphere. Murder is a child of darkness, a friend of night and storm, a dweller in ancient habitations where the rook and the raven keep watch. It seems oddly out of place in our neonlighted streets; it is reduced to journalistic triviality by gang warfare; it suffers from the tempo of modern life. Only by making use of its natural terrors and restoring it to its pristine dignity can we hope to see murder again made worthy of being considered one of the fine arts. Let us hope that the second century of the mystery story's development will witness its coming of age, for in its present condition the one quality it lacks above all others is maturity. It is surely strange that an age so deeply concerned with death as our own has not yet made its mark upon an art that deals only with death.

The Whodunit in World War II and After

By Howard Haycraft

The survey-and-summary which follows was published in the New York Times Book Review *for August 12, 1945.*

AT THE height of the Nazi blitz of London in 1940 special "raid libraries" were set up at the reeking entrances to the underground shelters to supply, by popular demand, detective stories and nothing else. No more dramatic illustration can be imagined of the singular appeal of the once lowly and scorned whodunit as the chosen escapist literature of modern times in general and wartime in particular. American readers have not been called on to give such convincing proof of their devotion. But corroborative evidence of a quieter sort is not lacking in this country, on the moving picture screen and the radio waves as well as in the bookshop and the library.

Unlike the First World War, when the detective story dropped nearly from sight, the present conflict has stimulated publication of the form to new highs. This is true despite a slight reduction in the number of new titles. For it is in the low price, pocket size reprint field that the whodunit—using the term in its widest and commonly accepted generic sense to include all related tales of mystery and crime with a perceptible thread of detection—has truly come into its own. One needs no dry statistics, but only to see the familiar gaudy paper covers in buses, railway coaches, and subway cars, to know that vastly more people are reading mystery-detective stories today than ever before. Meanwhile the pattern is being duplicated overseas, where hundreds of thousands of Americans in uniform are acquiring the habit by exposure to the widely popular hip pocket Armed Services Editions.

What this new audience means for the post-war period, when paper restrictions are removed, is a prospect that titillates the salivary glands wherever publishers, authors, and agents gather. Many of these are seriously convinced that the pocket size volume is the indicated physical shape of the detective story of the future, and that five years' time or less may see most mysteries published originally in low price paperback editions of 100,000 copies or more the initial printing. Time alone will prove the accuracy of these prophecies. If such a change from present practices does occur, it will in all probability come about gradually, not overnight.

The quality side of the whodunit balance sheet during the war years presents something of a paradox. On the one hand, the general level of technical and literary craftsmanship in the mystery-detective tale has never been higher. On the other, there have been relatively few individual efforts that can be called inspired, few exciting discoveries, in the period under consideration. A time of "static competence," one critic has called it. This is pretty obviously the result of the inevitable disruptions of war (and suggests the possibility of a post-war detection renaissance like that of the 1920's). How many brilliant performances in this as in all walks of literature have been postponed—at the least—by the physical fact of war can only be conjectured.

But if the martial years have produced few mystery landmarks (in the sense that the first stories of Dorothy Sayers and S. S. Van Dine and Francis Iles and Dashiell Hammett are hallowed ground to the true whodunit addict) there has been no dearth of competent and entertaining new blood (no pun intended). No span of years can be called sterile which introduced, in America alone, such capable or better newcomers (in approximate order of their appearance) as Raymond Chandler, A. A. Fair, Craig Rice, Hugh Pentecost, Dorothy B. Hughes, Cornell Woolrich, the Lockridges, Elliot Paul, Marion Randolph, Cleve Adams, Lawrence Treat, Frank Gruber, Elizabeth Daly, Barber and Schabelitz, David Keith, Frances Crane, David Dodge, H. R. Steeves, Virginia Perdue, F. W. Bronson, Mitchell Wilson, Katharine Roberts, Mary Collins, Richard Sale, William Irish, Vera Caspary, H. R. Hays, Margaret Millar, A. R. Hilliard, Stanley Hopkins, Jr., Lucy Cores, Ruth Fenisong, C. W. Grafton, Margaret Carpenter, Matthew

Head, Samuel Rogers, Doris Miles Disney, Hilda Lawrence, H. W. Roden, Bruno Fischer, Rosemary Kutak, Joel Townsley Rogers—to name only those who come first to mind.

British debutants during the period were naturally fewer. Arranged in the order that they became known to American readers, these include Raymond Postgate, Anne Hocking, E. H. Clements, Selwyn Jepson, Dan Billany, H. F. Heard, Manning Coles, E. X. Ferrars, Patrick Hamilton, Chris Massie, George Bellairs, Cyril Hare, Donald L. Henderson, P. W. Wilson, L. A. G. Strong, Nigel Balchin, and (to follow the Empire) A. W. Upfield and A. E. Martin, two promising beginners from Down Under.

The French *roman policier,* never widely translated in America, virtually ceased to exist after the fall of Paris and has not yet recuperated, so far as can be ascertained. But the translated Inspector Maigret tales of Georges Simenon (though published in the land of their origin well before the war) achieved their greatest and deserved American popularity during the period under review.

If I were compelled to nominate the three or four new writers of the years 1939–45 who are most likely to be bracketed by future historians with Sayers and Van Dine and Iles and Hammett—for distinction, originality, and influence in their chosen field—my vote would go to two Americans, one Englishman, and one Frenchman: Raymond Chandler, Dorothy Hughes, Raymond Postgate, and Simenon. (In addition to these, special "oscars" might profitably be awarded to Craig Rice and Mr. and Mrs. Lockridge for services above and beyond the call of duty in behalf of the light-hearted crime novel.) It is interesting, if possibly not indicative, to note that each of these writers made his initial bow in the early years of the period, before the serious military phases of the war began. It is considerably more significant that each in his own fashion represents an extension and advancement of the outstanding development which characterized the mystery story in the 1930's: the movement away from the mechanical formula whodunit and toward the novel of manners and character with a crime motif.

Aside from this continuation of an earlier movement, no major developments in detective-mystery technique have distinguished the war years. However, one or two topical trends are worth comment. As might have been predicted, the espionage theme has been used extensively and effectively. (Oddly enough, other than in variations of the espionage theme, the war has figured only casually as "material" for the whodunit.) In general the spy stories of this war have been agreeably free of the clichés of the old Oppenheim-Le Queux school of intrigue, following instead the naturalistic pattern established by John Buchan and developed by Eric Ambler and Graham Greene in the years between the wars. Two new writers whose espionage tales entitle them to rank with these undoubted masters are Manning Coles in England and Dorothy Hughes in America.

A related trend, possibly more lasting in its technical implications, is the augmented awareness of personal peril, both physical and psychological, to be found in an increasing number of mysteries today. This development is rapidly achieving the status of a distinguishable sub-species, called, with some ambiguity, the "suspense" story (often but not necessarily with an espionage background); and is regarded in some quarters as a logical and belated reaction against both the immobility and improbability so frequently complained of in run-of-the-mill detective stories.

As someone has remarked, detection as well as crime requires a motive. Too often in the pedestrian whodunit there is no plausible reason why the sleuth—whether "private eye" working for coffee and cakes, or meddling amateur working for nothing—should make himself a clay pigeon; and when he does, the reader yawns. (While if the professional police are involved, the action tends as a rule to be even more static.) Confronted with this dilemma, the "suspense" story restores, or attempts to restore, excitement, immediacy, urgency (one might almost say amateur standing) to the detective novel by the device of enmeshing the central character in a web of circumstance from which there is no escape save to fight (detect) his way out. The fact that the personal peril motif has been found well suited to moving pictures and the radio is not likely to lessen its future popularity.

One exception must be recorded to an earlier statement. Counter to the general rise in technical craftsmanship, the level of writing in the hardboiled whodunit has become disturbingly synthetic and desultory. Recalling the brave days of Hammett, it is a little sad to find the tough gentry (with the exception of Raymond

Chandler, A. A. Fair, and one or two others) mistaking activity for action, alcoholism for humor, and pornography for realism. Since the cause of this is nothing more serious than laziness, the cure is obvious and indicated.

Balancing this disappointing trend, there has been a gratifying decline in the coy and self-conscious style of American-feminine over-writing variously called the Had-I-But-Known or Terror-in-the-Attic school. Longsuffering readers need no reminder of the spinster-narrator who "forgets" (she was baking bread that morning) to tell the sheriff about the bloody axe she found in the woodshed with the murderer's fingerprints on it, thereby causing five more brutal deaths—and incidentally stringing out a wabbling plot another 200 pages. (Worse still the heroine who deliberately conceals vital evidence from The Law, with the same net result.) But happily the ridicule which has been heaped on this sort of mere-triciousness in recent years is beginning to bear fruit. And high time too!

In past years the translation of the detective story to the moving picture screen has been something less than successful. Recently, however, Hollywood has stopped underestimating the intelligence of its audience and has demonstrated that it can construct adult and exciting screen drama on the mystery framework, with emphasis on character and suspense. With such superior examples on record as "Double Indemnity," "The Woman in the Window," "Rebecca," "Suspicion," "Murder, My Sweet," "Laura," and "Phantom Lady" —to mention but a few—the film whodunit has definitely come of age.

No comparable maturity can be claimed for the American radio mystery, which for a variety of reasons is still relying largely on third-rate imitations of the "Thin Man" formula or juvenile melo-dramatics for its results. There are, of course, exceptions. Perhaps the most effective type of radio mystery to date is the simplified first-person "suspense" drama, as typified by the program of that name. On a purely quantitative basis whodunit addicts can have little complaint: I am told the coming autumn season will see no less than fifty separate programs of a mystery nature on the air.

The necrology of the years under consideration has not been extensive. In America, S. S. Van Dine, Carolyn Wells, Hulbert Footner, and Virginia Perdue were recorded in the obituary columns; in England, the beloved dean of the form, R. Austin Freeman, together with Ernest Bramah, Lord Charnwood, and Helen Simpson; in France, Maurice Leblanc, the creator of Arsène Lupin. Of these, only Miss Simpson died as the result of enemy action. (The only *character* to become a war casualty would seem to be Mr. Moto.)

Miscellaneous events during the war years which have affected or are likely to affect the reading and writing of whodunits include the founding of the Detective Book Club by Walter Black; the establishment of *Ellery Queen's Mystery Magazine,* the first successful "class" magazine in the field; and the recent organization of Mystery Writers of America, Inc., a professional group similar to the older London Detection Club.

By actual evidence of the printed word, more serious critical thinking has been devoted to the whodunit in the last few years than in any comparable period in its history. An imposing array of American, English, and French intellectuals have publicly pondered the causes, significance, and probable directions of crime fiction, among them Louise Bogan, Edmund Wilson, John Strachey, Joseph Wood Krutch, Jacques Barzun, W. Somerset Maugham, Raymond Chandler, Elliot Paul, Nicholas Blake, Vincent Starrett, Philip Van Doren Stern, Anthony Boucher, Harrison R. Steeves, Roger Callois, Jean Cassou, Mary McCarthy, H. R. Hays, Bernard De Voto, and George Orwell.

These critics and their opinions may be divided roughly into four principal categories: (1) the viewers-with-alarm, like Edmund Wilson, who have looked upon the whodunit and find it bad; (2) the seekers-after-truth, as typified by Krutch, Bogan, Callois, and Blake, who are primarily concerned with the still-unanswered "why?" of crime fiction; (3) the fundamentalists, the Barzuns and McCarthys, who, one infers, would restrict the form forever to the narrow confines of the "pure" detective story, unsullied by such heresies as style or thought; (4) the diametrically opposed camp, the non-fencers-in, led by Stern and Hays, who hold that the genre must have unlimited room for growth and expression if it is to retain the privileged position it now occupies.

Most serious well-wishers of the 'tec, I am convinced, adhere to the last view, if only for reasons of enlightened selfishness, and are in substantial agreement that the time has come for the whodunit to discard its dogmatism. Like all literary types, the detective story in the period of its development required a rather rigid and arbitrary set of standards to protect and guide its growth into ways that were good. With the arrival of maturity, these once sustaining molds have largely outlived their usefulness. This does not mean that the goals of the old disciplines (as, for example, the fair-play credo) need be lost; any more than the grown tree loses its strength when the stakes and wires which supported it as a sapling are taken away. But failing such removal at the proper time, both tree and literary form can be permanently harmed.

Fortunately for its admirers, the whodunit appears to be evolving in the advocated direction. More puzzle of character and less of mechanics, higher and unashamed literary value, more humanity, humor, and fear, less "plot" and more story, are quietly going into the making of detective stories today than a decade or even five years ago.

Vincent Starrett has suggested half-seriously that the day may come when the novel of manners will engulf the detective story, with the result that we shall ultimately have novels about detectives as we now have "novels about clergymen and physicians and peanut vendors." Possibly the alternative (*pace* Edmund Wilson!) is for the whodunit to take over the novel of manners.

ACKNOWLEDGMENTS

Gratitude has been expressed in the Foreword to those writers, editors, and critics who composed special articles and essays for this volume. Grateful acknowledgment is additionally made to the following individuals and firms for permission to reprint selections which originally appeared in other books or journals (such sources are indicated in the introductions to the individual selections):

To Dodd, Mead & Company, Inc. for G. K. Chesterton's "A Defence of Detective Stories"; R. Austin Freeman's "The Art of the Detective Story," copyright 1940; and Stephen Leacock's "Murder at $2.50 a Crime," copyright 1937.

To Oxford University Press for E. M. Wrong's "Crime and Detection."

To Charles Scribner's Sons for Willard Huntington Wright's "The Great Detective Stories," copyright 1927, and S. S. Van Dine's "Twenty Rules for Writing Detective Stories," copyright 1936.

To Ann Watkins, Inc. for Dorothy L. Sayers' "The Omnibus of Crime," copyright 1929, and "Gaudy Night" and John Dickson Carr's "The Locked Room Lecture," copyright 1935.

To Marjorie Nicolson for "The Professor and the Detective," copyright 1929.

To William Collins Sons & Company, Ltd. for H. Douglas Thomson's "Masters of Mystery."

To The Macmillan Company for Vincent Starrett's "The Private Life of Sherlock Holmes," copyright 1933.

To D. Appleton-Century Company, Inc. for Howard Haycraft's "Murder for Pleasure," copyright 1941.

To Joseph Wood Krutch for "Only a Detective Story," copyright 1944.

To A. P. Watt & Son for Monsignor Ronald A. Knox's "Detective Story Decalogue," copyright 1929.

To Sydney A. Sanders for Raymond Chandler's "The Simple Art of Murder," copyright 1944.

To James Sandoe for "Dagger of the Mind," copyright 1946.

To Marie F. Rodell for "Clues," copyright 1943.

To Rex Stout for "Watson Was a Woman," copyright 1941.

To Little, Brown & Company for Ogden Nash's "Don't Guess, Let Me Tell You," copyright 1940.

To the Estate of Christopher Ward for the late Mr. Ward's "The Pink Murder Case," copyright 1929.

To Lt.-Col. Richard Armour for "Everything Under Control," copyright 1941.

To Ben Hecht for "The Whistling Corpse," copyright 1945.

To Robert J. Casey for "Oh, England! Full of Sin," copyright 1937.

To Methuen & Company, Ltd. for E. V. Lucas' "Murders and Motives."

To Will Cuppy for "How to Read a Whodunit," copyright 1945.

To *Ellery Queen's Mystery Magazine* for the Editor's remarks in "Four Mystery Reviews," copyright 1946.

To Leland Hayward, Inc. for Dashiell Hammett's review of *The Benson Murder Case,* copyright 1927, and "From the Memoirs of a Private Detective," copyright 1923.

To Willis Kingsley Wing for Anthony Boucher's "The Ethics of the Mystery Novel," copyright 1944.

To Edmund Wilson and the *New Yorker* for Mr. Wilson's "Who Cares Who Killed Roger Ackroyd?" copyright 1945 The F.-R. Publishing Corporation.

To Peter Davies, Ltd. for Nicholas Blake's "The Detective Story —Why?"

To Ellery Queen for "Leaves From the Editors' Notebook" and "The Detective Short Story," copyright 1941.

To R. Philmore for "Inquest on Detective Stories."

To John Barker Waite for "The Lawyer Looks at Detective Fiction," copyright 1929.

To Constable & Company, Ltd. for John Carter's "Collecting Detective Fiction."

To James Sandoe for "Readers' Guide to Crime," copyright 1944.

To Harrison R. Steeves and *Harper's Magazine* for Mr. Steeves' "A Sober Word on the Detective Story," copyright 1941.

To Philip Van Doren Stern for "The Corpse in the Blind Alley," copyright 1941.

To the *New York Times Book Review* for Howard Haycraft's "The Whodunit in World War II and After," copyright 1945.

Index